FROM PSALM
TO SYMPHONY

Music advisor to Northeastern University Press

GUNTHER SCHULLER

FROM PSALM TO SYMPHONY

A History of Music in New England

NICHOLAS E. TAWA

NORTHEASTERN UNIVERSITY PRESS
Boston

Northeastern University Press

The photograph of Thomas Brattle's organ on page 49 is reproduced with
permission of the photographer, Richard Rozek, Senior Warden,
St. John's Episcopal Church, Portsmouth, New Hampshire. The illustrations on pages 96, 98, 128, 132, 152, 229, 307, and 383 are reproduced
with permission of the New England Conservatory of Music, with special
thanks to Jean Morrow, Director of Libraries.

Library of Congress Cataloging-in-Publication Data
Tawa, Nicholas E.
From psalm to symphony : a history of music in New England / Nicholas Tawa.
p. cm.
Includes bibliographical references and index.
ISBN 1-55553-491-0 (cloth : alk. paper)
1. Music—New England—History and criticism.   I. Title.
ML200.7.N3 T39 2001
780'.974—dc21   2001034529

Designed by Joyce C. Weston

Composed in Perpetua by Wellington Graphics, Westwood, Massachusetts. Printed and bound by Thomson-Shore, Inc., Dexter, Michigan. The
paper is Writer's Offset, an acid-free stock.

MANUFACTURED IN THE UNITED STATES OF AMERICA
04   03   02   01   5   4   3   2   1

CONTENTS

ILLUSTRATIONS

PREFACE

New England lacks a history of its music. Although the region contributed vitally to American music from the first Pilgrim and Puritan settlement on, no chronological account of its musical events exists. Yet New England's story requires telling. This is what the pages that follow intend to do.

At least five significant components to the story need recounting. First, the northeast corner of the United States has been preeminent in musical publication, beginning with the Bay Psalm Book of 1640, the first book published in British colonies, and including the music books and sheet music of the Oliver Ditson Company, America's dominant nineteenth-century music publisher. Second, it has made outstanding contributions to the improvement and manufacture of musical instruments, especially those involving Chickering and the piano. Third, in music education, New England was a leader for the nation, beginning with the singing schools of the 1720s, later with music in the public schools, still later with the new conservatories of music and the music departments of colleges and universities. Fourth, it fielded groundbreaking and first-rate musical establishments, among them the Handel and Haydn Society and the Boston Symphony Orchestra, which have long-established reputations in the nation. Fifth, it can boast admirable composers, from America's earliest practitioners of the art, such as William Billings, to some of the most skilled and artistically gifted of the nation, such as George Chadwick, Charles Ives, and Walter Piston.

The main concentration will be on art music (commonly known as classical music) as a subject, and on greater Boston as the New England center for the art. This is not to say that a coherent report on the different types of vernacular music would not be of value, simply that an examination of art music in New England seems urgent, since it is heading into a period of great difficulty, sent there through the domination of other forms of entertainment, a dropping off in audiences, and a shrinking of financial support. If we value artistic expression, that is to say, the conscious use of knowledge, taste, and creative imagination in the production of sounds, and if we prize sounds that afford some of the greatest sensory and intellectual pleasure known to humankind, then more than a passing scrutiny is due art music.

As for the great attentiveness given to Boston and its environs, it is here that more of the important musical events in the region took place. A cursory look at the authors who wrote about New England's music shows that a majority of them were located in and making use of what Boston and its suburbs had to offer. It was New England's largest urban district, with the richest opportunities for concert attendance, musical training, and amateur and professional music making. It provided the largest audiences for music. Composers found employment more easily here and conditions favorable for giving hearings to their compositions were more in evidence. A sizable number of discriminating listeners having considerable sophistication and musical understanding stood ready to encourage the efforts of creative artists.

The history that follows is an account of music in New England, comprising a chronological record of events and, when possible, an explanation of the cause and origin of such events. Historians are not scientists; neither am I. They cannot do what any scientist in chemistry, biology, and physics does, who investigates aspects of the physical world by means of hypotheses verified through experiments and resulting in hard, conclusive authentication. Instead, all historians, myself included, amass a number of facts and select what seem most significant, given their command of the subject under study. However objective they try to be, the selection is influenced by the attitudes prevalent in their era and the particular biases affecting them personally and their special field. These are reasons why few histories can stand for all time and why each succeeding generation may need to have fresh histories written on its own terms.

European writers on American culture have often demonstrated considerable ignorance combined with prejudice when writing about our music. American music historians, some of them quite respected, from time to time have espoused the cause of vernacularism, or nationalism, or originality and have selected and interpreted their material in accord with their leanings. For example, a prominent English writer has dismissed the general run of New England composers, beginning with Paine, as hacks specializing in the production of dull, trite, and unimaginative works. Unfortunately the book is often quoted. In a published history of music in the United States, written by someone outside the region, most New England composers disappear from sight because they did not create music that sounds as distinctively national to the author. In another history, they get short shrift because they are deemed not sufficiently original and innovative. Only composers who kicked over the traces, like Ives and Ruggles, receive sympathetic treatment. And the less-than-savory Puritans and the puritanical attitudes that are said to continue to afflict the six New England states persist as hostile stereotypes that crop up in newspapers and magazines, and on radio and television, though not to the extent they did seventy-five years ago. Some years back, John Rockwell, a *New York Times* music critic who had not previously been particularly fond of New England's music making, finally admitted that the dismissal of New England's composers and the disparagement of the region by outsiders were mainly political in nature and had little to do with the actual worth of New England's music.

I admit to a different agenda. This study may act as a counterpoise to the disparagement. Born a New Englander, I have a particular sympathy for the region, its problems, and its principal actors. Nevertheless, I do want to be evenhanded in my judgments and see clearly the faults as well as the virtues. Now, in the first decade of the twenty-first century, I detect a redirection of ideological positions concerning America's music. Originality, a national identity, and cutting-edge innovation are becoming less the deciding factors in evaluating American music of the past and present. The untrammeled freedom given artists to create is now seen also to have its attendant responsibilities to the audience. This is not to say that originality and freedom are to be swept aside; only that other issues are also involved that should be addressed.

The musical development of an area is intimately bound up with its geography, climate, economy, disposable income, educational opportunities, backgrounds of its immigrants, rural-urban dispersal of its inhabitants, and contacts with other regions and other nations. The recital that follows considers all of these factors. I hope that I do not unduly offend those critics who still adhere to one or another of the progressive orthodoxies of the recent past on questions involving what contemporary music should be about or what proper musicology should consider and avoid.

The study of music in the United States, and New England particularly, has involved me over several decades. I am fortunate in being able to avail myself of what I have previously written, especially those books listed in the bibliography. As I was reading again my notes about New England's music and also conducting fresh investigations into the subject, I felt increasingly convinced that the entire nation could benefit from the region's encounters with music. First, we can learn from the New England experience that art music is not necessarily lowered in quality when it holds the attention of large audiences agreeably and wins the favor of the general music public. We find that serious composers—whether Billings, Paine, Converse, Thompson, Piston, Schuller, or Harbison—do not have to compromise their principles and pervert the application of their skill and taste so that their compositions can prove attractive to more than a few people. One of the finest aptitudes of these seven composers, as with most of their New England colleagues, has been the ability to keep cultural disagreements under control. Unrestrained behavior and outrageous sound have not been part of the makeup of most of the artists. Therefore, they have garnered musical acclaim, which in the New England experience often indicates that a composer and his works have gained the devotion of not just the common run of listeners but also a broad spectrum of musically experienced men and women who are, each in his or her own way, sincerely desirous of seeking out the best in music. As a result, the musical history of New England has proven again and again that art music is relevant to the quality of human life and can engage the feelings of relatively large numbers of concertgoers.

Those musical compositions that may prove difficult to take in also exhibit redeeming features. Ives when most chaotic demonstrates recognition of the many unassimilated strands not yet plaited in the human spirit or a devil-may-care forward thrust that invites us to have a noisy and disorderly good time. Ruggles's striving to go beyond himself through the dissonancies of grinding seconds and sevenths promotes a cataclysmic vision that is nascent in all of us. The foxy insanity of Lucier on one level exploits the preposterous funning we have all yielded to at one time or another. In some works, Kirchner's and Schuller's atonal spin leaves us dizzy, but no one doubts the sincerity and expertise of these two men. Persistent listeners can eventually enjoy the rich emotional interplay resulting from the contraposing of apparently incompatible musical elements, which will show the way to a new level of meaning.

We must always keep in mind that in the best of times, most of our composers lead lonely, thankless lives, rarely befriended by patrons, performers, or the public. Their musical education has been intensively pursued at a great deal of expense over many years. Their creative efforts entail giving over thousands of hours and considerable exertion for what is essentially an unrewarding activity. Social, economic, cultural, and professional uncertainties abound. The practice of art music requires true devotion. It also generates a host of near martyrs who willingly suffer neglect rather than renounce their calling. Despite this, we hope they keep at it. We hope that eventually they can make their peace with performers and public and together sponsor a viable art.

The relationship between music and society has gone through countless changes year after year, since the Pilgrims landed in Plymouth in 1620. The rockbound wilderness confronted by the Pilgrims and Puritans, more than their attitudes, dictated severe limits on the sorts of music that could exist. When New England in the eighteenth century began to see the increased gathering of people in towns, most of them clustered around or within a close distance to Boston, then rudimentary music education and the first primitive concerts could take place. With the means now at hand for them to appear, the Yankee tunesmiths began to create homespun choral works to satisfy a homespun public.

After the arrival of the nineteenth century, improved communication with Europe brought in more sophisticated musical ideas and well-trained musical performers. It paved the way for more ambitious concerts that aired the latest musical works imported from abroad. The public, with greater leisure and disposable income, took to these concerts. Cultural leaders tried again and again to improve the quality of the performances. In midcentury, cultivated Germans abandoned central Europe and its political turmoil, bringing with them polished instrumentalists, vocalists, and music educators, and a fondness for the music they had known. They were the spur for more ambitious music making. The coalescing of towns into larger urban entities provided the resources for the formation of more cosmopolitan musical organizations, amateur mostly, succeeded by entirely professional ones after midcentury. Richer concert presentations and qualitatively excellent musical training were also the result of all these changes. By the last third of the century skilled and talented native art composers had appeared on the New England scene. For a while, Boston was the nation's center for art music, aside from opera, competing successfully with New York City and Philadelphia.

Boston lost its hegemony with the arrival of the twentieth century. New York City now became art music's epicenter. However, the city continued to harbor some of America's finest composers, music education institutions, choruses, and instrumental ensembles. The Boston Symphony, under Koussevitzky, turn out to be the principal orchestra in the

United States committed to the music of native composers, to whom the local public listened with interest if not enthusiasm—not just to Piston and Thompson, but also to Harris, Copland, Sessions, and others.

During the second half of the century, New England was second to none in holding to its commitment to music education in universities, colleges, conservatories, and music schools, and in presenting a varied diet of old and new music. What is more, attendance at many concerts were at nominal cost or free, especially those given under the auspices of schools, museums, libraries, and churches. Although the region surrendered composers to other areas of the country—Hovhaness, Bernstein, Adams, and so forth—it also gained outstanding composers—Kirchner, Schuller, Albert, and Harbison, among them.

In the last two decades of the twentieth century, a variety of listeners belonging to every social level sent lists of their favorite and most unforgettable recorded music to *Fanfare* magazine. Other, similar lists have been published in books, magazines, and newspapers. The number of American works cited was unexpected. Commonly named were compositions by composers active in New England—including those by Piston, Thompson, Kirchner, Schuller, and Harbison. In the future, not everything the composers write will meet with success. This has been true throughout history. However, the cultural pump needs continual priming. Eventually, if discouragement does not set in, effective compositions will flow out to a music public that will be eager for them.

FROM PSALM
TO SYMPHONY

1

TO SETTLE A WILDERNESS

W hen we ask where the real start of music in the British colonies took place, we are most apt to find the answer in New England, and in the rather severe, restricted, and somewhat ordinary singing of psalms, which must have seemed off-putting to non-Puritans. In order to place this New England music in its proper perspective, I start by glancing at what was happening in the rest of colonial America. Music marked by taste and refinement existed elsewhere in America, except among some of the Quakers, who shunned music for religious reasons. Yet even in Quaker Philadelphia, music seems to have captured the fancy of many residents.

English people were in Virginia and the Dutch in New York about the same time as the Pilgrims and Puritans and certainly enjoyed making music. Nor were they bound up as rigidly as the Puritans by religious restraints that censored certain forms of musical expression. The first arrivals in Virginia came in 1607, in the form of the Virginia Company, which was intended to operate somewhat as a military trading spot. Ten years later, the inhabitants were allowed to hold property, and tobacco became a leading commodity. Yet for a while, hardship was their lot. Cultivation of food products was neglected, and massacres by native Indians in 1622 weakened the colony. The mortality rate was appalling. Revival would begin only after 1624, when Virginia became a Crown Colony. The Dutch occupied the Albany area in 1624 and Manhattan in 1626. Again, the initial intent was profit through trade. Inept leadership left people unhappy and ready to welcome drastic political change. The English would take over in 1664.

Because the first arrivals in Virginia and New York were often seekers of fortune, many here on speculation, they failed to identify with the New World. Even after they were comfortably settled on the Atlantic seaboard, quite a few of them wanted only to replicate what they had known in their former lives, with no intention of moving away from it.

Thus, the music they produced was, insofar as circumstances permitted, identical with that of their place of origin. They tended, more than the Puritans, to compartmentalize their lives—certain hours given to God, certain hours to work, and certain hours to diversion, not excluding roistering.

Some fairly sophisticated music making would take place among the Spanish and Portuguese in Latin America and the French in Quebec, in the shape of masques, operas, masses, and motets. But these lands smacked more than a little of popery, with which none of the English colonists would have dealings, at least not until the next century. Only Maryland, to which Lord Baltimore had sent two ships in 1634, countenanced Catholic worship. Maryland's Toleration Act of 1649 gave emphasis to this openmindedness. Nevertheless, nothing of a more than primitive nature was possible in music owing to the sparse and scattered homesteads in the region and the shortage of wherewithal.

The launching of schools for musical study and the inauguration of a music that had the stamp of the New World upon it was left for New Englanders to accomplish. Admittedly, it was not an imaginative, inspired, or ingenious music that the New Englanders brought into being. Nevertheless, the sound, whatever its debt to Europe, gradually took on a homegrown quality and shifted step by step away from the characteristics of its original model.

The English Pilgrims and Puritans who crossed the ocean from Holland and England to what they called New England quickly learned that past experience alone would fail them in their raw surroundings. At first, they struggled to apply what they knew in any fashion they could. Almost immediately they realized that adjustments needed to be made. Out from the modes of living they had known in Europe, they carved those symbols, designs, and articles of faith that would help deal with and overcome the problems and difficulties encountered in the American wilderness. In their European lives, they had used traditional procedures for coping with vexing questions. Many of those procedures resisted transplantation. As the residents of Massachusetts Bay dealt with novel events and resolved unexpected crises, they would find themselves altering old usages and originating new ones.

The challenges were great along the flinty Massachusetts shore. Complete adherence to the old would not do. The emigrants who established themselves along the New England coast could not help but build a new society, set up a new civilization, and express themselves in individual cultural ways. And music was an essential part of those ways. From the beginning, they would sing and play musical instruments, though not during religious service.

Each phase of New England's history had failings and successes and showed nastiness and thoughtfulness, drudgery and inspiration. Men, women, and children submitted routinely to some limitations and endured others uncomplainingly, however discomfiting they might be. Music born in New England would always embody the unsettled contrariness that was behind its existence. Again and again we find that a part of its strength and uniqueness arose from tensions and dialectical oppositions in the society that produced it.

As a music historian I wish to pay close attention to the shifting nature of New England's cultural history, looking to the mind-set and circumstances that caused music to exist—to be sung, performed on instruments, composed, desired, and given a hearing. I agree wholly with Michael Kammen when he writes that each society is different and each culture exceptional in its own way.[1] I ask continually how and why New England society was different and in what ways was it exceptional.

I hope to steer clear of the major errors of judgment that have continuously popped up with the term Puritan. Those errors resulted from strongly marked biases and misunderstandings of the Puritan outlook on existence. They also resulted because it was mostly the religious leaders with strong convictions who wrote about their society and its moral stances. Unrecorded in history were the views of thousands of men and women below the rank of the highly educated and the economically better off.

The Puritan label itself is rather unfixed and applies to all classes and states of men's and women's affairs. Puritans held to a broad assortment of positions on religious and worldly matters. At the least, I want to do away with the common notion, not backed by any honest reading of history, that the Puritans were uniformly a narrow-minded bunch that discouraged every diversion related to this world and its pursuits, including music, rather than to religion or spiritual affairs. As will be shown, there were Puritan ministers open to the latest thing in law, politics, science, medicine, and philosophy. Ordinary people insisted on their secular amusements—including dancing, ballad singing, and musical games.

ARRIVING IN AN UNKNOWN LAND

The first English settlers disembarked on a seacoast barren of towns and empty of people to whom they could relate. Trees were everywhere and had to be cleared before crops could be planted. The soil was rockier and less fertile than they had anticipated. Winters froze them and afflicted them with snow, ice, and hunger. Summers left them stifled, overheated, and sticky with perspiration. They felt remote from Europe, and only small, slow ships with limited cargo space and precarious fragility provided links to the homes they had left behind. They struggled for food to survive, surrounded by potentially hostile American Indians and threatened by French Quebecers. The soil was shallow and grudgingly produced fruit, grain, and vegetables. The growing season was short and unpredictable. Game often proved illusive and required forays into intimidating forests; the ocean waited to swallow up fishermen. Given these circumstances, music could scarcely be of immediate concern, however much some men and women might love it.

On the other hand, the settlers were a determined lot and allowed nothing to faze them. Eventually music would indeed become a concern. The discouraging conditions would ameliorate and give way to enlightenment and music's cultivation. They would achieve both through education and training. There would also be a growing familiarity with a wide range of literature, other fine arts, and elements of science rather than just occupational and mechanical matters.

The Pilgrims were Separatists from the Church of England, with which they wanted nothing to do. They stressed the Bible as the source for spiritual value and the ability to read as the means for attaining spiritual knowledge. Common consent, on the congregational principle, selected those religious leaders who served the church in a public capacity. The implications for a future democratic society and for public education, including music education, are obvious. The Pilgrims left England for Holland in 1607–8, and 102 of them left Holland for America in 1620. A small settlement was established in what is now Plymouth, Massachusetts.

The Puritans, in contrast, did not break with the Church of England. Rather, they wished to work from the inside and purify it. They not only promoted education but also laid emphasis on it as necessary for salvation. Unhappy in an England where Bishop Laud was exerting pressure on them, almost one thousand men, women, and children formed the Massachusetts Bay Company, obtained a royal charter, and crossed the Atlantic in 1630 to settle along "Massachusetts Bay in New England." Aboard the ship *Arbella,* during the voyage, John Winthrop delivered a sermon entitled "A Model of Christian Charity," declaring: "For we must consider that we shall be as a city upon a hill. The eyes of all people are upon us, so that if we shall deal falsely with our God in this work we have undertaken, and so cause Him to withdraw His present help from us, we shall be made a story and a byword through the world." This sense of mission would imbue New England's educators, writers, musicians, and composers in later years. Lowell Mason's drive to introduce music into the public schools was bound up with it; Henry Lee Higginson's urge to accumulate the wealth to establish the Boston Symphony followed Puritan precepts; the composer Horatio Parker, gripped by a strong awareness of duty, echoed the values of New England; Henry Gilbert found his calling in the fight for an identifiably American music; and Charles Ives's dedication to emancipating music from its too well mannered fetters was a cause espoused from his youth.

Within half a decade, around ten thousand Puritans had arrived in New England. The nature of the land promoted small farms and discouraged a slave economy. Contiguous villages and towns formed around Boston. Their inhabitants bunched together to provide security from possible enemies, communal assistance in large tasks, and the fellowship of neighbors. They believed strongly in staying near each other as much as possible and erecting their homes about a church. Like a fan spreading out of Boston, community after community came into being. This would enable Thomas Ryan to state more than two hundred years later that the success of his chamber music ensemble was due to New Englanders' propensity for clustering together:

> In order to appreciate the environment of the Quintette Club during our early years [the 1850s], we have to remember that Boston, within a radius of one hundred miles, had a very large number of towns and cities of active working communities. With the exception of a few places like Providence, Worcester, and Portland, these towns had no theatres; their only entertainments were lectures or concerts and these were mostly given in churches; so we had all New England to ourselves (as far as supplying music was concerned) for many years.[2]

Immediately, the colonists took action to organize an association of towns with Boston as the center, rather than just as an outpost, where they could put their principles into practice. By 1637 the Puritan migration had dried up owing to political problems in England, not least of which were the struggles of Puritans against Royalists. Realizing they were on their own, the settlers established their first free grammar school in 1635 and

Harvard College in 1636. At Harvard's first commencement, the program's first paragraph stated: "After God had carried us safe to *New England,* and wee builded our houses, provided necessaries for our livli-hood, rear'd convenient places for Gods worship, and setled the Civill Government: one of the next things we longed for, and looked after was to advance *Learning* and perpetuate it to Posterity; dreading to leave an illiterate Ministery to the Churches, when our present Minsters shall lie in the Dust."[3]

The Puritan leaders agreed in 1647 that an urgent need existed to battle against ignorance. Education was seen as an essential means to understanding themselves and their relation to God, and to advancing the welfare of the Bay Colony. Therefore, they decreed that every town of one hundred families or more had to offer free grammar school education for all children. Boston Latin, Cambridge Latin, Roxbury Latin, and New Haven's Hopkins Grammar School soon achieved a reputation for excellence. Did not John Cotton (1585–1652), a very popular minister who had graduated from Cambridge University, in *Christ the Fountaine of Life,* explain, "Zeale is but a wilde-fire without knowledge?"[4] The accusations of irrational religious beliefs, closed minds, extreme conservativism, and moral self-righteousness hurled against the first settlers along Massachusetts Bay require at least some modification.

For much of the seventeenth century, clerics managed the Bay Colony. They controlled the meetinghouses, the political direction, and the schools. They repeatedly tried to amend the lives of their parishioners, believing to do them good in the ways that they saw the good. Egalitarianism was absent from their lexicon. Rebels against the Puritan orthodoxy had to move away from the Boston area. Thomas Hooker traveled to the Connecticut River in 1635 to practice his beliefs, although feeling cramped in his Cambridge quarters also encouraged the move. The next year, Roger Williams left for Providence. Anne Hutchinson was banished in 1638; she relocated near Williams. The next year, William Coddington had to move to Newport. Mary Dyer, a Quaker who was repeatedly expelled and kept returning, was finally hanged. Then came the witchcraft accusations and trials of the early 1690s, which remain one of the darkest blots on New England's history. Yet even this horrible phase of New England history must be put into the context of the period. Even into the next century, Europe was still burning witches. France did not stop until 1746; Germany, 1775; and Poland, 1793. Moreover, the Inquisition and its tortures continued in Italy until the century's end.[5]

At the same time, these same clerics, however preoccupied with maintaining the purity of their flocks, also refused to surrender to degrading circumstances created by the wilderness. Fallow minds and slackened morals loomed as dangers. A lapse into barbarism was not inconceivable. Therefore, even as their followings labored in the fields, forests, and small manufactories, the religious leadership demanded that they cultivate their intellects and tend their souls.

Clerical control, nevertheless, was bound to weaken. Seaports like Boston were openings on the world without. Rowdy sailors, cheap taverns, and sleazy brothels could not be excluded. Reports exist of drunkenness, unbuttoned merriment, and unseemly behavior, including wild fiddling and the bawling of lewd songs. Furthermore, the populace's love for brilliant colors, fine furniture, rich drapery, and modish clothes withstood repression. On 25 September 1638 John Winthrop (1588–1649) wrote into his *Journal:* "The court, taking into consideration the great disorder general through the country in costliness of apparel, and following new fashions, sent for the elders of the churches and conferred with them about it, and laid it upon them, as belonging to them, to redress it, by urging it upon the consciences of their people, which they promised to do. But little was done about it; for divers of the elders' wives, etc., were in some measure partners in this general disorder."[6]

Nathaniel Ward (ca. 1578–1652) was a minister who lived in what is present-day Ipswich, Massachusetts. He became upset over the way women were chasing after fashion, even from the first arrival of the Puritans. He wrote in 1647 in *The Simple Cobler of Aggawam in America:*

> To speak moderately, I truly confesse it is beyond the ken of my understanding to conceive, how those women should have any true grace, or valuable vertue, that have so little wit, as to disfigure themselves with such exotick garbes, as not only dismantles their native lovely lusters, but transclouts them into gant bar-geese, ill-shapen shotten shell-fish, Egyptian Hieroglyphicks, or at the best into French flurts. . . . it is no marvell they weare drailes on the hinder part of their heads, having nothing as it seems in the fore-part, but a few Squirrills braines, to help them frisk from one ill-favored fashion to another.[7]

Less strict members of the public countenanced the dancing to fiddled dance tunes not only of the sexes separated from each other but also of men and women together. Recognizing the prevalence of dancing, the righteous ones knew that some of it had to be approved. In 1684 the conservative minister Increase Mather, in *An Arrow Against Profane and Promiscuous Dancing*, gave his blessing to dancing and dance music so long as it was not "mixt or promiscuous dancing," that is to say, men dancing with women. And in the one conspicuous court trial of a dancing master, it was not dancing itself that was the transgression. It may also have been debts, arrogance, and serious blasphemy that were involved. Samuel Sewall's *Diary,* 12 November 1685, has the entry: "The ministers of this town come to the Court and Complain against a Dancing Master who seeks to set up here and hath mixt Dances; and 'tis reported he should say that by one play he could teach more Divinity than Dr. Willard or the Old Testament. Mr. Moodey said 'twas not the time for N. E. to dance. Mr. Mather struck at the Root, speaking against mixt dancing." On 17 December 1685: "Mr. Stepney, the Dancing Master, desired a Jury, so he and Mr. Shrimpton bound in 50 lbs. To Janr. Court. Said Stepney is ordered not to keep a Dancing School; if he does will be taken in contempt and be proceeded with accordingly." On 28 July 1686: "Francis Stepney the Dancing Master runs away for Debt. Several attachments out after him."[8]

Sewall (1652–1730) was extremely fond of music throughout his life and engaged in part-singing whenever he found partners. He was, too, a judge at the Salem witch trials of 1692 who openly repented his actions five years later. He would publish an antislavery tract, *The Selling of Joseph* (1700), and author the *Memorial Relating to the Kennebeck Indians* (1721), advocating the humane treatment of Indians.

Singing games, many of them round dances, were regarded normally as straightforward diversions for children and young folk of sixteen to twenty-five. The amusements regulated by the singing of the group, when they were set forth as games, appeased the officials responsible for moral behavior. Rules of propriety remained unbroken even when kissing redeemed forfeits at evening social gatherings, since it "was in honor given and taken before witnesses." Several of the dance tunes for the young have continued into the twentieth century: "Did You Ever See a Lassie," "The Farmer in the Dell," and "Go in and out the Windows," to name three.[9]

Many non-Puritans commenced migrating to New England after 1637 to better themselves economically. They disliked disenfranchisement in their new home and canvassed for change. Among the Puritans themselves, voices were raised against rule by only clergymen and theologians.

Indeed, as generation succeeded generation, a growing number of New Englanders became lukewarm Puritans at best and named themselves so only because they were willing to take on the colors of the ruling party, either for the sake of expediency or because they were indifferent to what religious labels they applied to themselves. They were not prepared to give the clerics their head on all matters. Moreover, their ethical and religious loyalties could be redirected if adjustments to changing circumstances made a change in direction advantageous. These ordinary people began to insist on representation on the General Court. In 1644 two legislative bodies representative of both sides, clergy and populace, came into being, each able to veto the legislation of the other. A voluntary synod of all New England churches met in 1648 and adopted the congregational form of church government.

King Philip's War broke out in the mid-1670s. During 1675–78 the Nipmuck, Narragansett, and Wampanoag tribes formed a loose confederation that ravaged the frontier villages and rolled back the settlements almost to the sea. After a decade's lull, Indians led by the French again wiped out frontier communities, especially in 1689. There was a growing conviction that secular leadership was required. This diluted domination by the divines. More devastating still was the English king's revocation of the Massachusetts Charter in 1684 and the imposition of a royal governor. Anyone with an annual income of forty pounds or having property worth one hundred pounds was allowed to vote. The first Anglican service took place in Boston in 1686. Afterward, as life grew more comfortable, the desire for material things increased. Slowly, the happier, more festive, and lighthearted customs of England underwent rebirth along Massachusetts Bay.

At the same time, the principled commonwealth, whose idea the Puritan ministers had tried to maintain, declined. The witchcraft trials of 1692 condemned fourteen women and six men to death. After the trials, the guilt-laden New England public lost faith in the judgments of the religious leaders and was skeptical about their devotion to the common good. Well might Cotton Mather call the years 1685–95 "Decennium Luctuosum," the decade of sorrow.

When the eighteenth century arrived, the makeup of New England society was fairly diversified, and the political system much less dominated by an oligarchy. The system of town government and town meetings expanded popular participation. Population growth never ceased. A little after the mid-eighteenth century, Boston alone could boast fifteen thousand inhabitants.

MUSIC ENTERS

We know that England's Puritans, whether Oliver Cromwell, John Milton, or John Bunyan, took pleasure in music so long as it was not offensive to morality or decency. During Cromwell's rule over England (1653–60) he maintained a private orchestra, allowed Italian opera into London for the first time, and sanctioned the publication of much secular music, including dance tunes. The English heard their first genuine native opera, *The Siege of Rhodes,* in 1656, with music by Henry Lawes and Matthew Locke. Only during worship did Puritans believe in limiting the music to the singing of psalms without help of an organ.

The New England Puritans had come from an England abounding in fine music. They had frequently heard, sung, or played compositions by William Byrd, Thomas Morley, John Bull, Giles Farnaby, Thomas Tomkins, John Dowland, Orlando Gibbons, Thomas Weelkes, and John Wilbye. All classes diligently applied themselves to music, from the aristocrat to the shoemaker. It was expected that any girl of refinement would sight-read songs and display a command of the virginals or perhaps the cittern. To sing a composition at sight was without question a widespread acquirement and a demonstration of gentle birth. Then, too, the barbershops customarily offered their patrons at least a guitar to play on while they waited their turn to come under the scissors. It was not unusual for a shop to keep a variety of instruments on hand.

Like their English counterparts, the better-educated New Englanders were well acquainted with all varieties of compositions, although owing to their transplanted condition the performance of any complex music was out of the question and concerts were impossible. Still, the furnishings they left behind at their deaths included musical instruments as well as secular and sacred music books published in England by Thomas Ravenscroft, John Playford, and Thomas d'Urfey.

Anne Bradstreet (ca. 1612–72) of Ipswich, Massachusetts, whose husband became governor, was the first American to publish a book of poetry, *The Tenth Muse Lately Sprung Up in America* (1650). Among her poems are several that show a firsthand knowledge of keyboard instruments and fine music. Another poet who made knowledgeable references to music and musical instruments was Edward Taylor (1645–1729), minister at Westfield, Massachusetts. He left behind a four-hundred-page manuscript entitled "Poetical Works," none of which was published until 1939. We also know that New England's Puritan leaders, such as Samuel Sewall, constantly satisfied their craving for secular and sacred music. Moreover, early on, music study formed a part of the Harvard curriculum. Thomas Symmes wrote in 1720 that music "was studied, known and approv'd in our *College,* for many years after its first founding. This is evident from the Musical *Theses* which were formerly Printed, and from some writings containing some *Tunes* with Directions for *Singing by Note,* as they are now sung; and these are yet in being, though of more than Sixty Years standing; besides no Man that studied Musick as it was treated by *Alstead, Playford* and others would be ignorant of it." Unfortunately, a fire demolished the Harvard Library in 1764, destroying the musical theses. Symmes also writes that his father, back in the 1650s, had studied "singing by note" at the college, enjoyed singing during adulthood, and had taught music to him.[10]

Samuel Sewall, in his *Diary,* mentions several times the part-singing by graduates of the college. For example, one classmate "catched" his friends a bass as they sang psalms during a picnic on Mount Wachusett. At another time, Sewall sorrowed over a dying classmate with whom he had often sung part-music.[11]

However intense the love for music and great the skill of singing, practical considerations and social disesteem barred taking it up professionally. This we know from a letter that Leonard Hoar, a Braintree, Massachusetts, resident who was visiting London, wrote to his nephew, Josiah Flynt, on 27 March 1661:

> Musick I had almost forgot. I suspect you seek it both to soon, and to much. This be assured of that if you be not excellent it will take up so much of your mind and time that you will be worth little else: And when all that excellence is attained your acquest will prove little or nothing of real profit to you unlesse you intend to take upon you the trade of fiddling. Howbeit hearing your mother's desires were for it for your sisters for whom tis more proper and they also have more leisure to looke after it: For them I say I had provided the Instruments desired, But I cannot now attend the sending of them being hurried away from London.[12]

In like vein, the Reverend Cotton Mather (1663–1728), son of Increase Mather and grandson of John Cotton, approved of music for "the

Refreshment of One that can play well on an Instrument," although he preferred "Regular Singing" because it would be "of Daily Use to you." He said
further about the pursuit of music: "Do as you please. If you *Fancy* it, I
don't *Forbid* it. Only do not for the sake of it, Alienate your Time too much
from those that are more Important Matters."[13] Mather, like Sewall, har-
bored many contradictions. On the one hand, he was of mystical bent and
believed in witchcraft; on the other, he had a modern scientific interest
that won him membership in the Royal Society of London.

The appreciation of music is established by the number of instruments
in Puritan homes and employed in community service. Virginals sounded
in parlors, trumpets and drums in militia parades and other street proces-
sions. Barbara Lambert reported in 1985 that she had found, for the years
1630–1730, the records of jew's harps; lutes, guitars, and citterns; virginals, spinets, and organs; violas da gamba and treble, tenor, and bass violins;
drums; trumpets, horns, flutes, and fifes; and dulcimers. Not counting the
jew's harps, 154 instruments belonged to men and women from all walks
of life: merchants, ministers, coopers, farmers, civic officials, seamen, and
so forth. More than half the owners were Bostonians; of those identified,
41 were Puritans, 27 of unknown religious affiliation, and 3 Anglicans.[14]

Nathaniel Rogers, of Rowley, died in 1664, leaving behind a "treble
Violl." The Reverend Edmund Browne died in 1678, leaving a "bass vyol,"
music books, and the accolade of excellent musicianship. Samuel Sewall,
who admitted he was "a lover of music to a fault," wrote in his *Diary,*
1 December 1699, about going to a shop to inquire about repair of his
wife's virginals. Harvard students were found idling their time with music
when they should have been studying. More than just one or two men and
women delighted in music. By 1716 Edward Enstone, the new organist at
King's Chapel, was able to advertise in the *Boston News-Letter:*

> This is to give notice that there is lately just come over from England
> a choice Collection of Instruments, consisting of Flageolets, Flutes,
> Haut-boys, Bass-Viols, Violins, Bows, Strings, Reeds for Haut-Boys,
> Books of Instruction for all these Instruments, Books of Ruled Paper.
> To be sold at The Dancing School of Mr. Enstone in Sudbury Street
> near The Orange Tree, Boston. Note: Any person may have all in-
> struments of Musick mended, or Virginalls and Spinnets Strung and
> Tuned at a reasonable Rate, and likewise may be taught to Play on
> any of these instruments above mentioned.[15]

Most New Englanders owned no instruments, though they did have
voices to use—and use them they did. Not surprisingly, secular songs, old

and recently coined, came often from their lips. To profit by the popularity for new songs, ballad mongers roamed town streets and country roads hawking ballad texts printed on broadside sheets of paper. Often a text, set down in doggerel verse, referred to some current affair, complete with a rough woodblock picture of the subject and a suggestion to sing the words to a widely known tune. The young Benjamin Franklin, while growing up in Boston, wrote and hawked ballads of this sort, two of them being "The Light-House Tragedy" and "A Sailor Song." John Cotton's son Seaborn, a Harvard student, wrote down such ditties as "The Lovesick Maid, or Cordelia's Lamentation for the Absence of Her Gerhard" and "The Last Lamentation of the Languishing Squire, or Love Overcomes All Things." Benjamin Franklin informed his brother Peter in a letter that he had met country girls in Massachusetts whose repertoire consisted of "psalm tunes or *Chevy Chase,* the *Children in the Wood,* the *Spanish Lady,* and such old simple ditties."[16]

These "old simple ditties" were often written down, and collections of them were handed down from generation to generation to the present day. Helen Hartness Flanders found many of them still extant when she sought them out during the mid-twentieth century. She entered New England farmhouses to record folk ballads that were orally transmitted and discovered ballad manuscripts put together by ancestors in the late seventeenth and early eighteenth centuries. These were present alongside published material from early times: sermons, orations, histories, Shakespeare's works, *Pilgrim's Progress,* Watts's hymns, and always, the family Bible. One manuscript collection, belonging to the Vermonters Edmund and Joseph Grandey, dated from the eighteenth century and was 1 3 2 pages long. Sea shanties, ancient chronicles, tavern songs, comic turns, tragic ballads—those brought over from England and others created in America—survived on paper and in the memories of descendants. Flanders says that some of the most ancient songs came from lumbermen.[17]

Leaders such as Cotton Mather grew concerned that the singing of sacred music would be neglected. He wrote into his *Diary,* 24 September 1 7 1 3: "I am informed that the Minds and Manners of many People about the Country are much corrupted by foolish Songs and Ballads, which the Hawkers and Pedlers carry into all parts of the Countrey. By way of Antidote, I would procure poetical Composures full of Piety, and such as may have a Tendency to advance Truth and Goodness, to be published and scattered into all Corners of the Land. There may be an extract of some from the excellent Watts's Hymns."[18] He need not have worried. The hymns of John Watts would become very popular by midcentury.

THE SINGING OF PSALMS

The Pilgrims who left Leyden, Holland, and crossed the Atlantic held in common the conviction that salvation could be won only on one's own, through personal deeds, mode of living, and obedience to biblical direction. Like the Puritans, they thought that worship required singing and that singing in the meetinghouse had to be confined to the psalms of the Old Testament. In this belief, they and the Puritans would agree with the Christian reformer John Calvin (1509–64), who also held that singing should be unaccompanied, plain, and exist as a handmaid to worship. Calvin published his first Psalter in Strasburg in 1539. In 1551 the influential Geneva Psalter came out, edited by Louis Bourgeois and containing many tunes he had composed, including the famous "Old One Hundred." The Dutch prepared their own Psalter based on that of Bourgeois, and the Englishman John Day published around 1562 a Psalter translated into English meter by Thomas Sternhold and John Hopkins. This was also modeled after the Geneva Psalter, with many tunes from the continent and some by English composers. Among the psalm tunes used were adaptations from popular and traditional songs, from Catholic hymns, and possibly from dance tunes. Contemporary observers, including Shakespeare, describe the psalms as being sung with dedication and delight, in rhythms related to jigs and hornpipes. Damon's Psalter, issued in 1579 for private use, was harmonized in four parts. Two other harmonized versions came out, meant for private use—East's in 1592 and Alison's in 1599.

Henry Ainsworth (1570–1623), a member of the Leyden exiles from England, published *The Book of Psalms Englished both in Prose and Metre* in 1612 for the congregation's use. Each psalm was set down to be sung in one of several systematically arranged and rhythmically measured verses, its meter determined by the number of lines in a stanza and the number of syllables in a line. All psalms of a certain meter could be sung to any tune designated as fitting that meter. He provided thirty-nine tunes taken from extant French, Dutch, and English Psalters, to which all 150 psalms could be sung. This was the book that the Pilgrims brought to Plymouth in 1620 and from which they sang until 1692. They would abandon the Ainsworth Psalter for the Bay Psalm Book because they found most of its tunes too long and hard to sing. About these men and women who were about to embark aboard ship, Edward Winslow wrote in *Hypocrisie Unmasked:* "They that stayed in Leyden feasted us that were to go to our pastor's house . . .

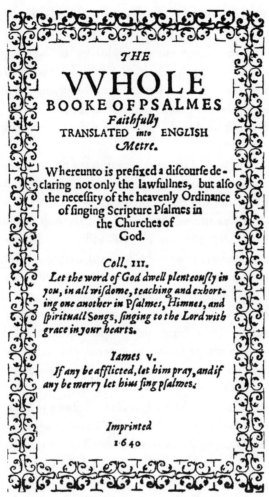

Title page of The Bay Psalm Book (1640).

where we refreshed ourselves, after tears, with singing of Psalms, making joyful melody in our hearts as well as with the voice, there being many of our congregation very expert in music; and indeed it was the sweetest melody that ever mine ears heard."[19] Apparently, by 1692 scarcely an "expert in music" was to be found.

The Puritans, a decade later, arrived with *The Whole Booke of Psalmes* of Sternhold and Hopkins. In all, seventeen meters were used, but most psalms appeared in common meter, also known as ballad meter, with a verse stanza of four lines, in 8-6-8-6 syllables. They also brought a collection of ninety-seven of these psalms in four-part harmony, the tunes harmonized by such important English composers as Dowland, Morley,

Farnaby, Tompkins, and Tallis. Ravenscroft published these as *The Whole Booke of Psalms* in 1621. These harmonized versions were intended not for liturgical use but for enjoyment and uplift in the home. John Playford issued a similar psalter in 1667. Nahum Tate and Nicholas Brady, disliking the crudeness of the verses in Sternhold and Hopkins, translated a new metrical rendering of the psalms and published it as *A New Version of the Psalms of David* (as opposed to the "old version" by Sternhold and Hopkins), in 1696.

The New England Puritans remained uncomfortable with the Sternhold and Hopkins psalter that had arrived with them in 1630. They thought that altogether too many freedoms were taken, so that the meaning of the original was altered. Moreover, the verse in this psalter, as with the Ainsworth Psalter, often lacked skill and grace. Thirty of New England's religious leaders, headed by Richard Mather of Dorchester and Thomas Weld and John Eliot of Roxbury, devoted themselves to providing a more literal English metrical translation of the original Hebrew. They reduced the number of meters to six, included no music, and referred worshipers mainly to the tunes printed in Ravenscroft's psalter. They assumed, too—overoptimistically, as it turns out—that their congregations would continue to remember the psalm tunes learned in England and pass them on from one generation to the next.

Fortunately, a printing press had arrived in 1639 and was installed in Cambridge, owned by Elizabeth Glover but managed by Stephen Day. His son, Matthew Day, probably did the actual printing. A first printing of seventeen hundred copies of the New England psalter was made in 1640. *The Whole Booke of Psalmes Faithfully Translated into English Metre,* better known as the Bay Psalm Book, was the first book printed in the English colonies. It is of considerable importance in itself, since the Puritans along with most of the English settlers in the other American colonies enthusiastically sang these psalms in their homes and churches. It was also important in its musical consequences. The absence of music as well as musical instruction led to the tunes being forgotten; singing schools were set up to remedy this shortcoming, which led to the rise of the first American composers.

On the title page is the admonition, "If any be afflicted, let him pray, and if any be merry let him sing psalms." The preface, attributed to Mather (although a case has been made for John Cotton) calls the singing of David's psalms "a moral duty" and summons all the faithful to sing them.

The reasons given for the publication refer to "the difficulty of Ainsworths tunes, and the corruptions in our common psalm books." Some people might find the versification crude and awkward, but "wee have therefore done our indeavour to make a plaine and familiar translation of the psalmes and words of David into english metre, and have not soe much as presumed to paraphrase to give the sense of his meaning in other words. . . . If therefore the verses are not alwayes so smooth and elegant as some may derive or expect; let them consider that Gods Altar needs not our pollishings."

Despite, or perhaps even owing to, the awkwardness, the psalms are clothed with a simple, austere dignity, as in Psalm 23, which is in common meter:

> The Lord to mee a shepherd is,
>   want therefore shall not I.
> Hee in the folds of tender grasse,
>   doth cause mee downe to lie.
>
> To waters calme he gently leads
>   Restore my soulle doth hee:
> he doth in paths of righteousness
>   for his names sake leade mee.
>
> Yea though in valley of death's shade
>   I walk, none ill I'le feare:
> because thou are with mee, thy rod,
>   and staffe my comfort are.
>
> For me a table thou hast spread,
>   in presence of my foes:
> thou dost annoynt my head with oyle,
>   my cup it over-flowes.
>
> Goodness & mercy surely shall
>   all my dayes follow mee:
> and in the Lords house I shall dwell
>   so long as dayes shall be.

The first settlers clashed over the singing of psalms. Some believed that Christians should sing them not aloud but only in their heart. Others said that sacred songs were appropriate to sing, but not the psalms of

David. Still others felt that only bonafide Christians should be allowed to sing the psalms. John Cotton moved to stop the controversy in 1647 with his sermon *Singing of Psalms a Gospel Ordinance*. He called on all men and women to sing psalms because it was "an holy Duty." He allowed that other spiritual songs from the Scriptures could be sung and that "any private Christian, who hath a gift to frame a Spiritual Song, may both frame it, and sing it privately. . . . Nor doe we forbid the private use of any *Instrument* of Musick therewithal; So that attention to the instrument, doe not divert the heart from attention to the matter of the Song." In the sense that Cotton uses it, the term "Spiritual Song" apparently includes a hymn, that is to say, a song with a text other than that of a biblical psalm. He concludes by stating that a person "with a spiritual gift" can "compose a Psalme upon any speciall occasion" and sing it before the Church for approval of the congregation.[20]

A second edition of the Bay Psalm Book came out that was actually a reprint. In 1651, however, a really fresh third edition was published, produced by Henry Dunster and Richard Lyon. They tried improving the texts and freeing the verse of some of its roughness. In addition, they included thirty-six new "Scripture Songs." No tunes were provided. This was the version of the Bay Psalm Book that achieved widespread acceptance not only in New England but also in the other English colonies and even in England and Scotland. Along with the Bible, it was the most universally owned book in seventeenth-century New England.

Yet many owners of the psalter were soon forgetting or unconsciously giving an individual shape to the original psalm tunes. Some worshipers stopped singing or mumbled their way through the verse. Those who tried to sing the psalms reproduced tunes from faulty memories. Music books were scarce. The skill to learn from those few publications that were available was negligible. The situation called for correction. As an aid to memory, an ordinance issued in 1644 advocated the practice of "lining out," that is to say, having a knowledgeable singer present the lines one at a time and having them repeated by the congregation: "For the present, where many in the congregation cannot read, it is convenient that the minister, or some fit person appointed by him and the other ruling officers, do read the psalm line by line before the singing thereof."[21]

The minister himself or a designated precentor was supposed to set the psalm tune by singing the first line in stentorian fashion, pausing, and letting the congregation duplicate what it had heard. The next line and the next, until the psalm's conclusion, were subjected to this double rendition. Regrettably, as the years went by the leader of the singing might exhibit a deficient memory, stumbling over the tune or starting off with the wrong melody. When the congregation responded line-by-line, different variations on the tune were heard all at the same time. Something further had to be done. As an example of the sort of problem that might arise, there is Samuel Sewall's diary entry for Sunday, 23 February 1718, when he was acting as precentor:

> Mr. Foxcroft preaches. I set York Tune, and the congregation went out of it into St. David's in the very second going over. They did the same 3 weeks before. This is the second sign [he had encountered the same difficulty a few weeks before]. I think they began in the last line of the first going over. This seems to me an intimation and call for me to resign the Precentor's place to a better voice. I have, through the divine Long-suffering and Favour done it for 24 years, and now God by his providence seems to call me off; my voice being enfeebled.[22]

The earliest known edition of the Bay Psalm Book that included tunes was the ninth, of 1698. (An unknown earlier version with music may have existed.) Thirteen psalm-tunes in two parts were printed along with simple directions about learning them. The tunes came from several of the editions of John Playford's *Brief Introduction to the Skill of Music,* which was first published in England in 1654. The edition of 1698 also contained "the ground and rules of musick for song." A "fasola" notation—that is to say, the letters *F, S, L,* and M—was inserted below the music with the hope that these letters would facilitate the learning of the notes, an idea borrowed from Playford's edition of 1672. As will be seen in the next chapter, this still was not enough to correct what the religious leaders saw as a desecration of the psalms of David, and it seemed to them imperative to take additional action before the situation deteriorated even more. That additional action would be the advent of the New England singing school in the 1720s. Until then, people got along as best they could. Alone, the singing was no problem; in concert with others, the singing was less than satisfactory.

In all, the Bay Psalm Book went through more than twenty-five editions in the colonies, seventeen in England, and nine in Scotland. Many of its verses would find their way into the Scottish Psalter of 1650. The last edition of the Bay Psalm Book was published in 1773. According to Irving

Lowens, the eminent scholar of America's musical history, the Bay Psalm Book mirrors a New England people trying to acclimate the forms of expression that had mattered to them in England. At the same time it illustrates the unwitting emergence of an entirely dissimilar society, with different requirements for music. The seeds were planted from which sprouted a "uniquely American music."[23]

CHAPTER 2

SINGING SCHOOLS AND TEACHER-COMPOSERS

Throughout the seventeenth century, the Puritans had packed off the tunes of psalmody to the haphazard transmission of oral tradition. It is true that in 1698 the ninth edition of the Bay Psalm Book had provided a few tunes and given rudimentary instruction in singing from notes, but no organized movement to teach those instructions came into being. Most New Englanders did not know how even to begin to learn their notes on their own. To do it by one's self meant to do it not at all.

Without a musical authority supported by general consent to regulate the singing, any inept, forgetful, or self-indulgent individual could adjust, change, distort, or cut out notes as he or she sang. Fancy, substitution, and error soon were dictating the sounds of worship. No two congregations and frequently no two churchgoers were singing alike. On the one hand, the situation was supportable and enjoyable to a person singing alone or with any other person familiar with his or her individual turns. An attractive musical folk art could well result from such oral transmission. Untrained and anonymous singers of varying degrees of skill, working within culturally unfettered situations, might create artistic works having sturdy shapes expressed in straightforward arrangements. On the other hand, when a hundred or more voices agreed to disagree, the sense of the psalms was obliterated in the resulting confusion. Nobody received the message of the Bible. And this alarmed the religious leaders.

The more rural, older, and lesser-educated classes were inclined to accept the situation. Conservation of things as they are was a part of their outlook. On the other hand, the discord dismayed the better-educated dwellers in towns. They found fault, too, with the lugubrious pace that the singing of psalms was assuming and with the way rustics time and again introduced new notes to bridge the pauses in the singing. They were not prepared to welcome the preliterate in artistic expression, or to defer to conflicting musical procedures. Younger men and women, from adolescents to those in their thirties, in particular, were eager for change and came down on the side of reform. The battles that ensued often shaped themselves as between the young and the old, the urban and the rural.

Religious leaders wished to amend the chaotic church situation by introducing a better course of action, namely, learning to sing together in an orderly manner, ruled by the tunes notated in music books. It was of paramount importance to hear clearly the word of God when sung and to create a worshipful atmosphere of harmony and concordance, rather than of discord and strife.

John Eliot, son of the famous preacher to the Indians, wrote that often, when "people of many congregations meet together, their ways of singing are so different that 'tis not easy to know what tune is sung, and in reality there is none. 'Tis rather jumble and confusion." The Reverend Thomas Symmes, of Bradford, Massachusetts, complained of a chaotic oral, rather than a trustworthy written, tradition, in 1720. He wrote of the complete disagreement, save for the title, of tunes sung in various churches. Everyone, he claimed, sang as he pleased, adding any ornaments one wished. It was sensible, he said, to ask that people learn to sing by note.[1]

Thomas Walter (1696–1725), who was born and died in Roxbury, Massachusetts, was upset over the musical problems that kept on arising during congregational singing. He apparently had known of Symmes's remarks from the year before when he wrote that music was

> miserably tortured, and twisted, and quavered in some Churches into a horrid Medley of confused and disorderly Noises . . . and there are no two Churches that sing alike. . . . Our Tunes are, for Want of a Standard to appeal to in all our Singing, left to the Mercy of every unskillful Throat to chop and alter, twist and change, according to their infinitely divers and no less odd Humours and Fancies. . . . There are no two Churches that sing alike. Yea, I have my self heard (for Instance) *Oxford* Tune sung in *three* Churches . . . with as much Difference as there can possibly be between *York* and *Oxford* or any two other different Tunes. . . . I have observed in many Places one Man is upon this Note, while another is a Note before him, which

provides something so hideous and disorderly, as is beyond Expression bad. . . . no two Men in the Congregation quaver alike, or together; which sounds in the Ears of a good Judge, like *Five Hundred* different Tunes roared out at the same time.[2]

Or, as an attendee at a church in Salem scribbled on a section of his pew:

> Could poor David but for once
> To Salem church repair,
> And hear his Psalmes thus warbled out,
> Good Lord, how he would swear.[3]

Obviously, two widely divergent customs were in conflict. Oral tradition, also called the "Usual Way," meant freedom to sing as one wished, without the tyranny of rules. Those advocating the Usual Way thought their singing was more melodious than what the reformers were trying to force on them. They made nothing of book learning or skill in understanding written music. If only a handful of tunes were imperfectly remembered, the musical pace slowed to a crawl, and a congregation depended on a precentor's forceful voice to line out the tunes (when he could remember them), it bothered no one. Reading music to them was uncalled for and seemed a "popish" act. Names given to notes were blasphemous. "It is a needless way since their good Fathers are gone to heaven without it." Too many hours were given to musical study, and the "young upstarts" so engaged "tarry out a-nights disorderly."[4]

A letter appearing in the *New-England Courant*, 20 March 1722, concerned a controversy in South Braintree between the adherents of singing the Usual Way, and the "Regular Singers," who wanted to "Sing by Rule." It illustrates what was happening in several of the hamlets and villages of New England in the 1720s. An Ephraim Rotewell warns: "The new Singers will bring in *Popery* upon us before we are aware of it. Truly, I have a great jealousy, that if we once begin to sing by *Rule*, the next thing will be to pray by *Rule*, and preach by *Rule*; we must have Common Prayer, Forsooth, and then comes *Popery*." The rival parties tried to overwhelm and render each other inaudible when joining in the psalmody in church, and pandemonium resulted. The Reverend Niles, advocate of the Usual Way, in August 1723 suspended seven or eight of the singers "by Rule." Those dismissed clamored for redress. The next month, a council of churches met to resolve the dispute. It agreed that Niles's act was unlawful. It

instructed the congregation to compromise and sing alternately by rote
and by rule. Strife continued. In December an intransigent Niles and his
followers began to worship at the minister's home. The "Regular Singers,"
led by a deacon, took over the meetinghouse. The *New-England Courant,* in
February 1724, printed a final report on the hullabaloo, saying the opponents to Regular Singing threatened to join the Anglicans, but nothing had
come of it.[5]

It was inevitable that the proponents of the Usual Way of singing
would lose out. As more and more towns formed, as communication with
Europe improved, and as New Englanders acquired greater sophistication,
the folk style was denied the isolation and lack of highly developed musical
knowledge that would allow it to survive handily.

TUFTS AND WALTER

In 1720 Symmes put the case for studying music in brief form after he
asked whether singing schools would not greatly promote the singing of
psalms. He was addressing all New Englanders, because in his time private
devotions continued to be a regular feature in daily living and psalmody a
significant part of congregational worship. Symmes wondered: "Where
would be the *Difficulty,* or what the *Disadvantages,* if People that want *Skill*
in *Singing,* would procure a *Skilful Person* to *Instruct* them, and meet *Two* or
Three Evenings in the Week from *Five* or Six a Clock, to *Eight,* and spend
the Time in learning to Sing?"[6] This was one of the first published pleas for
musical reform based on eliminating the haphazard manner of singing the
psalms by taking musical instruction and learning the tunes from written
notes.

Other writers joined Symmes in advocating correction through education. Cotton Mather, in *The Accomplished Singer* (1721), urged New Englanders to acquire "the Skill of Regular Singing" in order "to Serve God"
better when singing in meetinghouses.[7] The reform movement caught on
in New England and by 1730 had spread as far south as Charleston, South
Carolina. Singing schools began to appear in Philadelphia in 1753, New
York in 1754, and Maryland in 1765.

It remained for the Reverend John Tufts (1689–1750) to provide the
first instruction book in music. He was born in Medford, Massachusetts,
graduated Harvard in 1708, and was serving as pastor at Newbury, Massachusetts, when the volume came out. The *Boston News-Letter,* 2/9 January
1721, announced:

A Small Book containing 20 Psalm Tunes, with Directions how to Sing them, contrived in the most easy Method ever yet Invented, for the ease of Learners, whereby even Children, or People of the meanest Capacities, may come to Sing them by Rule, may serve as an Introduction to a more compleat Treatise of Singing [by Thomas Walter], which will speedily be published. To be sold by Samuel Gerrish, Bookseller; near the Brick Church in Cornhill, Price 6d.[8]

In March of the same year, Sewall wrote in his diary: "At night Dr. Mather preached in the School-House to the young Musicians from Rev. 14.3. 'No man could learn that Song.'—House was full, and the singing extraordinarily Excellent, such as has hardly been heard before in Boston. Sung four times out of Tate and Brady." On the same date, the Reverend Cotton Mather, the uncle of Sewall, wrote in his diary: "In the Evening I preached unto a large Auditory, where a Society of persons learning to Sing began a quarterly solemnity."[9] Learning had truly begun.

The earliest surviving edition of John Tufts's *A Very Plain and Easy Introduction to the Art of Singing Psalm Tunes* is the third, which appeared in 1723. By this edition, the number of psalm tunes had increased to thirty-seven, and they were given two-part settings (the fifth edition, of 1726, had three-part settings). Save for two tunes that may possibly have an American origin, all the music was found to have English antecedents. Eighteen of these tunes proved popular and continued in use into the twentieth century. A letter notation—*f s l m* to stand for *fa sol la mi* and placed on the music staff—attempted to make learning easier. A dot beside a letter signified a longer note. This sort of notation had already appeared about seventy-five years before and had been requisitioned for the ninth edition of the Bay Psalm Book. Apparently, the Tufts book pleased budding singers. By 1744 an eleventh edition had come out to meet the demand.

Walter's more substantial volume, *The Grounds and Rules of Musick Explained,* appeared in May 1721. It begins with concise instruction about singing. The selected English psalm tunes that follow are given as notes, not letters, in three parts. Eight editions would come out by 1764. Walter, the nephew of Cotton Mather and the grandson of Increase Mather, had obtained a Harvard M.A. in 1713 and immediately joined the effort of established religious leaders to get people to sing in some disciplined way. Not surprisingly, his book received the endorsement of several of the most eminent ministers. Most important to observe, teaching music had left the advocacy stage and entered the area of possibility with the Tufts and Wal-

ter books. Where before, learning to sing may have been an on-again-off-
again affair, it now became a regular offering in Boston, and from here a
regular offering in community after community as the movement expanded in an ever widening circle from Boston to New England and to the
rest of the English colonies.

FROM SINGING SCHOOLS TO CHOIRS

The feeling grew that congregational singing could stand improvement
and something needed to be done about it. A church or community might
well decide that musical instruction was desired and hunt up an instructor.
Or the music master himself could make a teaching proposal acceptable to
a church or community. The music teacher himself usually possessed only
a rudimentary knowledge of his subject. His own education had almost
always been limited to what he could glean on his own from music books,
that is to say, from music books that gave simple instructions comprehensible to him. Early on, he might have received the education offered at a
singing school. Complex music remained a mystery. Teaching for him
would always be a work in progress as experience increased his meager
musical knowledge and, in turn, that of his students.

Either a church or the students themselves would promise to reim-
burse the singing master for his services. Notices posted in public places
and printed in newspapers informed the village or town that a singing
school was about to begin. The peripatetic music teacher on a specified
date came on the scene and signed up learners. The novice singers would
then meet in a church or a public building, even in a tavern if it had the
necessary space.

Class lessons began. Students, men and women together, brought
commonplace books to copy music into or purchased a published volume,
usually oblong in format, containing basic singing instructions and a compilation of religious songs (psalms in the early years; hymns, anthems and
"set pieces" later; and at a later date, perhaps some secular pieces). A pitch
pipe gave them the pitch. They practiced vocal harmonization in three or
four parts for a few weeks. At the end they put on a public singing exhibition, sometimes with a sermon from the local minister added. Thus did
they acquire some ability to sing not only sacred music but also any secular
music they desired.

Boston may have had its first singing school as early as 1714. By May
1722 the town boasted a Society for Promoting Regular Singing in the
Worship of God, with almost one hundred members. This society, perhaps

the first of its kind in the English colonies, offered a presage of the Handel and Haydn Society to come a hundred years later. It was, of course, a direct outcome of the singing-school movement. On page 7 of the *New-England Courant* for 14 May 1722 a young reporter, Benjamin Franklin, writes that the society, numbering about one hundred persons, drew participants from the greater Boston area who performed by singing in three parts.[10]

In a letter dated 1 October 1723, Joseph Green wrote from Boston to Stephen Williams of Longmeadow about a singing exhibition: "On Friday last was ye delightful exercise of singing performed att the New Brick Church. . . . Ye singing was managed only by ye masters of it, viz, men and women, seated in the front Gallery on purpose for it; they sang four times, all which were performed with great dexterity and pleasancy."[11] By this date "Singing by Note" had taken the place of the Usual Way of singing in many towns in Massachusetts. Thirty years later town after town in New England was supplying the funding needed to hold singing schools.

The singing school was a singular American institution. In addition to providing instruction, it cheered the everyday activities of young people especially whose lives in other respects were often monotonous. It offered relaxation and enjoyment in a period when recreational alternatives were few. Adolescent boys and girls and unmarried young men and women looked forward to banter, gossip, flirtation, and possibly a little hugging and kissing on their way to and from and during evening classes. As for somewhat older people, town records show that men and women from all walks of life participated—from doctors and lawyers to housewives, carpenters, and tavern keepers. They too enjoyed acquiring some competency in singing and longed to get away from the grayness of everyday existence.[12]

The repertoires of the singing schools, though they started off with psalm tunes, soon went over to including hymns, that is to say, sacred songs whose texts were not biblical psalms. The hymn writer's intent was to convey the emotional meaning in God's message. Because lining out went on at a tiresome, painfully slow pace and was thought to detract from true worship, it was discouraged. Before the century's end, as choirs formed, it would disappear altogether. Unquestionably the most favored author of hymns in America was the Reverend Dr. Isaac Watts of England, an admired letter-acquaintance of Cotton Mather. Watts published *Hymns and Spiritual Songs* in 1707, *Divine Song* in 1715, and *The Psalms of David Imitated* in 1719. His hymns and psalm paraphrases struck contemporary Americans as lucid, emotionally communicative, and smoothly versified. "When I Survey the Wondrous Cross," "O God, Our Help in Ages Past," "Joy to the World," and "There Is a Land of Pure Delight" are four of them:

> There is a land of pure delight,
> Where saints immortal reign;
> Eternal day excludes the night,
> And pleasures banish pain.

Contributing to the changeover from psalms alone to the inclusion of hymns was the Great Awakening, a revivalist, evangelical movement that commenced in the mid-1720s and lasted through the 1740s. It began with the sermonizing of Jonathan Edwards (1703–58), a minister in Northampton, Massachusetts, and would spread into all of the colonies. Edwards had grown up in an inflexible Puritan environment, fed on a diet of exacting and doom-haunted Calvinism, and received an acute awareness of duty to God. Around 1725 he began to preach the need for the direct, personal experience of salvation to escape eternal damnation. Around 1734 he was advocating a change of attitude from one of relative indifference about religious matters to one of committed faith and wholehearted support of Christian principles. His preaching was filled with fiery warnings, such as "If God should let you go, you would immediately sink, and sinfully descend and plunge into the bottomless gulf. . . . The God that holds you over the pit of hell, much as one holds a spider or some loathsome insect over the fire, abhors you, and is dreadfully provoked. . . . He looks upon you as worthy of nothing else but to be cast into the bottomless gulf."[13] Listeners panicked. Hysterical fits of weeping seized terrified sinners. Men and women were urged to approach closer to divinity by the fervent singing of hymns.

Jonathan Edwards soon received help in his mission from George Whitefield, who had come from England. Whitefield traveled and preached eloquently about the need for God's mercy throughout the settled English territories. He also pressed people to adopt the Watts hymns. Since New Englanders, like most inhabitants of the other colonies, wanted to quit religion concerned with external appearances for that of the spirit and to achieve salvation, the preaching of Edwards and Whitefield swept through congregation after congregation, as did hymn singing. By mid-century, however, the Great Awakening had spent its force in New England, as the harshness of its underlying themes grew unacceptable to the next generation. Not so the hymns; they would live on.

During the years of the Great Awakening and after, the formation of singing societies, growing out of the singing schools, had taken place. The appearance of one in Boston has already received mention. Late in the century, societies would be active everywhere: the St. Cecilia Society of Newport; the Essex Music Association of Massachusetts, in Essex County; the Concord Musical Society; and later, the Beethoven Society of Portland, the Psallion Society of Providence, and the Massachusetts Musical Society of Boston.

The products of the schools or members of a society took to appearing as a group during church services and singing in accord with the music they had newly learned. At times they proved disruptive. They contended with and exerted themselves to overwhelm and render inaudible the advocates of the Usual Way. Some churches then allowed the first row in front of the pulpit or the first seats in the gallery to be reserved for the best singers. By 1770 a few of these singing groups had installed themselves as permanent choirs, leading the congregation in the newer music or performing on their own.

To give an example of the changeover, the parish of Rowley, Massachusetts, voted in 1762 "that those who had learned the art of singing may have liberty to sit in the front gallery." These singers stubbornly refused to support lining out. In 1785 the parish tried to defuse matters by voting to permit "the singers, both male and female, to sing in the gallery, and will allow them to sing once upon each Lord's day without reading by the Deacon." Five years later, lining out had ceased completely in the Rowley meetinghouse, and the choir dominated all the singing.

In Worcester, Massachusetts, a few parishioners had attempted to form a choir in 1773, but not until 1779 did the town vote to seat the proficient singers, most of them young, up front and stop the practice of lining out. The elderly Deacon Chamberlin persevered in the customary ways, however, abetted by some older people. Nevertheless, the young singers refused to pay attention to him or come in after his lead. Instead, they vanquished him by singing very loudly, without stopping at all. "The deacon, deeply mortified at the triumph of musical reformation, seized his hat, and retired from the meeting-house in tears."[14]

WILLIAM BILLINGS OF BOSTON

Talented painters, as fine and sophisticated as any that England had to offer, did appear in eighteenth-century New England—John Singleton

Copley, born in Boston, Gilbert Stuart, born in Rhode Island, and John Trumball, born in Connecticut. Charles Bulfinch, born in Boston, was an outstanding architect who merited his national fame. In the first half of the next century extraordinary New England writers would be active whose influence would be far reaching—Emerson, Hawthorne, Thoreau, and Melville. It took a long while for equivalent artists in music to appear. Sources of support and situations favorable for composers to emerge would slowly develop only over many decades. For composers to appear, they needed instruction beyond simple singing directions. Knowledge of musical theory and composition was essential, however elementary. In addition, budding composers found helpful the study of recent compositions, provided the music was easy to analyze and adaptable to suit American requirements.

England by midcentury had produced several composers able to satisfy the uncomplicated tastes of men and women living outside the more cosmopolitan and cultivated larger cities—William Tans'ur, Aaron Williams, William Knapp, Joseph Stephenson, and John Arnold, to name five. They composed unfussy vocal pieces whose parts moved more or less in lockstep. They also produced a newer kind of vocal music, with greater rhythmic variety, varying changes in the number of voices heard, occasional strings of notes in a melody sung on one syllable, and brief repetitions of a melodic phrase at different pitches or in different voice parts.[15] Their publications appeared in Great Britain and found their way to America.

John Lyon, born in New Jersey, had put out his *Urania* collection of selected British compositions in Philadelphia in 1761. *Urania* was an American musical milestone. Longer than any previous music book, it provided specimens of the new British styles, harmonized mostly in four parts, and even included one or two compositions by Lyon and Francis Hopkinson, a signer of the Declaration of Independence. Lyon provided compositional examples that could serve as models for the New England composers to come. One was the straightforward setting of a hymn or metric psalm: each voice moved in conjunction with the other voices as they followed the meter of the verse, and the melody was in the tenor. Alternatively, the text could be structured as a "fuging tune," in which a stanza of text was set to two musical sections: the first section went along with voices mostly together, and the second section opened with successive entries, normally starting in the bass and followed one by one in the upper parts, resulting in a polyphonic texture that continued briefly until all came together again to close the piece. The second section was then typically repeated. Still another type of composition was the anthem, a longer work comprising several sections, with frequent contrasts of tempo, meter, or texture. The composer selected his prose text from any part of the Bible or from nonbiblical prayers. Later, New England composers would take considerable liberties with the words to anthems, sometimes setting texts of a political nature. They also would turn to writing canons, works where voices entered one by one at fixed intervals, all on the same tune. Some compositions they called "set pieces," which were through-composed (without repetition) and, unlike anthems, had poetic texts. Among these set pieces were a few secular works. *Urania* contained ninety-six pieces in all, seventy of them psalm settings.

Urania had an influence on New England compilers of music, as they put together their own anthologies. Josiah Flagg published a *Collection of the Best Psalm Tunes in Two, Three and Four Parts,* engraved by Paul Revere in Boston in 1764, including many recent English tunes, though the composers are not named. Two years later, Flagg issued *Sixteen Anthems* by British composers. Just before the end of the decade, the *Universal Psalmodist* came out in Newburyport, a reprint of a book published by Aaron Williams in London in 1763. Musicians carefully scrutinized all of these works. However, the most influential music book in New England was *Tans'ur's Royal Melody Compleat,* published in Boston in 1767. Tans'ur became the accepted source of musical information for many of the early composers.

At last, in the fall of 1770 a most significant event in the musical life of America took place, the publication in Boston of William Billings's *The New-England Psalm-Singer,* with a frontispiece engraved by Paul Revere. This illustration shows seven men seated around a table. They are completely encircled by a music staff on which is inscribed "a canon of 6 in One with a ground, the words by Rev. Dr. Byles. Set to Music by Mr. Billings." With this one publication, the American musician had changed over from mere compiler of music to supplier of original compositions for singing schools and music societies. Of great significance, a single composer had added 126 original vocal compositions, mostly in four and some in five parts, to the dozen or so American pieces of music known to exist. A majority of these were brief psalm and hymn compositions. Four were anthems, three canons, and one a set piece. Billings tried out a variety of musical treatments, from the fixed movement of all voices together in

Frontispiece for William Billings's New-England Psalm-Singer.
Engraving by Paul Revere, 1770.

utter simplicity to voice parts moving in rather complex contrapuntal lines. Apparently he had been composing his pieces for several years, only now gathering them for publication.

The music is not uniform in quality. Notes sometimes awkwardly fit the words. Clumsy clashes occasionally occur in the harmony. While some pieces, such as "Chester" and "Brookfield," have excellent music, other pieces prove dull to the listener. Later Billings would admit to having made mistakes owing to inexperience. Yet, with this music book, the pattern was established for the scores of music books that would come out during the remainder of the century. Billings is a true democrat when he advises in his introduction "To all Musical Practitioners" that "Nature is the best Dictator. . . . I don't think myself confined to any Rules for Composition laid down by any that went before me, neither should I think (were I to pretend to lay down rules) that any who come after me were any ways obligated to adhere to them, any further than they should think proper. . . . Every Composer [is] to be his own Carver [of rules]."

William Billings (1746–1800) was born in Boston and seems to have grown up with little education. In 1760 he became an apprentice to a tanner, an occupation with which he continued during adulthood. At some point in his youth, he must have attended one or more of the Boston singing schools and certainly was acquainted with the music books available in Boston. He began as a singing master in and around Boston while in his early twenties, married at age twenty-eight, and had numerous children. Four churches in Boston provided spaces for his singing schools. He also traveled to other towns of New England to direct singing schools.

One of them, conducted in Stoughton, Massachusetts, in 1774, was the forerunner of the Stoughton Musical Society, set up in 1786 and still in existence. Interestingly, around 1790 a singing contest, possibly the first in America, was held when the singers of the First Parish of Dorchester grew irritated at the rising reputation of the Stoughton Musical Society and dared it to engage in a test of skill. The contest took place in a spacious hall in Dorchester, to which Bostonians came in large numbers to witness the affair. Each group sang anthems grandly and sonorously, but when Stoughton broke out in Handel's "Hallelujah Chorus" without the benefit of scores, Dorchester conceded defeat.[16]

For a while, Billings earned a good income, one that allowed him to purchase a house on Newbury Street for his family. He was also a patriot committed to independence from England and a friend of Samuel Adams. After the 1780s he ran into financial difficulties. He and his family began to live just above, and on occasion below, the poverty level. At one time or another he worked as a hogreeve, a minor city worker whose duty was impounding stray hogs. In 1790 friends found him in dire financial straits. They got up a concert for his benefit in Boston but to no avail. Shortly after the concert, Billings was hocking everything he owned to pay his debts. Billings died penniless and was buried in an unmarked grave in a corner of the Boston Common.

A contemporary described Billings as "a singular man, of moderate size, short of one leg, with one eye, without any address, & with an uncommon negligence of person. Still he spake & sung & thought as a man above the common abilities. He died poor & neglected & perhaps did too much neglect himself."[17]

One of his earliest singing schools was cited in a notice printed in the *Boston Gazette,* 2 October 1769: "John Barrey & William Billings Begs Leave to inform the Publick, that they propose to open a Singing School THIS NIGHT, near the Old South Meeting-House, where any person inclined to learn to Sing may be attended upon at said School with Fidelity and Dispatch."[18] He is known to have used a pitch pipe to launch the singing and may also at times have accompanied the vocalists with a violoncello.

His second book, *The Singing-Master's Assistant,* published in 1778, exhibits an extraordinary richness of content. Billings confesses that he has learned from experience, which he claims is the best teacher and far preferable to a person's being subjected to someone else's rules. The music book was highly popular after it came out, and other native composers freely borrowed from it. Fifty-one of the seventy-one compositions turn up in subsequent anthologies. One was the poignant "David's Lamentation." Another was the defiant "Chester," whose widespread popularity made it the national hymn of Americans during the Revolutionary War.

> Let tyrants shake their iron rod
> And slav'ry Clank her galling Chains,
> We fear them not, we trust in god,
> New englands god for ever reigns.

The reference to New England's God is interesting. Around 1763 Thomas Secker, Archbishop of Canterbury, had endorsed the appointing of bishops for America. The Congregationalists of New England and the Presbyterians to the south grew furious and denounced the suggestion, while the colonial Anglicans backed the archbishop. The radical but astute leader Samuel Adams, close friend of Billings, immediately took advantage of this example of English tyranny and kept the public constantly in a state of uproar over the threat to its freedom. Out of a background such as this came the words of "Chester."

A third piece in *The Singing-Master's Assistant* is "Lamentation over Boston," a patriotic anthem paraphrasing Psalm 137. The reference is to the British occupation of Boston during 1775–76:

> By the Rivers of Watertown, we sat down & wept when we remembr'd thee O Boston.
>   As for our Friends, Lord God of Heaven, preserve them, defend them, deliver and restore them unto us again.

A highly unusual "Jargon" answers his critics, who accused him of writing only consonant chords. He includes an address "To the Goddess of Discord," saying "some evil-minded persons have insinuated . . . that I am utterly unmindful of your Ladyship's importance." He then instructs the bass to bray like an ass, the tenor to sound like the filing of a saw, and the upper voices to produce sounds like a squeaking hog and an ungreased cartwheel. The music that follows contains endless dissonances in chord after chord, as he deliberately ignores conventional musical procedures and forces tones to collide with each other without preparation and resolution. Indeed, it might be mistaken for a twentieth-century neoclassical piece. The address, the admonitions to the singers, and the extraordinary impact of the music demonstrate his striking personality, his sense of humor, and his feistiness when attacked by censurers.

By 1778 it was clear from his two music books that Billings's religious beliefs were firmly held. They were in accord with those of most New Englanders and unhesitatingly stated in lucid, unequivocal terms. His allegiance to the cause of freedom is candid, unhedged, and militant. He stood up for Boston first, New England second, and all America third, as it fought to bring a new nation into being. He was obviously working with the musical materials he had on hand—untrained voices expected to sing without or with negligible instrumental support. He not only respected his musical compatriots' limitations but also owned to his own when it came to composing a "correct" musical composition. However, no authority on earth could bend him to its will—only practical wisdom gained from what he had observed and heard would guide him.

Four more of his books would come out in Boston: *Music in Miniature* (1779), *The Psalm-Singer's Amusement* (1781), *The Suffolk Harmony* (1786), and *The Continental Harmony* (1794). Publishing the last volume was not easy for Billings. In August 1792 the *Massachusetts Magazine* printed a public announcement stating that a large committee, representing several local musical societies, had formed to publish a volume of Billings's music, containing "Anthems, Fuges, and Psalm Tunes." Furthermore, "the distressed situation of Mr. Billings' family has so sensibly operated on the minds of the committee as to induce their assistance in the intended publication."[19]

The second and last of his publications contains longer, more complex works intended for knowledgeable choirs and singing societies. In none of the pieces is originality sought. Nevertheless, the sound is a counterpart of the rocky soil and questing spirit that typified many of his contemporary New Englanders. Billings's music held the attention of music lovers for its melodic expression, effortless vitality, and suitability to the requirements and limitations of amateur singers. No matter what the vocal part, it is not hard to sing and enjoy. All singers are given interesting lines to engage their attention. If some of the notes in a part do not please, the composer occasionally offers the singer "choosing notes" from which he or she can select.

The tunes are sturdy, reflecting the mental vigor of the composer. The titles of the psalm and hymn tunes are the names of New England towns and Boston streets. The vocal harmony sounds with a deep, resonant sonority that easily fills the enclosed space of a meetinghouse. The musical language of a much earlier era may be heard—the lowered seventh tone, some gaps in the scale, antiquated ways of moving to points of rest in phrases and strains, and piquant collisions (such as the same note simultaneously marked with a sharp and a natural). The listener hears tones moving in parallel fifths and octaves, and chords with the third omitted. Billings will not spoil a line for the sake of a correct harmonic progression.

His predilection for fuging tunes is aired in the "Commentary" that prefaces the music to *The Continental Harmony*. With inflections that sound as if the Revolutionary War was being fought in music, he says:

> It is . . . well known that there is more variety in one piece of fuging music than in twenty pieces of plain song, for while the tones do most sweetly coincide and agree, the words are seemingly engaged in a musical warfare; and . . . each part seems determined by dint of harmony and strength of accent, to drown his competitor in an ocean of harmony, and while each part is thus mutually striving for mastery, and sweetly contending for victory, the audience are most luxuriously entertained, and exceedingly delighted; in the mean time, their minds are surprisingly agitated, and extremely fluctuated; sometimes declaring in favour of one part, and sometimes another.—Now the solem bass demands their attention, now the manly tenor, now the lofty counter, now the volatile treble, now here, now there, now here again.—O inchanting! O ecstatic! Push on, push on ye sons of harmony and
>
> > Discharge your deep mouth'd canon, full fraught with Diapasons;
> > May you with Maestoso, rush on to Choro-Grando,
> > And there with Vigoroso, let fly your Diapentes
> > About our nervous system.[20]

A few pages after, he explains again his attitude toward musical rules:

> Musical composition is a sort of something, which is much better felt than described, (at least by me) for if I was to attempt it, I should not

know where to begin or where to leave off; therefore considering myself so unable to perform it, I shall not undertake the talk; but in answer to your question; although I am not confined to rules prescribed by others, yet I come as near as I possibly can to a set of rules which I have carved out for myself; but when fancy gets upon the wing, she seems to despise all form, and scorns to be confined or limited by any formal prescriptions whatsoever.[21]

He composed almost 350 works for chorus in four parts, most of them brief and all without instrumental accompaniment. Fifty-one pieces are fuging tunes; fifty-two are anthems or set pieces.

"Chester" was the first of his compositions known throughout America. The Continental Army marched to its strains. In the mid-1780s other works were heard outside New England. Andrew Adgate gave a concert in Philadelphia in 1788 where Billings's anthem "I Am the Rose of Sharon," from *The Singing-Master's Assistant,* was performed. It quickly became a local favorite, with one writer naming him "the rival of Handel." During the same year, Marietta, Ohio, was listening to his music. And in 1789 an English psalmodist, Thomas Williams, published in London a music book, *Psalmodia Evangelica,* that included Billings's "Marshfield" (from *The New-England Psalm-Singer*) and "New England" (the "Hartford" of *The Psalm–Singer's Amusement*).[22] A few years later, "Consolation" (from *The Singing-Master's Assistant*) came out in London.

Billings's music and commentaries about music would serve as beacons to the singing masters who became composers in the late eighteenth century and first decade of the nineteenth century.

OTHER EARLY NEW ENGLAND COMPOSERS

Almost thirty writers or compilers of psalmody came after Billings in New England. Among them were several highly regarded composers who followed the Billings model. The compositions in their music books, too, were designed primarily for singing schools and musical societies, although this did not preclude their use during a church service or for concert performance. We should keep in mind that during the latter part of the eighteenth century sacred music of this sort was popular with many in the general public, as well as esteemed and closely followed by leaders who counted—a genuine people's music. Around three hundred of their music collections, all in oblong volumes, would be offered for sale to the public by 1810.

Most of these musicians were born in Massachusetts. Their ancestry was Puritan; their educations were limited; their professions were humble. Their names alone smack of the New England soil. Among the best known were Justin Morgan (1747–98), Andrew Law (1749–1821), Supply Belcher (1752–1836), Jacob French (1754–1817), Daniel Read (1757–1836), Timothy Swan (1758–1842), Samuel Holyoke (1762–1820), Jeremiah Ingalls (1764–1838), Oliver Holden (1765–1844), Daniel Belknap (1771–1815), and Stephen Jenks (1772–1856). They all held singing schools and wrote and published music for chorus. Several of them would travel great distances for those times, extending the singing-school movement and disseminating its music throughout the United States. Morgan, for instance, born in West Springfield, Massachusetts, was a breeder of horses (the Morgan horse) who traveled to Pennsylvania around 1788 to hold singing schools and ended his years in Vermont.

Law, born in Milford, Connecticut, took a degree from Rhode Island College (now Brown University) and was a minister who traveled as far south as Alexandria, Virginia, and Charleston, South Carolina. For ten years he exerted himself in Philadelphia. Whatever else he may have been, he proved himself a resourceful and ambitious seller of his publications. He placed his music books in the bookstores of several of the larger towns in the New England states, then beyond New England, in New York, Philadelphia, Baltimore, and Charleston. In 1793 he devised a staffless shape notation, which he patented in 1802. *Fa* was a square-shaped note; *sol,* round-shaped; *la,* triangular; and *mi,* diamond-shaped. His attempt to advance his system through the publication of his *Art of Singing* (1803) was a failure: without placement on a staff, the notation left singers insecure.[23]

Belcher, born in Stoughton, Massachusetts, was a farmer and tavern keeper. He may have attended a singing school conducted by Billings. He moved to Farmington, Maine, in 1785. Here he held singing schools, directed choirs, taught school, worked for the town, and was elected member of the state legislature. He put out one ambitious anthology, *The Harmony of Maine* (1794), and was dubbed the "Handel of Maine" by a local critic.

French, a farmer, was also born in Stoughton and might also have studied under Billings. He would move to Medway, then Oxbridge, both in Massachusetts, and finally to Simsbury, Connecticut, two years before he died.

Read was born in Attleboro, Massachusetts, but moved to New Haven in 1782, where he managed a general store. He may also have learned his music under Billings. His *American Singing Book* (1785) was, after Billings, the first to consist entirely of music by one composer. "Sherburne," "Cavalry," "Stafford," "Windham," and "Greenwich" won a solid following in his day. Read was an astute salesman who attempted to sell his music in all parts of the country. A letter to Richard Atwell, 22 January 1793, reads:

> In short it is my wish that the American Singing Book, Columbian Harmonist, Child's Instructor be left with suitable persons in all the Capital Towns throughout the United States and that the friendship of the Teachers of music in every part be obtained as far as is possible. . . . It is not my idea to enter into the execution of this Business for the sale of a few dozens or a few Hundreds of Books only; but I have no doubt but we may extend it to thousands and perhaps to tens of thousands within a year or two.

On 12 March 1793 he wrote to his brother William:

> I expect that Richard Atwell will be at Attleborough in May or June and I think it probable he will go to the Southward towards fall with Books to teach music. By information I have had from the Southern States a young man capable of teaching music may do exceeding well that way. One Ives who studied music with me 18 months ago and has gone to Virginia has I have been informed cleared by one School only, 300 dollars in Six months.[24]

Swan, born in Worcester, Massachusetts, was a hatter and small merchant. He left for Suffield, Connecticut, around 1789, and then went to Northfield, Massachusetts, in 1807. He was perhaps the most melodically gifted of all the composers. Especially favored by the public was his "China," which became the preferred hymn for New England funerals during the nineteenth century. Well received also were his fuging tunes "Montague," "Bristol," and "Rainbow."

Holyoke, born in Boxford, Massachusetts, would die in East Concord, New Hampshire, after publishing 650 pieces and leaving another 200 in manuscript. He graduated from Harvard and was a schoolmaster.

Ingalls, born in Andover, Massachusetts, moved to Vermont around 1791, where he lived as a tavern keeper and farmer. Somehow and somewhere he had acquired the ability to play the bass viol. Certainly he knew the folk tunes prevalent in New England, for he borrowed some of them for his own compositions.

Holden, born in Shirley, would die in Charlestown—both in Massachusetts. At various times he was a farmer, carpenter, minister, and member of the state legislature. His "Coronation" continues to be sung.

Belknap, a farmer and mechanic, was born in Framingham, Massachusetts, though he died in Pawtucket, Rhode Island, to which town he had moved in 1812.

Jenks, another farmer, was born in Gloucester, Rhode Island, and moved to Ohio in 1829, where he continued farming, as well as teaching and writing music (including many fuging tunes).

The heyday of the New England singing-school movement and the music publications of the artisan-composers lasted from 1770 to the early 1790s. It began to wane in the mid-1790s and was over by 1810, as contemporary European influences seeped into American thinking. The American compositions were found to be primitive in conception and execution. Fuging tunes, in particular, came into disrepute. Law, as early as 1793, was calling for American composers to take their lead from the latest European composers. Oliver Holden, when old, apologized for his earlier musical indiscretions and advised American musicians to look to contemporary European rules for writing music and learn a correct "musical science." Daniel Read composed little music after the mid-1790s and also began to look toward Europe for musical enlightenment. Read, Holden, and Hans Gram, a Danish emigrant to Boston, would bring out *The Massachusetts Compiler of Theoretical Principles* in 1795. It was completely oriented toward Europe and contained musical examples of the "correct" and "scientific" manner of composing. Other like publications followed.

The new call for conforming to a correct, up-to-date musical science, which would occupy American reformers in the first half of the nineteenth century, has similarities to the proselytizing for singing by rule that engaged the energy of reformers in the 1720s. First the urban centers, then the smaller towns and villages, especially in the Northeast, would spurn the native musical growth and turn to transatlantic sources for its new music.

For a long while, however, the music of the first native school of composers would persist in country places. The music of the first New England composers would go southward and out to the western fringe of America's settled areas. Fuging tunes, hymns, and anthems would join sacred folk ditties, revival and gospel hymns, popular tunes refitted with devotional words, and other spiritual pieces in the throats of thousands of plain folks. With the transmission would go the notion of shape notes, especially via the notational scheme contained in William Smith and William Little's *Easy Instructor* (Albany, 1801). This New England music would also continue into the twentieth century, kept alive through the singing books and singing of southern and western shape-noters. In recent years, the musical literature of eighteenth-century New England has been revived and has won new appreciation. American music historians are studying the music and the composers who wrote it. Vocal ensembles are scheduling pieces by Billings and his colleagues for concert performance and church services.

CHAPTER 3

THE ROAD INTO THE
MUSICAL FUTURE

Although Puritanism weakened during the eighteenth century, the life of the mind and respect for learning remained embedded in New England thinking. When musical change took place, those carrying out the change were usually people who had thought hard about the desired transformation, had some knowledge about how to go about the switching of musical practices, and had the respect of the public. That was true for the psalms sung by rote, then by note; for the addition of hymn texts to psalms; for the rise of singing schools; and for the swing toward newly composed music written by the local composers who conducted the schools.

In the eighteenth century the means of maintaining life in New England grew easier, and the area took on a settled look. Discretionary income rose, and the demand for luxury goods, including music books and instruments, increased. Ships had grown larger, and the importing of nonessential products, including musical items, was now possible. Around 1720 merchants took to building mansions for themselves, equipped with sash windows and, oftentimes, Franklin stoves. New Englanders were less set in their religious ways and took greater interest in more worldly pastimes. No longer narrowly confined to isolated communities and things spiritual, men and women began to look outward from their neighborhoods and turned less suspiciously to secular entertainment. Songsters, containing verses only, and songbooks, containing both verses and the melodic line, came into demand. Local booksellers imported them in growing numbers for use in the home. They featured the secular songs of British theaters, pleasure gardens, and whatever was proving popular in London at the time of publication. Before the Revolutionary War, twenty-six songsters were published in America, six of them in Massachusetts. By 1800 publishers in

Massachusetts had issued forty-eight songsters. Of these, nineteen were for juveniles, eight involved the Masonic order, fifteen aired a wide range of subjects, and one concentrated on patriotic subjects.[1]

One of the most celebrated songsters was aimed at juveniles: *Mother Goose's Melody, or Sonnets for the Cradle.* Isaiah Thomas published it in Worcester, Massachusetts, in 1785. The volume is divided into two parts: "Part 1st. contains the most celebrated songs and lullabies of the old British nurses, calculated to amuse children and to excite them to sleep. Part 2d, those of that sweet songster and nurse of wit and humour, Master William Shakespeare." The book won fame throughout America. Thomas printed a second edition in 1794 and a third edition in 1799. Other editions have kept on coming out to the present day.

American publishers printed scarcely any songbooks in the eighteenth century, although a flood of them would come out in the next century. Without question, the most significant of those few published is the three-hundred-page *American Musical Miscellany,* "a collection of the newest and most approved songs, set to music." The volume was "printed at Northampton, Massachusetts, by Andrew Wright, for Daniel Wright and Company," in 1798. Most of the songs are traditional or recently composed English, Irish, and Scottish pieces, with verse and the melodic line given. Sentimental subjects, mainly centered on love, are to the fore. Some compositions, all of American origin (at least in their verse), are patriotic in nature. Occasionally, a bass part is added to the melody. The editors are not named, although I suspect that Hans Gram, the Danish émigré to Massachusetts, and Samuel Holyoke, a singing-school composer whose face was now turned toward contemporary Europe, had a hand in its compilation, since both are represented by pieces. A most intriguing number, as much political as patriotic, is "Adams and Liberty," the words by "T. Paine."[2] The tune is that of the British "To Anacreon in Heaven," which later would be applied to the equally political "Jefferson and Liberty" and to "The Star-Spangled Banner."

> Ye sons of Columbia, who bravely have fought,
> For those rights, which unstain'd from your Sires had Desended,
> May you long taste the blessings your valour has bought,
> And your sons reap the soil, which your fathers defended,
> > Mid the reign of mild piece,
> > May your nation increase,
> With the glory of Rome, and the wisdom of Greece.

(Refrain)
And ne'er may the sons of Columbia be slaves,
While the earth bears a plant, or the sea rolls its waves.[3]

A few songs already show the aversion to slavery growing in New England: "The Desponding Negro" and "I Sold a Guiltless Negro Boy."

> When thirst of gold enslaves the mind,
> And selfish views alone bear sway,
> Man turns a savage to his kind,
> And blood and rapine mark his way,
> Alas, for this poor simple toy
> I sold a guiltless Negro Boy.[4]

We know that an excellent vocalist, Mrs. Graupner, sang "I Sold a Guiltless Negro Boy" before a Boston audience in December 1799. What is of greater interest, Lawrence Hutton in an 1899 New York newspaper essay quotes Charles White, an old minstrel man, as saying that Gottlieb Graupner, the husband of Mrs. Graupner, appeared in the character of a black man at Boston's Federal Street Theater. Accompanying himself on a banjo, he performed "The Gay Negro Boy" at the close of the second act of *Oroonoko* on 30 December 1799. If this is true, it was a foreshadowing of the minstrel performances that would come thirty or forty years later. We know that Graupner had stayed in Charleston for a while. He may have learned about the banjo then.

The increasing attention to things of this world is also demonstrated by the upsurge of dancing and dancing lessons. Smelling profit to be made, European, especially French, dancing teachers were immigrating to America. Recently arrived English musicians augmented their incomes by opening dancing schools. By the 1720s Increase Mather was giving up the fight to limit dancing. Already in 1716 the *Boston News-Letter* had carried an unequivocal notice about "Enstone's Dancing School." When one June the headmaster of Boston Latin School addressed the parents of a graduating class, he complained bitterly of how much money went so freely for children's dancing lessons and how little for school and church support. Aware that the "People of Quality" were employing dancing masters to instruct their children, Mather wondered if "the Dancing Humour, as it now prevails, and especially in *Balls*" may lead to temptations like vanity and young people "of both Seces" taking "great Liberties with one another."[5]

Large formal parties featuring social dancing, sometimes given to benefit a charitable organization, were cautiously introduced at the beginning of the century and became more lavish as the decades went by. Dr. Alexander Hamilton of Annapolis supplied an interesting account of Boston's musical life in 1744. He had just come away from New York, which he found to contain too much bawdiness and too little wit:

> There is more hospitality and frankness showed here to strangers than either att New York or at Philadelphia. And in the place there is abundance of men of learning and parts; so that one is att no loss for agreeable conversation nor for any sett of company he pleases. Assemblys of the gayer sort are frequent here; the gentlemen and ladys meeting almost every week att consorts of musick and balls. I was present att two or three such and saw as fine a ring of ladys as good dancing, and heard musick as elegant as I had been witness to anywhere. I must take notice that this place abounds with pritty women who appear rather more abroad than they do att York and dress elegantly. They are, for the most part, free and affable as well as pritty. I saw not one prude while I was there.[6]

The enthusiasm for dancing seen in Boston extended to all of New England's towns. For example, Sir John Wentworth, governor of New Hampshire from 1767 to 1775, loved music and around 1770 completed "a great dancing room" in his mansion devoted to balls and to the mounting of musicals. In 1769 he had written to relatives in England requesting servants who could play the French horn and violin.[7] Newspaper notices increased that sought violinists to play for dances, as in the following item, in the *Newport Mercury,* 19 December 1758: "Any person who plays well on a VIOLIN, on Application to the Printed hereof may be inform'd where he will meet with proper Encouragement."[8]

Whether in Portsmouth, New Hampshire, or New Haven, Connecticut, or Newport, Rhode Island, well-to-do merchants wished their children to take on the sheen of refinement and modishness through dancing lessons. Town newspapers contained announcements of dancing schools throughout the century. Typical was one appearing in the *Newport Mercury* on 24 January 1774: "*William Selby* (organist of Trinity Church) informs the ladies and gentlemen that he purposes opening a Dancing School for teaching young ladies and gentlemen. N. B. Teaching days on Mondays and Thursdays at 4 o'clock P.M."[9]

Puritanism that demanded strictness in religious discipline and care in moral matters was no longer as powerful a voice in New England. The door had opened to a musical future that John Cotton and John Winthrop had never contemplated.

FRESH BEGINNINGS: ORGANS AND ORGANISTS

On 29 May 1711 the Reverend Joseph Green noted in his diary: "I was at Mr. Thomas Brattle's; heard ye organs and saw strange things in a microscope." Thomas Brattle, of Cambridge, had returned from a visit to England in 1689 and in all probability brought an organ back with him. Organs were excluded from churches because Puritans desired simplicity in worship and nothing that would confuse their worship with that of Catholics. This did not mean that organs were rejected for private use. Brattle's organ in his home stirred up curiosity but no censure. Brattle was forward thinking for his time—witness his opposition to the witch trials—and was fascinated by the world around him, whether as sound from an organ pipe or as magnified sight through a microscope. He died in 1713 and left his organ to the Brattle Square Church. The church refused the donation, but Brattle's act loosened eighteenth-century inhibitions on instrumental use and inaugurated an ongoing controversy on the part instruments should play in worship. The organ went instead to King's Chapel (also called Queen's Chapel and the Stone Church), in Boston. King's Chapel's Anglican congregation had no problem in accepting the gift. In 1756 King's Chapel installed another organ and sold Brattle's instrument to St. Paul's Church in Newburyport, Massachusetts. Eighty years later, the organ was at St. John's, in Portsmouth, New Hampshire. This was not the first organ to be used in an American church; that honor goes to an organ belonging to a small German religious colony near Philadelphia. It lent its organ in 1703 for use at a Lutheran ordination observance in the Swedish Church of Philadelphia.

Most meetinghouses did not have enough money to purchase organs anyway, and when any instrument did enter a church to assist the singers, it was at first usually the "church bass" or "God's fiddle," in size between today's cello and string bass. Other instruments might also cross the meetinghouse's threshold, depending on availability—a flute, bassoon, clarinet, or trumpet. Typically, the more liberal parishes led the others in taking this initial step. Because Anglicans felt no inhibitions about organs in church, affordability was the principle deterrent to their installing one.

Thomas Brattle's organ, imported ca. 1689.

Trinity Church in Newport, Rhode Island, boasted an imported one in 1733, and both Trinity and Christ Churches in Boston in 1736.[10] Anglican churches in Charleston, Philadelphia, New York, and elsewhere also permitted unrestricted use of organs. Indeed, Charles Theodore Pachelbel, son of the noted composer Johann Pachelbel and himself a capable composer, was organist at Charleston's St. Philip's Church from 1737 to 1750.

In the eighteenth century the Puritan church, taking its cue from the Pilgrims, became Congregational, each parish allowed free control over its affairs and able to cultivate a broader fellowship than heretofore had been the case. Despite the Great Awakening, many New Englanders, especially the urbanites, had not submitted to the frenzy. Reason ruled. God to them was more benign than the wrathful deity that Edwards preached about. In accord with the greater religious liberalism of the time, though not without controversy, organs did begin to make their way into Congregational worship. New England Protestantism was starting to unbind itself from tradition and authority and was adjusting religious belief to recent scientific ideas and to the changing spiritual needs of the congregation. The Congregational Church in Providence was at the forefront of musical change in 1770. On 10 July of that year Ezra Stiles noted in his diary:

> Last month an Organ of 200 Pipes was set up in the Meeting-house of the first Congregational Church in Providence; and for the first time it was played upon in Divine Service last Ldsday, as Mr. Rowland the pastor tells me. This is the first organ in a dissentive presby. Chh. in America except Jersey College [Princeton] or Great Britain.

On 16 May 1785 Stiles wrote of Boston's Congregationalists at last having an organ:

> They have lately determined to set up an Organ in Dr. Chauncey's Meetghouse being the old Brick or first Chh. in Bo. founded in 1629. The Doctor was against it, but Mr. Clark, his colleague, and the Congregn. in general were for it. This spring the Meetghouse was repaired and Dr. C. preached a consecrn. and farewell sermon on acct. of his great age. The people eager to get an organ waited on the Dr. who told them that it would not be long before he was in his

grave,—he knew that before his head was cold there they would
have an organ—and they might do as they pleased.[11]

American organ building did not start in New England. The first
known builder was Johann Gottlob Klemm, who constructed several organs after he arrived in America in 1733. Klemm installed one of these,
a hefty three-manual instrument, in Trinity Church, New York, in 1739.
The first New England–built organ was one tinkered together by a
resourceful amateur of Boston, Edward Bromfield Jr., in 1745. He gave it
two rows of keys and pipes to the number of several score. Unfortunately,
he died in 1746, before he could add all the pipes he had in mind. The first
proficient builder in New England was Thomas Johnston. He had belonged to the congregation of the Brattle Square Church until 1753 but
may have gone over to the Anglicans at King's Chapel after that. We do
know that he was a singer and an organ tuner and repairer. We do not
know when he started to build his own instruments. Apparently he was
self-trained. Christ Church, Boston, received a two-manual organ from
him in 1752. In 1754 he built an organ for St. Peter's Church, Salem, and
another for Boston's Concert Hall. Other fine organ builders followed
him—Dr. Leavitt, Henry Pratt, William Goodrich, and Thomas Appleton. Finally, in 1827 Elias and George Hook, who had apprenticed under
Goodrich, commenced manufacturing instruments comparable to the
finer ones from Europe.[12]

An organ in a church necessitated the locating of a person capable of
playing the instrument. The writer of *Observations Made by the Curious in
New England,* published in London in 1673, had commented that "no musicians by trade" could be found in Boston. That now changed. When Brattle's organ went to King's Chapel, the parishioners immediately realized
that they had to import a "sober person to play skillfully thereon with a
loud noise." For a few months they engaged a Mr. Price as organist. He was
supplanted in 1714 by a new arrival from England, Edward Enstone, who
was granted an annual salary of thirty pounds. The organist needed to supplement his meager salary. On 21 February 1714 he submitted a formal
written request "for liberty of keeping a school as a Master of Music and a
Dancing Master" to Boston's selectmen. He was refused, but not for long.
The *Boston News-Letter* made this clear in an advertisement that Enstone
placed in April 1716. By then he was not only playing the organ at King's
Chapel but also teaching dancing and importing an assortment of musical

instruments for local sale. He also offered to repair all instruments, tune virginals and spinets, and teach beginners to play any instruments offered for sale.[13] He had little competition for several years.

Apparently hiring an organist did not guarantee fine playing. In 1744 Dr. Alexander Hamilton of Maryland was visiting Boston and wrote, "I went to the English chapel [King's Chapel] with Mr. Lechmere and heard a small organ play'd by an indifferent organist."[14]

Thomas Dipper arrived from England via Jamaica and was the organist at King's Chapel from around 1755 to 1762. The *Boston Post-Boy*, 2 February 1761, announced that he had the intention of giving a vocal and instrumental concert on 3 February, assisted by two French horn players.[15]

A well-trained musician and composer of considerable importance to Boston, William Selby (ca. 1738–98), emigrated from London in 1771. For a short while he served Trinity Church in Newport, Rhode Island. Boston quickly gained possession of him, however, and there he remained until his death, assisting mostly at King's Chapel. He also was active in Boston music societies and in giving ambitious choral concerts. Indeed, his activities would eventually lead to the establishment of the Handel and Haydn Society.

Like Enstone, Selby sought to augment his salary not only as a teacher of keyboard instruments but also as a merchant purveying groceries and liquors. He wrote some keyboard, chamber, and choral compositions, among them an "Ode in Honour of General Washington" and "An Ode to Independence."[16] After the war he became the most eminent musical leader in Boston. During his incumbency, a debate was ignited about the denominational affiliation of King's Chapel, which had been Anglican for decades. The argument was settled in 1787 when the congregation turned Unitarian.

By midcentury the availability of instruments and imported music for sale increased rapidly. Portsmouth, New Hampshire, had "Italian violin strings and silver bases" for sale in 1757. In a decade or so, musicians had arrived to teach the violin and harpsichord. Newport, Rhode Island, was also finding instruments becoming more plentiful. The *Newport Mercury*, 26 June 1759, presented the following information: "*Imported in the last Ships* from London and Bristol, And to be sold by *Jacob Richardson*, Wholesale and Retail, At his shop in Brenton's Row in Thames Street, Newport, All sorts of Goods . . . [including] Brass and Iron Jew's Harps, ***English Flutes, Violins, Bows, Bridges, best Roman Violin Strings*."[17]

To give a final instance, John Harris came from London in 1768 and engaged in selling, repairing, and tuning keyboard instruments. The *Boston Gazette,* 18 September 1769, credits Harris, whose father was a spinet and harpsichord builder, with making the first spinet in America. By the eve of the Revolutionary War, it had become obvious that there would be no stopping New England's increasing call for trained musicians and musical entrepreneurs. Hostilities with England would slow things up, but that call would gather force at war's end.

THE FIRST CONCERTS AND PIANOS

The oldest notice of a concert in America was printed in the *Boston Gazette,* 3 February 1729. It promised a *"Consort of Musick* performed on sundry Instruments at the Dancing School in King-Street," a daring venture for the time. The next notice was printed in the *Boston News-Letter,* on 13–16 December 1731: "On Thursday, the 30th of this instant December, there will be performed a *Concert of Music* on sundry Instruments at Mr. Pelham's great Room, being the house of the late Doctor Noyes near the Sun Tavern. Tickets to be delivered at the place of Performance at *Five shillings* each. The Concert to begin exactly at Six o'clock, and no Tickets will be delivered after Five the day of performance. N. B. There will be no admittance after Six." Peter Pelham, a London engraver and mezzotinter, had come to Boston in 1726. He acted as "manager of the subscription assembly." He married the widow Copley, whose son was John Singleton Copley, the famous painter. Around 1732 Carl Theodor Pachelbel, son of the noted German composer Johann Pachelbel, appeared in Boston, did some concertizing, then left with Peter Pelham Jr. (by Peter Pelham's first wife), for Newport, New York, and Charleston. These were exciting happenings for music lovers who had been thirsting for concerts and who now would crave more.[18]

Faneuil Hall was built in Boston in 1742 and was hosting concerts by 1744, most of them with special permission from the selectmen because they were intended to benefit the poor. Eleven years later a new concert hall opened its doors on Queen Street. Concerts were growing in demand and emerged as another outlet for trained musicians from Europe. Possibly, the graduates of the singing schools were augmenting the number of music lovers who desired to be present at concerts. At any rate, both subscription and subscription-cum-public concerts were becoming common. It was a recreational direction being taken by all of British America.

Most concerts of necessity had to be simple affairs, with few instrumental chairs occupied and amateurs of varying abilities volunteering
their services. These amateurs played alongside one or two professionals,
if indeed these last were available. Impressive concerts were given in May
1771, when Josiah Flagg offered an evening of "vocal and instrumental
musick, accompanied by French horns, hautboys, etc. by the band of the
64th Regiment." On 13 May 1771 a detailed program was printed in the
Boston Evening Post:

Act I.	Overture Ptolomy	Handel
	Song "From the East breaks the morn"	
	Concerto 1st	Stanley
	Symphony 3d	[J. C.] Bach
Act II.	Overture 1st	Schwindl
	Duet to "Turn fair Clora"	
	Organ Concerto	
	Periodical Symphony	Stamitz
Act III.	Overture 1st	Abel
	Duetto "When Phoebus the tops of	
	the hills"	
	Solo Violin	
	A new Hunting Song, set to music by	Mr. Morgan
	Periodical Symphony	Pasquale Ricci[19]

Two years later, Selby was employing the same band to accompany his
chorus in a concert that included a Handel overture, the "Hallelujah" Chorus, and a Coronation anthem. After the war, Selby was again actively promoting concerts, beginning in April 1782 with airs, duets, and choruses of
Stanley, Smith, Handel, and T. A. Arne. A Boston "Musical Society" had
formed and was assisting him. Four years later, a performance at King's
Chapel, for the relief of prisoners, included a Handel overture, organ concerto, *Messiah* selections, and an aria from *Samson.* In 1789 George Washington appeared in Boston, and Selby was called upon to present a fitting
sacred concert. Washington sat through two anthems and an organ concerto, all by Selby, "Comfort ye" from the *Messiah* and "Let the bright Ser-
aphim" from *Samson,* by Handel, and the complete oratorio *Jonah,* by
Samuel Felsted.[20]

A hiatus in concert giving took place during the war years, at least for
the Americans. Although they continued to sing songs of British origin,

they also elevated two local compositions to high national status. One was Billings's "Chester." The other was a piece of uncertain origin, which the British, during their occupation of Boston, used to ridicule New England-ers: "Yankee Doodle."[21] Redcoats sang it in town squares, on village greens, and before churches to show their scorn for the native bumpkins. They marched jauntily to it on their way to Lexington and Concord. After the Battle of Concord and Lexington, however, the victorious Yankee Doodles took over the march as their own and hurled its tones back at the British at every opportunity. The earliest publication of "Yankee Doodle" was in England in the 1780s. It was offered to the English public as "Yankee Doodle, or (as now christened by the Saints of New England) The Lexington March. N.B. The Words to be Sung thro' the Nose, & in the West Country drawl & dialect." One wonders about the connection be-tween this English imprint and the droll "Yankee" New England caricature that began to emerge with Royall Tyler's play *The Contrast* of 1787, in which "Jonathan" portrayed a comic New Englander.

Other New England towns were enjoying their own local concerts after midcentury. Providence had its first known public performance in 1768, Newport in 1772, and Salem in 1798. Favorite songs, arias, concer-tos, and symphonies relieved the psalmody diet offered by the singing-school graduates, as musicians, mostly from Boston, traveled to near-by communities to present their wares. Before the century's close, Portsmouth and Concord, New Hampshire, and Portland, Maine, wit-nessed their first concerts.

Boston seemed to be almost catching up with and, in a couple of instances, coming abreast of the more advanced contemporary musical practices of Europe. On 7 March 1771 the *Massachusetts Gazette* mentioned that, during the intermission of a proposed concert, the Englishman David Propert would play "select pieces on the new instrument" called "the Forte, piano." Propert, organist at Boston's Trinity Church, also advertised himself as a teacher of keyboard instruments, including the fortepiano. From this, we must assume that at least one or two pianos were at hand. New the piano might be, but the wealthier Bostonians wanted to import it for their children, who then took instruction from the several keyboard players resident in the town. Jacques Pierre Brissot de Warville, a French lawyer, visited the town in 1788 and listened raptly to the piano playing of a few young women. Perhaps their physical attractiveness affected his judgment when he wrote: "This art, it is true, is still in its infancy; but the young novices who exercise it are so gentle, so complaisant, and so modest that the proud perfection of art gives no pleasure equal to what they afford. God grant that the Bostonian women may never, like those of France, acquire the malady of perfection in this art! It is never attained but at the expense of the domestic virtues."[22]

Three years later a newspaper estimated that around twenty-seven Boston families owned pianos, which had all come from London. The French visitor need not have worried about Boston's women acquiring "the malady of perfection in this art," if Susanna Rowson's assessment of young women's attainments has any truth in it. Born in England in 1762, she was an actress, dramatist, and author of the first best-selling novel in the United States, *Charlotte Temple* (1791). Also an educator, she opened the Young Ladies Academy, one of the first American schools for older girls, in Medford, Massachusetts, in 1797. She died in 1824. In the following verse, Rowson's reference is to the harpsichord, still the instrument more likely than the piano to reside in parlors:

> Behold Miss Tasty every nymph excel,
> A fine, accomplished fashionable belle.
> Plac'd at the harpsichord, see with what ease
> Her snowy fingers run along the keys;
> Now quite in alt, to th' highest notes she'll go;
> Now running down the bass, she falls as low;
> Flats, sharps, and naturals, together jumbled,
> She laughs to think how little folks are humbled.
> While some pretending coxcomb sighing, says,
> So loud that she may hear, "Heavens, how she plays."
> Then she speaks French. *Comment vouz portez vouz?*
> *Ma chere amie! Ma vie! Oh ciel! Mon dieu!*
> And dances—sink, chasse, and rigadoon,
> Or hops along, unheeding time or tune,
> As fashion may direct.[23]

This assessment of a typical girl's approach to music, while harsh, indicates the low priority placed on the arts during these years. People of limited means knew or cared nothing about the more elevated levels of musical attainment. People of affluence, even those who treasured music, felt that the professional production of music was best left to Europeans, whether abroad or on the American shore. In America, consensus held that it was men's duty to build a new nation and women's duty to bring up the future citizens of the new nation. "Miss Tasty" may have had a father who wished her not to go too deeply into music; her destiny lay elsewhere. In a revealing letter that John Adams sent from Paris to his wife, Abigail, in 1780, the thought that music had to be relegated to a secondary position for his and the next generation of Americans is made clear:

> I could fill volumes with descriptions of temples and palaces, paint-ings, sculpture, tapestry, porcelain, etc., if I could have the time, but I could not do this without neglecting my duty. My duty is to study the science of government that my sons may have the liberty to study mathematics and science. My sons ought to study geography, nav-igation, commerce, and agriculture in order to give their children a right to study philosophy, painting, poetry, music, architecture, sculpture, tapestry, and porcelain.[24]

Piano construction in America probably began when John Behrent, who had come to Pennsylvania from Germany, offered one of his own manufacture for sale in 1775. New England had to wait until native-born Benjamin Crehore went into production during the 1790s. Crehore, in turn, would train Alpheus Babcock. Babcock would later take out the first patent on a one-piece metal frame, an innovation that would later be taken over by all piano manufacturers. The instruments in these years were square pianos with a range of five to five and a half octaves.

THE EARLY MUSICAL THEATER

English "ballad" opera, not continental opera, had made a first appearance in Charleston, in 1735. After that year, English operatic troupes tried their luck in America, mounting works such as Charles Dibdin's *The Padlock,* William Shield's *The Poor Soldier,* and Thomas Arne's *Love in a Village.* These musical plays were easy to produce and had little resemblance to Italian grand opera. They contained down-to-earth plots, spoken English dia-logue, no recitative, and uncomplicated, tuneful songs whose music was beholden to the folk song of the British Isles. These were virtues that won them an enthusiastic American following. William Hallam was the first to arrive from London with an opera troupe, which was soon named the American Company and, later, the Old American Company. The year was 1752. Nevertheless, from the first appearance of English opera, the-atergoers were in constant battle with an almost fanatical group of con-servative critics, who wished to ban the stage productions altogether because of alleged moral and religious lapses. The antitheater camp outside New England won a few, temporary local victories. The suspension of theater performances throughout America would take place only during the war years, and even then did not apply to the British forces, whose officers got up several theater performances.

The critics of theater were more numerous and influential in Massachusetts than elsewhere in the country. Among them were persuasive social, political, and religious leaders. They did not need the war as an excuse for taking action. As early as 1714 Samuel Sewall had protested the acting of a play in the Council Chamber. In 1750 two young Englishmen and their local friends had put on Otway's *Orphan* in a Boston coffee shop, scandalizing many of the public. To put a stop to such amateur incidents and to ward off visits from the operatic troupes, powerful leaders had the legislature pass an antitheater blue law in 1750, banning all stage productions. Visits by Hallam's American Company were barred. Lovers of musical theater were in retreat, only occasionally able to sneak in an entertainment. In 1769 the more daring of Boston's inhabitants attended a "reading" of *Love in a Village*. The next year a "Mr. Joan" (possibly James Juhan), who "personates all the characters," appeared before a Boston audience and "read and sung" Gay and Pepusch's *Beggar's Opera*. He did the same with *Damon and Phillida*. A 23 March 1770 entry in the diary of John Rowe reads: "In the evening I went to the Concert Hall to hear Mr. Joan read the Beggar's Opera and sing the songs."[25] In June of the same year a notice announced "a vocal entertainment of three acts. The songs (which are numerous) are taken from a new celebrated opera, call'd *Lionel and Clarissa* [by Dibdin]." In short, despite the ban, occasional operas were done, though inadequately, with minimal forces and without presentation as a staged and costumed drama.

The move to repeal the blue law of 1750 gathered steam after the war. The war itself had weakened the old conservative coalition and had brought a more independent breed of citizen to the fore. By the 1790s a burgeoning number of men and women were actively pressing for revocation. Petition after petition was submitted. The state legislature refused to budge. The more consequential of these citizens decided to challenge the law. They sponsored the building of a "New Exhibition Room," which could hold five hundred people. It opened on 16 August 1792, managed by a Mr. Harper, Mr. Woolls, and Mr. and Mrs. Placide. A "Gallery of Portraits," which included songs, acrobatics, and dancing, and "Lectures, Moral and Entertaining" comprised the offerings. In truth, they were lightly camouflaged operatic performances. Bostonians were able to witness a couple of weightless French operas and a more steady diet of English operas such as *Devil to Pay, Love in a Village,* and *Thomas and Sally.* Governor Hancock, thinking it to his political advantage, arrested Harper for violating the ban in December 1792. The enraged supporters of the theater railed against the arrest. The protheater party added more people to their ranks, stirred up a strong public demand for theater, and soon gained the upper hand. During the following year they collected funds to build a new theater and at the same time continued the performances at the New Exhibition Room. They were spurred on by the example of New York, which had its Nassau Street Theater as early as 1750. Philadelphia had opened its Southwark Theater in 1766 and in 1792 built the magnificent Chestnut Street Theater. In 1792 Charleston also had its own theater building.

At long last, Bostonians had their own Boston Theater, better known as the Federal Street Theater, which made its first presentation in February 1794. The Federal Street Theater was a handsome edifice designed by the admired architect Charles Bulfinch. Its manager took to making visits to London to recruit performers. When the theater burned down in 1798 it was quickly rebuilt. One of its English singers, Catharine Hillier, would marry Gottlieb Graupner, who would have an extraordinary impact on Boston's music making during the first years of the nineteenth century. On a typical theater evening the doors opened at five o'clock and the curtain went up at six.

A second theater, the Haymarket, was launched in 1796.[26] Boston, with a population of around twenty-five thousand, was still too small to support two theaters. The Haymarket went bankrupt in 1799, and the building was torn down four years later.

Other New England towns were enjoying English opera by the 1790s, but none of their productions was ever as elaborate as those in Boston, and most made do with next to no resources. Portsmouth had heard its first performance in November 1769, when an actor-singer, probably Juhan, personated the songs from *Love in a Village* at Staver's Long Room. From September 1772 to January 1773 musical "exhibitions" were held there, directed by W. S. Morgan from Boston, assisted by four singers. The Bow Street Theater, once a warehouse, began presentations in 1792. Six years later an Assembly Room also offered entertainments. On 11 September 1769 the *Newport Mercury* told its readers that probably the same Juhan who had appeared in Boston and Portsmouth was visiting Newport and could be heard for the admission price of fifty cents: "This evening at Mrs.

Cowley's Assembly Room, in Church Lane, will be read the Beggar's Opera, by a person who had read and sung in most of the great towns in America. All the songs will be sung. He personates all the characters and enters into the various humors or passions, as they change from one to another throughout the Opera."[27] Salem, Worcester, Portland, Providence, New London, and Hartford underwrote opera performances. Troupes from Boston took to visiting New England towns and sometimes traveled as far south as Charleston. The Connecticut towns were as likely to receive visits from New York as from Boston.

In the 1790s musicians other than organists arrived in increasing numbers throughout the United States. The opening of theaters prompted such fine musicians as Graupner to come to direct their programs, conduct their orchestras, and assume leadership in every major musical enterprise that was afoot. Others came to provide a variety of musical services. For example, Peter van Hagen (1755–1803) left Holland and arrived in Charleston with his wife in 1774, where they became parents of a son. They moved up to New York in 1789 and finally settled in Boston in 1796. On arrival in Boston, Peter van Hagen established a musical magazine and Warranted Piano Forte Warehouse on Newbury Street. The following year the firm started to publish some music, mostly reprints of British pieces, some patriotic pieces, and works by van Hagen himself, who changed his name to von Hagen while he was living in Boston. He also directed the orchestra of the Haymarket Theater, arranged music for the stage, and played the organ at King's Chapel. Mrs. von Hagen taught piano in Boston, in Salem, and at the girl's academy in Medford, headed by Susanna Rowson. The son, Peter Jr. (ca. 1780–1837), was a skilled violinist who, like his father, played other instruments and wrote music. For a while he was organist at Trinity Church. He also directed a couple of greater Boston bands. After his father died, he operated the Newbury Street firm ineptly and had to sell it to Graupner in 1804.

Another all-around musician, James Hewitt (1770–1827), came from England to New York in 1792, where he published music, directed a theater orchestra, composed a battle piece, *The Battle of Trenton,* and wrote an anti-Federalist English-type opera, *Tammany.* He moved to Boston in 1812, conducted at the Federal Street Theater, played the organ at Trinity Church, gave lessons, and published music. His daughter Sophia grew up to be a fine local pianist and organist. His son John would compose one of the first American hit songs, "The Minstrel's Return'd from the War" (ca. 1828).

Before von Hagen's arrival, sheet music publication was rarely attempted in New England, and sheet music imports offered for sale were hard to come by. The earliest reference to such publication occurred in the *Boston Chronicle,* 17 October 1768: "The NEW and FAVORITE LIBERTY SONG, In FREEDOM *we're Born,* etc. Neatly engraved on COPPER-PLATE, the size of half a sheet of Paper, Set to MUSIC for the VOICE, And to which is also added, A Set of NOTES adapted to the GERMAN FLUTE and VIOLIN, Is just published and to be SOLD at the *LONDON Book-store, King-Street, Boston.* Price Six Pence lawful single, and FOUR SHILLINGS lawful, the dozen."[28]

Shortly after the war ended, Colonel Ebenezer Battelle arrived from Dedham to open the Boston Book-Store on State Street in 1783. He advertised in the *Massachusetts Centinel,* 6 November 1784, that in addition to stationery and books, including books of psalmody, he carried "MUSICK. Lately received, and SOLD at E. BATTELLE's Book-Store, STATE-STREET, A VALUABLE Collection of MUSICK BOOKS, consisting of Airs, Songs, Country-Dances, Minuets and Marches.—Symphonies, Quartettos, Concertos, Sonatas, Divertisementos, Duettos, Solos, Trios, Oratorios, &c. for the Organ, Harpsichord, Clarinett, French-Horn, Hautboy, Flute, Violin, Violincello [*sic*], Harp, Piano-Forte, Voice, &c." Battelle would sell his store in 1785 and, like the singing-master Jenks, move to Ohio.[29] It was not until the next decade that sheet music, whether imported or locally printed, was in steady supply.

TWO DISTINCTIVE MUSIC ESTABLISHMENTS

Gottlieb Graupner (1767–1836) was born in Hanover, Germany, the son of an oboist. He also became an oboist and mastered other instruments as well. A little after 1788 he relocated in London and played in the Haydn orchestra of 1791–92, where he gained an admiration for Haydn symphonies that never left him. Graupner immigrated to America in 1795, and the next year, in Charleston, married the singer Catherine Hillier, who was there with a Boston theater group. The couple made their way northward and by 1797 were settled in Boston. Soon in demand as a teacher on various instruments, Graupner augmented his income by managing a store at 6 Franklin Street that sold music and instruments obtained from London and from American sources. He also was a publisher, engraving and printing music on his own. Several songs composed by him still survive. He busied himself in all aspects of the town's musical life and contributed mightily to it by establishing the Philo-Philharmonic Society and having a finger in the founding of the Handel and Haydn Society.

Mrs. Graupner taught voice, had leading singing roles at the Federal Street Theater, and appeared in concerts with her husband. Later, after the birth of the Handel and Haydn Society, she would appear frequently in oratorios.

As early as 6 April 1799 an announcement in the *Columbian Centinel* read: "*Philharmonic Society.* A general and punctual attendance of the members is requested this evening, as business of importance will be laid before the society. By order, W. H. M'Neil, Secretary." No other report on this society exists.

Graupner commenced meeting with other, mostly amateur, players on Saturday nights to study and play the music of Haydn and his contemporaries. The first public notice of a meeting of the group calling itself the Philo-Philharmonic Society appeared in October 1809. The meetings proved congenial, and the members organized themselves by subscribing to a list of rules and regulations. No moneyed sponsorship, no cultivated aristocracy, no royal decree brought the orchestra into being. It was a democratic group relying on its own resources that saw to Boston's having its first real taste of orchestral music.

The leader of the violin section was Louis Ostinelli, the husband of James Hewitt's daughter Sophia and the father of Signora Biscaccianti, who trained in Europe and made a name for herself there as an opera singer. It was not long before members of the orchestra began inviting guests to come listen to them. Playing proficiency increased, as did attendance at the open rehearsals, until finally they were spoken of as concerts. No accounts of the earlier years of the society remain, except for meager meeting notices. Graupner chose the repertoire, obtained scores from London, and directed the players. Each year, the players renewed their membership. The size of the orchestra was variable, probably about fifteen to twenty players.

Before the creation of the Philo-Philharmonic Society, Boston was more familiar with the Baroque than the Classical repertoire. What concerts there were appeared irregularly, given by tiny pickup ensembles. Underrehearsed and unaccustomed to playing as a body, the instrumentalists could easily make a shambles of the music. This was changed now for the better. The Philo-Philharmonic met and rehearsed regularly. Players grew accustomed to each other's idiosyncrasies. The compositions played were recent symphonies and overtures. The performances, though not exceptional in quality, were more than satisfactory to a town hungering for music. In 1821 John Rowe Parker wrote in his *Euterpiad and Musical Intelligencer:*

> The Concerts of this Society are chiefly instrumental; the music is always heard with attention and oft times delight. The orchestra consists of nearly all the gentlemen of the profession in town, and its members are principally amateurs both vocal and instrumental; its support derived from an annual assessment of ten dollars upon its members, who gain admission by ballot. The public Concerts are always fully attended by a large assemblage of ladies and gentlemen, introduced by members who possess certain privileges of admission on public nights. [30]

After Ostinelli moved to Portland in 1822, the orchestra's playing went downhill. The orchestra would continue in existence until 1824, when a final concert was given on 1 May. This was the first of several orchestras that came and went over the years before the advent of the permanent Boston Symphony Orchestra.

An item clipped out of an old newspaper salutes Graupner: "Mr. Graupner's name was an honored one in the musical history of Boston. He was an eminent teacher of the piano-forte and of all orchestral instruments. He struck the first blow in the cause of true musical art, and continued the strife until taste for good music, and a fair understanding of its intrinsic value was established in Boston." [31] A few music historians have named Graupner "the father of the American orchestra."

A second musician also had a strong influence on musical life. George Jackson (1757–1822) was a composer, teacher, and keyboard performer who was born in Oxford, England, and may have studied at the Chapel Royal. He migrated to New Jersey around 1796 and served as a church organist and concertized there and in New York. He came to Boston to stay in 1812, working as a church organist. The War of 1812 caused officials to banish him to Northampton, Massachusetts, for failing to register as an alien. Despite the furor the banishment triggered, he remained exiled for three years.

He returned to become organist at Trinity Church and was also the proprietor of a music store. Not easy to live with, Jackson frequently entered into quarrels with other musicians and showed himself to be arrogant and having too high a regard for himself and his own judgment. On the other hand, he did enlarge the organ and choral repertoire of the town and help generate an environment that led to the founding of the Handel and Haydn Society. He agitated for higher choral standards of performance and goaded influential musicians to bring about improvement citywide. Jackson would also be the one to urge the society to publish Lowell Mason's influential anthology of sacred music as *The Boston Handel and Haydn Collection of Church Music* in 1822. Because Mason did not want his name to appear on the publication, Jackson himself is named as principal assembler of the volume.

On 22 February 1815 Jackson gave a concert celebrating Washington's Birthday and the Treaty of Ghent, which had recently ended the war with England. The massed vocalists and instrumentalists had a strong positive effect on musical thinking. Music lovers wished to perpetuate the experience. At last, on 20 April 1815, Gottlieb Graupner, Thomas Webb, Amasa Winchester, and Matthew Parker met to found the Handel and Haydn Society. The guidelines contain a passage attesting to the bigger objective at which these thoughtful men aimed:

> While in our country almost every institution, political, civil, and moral has advanced with rapid steps, while every other science and art is cultivated with a success flattering to its advocates, the admirers of music find their beloved science far from exciting the feelings or exercising the powers to which it is accustomed in the Old World. Too long have those to whom heaven has given a voice to perform and an ear that can enjoy music neglected a science which has done much towards subduing the ferocious passions of men and giving innocent pleasure to society; and so absolute has been their neglect that most of the works of the great composers of sacred music have never found those in our land who have even attempted their performance.[32]

The passage is permeated with the self-imposed sense of duty and the response to an inner calling that keep on rising to the surface in New England's history and that go back 150 years to the early Puritans. At the same time, the passage indicates how truly keen New Englanders were for learning about and listening to "good" choral music. This eagerness included Mainers, who as yet had no oratorio society to turn to. In May 1800 Portland heard Samuel Emerson of Kennebunk lecture on "Oratorio and Music"; twelve years later they heard Ammi Ruhameh of North Yarmouth give lectures "On Sacred Music." A Dr. Mitchell spoke about "Oratorio" and "Beethoven."[33]

The first concert of the society, with Webb as conductor, took place on Christmas Eve 1815. A chorus of one hundred men and women sang selections from Handel and Haydn at King's Chapel, accompanied by an organ and a dozen instrumentalists. The singers were members of the several church choirs in the Boston area, although the core was the entire choir of the Park Street Church. The musically inexperienced audience of almost one thousand people was transported by the music. The auditors took their religion seriously and revered the names of Handel and Haydn, whatever their acquaintance with their music. Their enthusiasm insured that the society would continue, as it has to the present day.

In 1817 the concerts moved to Boylston Hall, a gas-lit auditorium with a raised platform in the front. By this time, the society had achieved so great a reputation that the governor, members of the state legislature, and the city's councilors found it obligatory to attend. The next year, the complete *Messiah* was given; the year after, the complete *Creation* of Haydn. The orchestra at first consisted of members of the Philo-Philharmonic Society.

The singing and the instrumental playing never achieved anything close to perfection in those early years. The more discerning listeners complained of choristers off pitch and not having a thorough knowledge of their parts. Violins played out of tune or shakily. Cymbals were clashed together too enthusiastically; kettledrums thundered when they should have been quiet; trumpets blasted forth for no reason. If fast passages were overly difficult a player might lag behind. Conductors were not always well versed in their responsibilities. On the other hand, no one was used to or expected perfection. The listeners were happy to hear music that had been denied them for so long. Besides, for many in the chorus and audience, the performances were more a religious than an aesthetic experience.[34]

After the Philo-Philharmonic Society dissolved, the Handel and Haydn Society began slowly to replace the amateurs in the orchestra with professionals as the latter became more available. Thomas Ryan writes that when he arrived in Boston from Ireland in 1845 and played in the orchestra, one-third of its members were professional musicians who were paid two dollars an evening, whether for a concert or rehearsal. He says that among the oratorios performed were Handel's *Israel in Egypt, Samson,* and *Jephtha;* Haydn's *Seasons;* and Mendelssohn's *Elijah* and *St. Paul.*[35] The vocal soloists were usually talented amateurs or paid professionals such as Mrs. Graupner.

The hall of the Handel and Haydn Society in 1850.

An extraordinary event took place in 1823 that demonstrates how for-ward-looking the society's leadership was. Samuel Richardson, a member of the Handel and Haydn Society, and several other Boston gentlemen sent a request from a banker in Boston to one in Vienna, Herr Geymüller, to ask Ludwig van Beethoven if the society might commission an oratorio from him. Beethoven was delighted with the commission because it signified his far-flung renown but died before he could compose anything for Boston. On 5 November 1823 the *Morganblatt für gebildete Leser* gave news of the commission. A notebook of Beethoven survives that gives information on works he was contemplating before his death: "Eine Sym-phonie, quartetten, ein Biblisches oratorium ihm durch den Amerikan-ischen Consul, in Englischer sprache, aus den Vereinigten Staaten über-schicket." ("A symphony, quartets, a Biblical oratorio in the English lan-guage, which through the American Consul was received from the United States.")[36]

The Handel and Haydn Society set an example for the rest of New England at the time, and its presence was felt continuously thereafter. Sim-ilar oratorio societies, modeled after it, started up in the larger towns. If they faded away, the Society reminded local music lovers of what could be achieved, and fresh starts were made. For example, George Edwards stud-ied the music making in Maine and New Hampshire during the nineteenth century and concluded that the influence of Boston's Handel and Haydn Society was strong and constant in those states. For one, many of its sing-

ers moved from Boston to those two states and urged the study of compositions by Handel, Haydn, Mozart, Beethoven, and other excellent
composers. Edward Howe, a singer and clarinetist from Dorchester, Massachusetts, moved his upholstery business to Portland, Maine, and, mindful of the example of Boston's society, founded the Beethoven Musical
Society in 1819. Most members were mechanics, tradespeople, and manual workers. The vocalists and an orchestra comprising two violins, one
cello, one clarinet, one bassoon, four flutes, and an organ, studied and performed excerpts from the *Messiah* and *Creation,* as expected. However, they
also turned their attention to Beethoven's *Christ on the Mount of Olives.* By
1826 the Portland group had ceased to exist. The Handel and Haydn Society continued in the minds of Portland's music lovers, who in 1837
formed the Portland Sacred Music Society, which gave the first complete
Creation heard in Portland, with an orchestra of about five instruments
brought up from Boston. In a letter appearing in the *Portland Advertiser,*
signed "M," the writer tries to assure his fellow citizens that ignorant as
they may be about music, they should attend the performance and could
profit by it: "Many, we fear, will deny themselves the privilege of attending
the Oratorio from the simple fact that they have no conception of the
majestic grandeur of the piece to be performed; and many more perhaps,
from fear that they have no talent to appreciate its beauty. But to be
gratified and even enraptured with this production it is not necessary that
a man should be familiar with the laws of 'acoustics,' or with music as a science;—he only needs to have a soul."[37]

It is true that other areas of the nation had choral organizations and
instrumental ensembles from the earlier years of the eighteenth century,
most of them the result of German sects moving into the Pennsylvania
region. Though many of these Germans were musically knowledgeable,
they lived in seclusion, apart from the other settlers. The Pietists, led by
Johannes Kelpius, established Germantown (northwest of Philadelphia) in
1694, where Kelpius compiled a hymn book, *The Lamenting Voice of the Hidden Love at the Time when She Lay in Misery and Forsaken.* It contained ten
hymns, seven with a bass line. Conrad Beissel and his followers came to
Ephrata (near Lancaster) in 1732 and fifteen years later published *The Song
of the Lonely and Forsaken Turtle Dove.* This hymn collection was harmonized
so unceasingly with consonant sounds that it becomes tiresome to the ear.
The most numerous and significant of the sects were the Moravians, who
beginning in 1741 came to Bethlehem, Pennsylvania, and Salem, North
Carolina. They believed strongly in musical training for individuals from

all walks of life and built communities ardently devoted to music, which figured prominently in their worship and their leisure activities. Solo singers, choruses, and instrumental ensembles were heard in highly skilled renditions of sacred songs, anthems, and other religious music. Brass ensembles played for church services, christenings, weddings, and funerals. The Collegia Musica association met regularly to learn the latest contemporary music from Europe, many of the scores hand-copied abroad. Skilled instrument makers, such as the organ builder David Tannenberg, labored to satisfy the needs of the brethren. So also did such composers as Johannes Herbst and Johann Friedrich Peter. The latter even composed six string quintets (1789) for home use. The American-born John Antes (1740–1811) manufactured string instruments, composed sacred pieces, and, while in Egypt as a missionary, crafted three string trios (1770–81?) in the latest Classical style. Yet, during the eighteenth and nineteenth centuries, the Moravians remained on the fringes of the greater American society. The various city oratorio societies that came into existence in the nineteenth century tended to regard the Handel and Haydn Society as the most equal among equals.

CHAPTER 4

FOSTERING MUSICAL
IMPROVEMENT

New England until the last decade of the nineteenth century became the foremost region of the United States for education, literature, science, architecture, technology, and cultural life. Among its inhabitants were outstanding men and women in science, philosophy, literature, religion, and business enterprise. They provided remarkable instances of the capability of keenly motivated people to burst out of the limitations imposed by a quirky climate and inhospitable surroundings. For much of the century the six-state region was one of the most homogeneous in the United States, with Americans of British Protestant extraction predominating, even after a large influx of Germans and Irish Catholics in midcentury. New Englanders acquired the designation of Yankees rather than Puritans. Yet they manifested traits shared with their ancestors and extolled by such writers as Ralph Waldo Emerson: self-reliance, ingenuity, prudence, readiness to undertake projects of importance or difficulty, and energy to complete any undertaking. Their offspring bore these traits away with them when they left to trek west and south into northern New York and Pennsylvania, the Midwest, and, in lesser numbers, into early Oregon and Washington.

There was an obverse side to these qualities. The wealthy classes and conservative clergy tried to erect a fence of laws and economic and political patronage in order to keep out the new egalitarian ideas, the aspiration to live freer lives, the goal of equal rights, and the demand for full social and economic opportunity that entered during the era of Jacksonian democracy. They found the Irish after midcentury to be threatening their hegemony and tried to hedge them in, but could not subdue the Irish urge for success and power; nor could they decrease the Irish fertility rate. They fought against the political rise of ordinary people that began with

Andrew Jackson's election to the presidency, but found themselves unable to sustain the privileges to which they were accustomed. State after state amended its political ways in favor of a common citizenry entitled to elect representatives responsible to it and governing according to its laws.

This did not mean that the highest degree of democratic excellence was achieved. Ignorance, prejudice, and intolerance still existed, but in New England thoughtful men and women were learning to moderate these failings through education, discussion, and openness to the recent philosophies from Europe. For one, Unitarianism gathered force in New England at the same time that newly elected President Jackson launched his first attacks against the ambitions of an aristocracy manqué. Unitarianism tried to achieve a tolerant attitude toward those whose opinions, practices, race, religion, and nationality were different from one's own. The new Romantic movement infiltrating from Europe encouraged them not to rely completely on rational thought alone to explain all situations. At the same time, they rejected the ignorant hysteria that cause people to believe that an intolerant God stood ready to damn all humankind. The dressed-up Calvinism still lurking in the tenets of Congregationalism was no longer tenable.

One result of this questioning was the rise of Transcendentalism and its philosophical idealism. It swiftly became the first clamor of the spirit against the acquisitive, money-oriented aggravations of a commercial and industrial way of life. Warmth, imagination, and freedom from long-standing constraints became the new watchwords. And all three were essential to cultivate if ever New England was to see its first composers, that is to say, the first composers to carry major artistic weight. The Transcendental periodicals, the *Harbinger* and the *Dial,* were full of mention of music. John Sullivan Dwight applied Transcendental ideas to music, calling it a language of feeling, an expression of life's deepest mysteries, a binder together of people and nations, and a conduit to beauty, God, and eternity. The listener, wrote Dwight, received music intuitively and was elevated to the heights of experience when he heard the greatest music performed by the greatest artists. It was the duty of those able to bestow it to provide the best in art to all people.[1]

The Transcendentalists drew the notice of educated men and women because they held a dominant position in intellectual and cultural enclaves, and especially because they addressed a key strain in the nonmaterial side of American thought—a strain that has reappeared every so often. Contemporary young people yearned to explore all the dimensions of sentiment. The rebellious ones accused their society of being overly aloof, insensitive, profit minded, self-satisfied, conformist, or fearful of fresh ways of acting and doing. Most wanted to feel something and feel it gloriously. Van Wyck Brooks, writing of the antebellum years, observed: "In Boston, these new feelings had a focus in the various institutions of art and music that were appearing now on every hand. The C Minor Symphony of Beethoven was played in the Odeon in 1840. . . . The young men walked in from Cambridge in parties of three or four, deliciously thrilled by the darkness of the road and the chance of meeting a footpad."[2]

Emerson was offering contemplations of profundity, mystery, and beauty to the offspring of the Puritans. He saw the age-old protocols giving way. He detected warmness in people not before seen in New Englanders. Hawthorne was exposing images of evil and innocence, cruelty and torment, clothed in a glow of feeling and psychological insight. Melville brought in exoticism, adventure, and the need to understand men's motivations. Bryant was the consummate poet and political journalist, extolling New England scenes in his verse and national liberalism in his editorials. Longfellow was helping readers imagine the wonders of homely situations, historical events, and natural phenomena. He was the American favorite, raising men and women out of their mundanity, offering them poetry that carried them into a sphere of romance and loveliness. Fitz Hugh Lane of Gloucester painted celebrations of New England's ships and coastline. Adam Fischer of Boston was bringing country scenes and ordinary activities in the home and fields to life in his paintings. Sculptors such as the three Greenough brothers, Hiram Powers, and William Story were carving idealized figures to represent American and other images of nobleness as seen through New England eyes.

Conscience and duty would cause Dorothea Dix to crusade for better treatment of people with mental problems. Samuel Howe's concern for the blind drove him, with the help of Michael Anagnos, to found the Perkins Institute for the Blind. John Whittier and William Lloyd Garrison campaigned for the abolition of slavery. The Unitarian minister Theodore Parker preached for the improvement of prisons and the recognition of the civil rights of laborers and African Americans. These were all manifestations of the fresh New England spirit.

The amount and vitality of intellectual, artistic, and humanitarian activity was staggering in its variety. Whether the ones seeking for unprecedented change realized it or not, it was New England prosperity and riches mounting up from the profits of cotton mills, leather goods manufacture, and sea commerce that made new directions possible. When surplus wealth coupled with Puritan conscience was directed toward buttressing the arts more than just occasionally, then art music would really flourish.

MUSIC EDUCATION THROUGH
FOREIGN VISITORS

To provide knowledge in accordance with the latest standards was a primary aim of several influential leaders. In Massachusetts there were advances in education for the deaf, mute, and blind and the start of kindly meant reform schools for juvenile delinquents. Horace Mann, aware of the educational ferment around him, decided his mission was the improvement of normal education. He went on the road to every corner of the six states, holding conventions for teachers, school principals, and members of school committees. Not satisfied with what he himself had learned at home, he left for Germany to acquire the most progressive methods for educating the young. Mann was instrumental in advancing the Boston system of free public high schools and in establishing the first teachers' colleges, beginning in 1839.

Education was beginning to count culture among its dimensions. William Prescott stated in a letter written in 1840, "We are all becoming cultivated up to the eyes . . . *tiers état* and all. A daughter of an old servant of ours, whose father is an Irish bogtrotter that works on the roads, told me yesterday, she had nearly completed her English education, was very well into her French and should give one quarter more to her music and drawing."[3]

The Lyceum association for public instruction of adults in science, history, public affairs, and the arts had developed from the lectures given by Josiah Holbrook in Millbury, Massachusetts, in 1826. Nathan Hale and Edward Everett started a Useful Knowledge Society. The Natural History Society, Mechanic's Apprentices' Association, and Lowell Institute followed. As far back as the first Puritan settlements, New Englanders had prized knowledge and scholarship. Now, scores of townspeople and villagers in all New England states wanted to enroll in lecture courses. Workmen by the hundreds listened avidly to competent speakers tell them of worlds once considered beyond their horizons. Theodore Parker found it amazing that the lectures of people like Agassiz and Emerson, "men who do not spare abstruseness," were listened to and actually understood in

New England's towns and villages, not just by the well educated but "by large crowds of men of only the most common culture." It was a phenomenon "unknown in any other land or age," thought Parker.[4]

On his visit to the United States, Charles Dickens had turned a jaundiced eye on most of the country. He was quite taken with New England, however, and amazed at what he found in the boardinghouses where Lowell's mill girls lived. These young women, many of whom had come from farm families, read English literary magazines, wrote essays, stories, and poems, and put out their own periodical. They studied Latin, French, and German, enjoyed Shakespeare and Milton, and spoke knowledgeably about Longfellow, Wordsworth, and Coleridge. Pockets of this sort of learning would persist into the twentieth century. As an example, when I was in my last high school year, I went with my closest friend to meet his Yankee grandfather, an elderly man who had been a farmer in Franklin, Massachusetts, all of his life. The farm had been in the family since early times. Amazingly, the grandfather had written two novels in Latin. His frail wife, who was in bed dying of cancer, was eagerly reading *War and Peace* and insisted on our coming back twice to visit her in order to discuss Tolstoy's vision of the human condition.

Acquiring knowledge according to the latest musical standards rose in importance as the nineteenth century ventured on. Beyond the simple songs and dances they knew, there opened a world of art that astonished even the most educated New Englanders. A certain innocence was evident as they tried to process their novel musical experiences and systematically organize them in their minds.

When Ole Bull arrived in the United States from Norway in 1843, Americans rushed to listen to him to receive instruction on what they thought was the best in music played by one of the finest violinists of the time. Besides, Bull had quickly acquired a reputation for advocating personal liberty, social equality, and pursuit of the highest principles. Americans could not help admiring him. On 21 May 1844 he appeared before a full house at Boston's Melodeon, backed by an orchestra and helped out by a vocalist, Miss Stone. He played a concerto of his own, the "Carnival of Venice," and "A Mother's Prayer." Bostonians admired his principles, adored his playing ability, and felt elevated by his music.

Mrs. Longfellow called him "a divine musician" who put his soul into his instrument. She especially liked the "pleading tones" in "A Mother's Prayer," which deepened into "more passionate appeals at the end, as if a mother's heart was really speaking." Margaret Fuller went to two later concerts and said the music had "plunged" her into "anguish" and raised her "to rapture." Bull played a piece entitled "Adagio Religioso." Fuller was transported: "I felt raised above all care, all pain, all fear, and every taint of vulgarity was washed out of the world." Emerson, who was generally known for his tin ear, came to a concert at the behest of Margaret Fuller and wrote of the scene he had observed in rather skeptical terms: "Ole Bull had a dignified civilized influence. Yet he was there for exhibition, not as St. Cecilia incarnated. . . . Yet he played as a man who found a violin in his hand, and so bent to make music of that; but if he had found a chisel or a sword or a spy-glass or a troop of boys, would have made much of them. It was a beautiful spectacle."[5]

Once, in a more reflective mood, Margaret Fuller wrote, "Whether the arts can ever be at home among us; whether the desire now manifested to cultivate them be not merely one of our modes of imitating older nations; or whether it springs from a need of balancing the bustle and care of daily life by the unfolding of our calmer and higher nature, it is at present difficult to decide."[6] In 1844 Americans were musically uneducated, though willing to learn. John Sullivan Dwight had listened to Ole Bull's playing and found "it filled me with such deep, solemn joy." Ten years later, musical schooling had advanced apace. Dwight listened to him again, admitted to the virtuosity and tonal richness, but heard "lachrimosity" in the sound, and superficiality in slight pieces that were no substitute for Mozart or Beethoven. "Our audiences, after a whole winter of Mozart, Haydn, Beethoven, Mendelssohn, Schumann, etc., in symphony and quartet and sonata, are naturally slow to digest an entire programme of the concert giver's own composing, though he be ever so great a genius."[7]

New Englanders also had a chance to absorb the latest European developments in singing. In 1850 Jenny Lind, the "Swedish nightingale," came to America and toured under the management of P. T. Barnum. Through publicity generated by Barnum, she was admired for her purity, modesty, devoutness, and dedication to helping the poor: "the musical saint," "the second Santa Caecelia," "the angel of the stage," were epithets that Barnum applied to her and that soon were constantly on American lips. As much for what they saw as her virtue as for the genuine excellence of her singing, New Englanders took her to heart. She sang "I Know That My Redeemer Liveth" to a Boston public readily moved by appeals to faith. On one occasion, Daniel Webster watched her bow to the audience at the aria's close and solemnly stood up and bowed back.

Two incidents marred her otherwise perfect record in Boston. One was her first appearance at the Tremont Temple, when the first choice of seats was auctioned off and won by the popular entertainer Ossian Dodge for $640.00. He then proceeded to advertise the affair in every way possible to sell his sheet music and promote his appearances as a popular singer. The second involved her Boston farewell concert, a little before her return to Europe. Barnum oversold the concert; hundreds of ticket holders could not get in. A mob began a march on his hotel, but he was warned of the threat and escaped to New York.[8] On balance, when she finally departed from New England, Lind left behind listeners convinced that fine singing, fine music, and moral earnestness could be one.

Foreign orchestras also visited New England and played programs far superior to any that were locally attempted. Their performances allowed men and women of the Northeast to get a taste of excellent music presented by competent ensembles. Moreover, their American tours done, the departing orchestras almost always left behind admirable musicians, many of them locating in the Boston area. The Steyermark Orchestra, about twenty players led by Francis Riha, came to Boston in the winter of 1846, played nightly at the Melodeon, departed on a tour, and returned only to break up. Thomas Ryan speaks of "the delight with which we listened to the first fine orchestra that came to this country. It was called the Steyermarkische orchestra. It was not large, about twenty players, if I remember rightly, but they played *in tune,* and the smoothness so produced was a revelation" and an education.[9] Riha would later join Ryan in founding Boston's Mendelssohn Quintette Club.

The Lombardi Orchestra, its members at a former time engaged to play for Italian opera, came to Boston in 1848. August Fries directed it. The orchestra soon disintegrated, but Fries remained in Boston and also helped found the Mendelssohn Quintette Club. Next came the Saxonia Orchestra, conducted by Carl Eckhart. Financial difficulties arose, the orchestra foundered, and Eckhart and three other musicians remained in Boston. Little by little, Boston was becoming the home of well-trained instrumentalists who made their living by teaching, delivering public lectures, serving on arts advisory boards, directing local orchestras, and performing as soloists and in chamber groups.

Making the strongest impression was the orchestra conducted by Louis Jullien. Jullien came to America in 1853 with twenty-seven exceptionally fine musicians and added sixty more players to his orchestra from instrumentalists available in the United States. A flamboyant showman, though also an admirable musician, Jullien played light fare such as the notorious "Firemen's Quadrille" alongside such weighty pieces as Beethoven symphonies. His jeweled baton and throne set up in front of the orchestra were for effect. He supplied titillation in the "Firemen's Qua-drille," when flames seemed to leap out at the audience and firemen rushed down the aisles, fire hoses at the ready, as the orchestra sounded more and more agitated. At last, in the midst of pandemonium, "Now Thank We All Our God" boomed out and the relieved audience in full voice joined in—for the fire had been only a bit of legerdemain. In con-trast, his performance of symphonies was all it should be—subtle dynamic shadings, expressive interpretations, and first-rate ensemble playing. When Jullien returned to Europe, quite a few of the players he had brought with him chose to stay in the United States.

New Englanders were not rabid opera aficionados. Unlike New York-ers and New Orleanians, they felt no urge to found a sumptuous grand opera company locally until the end of the century and the creation of the Boston Opera Company. Throughout the nineteenth century, strong re-ligious sentiment continued against attending operatic productions. Thomas Ryan writes of the uncertainty caused by this hostility, saying that when the Howard Athenaeum was built, a huge church window was placed in its front so it could be converted into a church if the theater was unsuccessful. Moreover, local authorities were constantly trying to limit people's contact with theaters. For a long while, Massachusetts's theaters were barred from giving operatic performances on weekends. Not until 1850 was the ban relaxed, when the state legislature was finally forced to permit Saturday performances.

Fortunately the Howard Athenaeum thrived, and when Ryan was en-gaged to play in the house orchestra in 1847, he received a weekly salary of nine dollars. The ensemble was sizable for that day, consisting of two vio-lins, viola, cello, contrabass, flute, two clarinets, bassoon, two French horns, trumpet, trombone, and drums. For the most part, they played in the pit for dance companies and troupes presenting light musicals and also supplied incidental music for plays. Apples, oranges, and candy were ped-dled to the audience, who felt free to pelt the fruit onto the instrumental-ists' heads when displeased.[10]

A group that always pleased Bostonians visited the Howard Ath-enaeum regularly—the Seguin English Opera Troupe. Edward and Anne Seguin, thoroughly trained musicians with high standards of performance, made their first appearance in the United States in 1838 and remained popular through the 1840s. They had a varied operatic repertoire, all sung in English and often adapted to American likes and dislikes. "The list in-cluded most of the operas by Balfe, Wallace, Donizetti, Bellini, Auber,

Adam, and Boieldieu," writes Ryan. They also did the "comic *The Barber of Seville* [by Rossini] and the *Elixir of Love* [by Donizetti]."[11]

There were, of course, New Englanders who enjoyed Italian opera and wanted to attend authentic renditions of it in its original language. They knew of the Garcia Opera Company's stay in New York in 1825–26 and heard of the fabulous singing of Manuel Garcia's daughter, the future Maria Malibran. Yet they preferred to travel to New York for performances and made no move to bring the Garcias to Boston. Late in the decade, the resident New Orleans opera company visited Boston and presented a French repertoire. In the 1830s and 1840s small touring companies presented their wares to Bostonians. An excellent Italian troupe finally arrived from Havana in the summer of 1847. Some of Europe's leading singers and instrumentalists, led by Luigi Arditi, gave three performances a week at the Howard Athenaeum for about two months. They did the same the next summer.

Lastly, starting in the 1850s, New York opera companies organized by William Henry Fry, Max Maretzek, and others undertook yearly visits. Bostonians welcomed the visits but chose not to organize a similar company of their own. The snob factor that marred opera attendance in New York and offended Bostonians was at a minimum during these visits. Coming to see and be seen was a negligible consideration. Evening dress was not the rule. The gas lighting was never turned down in the auditorium during the performance, said William Apthorp, who also stated:

> We had opera in those days, too. Max Maretzek was the great operatic gun then, both as impresario and conductor; I think his company still kept up the old title of "Havana Troupe." The Boston Theatre was its battle-field; the dress-circle—that is, all of the first balcony behind the first two rows of seats— was cut up into open boxes, the partitions coming up no higher than the arms of the seats. But I never could discover that people "took a box"; the seats were sold separately, just as if the partitions did not exist. The entrance to the top gallery was fifty cents, though it was afterwards raised to a dollar. The opera orchestras were pretty small, and not of the best quality. . . . There was bass-tuba for *Robert le Diable,* and there were generally four horns.
>
> The music en scène was, for the most part, primitive enough. The scenery generally belonged to the theatre, and in those days the Boston Theatre had not launched out upon its gorgeous stage set-

tings. . . . The *"bujo loco"* of the septet in *Don Giovanni* was always represented by a blue-and-gold baronial hall, and who that ever saw it
can forget that street-scene, with the red brick wall, which figured in
almost every opera, no matter in what part of the world nor in what
age the scene was laid?

The costumes belonged either to the principal artists or to the
company, and were of varying degrees of splendour. There was one
fixed rule: the soprano heroine invariably wore a décolleté ball-
dress—white, if Fortune smiled; black, if down on her luck. Epoch,
country, in-doors or out-of-doors, rain or shine, made no difference.
The heroine—unless she was a peasant—stuck to that ball-dress as
for dear life.

In spite of these imperfections, the singing was usually excellent, said
Apthorp.[12]

POPULAR MUSICAL IDIOMS

What was just said about European soloists, orchestra, and opera companies pertained mainly to the largest urban areas, and they came and went
even to these places at irregular intervals, with time gaps of varying
but usually considerable size in between. However impressive was the
attendance of urbanites at their performances, the majority of New Englanders never saw these foreigners or, probably, never wanted to see
them. The larger number of city dwellers just stayed home. Town and village dwellers learned to do without. Those few men and women favorably
disposed toward these musicians had to look elsewhere for their common
musical fare. That "elsewhere," for one, was the wind band maintained
by almost every New England town and village. In the seventeenth and
eighteenth centuries it was connected with the company of local citizens
enrolled for military service, which was called out periodically for mus-
ters. At first the use of brass instruments was limited, but when valves
started to appear on them after the first two decades of the nineteenth
century, brass players became quite familiar on village greens and town
bandstands. Indeed, many New England bands were soon employing only
brass instruments. The selections the band men presented were a hodgepodge of marches, dances, overtures, variations, song arrangements,
and operatic excerpts adapted for band. On occasion a local musician's

contribution was aired. Bands gave concerts and played for dances, parades, and public celebrations. The open-air band concert in a warm summer evening was a regular feature in New England community life. The
usual village band contained eager amateurs varying in age from around
twelve to seventy.[13]

Edward Kendall formed his noted ensemble, the Boston Brass Band, in
1835. Other well-known bands from the antebellum period were the
Portland Band and the Providence Brass Band. The most prominent
bandleader of the time was Patrick Gilmore (1829–92), who had come
from Ireland. He would assume the directorship of the Boston Brass Band
in 1852, and in 1859 the Boston Brigade Band, which had a mix of brass
and woodwind instruments. After the Civil War he would organize two
gigantic "Peace Jubilees," involving hundreds of vocalists and instrumentalists, in Boston.

New Englanders could not very well bring bands into their homes.
They normally had to turn to their own resources for musical entertainment, which meant gathering around the parlor piano, if fortunate to have
one, and listening to keyboard pieces and singing undemanding songs.
Writing about his home in Portland, Maine, in 1817, Samuel Longfellow
observed that "in the home there were books and music. . . . In the home
parlor the sister's piano had replaced the spinet of his mother's youth. 'The
Battle of Prague,' 'Governor Brook's March,' 'Washington's March,' and
other music of the period were familiar and to such songs as 'Henry's Cottage Maid,' 'Brignal's Banks,' 'Bonnie Doon,' 'The Last Rose of Summer,'
'Oft in the Stilly Night,' Henry lent his voice and the training of the
singing school."[14]

Although the time was not ripe for the appearance of native composers of art music, the composers and performers of popular secular and
sacred song did appear in goodly numbers in the first half of the century,
some of the foremost from New England. Oliver Shaw (1779–1848),
born in Middleborough, Massachusetts, slowly went blind after a boyhood
accident. He studied music with a blind Newport organist, John Ber-
kenhead, later with Gottlieb Graupner, and then started teaching the keyboard and writing music in Dedham in 1805. Two years later he settled
permanently in Providence, where he was organist at the First Congregational Church. For several years Shaw also conducted singing schools. At
one time Lowell Mason was a student. As was usual for a New England
musician, he had an excess of energy. He sang, directed bands, and com-

posed songs, sacred choral pieces, dances, and marches. He participated in
founding the Psallonian Society of Providence in 1809 and influenced the
launching of the Handel and Haydn Society of Boston in 1815.

Shaw composed some of the earliest songs by an American to win
widespread favor—"Mary's Tears" (1817) and "There's Nothing True but
Heav'n" (1829). These two pieces are ubiquitous in the collections of
music made by private individuals during the 1820s and 1830s.[15] "Mary's
Tears," set to a verse by Thomas Moore, remained popular for around
twenty-five years. The title page of the sheet music states that it was
"sung at the Oratorio performed by the HANDEL & HAYDN SOCIETY, in
Boston, July 5th 1817, in the presence of the PRESIDENT OF THE UNITED
STATES."

Shaw's musical style was still guided by the British composers of the
previous century, which caused him to go out of date in the 1840s. Americans came to prefer a less complicated music with plain harmonies, fewer
sharps and flats, clear-cut and regular melodic phrases, and easy-to-sing
intervals. The folk tunes and dances of Ireland, Scotland, and England and
those modified for use or newly minted in the United States in accord with
American tastes became the main musical fare.

In 1839–43 a Tyrolean family of singers, the Rainer Family, toured the
eastern seaboard and created a furor everywhere they appeared. The
group consisted of two men and two women until 1841, when its personnel changed to five men and one woman. They sang songs traditional
among the Tyrolean people and marked generally by simple melody
and verse. These pieces were offered with a becoming modesty and in
a relaxed, natural manner. The voices were so smoothly integrated that
they sounded as one. Dressed in rustic Tyrolean costumes, they gave
the impression of a family unit healthy in body, mind, and morals. It
was not long before Americans, especially New Englanders, were forming similar ensembles that tried to portray themselves as mountain-grown
and attuned to the Rainer manner of singing. The most famous of
these ensembles was the Hutchinson Family Singers, from Milford, New
Hampshire.

Jesse and Mary Hutchinson had thirteen children, all of them musical,
all working on their parents' farm. After singing awhile in the church
choir, some of them turned to giving neighborhood concerts of secular
and sacred music. In the fall of 1841 Judson, John, and Asa Hutchinson,
modeling themselves after the Rainer Family, made a preliminary test of
people's reactions to their singing. They presented a few concerts not too

far away from Milford to decide whether it was feasible to embark on a wider tour. The results were encouraging. The next year, they added their sister Abby and began a singing career that took them to Boston in 1842, New York City in 1843, and eventually to the White House and the President of the United States. They concentrated on singing in close harmony and producing a euphonious combination of voices, which they projected with faultless intonation. John and Judson sometimes also performed on violins. Once in a while, John switched to the harmonium. Asa played cello, and Abby guitar. They caused a sensation wherever they appeared and grew accustomed to sold-out houses. In addition to their singing, the public responded to their uprightness, lack of airs, and high standard of morality. So great was their success that in 1845–46 they toured the British Isles, where they met with similar acclaim.

By the mid-1840s they had begun to embrace several causes, which won them the enmity of significant segments of American society—the abolition of slavery, the outlawing of alcoholic liquors, equality for women, and the right to vote for all Americans. They insisted on singing before desegregated audiences. They also sang at prisons and wherever they felt they could be a power for good. They tried charging modest admission fees or none at all to those with scarcely any money.

Although much of their repertoire was by other composers, especially the sentimental and dramatized compositions of Henry Russell, the Hutchinsons also shaped their own pieces, usually Hutchinson verses to extant sacred or secular tunes—"The Old Granite State" (1843), a celebration of their "mountain" home, "The Slave Mother" (1843), an antislavery sermon, "Excelsior" (1843), on a Longfellow poem, and "Get Off the Track!" (1844), telling of the emancipation that had to come. Abby married in 1849 and left the group, but the Hutchinson Family, with varying personnel, kept together for another twenty years.

Close on the heels of the Hutchinsons came the Baker Family, from Salisbury, New Hampshire: John, George, Sophie, and Henry and sometimes other family members. Aware of the success of the Hutchinsons, they imitated them as closely as possible. They were well received throughout much of the United States, in tours starting in 1844 and continuing for some thirty-five years. John Baker was also responsible for several songs regarded with affection by people in general: "Where Can The Soul Find Rest?" (1845),"The Burman Lover" (1845), "My Boyhood Days" (1848), and "My Trundle Bed" (1860). John Baker also tried his hand at a cantata, *Esther,* and an oratorio, *The Feast of Babylon.*

Unquestionably, the most famous antebellum composer from New England was George Root (1820–95). Born in Sheffield, Massachusetts, he grew up on a farm in North Reading, just a few miles outside Boston. The family was musical and did not stand in his way when he went to Boston to study music under Artemas Johnson and George Webb. In 1850 he traveled to Paris to study singing. On his return in 1851 he allied himself with Lowell Mason and engaged in teaching and reforming musical education. Five cantatas, of which the most renowned was *The Haymakers* (1857), came from his pen. They were equipped with unassuming music, delightful and easily sung choruses, and likable melodies.

The Haymakers depicts farm families and workers dwelling in an idealized countryside and brings them alive with music now veering toward popular secular idioms, now veering toward hymnlike intonations. After it was heard in Chicago in January 1860, a reporter in the *Chicago Press and Tribune* wrote:

> The operatic cantata of the "Haymakers" . . . bids fair to create as much of a furor here as it did in Boston. And there are good reasons why it should. Though as a musical production it is less difficult than the more pretentious works of foreign composers, it contains much that compares favorably with them. . . . But as we have hinted its chief excellence consists in the naturalness and success with which it gives expression, not to the exaggerated, violent and often baleful passions common to the Italian Opera, but the healthy sentiments of home and every day life. Mr. Root deserves credit for having struck out a new path in this respect. He has dared to appeal only to such sentiments as find their appropriate place at every happy farm fireside, and eschew all those intoxicating passions that excite only to harm.[16]

He won great fame as a song composer, close to that won by Stephen Foster. "The Hazel Dell" (1852), "There's Music in the Air" (1854), and "Rosalie, the Prairie Flower" (1855) were three early hits. Root's Civil War songs gained him even greater acclaim: "Just Before the Battle, Mother" (1861), "The Vacant Chair" (1861), "The Battle Cry of Freedom" (1862), and "Tramp! Tramp! Tramp!" (1864).

Root was quite aware that for most Americans it had to be a diet of song or hymn and nothing else. He said that he composed to satisfy the needs of his countrymen, hoping that what he presented to them would lead to a flowering of taste and appreciation of more complex works:

People change their musical homes, or rather add to them, as they progress in musical appreciation. At first they care only for the little way-side flowers and simple scenery of the land of tonic, dominant, and subdominant. They regard the musical world outside of that boundary as a kind of desert, entirely unfit to live in, and I may add once more, what has often been said in substance, that many people remain in this musical condition all their lives. But those who progress, begin, by and by, to see some beauty in the sturdier growths and the more varied scenery, and after awhile realize that the still unexplored regions beyond may be yet more beautiful when they are reached.[17]

He warned those men and women who enjoy artistic music, such as symphonies, not to grow conceited and despise the simpler songs of America:

The way-side flower has its place in the economy of God's creation as truly as the oak, and the little hill and the brooklet are as truly beautiful as the mountain and torrent are grand.

"But," some one says, "there is so much trash in the simple music of the day." There is trash at every musical grade, even to the highest. How much that is grotesque and senseless is seen in the ambitious attempts of those who follow Wagner, or would rival him in new paths, but have nothing of his transcendent genius. Such are usually among the despisers of the elementary conditions through which all must pass, and in which a majority of the music-loving world must always be.[18]

Other New England composers of noted songs in the antebellum years were Lyman Heath, born in Bow, New Hampshire, with "The Grave of Bonaparte" (1843); Marion Dix Sullivan, a New Englander married to a Bostonian, with "The Blue Juniata" (1844); Isaac Baker Woodbury, born in Beverly, Massachusetts, with "He Doeth All Things Well" (1844) and "Be Kind to the Loved Ones at Home" (1847); and John Ordway, born in Salem, Massachusetts, leader of Ordway's Aeolians, and composer of "Twinkling Stars Are Laughing" (1855) and "Silvery Midnight Moon" (1856). Later, the Connecticut songwriter Henry Clay Work (1832–84) would come along and take a musical stand against slavery and for temperance. His famous songs include "Marching through Georgia," "Kingdom Coming," "Grandfather's Clock," "Come Home, Father," and the minstrel number "Wake, Nicodemus."

REFORMING HYMNODY AND EDUCATION

City inhabitants soon found their cultural ideas and tastes permanently altered by education, experience, and intercourse with Europe at the beginning of the nineteenth century. The immigrant musicians in their midst condemned the psalmodic compositions of the New England singing masters, especially the fuging tunes, as the crude products of unlettered provincials. They persisted in advancing contemporary European styles, offering them as worthy of imitation. The hue and cry was taken up by urban cultural leaders who held up the harmonic practices of Handel, Haydn, Mozart, Beethoven, and other Central European composers, as well as those of the more sophisticated English composers, as admirable models for American composers. The native New England psalmody gradually gave way to this onslaught and soon existed only in some of the more isolated hamlets of the Northeast and in various locations in the southern and western states.

As early as 1793 Andrew Law of Connecticut was praising the variety in the harmonies of the more knowledgeable English hymn composers as contrasted with the "faulty" concords in the New England compositions. These last he found to be "languid and lifeless."[19] John Hubbard, a professor of mathematics and natural philosophy at Dartmouth College, agitated for change and recommended direct cultural action to bring about a rise in musical standards. A lecture delivered in Dunstable, Massachusetts, before the Middlesex Musical Society on 9 September 1807 was published the next year as "An Essay on Music." Native psalmody, he maintained, failed to come up to the "scientific" standards of Europe. He railed particularly against the "common fuge" because it detracted from religious observance. Hubbard quickly assembled an anthem collection intended to illustrate the proper approach to composition. In 1807, too, Elias Mann issued *The Massachusetts Collection of Sacred Harmony* in Boston, making it a point to say that he had left out the "wild fuges and rapid and confusing movements, which have so long been the disgrace of congregational psalmody."

These three critics failed to see the real merits of the New England works, instead judging them from European standards that had little connection with the efforts of Billings and his peers. They, of course, also wished to initiate an American music that would win the approval of Europeans here and abroad.

Thomas Hastings (1784–1872), born in Washington, Connecticut, was able to change taste even more than these three combined through the several compilations of sacred music that he published and through his widely known *Dissertation on Musical Taste* (1822), some of whose pages found their way into John Rowe Parker's Boston periodical, the *Euterpeiad.* Hasting's *Musica Sacra* collection came out in 1815 and included music arranged from Purcell, Handel, Burney, Croft, Madan, and Giardini. As Hastings grew older, he would turn more and more to the Germans for his borrowings.

In the *Dissertation* he denounced the singing school of the past:

> The art of singing is generally considered among us as a thing of so little difficulty, and so little importance, that almost any instructor, who will labor for a small compensation, can readily find employment. If he possess an agreeable voice, and understand well the nature of a pitch-pipe, and a six-penny gamut, he may readily pass for a competent man. A few giddy youths, perhaps, are wishing to spend their winter evenings together; and recourse is therefore had to a singing-school, as a convenient excuse. An insignificant, and too often a vicious, instructor is employed without the least hesitation. He, of course, supports neither order nor dignity in his school—his pupils are permitted to sing the most sacred words in the midst of unrestrained levity, without ever being reminded of their import. No real progress is made, either in the theory or practice of their art; but, on the contrary, a few indifferent pieces are committed to memory, and executed in the most wretched manner, without the least reference to the real nature of the song or subject. Owing to the low state of the art, however, such pieces will often afford *amusement* while their novelty lasts; and when this subsides, recourse is had to another similar instructor. Such pupils, after a few winter's [sic] attendance at school, where their tastes are necessarily vitiated, and their bad habits of execution confirmed, become, at length, too indifferent or too much occupied with business to pay any further attention to the subject.[20]

He wished to replace the works of Billings and his like with music more akin to that of the Germans, who "have given birth to a Handel, a Buck [Bach?], a Graum [Graun?], a Haydn, a Mozart, a Beethoven. . . . We are the decided *admirers* of modern German musick. We delight to study and to listen to it. The science, the genius, the taste, that every where pervade it, are truly captivating to those who have learned to appreciate it."[21]

Hastings was obviously not very familiar with the music of these Central Europeans. He himself favored a circumspect, strictly "correct," and simple hymn tune style. Some hymns that he wrote are still favored in churches: "Retreat," "Zion," and especially "Toplady," sung to the text "Rock of Ages."

Like so many other men devoted to bringing about reform in hymn writing and singing, Hastings would associate himself with Lowell Mason, the doyen of the group. Among the others associated with Mason were Henry Kemble Oliver, a Salem organist and choirmaster noted for his "Federal Street," and Benjamin F. Baker, for a time vice president of the Handel and Haydn Society, who would join Mason in the endeavor to bring music to public schools. William Bradbury, from York, Maine, would study with Mason and go on to make a name for himself as composer of music for Sunday school use. He sold 1.2 million copies of his *Fresh Laurels* (1867) and over 2 million copies of his *Jubilee* (1854). George Root would work with Mason on a number of teaching projects. All of these musicians would produce decorous, elegant-sounding hymn tunes, correctly harmonized and intended to replace the sacred music of the singing masters. Mason's contributions would include "Nearer My God to Thee" (tune: "Bethany"), "My Faith Looks Up to Thee" (tune: "Olivet"), and "From Greenland's Icy Mountains" (tune: "Missionary Hymn"). Often the verses came from noted writers, for example, Oliver Wendell Holmes's "Lord of All Being, Throned Afar," John Greenleaf Whittier's "Dear Lord and Father of Mankind," and E. H. Sears's "It Came upon a Midnight Clear."

Along with the dignified sort of hymn, the gospel song came into existence for use at rural camp meetings and urban gospel services and aimed particularly at Methodists and Baptists. These were more rhythmic and folklike compositions, appealing more unashamedly to the emotions and meant to excite worshipers. Bradbury and Root wrote many examples of this type of religious song. After the war, Philip Bliss and Ira Sankey would dominate gospel song writing and publication. One famous Civil War hymn resembled the gospel type: "The Battle Hymn of the Republic." Its tune came from a Methodist camp meeting song popular among black Americans from around Charleston, "Say, Brothers, Will You Meet Us?" The tune's composer is said to have been a William Steffe. Soldiers of the second battalion of the Boston Light Infantry Massachusetts Volunteer Militia, stationed at Fort Warren, on Boston Harbor, fitted it to the words "John Brown's body lies a-mouldring in the grave." The soldiers had in mind both John Brown, the militant abolitionist, and John Brown, an inept Scottish member of their battalion. Julia Ward Howe, while visiting in Washington, heard the Massachusetts soldiers singing "John Brown's

Body" in December 1861 and was inspired to write new words to the melody, after the Reverend James Freeman Clark had asked her to do so. It swiftly became a favorite among Union troops.

Lowell Mason (1792–1872), born in Medfield, Massachusetts, came from a musical family. His grandfather Barachias Mason had taught singing schools; and his father, Johnson Mason, had sung in a church choir and played several instruments. When thirteen years of age, Mason attended a singing school run by Amos Albee and went on to further musical study with Oliver Shaw. At sixteen years of age he was directing the Medfield church choir and, two years later, the band. In 1812 he left for Savannah, Georgia, with a Medfield friend, George W. Adams, and worked in a dry-goods store, later on becoming a partner. He married Abigail Gregory in 1817. Together, they parented Daniel Gregory and Lowell Jr., who would found the New York publishing house of Mason Brothers; Henry, who would start the reed organ and piano company of Mason and Hamlin; and William, who would become one of the finest pianists and chamber-music promoters of New York City.

Around 1819 Mason became a clerk at Planter's Bank. Meanwhile, he led the choir at the Independent Presbyterian Church and gained experience as a Sunday school singing teacher. While in Savannah, Mason continued his music studies with Frederick Abel, a German musician. Guided by Abel, he arranged hymn tunes based on melodies of the principal European composers and collected them into a volume patterned after William Gardiner's *Sacred Melodies,* a British collection that had put forth similar arrangements. Aided by George Jackson, Mason won the sponsorship of the Boston Handel and Haydn Society, and the collection came out in 1822 as *The Boston Handel and Haydn Society Collection of Church Music,* but without naming Mason as the author. It was an extremely well liked and influential hymn collection, most of it consisting of easily sung adaptations of music from Handel, Haydn, Beethoven, and other Europeans as well as some "corrected" versions of hymns by the New England singing masters.

The authorship did not remain a secret. The book's success was such that Mason was invited to return to Boston, which he did in 1827. At first he oversaw the music at three churches, until his appointment as music director of the Bowdoin Street Church in 1831. His choir of around six dozen members soon won a nationwide reputation for its superior merit. He achieved the same excellent results from the Central Church choir, which he took over in 1844. As a measure of its esteem for him, the Handel and Haydn Society named him its president and music director from 1827 to 1832.

It was around February 1831 that Francis Smith wrote the words of "America" in Andover, Massachusetts, and asked Mason's guidance on putting a tune to it. Mason advised him to examine a tune in a German music book and fit his words to it. The melody was the same as that for the British national anthem, "God Save the King"—an association that apparently was not voiced at the time. "America," beginning with the words "My country, 'tis of thee," was first sung in public at the Park Street Church on 4 July 1831.

Mason's interest in music education grew and was put on show in vocal music classes at the Bowdoin Street church and at private schools. Determined to promote musical literacy in children, he conducted singing classes in his churches and in 1829 published his *Juvenile Psalmist, or The Child's Introduction to Sacred Music* for them.

His approach to juvenile teaching, based on the Swiss educator Johann Heinrich Pestalozzi's theories about education, advocated moving from the known to the unknown, concrete ideas to symbols, and singing by rote to singing by reading notes from a page. Mason wanted children to exercise their curiosity about musical matters and to reason out their musical problems. Music, he insisted, was an avenue to physical, mental, and spiritual health. Following Pestalozzi's methods, he fixed the fundamentals of notation in pupils' minds through repetitive instruction and began with simple scales and scale patterns as the first stage in sight-reading. Unison and easy two-part singing of pleasant tunes were introduced to hold attention.

George Root says that William Woodbridge, recently arrived from Europe, introduced Mason to Pestalozzi's teachings. Woodbridge had already told Elam Ives Jr. of Hartford about Pestalozzi, and Ives had tried out the method. In 1831 Ives collaborated with Mason on the *Juvenile Lyre*. The next year, Ives would publish the *American Elementary Singing Book* employing the new approach. Mason kept pace with Ives and was the first to try applying the Pestalozzi teachings to an adult class:

> Wm. C. Woodbridge . . . called Mr. Mason's attention to Nageli & Pfeiffer's method of adapting Pestalozzi's idea of teaching to vocal music. Mr. Mason liked what he could see of it very much; then Mr. Woodbridge said to him: "If you will call together a class I will translate and write out each lesson for you (the work was in German) as

you want it, and you can try the method; it will take about twenty-four evenings." This was done, and the class was held in the large lecture room of Park Street Church, Boston. . . . The class was composed largely of prominent people of the city, who were interested in musical education, and all were greatly delighted with the new way.[22]

This was part of the gradual transition throughout New England from the old-style singing school to the "progressive" type put into practice by Hastings, Mason, and like-minded educators. Writing about this period in time, George Root said:

> I ought to say something about the condition of music in our part of the country [North Reading, Massachusetts] in those days. Not many years before, a singing-school had been held in the old red schoolhouse, where "faw, sol, law, faw, sol, law, me, faw" were the syllables for the scale—where one must find the *"me"* note (seven) to ascertain what key he was singing in, and where some of the old "fuguing tunes," as they were called, were still sung. I well remember how, shortly after, we heard that a new system of teaching music had been introduced into Boston, in which they used a blackboard and sang, "do, re, me," etc., to the scale. But how silly "do" sounded. We thought it smart to say that the man who invented that was a *dough-head*, and how flat were *fa* and *la*, in comparison with the dignified "faw" and "law." Later, however, when some tunes connected with the new movement came we changed our minds about the man who was at the head of it. Nothing before, so heavenly, had been heard as the melody to "Thus far the Lord hath led me on" (Hebron); and one of the great things [for me] in going to Boston was that I should probably see LOWELL MASON.[23]

Mason was aware that stubborn adherents to the older method of learning to sing and lovers of the older psalmody were unhappy about his reforms. He tried to explain himself to them, if only partially, in a letter dated 26 February 1860: "I am much dependent upon the good German writers—among whose works I find an exhaustless store of beautiful pieces—which are already—or may be by a little arrangement adapted to the wants of our people. . . . Now in doing this work, I fully believe that I am doing good, vastly more so, than as if I was composing myself."[24]

Lowell Mason would also participate in the promoting of musical conventions. In his 1854 *Complete Encyclopaedia of Music,* John Moore wrote that the idea of holding musical conventions arose in 1829, when members of the New Hampshire Central Musical Society at Goffstown held one, conducted by Henry Eaton, at Concord during two days in September. Another was held the next year, and still another in the following year, both conducted by Moore. The innovation caught on, and in 1836 Mason began to conduct them in Boston under the auspices of the Boston Academy of Music. The musical convention became the principal vehicle for the improvement of music teaching through the annual training of teachers over a period of several days, usually during the warmer months. [25]

THE BOSTON ACADEMY OF MUSIC

An important step in the nationwide advancement of music education was taken in 1833 when the Boston Academy of Music came into existence. Lowell Mason was the éminence grise behind the enterprise. The academy was founded after an association of about four dozen public-spirited community leaders, whose help was solicited by Mason, had advocated the expansion of opportunities for musical advancement for the public. The academy existed first, to promote the cause of music education for the general public; second, to set an example by initiating its own instructional classes; third, to train teachers of music; and fourth, to bring Bostonians meritorious music that would otherwise be denied them, by sponsoring performing groups and concerts.

George Webb, an English musician who had studied piano, organ, violin, and music theory, assisted Mason in realizing the academy's goals. When he came to Boston in 1830, he joined Mason in the work of the Boston Academy of Music. Webb was also the organist at the Old South Church and president of the Handel and Haydn Society for three years. The two men organized individual and group lessons in voice and instrument playing. They set up choral and instrumental ensemble groups and gave public lectures and concerts. They broke new ground with the music teacher training that took place annually during summer conventions. Soon, hundreds of teachers coming from most parts of the country were attending. They came for social pleasure and musical improvement—to study notation, learn to sight-read, engage in ensemble singing practice, exchange views with one another, and listen to lectures on the latest pedagogy. In later years, Mason would team with others to offer conventions in other New England states and beyond. When the sessions were expanded from a few days to three or more weeks, they were described as Normal Institutes. In 1853 Mason, Root, Bradbury, and Hastings held a three-month institute in New York. In 1856 the institute moved to North Reading, Massachusetts.

Published music, music books, and a magazine added to the academy's luster. Under the aegis of the academy Mason issued the *Manual of the Boston Academy of Music* in 1834, his inspiration coming from G. F. Kuebler of Stuttgart and his *Anleitung zum Gesang-Unterrichte in Schulen* (1826). Music teachers far and wide used the *Manual* and spread the word about music education for all. In the *Third Annual Report of the Academy* (1835) is the statement: "Letters have been received from persons in Georgia, South Carolina, Virginia, Illinois, Missouri, Tennessee, Ohio, Maryland, New York, Connecticut, Vermont, New Hampshire, and Maine, besides many individual societies in Massachusetts, asking for information relative to measures which they ought to adopt in order to introduce music as a branch of education into the communities where they live."[26]

The academy's first year attracted fifteen hundred students; its second year, twice as many as the first. An orchestra directed by George Webb, and varying in size from twenty-five to forty players, became an integral part of the academy. Seven Beethoven symphonies received local premieres, as did symphonies by Mendelssohn and Schumann. Ole Bull, Henri Vieuxtemps, and Henri Herz appeared as soloists at the concerts. Not that the orchestra members played perfectly. Yet, however flawed, it was an orchestra attempting to do major works that Bostonians had seldom or never heard. In general, each performance included an opera overture, an instrumental solo or two by members of the orchestra or visitors, a movement from an easy symphony, a musical potpourri, and a few vocal pieces.[27]

The Boston Academy of Music's *Ninth Annual Report, July, 1841*, submitted by Samuel Eliot, noted the need for improvement in the playing. An attempt to engage a more "efficient" orchestra was made: "Between twenty-five and thirty instruments were accordingly secured and were played by persons whose professional talent is well known in this city. Two or three amateurs with them, giving evidence of a zeal for improvement which we wish were more common. . . . This was the best orchestra ever assembled in Boston for an entire season." The orchestra, a mix of amateurs and professionals, had played works by Beethoven, Cherubini, and Mozart, plus dances and accompaniments for vocal numbers. It was obvious that more violins were needed, wrote Eliot. Unfortunately, too, public appreciation was unsatisfactory. Attendance was poor at concerts. Perhaps lowering admission prices and varying the programming even more would attract more people, he said.[28]

John Sullivan Dwight confirmed what Eliot saw as the problem. Writing in the *Dial,* July 1840, he reported a nucleus of around two hundred to three hundred subscribers and recommended "a series of cheap instrumental concerts" for improving turnout. Furthermore, he said, he wished that this largely amateur ensemble could stay together longer during the course of a year so that both its playing and its audience could improve.

One explanation for the poor attendance was the instrumentalists' unsatisfactory execution of the music. Thomas Ryan, who played in the academy orchestra, has written the first detailed description of a New England orchestra in action. He says that at one time he called Webb's attention to Mendelssohn's *Midsummer Night's Dream* Overture and all sorts of mishaps ensued:

> Well, we tried it. Our conductor was Mr. Geo. J. Webb,—an excellent general musician, but who had never heard the overture. He began by telling us that he had no score; so he stood up alongside of the first-violin desk and prepared to conduct. Rapping on the desk, he gave the signal to begin; out piped two flutes,—nothing else. He rapped again, implying that the players had not been ready to begin; then he said, "We will try again." He gave the signal—and out piped the two flutes. That caused a little titter of surprise, and we all looked quizzically at each other. Mr. Webb, however, dutifully gave the signal for the next "hold" or chord, when two clarinets joined the two flutes! More surprise. At the third hold (chord) the fagotti and horns were added, and at the fourth hold (chord) the entire wood and wind instruments all sounding most distressingly out of tune. This dissonant and unlooked-for result was followed by a dead pause; then every one of the players broke out with a hearty laugh of derision.
>
> I was on pins and needles and muttered, "Go on, go on!" After a while the people sobered down, and we tried to commence with the string part. The first and second violins (each relative part divided into two parts) began at an "accommodation-train" *tempo.* At the end of the violin passage, the wood and wind again held a very dissonant chord for two measures, which this time sounded so abominably out of tune that it really was as bad as if each man played any note he pleased; and it was so irresistibly funny they again everybody burst out laughing. But I buried my head under the music desk and cried; my idol was derided, every one poked fun at me.

That last dissonant chord ended the first rehearsal of the *Midsum-mer Night's Dream* overture. We never tried it again.[29]

Teaching matters at the academy did not always go smoothly, either. Mason and Webb had a brief falling out in 1841. In addition, two of Mason's former associates, H. W. Day and George Washington Lucas, accused him of favoritism in choosing instructors for the conventions and of trying to make money through whatever means he could. Mason did not take the criticism meekly. At one teachers' convention, Mason was addressing the assemblage when he spotted Day in the audience. He opened his Bible and proclaimed: "Now there was a day when the sons of God came together, and Satan also came among them." He shut the book firmly, walked in a deliberate manner up to Day, and forcibly escorted him out of the auditorium.[30]

Through the offices of the academy, Mason was also encouraging the teaching of music in the Boston public schools, in speeches and articles, and by rallying support from political, social, and religious leaders. He was convinced that music benefited a student spiritually, mentally, and physi-cally. It refined the mind and emotions, strengthened character, led to a harmonious social life, and gave aesthetic pleasure.[31]

Opponents arose who argued that the scarcity of musical aptitude among the public made teaching a waste of time, that at best music was an empty-headed subject, and that musical study served no useful purpose. The Boston School Committee rejected the petitions requesting music teaching in grammar schools. Mason gained a powerful ally when Samuel Eliot was elected mayor of Boston in 1837. Eliot immediately set up a committee to study the matter, and in August 1837 the Davis Committee Report came out recommending music in the public schools.

The school committee was forced to agree but refused funding. Mason then offered to teach gratis as an experiment and to supply all necessary materials. He was allowed to teach children, aged eight to fourteen, twice a week for thirty minutes each session, at the Hawes School in South Boston. In August 1838 the students put on a display of what they had learned, singing songs mostly from Mason's *Juvenile Singing School,* which had come out the year before. The audience was enthusiastic over the results. The impressed school committee decided to make music teaching permanent, hired Mason to supervise its introduction, and allowed him assistants. At the same time, music teachers attending the summer conven-tions wholeheartedly endorsed the cause of music in public schools and carried the idea back to their home states.[32] During the 1840s and 1850s Buffalo, Cincinnati, Chicago, Pittsburgh, Bangor, and New Orleans brought music into their public schools.

Mason and the Boston school committee still had their differences. In September 1845 he was suddenly discharged from the Boston public schools. No justification for the dismissal was given, though he asked for one. Five months later he was allowed to return but had to share his duties with Benjamin Baker.

The Boston Academy of Music was an influential musical presence for thirteen years. By 1847 its champions felt its mission was accomplished. The academy was dissolved. Mason now was known throughout the United States as the foremost music educator and hymn writer and compiler in America. His music publications bore such titles as *The Boston Academy's Collection of Church Music* (1835), *The Boston Academy's Collection of Choruses* (1836), *Carmina Sacra* (1841), and *Boston Collection of Church Music* (1850). He also put out several collections for children. They had brisk sales and made him a fortune.

Just before he died, Mason expressed his hopes for the future of America:

> May the future progress of music in this land be so directed and con-
> trolled as to insure its important aid to the highest degree of human
> culture, and thus to the attainment of a higher and more enduring
> happiness than that of the mere sensuous gratification which its per-
> formance does not fail immediately to afford. May its refining and
> elevating influence be experienced in private, in the family, in school,
> in social life, and may the house of worship be made to resound with
> the chorus of universal praise.[33]

AFTER THE ACADEMY

The Philharmonic Society, under Edward Riddle, coexisted with the Boston Academy of Music orchestra for some half a dozen years before it too went out of existence. Out of the ruins of both emerged the Musical Fund Society. It would live from 1847 to 1855. This new society represented another significant step forward in musical life. For the first time in New England history, an orchestra was organized on a cooperative basis. Certainly the planners had the similar structure of the New York Philharmonic in mind. Boston's Philharmonic Society eventually numbered from fifty to sixty instrumentalists, all of them professionals and committed to playing the best music. The musicians shared in the proceeds from the concerts. The performances started off at the Melodeon, which seated nine hundred. The orchestra got a reputation for rather decent playing, as compared with the previous academy and Philharmonic orchestras, and soon had a sizable subscription audience. Two years later, the Musical Fund orchestra moved to the Tremont Theater (later named the Tremont Temple), which seated fifteen hundred. Directed first by Thomas Comer, an Irish musician, and later by George Webb, the Music Fund Society played symphonies of Pleyel, Haydn, Mozart, Kalliwoda, and early Beethoven. Regrettably for it, after a few years the audiences shrank, and despite some small donations and a gift of one thousand dollars from Jenny Lind, it was headed toward extinction. One wintry evening, fate decided the issue. Owing to the freezing rain and dangerous ice condition of the streets, the instrumentalists left their instruments at the Temple building after the Saturday evening concert. A fire broke out that night and destroyed music, instruments, and other properties of the society.[34] It never recovered from the disaster.

Nevertheless, before that final day arrived, Boston had moved to correct what was generally seen as a major deficiency, the lack of an adequate hall for musical performance. The deficiency was remedied in 1852, when the Boston Music Hall opened. The new, up-to-date hall was built with the latest in gas jet lighting and seated three thousand people comfortably. What was more, all seats were readily accessible from the corridors. Wherever people sat, they could easily see and hear the orchestra. All that was needed was an orchestra of a quality commensurate with the hall. That was still twenty-six years down the road.

Another orchestra, the Germania Society, was contemporaneous with the Musical Fund Society. For a few years, some Bostonians thought it was the ideal ensemble everyone was awaiting. The Germania Society had formed in 1848, when twenty-four young, well-trained musicians left Berlin during a period of political turmoil in Central Europe and came to the United States. They appeared in New York and Baltimore, but found their most enthusiastic reception in Boston, where they gave twenty-two concerts and remained in 1849. Their first Boston concert excited enthusiastic admiration from the audience, when the Germania men played beautifully the very same *Midsummer Night's Dream* Overture that had eluded the academy orchestra. At times they augmented their ranks with additional musicians. The compact cluster of New England communities gave them a local performance venue. Under the leadership of Carl Lenschow and Carl Bergmann, they presented over eight hundred con-

The Germania Orchestra, ca. 1849.

certs in the Boston area and in tours to other cities of the United States. On 27 November 1852 the orchestra gave Boston its first sampling of Wagner by playing music from the opera *Tannhäuser*. Dwight said that it sounded "less strange than the fame of this bold innovator had led us to expect. . . . The melody was beautiful, not particularly original, but rather *Spohr-ish*."[35] The Germania Society also appeared thirty times with Jenny Lind and once engaged in a tour with Ole Bull. Carl Zerrahn, a flutist with the Germania, would conduct the Handel and Haydn Society in 1854.

The Germania also explored a popular vein. Under the direction of Carl Bergmann, a series of public afternoon rehearsals were opened to the public—a procedure that would continue with the Boston Symphony Orchestra. William Apthorp remembered one rehearsal where all the seats were taken off the Music Hall floor. The audience occupied the galleries. "Bergmann would announce the several numbers *viva voce*—often in the most remarkable English." Apthorp once heard the "Railway Galop," composer forgotten, "during the playing of which a little mock steam-engine kept scooting about (by clock-work?) on the floor of the hall, with black cotton-wool smoke coming out of its funnel."[36]

Over the years the orchestra members grew tired of touring. They began departing from the company, and by the 1853–54 season only fourteen of their original number remained. After a disastrous engagement under the management of P. T. Barnum, the suspension of its activities became inevitable. Although the Germania would disband in September 1854, most of its members would remain in the Boston area and generate other important musical endeavors.[37] For a few tantalizing years, these

Germans had given Bostonians a sample of what it was like to have a truly competent resident group of players entertain them with the finest in musical literature.

German instrumentalists were indispensable in every art-music sphere of activity, whether in Boston or in the rest of the United States. In 1849 four of them and Thomas Ryan formed the first truly important chamber music group in the United States—the Mendelssohn Quintette Club. August Fries and Francis Riha played violin; Edward Lehman, viola and flute; Thomas Ryan, viola and clarinet; and Wulf Fries, cello. At last, music lovers could hear the string quartets, quintets, and other chamber pieces of Beethoven, Mozart, Haydn, Mendelssohn, and others on a steady basis. The club would continue until 1895, with occasional additions of other musicians. Concerts took place mainly in Boston, where the players experienced their most notable successes. Little by little, however, the Mendelssohn Quintette Club expanded its touring circuit until in 1881 the group traveled to California and then to Australia, New Zealand, and Hawaii before returning home.

The foreign musicians constantly found their way into every new ensemble that was started. An indefatigable Carl Zerrahn, immediately after the dissolution of the Germania in 1855, established the Philharmonic Orchestra with fifty-four men. He and the orchestra would continue to give regular concerts until 1863, when the Civil War forced a stoppage. Sad to relate, the quality of its playing was not the equal of that of the Germania Society, although it was certainly better than that of the other ensembles previously mentioned. Writing about the concerts he had heard around 1860, William Apthorp said:

> The Orchestra was an exceedingly variable quantity: there were only two horns, and a second bassoon was not to be thought of. The second-bassoon part had to be played on a 'cello; and uninitiated visitors used sometimes to wonder what that solitary 'cello was doing in the midst of the wood-wind. Hamann, the first horn, had little technique, but a good tone. . . . I think there were hardly ever more than six first violins: I certainly remember one performance of Beethoven's A major symphony with only three first violins and two second. The solitary bassoonist was conspicuous by his singularity, not by his virtuosity.[38]

Not until 1865, when the Handel and Haydn Society put together a nearly one-hundred-piece orchestra, would Boston hear a full string section for the first time. Again, this was a one-shot deal and, save for the giant

The Mendelssohn Quintette Club, founded 1849.

orchestras amassed for the two postwar Peace Jubilees, not duplicated until the Boston Symphony Orchestra came along sixteen years later.

Zerrahn was back conducting symphony orchestra concerts in 1865, when he was asked to lead an orchestra formed by the Harvard Musical Association. By this time Harvard had had a fifty-seven-year connection with music. Early on in the century, Harvard students had expressed the desire to make music together and to present music for ceremonial occasions and the entertainment of friends. To this end, they established the Pierian Sodality in 1808, probably taking their name from Pope's *Essay on Criticism:* "A little learning is a dangerous thing; / Drink deep, or taste not the Pierian spring."[39] In 1856 the Harvard Glee Club began and soon was giving concerts aided by the Pierian Sodality.

Fifty of the alumni of the Pierian wished to continue their connection with the college and with music. Under the leadership of John Sullivan Dwight, Henry Oliver, William Wetmore Story, and Christopher Cranch, they organized the Harvard Musical Association at the Harvard commencement of 1837. Beginning in 1844, the association held regular chamber music evenings that eventually motivated the creation of the

Mendelssohn Quintette Club. The association would also be active in the start of *Dwight's Journal of Music,* the Cecilia Society, and in the eventual addition of music to the Harvard curriculum. Moreover, it would start to accumulate a music library, which would be second to none by the end of the century.

The orchestra under Zerrahn, for which the Harvard Musical Association was responsible beginning in 1865, would run from fifty to sixty players. Its programming was influenced by the exceedingly conservative tastes of John Sullivan Dwight and Otto Dresel, a German pianist and musical pundit resident in Boston, both of whom served on the planning board. They allowed no catering to "coarse" tastes by the orchestra, barred dances, marches, and operatic medleys, discouraged program music of every description, and would allow only "pure" music they deemed of the highest quality—usually symphonies of Mozart, Beethoven, Mendelssohn, and the like. Most music by contemporary composers was excluded from the repertoire. Hemmed in by these limitations, the orchestra was held to the "highest" ideals. Yet these exacting standards did not mean that the playing was now superior to that of the previous orchestras. Indeed, when Theodore Thomas took to bringing his well-drilled orchestra from New York to Boston in the 1870s, the Boston audiences grew dissatisfied with the local fare. In addition to feeling more and more unhappy about the restricted musical diet offered by the association orchestra, Boston music lovers felt embarrassed by the superior playing of the New York band, which put to shame the local musicians. More and more critics of the status quo arose to demand something better. And the clamor was continuous throughout the decade.

The Harvard Musical Association tried to put variety into its offerings, but too late. To add to the predicament, the Boston lot was unpredictable. It condemned the orchestra for the lack of new music, and when new music was played, the compositions proved unpopular.[40]

Bernhard Listemann organized another Philharmonic in 1880, in direct competition with the association orchestra. Previously, Listemann had acted as concertmaster in the Thomas orchestra. The Philharmonic played no better than its rival and succeeded only in dividing the relatively small audience, so that both ensembles operated at a loss. The quietus was given to both ensembles when the Boston Symphony Orchestra began life in 1881.

CHAPTER

5

TOWARD A NEW MUSIC ERA

There are two main thrusts to this chapter. The first concerns those elements in the environment that initiated the composition of American art music. Here we look to the encouragements developing from the American system. Throughout the century, it weighed heavily on Yankee minds that democracy needed to prove itself worthy of respect not only politically and economically but also socially and culturally. Only in this way could democracy be said to be truly successful. As George Bancroft wrote in the *Boston Quarterly Review* of October 1838, "If with us the arts are destined to be awakened into a brilliant career, the inspiration must spring from the triumphs of democracy. Genius will not create to flatter or decorate saloons. It yearns for larger influences; it feeds on wider sympathies; and its perfect display can never exist, except in an appeal to the general sentiments for the beautiful."[1]

The second concern involves the need for musical leaders to stop reacting to and only correcting what went before, instead of putting their energies to work exploring the potential for an altogether different musical approach. New England could not merely come into a musical legacy and add on to it with ideas drawn only from Europe; it had to add its own unique content to that legacy before handing it on to a future generation. Ralph Waldo Emerson, in his lecture "Historic Notes of Life and Letters in New England," delivered before the Concord Lyceum in 1880, spoke of two parties, one of the past and the other of the future. The latter represented forward movement in literature, philosophy, religion, politics, and social customs. Such a party, he said, had slowly gotten under way in the early part of the century and gathered momentum in the 1830s and 1840s, until by the 1850s it had taken over the thinking of most persons of authority.

Both concerns exerted a strong continuous pressure on the American music world, of which New England was a part, spurring it onward to press for the rise of music publishers and stores, to form a readership for the first music periodicals and criticism, and to participate in the proliferation of music associations and institutions during the antebellum period. From an important perspective, New England's music was constantly imagining itself anew, thus representing Emerson's party of the future. It had gone from the oral mandates of seventeenth-century Puritanism, to the singing-school psalmody of eighteenth-century pragmatic Yankeeism, and to the elevated musical sensibility of early nineteenth-century Transcendentalist modes of thinking that emphasized the intuitive and spiritual above the empirical. Yet, whatever the change, New England itself had retained its own identity.

Its identity would continue intact into the post–Civil War years, even as the Irish injected themselves into its political processes, and the Germans into its artistic processes. It would learn to accommodate both and make them a part of its distinctive character.

PIANOS, PUBLISHERS, AND PERIODICALS

An important cultural achievement for American democracy took place with the production in New England and elsewhere of keyboard instruments, making them inexpensive and plentiful enough to be available to ordinary people. At the beginning of the century, around six piano builders were active in the greater Boston area. One of the first, Benjamin Crehore, was originally a carpenter at the Federal Street Theater. He set up his own piano firm in Milton and around 1797 had begun to have Peter von Hagen sell ten to twelve of his instruments a year. Around 1813 John Rowe Parker had a Franklin Piano Manufactory that was assembling two pianos weekly by the end of the decade. He was also building church and chamber organs. The development of greatest consequence in piano building, however, came with Alpheus Babcock (1785–1842), who had worked at the Franklin shop and in 1821 affiliated himself with John MacKay. New England's climatic extremes of temperature and humidity were raising havoc with pianos imported from Europe and with American productions based on European designs. About the year 1825 Babcock evolved a complete iron frame cast in one piece to withstand the weather conditions prevalent around Boston and began to equip a square piano of his design with this innovation. Babcock's invention would after a few years become standard in all piano manufacture, American and European.

Jonas Chickering (1797–1853) commenced his career as a cabinet-maker in Ipswich, Massachusetts, then came to Boston and learned piano making during an apprenticeship to John Osborne, who had learned his trade from Benjamin Crehore. Chickering eventually formed a partnership with MacKay in 1829. He would take over the entire business after MacKay was lost at sea in 1841. Chickering did not hesitate to adopt and improve on the Babcock innovation. In 1837 he applied for a patent for a full metal plate for square pianos; in 1840 he patented a more advanced one-piece iron frame design for square pianos; the next year he patented this advancement as applied to grand pianos; and in 1843 he patented the full metal plate for grand pianos, together with a device for casting agraffes in the plate.[2] The firm of Chickering and Sons would thrive for several decades.

Jonas Chickering would also win admiration for his benevolence to musicians, helping them financially when in need, and for his generous support of whatever enrichment of the Boston music scene was taking place. Chickering and Sons also gave the Boston community a new music hall, seating four hundred people, located in one of his warehouses. The piano virtuoso Louis Moreau Gottschalk spoke of it as "a perfect gem, which he graciously places at the command of artists who visit Boston."[3]

After Jonas Chickering's death, his sons took over. Charles Frank Chickering, the second son, continued to contribute vitally to improvements in piano design. Chickering and Sons' only direct competitor in quality was the Steinway firm of New York, which adapted the metal frame for its own use. Both Chickering and Steinway pianos won gold medals at the Paris Exhibition of 1862. In 1876 Charles Chickering was awarded the French Légion d'Honneur. When Chickering pianos secured the approval of Franz Liszt, the European piano makers moved quickly to take over the New England refinements in piano design. Unfortunately, the firm slipped up financially in the century's final decade and was bought by the American Piano Company.

Another contribution to keyboard manufacture was made by the Mason and Hamlin Organ and Piano Company. They helped make keyboard instruments affordable to the common people as a whole. Founded in 1854 by William Mason, son of Lowell Mason, and Emmons Hamlin, Mason and Hamlin began as a reed organ factory. In the first year, 459 small instruments, called melodeons, were built to an improved design by Hamlin. These were perfect for small parlors and for musicians and circuit ministers constantly moving from place to place and in need of a portable instrument. In 1861 the firm introduced the cabinet or parlor organ. Prices were pegged so low that most families could find the money for an instrument, thus achieving a democratic objective. Its models, in every configuration, ranged from $22 to $1,500 each. By 1882 the firm had added pianos to its reed organ offerings, ranging from uprights to grands.[4]

The availability of music in print was also advanced. Following up on von Hagen and Graupner, John Rowe Parker offered buyers a good selection of sheet music and other music publications, much of it imported, at his Franklin Music Warehouse. However, the first real impact on New England music publishing and retailing came with Oliver Ditson (1811–88). He had apprenticed himself to Samuel Parker, music publisher, from 1823 to 1826 in order to learn the trade. He worked for other firms until he struck out for himself in 1835, allying himself with Parker until 1842, then later with John Haynes. Under the guidance of Ditson, the firm Oliver Ditson and Company grew enormously, increasing its own production of sheet music and music books. For example, in a two-week period—the last week of February and the first week of March 1856—Ditson published thirteen vocal and eleven piano works; two weeks later another thirty-one works came out. The establishment as it existed in 1857 dazzled a reporter for the *New York Musical Review*. Ditson by then had moved to new quarters at 277 Washington Street. The vast basement was given over to the wholesale end of the sheet music business. The ground floor showed off and retailed a huge amount of music publications. The floor above made room for the engravers and stampers as well as an enormous supply of paper. The next floor had twenty-five to thirty men running twelve printing presses. The firm was reputed to have an inventory of 9 million sheets of music and fifty thousand engraved plates and to use about one thousand reams of paper yearly for sheet music publication alone.[5]

The Ditson firm bought up competitor after competitor in other American cities. In 1865 Ditson funded the establishment of a veritable music supermarket in Chicago, Lyon and Healy. At the end of the century, Ditson had become the largest music publisher in the United States, its catalogue offering over 100,000 titles for sale. Oliver Ditson and Company also sold an array of music education books, a song and piano "masterpiece" series edited by authorities in music, and instructional material to facilitate the layman's understanding of fine music. After World War I its glory days were over, and the Great Depression aggravated financial matters even further. In 1931 Theodore Presser took over the entire Ditson catalog.[6]

New England also contributed several critics of music and musical life who were out of the ordinary. Joseph Tinker Buckingham, born in Windham, Connecticut, in 1779, provides an example of the contentious, independent-minded Yankee unwilling to take any authority's pronouncements about music or the inflated reputation of a performer at face value. Without much formal education, he worked on a farm as a boy, then for a printer, before opening his own printing shop in Boston. He also became an omnivorous reader. His early experience in music was hymn singing at home and printing broadside ballads for street hawkers. Yet somehow he acquired some musical knowledge and a tremendous love for music.

From 1806 to around 1834 he wrote music reviews and commentaries in the several Boston periodicals he edited: the *Polyanthos* (1806–7), the *New-England Galaxy* (1817–28), and the *New-England Magazine* (1831–34). In the *New-England Galaxy*, March 1818, he censured the Handel and Haydn Society for its sloppy performance of Handel's *Messiah*. In 1820 he complained in the *Galaxy* about "the refined childishness and scientific frippery" in Haydn's *Creation* music and asked that the society give the composition a rest for a few years.

His barbs spared no performer. If a singer was drunk onstage or had egotistically preened himself or herself before an audience, Buckingham was unforgiving. New York writers, he argued pugnaciously, might let them get away with such antics, but all New York's critics could do was to puff performers for a fee, not judge them at their true worth. Needless to say, he won himself more than a few enemies.

Mrs. Poe, the mother of Edgar Allan Poe, gave musical performances in Boston during the winter of 1806–7. Buckingham complained, "The publick were compelled to listen night after night to the 'childish treble' of Mrs. Poe, who has never before ranked higher than a third or fourth rate singer." An angry Mr. Poe is reported to have confronted Buckingham in his office over the insult to his wife, but no record remains of what took place behind the closed door.[7]

Alexis Eustaphieve, Russian consul in Boston, once sued Buckingham for libel, though he got nowhere with his suit. The editor had detested what he described as Eustaphieve's antidemocratic airs, writing, "He supposed himself to be the autocrat of the fashionable world of Boston." Buckingham also hated how the consul was force-feeding music to his daughter, compelling her to practice endless hours at the piano in order to make a virtuoso out of her. Buckingham reviewed her playing and admired its facility. However, "intricate passages and novel combinations of double demisemi quavers, with almost endless chromatics" are not by themselves signs of real talent, he observed. He was listening to a "lifeless automaton whose haggard cheeks and feeble frame evince the daily drudging to which it has been subjected." Better she should learn to play a simple melody "with real taste, feeling, and expression."[8]

The *New-England Magazine,* December 1831, had Buckingham explaining that music to him was not "a mere luxury, a mere parlor ornament." It was a recreational necessity for all humanity and a channel to morality and civilized pleasure for his fellow citizens. It thus sustained the principles on which the nation was based. For these reasons, he had to attack anything that sapped music's potency and anyone who made a superficial amusement of it:

> I greatly love, and I must say too, respect, the art of Music. . . . There are not many who will allow it to be any thing more than the source of a momentary, perishing enjoyment—at most, and at best, a mere luxury, doing little in any condition of society to advance or secure its more valuable and permanent interests. To this opinion, however, I cannot assent. . . . For my own part, I cannot but think that the cause of civilization, of intellectual progress and refinement, even of morals and religion itself, lie under serious obligations to the science and art of music.[9]

Buckingham's published commentaries were the subject of conversation in the homes of more than a few New Englanders. His blunt language alerted readers to an art whose meaning went deeper than the idling away of a leisure moment. He is important because he was readying a new generation of Yankees to listen to music seriously, to demand the best in themselves by demanding the best in music, and to think independently. And for him, there was a best in all types of music from the plain hymn and ballad to the exalted symphony and oratorio. Buckingham's was the spirit of a striving democrat trying to broaden his and his colleagues' musical horizons, urging them out of their lethargies and ready acceptance of anything put before them that unsound critics denominated as art.

John Rowe Parker tried to further the cause of music by publishing the *Euterpeiad* in 1820–22 out of the Franklin Music Warehouse on Milk Street. The first periodical published in America that was given over to musical matters, it was oriented toward Europe and contained none of the acerbic challenges issued by Buckingham. Music histories, biographies, articles, and news items were liberally borrowed from European, mostly

English, sources. Happenings on the local scene were dutifully reported on. Contributions by various "gentlemen" and "ladies" found space on the pages. Since the *Euterpeiad* did not have the sales for which Parker had hoped, after a year he included a "Ladies' Gazette" with the publication. This soon became independently printed as the *Minerviad.* Both journals folded early in 1823.

Another significant first came in 1854, when Oliver Ditson published John W. Moore's *Complete Encyclopaedia of Music.* Again, as with the *Euterpeiad,* there was a great deal of borrowing "from the best foreign authorities." Moore added more information to some entries, however, and also inserted a few of his own. He is usually most tempted to refashion an entry or insert a new one if he can illumine the nature of the American musical condition, the connection between music and the American democracy, and the direction toward which both should head. For example, under "Oratorio" he writes:

> Like all other tastes, the love of music may be nourished from the smallest germ into large and vigorous life; the habit of attending to its beauties, and the desire of appreciating them, lead to a conviction of its truth; whilst its effect upon the mind is to elevate and refine, perhaps beyond all other sensuous enjoyment. If you doubt, go listen to the "Creation," or any other sublime oratorio, and mark the potency of many impassioned scenes upon a people who, as yet, are but in the first chapter of what may become to them a noble volume. Listen to the heavenly sounds, and acknowledge that it is in moments like these that the heart expands its sympathies, stretches out the hand to the weak, whispers encouragement to the depressed, and applauds the strong; that men grow gentler and better, determine upon goodness, and build upon hopeful resolves. It is in moments like these that they catch glimpses of pure taste and brilliant fancy, and make for themselves a world of beauty; and the dream becomes a rest and solace after the hard buffets, and anxious cares, and gloomy realities of daily life. It is in looking at art with such feelings that we desire to see it encouraged in the midst of a population whose labors, in spite of their noble tendencies, are apt, without recreation, to lower the tone of the mind; and because we are anxious that every attempt should be in a right direction—emanate from the best feelings; not a mockery of art, but a true worship.

Moore claimed in his preface that the book entered "an unoccupied field, no such work having been compiled before either in this country or in England, and nothing like it existing in the English language excepting a small Lexicon published by the author of this work in 1845." Indeed, its more than one thousand pages on almost all conceivable musical matters was unprecedented for the time. For English-speaking music lovers, it provided a wealth of information, some of it inaccurate, that had hitherto been unavailable.

The author was born in Andover, New Hampshire, in 1807 and began putting out periodicals in 1828, with his weekly *Free Press* of Brunswick, Maine. He sold the weekly in 1831 and founded the *Concord Advertiser* in Concord, New Hampshire. Six years later he was in Bellows Falls, Vermont, and publishing the *Bellows Falls Gazette.* It was in Bellows Falls that he compiled the *Encyclopaedia,* allowing Ditson to print the volume after having labored over it for eighteen years. In 1875 a brief appendix was added to the original work. Only *Grove's Dictionary of Music and Musicians,* which came out in London in 1879, would supersede it. Even then, the content was shaped to suit English interests, and not until an *American Supplement,* edited by Waldo Selden Pratt, came out in 1926 would American interests be adequately addressed.

Another publication, *A Handbook of American Music and Musicians,* edited by F. O. Jones, was published in Canaseraga, New York, in 1886. Jones says in his preface that he tried to include in it "everything relative to American music, musicians (both native and foreign born), and musical subjects." The book's 182 pages are notable for their aim at accuracy and for their conveyance of information about the American musical world hitherto unavailable from one source.

Unquestionably the most important music periodical to come out in nineteenth-century America was *Dwight's Journal of Music,* which lasted from 1852 to 1881. At first John Sullivan Dwight was not only editor but also owner and publisher of the journal. Six years later, Oliver Ditson was its publisher, although Dwight continued as editor. Dwight would also publish a *History of Music in Boston* as the fourth volume of Justin Winsor's 1880 *Memorial History of Boston.*

Dwight was the quintessential musical Transcendentalist. He was born in Boston in 1813 and graduated Harvard College in 1832 and Harvard Divinity School in 1836. While at Harvard he became fluent in German, even translating Goethe and Schiller. He was one of the graduates who founded the Harvard Musical Association as a means for elevating the standards of musical taste. He collected a worthwhile music library for the association and through it proselytized for a Harvard faculty appointment in music.

For a short while he was a Unitarian minister but gave that up to join the Transcendentalists' Brook Farm experiment in communal living in 1841. Though lacking in formal musical training, he was passionately devoted to the art, wrote articles about it in the *Harbinger,* a Transcendentalist periodical, and lectured to his fellow Transcendentalists at Brook Farm about its appreciation. Like Buckingham and Moore, he gave music a high position in the conduct of life. He wrote in 1849, "Music is both body and soul, like the man who delights in it. Its body is beauty in the sphere of sound,—*audible beauty.* But in this very word *beauty* is implied a soul, a moral end, a meaning of some sort, a something which makes it of interest to the inner life of man, which relates it to our invisible and real self."[10]

In the 1850s all of the arts, including music, were on a number of New England minds. Music took on increased value, and listeners showed sensitivity to its productions heretofore unknown. At the beginning of 1852 Dwight issued a notice describing how he would run the contemplated *Journal:* "The *tone* [is] to be impartial, independent, catholic, conciliatory, aloof from musical clique and controversy, cordial to all good things, but not eager to chime in with any powerful private interest."[11] After it came out, William Apthorp summarized informed American musical opinion about Dwight and his *Journal*:

> [*Dwight's Journal of Music*] certainly was the highest-toned musical periodical of its day, all the world over. In it Dwight's fineness of artistic instinct and his unflinching intellectual honesty found adequate expression. He has often been praised for the courage he showed in standing to his guns as he did, through thick and thin. Indeed, his moral courage was something wonderful, and all the more so for being wholly unconscious; for it never occurred to him that it took any "courage" to say what he thought, utterly regardless of consequences.[12]

Dwight himself wrote a good deal of the *Journal;* correspondents from around the country also contributed, among them Alexander Thayer, George Curtis, William Apthorp, and W. S. B. Mathews. He published reviews, theoretical information, studies of compositions, composers' and noted performers' biographies, histories of past musical periods, and intelligence of contemporary American and European musical life. He did not worry about getting Europe's approval, although he did win it. He was more intent on improving the musical discrimination of a diverse conglomeration of citizens whose tastes were still only half-formed. For many years, the *Journal* set the criteria by which music was judged and was at the forefront of musical thought for all sophisticated Americans.

Ryan called Dwight "a spur and a whip" to all artists, unforgiving if they catered to corrupt tastes or aimed only to win popular approval. It was not in his nature to compromise with anything he considered mean or common in music.[13] His musical preferences were conservative and oriented toward Germany and Austria. It is unfortunate that he would look no further than Beethoven, Mendelssohn, and Schumann. In May 1852 he praised the New York Philharmonic for playing Mendelssohn: "The Philharmonic Orchestra is admirably drilled. The members are all inspired by the same sympathies,—mostly Germans, they believe in the German composers, who would not regret to sit among the audience and hear their own immortality so assured." He gave advice to the Mendelssohn Quintette Club in 1852, when it was playing to less than full houses:

> Dear especially and justly to the lovers of good classic music is this fraternity of five young artists. . . . To them we owe our *sphere* of periodical communion with the great German masters in their most select and genial moods. . . . Think how much of Haydn, Mozart, Beethoven, and Mendelssohn—of masters, who used to seem so far off, unapproachable to us novices in music—they have this winter opened to us in their eight subscription concerts. . . . We earnestly trust that the Messrs. Fries, Riha, Ryan and Lehmann will not abandon the high ground they have taken, from any dismay at a momentary fluctuation in their outward success. . . . there is but one ground on which such a Society can stand and outlive temporary discouragements, and that is the ground of almost strict adherence to classic chamber compositions, in their original forms.

Note the "strict adherence" to the classics. To him, Romantic program music was an annoyance. He disliked the music of Berlioz, Liszt, Brahms, and Wagner. He considered Italian opera to be drivel. American popular music, especially the songs of Stephen Foster, was anathema to him. In 1853 he described Foster compositions like "Old Folks at Home" as

> erroneously supposed to have taken a deep hold of the popular mind; that the charm is only *skin-deep;* that they are hummed and whistled *without musical emotion,* whistled "for lack of thought"; that they persevere and haunt the morbidly sensitive nerves of deeply musical persons, so that they too hum and whistle them involuntarily, hating

them even while they hum them; that such melodies become catching, idle habits, and are not popular in the sense of musically inspiring, but that such and such a melody *breaks out* every now and then, like a morbid irritation of the skin.

He was certainly instrumental in impeding the independent development of American composers—always measuring their works, when they tried to take hold, against the works of Beethoven and allowing no novel or national idiom to be cultivated. When the Philadelphia composer William Henry Fry had a *Santa Claus* Symphony premiered in 1853, Dwight suggested that the composer allow "the world's impression" to determine its merit. He also warned Fry:

> Of course the bulk of our public concerts and musical entertainments must consist of pieces of a guaranteed excellence, of works that the world *knows* to be good, sure to give pleasure, sure to inspire and reward attention. It will not do to invite the public to perpetual experimental feasts of possibilities; to assemble a concert audience, like a board of jurors, to listen to long lists of new works and award prizes. . . . It is of no use to tell us why we ought to like *Santa Claus,* the thing is to make us like it.

What was interesting was the *Journal*'s report in June 1853 on two Bostonians who had gone to Leipzig to study music. A correspondent wrote that Charles C. Perkins was "pursuing his studies with much diligence and has recently finished another Quartet for stringed instruments, which is considered above par." And James C. D. Parker was "making rapid progress . . . in composition. It will interest his friends to know that he has also composed a Quartet for strings, which is pronounced very clever."

After the Civil War, Boston's music lovers gradually wearied of Dwight's inflexible opinions, however sincerely intended, and grew impatient with his opposition to any innovation in the orchestral repertoire. His pronouncements were increasingly ignored, and his *Journal* was no longer accepted as a disseminator of musical truth and an authority of last resort. Though considered a relic of the past, he was still honored for his accomplishments in keeping Bostonians' focus on the highest in music during years when they exercised little discrimination in their musical preferences. Dwight retired to a room at the Harvard Musical Association and was its librarian until his death in 1893.

POST–CIVIL WAR CONDITIONS

Boston's atmosphere pleased the German musician George Henschel when he came to the city in 1880. He would be the Boston Symphony Orchestra's first conductor. Looking about him, he said:

> How different the impression Boston made on me as compared to that of New York. In the first place the streets had names, not numbers. . . . And then the "down-town," i.e. business part of the city: narrow-streets and crooked lanes, a dear old church with a beautiful portico, still called the "King's Chapel," the old Statehouse, with the Lion and Unicorn still in its gable, the "Old Corner Book-store," and numerous other old-world landmarks—all this made me feel quite at home.[14]

Postwar Boston had other attractive features for sophisticated and knowledgeable European visitors. The city struck most of them as less subject than other American cities to an aggressive, money-dominated mentality and more preoccupied with learning, literature, and the arts. To think of it was to think of the older writers—Emerson, Thoreau, Hawthorne, Whittier, and Longfellow—and those who were active in Boston and its environs during the latter part of the century—Holmes, Howells, Aldrich, and Lowell. The highly regarded *Atlantic Monthly* was published here; the illustrious Harvard, now being made over into a major university, was across the Charles River. Painters, sculptors, and architects found encouragement when they lived and worked in and around Boston. Local cultural leaders were aware that elsewhere in the country, in Emerson's words, "things are in the saddle, and ride mankind." They did not want it to be said of them. The Civil War had pulled away almost every traditional prop that held society together. They hoped to reinterpret tradition so it could adapt to contemporary conditions and accommodate contemporary demands. They were delighted in 1901 when Tolstoy dispatched a "Message to the American People," asking why they did not take to heart the words of Emerson, Thoreau, and Theodore Parker.

Though the Massachusetts Bay area could not boast about a long-standing symphony orchestra, like New York's Philharmonic, until 1881, nor an outstanding opera company, like New York's Academy of Music or Metropolitan, until 1909, it did harbor numerous choral societies, generate public concert after concert, and see more than a few vocal and instrumental performances in private homes. Men and women listened enthusiastically to the visiting Fisk Jubilee Singers and their presentation of black musical literature. They seconded Boston-born Alice Cunningham Fletcher's many studies of American Indian music, which had won the support of the Peabody Museum in Cambridge. Operetta became the rage, especially after an unauthorized version of Gilbert and Sullivan's *H.M.S. Pinafore* was staged in 1878. Not yet frozen into different taste groups, the same people who listened to a Beethoven symphony or Haydn mass on one day might attend a vaudeville or minstrel show on another. In 1892, when Antonín Dvořák arrived to lecture Americans on what their national music should be and soon was offering the Symphony *From the New World* as an example, an intense debate was set off among Yankees over the proper place of indigenous music and originality in the writing of an American music.

With regard to women's cultural liberation, New England could proudly point to such firsts as the well-received art music composers Margaret Ruthven Lang and Amy Beach, and the Fadette Ladies' Orchestra of Boston. The orchestra, founded in 1888 by Caroline Nichols, started off with six members. Within a decade it grew to forty players and became the first professional all-women's orchestra to tour the United States and Canada. It would disband in 1920.

Even Louis Moreau Gottschalk, a New Orleans pianist and composer who had often fared roughly at the hands of Boston critics, had to admit on 26 February 1864:

> Boston . . . is par excellence the aristocratic city. It pretends to be the most intellectual in the United States. It is not to be denied that it has made enormous progress in the sciences and arts. The university at Cambridge is the most celebrated in the United States. Her poets are known the world over. She has for eight years possessed the largest organ in America. . . . Boston has six theaters and three concert halls, two of which can seat thirty-five hundred persons. It is in one of these, the Tremont, that I gave my concerts. It is in my opinion the best for hearing and the most magnificent concert hall in the world.[15]

Gottschalk had undergone criticism, especially from Dwight, because he did not adhere to the most serious and highly regarded musical repertoire but insisted on playing pieces meant to dazzle or to appeal to sentimentality. The highly original piano compositions by Gottschalk that featured popular and traditional tunes and dances of the United States and Latin America did not seem to aim at the sublime so cherished by Dwight.

Still dominant in local thinking was the Transcendentalist endeavor to make Americans deserving of their freedom and raise them to a respected standing among civilized people. Dwight and others like him felt that Gottschalk had failed to contribute to this endeavor.

When the first significant New England art composers came along, they would not seek to dazzle or sound sentimental or chase after the most up-to-date musical idiom, just for the sake of making a sensational impression. Nor would they adopt the musical vernacular of American Indians and African Americans, as Dvořák thought they should. Neither, they claimed, was their vernacular. At the same time, the sublime would be very much on their minds. As William Kearns wrote of two of the composers, "Although their immediate environment and careers caused them to write quite different kinds of music, Ives and Parker did share broader philosophic concepts: faith in social progress and belief in the ethical basis of art. . . . This sense of social mission was an outgrowth of the Puritanical-Transcendentalist-Victorian heritage that Parker shared with his generation. Moral values were cited as reasons for almost all activity."[16]

If and when a symphony was composed in New England, it would correspond not necessarily to a code of genteelness but to the function that people had assigned to it and for which they would value it—to improve them morally, to exalt them spiritually, to bring out the best in them, and to aspire to something above and beyond them.

CELEBRATING PEACE

What were the ingredients that went into the Peace Jubilees that were held in Boston and attracted national, even international, attention?

First, thanks to the singing schools, normal institutes, music classes in the public schools, numerous church choirs, and proliferating choral societies of New England, a huge cadre of singers was available to anyone wishing to make use of it. Meanwhile, the giving of music festivals had taken hold in Europe. These were musical events each consisting typically of a series of performances over a period of days, sometimes in celebration of a composer or event. In an effort to equal Europe, the Boston Handel and Haydn Society in May 1856 experimented with a festival over a few days during which a chorus of six hundred and an orchestra of almost eighty instrumentalists (some brought in from New York) presented Handel's *Messiah,* Haydn's *Seasons,* and Mendelssohn's *Elijah,* plus some concerts of a diversified nature. Boston tried again at the war's end, in May 1865, when a chorus of seven hundred and an orchestra of one hundred presented an even more impressive festival. A third festival, held three years later, included Mendelssohn's *Reformation* Symphony and Beethoven's Ninth Symphony.[17]

Second, the idea of a "jubilee" was also in the air, a period for rejoicing and festivity. Witness the Jubilee Concert of 1 January 1863, held in Boston's Music Hall in appreciation of Lincoln's putting forth the Emancipation Proclamation. Emerson, Longfellow, Whittier, Holmes, Edward E. Hale, and James Fields placed their names on the notices, and Dwight involved himself in the planning for the concert. The music was by Beethoven, Mendelssohn, Handel, and Rossini, and the singing came from excellent local vocalists. It opened with Emerson's "Boston Hymn." Later, Holmes's "Army Hymn," which Otto Dresel set for soloist and chorus, was presented. The audience was carried away by the music and feelings of patriotism.[18]

Third was the involvement of Patrick S. Gilmore. Born in Ireland, he traveled to Boston in 1849 and in 1850 joined John Ordway's minstrel troupe, the Aeolian Vocalists, as cornet and tambourine player and songwriter. His best-liked song was "Good News from Home" (1854). He also is supposed to have composed "When Johnny Comes Marching Home" (1863), under the pen name Louis Lambert.

Gilmore made a name for himself as a band director of first the Charlestown Band, next the Suffolk Band (1852), then the Boston Brigade Band (1853), and last the Salem Brass Band (1855). The Salem Brass Band, under his direction, won a national reputation after it was invited to Washington and participated in President James Buchanan's inauguration-day parade in 1857. Gilman then left the Salem band and turned his attention completely to establishing his own Gilmore's Band, giving a first concert in 1859. This band became even more famous than the Salem one, performing in 1860 at both the Democratic convention at Charleston and the Republican convention in Chicago, which nominated Lincoln for the presidency. During the Civil War, Gilmore's band was attached to the Twenty-fourth Massachusetts Regiment.

Gilmore found himself in New Orleans in 1864, where General Banks gave him the responsibility of organizing a colossal concert to celebrate Michael Hahn's assumption of the governorship of Louisiana. His performers included five hundred instrumentalists, six thousand adult and juvenile singers, fifty cannons, and forty men striking anvils.

After the war and his return to Boston, he sold the idea of a jubilee to local business leaders, politicians, and the press. Eben Jordan, whose son would support the building of the New England Conservatory of Music's Jordan Hall and the construction of the Boston Opera House, was a backer of the jubilee. After gaining approval, in 1869 Gilmore organized the National Peace Jubilee and Musical Festival in Boston, a five-day celebration of the Civil War's end that gathered five hundred orchestral players, with Ole Bull as concertmaster, ten thousand singers, and six bands. A vast audience crowded into a specially built auditorium, three hundred feet long, one hundred feet wide, and one hundred feet high. It was erected on three acres in the Back Bay, at the corner of St. James Avenue and Clarendon Street. Special excursion trains brought people in from all over the United States. President Ulysses Grant and political and military figures from around the country attended. The program for the first concert, on 15 June, according to Thomas Ryan, was as follows:

1. GRAND CHORAL, "A Strong Castle is our Lord," Luther
2. TANNHAUSER OVERTURE, Select Orchestra of 600, Wagner
3. GLORIA from the Twelfth Mass, Mozart
4. AVE MARIA, Bach-Gounod
    Sung by Madame PAREPA-ROSA
    The violin obbligato played by two hundred violinists.
5. NATIONAL AIR, "The Star Spangled Banner," Key
    Sung and played by the entire force with Bells and Cannon

Intermission fifteen minutes

6. AMERICAN HYMN. Keller
7. OVERTURE, "William Tell" Rossini
8. INFLAMMATUS from the "Stabat Mater," Rossini
    Madame PAREPA-ROSA
9. CORONATION MARCH, from "Le Prophete," Meyerbeer
    1000 performers
10. ANVIL CHORUS, from "Il Trovatore," Verdi
    All the forces; 100 anvils, performed on by 100 members of the Boston Fire Department; Bells and Cannons.
11. MY COUNTRY, 'TIS OF THEE, words by REV. S. F. SMITH, D.D.
    All the forces; the audience requested to join in singing the last stanza.[19]

Ryan reported further:

> At the termination of the "Anvil Chorus" there was enormous
> applause. The whole mass of people rose to their feet, jumped up
> and down, and nearly dislocated their arms by waving handkerchiefs,
> fans, hats, parasols, even babies. . . . Fifty thousand people in a
> wooden building can make some noise. . . . When the piece was
> ended, the gentlemen firemen would march out; and, the applause
> continuing, they would march back again and go through the whole
> exciting performance once more.[20]

John Sullivan Dwight hated the element of the jubilee that blew it up
into a showy extravaganza. His *Journal,* of 19 June, spoke of it as "a plan
so vain-glorious in the conception, so unscrupulously advertised and
glorified before it had begun, and having so much claptrap mixed up with
what there was good in the program." Yet Americans felt that the jubilee
had given the United States standing in the musical world and had forced
Europe to rethink its accusations that all America was good for was
mechanical innovation and the making of money.

It was so successful that a second event, the World Peace Jubilee and
International Musical Festival, was organized on an even larger scale, from
17 June to 4 July 1872, the excuse being the end of the Franco-Prussian
War. Ensembles from Europe came to participate—Johann Strauss's
orchestra from Vienna, the French Garde Républicain Band, the English
Grenadier's Guards Band, and the German Kaiser Franz Grenadiers Band.
Some 19,000 instrumentalists and singers presented the music to an audience accommodated in an immense 100,000-seat structure. There was a
day each given over to England, Germany, and France, with the music tailored to match. Kindling popular enthusiasm for the spectacle proved
impossible, however; owing to the huge musical forces, chaos often
afflicted performances, and people stayed away. The sponsors lost a great
deal of money.

In 1873 Gilmore would organize a third jubilee, now in Chicago,
meant to celebrate the rebuilding of the city after the disastrous fire of
1871. He would leave Boston for good in 1874, going to New York, where
he would organize a new band.

The two Boston jubilees were crucial in laying the groundwork that
would make the existence of New England composers possible—they
would build the audience for art music. As one of those composers,
Arthur Foote, said: "These monstrosities were counterbalanced by the

immense amount of good done through the formation of choruses in towns everywhere, that came together and spread familiarity with works like the 'Creation' and 'Messiah.' . . . I sang in the Salem [Oratorio Society] chorus, and, as one of it, was present at the concerts of this Jubilee [of 1869], as also at those of its successor in 1872. . . . They had a marked effect in awakening a real interest in good music."[21] Or, as Louis Elson wrote: "Of course, this was not art. Groceries or dry goods may be wholesaled but not music; yet the second Peace Jubilee was a factor in the advance of music in the eastern part of America. The chorus was made up of innumerable societies from all parts of New England and the Middle states. Many of these societies had been content with practicing weak sacred selections. . . . If the Peace Jubilee of 1872 did nothing else, it at least left a better repertoire to the country societies as a legacy."[22]

THE FESTIVAL IDEA

The music festival initiative was not destined to fade away with the end of the jubilees. Outside Boston, at least four New England festivals took on some importance, especially since they were annual events. None, as with the jubilees, had a specific rationale for its existence. Each came into being because men and women wanted to gather together in a musical setting to perform and listen to music. At least three of the four would take advice from or offer directorships to native composers, and all four would perform original New England compositions. Without question, they increased the audience for art music and helped along the notion that New England composers should be encouraged and their works heard.

One of the oldest festivals in the United States was the Worcester Festival. It emerged from a musical convention held in Worcester, Massachusetts, in 1858. At first it resembled a musical convention, relying on teachers and singers to meet, study, and perform oratorio selections. In 1863 the Worcester County Musical Association was formed, and shortly after, the festival departed its convention moorings. The concerts increased in number and were designed after those of English festivals. Carl Zerrahn was appointed conductor from 1866 to 1897. One of the first steps he took was to commence presenting complete oratorios with an orchestra instead of only selections. The Boston-based composer George Chadwick would take over the directorship from 1897 to 1901, and during these years compositions by the New Englanders Chadwick, Horatio Parker, Frederick Converse, and Henry Hadley were performed. During the twentieth century, the Philadelphia and Detroit symphony orchestras would pay visits during festival time. In the post–World War II period the festival would be instrumental in the birth of the Worcester Symphony Orchestra.[23]

A second festival began in 1889 and was held annually until 1910, with the exception of the year 1900. The Springfield Music Festival, sponsored by the Hampden County Musical Association, had Chadwick and Victor Herbert as directors for at least half its existence. As with the Worcester Festival, the Springfield Festival encouraged American composers to submit their works for performance. Among the works presented were Chadwick's *Phoenix Expirans* and Parker's *Hora Novissima*.[24]

The Maine Music Festival began in Portland in 1897 and lasted until 1926. The aim of its organizers was to study and sing the more difficult choral compositions, to listen to the greatest musicians of the world, to support local musical talent, and to give hearings to Maine's composers. Two years later, the festival took place for three days in Portland (called the Western Festival) and three days in Bangor (the Eastern Festival). When the Lewiston Armory was completed, two evenings and one afternoon of the Maine Music Festival took place there. Choruses from around the state participated in the performances, and for around ten years the Maine Symphony Orchestra, organized by William Chapman, provided the instrumental backing and also gave its own concerts in Maine and New Hampshire. During the last five years of the Maine Festival, fully staged operas were heard, among them *Faust, Carmen, Aida, Il trovatore,* and *Martha*.[25]

The fourth series of annual festivals began in 1899, sponsored by the Litchfield County Choral Union, in Connecticut. In the first half of the nineteenth century there had been a Litchfield County Musical Association, frequently directed by Robbins Battell. It performed "the best works" to piano accompaniment in Litchfield, Winsted, and Norfolk. In 1878 a Winsted Choral Society was formed, and four years later Battell began summer concerts on the Norfolk Green. Battell's daughter Irene, wife of Carl Stoeckel, then founded the Norfolk Glee Club in 1897.

Mr. and Mrs. Stoeckel, finding local music lovers receptive to a coalition of their musical forces, then went ahead to establish the Litchfield County Choral Union in 1899. A chorus of seven hundred local singers, plus an orchestra of around fifty instrumentalists from New York and various distinguished soloists, began to participate in the festival each June at Norfolk by offering "free music of the highest class to 70,000 residents of

Litchfield County." A small fee was later charged. By 1902 a music shed sheltered the performances. Several American composers received either first performances of one of their works or commissions to write new music. Among the works heard at Norfolk were Horatio Parker's *King Gorm the Grim* (1908) for chorus and orchestra and *Collegiate* Overture (1911) for orchestra and male chorus; George Chadwick's *Noel: A Christmas Pastoral* (1909) for soloists, chorus, and orchestra and *Aphrodite* (1912), a symphonic fantasy; Henry Hadley's Fourth Symphony (1911); E. S. Kelley's *New England Symphony* (1913), and Henry Gilbert's *Negro Rhapsody* (1913) for orchestra.[26]

In 1996 a complimentary Litchfield Jazz Festival would start up and quickly win the reputation of being one of the top jazz festivals in the country.

SOME FORWARD-LOOKING MUSICIANS AND MUSIC LOVERS

Several men and women played significant roles in the encouragement of local music enterprises and the rise of local composers. Foremost among them was B. J. Lang (1837–1909), born in Salem and making his debut as a pianist with the Mendelssohn Quintette Club, at the age of fifteen. He left for Germany in 1855 to study composition with Alfred Jaël and piano with Franz Liszt. He returned to live in Boston in 1858 and quickly made a name for himself as a pianist, organist, and conductor. The composer Margaret Ruthven Lang was his daughter.

Lang's organ playing was a feature in the services at South Congregational Church for many years and was also heard at Old South Church and King's Chapel. A proponent of contemporary music, he was a needed antidote to the conservatism of John Sullivan Dwight and Otto Dresel, a German who preached the virtues of the Austro-German musical classics and rejected all that came after. Lang succeeded in giving hearings to Tchaikovsky's First Piano Concerto, Johannes Brahms's Second Piano Concerto, Berlioz's *Damnation of Faust,* and Wagner's *Parsifal* before audiences that had been advised to approve none of these composers. Richard Wagner especially won his admiration, and he urged Bostonians to attend the Bayreuth Festival and take in the *Ring* cycle and other Wagnerian operas. When Arthur Foote was still a youth, Lang was convinced of his musical gifts and persuaded Foote to give up an accepted profession in favor of a more uncertain musical career. Lang would also bring him along to hear Wagner's music at Bayreuth.

Lang served as director of the Apollo Club, a men's singing society started in 1868; the Cecilia Society, a choral society started in 1874; and the Handel and Haydn Society. As a choral conductor, he introduced several American compositions, two of them being Buck's *The Nun of Nidaros* and Chadwick's *The Viking's Last Voyage*. Thomas Ryan summed him up as a "progressive" musician "of marked character, a typical American, ambitious and industrious."[27] He was an influential guide. His teaching and beliefs affected such composers as Arthur Foote, Ethelbert Nevin, and Lang's daughter Margaret, as well as writers such as William F. Apthorp.[28] Foote wrote Lang's obituary for the *Boston Evening Transcript* in 1909:

> It was in the summer of 1874 (just after graduating at Harvard) that began for me a long and close companionship with B. J. Lang. That summer, as sometimes in subsequent years, he came into town once or twice a week, and gave a few lessons. We used to meet for organ lessons at Dr. Hale's church on Union Park street. . . . When any of us younger people went to him with our manuscripts, we never came away without keen and sympathetic criticism that had to be heeded. He had a remarkable feeling for perfection of detail (the absence of which is the great defect of most of our music here); for him there were no trifles, for they make perfection. . . . In his lessons, it was not only the music and the playing, but other things quite as important, that we got. He was willing to take the trouble and the risk of giving advice and direction about outside things: about manners, habits, business questions . . . so that we felt the friend as well as the teacher. . . . He was by nature an optimist; and he taught us . . . that encouragement is better than fault-finding, and that achievement comes partly from a belief that the thing can be done.[29]

Along with sympathetic music directors, wealthy or influential supporters helped advance native composition. Patrons were essential to native composers, wrote Daniel Gregory Mason. To genuinely benefit artists, the benefactor had to have delicacy, a capacity for appreciating differing points of view, and a great love for art: "Otherwise, however you may try to gloss the matter, you are a dispenser of benefits, a king without a court, a patronizer rather than a patron. You are substituting a feudal relation of lord and vassal for the democratic one of the cooperation of equals variously endowed for the realization of ends desired by all."[30]

Boston's musical life was immeasurably enriched when Henry Lee Higginson (1834–1919) founded the Boston Symphony Orchestra in 1881, at the same time adding an endowment of around one million dollars. Each year he covered whatever deficit arose. Higginson was a banker who had also studied keyboard, voice, and music theory in Vienna. He had received an admonishment during the Civil War from Charles Lowell, just before his death, who warned him: "Don't grow rich; if you once begin you'll find it much more difficult to be a useful citizen. Don't seek office; but don't 'disremember' that the useful citizen holds his time, his trouble, his money, and his life always ready at the hint of his country. The useful citizen is a mighty, unpretending hero, but we are not going to have a country very long unless such heroism is developed."[31]

Higginson did grow rich but also wanted to be a "useful citizen." His purpose in underwriting Boston's first ongoing professional orchestra, with an initial membership of seventy instrumentalists, was "to give Boston as many serious concerts of classical music as were wanted, and also to give at other times, and more especially in the summer, concerts of a lighter kind of music, in which should be included good dance-music . . . to keep the prices low always, and especially where the lighter concerts are in question, because to them may come the poorer people, 50 cents and 25 cents being the measure of prices."[32]

Additionally, Higginson aimed to promote cultural equality by keeping a large number of seats unreserved and available at low cost to wage earners. He also desired the constancy of quality that occurred when professional musicians played solely for the one orchestra. In 1885 he would institute a summer season of light music, called the promenade concerts, which would lead directly to the present-day pops concerts.

The Boston Symphony Orchestra, though beholden to the generosity of one man, was entirely committed to public, not private, performances. It was steered by an aesthetic principal that decreed that the musical director, not Higginson, would have sovereign control over musical matters, with no meddling from outsiders.[33] This policy Higginson maintained until his resignation in 1918, when a board of directors replaced him. Gustav Mahler considered the turn-of-the-century orchestra to be in the "ersten Ranges," while the New York Philharmonic, which he conducted in 1909, was "talentlos und phlegmatisch."[34]

It was not always easy for Higginson to keep up his sponsorship of the orchestra. Yet he rarely weakened. As he said in 1889:

> Several times when I have faltered in my plans for the future, I have taken heart again on seeing the crowds of young fresh school girls, of music-students, of tired school-teachers, of weary men, of little old ladies leading gray lives not often reached by the sunshine, and I have said to myself: "One year more anyway." . . . . Considering these things, can I have done harm by the concerts? Are they not worthwhile. . . . We are all bound in our day and generation to serve our country and our fellow-men in some way.[35]

The support given American musicians through concerts given in private homes helped native composers, although generous financial aid rarely accompanied the private concerts. Clara Kathleen Rogers, a highly praised professional singer before her marriage to the Boston lawyer Henry Munroe Rogers, also had tried her hand at musical composition. More important, she and her husband dedicated themselves to the nurturing of music in their home. She writes that the musical evenings were to some extent meant to lend a hand to unknown American musicians by giving them a hearing before people capable of advancing their careers. Attending her soirées were musicians like Lang and Julius Eichberg, critics like Dwight and William Foster Apthorp, the several music directors of the Boston Symphony, writers like Julia Ward Howe, and composers like Chadwick, Foote, and MacDowell. Louise Moulton and her husband held similar evenings, to which came academics, novelists, musicians, and of course, composers. They welcomed "the socially unknown guest," and the Moultons' sympathies "had little relation to social standing."[36]

Celia Thaxter, the friend of John Knowles Paine, actively worked to benefit MacDowell and his music. William Mason speaks of the summer concertizing at Appledore, her home on the Isles of Shoals, with "doors wide open to the sun and salt breezes, the people sitting in the room and grouped on the piazza, shaded by its lovely vines, the beautiful vistas of gaily colored flowers, sea and sky beyond." Appledore in the 1890s became a center for vacationing artists. MacDowell introduced his Sonata *Tragica* here. Listeners' responses were cool at first, and then, after repeated playing of the work, quite affirmative. On another occasion, MacDowell presented the Sonata *Eroica* at Appledore, this time to a highly appreciative audience. Mason concludes: "This incident [MacDowell performing his newly composed sonatas] is related to illustrate the remarkable effect of musical surroundings and the great advantage of living in a musical atmosphere. Here were people of intelligence and culture who, under adverse circumstances, would not have appreciated the beauty of these intellectual works, but who after closer association were led to perceive their beauty and who learned to love them."[37]

Paine's advancement was greatly indebted to John Fiske, a philosopher and historian on the Harvard faculty. Fiske smoothed Paine's social manners, introduced him to a choice group of people—among them William James, Chauncy Wright, and William Dean Howells—shored up his standing among the Harvard faculty, and wrote enthusiastically about him in newspapers and periodicals. Paine went along with Fiske and his children on leisurely walks around Spy Pond, had discussions on Darwinian evolutionary theories with intellectuals in Fiske's library, and involved himself in Fiske's numerous musical evenings.[38]

One or two professional American musicians tried to move native music forward in the cultural world. David Bispham, the renowned Philadelphia-born singer, brought about the premiere of Horatio Parker's *Hora Novissima* at Worcester, in England. Bispham submitted the score to Hans Richter, director of the Birmingham Festival, in 1898, which brought about the performance. Emma Eames, a celebrated singer born in Bath, Maine, performed the songs of Amy Beach at every opportunity. One recalls the remark that Finck ascribes to Foote: "Mr. Foote thinks—and here I again agree with him—that the popularity of songs depends very largely on their being taken up by concert-singers." The famous Venezuelan concert pianist Teresa Carreño responded favorably to MacDowell, playing his works before audiences in the Americas and Europe. MacDowell's Second Piano Concerto, dedicated to her, was frequently performed with orchestras.[39] The opera singer Louise Homer provides an example of a friendly performer, one loyal to Parker and his music. When Parker's opera *Mona* was to be mounted at the Metropolitan Opera, she took on the title role and dedicated herself to gaining a thorough understanding of it: "Her passionate desire to make a success of this work was most touching. It occupied her thoughts, almost exclusively, for several months."[40]

Once in a while a composer received financial assistance. For example, when Horatio Parker was a youth living in Auburndale, just outside of Boston, a Mr. Burr furnished him with the money needed to travel to Germany for his musical education. The benefactor has not been identified beyond his name. The affluent J. Montgomery Sears befriended

MacDowell in Boston and promised him ample subsidy to cease his teaching and compose an opera. Though stirred by the offer, MacDowell refused it, not desiring to write at someone else's say-so, and worried that the projected opera might not represent him at his best.[41] These examples notwithstanding, seldom did a composer receive money to help provide him with a living or to commission a work during the second half of the nineteenth century.

Perhaps the most renowned Boston patron of the arts was Isabella Stewart Gardner. Her advocacy of music by Charles Loeffler, the Alsatian composer and violinist, is well known. Loeffler joined the Boston Symphony in 1882 and dwelt in the Boston area until he died in 1935. The Gardner home constantly echoed to the sound of music, usually European and played by Europeans. Some of the music was American and, if practicable, played by Americans. Foote played the piano for her and heard his own music (the Trio in B Flat, op. 65, for one) at the Gardner home. She helped Evelyn Ames establish the Manuscript Club of Boston in January 1888 to assist local composers in providing opportunities for them to hear their music at her home. Some compositions thus performed were Foote's Suite in E for Orchestra, op. 12, Parker's Quartet in F for Strings, op. 11, Clara Rogers's Violin Sonata, Margaret Ruthven Lang's *Petite Suite,* and Clayon Johns's songs. A year later, interest in the club decreased when Ames was absent from Boston, and it disbanded.[42]

The Music Teachers National Association had George Chadwick among its founders in 1876. Its focus was on music education, but it was also committed to the support of American music. At its eighth annual meeting (1884) in Cleveland, the association sponsored the first known all-American concert—songs, piano pieces, and chamber works by Paine, Chadwick, and Foote. The next year's meeting scheduled Paine's Violin Sonata, among other works. The chief planner for its concerts was Calixa Lavallée, a Canadian composer and pianist who came to Boston at the beginning of the 1880s. Arthur Foote states: "Two things of value came from my interest in the society. First, I thus became acquainted with most of the best musicians not living in New York or Boston, thereby broadening my ideas, and doing away with a certain provincial conceit that we are apt to have here. Second, through their concerts came the first real chance of a hearing of my compositions in large form. At that time an American writing serious music was a rare bird, opportunities for a hearing being hard to get. To these concerts I thus owe the beginning of what reputation I may have."[43]

The standing of composers was enhanced by reports and reviews published in newspapers and magazines, which the music public read and discussed with great interest. Most of New England's reporters had musical instruction, unadventurous tastes, and a liking for German music. John Sullivan Dwight, influential editor of *Dwight's Journal of Music* during the years when Paine, Chadwick, and Foote were trying to establish themselves, was disposed to write approvingly about their compositions, so long as they adhered to classical models, and urged the public to take heed.[44] As these composers were quite aware, Dwight believed in musical orthodoxy and loathed innovation. He loved the music of Bach, Mozart, and Beethoven and disliked operatic works (save for those by Gluck, Mozart, and Beethoven), program music, and concertos emphasizing virtuosity. Most contemporary compositions left him cold. According to William Apthorp, Dwight's "naïveté of perception, his ever youthful enthusiasm, his ineradicable power of enjoyment, held out unimpaired to the end [Dwight died in 1891]. What he was, he would be genuinely and thoroughly; fashion had no hold on him, and his refinement never had a touch of dandyism nor finical affectation."[45] Dwight praised Paine's First and Second Symphonies when they were premiered. He criticized Paine's programmatic Symphony Fantasy, *Shakespeare's Tempest,* in D Minor, op. 31, when Theodore Thomas premiered it in 1877. Dwight's conservative tastes were in evidence when he pronounced it to be a post-Classical, excessively Romantic symphonic poem à la Liszt.[46]

Other writers contributed articles about and reviews of native art music. Benjamin Edward Woolf's writings appeared in the *Saturday Evening Gazette,* the *Boston Globe,* and in 1894 the *Boston Herald.* Louis C. Elson wrote for the *Musical Herald,* the *Boston Courier,* and the *Boston Advertiser.* William Foster Apthorp's writing appeared in the *Boston Evening Transcript,* the *Atlantic Monthly,* the *Sunday Courier,* the *Boston Traveler,* and the program notes of the Boston Symphony from 1892 to 1901. Howard Malcom Ticknor was for a time an assistant editor of the *Atlantic Monthly;* his articles appeared here and also in the *Boston Advertiser,* the *Boston Globe,* the *Boston Herald,* and the *Boston Journal.* Henry Taylor Parker wrote principally for the *Transcript.* Philip Hale's commentaries appeared in the *Home Journal,* the *Boston Post,* the *Boston Journal,* the *Musical Courier,* the *Boston Herald,* the *Musical Record,* the *Musical World,* and the program notes for the Boston Symphony concerts from 1901 to 1934. The many writers on music and the numerous publications issuing their commentaries bear witness to Boston's high interest in art music.

THE FOREIGN IMPACT

The natives of Germany and Austria who immigrated to Boston strove to awaken an interest in the art music of their native countries and were both a support and an impediment to the American composer. Undoubtedly they were influential in creating organizations that would insure art music's continuing existence. By so doing, they encouraged the appearance of New England's second wave of composers. The musicians among them functioned as performers, orchestral and choral directors, music educators, and music publishers. From 1848 on, Boston experienced a great influx of these German immigrants. They had fled from the unrest occasioned by the futile democratic revolt in Central Europe. Already mentioned was the appearance of the Germania Musical Society. From this orchestra came Carl Zerrahn and Bernhard Listemann, the foremost orchestral directors in Boston before the arrival of the Boston Symphony in 1881. The Boston Symphony Orchestra consisted wholly of proficient Central European instrumentalists. George Henschel, its initial conductor, was born in Breslau and trained in Leipzig and Berlin.

With these influences operating on them, Bostonians learned to believe that the greatest music was that of Mozart, Schubert, Beethoven, Mendelssohn, and Schumann. As attraction to musical study grew, New Englanders engaged resident German instructors or left for extended sojourns in Germany and Austria, where they studied music and immersed themselves in cultural life. After the war, four additional Germans came conspicuously into musical view: Julius Eichberg, Franz Kneisel, Wilhelm Gericke, and Arthur P. Schmidt. Eichberg was a violinist, conductor, composer, and in 1867 founder of the Boston Conservatory of Music. Kneisel arrived in 1885 to become concertmaster of the Boston Symphony and found the Kneisel String Quartet—a stroke of luck for American composers who wished to hear their chamber works in concert. Gericke gave first performances of several orchestral compositions by New England composers when he conducted the Boston Symphony from 1884 to 1889 and from 1898 to 1906, as did other Boston Symphony conductors—Arthur Nikisch, 1889–93, and Emil Paur, 1893–98.

Arthur P. Schmidt arrived in 1866. Not later than 1877 he had launched a music-publishing firm that would issue the compositions of New England composers, especially those of Foote and MacDowell. Schmidt published the music in Boston or, if that proved unfeasible, in Germany. He placed his publications with many European retailers and pressed for performances in Europe's principal cities. Thanks to Schmidt, Paine's Second Symphony was the first sizable native score to be published in the history of the United States (1880), the expense of publication met by a subscription fund-raiser. Eight years later, Schmidt published Chadwick's Second Symphony, the first large American work to be issued without a subvention. Foote acknowledges the great debt the New England group of composers owed Schmidt, stating: "When it is remembered that before Schmidt there had been published in this country no music other than such as was of comparatively small consequence, it is obvious that what he did was of far-reaching importance."[47] Foote praised him as a dedicated exponent of American music, publishing American scores every year of his life. He had high principles, definite opinions about music, and generosity in helping American composers.[48]

Franz Kneisel arrived in Boston in the fall of 1885 to become concertmaster of the Boston Symphony under Gericke. He was immediately encouraged by Higginson to form a first-rate string quartet. To this musician's sponsorship, encouragement, and advice, Foote owed a great deal. He wrote:

> I played with [the Kneisel Quartet] a good many times, chiefly at first performances of my own compositions. Not only had I the honor and happiness of having a hearing of my Violin Sonata, Piano Trio in B-flat, Piano Quartet and Quintet, and String Quartet, but also learned much from Kneisel through his suggestions as to practical points in composition, and I became aware of a different and higher standard of performance through my work with him in rehearsal. . . . When Kneisel died, in 1925 [he actually died 26 March 1926], the grief was accompanied by the old feeling of thankfulness and a never-to-be-forgotten appreciation of his encouragement.[49]

Theodore Thomas, although not a Boston resident, was another German who furthered the cause of New England's composers. In 1869 he formed a superb New York orchestra and traveled with it to Boston. Three years later, in 1888, Thomas became the founding director of the Chicago Orchestra. He had an unshakable faith in America's own music and performed many works by New England composers. Immensely consequential was his premiere performance of Paine's First Symphony at Boston's Music Hall, in January 1876. He then brought it out in New York. The superb quality of his orchestra's playing spurred the call for a permanent professional ensemble in Boston. The top-quality presentation of Paine's work persuaded audiences that native works were worth taking seriously.

Eben Tourjée, not German but influenced by them, came from Rhode Island to reside in the Boston area and, with the help of Robert Goldbeck, founded the New England Conservatory of Music in 1867, modeling it after the German conservatories. After a decade, the school would have almost fifteen hundred students enrolled. Tourjée would also found the College of Music of Boston University in 1872, its faculty consisting mostly of teachers from the conservatory.

Boston was not alone in the move to establish conservatories of music after German models. By 1867 the Cincinnati Conservatory and the Chicago Academy of Music had opened their doors. The next year, the Pea-

An early print of the New England Conservatory of Music.

body Conservatory of Baltimore and the New York College of Music took in their first students.

Foreign backing of music had a harmful side to it. Central European tastes dominated New England thinking and were centered on Central European composers, whose works were revered far above those of Americans, and on Central European performers. It follows that a patronizing attitude was ordinarily apparent even when foreign musicians commended an American performer or composer. This attitude, needless to say, was communicated to the Americans who controlled the cultural purse strings. The partiality toward European singers, instrumentalists, and compositions, some of them second-rate, was obvious in America, including New England, during the second half of the century. For many years few American instrumentalists would find employment in New England's all-professional orchestras and few native composers would be able to have consistent exposure of their new works before concert audiences, let alone repeated presentations of old ones, the few performances by the Boston Symphony and the Kneisel Quartet notwithstanding.

CHAPTER

PAINE AND CHADWICK

T he first New England art music composers to establish national and, to some extent, international, reputations—John Knowles Paine, George Chadwick, Arthur Foote, Horatio Parker, and Amy Beach—shared similar values in the music they created. They found nothing wrong in gratifying their listeners with enjoyable sounds. In doing so, they felt their music should measure up to the cultural standards subscribed to by the music public, which for the most part the composers accepted. The mandates to evoke the sublime in musical speech, to impress the mind with a sense of nobility, and to suggest emotions beyond the personal were constantly on their minds. At the same time, they hoped to go beyond the furors and fashions of their day and create works that might stand up to future decades.

During the latter part of the nineteenth century, no one insisted that a composer's music sound completely different from anyone else's. Composers like Paine and Chadwick respected tradition. We must understand this to mean that they had an acute awareness of it and not an unquestioning adherence to it. They knew that music past and present had an existence in the present, where both were heard side by side. If they used traditional triadic harmonies and traditional structures such as variation and sonata form or fugal procedures, they did so because they appreciated orderly arrangements of tones and respected time-honored designs, drawing on them until something they thought was an improvement came along.[1]

Other composers existed in America slightly before or simultaneous with the New Englanders with whom we are concerned, but none had an ongoing influence, whether Gottschalk of New Orleans, Fry of Philadelphia, or Bristow of New York. A few composers were born in New England but led their professional lives elsewhere—William Mason, Silas Pratt, and Frederick Gleason, to name three.

Dudley Buck (1839–1909) requires more extensive discussion. He was born in Hartford, studied in Leipzig, Dresden, and Paris (1860–62), returned to Hartford, went for a short while to Chicago, and then located in Boston, where he worked as an organist and taught at the New England Conservatory. At the Peace Jubilee of 1872 the audience heard his undemanding, diatonic, and tuneful *Festival Hymn*. Two years later, he composed his first successful large-scale work, *The Legend of Don Munio,* for solo singers, chorus, and orchestra. This was followed by *The Forty-Sixth Psalm,* which the Handel and Haydn Society premiered in 1874. By 1875 Buck was in New York. His cantata *The Golden Legend* (1880), based on Longfellow, won an award from the Cincinnati Festival Association. He liked writing for the quartet-choir of his day, and composed many cantatas and the first organ sonata by an American composer. In his time, his compositions were recognized as well put together, easily accessible, and in a melodious style that often veered toward popular music. He left no lasting impression on future composers, as would Paine and Chadwick.

JOHN KNOWLES PAINE

John Knowles Paine (1839–1906) was born in Portland, Maine. His father was a bandmaster and proprietor of a music store. His sister Helen taught voice and piano and appeared in public as a contralto soloist. During boyhood, he commenced his musical education with Hermann Kotzschimar, a German musician living in Portland. At the age of sixteen he completed a string quartet and at eighteen made his first public appearance as an organist.

Never accepting defeat, Paine managed to become a composer to be reckoned with despite the obstacles of time and place. He achieved success through his own considerable efforts and triumphed over all obstacles that stood in the way of thorough musical training, among them lack of funds and local educational opportunity. He was always ready to seize any opportunity that came his way, to pry open doors that remained shut, and to continue writing no matter how poorly the public responded to his music.

Paine departed Portland, Maine, and abandoned any pursuit of a socially approved vocation in 1858, when three subscription concerts enabled him to travel to Berlin to further his musical education at the Hochschule für Musick. He studied organ with Haupt and theory and composition with Wieprecht and Teschner. He then returned to Boston to

Inside the early New England Conservatory: parlor, library, dining hall, and music room.

advance his career. He saw that Harvard University might be receptive to music instruction and called upon supporters to back his application for an instructorship. He achieved his goal in 1862, and eventually, in 1876, garnered a professorship. He struggled doggedly against such influential foes as the historian Francis Parkman, who was constantly trying to wipe out the music department: "Francis Parkman, the historian, a member of the Corporation . . . is said to have ended every deliberation of that body with the words 'musica delenda est'; and . . . for many subsequent years, when the College was faced with a need of funds, was always ready with a motion to abolish the musical department."[2] Paine's further aims were to command respect as a symphonic composer and to educate young composers and make the start on their own careers easier.

Daniel Gregory Mason complains that he found Paine to be a tyrannical teacher who denied him the freedom to experiment in his compositions.[3] His instruction was thorough; his manner was dry; his criticisms were relentless but just. Students like Clayton Johns, Walter Spalding, Arthur Foote, and Frederick Shepherd Converse testify to this.

Critics of his day bear out his importance as a composer. When Theodore Thomas performed Paine's First Symphony in Philadelphia in August 1876, an unnamed writer in *Dwight's Journal of Music* said that the symphony was heard along with a work by a Philadelphian, William Fry. Fry, the reporter decided, wrote pleasing melodies yet was nothing but a second-class composer: "Fry's symphony, *A Day in the Country,* has uninteresting music and is not in any way on a level with Paine's." In contrast, Paine's music was equal in quality to any in Europe. He applauded Paine's superb thematic construction, first-rate instrumentation, and telling musical ideas. The First Symphony was "unquestionably the best large orchestral work yet produced by any native composer." By 1893 the Chicago writer on music W. S. B. Mathews was insisting that Paine was "a composer of the very highest rank among those in America and the world at large." Rupert Hughes in 1900 commented: "The most classic of our composers is their venerable dean, John Knowles Paine. It is an interesting proof of the youth of our native school of music, that the principal symphony, 'Spring,' of our first composer of importance, was written only twenty-one years ago. Before Mr. Paine there had never been an American music writer worthy of serious consideration in the larger forms." "Nothing can better prove the rapid advance of music in America," wrote Louis Elson in 1904, "than the fact that when Professor Paine began his career he stood alone, the one classical composer of America; while today there are at least three men, Chadwick, MacDowell, and Horatio W. Parker, who might dispute the field with him."[4] The statements of these writers demonstrate his contemporaries' high estimation of Paine and their viewing of every premiere of a large Paine composition as a significant event in the progress of American culture.

At a time when the writings of Mark Twain and William Dean Howells, the paintings of Winslow Homer, and the sculptures of Daniel Chester French were introducing a new view of how Americans saw themselves, Paine was producing his Mass in D, *St. Peter* oratorio, and two symphonies. He banished from them whatever was run of the mill or without substance. He steered clear of showy orchestration and luxurious harmonies for their own sake. Paine composed each major work meticulously and after considerable planning, aware that he would inevitably have to stand comparison with the greatest European composers and that uncompromising evaluators like Dwight had him under their microscope.

He devised themes that lent themselves to musical development and at the same time remained melodically attractive.[5] John Lathrop Mathews visited Paine in March 1896 and found him at the piano playing an ear-catching passage, something "with a decidedly oriental flavor [*Azara?*]." Asked how he went about composing, Paine replied in rather terse fashion: "Why, I have an idea—and jot down a sketch of it. Then bit by bit it grows and gets plainer and I increase my sketch, until at last I have the thing complete. Then when I feel in the mood I sit down to it and write the full score."[6]

In his first-movement sonata forms, the short and cogent subjects are constantly enlarged upon, an aim being to keep ideas always fresh and interesting. When developments take place they sound organic, with learning concealed. Eventually, there is a return to the initial themes in forms that are readily recognizable. The slow movements bring out thoughtful romantic moods, usually as elegiac melody injected with a degree of yearning. Dance movements are not the bumptious "jokes" of Beethoven scherzos but are amiable and weightless in character. Finales regularly summarize the music that went before, sounding broader and more hymnlike.

Although he grew more flexible later, Paine at first felt no urge to explore the radical innovations pointing to the future that were propounded by advanced European composers of the time. His compositions usually make only cautious nods in the direction of the word-sensitive expression found in Wolf's songs, the complicated leitmotif procedures of Wagner's operas, and the fantastic excessiveness of Liszt's and Strauss's tone poems. He integrated into his music whatever practices he found adaptable to his own style but never sought novelty for its own sake. He did warm up to Wagner by the 1880s. In a letter to Henry Finck dated 31 January 1882 he wrote: "I want to take this opportunity to say that my opinions regarding Wagner and his theories have been modified since you were in College [class of 1876]. I consider him a great genius who has had a wonderful influence on the present day." While working on the opera *Azara,* Paine sent Finck a letter dated 25 March 1900 that stated: "I wish I could play you the whole opera. You will find that I have entered upon a new path in all respects—in form, thematic treatment, instrumentation, etc. All dramatic composers must learn from Wagner, yet I have not consciously imitated him in style, etc." A month later: "I have followed throughout the connected orchestral rhythmical flow, and truth of dramatic expression characteristic of Wagner."[7]

Paine likes clear-cut statements either as a spaciously rounded melody or as a brief memorable musical theme achieving its total impression cumulatively over a period of time. Phrases are free from awkwardness, rhythms unambiguously clear, tonal areas plainly set apart, transitory modulations numerous, harmonic progressions logical, orchestrations fitting, climaxes convincing, and design of the whole expertly realized.

The warmth and richness of Romanticism merge with the disciplined contrapuntal procedures gleaned from the Baroque.

American listeners of his era could easily enjoy and satisfy their expectations in his music, knowing that a striving for originality would not get in their way. If he reminded the listener of Beethoven, Mendelssohn, and Schumann in his earlier works, or Brahms and Wagner in the later ones, it concerned neither him nor his audience; saying something sincerely and directly was more his concern. Nevertheless, he kowtowed to no composer. He did leave music lovers of his time persuaded that a distinctive personality had revealed itself, that he had his own expressive manner, and that this manner signified a musician firm in his beliefs.[8] "The best of Paine's works," wrote Richard Aldrich, "show fertility, a genuine warmth and spontaneity of invention, and a fine harmonic feeling, as well as a sure touch in instrumentation." This was music "held up to a high standard."[9]

Paine was no nationalist composer dedicated to writing a recognizably American music. He claimed composers "are great because they are individual, not because they are local or patriotic. . . . It is barely possible that we may at some time have a representative American school. But I doubt it very much. The time for such a thing is past. We have now not national, but international music, and it makes no difference whether I compose here or in St. Petersburg, so long as I express myself in my own way."[10]

When Paine was in his forties, music writers were already placing his works in three periods. For instance, Louis Elson in June 1882 mentioned a first period (the time of his Mass in D), when works contained a free expression of imagination and emotion, revealing Paine's true nature. He pointed to a second period, concurrent with the *St. Peter* oratorio, when Paine's music sounded more dried out and forced. Perhaps, Elson guessed, Paine thought he should make his learning obvious. Lastly, Elson said, came the third period, centered on the *Spring* Symphony and the music to *Oedipus Tyrannus*. The virtues of the first two periods were integrated. The learnedness now served the composer. By this time, the public's esteem of Paine had grown: "As many as thirty performances of his works have taken place this season," Elson stated.[11] The opera *Azara* had not yet been written at the time of Elson's commentary.

Intimate Music for the Chamber

Although Paine's main interest was not in brief and intimate vocal works, he wrote several charming vocal pieces. In 1879 the publisher Ditson issued four of them as opus 29: "Matin Song" (B. Taylor), "I Wore Your

Roses Yesterday" (C. Thaxter), "Early Springtime" (T. Hill), and "Moonlight" (J. von Eichendorff). In 1885 the publisher Schmidt announced he was issuing four more, as opus 40: "A Bird upon a Rosy Bough" (C. Thaxter), "A Farewell" (C. Kingsley), "Beneath the Starry Arch" (H. Martineau), and "Music When Soft Voices Die" (P. Shelley). The Shelley song has not been found and probably was never issued. Three more songs exist in manuscript.

In general, these compositions unfold with an easy grace. Paine is careful of word accents, treats the voice idiomatically, and provides tidy piano accompaniments. They strike the ear as appealing serenades, but rarely more than that. The strophic "Matin Song," in two stanzas, was the most popular of the lot. It was first sung publicly in January 1877 by the English singer Clara Doria, a year before she married Henry Munroe Rogers. William Treat Upton, who praises the song's charm and lack of pretension, finds its tune noteworthy because twelve of the measures have different rhythms, yet all sound unforced.[12] Other songs praised by contemporaries are "I Wore Your Roses Yesterday," "Moonlight," and "A Bird upon a Rosy Bough." One song, "Early Springtime," is surprisingly atypical of Paine's usual manner of writing. "Most curiously original," wrote Rupert Hughes at the turn of the century.[13] This song, set to a serious prose text by the Reverend Thomas Hill, modulates twice from C-sharp minor to E major, and the piece ends on the dominant of C-sharp minor.

On his return from Germany, Paine became organist at Boston's Old West Church and gave recitals that emphasized Bach's music and included some of his own compositions. These last are minor and mostly early works, among them preludes, fugues, fantasies, and concert variations. Some draw on known melodies. Variations on "Old Hundred," "The Austrian Hymn," and "The Star-Spangled Banner," and the fantasy on "Ein Feste Burg" are four examples.

Barbara Owen, who is knowledgeable about New England's organs and organ literature, reveals that American composers evolved a distinctive style of organ music because of smaller halls with less reverberation and drier acoustics than those of Europe, the simpler instruments available to them, and the different use for organ music. Composers like Paine designed organ pieces to be heard in public recitals and in homes equipped with modest organs.[14] As attractive and workmanlike as they may be, Paine's organ compositions rarely adventure beyond the conventional.

Paine, though a pianist, wrote little for piano, mostly pleasant, inconsequential, Schumann-like efforts. During his youth, he had written two piano sonatas, one of them now lost. Then, in the mid-1860s, he came out with "A Funeral March in Memory of President Lincoln."[15] The music is in a cautious style, melancholic, and similar to the *Marcia funebre sulla morte d'un eroe* of Beethoven's op. 26 Piano Sonata. Somewhat better in quality is opus 11 (1868), *Vier Character-Stücke für Piano-forte.* An unnamed writer gave the four movements "unqualified praise" in 1872 for their "genuine, unforced, at times almost startling originality." He makes one criticism: "The only point at which we can take exception is that they do not lie quite so easily under the fingers as might be desired, though where there is so much genuine merit, such a consideration becomes of secondary importance."[16]

With the Romance, op. 12, of 1869, Paine expanded his harmonic vocabulary and wrote with increased confidence.[17] It is a ternary march in E-flat minor. Regardless of the indications to play in a sweet singing fashion, a feverish tightness invests the first division. The piece seems a bit lacking in continuity. Robert Schumann's music comes to mind, although the opening phrase of the B section suggests the slow movement in Paine's First Symphony.[18]

Four Characteristic Pieces, op. 25 (1876), comprises a Dance, Romance, Impromptu, and Rondo Giocoso.[19] The music is more assured, unveils personal emotions from affectionate to ardent, and favors ternary form. The opening of the Dance, in triple meter, again resembles the start of the First Symphony's slow movement. The Romance is appropriately songlike, although unobtrusive short-lived modulations do take place. The expression is fastidious yet intimate. The Impromptu goes its way in the manner of Schumann's *Novelettes,* op. 21, that is to say, vigorously and with fire, and with a prettily expressive middle section. The Rondo Giocoso bears an 1893 copyright and the designation "new edition." All four pieces of opus 25 contain creditable music—none run of the mill, and all worth hearing today.

In the Country, op. 26, is made up of "ten sketches for the piano."[20] Each piece bears an evocative title: "Woodnotes," "Wayside Flowers," "Under the Lindens," "The Shepherd's Lament," "Village Dance," "Rainy Day," "The Mill," "Gipsies," "Farewell," "Welcome Home." The first number hints at birdcalls; the flowers are delicately Mendelssohnian; the lindens are depicted through descending arpeggios and syncopated melody; the lament sorrows in a minor key complete with diminished seventh chords and biting cross-relations; the dance has a nimble bounce to it; the rainy day brings on momentary sadness (its music resembles Schumann's

Albumblatt No. 2 from his *Bunte Blätter,* op. 99); the mill's running water is realized with fast sixteenth-note figures in the left hand. Paine attempts scarcely a gypsy effect in "Gipsies," except for the obvious augmented second in measure 25; the farewell is poignant, and the welcome festive. All ten pieces are pleasurable, with no deep probing of the emotions. Ditson published the Romance, op. 39, in 1883. The piece, an *andantino* in D-flat major, is surprisingly eloquent and brings Liszt to mind. The Romance is one of Paine's most commendable compositions for piano.

Trifles in comparison are the Three Piano Pieces, op. 41, which Schmidt published in 1884: "A Spring Idyl," "Birthday Impromptu," and "Fuga Giocosa." The last, in three parts, is based on the tune of an old baseball song, "Over the Fence Is Out, Boys."[21] Although witty and prefaced with the indication *Allegro scherzando,* no hearty laughter sounds, in part due to the fugal structure. Paine will not play the clown.

A Nocturne, op. 45, which Schmidt published in 1889, concludes the piano works. Nothing of Chopin is hinted at. Louis Elson reviewed it immediately on publication in the *Boston Musical Herald,* writing: "A shade more difficult than the nocturnes of Field, and it resembles these somewhat in not being too sentimental. It is good, healthy music, free from the morbid character that is in many of the nocturnes today, yet affording opportunity enough to the musician to display sentiment and refined shading."[22]

Paine wrote little chamber music. An early String Quartet in D Major (1855), a Piano Trio in D Minor (1874), a Violin Sonata in B Minor (1875, revised 1905), a Romanza and Humoreske for cello and piano (1875), and a Larghetto and Scherzo for violin, cello, and piano (1877) lists all of it. Paine published none of these compositions. Most of their performances were in private homes, like the one at Fiske's home, in December 1874, when around one hundred people heard the trio.[23] Newspapers and periodicals did not review such performances, and information about them, scarce as it is, must come from letters, diaries, and reminiscences of those attending the concerts.

The quartet, a student work from his Portland days, reveals a promising musician learning how to handle sonata, dance, variation, and fugal forms. The trio shows the composer managing his material with assurance, albeit in unadventurous fashion. Its first movement projects emotional struggle; the second movement has plain and occasionally plaintive lyricism; and the finale introduces brash and assertive rhythms. The music of the trio is persuasive and continues to merit performance.

In the next three works, Paine stresses poetic melody and direct communication. Motives undergo extended development. Contrasts are skillfully managed. Whatever structure Paine chooses to assign a movement is handled with assurance. Expression runs from calm to passionate. The music is imaginatively realized and sounds individual and captivating. These three compositions strike the ear as Romantic, with some hints of the Classical.

The audience responded enthusiastically when it heard the earlier version of the Violin Sonata at Boston's Mechanics Hall in May 1876. A Boston newspaper reviewer said the first movement's *allegro con fuoco* was "in a strong spirited style" and rich in melody. The second movement's canonic *larghetto,* "though less absorbing," had "a grave and tranquil beauty." The finale, an *allegro vivace,* had an "excitingly . . . fierce dramatic quality which also characterized the [first] symphony of Mr. Paine."[24] The New York critic H. E. Krehbiel heard the sonata in November 1887 and wrote that it was beautifully written. He wished that the slow movement's principle theme had more warmth.[25] The 1905 revision resulted in a bolder composition having subtler textures, more chromaticism and dissonance via nondominant sevenths and altered chords, and less conventional harmonic progressions. A polished craftwork, containing strong and vital expression, the sonata's merits are similar to those of a chamber work by Brahms.

Both the Romanza and Humoreske and the Larghetto and Scherzo deserve similar praise, and listening to them is eminently gratifying.

Two Grand Gestures

Two of the three choral works that Paine composed in the early sixties were for Harvard, the straightforward, appealing "Commencement Hymn" in C major (1862), to a Latin text by James Bradstreet Greenough, and *Domine salvum fac Praesidem nostrum* in D major, op. 8, for men's voices and orchestra, written for the inauguration of Thomas Hill as president of Harvard in 1863 and performed again at the inauguration of Charles William Eliot in 1869. The *Domine salvum* is essentially a homophonic hymn, and well suited to its purpose. Paine remains within traditional bounds—modulations are cautious, dissonances properly conducted, and vocal lines sung without trouble.

The third work, "Radway's Ready Relief" for bass solo and men's chorus (1863), is atypical for Paine. This comical trifle, written for some friends, turns to parodies on composers' styles, among them Handel and

Beethoven, and injects five absurd flourishes from a piccolo into the last five measures. The text comes from a newspaper advertisement for a patent medicine. A "William Henry Myers, Esquiah," desires relief from his "acute and chronic rheumatiz." A tongue-in-cheek recitative for bass solo swears the medicine "immediately gave him rest," and the ecstatic chorus counsels everyone to "ask for Radway's Ready Relief." For twenty years the piece was sung privately. The Apollo Club, conducted by B. J. Lang, finally presented it to the general public in April 1883. The reviewer in the *Advertiser* for 26 April 1883 found it

> exceedingly ingenious and one of the most genuinely humorous bits of music that we have heard for a long time. It is serio-comic, of course, and nearly all the chief forms of the most sedate composers are used in turn with droll effect. In the solo . . . the series of roulades is very comical, but even that is not so funny as the steady melodic sweetness and dynamic softness that characterizes the music which directly follows, and is fitted to the words, "The continued use of Radway's Ready Relief cured him." The closing phrases are very involved and intricate, abounding in runs and roulades, and written sometimes in the mode of a fugue, sometimes in that of the canon, but all have a very humorous effect, which reaches its height with the help of some unexpected notes from the piccolo.

A *Courier* writer on 26 April 1883 states it was held back from the public "for fear that it might be misunderstood or misemployed." The public on the whole enjoyed the musical joke. One hostile auditor, after a performance by the Mendelssohn Club, said the singers "blotted" an otherwise fine program "with the words of Mr. J. K. Paine's song" and criticized the club for having "given its attention to such trash."[26] This unfriendly remark calls attention to the sort of reception that Paine had feared and that would dissuade him from writing compositions of a light nature.

None of the three compositions prepared contemporary listeners for the extraordinary Mass in D Major, op. 10, for soloists, chorus, and orchestra that he may have begun at age twenty and did complete at age twenty-six, in 1865, an astonishing achievement for someone lacking the help of American precedents. Though guided by the choral works of Handel, Mozart, and Beethoven, the Mass teems with original details and rises to stirring expressive heights. It is a major contribution to Western musical culture.

A presentation of three movements with organ accompaniment took place at Harvard's Appleton Chapel in June 1866 before transported listeners. The composer conducted the first complete performance in Berlin, 16 February 1867, before a large audience that included the royal family. Paine won praise for his discriminating judgment, technical command, and sincerity. Not least, he was identified as an important composer. A critic or two thought some passages difficult to sing and wished for more "poetic originality." Especially liked were the "Dona nobis pacem" and the "Crucifixus."[27] Indicative of the problems facing native art music's future, the local Handel and Haydn Society refused to perform the work when proposed for its April 1868 concert.

The Mass in D is in eighteen segments and requires an orchestra with woodwinds, horns, and trumpets by twos, three trombones, organ, timpani, and strings. The "Kyrie," a deeply felt supplication, goes from a stately introduction and a choral fugato in D minor to a majestic and homophonic choral "Christe" in F major, and a return to the "Kyrie."[28] The "Gloria," a lively *allegro vivace,* is mostly loud and outgoing—an effective contrast to the pleading of the "Kyrie." The "Qui tollis," for alto solo and chorus, is a moving *adagio* that reaches an emotional climax just before the return of the opening music, which is set to repeated cries of "miserere nobis." The "Quoniam" for tenor solo that follows this movement replaces gloom with conviction. Next, the "Cum sancto spiritu" leads into an exciting four-voice fugue on "In gloria Dei Patris." With this, the first part ends.

The second part opens with a clear-cut and firm "Credo." Then comes one of the most beautiful sections of the Mass, the "Et incarnatus" in G minor for soprano solo and a "Crucifixus" in C minor, sung as a slow fugue by a grief-stricken chorus. After the "Crucifixus," a fittingly euphoric "Et ressurexit" sweeps away the gloom. Every segment that follows attests to the technical skill and musical gift of the composer. The conductor and composer Gunther Schuller, who recorded the Mass, finds the finest portions of the Mass in the work's close—the "Benedictus," for quartet and chorus, the "Agnus Dei," for soprano-alto duet and chorus, and the "Dona nobis," for chorus. He praises the melodic quality, the rhythmic variety and syncopations, and the unfailing wealth of fresh ideas.[29]

The oratorio *St. Peter* was Paine's next large choral composition. Paine himself compiled the text from the Bible. He also used the melodies of three Lutheran chorales, after the example of Bach and Mendelssohn. Indeed, works like Bach's *St. Matthew Passion* and Mendelssohn's *St. Paul* guide the course of many sections of the work. The sure management of the chorus from intricate fugal passages to simply harmonized chorales owes much to his models. Instead of the traditional bass voice, however, Paine assigns the part of Jesus to the tenor. The bass takes on the part of St. Peter. Paine's music is less substantial and erudite than Bach's and more full-bodied than Mendelssohn's. His harmonic practices are of his own era: diminished seventh chords, unanticipated modulations, vivid tone painting by means of augmented sixths and nondominant sevenths, and excitement generated by deceptive cadences and flights into remote keys.

Ditson published its piano score in the same year the piece was completed, 1872, and the first performance took place at Paine's birthplace, Portland, Maine, in June 1873. The next year, the Handel and Haydn Society, owing to much prodding, produced it in Boston. After examining the Ditson score, a critic writing in the *Nation*, 13 February 1873, found *St. Peter* dry and deficient in emotion and melody. Paine's friend John Fiske quickly rebutted in the *Atlantic Monthly* of April 1873, saying the writer knew only the piano score and had a ridiculous idea that an oratorio should serve as an amusement. On the contrary, Fiske said, Paine deserved praise for his religious rather than sensuous melodies, and for music that refused merely to please. "An artist does not work for years putting his whole heart, soul, and being into his work, merely to furnish people with an aesthetico-intellectual anodyne,—to give them music which they can passively enjoy without the exertion of thinking. . . . Throughout the whole of Mr. Paine's *St. Peter* the music is persistently of a religious character, never inclining to sentimentality."[30]

Paine divides the work into two parts, the first in nineteen numbers, the second in twenty. The oratorio's first section, "The Divine Call," begins with an orchestral introduction sounding impressively in B-flat minor. This leads into the stately "The time is fulfilled," a strong affirmative choral statement. An ominous call to "repent" and a more hopeful consequent, "and believe in the glad tidings of God," follow. Next one hears the serene summons of Jesus, telling Simon and Andrew to follow him. This in turn leads to a pensive and lyrical air for soprano, "The spirit of the Lord is upon me." A nice coloristic touch enters when, with "We go before the face of the Lord," twelve tenors and basses take the part of the twelve disciples. After that appears the simply harmonized chorale "How lovely shines the morning star." Paine proceeds from number to number conscious of the need to provide musical and expressive variety in order to keep listeners attentive.

The next two large sections of the first part involve Christ's life and message, up to his betrayal by Judas, followed by Peter's denial of Jesus and subsequent repentance. These are also the most dramatic and fascinating segments of the oratorio. Especially effective is the bold declaration of Peter to Jesus' question "But who say ye that I am?" Peter, accompanied by trombones, answers with an emphatic octave leap downward and an upward skip on "Thou art the Christ." The most beautiful numbers come after Peter's denial and the crowing of the cock ("And while he spake the cock crew. And the Lord turned, and looked on Peter: and he remembered the word of the Lord; and he went out and wept bitterly."). A "Lament" follows, in part a dramatic recitative, in part a sorrowing arioso. Peter comes after with the air "O God, my God, forsake me not!" Unexpected yet marvelous is "Remember from whence thou art fallen," where a small group of women, representing a chorus of angels, sings a capella and in chordal fashion. Three numbers later, a magnificent choral number, "Awake, thou that sleepest," completes the first part.

The second part, "The Ascension" and "Pentecost," has more contemplative music than the first. Drama has vanished. Contrasts are fewer. Erudition sometimes gets in the way of imagination. Yet John Fiske considered the second part the musical climax of the oratorio. The opening chorus, "The son of man was delivered," he found deeply pathetic; he pointed to the inwardness and superb meditative qualities in the quartet "Feed the flock of God." He continued: "The wave of emotion answering to the sensuously dramatic element having partly spent itself, the wave of lyric emotion gathers fresh strength, and one feels that one has reached the height of spiritual exaltation."[31]

Writing at the turn of the century, Rupert Hughes was of two minds about the oratorio, commending its great power and dramatic strength, praising the air of Peter "O God, my God, forsake me not," and also stating: "While containing much of the floridity and repetition of Händel at his worst, [the oratorio] is also marked with the erudition and largeness of Händel at his best."[32] Most contemporary critics agreed that *St. Peter* was carefully and competently written, praiseworthy for several sections of great depth and loveliness, but at times more an exhibit of "ingenuity than inspiration."[33]

One more choral work from the 1870s requires mention, the "Centennial Hymn," mostly a one-note-a-syllable setting of a Whittier text. Theodore Thomas commissioned Paine to compose it for the opening of the Centennial Exposition at Philadelphia in May 1876. However simple it seems, the hymn's serene, leisurely paced, and pleasant music ranks it high among occasional pieces of this type. Without question, it is superior to Richard Wagner's "American Centennial March," also composed for the exposition.

Orchestral Music

After completing *St. Peter,* Paine became more concerned over musical expression, apparently troubled by the charge of not communicating warmth. From 1872 through 1875, he labored on a work that would reposition him with critics—the Symphony No. 1 in C Minor, op. 23. Theodore Thomas and his orchestra introduced the symphony on 26 January 1876 at the Music Hall and then took it to New York and Philadelphia. Music lovers received it with long-drawn-out applause at the close of each movement. A report in the *Atlantic Monthly* spoke for most members of the audience: "Whatever anxiety or lack of entire faith anyone may have felt beforehand must have been removed by the very first phrase, which with its rushing bass and powerful stroke of chords . . . proclaims at once the technical skill and boldness of design that belong only to masters of symphonic writing."[34]

According to a statement in the *Boston Saturday Evening Gazette,* 29 January 1876, those who heard the symphony considered it a great work, one of strength. Paine had surprised even close friends with the "fluency of idea, freedom from dryness, apparent spontaneous flow of thought, and the graceful flexibility of style." The following comment on the *adagio* movement is surprising, because of Paine's alleged aversion to Wagner: "It flows calmly and sweetly after the manner of those continuous melodies with which Wagner has made us so familiar and it has much of the rich sensuousness that marks that composer in his more placid moods."[35] The symphony had erased the blemishes seen in the oratorio. George Chadwick in 1908 said that the First Symphony won Paine real recognition "as a romantic composer of high ideals and genuine imagination." It "at once attracted attention by its interesting melodic material, its masterly use of symphonic form and its sonorous orchestration." He adds that this work (and later Paine's Second Symphony), far more than any other native music, encouraged other American composers to add to the symphonic literature. Chadwick then bitterly closes with: "The simple and benighted music lovers of those days had not been taught by blasé critics that the sonata form was a worn-out fetish, that noble and simple melody was a relic of the dark ages, and that unresolved dissonance was the chief merit

of a musical composition."[36] Chadwick was referring to the cultural politics of modernism versus traditionalism emerging in the twentieth century.

The symphony calls for woodwinds, trumpets, and timpani by twos,
plus four French horns, two tenor trombones and bass trombone, and a
large complement of strings.[37] It commences *allegro con brio* on a powerful,
dramatic, elemental main motive designed for a movement in sonata
form. The subordinate theme, in the relative major key, is a gracefully lilt-
ing tune in the first violins. The development section is not dramatic. It
acts more like a lull in a storm, so that the recapitulation of the main idea
will again have a gripping effect. The model coming to mind is Beethoven's Fifth Symphony. One also hears rather Brahmsian passages, although
Brahms's First Symphony was still in the future.

The second movement, an *allegro vivace* in triple meter, assumes a
genial, leisurely pace, and the poetic duo for French horn and clarinet in
the middle trio reveals Paine's new grasp of orchestral colorations. The
trio, *meno allegro,* is a woodwind serenade, cheerfully yet tenderly lyrical.
The third movement is an expressive and songlike *adagio.* Beautiful and
moving, it constitutes the emotional peak of the symphony. A writer in the
Boston Journal writes of the entire symphony and particularly of this movement as sounding "entirely free from common-place thought or expression," and praises "its expression of fine shades of tone, corresponding,
indeed, to the delicate tints of an expert painter, and producing in the
mind a similar pleasure."[38] The finale, in C major, is in a sonata structure
and sounds muscular, spirited, at times celebratory and at times majestic.
It fittingly concludes the symphony.

In November 1876 Thomas played another new Paine work, the
Overture to Shakespeare's *As You Like It,* op. 28, in F major. Music lovers
thought it a valuable addition to musical literature. The reviewer in
Dwight's Journal of Music wrote that the play dictated the musical moods,
but listeners did not need to tie the music to the play. The piece was enjoyable in itself, simply as music—full and mellow in tone and never monotonous. Some people claimed they sensed the Ardennes forest and the love
plot in the expressive *andante* introduction. Furthermore, they said, the
allegro vivace that followed contained sounds of the hunt and other woodsy
music. Jollity reigned, but with a hint of the "winter wind" and of "man's
ingratitude."[39]

In the fall of 1877 Thomas presented Paine's first bow to Liszt, the
Symphonic Poem *Shakespeare's Tempest,* op. 31, in four connected parts.

Part 1, *allegro furioso,* depicts the storm; part 2, *adagio tranquillo,* the calm
scene before Prospero's cell and the appearance of Ariel; part 3, *allegro
moderato e maestoso,* Prospero's tale; and part 4, *allegro moderato e maestoso,*
the love of Ferdinand and Miranda, an incident involving Caliban and
Ariel, and the victory of Prospero's "potent art." A *New York Tribune*
reviewer declared the work to be strong and original and showing authori-
tative craftsmanship. Dwight, conservative as usual and hostile to the
Liszt-Wagner approach, complained about the realistic allusions ("Then,
among passages of grave or tender beauty, where indeed we could think of
Prospero and of Miranda, there were salient phrases like Wagner's Leit-
motive, to say this is Ariel, Trinculo, Caliban, etc. Ariel's motive we con-
fess we thought not worthy of so delicate a sprite. It was a pert little fillip
on the piccolo, and by most was recognized as Ariel."). He wished Paine
had written an overture instead.[40]

Fiske rebutted, saying that the composition revealed originality in
form and ideas, an orderly treatment of themes, and a lucid structure.
Part 1 was in a regular prelude form; part 2 was mostly a cantabile song,
followed by quiet harp chords under Ariel's flute motive. A "grotesquely
capering bassoon" aptly depicted Caliban. Part 3 was in rondo form with
some thematic development; and part 4 had elements of sonata form. The
conclusion reintroduced reminiscences of Prospero's theme from part 3,
in the manner of the finale of Beethoven's Fifth Symphony.[41]

Paine revised the score, and the revision was played several times. In
1885 the *Boston Evening Transcript* reported: "We were heartily glad to hear
Mr. Paine's 'Tempest' again. . . . Not because it is American music—that
consideration, per se, leaves us quite cold—but because it is American
music thoroughly worth hearing at a symphony concert." The revised
work, the reviewer wrote, was never trite, filled with beautiful and
charming ideas, and on a high plane. The *Tempest* exists today only in its
1907 revised version.[42]

On 23 April 1878 Bostonians heard the Thomas orchestra perform a
Duo Concertante in A for violin, cello, and orchestra by Paine. The audience warmly applauded the three movements. Dwight found the music
brilliant and richly scored. The *adagio* movement was especially melodious, the finale's *allegro* satisfying.[43] After its first performance the composition remained ignored and unpublished.

The Symphony No. 2 in A Major, *In Spring,* first played in 1880, had
been preceded by the "Spring" symphonies of Robert Schumann and
Joachim Raff. Only one or two correspondences with Schumann's style

are found, and none with Raff's. The composition displays outstanding qualities. By this time, Paine's style had completely matured and become more completely Romantic. Orchestral blends and coloristic harmonies are skillfully deployed for expressive purposes. Richard Aldrich describes Bostonians as making their stormy enthusiasm obvious at the premiere: women's handkerchiefs waving, men yelling admiringly, and Dwight's umbrella wildly snapping open and shut. Dwight wrote that the symphony was worked out with great care and nicety of detail. Its outstanding qualities made a profound impression on "a great majority of listeners." The music was alive with ideas, though based on only a few motives. Its nobility earned it a place "among the works of the masters." After the first hearing, the reviewer in the *Boston Transcript* wrote of the enthusiastic audience and lauded "the very great power" and "exalted artistic character" of the work. After hearing it again almost a year later, the *Transcript*'s reviewer (perhaps the same writer) wrote that the symphony had won greater public favor and sounded more and more imposing with each new performance. "Fresh musical ideas" gave "expression to deep and genuine artistic inspiration and emotion, and this in a pure, serious, elevated style—not a scholastic imitation of the classic masters, but a manner natural to the modest, reverent, studious nature of the composer." When done in Chicago in April 1892, it was considered "without doubt, the most important orchestral composition that has been issued from the pen of any American composer."[44]

Schmidt, assisted by Paine's admirers, found subscribers to underwrite the publication of the full score in 1880, a first for a large orchestral work by an American.[45] In 1889 Alfred John Goodrich invented a poetic title for each movement of the symphony, which may have come to him from the composer—1: "Departure of Winter; Awakening of Nature"; 2: "May-night Fantasy"; 3: "Romance of Springtime"; 4: "The Glory of Nature."[46] Paine himself suppressed any detailed description of the scenes he may have had in mind.

The instrumentation is the same as the First Symphony, minus the bass trombone. The first movement begins with an introduction in A minor, *adagio sostenuto,* in common time. The cellos and violas announce a germinal motive that figures throughout the entire work.[47] Eventually, the tempo quickens to an *allegro ma non troppo* in A major, and the main subject sounds. The germinal motive recurs in the subordinate theme and plays an important part in the development. It returns in the coda to mix with all of the other musical ideas. The second movement, a scherzo in triple meter, is a brisk impish dance. The slower trio turns into a woodsy "May night fantasy," as woodwinds intone a rustic melody that hints at the germinal motive.

The intensely felt *adagio* has a rondo structure. The germinal motive activates many of the melodic lines. A horn countermelody against the main melody in the divided first violins is especially enchanting. The music next achieves Tchaikovskian intensity with a syncopated theme in the minor mode. Later the main theme returns reorchestrated to give it greater eloquence. The fourth movement, an optimistic *allegro giocoso,* is in sonata form. Variants of the germinal motive weave in and out of the fabric, their message a joyful one. The second theme emerges as a broad, hymnic song of thanksgiving. Could New England psalmody have been the inspiration for this song? The hymn returns in more majestic fashion at the end of the movement and makes a fitting close to the entire composition.

Rupert Hughes sums up contemporary opinions: "Paine's symphony, though aiming to shape the molten gold of April fervor in the rigid mold of the symphonic form, has escaped every appearance of mechanism and restraint. It is program music of the most legitimate sort, in full accord with Beethoven's canon, 'Mehr Ausdruck der Empfindung als Malerei.' It has no aim of imitating springtime noises, but seeks to stimulate by suggestion the hearer's creative imagination, and provoke by a musical telepathy the emotions that swayed the nympholept composer."[48]

Paine's Final Works

In May 1881 audiences at Harvard's Sanders Theater witnessed performances of Sophocles' *Oedipus Tyrannus,* given in Greek and intensified with music of Paine—an orchestral prelude, six choruses for male voices, and a postlude. Now, at the height of his powers, Paine was illustrating the tragedy of a king, unsuspecting slayer of his father and husband of his mother, who brings suffering to his people and ultimately must confront the horror he himself has produced. Paine made no attempt to reproduce archaic music, since no one knew how the ancient music had sounded.[49] The great majority of reviewers loved the music. The prelude and the second, third, fifth, and sixth choruses received the highest approval possible. The writers praised "Mr. Paine's own individuality," "lofty, tragic sentiments," "strong imaginative appeal," "an atmosphere . . . distinctly noble," and "a work that ranks as a masterpiece."[50] On 18 November 1903, while Paine was visiting Germany, the prelude was performed in Berlin. Amy Fay says that an appreciative audience insisted on recalling the composer thrice.

Berliners presented him with a medal and diploma and treated him with great honor.[51] The instrumental prelude, in particular, is an exceptional composition, of which New Englanders can be proud.

After completing *Oedipus,* Paine composed several cantatas, hymns for official celebrations, and incidental music to Aristophanes' *The Birds.* His last orchestral composition was a symphonic poem, *An Island Fantasy,* completed in 1888. Two paintings by J. Appleton Brown inspired this absorbing idyll of the ocean at Summer Island, in the Isles of Shoals, off the New Hampshire coast, one painting serene and sunlit, the other stormy. Paine set down moods, not programmatic incidents, within a rondo structure. He abstained from indicating his extramusical intentions. Daniel Gregory Mason and others have unjustly accused the composer of being unable to depict a real ocean and a real island.[52] They failed to understand that Paine was attempting to give voice to his own reactions, not unlike Beethoven's comment on the score of his *Pastoral* Symphony, "more an expression of feeling than of painting."

Paine worked on his last major composition from 1883 to 1898, his opera in three acts, *Azara.* The libretto, the composer's own, draws on a thirteenth-century French *chante-fable,* the love-romance *Aucassin and Nicolette.*[53] The Boston Symphony presented its ballet music, the three Moorish dances, on 10 March 1900. Ephraim Cutter Jr. gave the opera an incomplete concert performance with piano accompaniment in 1903. The Cecilia Society conducted by Lang tried a concert performance with several cuts in the music, but this time with an orchestra, in 1907. Paine and several prominent musicians attempted to get the Metropolitan Opera, then under Heinrich Conried's management, to mount it. Conried claimed that he could not find contralto and bass soloists capable of singing in English. Nor could the chorus sing in English! The excuses sound weak. The opera never received a staged performance.[54]

The language of the libretto is stilted. The dignified yet lovely heroine, Azara, has her counterpart in Horatio Parker's opera *Mona,* in the Boston novels of William Dean Howells, and in such paintings by local artists as Abbott Thayer's *Caritas,* now in Boston's Museum of Fine Arts.[55] The design of the acts admits no obviously distinct set pieces, with independent intermezzi, arias, and the like, although the listener can easily identifies those explicitly melodic sections that stand in the place of set pieces. Paine employs the more advanced melodic, harmonic, rhythmic, and instrumental devices of the late nineteenth century. The flexibility in shaping dramatic forms owes a debt to Wagner, but Wagnerian musical style is absent. *Azara* contains a great deal of engaging music. Thought and effort went into its composition. The libretto does need revision to make the language less like a cumbersome translation from the German. The vagaries of plot are no better or worse than those of most operas that have achieved great popularity. It still awaits a fully staged performance by topflight singers and an orchestra.

Twentieth-century writers have abused Paine with criticisms of excessive gentility. Yet his pieces have grit. All are well crafted. His music is always enjoyable. In his day, his works were admired and played throughout the United States and in Europe. He won a place above all previous composers as America's first celebrated symphonist and persuaded other musicians to take up serious musical composition. His creative ideals and high standards of workmanship served to guide younger composers. Music courses as part of a university's curriculum became nationally acceptable after he initiated them at Harvard. He educated several distinguished composers and writers on music. Clearly, Paine was a composer of foremost significance for his own time and for American civilization.

GEORGE WHITEFIELD CHADWICK

Like Paine, George Whitefield Chadwick (1854–1931) was determined to become a composer and became one despite his father's opposition. After his mother died, the small boy grew up with little direction from anybody. He quit public school without graduating to work briefly in his father's insurance office. An older brother gave him music lessons, and soon he was able to earn money as an organist. When fifteen years of age, he enrolled as a special student at the New England Conservatory, his own savings financing the action. In 1876 Chadwick left Boston to become a music teacher at Olivet College, in Michigan. He left this position to further his musical education in Germany, where he remained from 1877 to 1879. Two student works, the Second Quartet for Strings and the Overture *Rip Van Winkle,* received European performances in 1879. European critics detected excellence in the music and acclaimed the composer's exceptional talent. He took some time off while in Europe to roam France with some young fancy-free American painters. This tour may help explain one source for the French influence that some writers detect in his music.

Chadwick returned to Boston in the spring of 1880 and joined the faculty of the New England Conservatory two years later. He became its director in 1897. At the same time, he conducted choruses and orchestras of local music clubs, the New England Conservatory, and the annual festivals at Springfield and Worcester. He became familiar with a variety of musical styles through conducting such works as Berlioz's *Damnation of Faust,* Franck's *The Beatitudes,* Glazunov's Sixth Symphony, Saint-Saëns's *Samson and Delilah,* and Brahms's *German Requiem.* He carved out some leisure for music composition, especially in summers. The composer Arthur Shepherd, Chadwick's student in 1896–97, describes his teacher as "an independent, virile, American spirit and a self-confident, peppery man of great charm."[56]

One finds dualities in George Chadwick's creativity—the advancing of old and inquiry into new musical techniques, the loyalty to serious art and the turn to popular and folk music, and the confidence in established styles and the stimulation of novelty. In one work, phrasing is brief, tune diatonic, and harmony consonant; in another, phrasing is lengthy, tune full of accidentals, and harmony lush and dissonant. He refused to be frozen into one procedure. He pioneered the introduction of humor and the vernacular into music. Chadwick's finest works, such as the Second Symphony, Fourth String Quartet, *Symphonic Sketches,* and *Tam O'Shanter,* present him as an astute artist enriching the meaning of his subject matter through a unique approach to its development and integration. To bring musical scenes to life, he sometimes applies rhythms and harmonies like the discontinuous brush strokes and thick palette-knife applications of some Impressionistic painters. At the same time, the unassailability of his structures marks him as a New England composer committed to logical discourse. Even when his orchestrations catch fire or startling successions of passages far removed from each other occur in his music, he still is watchful of his tonal organization.

John Tasker Howard comments that only in young manhood was Chadwick subject to the "academic-romantic tradition" of his German teachers. Eventually, his enquiring mind, brilliant aptitude for his craft, and undeniable emotional sincerity toned down this influence.[57] Edward Burlingame Hill, a younger contemporary free of the German academic tradition, had studied music with both Paine and Chadwick. He was already an eminent composer favoring French Impressionism when he stated that Chadwick's main attributes were effortless and pleasing melodic inventiveness, skilled part-writing, and coherent structures. Harmony was solid and captured effects that were romantic, poetic, or dramatic in color without employing "the devices of ultra-modern

George Chadwick in 1924.

eccentricity." Hill found the instrumentation brilliant, resourceful, and idiomatic. Chadwick's contrapuntal adroitness was outstanding, his grasp of chamber and symphonic styles incomparable, and his spontaneity of expression extraordinary. In addition, Chadwick "has shown most convincingly in the overture to '*Melpomene*' that he can depart from the strict letter of the poem and justify the result." Finally, Hill states, Chadwick supplies a secure framework to his substantial works, so that he can freely elaborate details as he chooses.[58]

The vernacular in Chadwick's music draws on the hymnody and the traditional tunes and dances of New England. Occasionally, hints at popular ballads and minstrel songs suggest themselves. Once in a while, allusions to contemporary cakewalk, ragtime, and novelty songs appear. Melody may be syncopated and centered on a scale with half-step intervals avoided or omitted. His music can sound modal owing especially to the use of the lowered seventh degree of the scale. The evocative French horn solo that begins the Second Symphony, for instance, grows from a gapped Dorian mode—the second and sixth tones are omitted, and the seventh is lowered. Syncopation sounds on the second beat of each of the first three measures. The passage is quintessentially American, whether one associates it with the music of African Americans or Anglo-Celtic Yankee Americans. In addition, the opening phrase permeates all of the movements of the Second Symphony, making it a cyclical composition. The composer completed this symphony seven years before the visit of Antonín Dvořák to the United States. Some recent critics are therefore mistaken to write that Dvořák lead Americans, Chadwick among them, toward adding native musical materials to their art music. In truth the opening phrase of this symphony may well have inspired the second-movement melody of Dvořák's Symphony *From the New World,* completed eight years later. In addition, the Second Symphony's cyclical nature could have given Dvořák the idea to do something similar in his symphony.

Other passages in Chadwick's music capture the cracker-barrel humor and tall-tale telling of New England rural folk sitting around the potbellied stoves of village general stores during winter—as in the second movement of the Second Symphony, the third movement of the Fourth String Quartet, and "Jubilee," "Hobgoblin" and "A Vagrom Ballad" from the *Symphonic Sketches.* Chadwick's musical Americanisms, states Carl Engel, are less the sound of American Indian, African American, and contemporary popular music, more that of the New England Yankees. He continues: "Mr. Chadwick can write naïvely, even rustically; he has the courage to set on paper tunes that are unblushingly amiable. But when he puts these tendencies to better purpose, he blends the simple with the touching, he writes a melody like that of the final chorus in his 'Land of Our Hearts,' which is both hymn and folk-song, straightforward, perfect and abiding."[59]

For Keyboard, Voice, and Chamber Ensemble

Like Paine, Chadwick wrote few works for the keyboard. Some are teaching pieces; most are pleasant. Six Characteristic Pieces for Pianoforte, op. 7, from the early 1880s, is mostly lighthearted. The best of the six pieces is the "Irish Melody," an attractively guileless work yet having some substance. Later came Two Caprices (1888), Three Waltzes (1890), a Chanson Orientale (1895), a Nocturne (1895), and Five Pieces for Pianoforte (1905). None was a major effort.

In contrast to his small body of piano and organ music, Chadwick wrote over 125 art songs. Early on, Chadwick explored several manners of expression in song, all of which were fused into his mature style. First was that of Schubert and Schumann, as in "Thou Art So Like a Flower" (1885), op. 11, no. 3, on a text after Heine. Second, in "A Bonny Curl" (1889), text by Amelie Rives, he turns Anglo-Celtic Yankee, with use of the Scotch snap and a melody hovering around the third and sixth tones of the scale and shunning half-step progressions. Third, "In Bygone Days" (1885), op. 14, no. 3, is a semi-artistic American sentimental ballad, a type popular during the late nineteenth century. Possibly because he detected these connections to the music of the masses, Rupert Hughes called the song "trashy."[60] Another song of this type, "Before the Dawn" (1882), op. 8, no. 3, has its equivalences in the well-liked songs of Reginald DeKoven, Carrie Jacob Bond, and Ernest Ball. A song conveying passionate desire, "Sweetheart, Thy Lips Are Touched with Flame," is excitingly set forth. "The Danza" (1885), op. 14, no. 1, to a poem of Arlo Bates, on the other hand, is easygoing. Its catchy tune, supported by a nimble accompaniment in triple time, takes after a Spanish American waltz.

Still another side of Chadwick is shown by his fascination with the Middle East. The fascination was common to many artists of his era, whether in the United States or Europe—composers, poets, painters, novelists, sculptors, and authors of travels. Yet Chadwick's interest is limited usually to the poetry he selected for musical setting. Less often is the Middle East influence found in the music. "Song from the Persian" (1886), words by Thomas Bailey Aldrich, does at least suggest an exotic atmosphere through its music. The minor mode, half-step intervals (none from leading tone to tonic), characteristic augmented-sixth harmony, and languorous curves of melody often convey this special aura. More typical, however, is the fine "Bedouin Love Song" (1890), to a poem of Bayard Taylor. The music makes no attempt at the exotic. An equally excellent song, "Allah" (1887), to a poem by Henry Wadsworth Longfellow, also spurns the exotic in its music. In fact, the dignified and diatonic melody could be taken as Celtic American.

Songs that received much praise from contemporary and later critics include "The Miller's Daughter" (1881), "The Sweet Wind That Blows" (1885), "He Loves Me" (1885), "The Lily" (1887), "Sorai's Song" (1888), "Green Grows the Willow" (1888), "Love and Joy" (1892), "A Ballad of Trees and the Master" (1899), "When I Am Dead" (1910), "The Daughter of Mendoza" (1914), and the late *Three Nautical Songs* (1920). The publication of a Chadwick song was always greeted with pleasure. In 1890, when Schmidt published his twelve *Songs of Brittany,* Louis C. Elson wrote in the *Boston Musical Herald:* "The eminent composer has here set, to ancient Breton themes, a series of graceful poems by Arlo Bates. All are short, simple and interesting. At times one of the old church scales with flat seventh shows itself and whether the songs be ancient or not (the reviewer is not familiar with the music of Brittany) they have a quaint and very agreeable flavor."[61] If Paine stands as the pioneer of the American symphonic tradition, surely Chadwick deserves like status for his contributions to American art song.

The number of chamber works that Chadwick composed, like his songs, is larger than Paine's. One early string trio in C minor, now lost, was completed before he left for Germany.[62] The chamber works that are extant, five string quartets and one piano quintet, were composed between 1877 and 1898. Later he would add a couple of inconsequential pieces. All of these compositions radiate warmth and disclose a great deal of harmonic variety, a solid grasp of counterpoint, and a command of motivic development. Carl Engel praises the chamber works for their alert vigor, natural unforced melody, able instrumentation, confident management of the musical fabric, and evoking a native sound analogous to American folk music.[63]

The First Quartet for Strings in G minor was written in Leipzig. He told a friend in February 1878 that the quartet was "going to be pretty good; I have introduced . . . 'Shoot the pipe' [a traditional American dance tune] in the Scherzo; nothing like economy you know." Later, he wrote to the same friend, "I think that I have some original things in it."[64] More Americanisms are hinted at in the last movement—American two-step and gospel hymn. No known contemporary American performance of the complete quartet took place. After Chadwick returned to the United States, he arranged the slow movement as an Andante for String Orchestra, which was premiered in 1882 at a Philharmonic concert. In November 1878 Chadwick completed his Second Quartet for Strings in C Major. Melody is more folksy, harmony richer, rhythm more ear catching. After examining it, his teachers discovered "a quite extraordinary talent in composition," well above the student level. When fellow students at the Leipzig Conservatory heard the work privately performed, Chadwick says, they clapped and clapped until the director stopped them. In the spring of 1879 it had a public performance at a students' examination concert, where, Chadwick says, "Each movement was much applauded and in the end I was vociferously cheered."[65] On 5 January 1881 the Beethoven Quintet Club presented the quartet in Boston with Chadwick present. He experienced a triumph. The *Boston Advertiser* commented: "Mr. Chadwick has succeeded in his work, and placed himself before the public in a very favorable light. This fact the very critical audience present expressed by calling him upon the platform to bow his acknowledgements to their approbation and receive the cordial grasp of the hand from each of the players." Reviewers thought he showed some affinities to Mendelssohn, but agreed that the composer was in no way a novice. The quartet and the *Rip Van Winkle* Overture, also composed in 1879, demonstrated individuality to Bostonians and had sufficient family resemblances to identify them as the work of the same composer.[66]

The Beethoven Quintet Club performed Chadwick's Third Quartet for Strings in D Major on 9 March 1887, almost a year after it was completed. On the evidence of this composition, Chadwick seems to have become more truly himself. Local reviewers found it equal to the best contemporary quartets anywhere and called Chadwick "our junior Haydn." To them, it showed an advance in style over the Second Quartet. The New York critic H. E. Krehbiel heard it on 22 November in New York City and described the work as straightforward, of modest length, and with no superfluous notes. He felt the second movement, a theme and variations in D minor, owed a debt to "the posthumous quartet by Schubert [the *Death and the Maiden* Quartet in D Minor]." The broad melody sounded especially fine in its opening presentation and in the first and third variations.[67]

The Quintet for Piano and Strings in E Flat was finished in October 1887. It was presented in company with the Third Quartet and a few songs on 23 January 1888 before a small audience. Reviewers liked the quintet. Over the next few years it gained enough public favor for Schmidt to have it published in 1890. Writing about the quintet many years after its first performance, Olin Downes said that it deserved its popularity. "Melodic invention, the hand of a sure craftsman, and an engaging and vigorous personality are shown in Chadwick's best music," where this quintet belongs, although he thought the Americanisms were "old-fashioned."[68]

The Fourth Quartet for Strings in E Minor, first performed in December 1896, makes clear what was usually hinted at in the earlier chamber music, an obvious American sound.[69] Its chief musical antecedent was Chadwick's own Second Symphony in B Flat, dating from 1885, whose idiom is solidly American. By this date, Chadwick would also have known the Dvořák contributions—the Symphony No. 9 in E Minor, *From the New World,* op. 95, the "American" Quartet for Strings, op. 96, and the "American" Quintet for Strings, op. 97, composed during Dvořák's stay in the United States in the early 1890s. Chadwick turns to traditional American usages, often using melodies similar to those found in Yankee churches and the hinterland, which he rendered in the Mixolydian or Dorian modes. The work is clearly cyclical. Musical ideas in later movements continually grow out of the initial one in the first movement. The rhythms concur with those of New England psalmody and country dance. In the first movement, after a touching slow introduction and a brisk first theme, we hear a pentatonic tune of pleasing character and undoubted American origin. Later in the movement a melody materializes as if from a worship service in a New England meetinghouse. The slow movement begins with a stately American dance, guileless and effective. The middle part, on the other hand, is unexpectedly fast, in the minor, and more emotional. The third movement starts like an agile banjo tune from a minstrel show; its trio, in sharp contrast, resorts to American psalmody, with a simple, folklike melody. The main theme of the last movement supplies the framework for a set of variations; then comes a brief *lento espressivo* middle section and finally, a fugue. The coda of the finale, *presto con brio,* serves as a magnificent finish to music of considerable merit.

The quartet became possibly the most widely performed of Chadwick's chamber works. Most contemporary listeners thought it was in a modern idiom and with a character all its own. In 1904 the quartet was heard in Boston at an Arbos Quartet concert that also presented Franck's Violin Sonata in A and Brahms's Sextet, op. 18. The reviewer for the *Boston Advertiser,* 12 March 1904, presented the majority view when he wrote that Chadwick was "easily the peer of all American composers in string quartette music. His appreciation of the possibilities of the quartette is well shown in this splendid work. The beautiful harmonies throughout and the strong and vigorous fugue of the finale will satisfy the most exacting from an intellectual standpoint. Then the melodious themes, some of them quite jovial in character, cannot help but interest even the layman. The fact that the work of one of our own composers can stand equally on a programme without being overshadowed in the least by some of the best compositions of such men as Franck and Brahms is the highest proof of its worth. As has often been said in these columns, the real test of our American music is to give it a place in the programme with that of the greatest masters."[70] Cultural politics is one reason why this composition has been prevented from entering the standard repertoire.

The Adamowski Quartet premiered the Fifth Quartet for Strings in D Minor in February 1901. Steven Ledbetter quotes Chadwick as remarking twenty years after the event: "It was very warmly received, perhaps because the 'soil music' as Cadman calls it, that it contains makes a special appeal to our American ears. But otherwise it is pretty well made for the instruments & has a lot of 'good sound.' . . . The Adamowskis were quite proud of it and played it with lots of fire and enthusiasm." Chadwick revised parts of the first and slow movement two years later.[71] The quartet, like its predecessor, smacks of the New England soil, but less obviously. Its four movements proclaim, said a writer in the *Boston Globe,* 28 January 1910, the composer's powerful individuality, constant inventiveness, and stylistic lucidity; what is more, the quartet is highly pleasing to hear.[72] A staid first movement precedes a meditative slow movement; after that come a carefree scherzo and a finale that is both folklike and sometimes marchlike. The creative level is high. It was his last large chamber work.

Part-Songs and Choral Music

Chadwick composed many choral pieces, among them anthems, part-songs, and arrangements of his solo songs. All are enjoyable; hardly any are unusual. Of the music to piano accompaniment, Rupert Hughes commends "Jabberwocky" (1886), to the Lewis Carroll text, for its irresistible humor, and "Reiterlied (Trooper's Song)" (1889) for its superb joyousness. Vocal compositions with orchestra are also enjoyable but rarely remarkable. On 22 April 1881 the Apollo Club, in recognition of the young composer's growing fame, presented Chadwick's "The Viking's Last Voyage" for baritone solo, male chorus, and orchestra. A brooding, dramatic subject, expressive melodies, stormy emotions, and heroic weltschmerz—the composition matched the tastes of the audience. A year later, Chadwick followed up his winning piece with a burly "Song of the Viking" for male chorus and keyboard. He arranged the keyboard part for orchestra in 1914. Although Rupert Hughes liked "The Viking's Last Voyage," he had to kid Chadwick: "What would part-song writers do if the Vikings had never been invented? Where would they get their wild choruses for men, with a prize to the singer that makes the most noise? Chadwick falls into line with

'The Viking's Last Voyage,' . . . which gives him a very high place among writers in this form."[73]

The cantata *Phoenix Expirans* (1891) employs a Latin hymn text and calls for four soloists, mixed chorus, and orchestra. After the Handel and Haydn Society premiered it, a writer reporting on the musical season of 1892–93 in Boston's *Home Journal* named it the "marked event of the season. The eroticism of the text did not disturb the bulk of the congregation, as the burning lines were cooled in the obscurity of the original Latin." H. E. Krehbiel, who heard it in New York City on 15 December 1892, considered it Chadwick's finest choral work up to that time. He found its melody fresh, its impression dignified, its orchestration colorful, and its harmony warm.[74]

Noël, A Christmas Pastoral, for four soloists, mixed chorus, and orchestra, was completed in 1908 and performed at the Norfolk Festival in 1909. It consists of a prelude and twelve vocal numbers. The prelude, entitled "The Star," sets the mood of the composition by projecting the peaceful depictions to come. The first number, "This is the month," is set for a capella chorus singing homophonically and makes an excellent effect. The second number, "From the eastern mountains," is successfully set for soprano soloist and chorus. Number three, "O long and darksome was the night," for alto solo, blends two musical approaches, ancient and contemporary, until the music grows animated on the words "When Thou, O Christ!" Unexpectedly, and for a short while, Chadwick thrusts us into the domain of late Wagner. *Noël* ends grandly with the solo quartet singing "Hither come, ye heavy hearted," followed by the chorus on the chorale "How lovely shines the morning star" and then an elaborate choral fugue on "Wake, wake your harps to sweet songs!" At the beginning of the century, *Noël* was well liked. When done in Baltimore in December 1916, for example, it won rave reviews for its musical beauty, deep devotion, and moving evocation of a pastoral atmosphere.[75]

Given Chadwick's flair for the dramatic, it is disappointing that he wrote few works for the musical stage. A contributing factor to the small number was beyond question the reluctance of impresarios in the United States to take a chance on native compositions however deserving of esteem. Chadwick's two serious operas, *Judith* and *The Padrone*, would join Paine's *Azara* in never receiving staged performances.

In 1884 and 1892, respectively, he had completed the two-act operettas *The Peer and the Pauper* and *A Quiet Lodging*, designed for private club entertainment. Then in 1894 came the two-act *Tabasco*, a "burlesque opera" with a libretto by R. A. Barnet, which made provision for amateur performance. After its first presentation, in January 1894, Philip Hale wrote in the *Musical Courier:* "He of our American composers has certain peculiar advantages in this undertaking new to him. He has not only melody, rhythm, color, facility; he has a strong sense of humor, an appreciation of values, and that quality known as horse-sense."[76] Three months later, a professional performance made *Tabasco* so popular that the Seabrooke Opera Company decided to tour with it. The publisher B. F. Wood issued the music in piano score. *Tabasco* side-splittingly lampoons the popular song and operetta styles and the vaudeville routines of the day. Everything is turned on its head. Illogic is the governing logic. The locale is Tangiers. The first act opens on a bustling harborside scene with the obligatory chorus of commoners mixed together with the cries of street vendors advertising their wares ("Cucumbers and fresh Tomater, Epsom salts and Cream of Tartar," "Coffee, coffee, all male berries," etc.). Next, the grand vizier, Ben-Hid-Den, weeps over his destiny "to be society's door-mat." Later, Fatima's song "O Lovely Home" is a mock sentimental ballad on a done-to-death topic. One hears a suspicion of "Auld Lang Syne" harmonized in the manner of a sentimental ballad by Paul Dresser with a barbershop twist at the end. The audience also is introduced to a Spanish bolero, a French rigaudon, and a Viennese waltz, the last carried out to the patter of the harem women's feet.

A French chef, François, sings his hilarious "Ditty" in an Irish brogue and longs for the "blossoms in Ireland the shamrocks between." Even more absurdly incongruous is the plantation ballad, "O darkies don't yer 'member de ole Kentucky farm," complete with the four-part choral ending of blackface minstrelsy. Finally, the "March of the Pasha's Guard" would easily fit into a Mulligan Guard routine of Harrigan and Hart. No other New England composer had such a capacity for musical tongue-in-cheek. At the same time, his dazzlingly varied musical numbers are entertaining in their own right.

Different from top to bottom is the Biblical drama *Judith,* to a libretto by William C. Langdon, which Chadwick completed in 1900. Chadwick conducted it in concert version the next year at a Worcester Festival, and later in Boston's Symphony Hall. The plot is built around Judith, a stunning Hebrew woman single-mindedly intent on avenging her people and her God. She comes into an Assyrian camp where a multitude is blaspheming against Jehovah. She bewitches Holofernes, the Assyrian leader, with her comeliness and beheads him after he has become helplessly drunk. Steven Ledbetter and Victor Yellin, in their article on Chadwick for the *American Grove,* say that some dramatic action and orchestral sonorities are indebted to Saint-Saëns's *Samson et Dalila,* which Chadwick had conducted just before composing *Judith,* and that some choral writing shows the influence of Mendelssohn. The article goes on to praise the "colorful, large-scaled opera, much of which could be acted to telling effect," and calls the act 2 scene where Holofernes succumbs to Judith's beauty and dies by her hand "one of the most expertly constructed and tautly lyrical passages in American dramatic music."[77]

A contemporary of Chadwick, the conservative critic Louis C. Elson, admired *Judith:* "Splendid contrasts occur between the religious loftiness of the old Hebrews (chiefly broad chorales or contrapuntal choruses) and the brutal sensuality of the Assyrians, expressed in dances or in bombastic marches. A combination of these two elements, in the second part, gives a most skilful display of the composer's ability; and the simultaneous presentation of the sighs of the prisoners and the laughter of their conquerors is supported with some of the most graphic orchestration imaginable."[78]

Chadwick seems never to have settled in his own mind whether he was writing an oratorio or an out-and-out opera calling for stage action. Leading motives are employed charily. The music, splendid as it is, provides hardly any sense of forward movement, and the scenes come across as static. Act 2 is the most "operatic" of the three, with abundance of movement, color, and contrast. Its magnificent final scene describes the dissipated Assyrians, Judith's struggle of conscience, and her gory action with extraordinarily suitable music. Act 3, given over to the victorious Judith and the exultant Israelites, is more oratorio than opera. With no opening for suspense or dramatic changes in mood and feeling, the act remains lifeless for most of its length.

Chadwick's opera *The Padrone,* written in 1912 and 1913, lets slip an appreciation of Puccini and *verismo.* The story is about recent Italian immigrants to the United States and a criminal boss's tragic dominance over their lives. The unidentified city setting was probably modeled after Boston's Italian section, the North End. The opera has thrilling action, luminously orchestrated music, and plentiful occasions for vocal display—all that an opera enthusiast could desire. Yet it has never been brought to life on the stage. It appears that the protagonists were considered of no account and too common. Besides, the text was in understandable English, not in a happily unintelligible foreign language, sung by quaint peasants dancing tarantellas or brandishing wine glasses and singing in celebration of love of some sort. The opera remains in manuscript at the New England Conservatory of Music, ignored.

Orchestral Compositions

Chadwick won his highest esteem as an orchestral composer. His expertise was such that orchestra conductors and members of symphony orchestras delighted in his idiomatic feel for instruments.[79] The orchestral tone images he invented show mastery similar to that of Berlioz, Wagner, Strauss, and contemporary Russian and French composers. His earliest compositions had confined themselves to Classical limits. As he grew older, his orchestrations increased in brilliance and in revealing atmosphere and feeling. Carl Engel, a Chadwick devotee, states: "For 'Tam O'Shanter' chased by the host of devilish imps, for the 'Angel of Death' spreading his wings protectingly, for the impassioned worshippers of 'Aphrodite,' for pictures as varied as they are vivid, Mr. Chadwick finds an orchestral representation that is definite and telling. His orchestra can sing; it can roister. It can be droll without being grotesque. It can be graphic and yet escape being flatly imitative. Here then are paired consummate technic and real originality."[80]

His student work the *Rip Van Winkle* Overture was performed in Leipzig in March 1879. The Harvard Music Association's orchestra presented it later that year in Boston. Approving audiences and reviewers endorsed the composer's abilities and put him in Paine's class. From the beginning he handles structure, orchestration, and emotional range with assurance. In the person of Rip one supposes that Chadwick is already making an effort to understand the illogicality of the human condition, with its unavoidable cycles of misery, foolishness, and hope. Sensibly, he declines to provide a program, although a writer or two tried to supply their own: the cello in the introduction is the sleeper awakening; weird and strange sounds depict the mountain scene; the stirring coda represents the bright excitement of the village, and so forth.[81]

Chadwick's Symphony No. 1 in C major received its first performance in February 1882 at a Harvard Music Association concert. Again, the audience approved of the music. According to the *Boston Sunday Herald,* 19 February 1882, this aspiring work was begun in Leipzig in 1877, and the first movement was heard in Munich in 1880. The composition was completed in Boston. Most reviewers described the symphony as attractive and imaginative, dramatic and heartfelt, and wholesome.[82]

The first movement starts with a quiet four-measure introduction, leading to the awaited *allegro molto e sostenuto,* whose first theme makes the most of a syncopated four-note motive. The scherzo that follows is pleasingly optimistic. The *adagio* dispenses a broadly singing melody. Especially pleasing is the passage toward the end, when the English horn chants plaintively alongside a gentle countermelody in the violins, after which an arresting culmination of the entire movement occurs. The finale, after a majestic introduction, speeds up for a vigorous main theme. The melody from the *adagio* movement is reintroduced in the coda.

His next orchestral composition, the *Thalia* Overture, subtitled an "overture to an imaginary comedy," had a first performance from the recently founded Boston Symphony Orchestra in January 1883. The Boston audience prized it. The work sounded strong and dignified, even though the composer considered it comic. Zesty music takes over after an elegant slow opening. The main body of the work is at one moment humorous, at another glowingly bold.

The Boston Symphony presented the scherzo from a symphony in progress in March 1884. An Apollo Club concert unveiled an Introduction and Allegro from this same work in April 1885. Finally the Boston Symphony, 10 December 1886, premiered the entire Symphony No. 2 in B-flat Major. Here was a symphony worthy of place beside the two Paine symphonies as one of the most outstanding American symphonic works of its time. The opus was immediately welcomed as the long awaited and convincingly "American" symphony in melody, rhythm, and overall spirit. Nevertheless, Chadwick did not envision himself here, or in the Fourth Quartet, as having initiated a clear-cut "American" style. His aim was universality. That his personal style incorporated "Americanisms" was very well so long as this alone did not entirely define his creative manner. His personality being what it was, he could not help employing Americanisms. The danger, he thought, was to have his music understood as only regional, colloquial, and therefore provincial. Before Dvořák's advocating the use of Indian, African American, and Stephen Fosterish melodies in art music, nobody likened Chadwick's use of the vernacular in this symphony to the music of Indians or African Americans or Foster. When the scherzo alone was performed in 1884, critics spoke of its tangy originality, irresistible color, and closeness to Celtic humor. A *Boston Transcript* critic said it "positively winks at you." The *Boston Courier* reviewer spoke of its unconventionality and pronounced the movement splendid. When the complete symphony was heard in 1886, it had such an unprecedented character that a comparison with any other work was impossible for his contemporaries. Nobody connected it with African American music, as would be done in the next century. Nobody spoke of the influence of Dvořák, as some twentieth-century writers have done, ignoring the fact that the Bohemian composer's arrival in the United States was still some years in the future. After a February 1891 performance, Philip Hale spoke of the symphony's smelling of the American soil, the scherzo as clothed in delightful vulgarity. Finally, in 1906 we find Hale, in the *Boston Sunday Herald,* saying that to speak of an Indian or Negro flavor is unsatisfactory: "The scherzo of Mr. Chadwick's Symphony in b flat is much more American as far as 'Americanism' is concerned, for it breathes the spirit of devil-may-care independence, it snaps its fingers at judicious and conventional comments, it is good-natured, and it is cheerfully irreverent. The same composer's 'Vagrom Ballad' [from the *Symphonic Sketches*] has also an American flavor—and yet a conductor of symphony concerts might well hesitate before putting it on a programme."[83]

The scoring is for woodwinds, trumpets, and timpani by twos; four French horns; three trombones; and strings.[84] The first movement opens on an *andante non troppo,* in common time, with the first horn intoning the principal motto for the entire symphony. A poetic atmosphere is soon established that pervades the remainder of the movement. The ensuing *allegro con brio,* in sonata form, has an intrepid first theme derived from the motto. The subordinate theme, in F major, begins as a soft cantabile horn solo backed by open fifths and octaves in the strings. A rousing codetta concludes the exposition. The development section centers prominently on the motto. In the recapitulation the subordinate theme, now played by a muted trumpet, sounds as if Chadwick had the sound of a New England village band concert in mind.

The second movement, in F major, is an *allegretto scherzando* in duple meter and rondo form (ABACAB¹A). The frolicsome main subject is based on the motto. The third movement, a *largo e maestoso* in D minor and triple meter, opens on still another variant of the motto, after which the lower strings enter to sing in warm, rich fashion. The middle section, *allegro non troppo,* turns much more dramatic. The recapitulation of the opening melody in the woodwinds sounds ardently in 9/8 time and is intensified by chromatic figures in the strings. The finale is an exuberant and festive *allegro molto animato* in common time. As expected, the motto underlies much of the movement; less expected, themes from the other movements return, confirming the cyclic nature of the symphony. The entire work concludes with allusions both to the motto and to the main theme of the allegro in the first movement. The symphony is one of Chadwick's master-pieces.

The *Melpomene* Overture, a dramatic overture devoted to the muse of tragedy, is an obvious companion piece to the *Thalia* Overture. The Boston Symphony gave the work its first performance in December 1887. A prevalent interest among composers of his era was the composing of dramatic or tragic overtures. In 1870 Dvořák had completed a *Tragic (Dra-matic)* Overture, originally intended for his opera *Alfred*. This and the Brahms *Tragic* Overture of 1880 may possibly have motivated Chadwick into writing *Melpomene*. Chadwick supplies no detailed program for his overture. The orchestra is larger than that of the Second Symphony. He adds a piccolo, English horn, tuba, bass drum, and cymbals. Americanisms are absent. Throughout, he exploits the coloristic possibilities of the instruments. The use of appoggiaturas and dissonance to increase and less-en tension is skillfully managed. The music public was completely won over. The overture quickly found its way into the repertoire of several American and a couple of European orchestras. Critics praised its honesty, power of expression, and lack of overcharged depressive elements. Writ-ing in the *Boston Journal,* 15 March 1896, Philip Hale states: "Mr. Chadwick . . . did not attempt to exploit musically a strange family tree. His music is indeed tragic, nobly tragic. The very introduction prepares for the black curtain. Yet the gloom is neither peevish nor pessimistic. The mourning is a loud lamentation. There is the thought of heroic life and heroic death. His tragedy does not hint at Helen of Troy or her successors. There is no amorous parley in life; there is no sensuous regret when Death enters and dominates the scene."[85]

A Symphony No. 3 in F Major, his last symphony, was offered the pub-lic in 1894. It won a composition prize of three hundred dollars from the National Conservatory in New York. Gapped scales, modal passages, and Americanisms are less in evidence than they were in the previous sym-phony. The music not only entertains but also rewards the listener with real musical ideas, though these are not so powerful and expressive as they are in the Second Symphony. The third movement has an especially lovely melody in the French horn and, later, the low strings.

Percy Shelley's poem *Adonais* (1821) inspired Chadwick's next orches-tral work, *Adonais,* "an elegiac overture, in memoriam Frank Fay Marshall (amici probe et fidelis)," which the Boston Symphony premiered in February 1900. Mr. Marshall had died in 1897. Here, personal grief is underlined. The boundaries of sonata form are more frequently abandoned than in earlier overtures. The work gives off persistent gloom. Melancholy close to sentimentality mingles with passionate protest. *Adonais* failed to win a following and had few performances.

For several years (1895–1904) Chadwick worked on the four compositions that together would be given the title *Symphonic Sketches,* Suite for Orchestra. The Boston Symphony performed them in February 1908. American audiences immediately regarded the *Sketches* with special favor. In a note appearing on the title page of the score, Chadwick states: "Although these pieces are intended to be played in succession, they may be performed separately if more expedient."[86] The first sketch, "Jubilee," was completed in 1895; the second, "Noël," in 1895; the third, "Hobgoblin," in 1904; and the fourth, "A Vagrom Ballad," in 1896. The glumness of *Adonais* has vanished. The four pieces radiate only light. The style revisits the distinctive expression found in the Second Symphony and the Fourth Quartet. The underlay of Central European romanticism is less in evidence than in previous compositions.

The greatest favorite of the four pieces was the first. Prefaced to the "Jubilee" score is a poem by "D.R.," which begins:

> No cool gray tones for me!
>> Give me the warmest red and green,
> A cornet and a tambourine,
>> To paint My Jubilee!

The orchestra is large. The music, abrim with Yankee spirits, jumps off in full voice with the first theme. Syncopations abound and energize several melodic phrases. Rhythms here and there seem to have origins in the Caribbean. A subsidiary idea (fourth and seventh tones missing) has the four horns mimicking the prancing steps of rustic dancers. The strings answer with a smooth, diatonic tune in popular ballad style.

"Noël" also has a verse appended to it:

> Through the soft, calm moonlight comes a sound;
>> A mother lulls her babe, and all around
> The gentle snow lies glistening;
>> On such a night the Virgin Mother mild
> In dreamless slumber wrapped the Holy Child,
>> While angel-hosts were listening.

Conceived as a pastorale, the music, *andante con tenerezza,* is mostly a hushed hymnlike meditation on the Nativity. The effect is haunting.

Shakespeare's "That shrewd and knavish sprite called Robin Good-fellow" heads the score to "Hobgoblin," subtitled "Scherzo Capriccioso." A horn call begins the movement; a clarinet then plays a syncopated melody. Other instruments rework the same melody. A new syncopated idea begins in the horns. This melody and the music that follows even more clearly belong to the New World. Extroverted and buoyant, the composition often turns rascally and irreverent like that figure in English and New England folklore, Robin Goodfellow.

"A Vagrom Ballad," to be played *moderato, alla burla,* is:

> A tale of tramps and railway ties,
>   Of old clay pipes and rum,
> Of broken heads and blackened eyes
>   And the "thirty days" to come!

Yellin states that Chadwick was thinking about a camp of homeless vagrants, which he had seen as he traveled back and forth to Worcester. He also was recalling the soft-shoe vaudeville routine of the stage hobo, a tragicomic symbol of the entirely liberated man.[87] The percussion section adds a xylophone and snare drum. The piece begins in a mock-serious A minor, yet with some pathos. The main theme, in the bass clarinet and bassoon, is marked *cantando.* They play a good-natured yet eccentrically moving ditty. No information has come to us about why Chadwick saw fit to throw in a snatch of a Bach fugue. This tune lays the groundwork for the free variations that follow. Lastly, the coda, based on the tune, goes faster and faster until the final measure. Speaking about "A Vagrom Ballad," Oscar Sonneck states: "This gem of American musical humor, worthy of a Mark Twain, was composed in 1896, though not published until 1907! If certain of our younger composers brush aside such a piece as 'old foggish,' they are welcome to this opinion as they are to their naïve preferential belief in the efficacy of French as against German measles as a musical beautifier."[88]

Other orchestral compositions came from Chadwick during these productive years. The *Euterpe* Overture, completed in 1903 and premiered in 1904, mulls over the muse of music. Sounding fresh and lyrical, it starts in an unhappy D-minor mood but later achieves some of the exhilarating syncopated feeling found in the *Symphonic Sketches.* Alternations between melancholy and joy encompass the two aspects of the muse.

In 1904, also, the Sinfonietta in D Major was heard for the first time. Less demanding than a symphony, the music is instantly enjoyable. It is undoubtedly one of Chadwick's most felicitous scores. The first movement, *risolutamento,* begins with a frank and confidently affirmative statement. Leading tones are avoided. Continuous syncopation imparts a characteristically American swing to most measures. The second movement, a *canzonetta,* sounds like a modal folk song and has some connection with the slow movement of Mendelssohn's *Italian* Symphony. The syncopated *scherzino* movement surrounds a smooth and bucolic trio. The finale is brisk and marchlike. Only once does the sound of deep sadness break in on the usual optimism.

Completed in 1904 and heard in 1905, *Cleopatra* was Chadwick's first symphonic poem and comes with a program based on the *Cleopatra* of Plutarch, not Shakespeare—her journey on the Nile, the coming of Anthony, the lovers' obsession with each other, the woeful end of Anthony, the lamentation of Cleopatra followed by her death, and the entombment of the two lovers. A strange sensuousness and exoticism, not normally encountered in Chadwick's instrumental music, pervade the melodies and harmonies. The Symphonic Fantasie *Aphrodite* received its first performance in 1912. Added to the score is a verse, which begins:

> In a dim vision of the long ago
> > Wandering by a far-off Grecian shore
> Where streaming moonlight shone on golden sands
> > And melting stars dissolved in silver seas,
> I humbly knelt at Aphrodite's shrine.[89]

Impressionistic splashes of tonal color occur alongside linear movement in the music, sometimes grave, majestic, or mysterious.

Finished in 1909, a Suite Symphonique in E Flat had its premiere in 1911. Its American spirit and sound have a decided connection with those of the *Symphonic Sketches.* Although this suite never achieved the reputation of the earlier composition, especially winning are the "Romanza," in particular the haunting saxophone solo, and the "Intermezzo e Humoreske," with its cakewalking section in 5/4 time.

A symphonic poem, *Angel of Death,* inspired by the Daniel French sculpture, was heard in February 1919. However, it was *Tam O'Shanter,* a Symphonic Ballade, completed and performed in 1915, that was his last work to make an immense impression on the public and critics. The composition derives from the poem of Robert Burns, written in 1790. The published score comes complete with a detailed program explaining the different sections of the music.[90] A first hearing offers a lesson on how problematic it is to label any music as exemplifying a specific sort of Americanism. Here is a work illustrating an inebriated Tam O'Shanter, a Scotsman, riding through a Scottish countryside at night. We hear the gapped scales, modal progressions, psalmody, folklike balladry, and dance tunes already present in other Chadwick works. Various writers have said they accentuate Chadwick's individuality or his sensitivity to things American. When one or more of these musical characteristics occur in other contexts, writers have claimed them to get their inspiration from the Celts, English, African Americans, or American Indians. For example, at one point in *Tam O'Shanter* the double reeds and a trumpet play a "horn-pipe dance tune," and at the close, the first violins execute a *crescendo molto*. Both of these sound not unlike parts of MacDowell's *Indian Suite*.

A tipsy Tam O'Shanter rides home through storm and darkness. "A jocund, roistering chorus in the style of a Scottish folk-tune, given to the horns and trombones, sometimes in different keys simultaneously," delineates him. Shortly, an insistent eighth-note figure in the lower strings indicates the horse's canter, and above occur fragments of Tam's tune. Later, he nears Kirk Alloway and part of an old Scottish tune, "Martyrs," materializes. To Tam's amazement, he glimpses an orgy taking place in the church, "described in a series of dances very much in the Scottish style." One dance is the hornpipe tune already mentioned. Bagpipes squeal in the oboe and bassoon; bones rattle in the xylophone; "unearthly shrieks" come from the clarinets and muted horns; the trombones groan. The dance gets faster and faster, developing into a wild and "furious reel." Two threatening booms of a gong unleash screaming witches who dash after Tam. The furious pursuit ends with Tam hurtling over a bridge to his home and safety. Quietude descends. The prolonged coda is meditative, with soft sustained melody and simple harmonizations. The composition dies out on Tam's own theme.

Tam O'Shanter is one of the most colorful scores by any American until that time. There is nothing academic about it. After the Chicago Symphony presented the composition in January 1916, a correspondent in the *Boston Transcript* praised its "sense of the sardonic." The music to him was "quizzically humorous," "imaginative," "at once wry and picturesque." Chadwick, the writer said, had a sure sense of the Scottish, especially in the rhythms and in "a quirk of cadence." Nevertheless, he found the Scottish tunes "closely akin to prevalent 'Americanisms' of music."[91]

Beginning in the 1920s, Chadwick's music suffered continuous attack from modernists and soon went out of fashion. With Chadwick's death, whatever vogue existed for his music departed. Yet his compositions are too fine to remain unheard. Chadwick is indisputably an *American* composer. His orchestral writing glows. The melodies cheer the spirit. He sees the value of musical glee as well as grief. Chadwick remains an artist of sturdy integrity and splendid individuality.

PARKER, FOOTE, AND MACDOWELL

Contemporary music lovers considered Horatio Parker (1863–1919), Arthur Foote (1853–1937), and Edward MacDowell (1860–1908) to be wonderful composers in their own right. Each man played an important part in America's cultural life as music educators, performers, and composers. Each man created musical compositions of the first rank: Parker's oratorio *Hora Novissima* and opera *Mona;* Foote's Suite for Strings in E Major, *Four Character Pieces after the Rubáiyát of Omar Khayyám* for orchestra, and *A Night Piece* for flute and strings; and MacDowell's *Indian* Suite, piano sonatas, and last three piano suites.

HORATIO PARKER

Parker was born in Auburndale, a few miles out of Boston. His commitment to music began in his teenage years. It was so total that he wished to take part in no other activity, whether in school or on the playing field.[1] His father was a prominent Boston architect, his mother a pianist, music teacher, and poet. She also was familiar with Latin and Greek. As one might expect, his mother supported his musical interests. She would later translate the Latin into English for his impressive *Hora Novissima* and write texts for his *The Holy Child* and *St. Christopher.* Chadwick, who instructed the budding composer, writes that by eighteen years of age, Parker already was showing an aptitude for songful melody and had a respectable command of harmony and modulation. The winning works of Paine and Chadwick served to fuel Parker's own fledgling efforts at composition.[2] Before he was twenty, he had composed songs, keyboard pieces, and chamber and orchestral music.

Like the two older composers, Parker felt a need to continue his musical education abroad. He left the Boston area to study music from 1882 to 1895 in Munich, where Josef Rheinberger instructed him in composition. Soon after returning to the United States, Parker was active as teacher, organist, and choir director in New York City. In 1893 he took over the music direction of Boston's Trinity Church. The next year he added a professorship at Yale University to his responsibilities, constantly commuting between Boston and New Haven until 1902. He then gave up the Boston position to take up similar duties at New York City's Church of St. Nicholas.

Throughout these years, Parker turned out musical composition after musical composition, most of them for solo voice or chorus—art songs, anthems, sacred services, cantatas, oratorios. He wrote few symphonic, chamber, and keyboard works. After the turn of the century, he would contribute several compositions for the stage, the most ambitious being his two operas, *Mona* and *Fairyland*. Little about Parker's musical style, early or late, is audacious or unusual. Charles Ives, Parker's best-known student, thought him a strict and commendable teacher and admired a great deal of his music, finding dignity and depth in the choral works especially. On the whole, Parker's compositions, Ives said, demonstrated a fine intellect, high ideals, and technical mastery. On the other hand, no spirit of adventure was apparent.[3]

For counterpoint and some overall designs, Parker looked back to Handel and Bach. In melody, Mendelssohn was a stimulus. For harmony, he took note of the rich chord formations and varied harmonic progressions favored by Liszt, Wagner, and Strauss. Furthermore, he appreciated the compositions of Brahms, Franck, Gounod, d'Indy, Elgar, and Dvořák.[4] (During 1892–93 Parker taught at New York's National Conservatory of Music, where Dvořák was director.) Nothing "American" appears in his music except for passages in his choral works that echo his Puritan psalmodic heritage. A few critics of his time described his music as sometimes overly severe, too intellectual, or lacking appeal. Yet he composed music because of a ceaseless craving to create in sound. He perceived in himself a God-given talent that it was his duty to use. Indeed, a sense of duty was incorporated into his makeup. He felt obligated to give the best in him. It meant dedication to his vocation and to producing worthy works that the music public might find of value. In this dedication we find the key to his artistic merits.

Like his teacher Rheinberger, he was an exceptional craftsman. An article in the *New York Musical Courier,* 5 April 1893, possibly written by H. E. Krehbiel, describes him as keeping "copious notes" and having "quantities of books laden with rhythmic morsels. Some he uses later, some rejects, some recalls without reference." The article goes on: "His greatest difficulty lies in determining upon the value of ideas. . . . The final chorus of 'Hora Novissima' troubled him extremely, varying in its impression upon him each time it was examined, and finally receiving his unqualified approval as a fit ending to his big work. He wishes there might be a standard for this 'worth of an idea'; but that would restrict taste and limit invention."[5] Although a master of orchestration, Parker rarely tried to exploit the orchestra's coloristic possibilities, contenting himself with orchestrations resembling translations of organ passages into the instruments. Nor did his employment of harmony, skillful as it was, call attention to itself or venture beyond established parameters. Scarcely ever does boldness characterize his sound, despite Parker's increasing use of elusive tonalities and dissonances as he grew older.

Parker's strength is in melody. Most tunes sound cohesive, balanced, and comprehensible. Increasingly, from the 1890s on, they grew longer, more chromatic, and suppler. In one or two later works, like the grand opera *Mona,* a few strains do occur that lose their lyricism by skipping about a great deal. Yet in several works, including *Mona,* other strains do exude a melodious warmth like that of Italian arias. In the *New York Musical Courier* article just quoted, the author says that Parker believed in melody that would catch the ear. This it assuredly does in works representative of his best efforts, such as *Hora Novissima* and the Concerto for Organ and Orchestra.

Concerning his solo keyboard and chamber compositions little need be said. "They seem rather the incidental byplays and recreations of a fancy chiefly turned to sacred music of the large forms," comments Rupert Hughes.[6] They are mostly short characteristic pieces identifiably Romantic and invariably well put together. (The String Quartet of 1885, the String Quintet of 1894, and the Organ Sonata of 1908 are exceptions, both in their length and their blend of the Classical with the Romantic.) These pieces fall pleasantly on the ear, then are soon forgotten. Almost all of them owe a debt to Mendelssohn and Schumann primarily and Beethoven occasionally. For example, in *Four Sketches* for piano (1890), the "Romanza" is charmingly Mendelssohnian, while the brisk "Scherzino" veers toward

Schumann. Similar things can be said of the organ compositions, for example those of opera 17, 20, 32, and 36, composed from 1890 to 1893. In
the main, they charm the listener. When most serious, as in the Fugue in
C Minor, op. 36, no. 3, Parker's music impresses us, as Barbara Owen says,
for its skillfully written counterpoint, easy flow of the horizontal lines, and
underlying technical reasoning.[7] Nevertheless, the piece stays only briefly
in the memory. As for chamber music, the Suite for Piano, Violin, and
Violoncello of 1893 certainly illustrates the characteristic-piece (brief and
lyric) approach and Parker's affinity to Mendelssohn. The four movements
are a prelude in A major, menuet in D minor, romance in B-flat major, and
finale in A major.[8] A prominent melodic line plus a modest homophonic
accompaniment describes the usual musical treatment. Nothing of fundamental importance transpires.

His songs are more compelling, their melody finer and rhythm wider
ranging. Harmony is less perfunctory and accompaniment more inventive.
Parker composed over seventy songs, several of them excellent. His pri-
macy as a songwriter was apparent in 1886, with his *Three Love Songs,*
op. 10, especially no. 2: "Night Piece for Julia."[9] It captures the feeling of
love nourished by the setting of stars and moonlight. At an opposite
extreme, but also effective, are the charming *Six Old English Songs* (1899),
all deliberately simple in technique, direct in expression, and restrained in
emotion. No. 6, "The Lark Now Leaves His Watery Nest," was once quite
popular. Other worthy Parker songs are "Pack, Clouds Away" (1891),
"O Ask Me Not" (1891), "I Know a Little Rose" (1893), "Love in May"
(1901), "Serenade" (1904), "Good Bye" (1904), and "Only a Little While"
(1910).

He wrote scarcely anything for orchestra. The Overture *Count Robert
of Paris* (1890) won him esteem as a serious composer but now seems a
competent effort only. When Thomas and the Chicago Orchestra performed it in 1893, Parker wrote a brief program note establishing it as
similar to overtures by Paine and Chadwick: "Count Robert of Paris is a
symphonic picture of the trials and triumphs of Count Robert, as told in
Sir Walter Scott's romance of the same title. The connection between the
romance and the overture is rather one of sentiment than of accurate
detail. The second theme is in strong contrast to the first, and indicates the
womanly element on the story. The work is not intended as program
music strictly."[10]

Chadwick writes that Parker usually needed words to rouse him, thus
the few purely instrumental works. He considered the symphonic poem

A Northern Ballad (1899) worthy of praise and said it was Parker's most important orchestral work.[11] The New Haven Symphony premiered *A Northern Ballad* on 7 April 1899, and in the next few months it was performed in Boston, Chicago, Cincinnati, and New York City. Why "Northern"? Parker failed to explain. A moderately fast piece in sonata form, the composition draws most of its themes from the introduction. Possibly the melody of the introduction is folklike, as claimed in the Chicago Symphony program notes for 10 February 1900. The work's one bold stroke is the tonality. It starts in E minor and closes in D flat. Most critics thought the composition owed something to Dvořák and Tchaikovsky. They found the harmony rich, the melodies persuasive though not unusual, and the scoring effective despite the mostly "cloudy grey colors," to quote W.F.A. of the *Boston Transcript*.

Three years later, Parker completed his Concerto for Organ and Orchestra (premiered by the Boston Symphony Orchestra on 29 December 1902), which is qualitatively equal if not superior to the *Ballad*. William Kearns, in his study of Parker and his music, declares it the best of Parker's instrumental works, praising the unusual structure, quality of ideas, inventive development of them, and idiomatic writing for organ and orchestra.[12] After hearing the concerto at a concert, which also featured *Hora Novissima,* in Boston's Trinity Church in 1989, I came away convinced that Kearns's assessment was correct. Unlike those of *A Northern Ballad,* the concerto's ideas belong more to Parker and less to other composers. The work is tuneful and about twenty-four minutes long. It honestly and unequivocally communicates the composer's inner feelings. The organ is not a contender with the orchestra, nor usually heroic, except possibly in the finale. The orchestra itself consists of strings, brass, harp, and drums.[13]

One other orchestral work requires mentioning, the symphonic poem *Vathek,* of 1903. Brooks Shephard Jr., a Yale music librarian, wrote to the conductor Karl Krueger: "The inspiration [for *Vathek*] was William Beckford's picaresque romance by the same title, and Parker himself oddly suppressed the title in his list of works submitted to Grove's Dictionary. We have been unable to find that it was ever performed, even by the New Haven Symphony."[14] Beckford, an Englishman, lived from 1760 to 1844. The work calls for a large orchestra. It fails to achieve the quality of the concerto or *A Northern Ballad.*

The branch of composition to which Parker devoted most of his energy was choral music, ranging from the modest to the complex. Kearns observes that of the more than twenty-five anthems written by

Parker, "Bow Down Thine Ear," "The Lord Is My Light," "Give Unto the Lord," and "I Will Set His Dominion in the Sea" were admired in his time and continue in the church repertoire.[15] Before writing *Hora Novissima,* Parker produced six secular cantatas for various soloists, chorus, and orchestra: *Ballad of a Knight and His Daughter* (1884), *King Trojan* (1885), *Idylle* (1886), *The Norsemen's Raid* (1888); *The Kobolds* (1890), and *The Dream King and His Love* (1891). He was aware of the sturdy choral-society movement in the United States and knew that his cantatas would be welcomed and receive repeated performances. Central Europeans usually provided Parker's texts, with one exception, *The Kobolds,* which Boston's own Arlo Bates wrote. All of the subjects went well with nineteenth-century American tastes—elves, fairies, knights, and beautiful maidens, and portrayals of duels, battles, wild nocturnal rides, and love consummated and unconsummated. Immaculate workmanship sets apart the choral writing. Homophony takes over most measures. Harmony is rich. Parker strikes a balance between the lyrical and the dramatic.

The oratorio *Hora Novissima* is indisputably Parker's best work of art and an important addition to musical literature. It was written for the Church Choral Society of New York and had a first performance on 3 May 1893. Fame came quickly. It even gained performances in England, the most significant of which was at the Three Choirs Festival of Worcester. The oratorio also earned him an honorary Musical Doctorate from Cambridge University. Trying to characterize its meaning for his time, Chadwick says: "The solid musical worth of 'Hora Novissima,' its skillful and impressive choral writing, the poetic beauty of the solos, and the varied and colorful instrumentation, endear it to musicians, while its lofty spiritual atmosphere, its fervent religious expression, although tinged with a romantic mysticism, make a strong appeal to the general musical public."[16] Parker's mother translated the original Latin poem by a twelfth-century monk of Cluny into English. The text contrasts the evils of earthly existence and visions of the longed for "Golden Jerusalem" that one arrived at only after death. *Hora*'s eleven sections contain selections for soprano, alto, tenor, and bass soloists, for solo quartet, and for chorus. A master who put his strongest feelings into the music fashioned all the parts with skill and care. Expression is candid and honest. Recurring melodic and rhythmic motives are noticeable unifying devices. Throughout, a warm lyricism makes itself known.

The opening, an instrumental introduction and the choral "Hora Novissima," alerts listeners to earth's last hour and the judgment to come. A motto sounds that will receive wide-ranging employment in its initial shape, and in inversion, retrograde, and retrograde inversion. The second movement, "Hic breve vivitur," for solo quartet, contrasts the brevity of earthly life with future eternity. The third is the well-liked bass aria "Spe modo vivitur." A prelude and double fugue for chorus follows, "Pars mea, Rex meus." The fifth number, "O bona patria," for soprano solo, beautifully conjures up a vision of heavenly bliss. The music portrays the intense yearning for the promised land. Part 1 concludes on the fine "Tu sine littore" for solo quartet and chorus.

Part 2 starts with the tenor solo "Urbs Syon aurea," followed by the double chorus on "Stant Syon atria," and the alto aria "Gens duce splendida." Number 10, an unaccompanied chorus singing "Urbs Syon unica," is beholden to the New England psalmodic tradition. Quartet and chorus sing a closing song of praise to the heavenly city, "Urbs Syon inclyta." It is not entirely joyous, especially when the music expresses world-weariness and personal contrition and the singers cry out "Burdened with guilti-ness, / Weary and comfortless, / Help, I implore Thee," then plead with God to make "His light to shine / In this dark soul of mine."

Philip Hale was completely taken with *Hora Novissima*. "Pars mea" he labeled "a masterpiece, true music of the church." "Urbs Syon unica," he said, is so characteristic of the composer that "no one in the country or in England . . . could by nature and by student's sweat have written those eleven pages." Hale continues: "I have spoken of Mr. Parker's quasi-operatic tendency. Now he is a modern. He has shown in this very work his appreciation and his mastery of antique religious musical art. But as a modern he is compelled to feel the force of the dramatic in religious music."[17]

Other vocal works with orchestra followed. They share the same communicative inclination as does *Hora*. They merit reviving, but unlike *Hora*, none brings completely to fruition the composer's intentions: *Cáhal Mór of the Wine Red Hand* (1893), a rhapsody for baritone; *The Legend of St. Christopher* (1897), an eloquent and dramatic oratorio; *A Wanderer's Psalm* (1900), a cantata for chorus; *A Star Song* (1901), a rhapsody for chorus; *King Gorm the Grim* (1907), a ballad for chorus; and *Morven and the Grail* (1915), a final oratorio. Just before the end of his life, Parker completed two more compositions: *The Dream of Mary*, a morality for adult and children's chorus and congregation; and the cantata A.D. *1919*.

Earlier, I had described Parker's mature style as a bit dramatic. Regrettably, it never developed into a musical speech able to take hold of an audience's attention when joined to stage action. The grand opera *Mona*, completed in 1910, evidenced this deficiency, despite its winning Parker a temporary fame.[18] Parker had set out to write an opera that he hoped would win the ten-thousand-dollar prize that the Metropolitan Opera was offering for the best opera with libretto and music by an American. Brian Hooker provided him with a libretto, and Parker began setting it in July 1909. *Mona* was completed the next year and did win the prize. The Metropolitan first performed the opera on 14 March 1912. Nine days later, at a dinner given by the Metropolitan's directors, the composer said: "The result of our labors is not Italian opera or French opera or German opera. I believe it is American opera, for it certainly is nothing else, and whether one likes it or not is a matter of taste concerning which others may dispute."[19]

The plot spotlights the self-destructive fanaticism of Mona, a British princess who led a revolt against Roman rule around 100 A.D. She complicates matters by also loving Gwynn, the disguised son of the Roman governor. Patriotic fervor and passion for her lover compete for dominance within her. When, in the third and final act, Gwynn reveals his identity, Mona assassinates him. The Romans quickly get hold of her, condemn her to die, and lead her away to her death. Hooker's verse libretto is bookish, wooden, and occasionally incomprehensible. Scarcely any stage action takes place. Parker's score could do with more arresting music. Although sincerity invests its measures, so also does an overload of gloom. Leading motives are meant to identify characters and shed light on convictions and feelings. Audience-pleasing tunes and sentiments to warm the heart are hard to find. Chadwick, a champion of Parker's music, had to conclude: "He had little sympathy for the conventions and the artificialities of the stage, and perhaps he was lacking in what the Germans call theatre *blut*. This, combined with inexperience in composing for the stage and plots which made little appeal to the average theatre-goer, militated against the popular success of these works [*Mona* and a later opera, *Fairyland*], but they proved his complete mastery of modern harmony and modern orchestration."[20]

Musicians can admire the quality of the musical details, the music's readiness to adjust to the actions on the stage, and the moments of inspiration, no matter how fitful. More an oratorio than an opera, *Mona* strikes us as a creative work of moment and deserving respect. Its weakness is an inability to come alive on the stage.

In 1914 Parker completed a second opera, *Fairyland,* the libretto again by Brian Hooker, which won a prize of ten thousand dollars from the

National Federation of Music Clubs. Los Angeles gave it six performances. The libretto was short of energy; the characters were short of believability. The opera failed. As Parker's daughter confessed, it was "not generally considered so unified, vigorous or important a work as 'Mona.'"[21]

Around the time that he was composing *Mona,* Parker found himself becoming less admired. He was being criticized for adopting standards so high that they made few allowances for entertainment and popular appeal. *Hora Novissima* continued to be his most approved composition for voices and orchestra. This oratorio, *A Northern Ballad,* the Organ Concerto, and several songs are among the top-quality works that the New England group of composers bequeathed to posterity.

ARTHUR FOOTE

Arthur Foote was the first noted American art composer to receive his musical education entirely in the United States. He was born in Salem, Massachusetts, where his father was editor of the *Salem Gazette.* He began piano lessons with a local teacher at the age of fourteen. Shortly, he started to study theory with Stephen Emery and keyboard playing with B. J. Lang. In 1870 he enrolled at Harvard and had John Knowles Paine as his teacher in composition. He eventually earned the degree of Master of Arts in music from Harvard University, the first such degree granted by an American university. An admiration for Wagner's operas began with a visit to Bayreuth in 1876, although Wagner never had much influence on Foote's own style. He derived more creative sustenance from Beethoven, whose symphonies frequently figured in local performance. He states that in the 1880s "it seemed natural to have all . . . [the Beethoven] symphonies in one season of the symphony concerts."[22] From the evidence of his music, Foote also cherished Brahms's compositions. Although later he became well acquainted with the innovations of Debussy, Stravinsky, and Schoenberg, he would find the vague tonality, steady dissonance, and untamed rhythms in much of the twentieth century's innovative music to be alien to his unassuming nature.

Foote earned a living in Boston as a keyboard teacher, church organist, choir director, and pianist appearing mainly in chamber music concerts. He was a cofounder of the American Guild of Organists and its president for four years.

During his entire life he remained self-effacing about his keyboard and creative abilities. Reading his autobiography and his *Musical Quarterly* article, "A Bostonian Remembers," one must believe that the self-effacement grew out of inborn modesty and a reverent regard for music.[23] He worried that he might not be worthy of following in the footsteps of the masters he admired. At the time of his death, Redfern Mason's obituary in the *Boston Transcript,* 17 April 1937, read: "Arthur Foote had a trait which, in the eyes of the world, is a fault. He never blew his own trumpet; he was utterly unskilled in the art of crying up his own wares. Chadwick would try to stir him up. 'When I want a work produced I go to Chicago and get Stock to do it,' he would say. But Foote would shake his head. . . . The art of self-advertisement was something he was ashamed to learn."[24]

One must respect Foote the composer. His music speaks directly without elaborate artifice. It can sound movingly beautiful or guarded yet refined, but never mawkish or extravagant. His talent lay in melody, not in dramatic statements. He was aware of his limits and never tried to move beyond them. Foote's uniqueness is found in the turn of a phrase, in a subtle harmonic change. The practice of restraint, a New England tradition, governed his art. Still, contemporary audiences came to admire his music for its own sake and not for its Americanisms or modernity.

Foote composed about one hundred songs, several achieving celebrity in America and abroad—among them the "Irish Folk-Song" and "I'm Wearing Awa' to the Land o' the Leal."[25] An enticing tune and a fitting accompaniment are common to most of them. The strophic "It Was a Lover and His Lass" (1885), to Shakespeare's poem, is a beguiling piece that shows Foote's knack for inventing memorable vocal lines, sensitive piano accompaniments, and attractive harmonies bordering on the modal. "I'm Wearing Awa' to the Land o' the Leal," poem by Lady Nairn (1887), is straightforward. The individual singing is worn down by life and looking forward to death. The music is in two strophes, with a softly rocking tune consisting of an eight-measure strain. In the cheerless "A Roumanian Song," poem by "The Bard of the Dimbovitza" (1899), the music becomes unusually striking on the word "Ah!" vocalized with long tones as the piano sounds the melody.

Foote composed around fifty part-songs and thirty-five anthems. The anthems "God Is Our Refuge," "And There Were Shepherds," and "Awake, Thou That Sleepest" were extolled in Foote's time. Three compositions for chorus and orchestra make use of secular texts by Longfellow: *The Farewell of Hiawatha* (1885), *The Wreck of the Hesperus* (1888), and *The Skeleton in Armor* (1891). All three are respectable pieces of music, expressive in some sections and, regrettable to say, dull in others. The listener hankers after soloists to alleviate the choral singing. The music often fails to high-light the points of climax.

On the whole, the solo keyboard compositions for piano or organ are skillfully made and flow easily. Most adhere to the values of romanticism and do no adventuring beyond. They only occasionally take advantage of the full resources of the keyboard; Foote introduces nothing dramatic, pic-turesque, or exploitive of piano coloring. On the other hand, the music public took pleasure in the composer's expertise, his fascinating treatment of the material, and, not least, the articulate and moving melodic lines. His best-known piano composition, *Five Poems after Omar Khayyám,* op. 41 (1898), did not really come into its own until he orchestrated four of the five pieces and released them as *Four Character Pieces after the Rubáiyát of Omar Khayyám,* op. 48 (1900), with the third of the five piano pieces omit-ted. His best organ works are the Suite in D Minor, op. 54, and Seven Pieces, op. 71. Opus 54 corresponds to a contemporary interpretation of a Baroque suite, closing with a sparkling toccata. Opus 71 begins with a Cantilena in G that comes over as a long uninterrupted song without words, not too distant from the "aria" movement found in many Baroque suites. The most evocative piece is no. 7, a Canzonetta. Its high treble mel-ody is a movingly expressive idea.

Foote was a masterful composer of chamber music. Franz Kneisel and his quartet, drawn from members of the Boston Symphony, did a great deal to encourage him. Foote states that the Kneisel Quartet performed much of his chamber music in Boston and that he "learned much from Kneisel through his suggestions as to practical points in composition."[26] Despite his contrapuntal skills, he continued to favor writing outright tunes without the complications of counterpoint. Strong feeling stays beneath the surface and often breaks through.

The Three Pieces, op. 1, for cello and piano, and the Three Character Pieces for violin and piano, op. 9, date from the early 1880s. Plain ternary constructions and pretty tunes categorize them. The First Piano Trio in C Minor, op. 5, was premiered in 1882. Disarmingly attractive melody prevails. The First String Quartet in G Minor, op. 4, was performed in 1883 and again in 1887. Critics said that the most appealing movement was the third, the Andante in B flat. They wrote that a gift for melodic writing was evident throughout the quartet. Contrapuntal textures are few. The entire piece shows more unity than did the Trio in C Minor.[27]

Foote introduced greater vigor, contrast, harmonic sophistication, contrapuntal activity, and emotional scope into the chamber compositions written in the late 1880s and the 1890s: the Violin Sonata in G Minor, op. 20 (1889), the Piano Quartet in C Major, op. 23 (1890), and the Second String Quartet in E major, op. 32 (1893). These three are outstanding compositions and worthy of entering the standard repertoire.

Possibly his finest chamber work is the Piano Quintet in A Minor, op. 38 (1897).[28] In the first movement, *allegro guisto: appassionato,* all five players share important thematic material. Shifts in mood occur frequently— for example, the dramatically passionate opening theme changes to wistful dreaminess in the brief two-measure phrases of the transition passage. Next comes a gypsy-like *più allegro* that links up with the subordinate theme. This new melody sounds majestically and with Brahmsian breadth. The fast-moving development of the first theme builds to a satisfying climax by means of a fugato. In the recapitulation, the second theme reappears in A major, a whole step higher than its key in the exposition, with the music thus acquiring a needed brightness.

The second movement, an intermezzo with a trio moving along at moderate tempo, is in a pensive mood. Modal references give subtle colorings to the first section. The trio goes faster but sings melodiously. The next movement, a vivacious scherzo, comes alive with a rhythm like that in the second movement of Beethoven's first Razumovsky string quartet, though Foote's manages it quite differently. The finale in A major is in rondo form. A lively, dancelike first theme has an intimation of the gypsy about it. The first episode features a running sixteenth-note figure in the piano; the second episode has the brooding lyricism usually associated with Brahms.

Three marvelous compositions worthy of high praise followed: the Second Piano Trio in B Flat, op. 65 (1908), the Third String Quartet in D Major, op. 70 (1911), and the Cello Sonata, op. 78 (ca. 1913). Contemporary audiences found them clear and strong in structure, astute in detail, and noble in expression. In 1918 he completed his Nocturne and Scherzo for flute and string quartet. When Pierre Monteux later suggested arranging the Nocturne for flute and string orchestra, it became one of Foote's most loved compositions, *A Night Piece.* There is much that is French in its style.

Foote's first important venture into orchestral music came with the writing of the Overture *In the Mountains,* op. 14, in 1886.[29] When the Boston Symphony gave it a first performance, in 1887, audience and critics hailed it more for its ear-catching sound; less for its originality. No connection between title and music was apparent.[30]

The Boston Symphony also premiered a Suite for Strings, op. 12, in 1886 and a Suite for Strings, op. 21, in 1889, both works glancing back to the Baroque era of Bach and Handel. The first suite is in three movements: Allegro Commodo, Andante, and Gavotte. The second suite contains a Prelude, Minuetto, Air, and Gavotte. Foote resorts to Baroque practices not as an antiquarian but as a poet wishing to evoke certain distinctive sound characteristics. The results are never academic and always unlike the music of Bach and Handel. Romanticism with its warm lyricism and an expanded harmonic palette invests the measures. The Serenade for Strings in E Major, op. 25, is an 1891 reworking of movements from both of the previous suites.

The next work, the symphonic prologue *Francesca da Rimini,* op. 24, dates from 1890. It is quite different from the Tchaikovsky work of the same title. In a free sonata form, the composition is solidly written, eminently likable, and captures qualities in the Dante original not encompassed by Tchaikovsky's treatment. For much of its length, the piece shows the composer reflecting on the lovers' inner feelings rather than trying to capture pictorial gestures of conflict and passion. Nevertheless, intensity of feeling does arise. Writing in the *Boston Musical Herald,* March 1891, George H. Wilson praised *Francesca da Rimini*'s convincing musical frame and vital ideas: "It is a concise and telling composition, a little freer in form than an overture, but at no point radical in treatment. It tells us how near we are in this country to forming a school, and recalls with pleasurable excitement the fact that right here among us is the nucleus of this school!"[31]

A Cello Concerto, which Foote began in 1887 and finished in 1893, is one of his least-known major works. The one or two contemporary musicians familiar with it claim it to be a fine composition worthy of resurrecting. A cassette tape that I heard of a performance by Douglas Moore confirms that contention.[32]

The composer completed the Suite for Orchestra in D Minor, op. 36, in 1895. Its premiere by the Boston Symphony came the next year. Some years later, Foote commented: "It was only fairly successful, but with two really good movements. . . . Its fortune has been the usual one of American compositions of its sort. It had a few performances by orchestras here (and one in England by Henry J. Wood) and afterwards little chance. The movement in variation form really satisfied me."[33]

The first movement, *Allegro energico, con brio,* begins vividly with an intrepid, driving theme. This theme in turn is followed by two quiet subsidiary ideas, with woodwinds and horns prominent. Development centers on the principal theme, and the recapitulation reproduces both secondary ideas before returning to the principal theme. The deeply searching second movement is headed *Expressivo, non troppo adagio*. Its first section lingers over a long legato melody, marked *dolce*, in the first violins. An episode presented by the brass section offers a colorful and effective contrast. The second theme is a fresh, gracefully syncopated melody. Before long the melody of the first section returns in the cellos and receives a lovely new accompaniment. Especially dramatic is the return of the episode material now heard in the full orchestra and supported by abrupt syncopated rhythms. The third movement, *Andante espressivo, con moto*, states a calm, mildly syncopated theme and follows it with a chain of imaginative variations. The buoyant finale is labeled *presto assai*. Continual syncopations suggestive of dance give a festive character to the first theme, which later breaks away into a fugato. The second theme continues with syncopations. It even sounds as if Chadwick might have written it when it is eventually heard against a descending French horn phrase, also syncopated. The recapitulation commences with a fugato on the first theme, followed by a standard return of the second theme and a fine coda.

The *Four Character Pieces after the Rubáiyát of Omar Khayyám*, op. 48, came out in 1900 and proved instantly popular. A friend, the Scottish pianist Helen Hopekirk, had urged him to recast the piano original. The composition demonstrates an individual character that easily distinguishes it from the rest of Foote's output. Shifting harmonic nuances and diverse orchestral colors often suggest musical Impressionism. The first piece, *andante comodo*, is prefaced by the following verse:

> Iram indeed is gone with all his Rose,
> And Jamshyd's Sev'n-ring'd Cup where no one knows;
> But still a Ruby kindles in the Vine,
> And many a Garden by the Water blows.

A long, languorous clarinet solo conjures up a nocturnal atmosphere, and delicate modal references obliquely (never directly) intimate a setting in a Persian garden.

The second piece, *allegro deciso*, has the following verse:

> They say the Lion and the Lizard keep
> The Courts where Jamshyd gloried and drank deep:

> And Bahram, that great Hunter—the Wild Ass
> Stamps o'er his Head, but cannot break his sleep.

Later, when the tempo changes to *più moderato,* the verse reads:

> Yet, ah, that Spring should vanish with the Rose!
> That Youth's sweet-scented manuscript should close!
> The Nightingale that in the branches sang,
> Ah, whence, and whether flown again, who knows!

The first division displays an assertive, driving theme in the full orchestra, with the brasses to the fore. Suddenly the mood changes to one quieter and more pensive; clarinet and flute solos are featured. The movement concludes with a return to the opening material boldly and vigorously stated.

The third piece, *comodo,* interprets the following:

> A Book of Verses underneath the Bough,
> A Jug of Wine, a Loaf of Bread—and Thou
> Beside me singing in the Wilderness—
> Oh, Wilderness were Paradise enow!

The movement has the feeling of a pastorale. A mellifluous theme steadily unfolds in the strings, mounts to an eloquent climax, and then returns to tranquillity.

The last piece begins *andantino ben marcato,* interpreting the following verse:

> Yon rising Moon that looks for us again—
> How oft hereafter will she wax and wane;
> How oft hereafter rising look for us
> Through this same Garden—and for one in vain!

The tempo then shifts to *molto allegro:*

> Waste not your Hour, nor in the vain pursuit
> Of This and That endeavor and dispute;
> Better be jocund with the fruitful Grape
> Than sadden after none, or bitter, Fruit.

For this final movement, Foote has a solemn tune start on a low pitch. Gradually it grows richer in texture as instruments are added. Next, the tempo picks up. Strings playing *tremoloso* produce a scurrying effect. A new melody enters, which refers back to the theme of the first piece and goes from loud to very soft before ushering back the solemn tune of the movement's beginning. Melancholy music then ends the composition.

The immensely successful Suite for Strings in E Major, op. 63, was completed in 1908. Throughout his tenure with the Boston Symphony, Serge Koussevitzky would sponsor and Boston audiences would enjoy it. The work consists of three movements: a Praeludium, Pizzicato and Adagietto, and Fugue.[34] The composition as a whole gives an impression of effortless musical flow, restrained grace, and stately beauty. A few ideas are thriftily elaborated. When counterpoint occurs, it is more or less in compliance with and generated by the harmonic progressions. The style of Bach and Handel is the point of departure, but a kinship with the music of Brahms and Tchaikovsky cannot be denied. Nevertheless, the expression is totally Foote's own.

One last composition requires mention, *A Night Piece* for flute and strings with optional bass, from 1922, a new rendering of the first movement of the Nocturne and Scherzo for flute and string quartet.[35] Pierre Monteux and the Boston Symphony Orchestra gave it a first performance on 13 April 1923. As with the previous suite, widespread appreciation came quickly. Few other compositions by American composers can equal it for absolute musical attractiveness. Its virtues are transparent harmonies, gently patterned harmonic rhythms, sensitively placed dynamic inflections, and above all an ethereal melody for the flute. The heading *andantino languido* gives an indication of its character.

A closer acquaintance with "A Night Piece" and the Suite for Strings in E offers a profound and touching perception of Foote's nature. As in so many of his compositions, the music is managed with a fragile self-effacement. The writing is extraordinary for its lack of clichés. Although content with traditional practices and indisposed to experiment, Foote creates sounds at once vivid, sincere, and peculiarly original.

Waldo Selden Pratt summed him up in the *American Supplement* to *Grove's Dictionary* as follows: "Few American composers [up to 1920] have won such high esteem. The uniformly high quality of his work in diverse forms has been coupled with a surprising uniformity of success. His orchestral works are played by leading orchestras, his chamber-music has been a staple in American programs, his organ-music is everywhere popular, and his songs are prized by singers, accompanists, and audiences. . . . On Thanksgiving Day in 1914, organists throughout the country, by concerted arrangement, played his Festival March in F as an expression of gratitude for his recovery from a serious illness—a tribute seldom paid to any musician."[36]

EDWARD MACDOWELL

Edward MacDowell was born in New York City. His mother and his wife were New Englanders, however, and he lived in Boston during his most productive years, 1888–96. After he left to teach at Columbia University, Boston's sponsorship of his music continued to exceed that of any other city. MacDowell would also purchase a home in Peterborough, New Hampshire, where he would spend some of his happiest days. Beginning with his earliest compositions, he revealed himself as a complete Romanticist, with negligible Classical leanings. He gave free rein to his creative imagination. The capturing of a mood or an emotion was his primary consideration. At the same time, he subscribed to the civilized musical discourse and good taste of his generation.

As a boy, he studied piano with the excellent Venezuelan virtuoso Teresa Carreño. Later, he went abroad, and his instructor in composition was the composer Joseph Joachim Raff, a friend and admirer of Franz Liszt. MacDowell came to admire the music of Raff, Liszt, and Wagner. Grieg and Tchaikovsky also interested him. The more classically oriented Brahms usually left him indifferent, and French music held no attraction for him.[37] Every now and again (as in the first movement of the First Piano Concerto), a musical theme sounds similar to Grieg's. Yet, as John Tasker Howard correctly points out, MacDowell's music is significantly different from that of Grieg. More frequently than Grieg, he sought to make big, heroic statements. Unlike Grieg, he did not desire to be taken as a nationalist composer.[38] He read omnivorously and relished widely differing literatures, including poetry, mythology, medieval tales, and the writings of Mark Twain and Joel Chandler Harris. He enjoyed paintings and sculptures and loved the myriad aspects of nature.

He returned to the United States from Germany after failing to find a permanent position abroad and went to live in Boston in September 1888. Students flocked to him to study piano or composition, among them Henry Gilbert and Ethelbert Nevin. MacDowell's piano performances featuring his own composition (fantasy pieces, idylls, poems, nocturnes, mood pictures, virtuosic studies, and sonatas) soon became important musical events for Bostonians. The Boston Symphony Orchestra performed his orchestral works regularly: concertos with the composer at the keyboard, orchestral suites, and symphonic poems. Leaving Boston in 1896 for New York City and a teaching post at Columbia University was a tragic mistake for him. Later visits to Boston and the purchase of a much-loved summer home in Peterborough, New Hampshire, could not relieve the mental strain brought on by overwork and battles with administration over funding the music department and recognizing the academic worthiness of musical studies. He resigned in 1904, succumbed to acute nervous prostration, and died in 1908.

John Erskine, a MacDowell student at Columbia, sheds important light on MacDowell's attitude about introducing identifiably American sounds into a music composition:

> In the composition class one day he spoke his mind about the material we used. Our work, when of good enough quality, he said might pass for that of Europeans. Neither our themes nor our rhythms suggested that we lived in New York. He hastened to add that he set no value on conscious or deliberate nationalism, but an artist must accept himself for better or for worse. What we whistled, sang or played in moments of relaxation more often than not was ragtime. Well, if syncopated rhythms were natural to us, why not try to make them something important? "I would do it myself," he went on, "if I had not lived so long in Europe. Ragtime is not instinctive with me as it is with you—though I did make an attempt at it in the scherzo of my Second Concerto."[39]

Jo Shipley Watson amplifies the Erskine statement in an article, "MacDowell as a Teacher," in the *Boston Transcript,* 14 September 1907: "'Harmony,' Professor MacDowell used to say, 'gives atmosphere for the melody; it is the tone background for melody; it enforces the melodic trend; but the main thing is the melodic trend. . . . Nationalism must be based upon the spirit of the people, not upon the clothes they wear. . . . Out of our idealism, our music will grow.'"[40]

MacDowell's music is usually serious, atmospheric, and shaped by remembered experiences. He considered himself a poet-singer and invariably wrote around poetic ideas. He depicted aspects of the natural world, myth and fairyland, and chivalry and heroism. Except for an evocative title, MacDowell rarely supplied a detailed program for a composition. His wife, Marian, once explained that her husband "held that a poetic name given a piece helped the performer in his interpretation, without limiting his imagination. Furthermore his writing was never descriptive in a realistic sense; it was the expression of a mood which might be awakened by a scene, a poem, an idea, or an experience." She also stated, "His music can seldom if ever be considered pictorial or imitative. It presents the spirit of a picture rather than the picture itself."[41]

Most melodies sound unlabored, pliant, and directly appealing. Harmony shows individuality. Dissonances increase or decrease to suit his coloristic or expressive purposes. Chromaticism, frequent modulation, and forceful contrasts abound. The entire paraphernalia of rhythmic devices exploited by the late Romantics and some rhythms unique to America were at his command. His piano miniatures display an assortment of charms. His piano sonatas exhibit both dramatic power and great tenderness. MacDowell stated that the structures of his compositions were intended to give "poignant expression" to his poetic thought. He arranged sounds "so that they constituted the most telling presentation of a musical idea." The miniatures were normally cast in a simple ternary design. The sonatas employed traditionally structures, such as sonata allegro, rondo, and sonata-rondo, but adapted for his purposes. Symphonic poems received unique designs. Whatever the form, it was not a matter of periods, sections, and main and subsidiary themes. It had to be the "most telling presentation of a musical idea." Ultimately, form was "nothing more than a synonym for coherence."[42]

Like Foote, he was uninterested in experiment for its own sake. He worked within clearly marked confines with a continual return of certain interrelationships of sound and with a circumscribed range of expression. He wanted all artistic compositions to involve the general music public, not just a small group. He felt the composer was answerable to his society and at the same time had a claim on the attention of his society.

Songs

MacDowell composed forty-six songs for voice and piano. In several of them the melody shows a kinship to American folk song of Anglo-Celtic origin in its simplicity and stylizing. Above all else, he wanted a graceful, emotionally convincing, and rhythmically attractive tune that would approximate the main expression of a poem. Melodic logic came before accurate declamation. Music engendered its own inflections, he said, and a composer erred if his music was completely subservient to the verse. He opted for flexibility and a chordal approach in the accompaniment. Few American composers had MacDowell's facility for detecting the principal mood of a poem and replicating it in music. Henry Finck says that MacDowell's own characteristic song style came with his opus 26, *From an Old Garden,* a set of six songs composed in 1886–87. He claims that "Menie" (the verse by Robert Burns), from Two Songs, op. 34 (1887), projects an "exquisite melancholy" and should be numbered among his best songs.[43]

In 1890, now living in Boston, MacDowell composed Six Love Songs, op. 40, to poems by W. H. Gardner. The American public found no. 3 of this set, "Thy Beaming Eyes," the most pleasing of all the songs that he wrote during his lifetime. As in a majority of the poems that the composer set, the subject is love. An agreeable and easily remembered tune and an undemanding accompaniment of slowly changing chords give reasons for much of its popularity.

Eight Songs, op. 47, finished in 1893, were set to three poems by MacDowell, three by William Dean Howells, and two by Goethe. All are likable illustrations of his mature style. No. 1, "The Robin Sings in the Apple-tree," words by the composer, has music with a fragile, yearning quality to delineate love that has died. No. 2, "Midsummer Lullaby," is given a quiet grace. No. 3, the slow-moving, pathetic "Folksong" to Howells's verse, is not really folklike, its use of the Scotch snap notwithstanding. Possibly the finest song that MacDowell wrote is no. 7, to a Howells poem, "The Sea." The subject concerns a lonely woman standing on the seashore and awaiting the return of her lover, not knowing he has drowned. The composer provides neither prelude nor postlude, preferring to have the singer tell the story from the start, while the pianist underlies the vocal line with tones that heighten the perception of calamity.

MacDowell later wrote at least three other sets of songs worthy of attention: Four Songs, op. 56 (1898), Three Songs, op. 58 (1899), and Three Songs, op. 60 (1901). The fine "Constancy (New England A.D. 1899)," op. 58, no. 1, verse by MacDowell, dwells on a deserted house and garden to bring out the theme of neglect, decay, and mortality. It ends on lines prophetic of the future of the composer's own music: "For house and ye shall pass away, / Yea! even as my song."

Music for Orchestra

The Piano Concerto No. 1 in A Minor, of 1882, was MacDowell's first large work. Written and premiered in Europe, this bold and appealing composition was praised by Franz Liszt, who urged the young musician to devote himself to musical composition. The first movement begins with a solemn solo piano introduction of thirteen measures that anticipates the main theme. Then the *allegro* proper presents the theme piecemeal in the woodwinds, next as a melody in the strings while the piano adds ornate embellishments, and finally as a complete statement in the full orchestra. The impression is one of conflict and confrontation between piano and orchestra. The subordinate theme supplies a welcome lyrical relief to the strife. The second movement presents a serene, discreetly orchestrated melody, and the finale is fittingly exuberant.

His only other piano concerto, No. 2 in D Minor, was also composed in Germany, between 1884 and 1886, and had its American premiere in New York City on 5 March 1889, with Theodore Thomas conducting and the composer at the keyboard. Most critics who heard it then and over the next two decades described it as skillfully written, virtuosic, and with outstanding musical ideas. A few found it too modern for their tastes, too prodigal in its proliferation of ideas, or too diffuse in structure.[44] One of the most enthusiastic reviews came from H. E. Krehbiel, in the *New York Tribune,* March 1889, who wrote that the concerto was a "splendid composition, so full of poetry, so full of vigor, as to tempt the assertion that it must be placed at the head of all works of its kind produced by either a native or adopted son of America. But . . . it can stand by itself and challenge the heartiest admiration for its contents, its workmanship, and its originality of thought."[45]

The first movement dwells on a disarmingly elegiac melody in muted strings, which leads to an impassioned declamatory statement in the piano, then back to the elegy, now played by the flute. The middle movement is a *scherzo presto giocoso.* The finale recycles ideas from the first movement, heard in a variety of transformations. On the whole, the music sounds brilliantly, yet with elements of regret and heartache.

The two piano concertos elicited the best in the young composer. His several symphonic poems do not portray him at his best. The first, *Hamlet and Ophelia,* dates from 1884–85. The premiere took place in Boston on 28 January 1893. No program is supplied. It exists as two movements: the first, "Hamlet," in D minor, the second, "Ophelia," in F major. Both share the same material. Although romantically warm and richly scored, the dramatic moments sound bombastic and the tragic, bathetic. The second symphonic poem, *Lancelot and Elaine,* inspired by the poem of Alfred, Lord Tennyson, dates from 1886. The Boston Symphony Orchestra gave its American premiere on 10 January 1890. Again, the composer failed to supply a program. Presumably the chivalric nature of Lancelot and the tender loving one of Elaine were considered. Regrettably, the composition is only a small improvement over the first tone poem. The work is episodic and ambiguous in musical character and lacks a compelling vision.

A poem by John Keats is behind the third symphonic poem, *Lamia* (1887). A preface to the score, published by Schmidt in 1908, gives a program. The serpent-enchantress Lamia loves Lycius, and in the form of a beautiful young woman gets Lycius to marry her in her enchanted palace. The magician Apollonius comes on the scene and exposes the sorcery. Lamia reverts to serpenthood, the palace vanishes, and Lycius dies. The piece starts off well, with a sad theme in cellos and then violins that represents the yearning Lamia, followed by chromatic slithering about in the lower strings and bassoons. What follows is unconvincing. The structure is wobbly. MacDowell's last attempt at symphonic poetry was *The Saracens and the Beautiful Alda,* two fragments after the Song of Roland, first performed in 1891. Two excerpts from the epic tale *Song of Roland* head the score, published by Breitkopf & Härtel in 1891. The music seems more solid than that of any of the previous tone poems and its working-out more persuasive, but the two movements are over almost before they are begun.

Perhaps by 1891 MacDowell wanted relief from the seriousness, angst, and opposition of *eros* and *agape,* physical and idealized love. He ceased writing symphonic poems and composed a less weighty but completely delightful First Suite for Orchestra, op. 42. An additional movement, "In October," was added two years later.[46] The creation of mood and evoking of atmosphere replace programmatic storytelling. The composition as it now stands has five movements: "In a Haunted Forest," "Summer Idyll," "In October," "The Shepherdess Song," and "Forest Spirits." The Boston Symphony Orchestra played the suite without the added movement on 24 September 1891 and the completed suite on 25 October 1895. The work has a good deal of charm. The A-minor first movement opens slowly and mysteriously. After thirty-four measures, the music begins a tumultuous allegro that sketches the night-obscured activities of forest sprites. The "Summer Idyll" is a captivatingly graceful dance in 6/8 time. The American dance hall is close by. "In October" begins with a French horn motive that instantly conjures up an autumnal forest scene. This motive dominates the movement. The next movement, a brief "Shepherdess Song," is based on a version of the melody heard in the oboe during the previous movement. The most American of all the movements is "Forest Spirits," which could easily be relabeled "High American Spirits." A blithely syncopated tune starts it off. In the middle, MacDowell introduces a second tune heard in the violins and violas that would be right at home in an Aaron Copland composition of the late 1930s. The coda ends with variants on the opening theme of the first movement.

Between 1891 and 1895 MacDowell worked on one of his most important compositions, the Second (*Indian*) Suite for Large Orchestra, op. 48. H. E. Krehbiel maintains that the composer had fully sketched the piece before Dvořák wrote his *New World* Symphony. On the other hand, T. P. Currier claims that he heard MacDowell mention a connection with the Dvořák work, although he is uncertain what that connection was.[47] The Boston Symphony Orchestra introduced it during a performance in New York City on 23 January 1896 and played it in Boston a week later. At its conclusion, the Boston audience recalled the composer a dozen times, according to his wife, Marian. She adds: "It is a symbol of his love for Boston that of all the many trophies he received throughout his life, the great laurel wreath that was given him on this occasion was the only one he cared to preserve."[48] Philip Hale, in the *Boston Journal,* stated that composers are not Indians and cannot build a national school on Indian or, for that matter, African American music. Nor does MacDowell attempt to do so. Hale praised MacDowell's sincerity, original use of instruments, and avoidance of conventional procedures. The Second Suite had rare beauty for him, Hale said, and deserved the designation of masterpiece.[49]

Like the First Suite, it has five movements: "Legend," "Love Song," "In War-time," "Dirge," and "Village Festival." A prefatory remark by the composer explains that the thematic material was suggested by melodies of the North American Indians, which occasionally show similarities to northern European themes.[50] He handles these melodies freely and adds several of his own. All of them bear a likeness to each other, thus helping to unify the several movements. MacDowell had in mind the emotions arising out of a contemplation of Indian life. The tunes had probably been taken from Theodore Baker's 1882 *Über die Musik der nordamerikanischen Wilden.* Charles Wakefield Cadman, a composer deeply interested in Indian music, found the Second Suite not to be "a mere ethnological report set to music." He heard a happy balance of musical values, "of atmosphere obtained, of triumph, of dignity, even of melancholy, wedded to finely conceived contrasts and dynamics."[51]

The "Legend" movement uses Iroquois and Chippewa melodies. No story is told. It begins with an evocative horn call, sounding "with much dignity and character." The movement soon doubles its speed, and clari-

nets and bassoons present a resolute principal theme played staccato and in
a modal E minor. A secondary theme given to the violins enters, which has
grown out of the principal theme, except that the expression is now pensive rather then detached and decisive. The principal theme returns and
reaches a climax. The secondary theme returns. It swells in intensity and
closes the movement.

The second movement, "Love Song," to be played "tenderly," uses a
melody of the Iowas. A flute tune with the third and seventh tones of the
scale missing starts it up. Thirty-three measures later a second tune
sounds, which has obvious affiliations with the principal theme of the first
movement. The clarinets return to the opening tune while the strings play
a countermelody that suggests this movement's second melody.

The third movement, "In War-time," borrows themes of the Atlantic
coast Indians. MacDowell wants the music played "with rough vigor,
almost savagely." An Iroquois war song begins in the flutes. When the violins take up the idea, twenty-nine measures later, the melody resembles
the sort of English folk tune that Ralph Vaughn Williams and Gustav Holst
would later introduce into some of their compositions. Suddenly activity
ceases. A very soft pizzicato string chord brings in a clarinet playing in the
low chalumeau range. The melody is an anguished wail. A feeling of desolation prevails. The first part of the war dance then returns.

MacDowell requests that the orchestra perform the "Dirge" slowly
and mournfully. The theme is the bleak one that had appeared briefly in
the middle of the previous movement. Based on a Kiowa melody, it is
heard against poignant dissonances that generate the desired expression
with a masterly economy of means. The movement ends with a hushed
trumpet behind the scene murmuring a final lamentation. Gilman recorded MacDowell's own comment on the "Dirge": "In 1903 . . . he
expressed a preference for the 'Dirge' . . . above anything that he had
composed. 'Of all my music,' he confessed at this time, 'the "Dirge" in the
"Indian" suite pleases me most. It affects me deeply and did when I was
writing it. In it an Indian woman laments the death of her son; but to me,
as I wrote it, it seemed to express a world-sorrow rather than a particular-
ized grief.'"[52]

The last movement is the fast and light "Village Festival" in E major.
Although the material is supposedly of Iroquois derivation, the initial melody is a mutation of the lamentation theme and also has a link to the second theme of the first movement. Brisk dancing rhythms hint at revelry,
but MacDowell leaves everything to suggestion with no pictorialism at-

tempted. In his notes for the Boston Symphony program booklet, Philip Hale spoke of the Second Suite's force and tenderness. He thought it unnecessary to wonder if the composition consisted of distinctively American music, "for the best pages of the suite are not parochial—they are not national. They are universal in their appeal to sensitive hearers of any land."[53]

Piano Miniatures

MacDowell, a professional pianist, produced a far greater quantity of works for the piano than did Paine, Chadwick, and Foote. MacDowell once confessed to T. P. Currier that he preferred to write for piano than for orchestra, because getting an orchestra to perform a work was a headache, and usually such a work was played perhaps once every two or three years, at best. On the other hand, he himself could play any of his piano compositions whenever he wished.[54] Whether miniatures or lengthy sonatas, his piano music had an immediate appeal for music lovers of his time. His finest keyboard works struck several contemporary reviewers as supreme artistic achievements. They also savored MacDowell's playing of his own works, which was definitely impressionistic, according to Currier. The music could sound "vague, far off, floating in space. Pieces clearly written and 'splendid for practice,' became streams of murmuring or rushing tone. Delicate chord-groups, like his melodies, floated in air; while those in fortissimi resembled nothing so much as full orchestral bursts."[55]

The range of moods heard in most of the miniatures is restricted mostly to three: (1) the tender song without words with the tune in the upper part—melodious, legato, and the fingers of both hands playing a chordal accompaniment; (2) the majestic statement, somewhat declamatory in nature—sonorous, thickly textured, melody often in octaves, and the deep bass utilized; and (3) the high-spirited, playful bagatelle, such as the pieces depicting autumnal scenes or "Uncle Remus" or "Bre'r Rabbit"—where texture is less dense, syncopations often introduced, and sixteenth notes dart about in whimsical fashion. Contrapuntal activity is nil. Interestingly, most miniatures, even many of the études, pose no great technical difficulties. Their challenge lies in the realization of the poetic expression. He loves to muse upon things and tell in music how they affected him—lovers, sunset, a flower, an abandoned building, an ocean scene, the New England of Pilgrim and Puritan times, and so on. Titles and sometimes a line or a brief poem indicate the direction of his thought. Otherwise, he lets listeners read in their own interpretations.

The piano compositions written in Germany cannot, of course, compare with the consummate works of his maturity. The young musician modeled his music after the examples of his European mentors and Raff in particular. Piece after piece shows the artist gaining command of his craft but still reluctant to strike out on his own. Nevertheless, several of the early compositions are satisfying in their own right, especially when heard in their revised versions. Indeed, the older MacDowell had an inveterate tendency to rework almost all of his earlier music, normally for the better. When a year is cited for the compositions that follow, they represent the original date when a work was completed, not the date for any revision.

The First and Second Modern Suites (1881, 1882) encouraged such masters as Franz Liszt to take notice of the aspiring composer. Breitkopf and Härtel of Leipzig published the suites at Liszt's urging. The unassuming Serenade, op. 16 (1882), has a fetchingly subdued melody to a guitar-like accompaniment heard before and after a succinct but bright middle segment. The "Witches' Dance" from Two Fantastic Pieces, op. 17 (1883), proved popular in its time although the composer later came to scorn it. The four pieces in *Forest Idyls,* op. 19 (1884) suggest the composer is beginning to find his own voice through a poetic rendition of mythological outdoor scenes. Reality replaces myth as starting points for his mood pictures in Six Idyls after Goethe, op. 28, and Six Poems after Heine, op. 31 (both finished in 1887). The poems refer to tangible objects, people, and settings. His skill in distinguishing subjective states of mind has grown. Commenting on "Scotch Poem," op. 31 no. 2, Marian MacDowell observes: "In so much of his music one feels the strong influence of his Scotch-Irish (Keltic) blood. I may say that throughout all of his compositions from the very first of his works to practically the last things he wrote—and especially in the Keltic sonata—one feels strongly a certain Northern atmosphere. So distinctive is this characteristic that he would never be mistaken as having been, for instance, of Latin birth."[56]

Four Little Poems, op. 32 (1887), contains two particularly fine pieces: "The Eagle" and "Winter." The former sounds with fitting grandeur as full chords high in the piano commence an interpretation of Tennyson's poem on the eagle that "clasps the crag with crooked hands." In the second half of the piece, the melody sounds solemnly in octaves low in the bass against faster-moving chords heard four octaves above. The wide void between the two hands perfectly symbolizes the space between an eagle's aerie and

the earth below. The latter piece, on a poem of Shelley, captures the still-
ness of a frigid landscape. *Marionettes,* op. 38, was originally published in
1888; an improved revision in 1901 added two new items, a "Prologue"
and an "Epilogue." Caprice, humor, sardonicism, and an odd sort of sadness mingle in these little pieces. The "Prologue" is very much in the style
of an American stage musical à la Victor Herbert and a fitting curtain
raiser. "Soubrette" becomes a manipulated doll dancing without supple-
ness. "Lover" exhibits a similar expression. "Witch" and "Clown" move in
rigid staccato motion throughout. The figures are entirely artificial. The
witch never threatens; the clown never cries. All is pleasant make-believe.
The "Villain" is to be played "with sinister emphasis," obviously a tongue-
in-cheek direction. For a couple of minutes, in the winsome "Sweetheart,"
the marionettes are allowed to appear human. The lover sings "simply" and
"sweetly" about the charms of his beloved. The brief "Epilogue" reveals the
feelings of the composer as he ruminates for a last moment on his characters. The curtain closes with a final compassionate glance at the marionettes.

MacDowell published two sets of studies, twelve in 1890 (opus 39)
and twelve more in 1894 (opus 46). Each étude is prefaced with a title. All
twenty-four numbers are enjoyable. Possibly the subjective "Novelette" is
the most outstanding of the twenty-four. The puckish "Burlesque" is entertaining; the more conventional "Polonaise" is agreeably rousing.

The finest of his short pieces are collected in four suites: *Woodland
Sketches,* op. 51 (1896); *Sea Pieces,* op. 55 (1898); *Fireside Tales,* op. 61
(1902); and *New England Idyls,* op. 62 (1902). New England's landscapes,
seascapes, and stories emerge from most of the pieces. Each work is
clearly structured and compact. Each is an individual tonal painting
limned with a sure hand. Most conform to the three stylistic approaches
mentioned earlier. Ternary form prevails. Gilman, a MacDowell enthusiast, wrote of the ten *Woodland Sketches* as follows: "The method is the
method of Shelley in the 'Sensitive Plant,' of Wordsworth in 'The Daffo-
dils,' as it is the method of Raff rather than of Wagner—although Raff
could never have written with precisely that order of delicate eloquence. . . . Always he is the admirable poet, intent upon realizing through
the medium of tones rather than of words, a deep and intimate vision of
the natural world."[57] The natural world was that surrounding his Peterborough summer home, purchased in 1895, and it was in Peterborough
that he wrote all of them. His wife Marian explains how "To a Wild Rose"
found its way into *Woodland Sketches.* She explains that every morning her

husband wrote a short melody, which he later threw away, because as a composer he wished to keep up the technique of composition. She saw one of the tunes and said that its charm reminded her of the wild roses growing close to his log cabin in Peterborough. He retrieved the tune and made it into a composition.[58] It is the epitome of his tender song-without-words style, novel in expression, comely in sound, and deceptive in its art-lessness. "To a Wild Rose" soon became one of the most popular composi-tions he wrote in his lifetime.

No. 2 of the *Sketches,* "Will o' the Wisp," provides an example of his brisk, seemingly effortless bagatelle style. "At an Old Trysting-Place," according to Mrs. MacDowell, reveals her husband's interest in the Peterborough émigrés, who went westward in search of more fertile farmland. The title refers to them, not to lovers: "He was trying to express the wistful homesickness that might have enveloped these people."[59] The composition is gentle and warm from beginning to end and comprises a single likable melody. The next number, "In Autumn," vibrates with the cheer of brisk harvest days after the summer's languor. "From an Indian Lodge" opens in MacDowell's majestic, declamatory style. The austere octaves followed by the low tremolos in the first five measures have a blunt, raw strength to them. The main body of the work is a touching yet dignified slow dance.

"To a Water-Lily," in ternary form, has "a dreamy, swaying rhythm" in its first section and a gradually accelerating and crescendoing middle, to be performed "questioningly." Marian MacDowell, who says that her husband first smelled the scent then caught sight of a water lily alongside an old deserted road, further explains the expressive indication as follows: It was the first time he had seen one growing out of a coal-black pool. His com-ment was, "I have been thinking of the resemblance between that pool and the tenements I found when I went to look for my birthplace. Suddenly I realized that the slums are a great deal like that black pool. Some of our finest citizens have come out of that environment, just as the water-lilies force their stems to the surface to flower in great beauty."[60] No. 7, "From Uncle Remus," is a marvelous tribute to Joel Chandler Harris and his folk tales. This jolly, American-sounding movement contains eccentrically jumping figures gathered in off-balance five-measure phrases. Next come the withdrawn and forlorn tones of "A Deserted Farm." MacDowell found the empty homestead as interesting and romantic as the ruins of an old castle. It called to his mind the New England families that had left the homes they loved, often meaning to return but seldom doing so.[61] The music to "By a Meadow Brook" never babbles. It does radiate charm and blitheness. The last number, "Told at Sunset," is an epilogue; witness its title and references to themes from "A Deserted Farm" and "From an Indian Lodge."

Sea Pieces contains eight numbers, all superb, all prefaced not with just a title but also a line or a short stanza of verse. An affinity for oceanscapes and wonder at the mystery and might of the vast waters are unmistakable in the music. The full-textured, sonorous type of composition is well represented in no. 1, "To the Sea"; no. 2, "From a Wandering Iceberg"; no. 3, "A.D. MDCXX"; no. 6, "From the Depths"; and no. 8, "In Mid-Ocean." The delicate, tender type is heard in no. 4, "Starlight"; no. 5, "Song"; and no. 7, "Nautilus." None of the high-spirited bagatelle type is included.

Fireside Tales, composed about the same time as the Fourth Sonata (*Keltic*) for Piano, has a flavoring of Celtic melody, especially in no. 1, "An Old Love Story." No. 2, "Of Br'er Rabbit," is another tribute to Joel Chandler Harris. The melody of the first piece begins like the old Irish air that Fred E. Weatherly would later adapt for use in his well-known song "Danny Boy." The second has the humor, syncopations, and brusque gesturing that one associates with minstrel show dances. John Tasker Howard writes that MacDowell built himself a log cabin in Peterborough and there composed the *Fireside Tales* and the *New England Idyls.*[62] The ten numbers of the latter are entitled "An Old Garden," "Mid-Summer," "Mid-Winter," "With Sweet Lavender," "In Deep Woods," "Indian Idyl," "To an Old White Pine," "From Puritan Days," "From a Log Cabin," and "The Joy of Autumn." The nature of their contents is shown by their titles. Only the last exemplifies the fast, buoyant type. "Mid-Winter," "In Deep Woods," "To an Old White Pine," and "From Puritan Days" are outstanding examples of the majestic, thick-textured kind of composition. The remainder record dreamlike fantasies, mostly of a tender nature.

Piano Sonatas

MacDowell's four piano sonatas are the weightiest statements to come from his years of maturity. A complete understanding of MacDowell's contributions to musical literature is impossible without them. Nobility is the first word that came to the mind of writers when trying to characterize them.[63] All four sonatas resonate with the bardic tones of an American proud of an ancestry going back to the Celtic poet-singers. Like them, he tried to capture epic thoughts and sing of heroic struggle, courage, love, and suffering. The sonatas explore areas of expression untouched in his other works. Contrasts within and between movements are conspicuous and frequent. Specific melodic, rhythmic, and harmonic patterns are shared by all sections of a movement and all movements of a sonata, thus giving structural coherence. Striking command of musical rhetoric, intricacies of feeling, dramatic drive, and variety of means for attaining creative ends distinguish all of the sonatas.

The first sonata, his opus 45, the Sonata *Tragica* in G Minor, has a slow movement that was begun shortly after and in memory of the death of Raff in 1882.[64] Bostonians heard the slow movement alone in March 1892 and the entire sonata in March 1893. The sonata proved to be deeply moving and like nothing that any American had composed until that time. The contemporary writer on music James Huneker, carried away by its beauties, declared it "the most marked contribution to solo sonata literature since Brahms' F-minor piano sonata."[65] As the music of the first movement evolves, the listener easily experiences the anguish that the composer wishes to communicate. The second movement, *molto allegro, vivace,* is not designated a scherzo, and nothing joyous enters into it. It has a granitic quality about it that bespeaks endurance under stress. The center of gravity for the entire work is the third movement, a *largo con maestà.* Its lamentation is an exalted outpouring of feeling from beginning to end. The movement was a favorite of the composer and requires a real dramatic sense to perform it properly, according to Percy Scholes.[66] The last movement, *allegro eroico,* is derived from the first two measures of the first movement. It supplies a heroic peroration to the sonata

The second sonata, the Sonata *Eroica* in G minor, op. 50, was finished in 1895 and displays the motto "Flos regum Arthurus."[67] MacDowell insisted that the sonata was not descriptive of the Arthurian legend in the usual sense. He said the first movement contemplated the coming of Arthur; the second, a scherzo, was suggested by a Doré picture of a knight surrounded by elves; the third, an interpretation of Guinevere; and the last, a commentary on the passing of Arthur.[68] The third movement is one of MacDowell's most inspired creations. In it, the composer tries to bring out the softness, longing, and ardor that constituted the nature of Guinivere.

The composer's love for North European myth and his rapport with Edvard Grieg found expression in the Third Sonata, op. 57 (called the *Norse*), in D Minor, which MacDowell completed in 1899 and dedicated to Grieg.[69] He wrote three movements only. One does not find the interior fast movement of the first two sonatas. Heading the score are these lines of verse:

Night had fallen on a day of deeds.
The great rafters in the red-ribbed hall
Flashed crimson in the fitful flame
Of smouldring logs.
And from the stealthy shadows
That crept 'round Harald's throne,
Rang out a Skald's strong voice,
With tales of battles won;
Of Gudrun's love
And Sigurd, Siegmund's son.

Nevertheless, nothing truly Nordic sounds in the music.

The composition has an unusual potency, a unique approach, and highly personal shifts in meaning. All musical passages in all three movements share the same basic idea. This is apparent in not only the themes but also the harmonies and even rhythms. Each new representation of the basic material appears as a metamorphosis of both the music and expression. The first movement begins with the slow mournful tolling of bells against a lugubrious melody sounding deep in the bass. Later, the music accelerates and increases in volume until a faster second theme enters very loudly. The first two notes of this theme, in the rhythm of a Scotch snap, grab the listener's attention. The music continues in a spirited, robust, and impetuous manner.

MacDowell describes the slow middle movement as mournful yet tender. The last movement, as expected, recycles the material introduced in the first movement. The initial theme in D major abounds in "character and fire." The movement grows increasingly perturbed, the composer allowing no technical resting place for the pianist and no emotional respite for the listener. Then abruptly the fast pace ceases, and the slow mournful tolling of bells heard at the beginning of the composition recurs. In the last four measures, the first theme of the first movement reappears to end the work as it began—in the gloomy D minor tonality.

In 1900 MacDowell completed his fourth and last sonata, the *Keltic,* op. 59, in E minor. This was, like the Third Sonata, a work dedicated to Grieg. As in the previous sonatas, the essential musical ideas are stated from the first and find their way into the themes of all three movements. Here and there, MacDowell introduces a moment of gentleness, but the ambiance is primarily epic, with an atmosphere of imposing grandeur set from the beginning. Again his love for myth finds expression. The stimulus to creativity came from Irish legend, the *Cycle of the Red Branch,* and the

Gaelic tales of Fiona MacLeod (pseudonym of William Sharp).[70] The first movement involves the feats of the hero-warrior Cú Chulainn. The middle movement depicts Dierdre, the most beautiful woman in all of Ireland, whose great love for Naisi leads to their tragic deaths. The finale concerns the death of Cú Chulainn, who falls a victim to magic during single-handed battle against an army. Heading the score are the following lines:

> Who minds now Keltic tales of yore,
> Dark Druid rhymes that thrall,
> Deirdre's song and wizard lore
> Of great Cuchullin's fall.[71]

To Gilman MacDowell said, "The music is more a commentary on the subject than an actual depiction of it." To N. J. Corey, he wrote: "Like the third, this fourth sonata is more of a 'bardic' rhapsody on the subject than an attempt at actual presentation of it, although I have made use of all the suggestion of tone-painting in my power,—just as the bard would have reinforced his speech with gesture and facial expression."[72]

The first movement starts with a majestic theme stated like a psalm tune. It progresses to an immense culmination of extreme loudness. With the secondary theme, texture thins, tension lessens, and tones brighten. Here and there, a Scotch snap appears in the music. The development of the material, as is usual for MacDowell, is less a manipulation of ideas for musical purposes, more a contemplation of different aspects of the heroic state, using the main theme as a point of departure. The directions for the slow movement call for an expression of "naive tenderness." Yet only at the beginning and end is tenderness found and a connection with Deirdre recognizable. During the middle fifty-four measures the mood is ardently heroic or darkly bardic, the music referring to the main theme (Cú Chulainn) of the first movement. The last movement requires "swift and fierce" performance. Magnificently muscular and decisive in gesture, the movement is one of the most impassioned composed by any American until that time. The main theme, mostly in detached eighth notes, has a spectacular urgency and forward propulsion. The lyrical secondary theme offers some relief. The main theme and its relentlessly driving energy returns, however, first in a free-fantasy elaboration, second in a recapitulation that gradually increases "in violence and intensity" (the composer's direction). Without warning, the Cú Chulainn theme of the first movement comes back, now tragic. References to the Deirdre movement enter, and the music closes quietly.

MacDowell liked the Fourth Sonata best of all the sonatas, followed by a liking for the Second Sonata. In addition, he loved the slow movement of the First Sonata. He felt that not a measure of the *Keltic* needed revision and thought, as Gilman explains, that "he had scarcely ever written anything so rounded, so complete, in which the joining was so invisible. He played it con amore, and it grew to be part of himself as no other of his works ever did."[73]

The four sonatas are among the most notable musical compositions written by any American until the turn of the century. They confirm what was also evident in the *Indian* Suite and the piano miniatures of his adult years—that he had an identifiable style, a musical imagination, and sufficient command of form to render his poetic concepts convincingly. Unlike Paine and Chadwick, he wrote no operas, no oratorios, no symphonies, and very little choral music. His symphonic poems are beautiful in spots but less interesting as a whole. His expertise lay principally in solo piano music. The flame of personal emotion kindled the musical ideas he invented for the piano and made him the exemplar of the pure Romantic among American composers.

CHAPTER

BEACH AND IVES

Amy Beach (1867–1944) and Charles Ives (1874–1954) were younger than the composers already discussed, and they were different. They did not share in the camaraderie that the older New Englanders, save for MacDowell, enjoyed with each other. Each went her and his way. Neither accepted the precepts of their society—that a woman's main, if not only, goal should be marriage and motherhood, or that a young musician's guiding principle should be fulfilling the expectations of his mentor and community. Beach, as a serious composer breaking her way into a man's world, was a nonconformist. Ives, as a rebel questioning the reverence extended to all musical conventions, was an iconoclast. Neither went abroad to study. She was mostly self-taught in composition; he taught himself new musical procedures well beyond those imparted by Parker, his teacher at Yale. Both had completed most of their major works by the end of the second decade of the twentieth century. Neither was a teacher. Beach had some private income and earned money as a concert pianist; Ives operated an insurance business. Both had to carve time out of their busy lives to create their musical works.

NEW ENGLAND COMPOSERS WHO WERE WOMEN

Long before Amy Beach, New England had been the home of independent-minded women who cherished a good education for themselves and their daughters, and who played no small part in the careers of their husbands or at times pursued their own callings. A major export from New England to other states was the educated young woman setting out to teach school throughout the United States, including newly settled areas. She has become part of the American myth, in literature, motion pictures, and television. One notes that a small, enlightened part of American society, all of its members made liberal by education and experience and some with Transcendental leanings, inhabited New England and especially the greater Boston area. It produced and had high respect for women with outstanding literary, intellectual, and artistic abilities. Margaret Fuller, Elizabeth Peabody, Dorothea Dix, Harriet Beecher Stowe, Emily Dickinson, Louisa May Alcott, and Amy Lowell were seven such women. Other women had gone on to musical careers and won respect as musicians— Sophia Hewitt, Eliza Biscaccianti, Elise Hensler, Adelaide Phillips, and Emma Osgood. Boston was a place ready for women composers.

In 1878 Clara Doria married a Boston lawyer, Henry Munroe Rogers, and came to live in Boston. She had been born into a musical English family in 1844, had studied at the Leipzig Conservatory of Music, and at age fourteen had already composed a string quartet. After graduating from the conservatory in 1860, she continued to write music but concentrated mainly on a singing career. She traveled to the United States in 1871 to tour with the Parepa-Rosa Opera Company. After marriage, she ceased touring as a singer. Her husband came to an understanding with her that she should keep on with music. She turned to teaching at the New England Conservatory and composed as never before. At the same time, the Rogers home became noted for its musical evenings.

When Arthur P. Schmidt published her Six Songs in 1882 and critics judged them eloquent and attractive, she began to win praise as a composer. She wrote many songs, piano pieces, a Cello Sonata, and a Violin Sonata. The Violin Sonata, Sonata *Dramatica,* op. 25, was premiered on 9 January 1888 at Isabella Stewart Gardner's home, during the first meeting of the Manuscript Club of Boston, with Charles Loeffler playing the violin and the composer at the piano. Its first movement is forceful, frankly emotional, and striking in effect. The slow movement supplies the violin with lovely poetic melodies. The finale has exciting passages verging on the theatrical. Most of her compositions were never published, although she did bring out two books on her musical life: *Memories of a Musical Career* (1919) and *The Story of Two Lives* (1932).

Another musician who came to Boston was Helen Hopekirk. Born in Edinborough in 1856, she also studied at the Leipzig Conservatory, training as a pianist. She toured the United States, starting at the end of 1883, and made an appearance with the Boston Symphony. She undertook a second tour at the beginning of the 1890s, playing the piano at a Boston concert featuring her own Violin Sonata No. 1 in E Minor in 1891. In 1897 she and her husband came to live in Boston, and in that year Ditson published several songs that she had written. She kept herself busy teaching piano at the New England Conservatory and giving piano recitals. The Boston Symphony presented her Piano Concerto in D in 1900. Hopekirk was a close friend of Arthur Foote and befriended women pursuing musical careers, among them the composers Margaret Ruthven Lang and Mabel Daniels. Women's rights and women's suffrage, whether in America or Great Britain, preoccupied her. Hopekirk was also a champion of contemporary French music, introducing Bostonians to new works by D'Indy, Fauré, and Debussy. Most of the pieces she composed were songs, often reflecting a Scottish idiom, and piano and violin pieces. In addition to the concerto, she wrote a *Concertstück* for piano and orchestra and a second Violin Sonata.

Born the same year as Beach and also a composer, Margaret Ruthven Lang (1867–1972) was fortunate to have an influential Boston music leader as her father, B. J. Lang. Until his death in 1909 he helped her every step of the way, from facilitating her musical study, first in Munich and then in Boston with Chadwick and MacDowell, to getting soloists, choral and chamber groups, and orchestras to perform her compositions. Her debut as a composer took place in 1887, when Myron Whitney sang some songs at a recital. Five songs were sung at the 9 January 1888 meeting of the Manuscript Society. The next year, her song "Ojalà," with words by George Eliot, won widespread popularity and was heard at the Paris Exhibition. Noted singers such as Ernestine Schumann-Heink, Alma Gluck, and John MacCormack included her music in their recitals. Mrs. Gerrit Smith even went so far as to present all-Lang recitals. Two other songs that won fame were "Oriental Serenade" (1892) and "An Irish Love Song" (1895).

The Cecilia Society and the Apollo Club, both directed by her father, immediately took up whatever choral numbers she turned out. For example, in 1890 the Apollo Club did her very fine *The Jumblies,* a setting of Edward Lear's limericks for baritone, men's chorus, and two pianos. In 1893 the Boston Symphony premiered her *Dramatic* Overture, and in the same year her *Witichis* Overture was heard at the World's Columbian Exposition in Chicago. Six more works calling for orchestra followed: *Sappho's Prayer to Aphrodite* (1895), for mezzo-soprano and orchestra; *Armida* (1896), for soprano and orchestra; *Phoebus' Denunciation of the Furies* (1901), for baritone and orchestra; the *Totila* Overture (1901), Ballade

(1901) for orchestra; and incidental music to *The Princess Far Away* (1906). Unfortunately, we can have no idea how the orchestral works sounded. They no longer exist and were possibly destroyed by her. In addition, she decided to stop composing around 1917, although she had fifty-five more years of life ahead of her.

Another New England composer, Mabel Daniels (1878–1971), was born in Swampscott, Massachusetts. She acquired her parents' and grand-parents' love for music and decided on a musical education. George Chadwick in Boston and Ludwig Thuille in Munich were her principal music instructors. In addition, she earned her B.A. degree *magna cum laude* from Radcliffe College. The Radcliffe Glee Club was under her direction during 1911–13. She taught at Simmons College from 1914 to 1918.

Daniels first gained notice beyond Boston in 1911, when she won two prizes offered by the National Federation of Music Clubs, for her song "Villa of Dreams" and for two three-part songs, "Voice of My Beloved" and "Eastern Song." Though she often obscured tonality, made liberal use of dissonance, and borrowed certain congenial practices from Impression-ism, she was essentially a musical moderate who honored traditional prac-tices.

Her interest lay mainly in writing for voice. Her first consequential work was *The Desolate Cry,* a cantata for baritone solo, chorus, and orches-tra, on a poem by Wilfred S. Blunt. It was premiered at a MacDowell Col-ony summer festival in 1913. Reviewers praised the sympathetic vocal writing and the dramatic qualities of the whole work.[1] Another celebrated composition, *Exulatate Deo,* a motet for chorus and orchestra, was com-posed for the fiftieth anniversary of Radcliffe College in 1929. The sev-enty-fifth anniversary of Radcliffe was commemorated with her *Psalm of Praise,* for chorus, trumpets, percussion, and strings.

Daniels heard one of her most ambitious compositions premiered at the Worcester Music Festival in 1940. *The Song of Jael,* a large cantata for dramatic soprano, chorus, and orchestra, text from Edwin A. Robinson's poem "Sisera," enlightens us about Jael, a Jewish woman, who slew the tyrant Sisera. It begins and ends with triumphant religious music; the mid-dle is a brief pastoral *andante.* In the piece, Daniels boldly goes beyond her usual musical conservatism. Powerful and sinewy musical rhetoric, rest-less chromatic progressions, and moments of eloquent spiritual probing give it a great deal of consequence. David Ewen found the melody and har-mony close to that of Honegger. Warren Storey Smith is quoted as writing, in the *Boston Post,* that *The Song of Jael* was "a prolonged hymn of triumph that comes to a mighty climax. . . . The outstanding feature . . . is the striking and frequent highly original handling of the chorus. There are, nevertheless, many effective moments in the orchestral score, while the long soprano solo is dramatic and impressive."[2]

Among her few orchestral pieces was the knowledgeably composed *Pirate's Island,* premiered in Harrisburg, Pennsylvania, in 1935. It gained instant approval for its accessibility and cheerfulness. Its out-of-the-ordinary rhythmic qualities inspired Ted Shawn to choreograph a theatrical dance to the music. The *Pastoral Ode* for flute and strings of 1940 is in the more up-to-date style of *Jael* but is less tonally ambiguous and more charming in its expression. Daniels's most appealing instrumental work, *Deep Forest,* a prelude for a small orchestral ensemble, was composed in 1931, then rewritten for a large orchestra in 1934. Daniels said of it: "This little piece makes no pretense at being other than a simple prelude, frankly impressionistic in style."[3] The musical consideration of the sights and sounds of nature has no harshness or emotional intensity. It peacefully evokes the ever-present New England countryside that was so dear to her.

Like other women who wished to be composers, Mabel Daniels had to battle her way through a male-dominated territory. She once complained that because their obligations were more time-consuming than men's and because they normally lacked the stamina to compose many lengthy and ambitious works, women tended to compose briefer, more modest pieces.[4] She had the qualifications to create more than modest works, but did not do so as often as her talents warranted.

AMY BEACH

Musical precociousness, a well-disciplined mind, and an active promotion of her compositions distinguished a young Amy Cheney determined to make her mark as a composer. She was only a year old when she first surprised her family with her musical feats. She had absolute pitch, a facility for memorizing countless melodies, and an ability to sing an accompaniment to any given tune. By the age of four, she was exploring the piano keyboard and shortly was trying to compose brief pieces.[5]

Born in Henniker, New Hampshire, Amy Cheney was about four years of age when her family moved to the Boston area. Her mother, a singer and pianist, gave her early piano instruction. Further instruction came from

Ernst Perabo, Junius Hill, and Carl Baermann. At sixteen years of age (1883) she debuted as a pianist, performing a Moscheles concerto and a Chopin rondo. Yet, in composition, she was mostly self-educated, translating and studying the musical treatises of Berlioz and Gevaert and living with the musical scores of the finest composers. She married Henry Beach, a prominent Boston physician, in 1885. Nine years later, Boston's Arthur Elson, impressed with her outstanding ability, was saying that women should compose music without inhibitions if they wished to do so. He added: "In our country, Mrs. Beach holds the foremost position at present, with Miss [Margaret] Lang a good second."[6] A few years later, the New York music critic Richard Aldrich was crediting Amy Beach with a command of technique, a real talent for composition, and a number of consequential works that commanded respect. Even so, he criticized the reminiscences of other composers and lack of originality and distinction in her music. He said her Violin Sonata, op. 34, had warmth and brilliance but owed much to Wagner; her Piano Quintet, op. 67, was eloquent but too obviously so; and her Prelude and Fugue for piano, op. 81, derived from Rachmaninoff.[7] Her response to the criticism was that men could not forgive her for being a woman. Luckily for Beach, she lived in a city where music was seriously cultivated, where cultural and educational institutions abounded, and where, more than in any other section of the United States, women had freedom to pursue artistic interests. Also of infinite value was her husband's prominence in Boston's social circles. Beach, more than the women already mentioned, became noted for her major compositions in several genres. Her reputation grew nationwide and eventually spread to Europe. She persisted as a virtuosic performer and composer throughout her life. In addition, she was a force in the Music Teachers National Association and, in 1926, cofounder and first president of the Association of American Women Composers.[8]

The compositions of Amy Beach normally contain melodies of expansive length. A few sound naively lovely, especially when she uses folk tunes (Gaelic, Afro-American, Indian, Eskimo, Balkan) or their equivalent. Her harmony features chromatically altered chords of every description. Texture tends to opulence. Tonality is obscured by persistent secondary-key references and enharmonic twists. She enters into vehement climaxes, which can be lengthy and occasionally over the top. Her structures are employed flexibly and may tend to prolixity. The influence of Brahms, Liszt, Wagner, Franck, and MacDowell is detectable. French Impressionism enters some later compositions. Her compositions can sound strongly passionate, sometimes close to frenzy, or delicately refined, sometimes burdened with sentimentality. Certainly her music is more intensely emotional than that of any other New England composers taken up so far.

Beach, like all of the women already discussed, wrote art songs, producing over 120 of them. They proved popular and found frequent performance in her lifetime. Her most celebrated songs include "Ecstasy" from opus 19 (1893), and "The Year's at the Spring" and "Ah, Love, but a Day!" from opus 44 (1900). In a majority of songs, expression is clear-cut, distinctive, and economically established. By the turn of the century, music critics considered her one of America's foremost song composers. One reviewer remarked about a song recital featuring her songs (some still in manuscript) that was given on 18 March 1903: "Covering as these pieces do, a period of years, it was interesting to mark the progress toward liberty which they indicate. The earlier are elegant, well studied, nicely balanced between voice and instrument. . . . But the later ones, while losing nothing of thoughtful studiousness, yet have the spring, the warmth and the independence which one describes in the common phrase, 'letting go.' They have a ring of their own and they encourage enthusiasm in the singer as the manuscript songs made particularly plain."[9]

Her sacred and secular works for chorus were well received during her lifetime. Although competently written, pleasant to hear, and favored by contemporary choruses, none achieves the distinction of her best songs. Her most ambitious vocal work, the Mass in E-flat Major for chorus, vocal quartet, and orchestra, was completed in 1890, when she was in her early twenties.[10] Though a remarkable achievement for one so young and almost entirely self-taught in composition, the Mass lacks the necessary distinction to make it one of her choice compositions. When first performed in 1892, it brought Beach favorable criticism but little popular success. She tends to linger too long on an idea, preferring to repeat rather than to develop it. Solo passages tend toward the operatic, and chromatic harmonies are overly sensuous.

Amy Beach's pieces for solo piano baffle characterization. The earlier ones normally are brief compositions that are quickly consumed and digested. They descend from Chopin's piano compositions. Later works turn more Lisztian. Some use the techniques of Debussy and Ravel. These last may be leaner in texture or bolder in their dissonance. The Ballad, published by Schmidt in 1894, is one of the more outstanding early pieces. It begins on a tranquil *andantino.* The lyric theme expands emotionally and reaches a fast middle section. Finally, it returns to the original theme now fashioned into a grand heavy-textured peroration. The *Variations on Balkan Themes* of 1904 show her in a style more like Liszt's and MacDowell's. *Eskimos,* four characteristic pieces based on Eskimo themes (1907), reveals her employing a leaner style. "Les Rêves de Colombine" (1907), "By the Still Waters" (1925), and Three Pianoforte Pieces (1932) have her looking toward French masters, and Five Improvisations (1938) show her more dissonant than usual. All are effective and idiomatic works diverse in expression and resourcefully exploiting the keyboard.

Among the chamber works are a Violin Sonata in A Minor (1896), a Piano Quintet in F-sharp Minor (1907), a Theme and Variations for flute and string quartet (1920), a String Quartet in one movement (1929), and a Piano Trio (1938). The rewarding four-movement Violin Sonata, op. 34, exhibits sincerity, inventiveness, and fine craftsmanship in all of its movements. Writing about the sonata in *Cobbett's Cyclopedic Survey of Chamber Music,* the composer Arthur Shepherd observes that it was once enthusiastically received in the United States and Europe. Audiences found "genuine creative power" and "glowing fancy" in the music.[11] The composition is certainly one of Beach's finest efforts.

Throughout the first movement, Beach's rhetorical gestures and climaxes are convincing because, however passionate and rhapsodic they are, they take place within a controlled and lucid structure. One finds balance, imagination, disciplined sentiment, and a fascinating variety of ideas. The second movement is a sprightly scherzo in G major, with a slower, more melodious trio. The highly effective third movement, *largo con dolore,* is in ternary form. The violin engages in a long soliloquy whose beginning has an elegiac Brahmsian quality to it. The last movement has a fast and impetuous first theme and a top-notch subordinate theme that resembles the Wagner of the *Siegfried Idyll.* The close is brilliant in effect and ardent in feeling.

Compared to the Violin Sonata, the Quintet in F-sharp Minor for piano and strings, op. 67, seems more overwrought and more loaded with chromaticisms, complicated harmonies, and blurred tonalities.[12] Unresolved dissonances get in the way of relaxation. When the composer is not dispensing restless energy, she may tend toward the sugary, as in the slow movement. The listener is not always convinced that the parts are integrated into the structure as a whole. The movements are freer in form and jumbled in their collective effect. Yet Beach is attempting to achieve a musical discourse more potent in force and persuasiveness than that of the

Violin Sonata. "Rhapsodic" is the term critics frequently use to describe the quintet's character. Beach meticulously elaborates her motifs and tries for coherence by having the mournful music in the *adagio* introduction to the first movement return in the final movement. The work's romantic sentiment appealed to contemporary audiences, for the work was well favored in its day. Late chamber compositions, such as the Theme and Variations for flute and strings and the String Quartet, are less heated and go for more transparent textures.

Two of her most ambitious compositions remain to be discussed, the *Gaelic* Symphony in E Minor (1894) and the Piano Concerto in C-sharp Minor (1899). The symphony is the first composed by an American woman to be performed by an American orchestra, the Boston Symphony. It is notable for its gravity, dynamism, and innate power. When premiered in October 1896 and performed again in February 1898, reviewers, all of them male, were not quite sure how to take it. They were upset by its energy and drive, which they considered typical of men and not appropriate to women. Philip Hale, in the *Boston Journal,* praised Beach's indisputable talent and declared the work superior to her Mass. He criticized her for feeling she had to be virile at any cost and found the slow movement weak and too long. Louis Elson, in the *Boston Advertiser,* named her America's foremost woman composer, but chided her for her "meaningless chromaticism," "heavy scoring," and "determination to sound powerful." The consensus was that she excelled in the lighter second movement and resorted to excessive repetition in the slow third movement. Everyone recognized the sincerity and craftsmanship of the composer.[13] The attractive first movement is cast in a sprawling sonata structure. It opens *allegro con fuoco* with a grand, impassioned first theme. Nothing Gaelic appears. The peaceful subordinate section begins as a clarinet solo, but later the oboe and flute present a new melody of decided Celtic flavor, based on a gapped scale with fourth and seventh tones missing. The development elaborates on the first theme. The expected climactic outbursts occur both in the development and the coda. The ternary second movement is labeled *alla siciliana,* with a faster middle section. This is the most winning music of the symphony, steering clear of passion, chromatics, and big orchestral effects. The bucolic *siciliana* melody, heard in French horn and oboe, is without doubt a Celtic-like song without words, and the *allegro* middle presents a spirited dance of like origin. Again, in the slow movement a Celtic-oriented melody turns up. Here the manner is unassuming, complexity down to a minimum. The finale, the least "Gaelic" of all the movements, rewards the listener with clear and cogently expanded musical ideas. The symphony represents the composer at her best.

The Piano Concerto was premiered in April 1900, with the composer as soloist. Though regarded as a magnificent contribution to concerto literature, the work was found less attractive than the symphony. Reviewers complained about noisiness, muddy orchestration, superfluous ideas, excessive ornamentation, and passionate discourse that led nowhere.[14] The first movement, alternately lyric and impassioned, is more or less in sonata form and very long.[15] The scherzo, *perpetuum mobile,* introduces tantalizingly brief ideas against the constant sixteenth-note motion of the piano. It strikes the ear as music waiting for something to happen. That something is the *largo,* an affecting lament that links up directly to the finale, where sweeps of ardor are relieved by moments of tender lyricism.

Four instrumental works—the Violin Sonata, Piano Quintet, *Gaelic* Symphony, and Piano Concerto—were the principal reasons why the music world of America and Europe took Amy Beach seriously as a composer. She traveled everywhere playing her concerto with different orchestras and presenting her songs and piano compositions in recitals. Musicians avidly took up the sonata and quintet, at least for a few years. Regrettably, changes in musical styles and tastes made her music seem dated, even obsolete, to a younger generation. Her eclipse began to end at the end of the twentieth century, however, owing in part to the determined women's movement and to the revaluation of Romanticism.

CHARLES IVES

Ives had a bandmaster for a father, as did Paine; Ives chafed at the strictures of his teacher Parker, as did Parker at Chadwick's admonitions; Ives worked in insurance, as did Chadwick for a short while; Ives admired Beethoven and the New England Transcendentalists, as did all of the older composers. In short, he had several things in common with his fellow New England composers. What is more, a great deal of his music has correspondences with their music, so much so that one must conclude that their compositions formed the matrix out of which Ives's music emerged.[16]

He was born in the town of Danbury, Connecticut, and lived there until he went to Yale. His grandparents adhered to Transcendentalist tenets and may even have housed Emerson during a visit to Danbury. His father, George Ives, had a broad foundation in music, a questioning mind, and a willingness to explore in experimental directions that seemed bizarre to nineteenth-century Danburians. Danbury was not Boston and had much less sophistication about, tolerance for, and exposure to any of the arts. Life as a musician was held in low esteem, and life as a composer, even lower. Young Charles witnessed his adored father acting as a jack-of-all-music—teaching, directing church music, rehearsing his band, conducting ensembles, arranging pieces for local groups, learning to play a variety of instruments, leading the singing at camp meetings, and providing music for public celebrations and private dances. The boy soaked up what he heard—hymns, gospel songs, traditional and folk melodies, popular ballads, and syncopated minstrel and rag rhythms—into his very being. At age twelve he was writing his first music and playing the drum in his father's band; at age fourteen, he had a job as church organist.

When Charles and his father tried writing in quarter tones, duplicating realistic bell sounds on the piano, letting music in two keys clash together, and reproducing the effect of two bands simultaneously playing different pieces, they were making trial of new possibilities, attempting to "stretch the ears," and going well beyond the bounds of traditional music. Curiosity, an open mind toward any sounds, and a willingness to experiment were qualities that the father passed on to his son. One of Ives's earliest works, the Variations on "America" for organ (1891–92), already has surprising elements in it, including deliberate note collisions and bizarre stylistic twists.

At the same time, the father insisted that the son ground himself soundly in the musical fundamentals and learn to discipline himself. "Charlie, it will be time enough to write an improper fugue and do it well when you can write a proper fugue and do that well," was his advice. He was adamant that Charles have a command of harmony, counterpoint, musical forms, sight-singing, and the keyboard, and that he have an appreciation of such important musical literature as the works of Bach and Beethoven.

The grounding in fundamentals continued when Charles Ives enrolled at Yale in 1894 and took music courses with Horatio Parker, a thorough and exacting teacher. It was in 1894, too, that his father died. The distraught Charles would make overtures of friendship to his teacher but find that the otherwise amiable Parker was not able to accept the role of father-substitute, owing to grave problems of his own. The student did try showing his radical compositions to him. Once it was two fugues, "with the theme in four different keys, C–G–D–A—and in another, C–F–B♭–E♭. It resulted, when all got going, in the most dissonant sounding counterpoint.

Parker took it as a joke (he was seldom mean), and I didn't bother him but occasionally after the first few months. He would just look at a measure or so, and hand it back with a smile, or joke about 'hogging all the keys at one meal' and then talk about something else."[17]

Experimentation was put in cold storage, as Charles turned to mastering the basic principles that served as the foundation for composition. It was an essential preparation for the composer, despite Parker's being thrown off balance by the youthful Ives pieces that went far beyond orthodoxy in their sound. At the same time, Ives maintained an active social life, played organ at a church, and tried out some of his music with the orchestra at the local Hyperion Theater, where he sometimes helped out at the piano.

After graduation in 1898, Ives began the double life that would continue over the years: weekday employment as an insurance man in New York, eventually forming the firm of Ives and Myrick, and weekend, holiday, and vacation activity as a composer. After leaving Yale, he decided that his music was not practical and that he "could keep his music-interest stronger, cleaner, bigger, and freer, if he didn't try to make a living out of it."[18] He never seriously thought about entering a musical profession, especially after the failure of a cantata, *The Celestial Country,* to achieve wide appeal. Two deterrents weighed against the move. First, he had learned during boyhood that his playmates and their parents thought music a "sissy" undertaking, and he was ashamed to reveal his interest. Second, his father had preached to him that making a living out of music might compromise his creativity. By 1906 his heart had begun to give him trouble, but he pushed his problem to one side as he courted Harmony Twichell, a nurse, singer, and reputedly one of prettiest young women in Hartford. In 1908 they married. She stood loyally by him ever after as he pursued his lonely cultivation of music and cared for him during his many years of illness. While working in New York, both of them had cast longing eyes toward New England. Following the precedent of MacDowell and his wife, after four years of married life they purchased a farm in West Redding, Connecticut, which had a lovely view toward Danbury. Soon they were living at the farm from May to November and had adopted a baby, Edith Osborne, to live with them.

For twenty years, until around 1919, he devoted all of his spare time to composition, usually working on several works at once, and often leaving pieces unfinished. After 1919, owing to heart attacks coupled with disturbance over World War I and its aftermath, he reduced his creative efforts to a trickle and soon, save for some revisions, ceased composing altogether. Perhaps the absence of public performance for his music also proved discouraging. He would retire from the insurance business in 1930 owing to his poor health. On his own, he published his Second Piano Sonata, *Concord,* and separately the *Essays before a Sonata* in 1920. The solitary other private publication was the *114 Songs* of 1922. He deliberately copyrighted nothing and mailed the publications gratis to musicians, music teachers, music institutions, libraries, and periodicals. He also gave away free copies to whoever asked for them.

From 1928 to 1934 he helped support the Pan-American Association of Composers. At last, in 1931 and 1932 Nicolas Slonimsky conducted an Ives orchestral piece, *Three Places in New England,* in America and Europe. Aaron Copland scheduled seven of his songs for the first Yaddo Festival, in 1932. Ives, too, found musical colleagues to advocate his music, among them Henry Cowell, Elliott Carter, and Lou Harrison. The composer Carl Ruggles, who had a reputation for being cantankerous and profane, became a good friend. But the real breakthrough to recognition as a composer and to performances of his music took place when John Kirkpatrick played the *Concord* Sonata in New York at a Town Hall concert on 20 January 1939.

Post–World War II listeners in general found some of his earlier compositions, more or less based on traditional practices, easy to accept (Variations on "America" for organ, the cantata *The Celestial Country,* the song "The Circus Band," and the first two symphonies), but many of the later ones, which seemed to cross the threshold into chaos, they found difficult to assimilate. Few music lovers subscribed to his view that manliness had a musical equivalence in dissonance (and it was important for Ives to sound manly). Ives had absorbed Parker's idealism, had faith in his New England heritage, and showed a marked interest in Transcendentalist concepts when writing music. He wanted to direct his efforts toward expressing the deeply moral and spiritual side of humanity. His music is inseparably connected with the Yankee character and shows the "rough-hewn independence of the New Englander." For him it was New England's past and present, not Europe's, that fascinated him, writes Rosalie Perry, who adds, "God must be everywhere, so Ives concurred with Emerson's Transcendentalism, but he was especially located in New England."[19]

Until the 1980s Ives was considered a modernist whose music led the way to the contributions of Stravinsky and Schoenberg. Yet a true grasp of the meaning of Ives's music comes only through recognizing its embodiment of time-honored native principles. One discovers this not only, as expected, in his more conventional works, but also, and more important, in the unorthodox, radical works. The latter he saw as further advances along the road he had always been traveling. In his maturity, he used the word "nice" as a bludgeon with which to slam music that he thought too pretty, finicky, worn-out, or empty in meaning. His later music would not be nice. It would club the ears with fistfuls of clashing notes and simultaneous rhythms, each going its own way.

Ives's music, even when without an explanatory title, note, or program, invariably grew out of personal experience, whether related to an aspect of small-town life and habits, a slice of American history, or a New England landscape. He is alive to memories from adolescence and his wistful desires to return in thought to an idealized former moment in life—to home, family, and friends. Ives the composer yearns for the happiness embodied in a dimly recalled time past, which simmers in his consciousness. "The Circus Band" describes the circus coming to Danbury during his boyhood. In "Putnam's Camp" he imagines himself a boy sitting on a hillside watching the encamped Continental soldiers below. His Second String Quartet is about Yankee neighbors who heatedly argue with each other but, at the end, reconcile and arrive at quietude.

He had learned from observation and, like William Billings before him, believed that experience was the best teacher. His musical approach was to dismiss the need for an individual style. Any technique was employed if it was to his music's advantage, even if it meant using the most conventional or off-putting methods. Oftentimes his music seems to develop without regard for logical sequences or an overall structure. Into his curving, twisting lines he injects fragments of those traditional, patriotic, popular, and hymn tunes that had surrounded him as he grew up. In one sense, they represent a melodic collage layered onto his music; in another sense, they are the means for surmounting the disconnection of art from everyday life. There are also musical bits from Beethoven and other European art composers whom he admired. He would not usually use American Indian or African American melodies, because they were foreign to him. Ives felt that to write music of substance he had to use the distinctive characteristics of the music natural to him as a springboard to go from the American to the universal.[20]

In *Essays before a Sonata,* the accompanying document to the *Concord* Sonata, he makes clear that he is wary of "manner," which he considers musical technique that signifies nothing in itself. It is "substance," which is "spiritual consciousness," that he believes his music must acquire in order to have meaning. This substance "comes from somewhere near the soul, and the manner comes from—God knows where." Composing is like walking up a mountain with the downward and upward view changing with every step. At the top, the composer-climber "looks toward Heaven and Earth, he is not in just the same key he started in, or in the same moment of existence." He states disdainfully that beauty "is too often confused with something that lets the ears lie back in an easy chair." If the music doesn't bother us, we call it beautiful. A new work accepted immediately as beautiful is one "that tends to put the mind to sleep." Like a narcotic, such music "is seldom the basis of progress—that is, wholesome evolution in any creative experience."[21] In believing all of this, Ives would remain at variance with the general music public.

Vocal and Keyboard Music

While still an adolescent, Ives composed several extraordinary psalms at his father's urging. John Kirkpatrick writes: "Each explores different ideas: the 150th, parallel triads in close dissonance and pandiatonic fugato; the 67th, polytonality; the 54th, whole-tone triads and dissonant chordal canon; the 24th, free mirrors radiating from a stable center."[22] Most psalm settings come from the year 1894. He would quit composing them soon after graduating from Yale. To the psalms should be added the three *Harvest Home* chorales (1898–1901) for chorus, brass group, and organ. Ives called the chorales music of the outdoors, in which the parts coexist independent of each other in the same way as natural objects. An opaque texture and ponderous motion are the musical result.

Ives composed around 150 songs, the earliest ones more traditional, the later ones often quite advanced in their sound. In even the seemingly more orthodox settings, however, quirky passages are apt to occur. The amiable "A Christmas Carol," effortless to sing and hear, was composed in 1897. In 1902 he wrote a song, "There Is a Lane," that would fit comfortably into Tin Pan Alley, save for some odd sounds in the piano. To his wife's poem "Two Little Flowers" (1921) he added straightforward, engaging music. "At the River" (1916) quotes Robert Lowry's hymn tune but surrounds it with a remarkable harmonic fabric. "Charlie Rutlage" (1920) sometimes hints at a cowboy ballad, sometimes sounds like a theatrical piece employing snippets of tunes while the voice declaims in rhythmic speech. "Like a Sick Eagle" (1913) engages in microtonal embellishments.

"Majority" (1921) clouts the listener with strongly jarring tone clusters. Confronted by Ives's *114 Songs*, Aaron Copland writes with an exclamatory pen:

> Almost every kind of song imaginable can be found—delicate lyrics, dramatic poems, sentimental ballads, German, French, and Italian songs, war songs, songs of religious sentiment, street songs, humorous songs, hymn tunes, folk tunes, encore songs; songs adapted from orchestral scores, piano works, and violin sonatas, intimate songs, cowboy songs, and mass songs. Songs of every character and description, songs bristling with dissonances, tone clusters, and "elbow chords" next to songs of the most elementary harmonic simplicity.[23]

One of the most extraordinary and stirring songs is "General William Booth Enters into Heaven" (1914), which sets portions of a poem by Vachel Lindsay. Ives's music recreates the frenzied, aggressive evangelism attending the first general of the Salvation Army. A magical juggling of rhythms furthers the dramatic delineation. Dissonant tone clusters pound out a street-march beat depicting the relentlessly advancing army. With the line "Are you washed in the blood of the Lamb?" we hear a snatch of the Lowell Mason melody "There Is a Fountain Filled with Blood" (and not the melody that Lindsay had in mind). With the mention of a banjo, James Bland's "Golden Slippers" starts up. A wonderfully moving section has the singer on a three-note figure for the line "Jesus came from the court house door," while the hymn tune consoles us from the accompaniment. Then again the strident march beat sounds, only to fade away gradually into the distance as the army marches away.

Ives's longest vocal piece is the cantata *The Celestial Country*, which had its stimulation and starting point in the successful oratorio *Hora Novissima* of his teacher Horatio Parker. Some passages in the cantata have parallels in the music to the oratorio. In all probability Ives hoped to approximate the achievement of the older composer. He began working on it in 1898 and tried it out in a performance at New York's Central Presbyterian Church in 1902, with Ives at the organ. The audience's response was no more than cordial. The performance received two newspaper reviews that commended the music without much warmth. The cantata was never performed again while he lived. Let down by the reception of this major effort to communicate with an audience, Ives gave up on trying to please the public, retreated into isolation, and wrote only to please himself.

Oftentimes what he would then write would be incomprehensible to the eye and ear and close to impossible to perform.

The Celestial Country, for tenor, baritone, chorus, and small instrumental ensemble, is about thirty-nine minutes long and in seven sections. Like Parker's *Hora,* it is a fervently romantic composition whose text, by Henry Alfred, contemplates the heavenly home that people hope to achieve. Although the score is well written and the music is attractive, nothing truly special distinguishes it from the herd of like works written by many other competent composers during the nineteenth century.

Ives composed a number of short piano pieces, which explore a variety of styles, some extremely advanced. In 1905 a *Three-Page* Sonata, lasting around eight minutes, was completed. Its histrionic first section leads to a slower, more singing middle section and concludes with a noisy, rhythmically spasmodic finale, part march and part rag. The First Piano Sonata, written between 1901 and 1909, already reveals his fondness for quotation and highly idiosyncratic conduct of melody, harmony, and rhythm, including touches of ragtime. Ives says the music is about the remembered outdoor life in Connecticut villages—farming, baseball games, and the barn dances of winter nights: "In the summer time, the hymns were sung outdoors. Folks sang (as *Old Black Joe*)—and the Bethel Band (quickstep street marches)—& the people like[d to say] things as they wanted to say, and to do things as they wanted to, in their own way—and many old times . . . there were feelings, and of spiritual fervency."[24]

In the Second Piano Sonata, *Concord, Mass., 1840–60,* Ives paid homage to the Transcendentalists and to Beethoven, whose Fifth Symphony opening serves as an expressive and organizational motto through much of the work. Simeon March's hymn "Jesus, Lover of My Soul" is also prominent in the score. Thick densities and inharmonious sounds stretch the ears. He paints a first movement entitled "Emerson" (1911–12) with a powerful Impressionistic brush. The fanciful second movement, "Hawthorne" (1911), is mostly a rush of sound, with a slower, quieter interlude interrupting twice. Soft clusters of tones are sounded by means of a fourteen-inch board placed on the keyboard. The third movement, "The Alcotts" (1912–14), thins out the density of the previous two movements and adds Scottish melodies and a hymn tune. The last movement, "Thoreau" (1910–15), to which he tagged on a flute part, wears a mask of serenity and has an unsettled ending that lingers in one's consciousness. For the most part the sonata is the outcome of stream-of-consciousness writing that represents the inner thoughts of the composer.

Chamber Music

Ives's First String Quartet, its secondary title *From the Salvation Army,* dates from 1896, when he was still at Yale. It has four movements: Chorale, Prelude, Offertory, and Postlude, in tonal, late-Romantic style. Much of this music stems from organ pieces he had played at New Haven's Centre Church. Already we find Ives's propensity to include hymn tunes in his larger compositions. It begins with a dignified fugue based on Lowell Mason's hymn "From Greenland's Icy Mountains" as main subject and "All Hail the Power of Jesus' Name" as countersubject. The next movement is a cheerful redeployment of "Beulah Land" and "Shining Shore." Next comes a meditative third movement based on "Nettleton" and drawing on the previous two hymns. The finale bonds the "Coronation" hymn to "Stand Up, Stand Up for Jesus."

The Second String Quartet (1907–13), although still romantic in tendency, follows a program and is unrestrainedly unlike the First. It has a first movement entitled "Discussions" (slow and dissonant), in which "Columbia, the Gem of the Ocean" is asked to arbitrate between "Dixie" and "Marching through Georgia," with the ultimate reconciliation being "Hail! Columbia." The next movement, "Arguments," picks up speed and intensity as the four players forgo a tonal anchor and squabble over what to play. "The Call of the Mountains" starts off quietly but dissonantly and reaches a superb peroration on "Nearer, My God, to Thee." Ives said the quartet was about four men who talk, argue, fight, make up, and "walk up the mountain side to view the firmament."

Ives apparently liked writing violin sonatas. What is more, although the four that he wrote cover a number of years, from 1902 to 1916, there is a consistency in their use of American tunes, relatively unproblematic sonorities, and adherence to a traditional three-movement organization. Between 1902 and 1908 Ives worked on his First Violin Sonata: *andante-allegro, largo cantabile,* and *allegro.* It opens ecstatically and contrapuntally, then shifts into renditions of "The Shining Shore" and "Bringing in the Sheaves" before returning to the opening material. The *largo* brings in "The Old Oaken Bucket" tune and its bright reminder of "How dear to my heart are the scenes of my childhood." In contrast, the last movement is clothed in darkness, symbolized by the Lowell Mason hymns "Work for the Night Is Coming" and "Watchman, Tell Us of the Night."

The Second Violin Sonata (1907–10) bears titles for its movements: "Autumn," "In the Barn," and "The Revival." "Autumn," related to a hymn of the same name, is in relaxed double-variation form. A barn dance enlivens the middle movement, with Root's "The Battle Cry of Freedom" thrown in gratis. The finale begins transcendentally with Wyeth's "Nettleton" ("Come Thou Fount of Every Blessing") and grows more animated and intense in camp meeting fashion, with a concluding fade-out on the hymn.

Around 1913–14 he completed his much longer Third Violin Sonata, an *adagio, allegro,* and *adagio cantabile.* The hymnic first movement turns to the tunes "Beulah Land," "I Hear Thy Welcome Voice," and "I Need Thee Every Hour." The middle movement jubilates with a syncopated "There'll Be No Dark Valley" and "O Happy Day." The sonata's finale is a stately rendition of Lowry's "I Need Thee Every Hour."

The brief Fourth Violin Sonata, *Children's Day at the Camp Meeting,* was completed around 1916 and has three movements based on hymn tunes, *allegro* ("Work for the Night is Coming" and "Tell Me the Old, Old Story"), *largo* (Bradbury's "Jesus Loves Me"), and *allegro* ("Shall We Gather at the River").

Orchestral Music

Ives wrote a great many programmatic pieces, all given titles, like *Hallowe'en,* a 1906 musical joke; *Central Park in the Dark* (1906), an impressionistic fantasy with the sound of pop and rag tunes and the noise of passersby; *The Gong on the Hook and Ladder of Firemen's Parade on Main Street* (1911), another musical joke about the now fast, now slow motion of his hometown's hook and ladder truck; *Tone Roads* No. 1 (1911) with its absence of key centers to depict the rough and rocky journeying of the "Forefathers" to reach home, church, and town meeting; and *The Fourth of July* (1913) a boy's view of the celebration told through "Columbia, the Gem of the Ocean," "The Battle Hymn of the Republic," and "Yankee Doodle" heard separately, then all at the same time, in one stupendous cacophonous moment. Such pieces are meant to capture slices of reality and may well have served as studies for his more ambitious compositions. Several of them illustrate the composer in his most exaggerated and immoderate moments.

The disarming First Symphony (1895–98) is a student work of much merit, written in a Romantic style under Parker's direction. It is in four movements: *allegro, adagio molto, scherzo: vivace,* and *allegro molto.* In his *Memos* Ives says, "The first movement was changed. It (that is, the symphony) was supposed to be in D minor, but the first subject went through six or eight different keys, so Parker made me write another first movement. But it seemed no good to me, and I told him that I would prefer to use the first draft. He smiled and let me do it, saying 'But you must promise to end in D minor.'"

From 1900 to 1902 Ives worked on his Second Symphony, a far more moving work than the First: *allegro maestoso, allegro, adagio cantabile, lento maestoso,* and *allegro molto vivace.* He gives symphonic treatment to tunes like "Massa's in de Cold, Cold Ground" and "Pig Town Fling" in the opening movement and also inserts music from an earlier organ sonata. The next movement includes "Wake, Nicodemus," "Bringing in the Sheaves," and a college song. "Beulah Land," "Come Thou Fount of Every Blessing," and "From Greenland's Icy Mountains" come into the third movement, also music from an earlier organ prelude. The fourth movement has "Massa's in de Cold, Cold Ground" and "Pig Town Fling." In the final movement he draws from an earlier *American Woods* Overture.[25] The finale is characteristic of Ives, with its liberal dollops of fiddle tunes, "Camptown Races," "Old Black Joe," "Long, Long Ago," "Columbia, the Gem of the Ocean," and "Reveille."

Years after he finished the symphony, he would eliminate the harmonious tonic-triad ending and substitute an unconvincing screech instead. This brings up the question that several musicians have asked—to what extent did Ives in his later years alter the traditional passages in his music to conform to the viewpoints of his friends who favored radical, post-triadic musical ways? Elliott Carter has claimed that he actually saw Ives altering passages in his manuscripts so they would sound more up to date. On the other hand, Ives's two publications, of 1920 and 1922, show that his use of dissonance was of long standing. Moreover, the dissonances heard in many of his works belong there and aid in strengthening the form.

The generally hymnlike Third Symphony, *The Camp Meeting,* dates from 1904 and has three movements: "Old Folks Gathering" *(andante),* "Children's Day" *(allegro),* and "Communion" *(largo).* Its effect is very different from that of the previous symphony. Nonfunctional harmony, extensive chromaticism, and two or more keys sounding simultaneously challenge the music lover. The outer movements are devotional in character, using the hymn tunes "What a Friend We Have in Jesus," "There Is a Fountain Filled with Blood," and "Just as I Am, without One Plea." The lively middle movement, drawing on an earlier piece, *Children's Day Parade,* goes from simple folk melody to a march and back to the melody. The symphony waited until 1946 for a first performance, and to Ives's amazement won a Pulitzer Prize.

Two Contemplations for small orchestra came next, in 1906, and had "The Unanswered Question" and "Central Park in the Dark" as movements. The first is one of Ives's most original and celebrated compositions. Slowly intoned string harmonies represent "The Silence of the Druids— Who Know, See, and Hear Nothing." A trumpet keeps on asking "The Perennial Question of Existence." And woodwinds represent the pundits who try to give answers seven times, but end up quarreling among themselves. The question is asked one last time; only silence follows.

The First Orchestral Set, known as *A New England Symphony* or *Three Places in New England,* was completed around 1912. The movement entitled "The Saint-Gaudens in Boston Common" imagines the ghostly black 54th Regiment of Massachusetts Voluntary Infantry marching toward, by, and away from the onlooker to the slow pulse of spirituals, Foster's "Old Black Joe," George Root's "Battle Cry of Freedom," and Henry Clay Work's "Marching through Georgia." Ives prefaces the music with allusions to "Generations of pain," "Images of Divine Law," and "the drum-beat of the common-heart." The Charles William Eliot inscription on the bas-relief of Robert Gould Shaw and his black troops reads: "The black rank and file volunteered when disaster clouded the Union cause, served without pay for eighteen months till given that of white troops, faced threatened enslavement if captured, were brave in action, patient under heavy and dangerous labors, and cheerful amid hardships and privations."

The next movement, "Putnam's Camp, Redding, Connecticut," depicts the confusing commotion of a Revolutionary War army encampment to the sound of "The British Grenadiers," "Yankee Doodle," and a march of Ives's own composition. It represents the fantasy of a child during a Fourth of July picnic at the site.

"The Housatonic at Stockbridge" illustrates a quiet morning scene, with the misty drone of a hymn and distant church bells sounding faintly over a riverside meadow. Ives said that it was "suggested by a Sunday morning walk that Mrs. Ives and I took near Stockbridge the summer after we were married. We walked in the meadows along the River and heard the distant singing from the Church across the River. The mist had not entirely left the river bed, and the colors, the running water, the banks and trees were something that one would always remember."[26]

His last completed symphony, the Fourth, worked on between 1909 and 1916, has four movements: *prelude: maestoso, allegretto, andante moderato,* and *largo* with optional mixed chorus. Ives provided a word or two about the music: "The aesthetic program of the work is . . . the searching questions of What? and Why? which the spirit of man asks of life. This is particularly the sense of the prelude. The three succeeding movements are the diverse answers in which existence replies."[27]

The above would appear to be an extensive new examination of the problem posed in "The Unanswered Question," this time with resolution offered. At least fifteen earlier pieces were reworked for the symphony. An immense orchestra is required. Setting two to four independent groups against each other produces thickly layered surfaces. Each group is fixed in its own tonality and proceeds in its own metrical pattern and speed, sometimes synchronizing with another group and sometimes linked to none. A complexly woven fabric of contrapuntal lines results. Lowell Mason's "Watchman, Tell Us of the Night" leads off, followed by marches, fiddle tunes, and patriotic and popular songs entering and leaving in unpredictable fashion. We also hear "Nearer, My God, to Thee" and "The Sweet By and By." But it is the Mason hymn that dominates in the music, as Ives keeps in mind the text's promise of a guiding star and arrival at the promised day.

> Watchman, tell us of the night
> What its signs of promise are.
> Trav'ler, o'er yon mountain's height,
> See that glory beaming star.
> Watchman, does its beauteous ray
> Aught of joy or hope foretell?
> Trav'ler, yes; it brings the day,
> Promised day of Israel.

Ives states that the second movement "is not a scherzo in an accepted sense of the word, but rather a comedy—in which an exciting, easy, and worldly progress through life is contrasted with the trials of the Pilgrims in their journey through the swamps and rough country. The occasional slow episodes—Pilgrims' hymns—are constantly crowded out, overwhelmed by the former. The dream or fantasy ends with an interruption of reality—the Fourth of July in Concord—brass bands, drum corps, etc."[28] There are quotes from "Columbia, the Gem of the Ocean," "Yankee Doodle," "Turkey in the Straw," "Camptown Races," "Marching Through Georgia," and "The Sweet By and By."

The third movement is a double fugue, with material taken from the First String Quartet. It has as subjects phrases from "From Greenland's Icy Mountains" and "All Hail the Power of Jesus' Name."

The finale is meant to contain the quintessence of the entire symphony. "Nearer, My God, to Thee" forms much of the argument. The work ends mysteriously, as the music dies away to nothing, leaving behind a sense of serenity and fulfillment.

There was also a Universal Symphony that Ives started but left unfinished.

In conclusion, we must admire the man who stood firm for what he believed in and the composer who would try to reach his expressive goals even if it meant challenging the limits set by tradition. His intentions were good, but the music does not always come up to the intentions. He needed the discipline that his father and Parker had urged him not to forgo. Quality is uneven. More performances along the way would have helped him realize whether he had achieved in actual sound what looked fine on paper. This corrective was never offered him. Some compositions just do not hang together as music or as artistic expressions. His many interior-monologue kinds of compositions require a stream-of-consciousness sort of listening that not everyone is able or willing to supply. His music is not well suited to every person's experience, taste, or liking. Sometimes one comes away feeling that a mainstream configuration, hidden from view by a lot of extraneous, clashing notes, is struggling to make itself known.

Yet when Charles Ives hit his mark, as he so often did, the result could be unimaginably rewarding. His was a fresh, original voice calling attention to the gold to be mined from the American vernacular and psalmodic tradition. He was constantly urging listeners to dare venture along less charted ways. American culture and humanity have become richer through possession of works like the Second Symphony, the Fourth Symphony, *Three Places in New England*, "The Unanswered Question," and the *Concord* Sonata.

CHAPTER 9

TRANSFORMATIONS

The first well-known American composers connected with New England had emerged during the last third of the nineteenth century: John Knowles Paine, George Chadwick, Edward MacDowell, Horatio Parker, Arthur Foote, and Amy Beach. They had achieved international reputations with their highly crafted compositions that demonstrated mastery of the Classical-Romantic musical idiom. What is more, contemporary American audiences from the eastern to the western seaboards had delighted in their music. Then a younger generation of American composers came along, born in the 1870s and early 1880s, whose main creative years spanned the first third of the twentieth century. Unlike Ives, they were not given to experimentation and had little interest in advanced techniques beyond the accepted common-practice usages. Among the best known in their time were Frederick Shepherd Converse, Daniel Gregory Mason, Henry Hadley, Edward Burlingame Hill, and Henry Gilbert. Although most of their early works grew from academic Germanic roots, their mature compositions reveal the influence of Richard Strauss, Piotr Ilyich Tchaikovsky, Modest Mussorgsky, contemporary French composers (d'Indy, Debussy, Ravel), and also one or more American musical dialects (minstrel, British American folk, American Indian, African American, and contemporary ragtime and jazz).

A composer friend of Gilbert, Arthur Farwell, in 1914 saw this generation of composers working in a "transitional period," suspended between the older stylistic era and the new.[1] The New England composers about to be discussed would create their compositions during a period when advanced artists such as Arnold Schoenberg, Edgard Varèse, and Igor Stravinsky were engaged in ceaseless stylistic explorations, some far-reaching in nature. Although they continued to cultivate the genres favored by the older New Englanders, most of them wrote fewer chamber works and more tone poems and other types of descriptive music.

It would not be long before a new wave of American composers would come along who would venture far beyond the boundaries of tradition and supplant this generation in the early 1930s. In 1933 the composer Marion Bauer reported: "To many, the present day music seems to break completely with the past, to have no logical connection with former accepted methods. . . . It must be acknowledged that we are in a stage of transitional upheaval."[2]

PARADOX

Was New England (and more particularly Boston) living through a "Golden Age" at the beginning of the twentieth century, or was it in the stifling grips of "Puritanism," or paradoxically both? The pianist Heinrich Gebhard remembered the first two decades of the century as indeed the "Golden Age of Music" in Boston. He pointed out that the foremost resident and visiting musicians, including the conductors Muck, Nikisch, and Monteux, brought the best art music, including the newest compositions of Debussy and Strauss, to the city and unfailingly presented works by America's own composers.[3] On the other hand, critics outside New England attacked this image. They accused Boston of being the center of a stifling Puritanism, defined as smug, arrogant, and small-minded. No vital artistic activity could go on under such a condition, they insisted, because the dedication to the arts was superficial and genteel at best. Yet a blanket condemnation of this sort cannot hold water. Of course, New England, like other regions of the United States, contained men and women who were affluent, self-satisfied, morally conservative, philistine in taste, and perfunctory in their commitment to art. To be sure, some New Englanders were strict in moral matters, often excessively so, and adhered to a spiritual austerity that took little joy in secular musical sounds. Not surprisingly, they tried to impose their views on others. Surely, such people lived in all sections of the nation. On the other hand, New England also was rich in informed and responsible people committed to the public good. They built progressive institutes for the blind, the deaf, and the mentally disordered, sponsored hospitals, museums, and libraries open to the public, and liberally supported musical organizations and composers. When we think of the Handel and Haydn Society, the Boston Symphony Orchestra, and the several New England composers who had won and were winning the respect of the nation, the allegation of artistic barrenness cannot stand up to scrutiny.

Three music directors of the Boston Symphony Orchestra—Pierre Monteux, Serge Koussevitzky, and Charles Munch.

Michael Kammen quotes a flabbergasting *New York Times* editorial from 1889, which was an early attack against Puritanism. It stated that anti–New England sentiment had increased, because "the New England temper had been dour and artistically stifled for more than two centuries." As a result, many "worthy and noble souls" had chosen to "escape from the sad shores of Cape Cod." They found in New York "quite as much godliness and far more liberality than in Plymouth or Boston." (The editorial, of course, reeks with prejudice.)

Kammen goes on to explore the history of "anti-Puritans," directing attention, for example, to the influence of H. L. Mencken and his remark "Puritanism is the root of all that's unattractive about American culture, compounded over time by evangelism, moralism from political demagogues, and relentless money-grubbing." Another writer, Warren Susman, tells of how Van Wyck Brooks, in *The Wine of the Puritans* (1908), spoke of stifled emotion and imprisoned self-expression, and of how George Santayana in 1911 found himself rejecting New England culture owing to the "pale and ineffectual" Puritanism it reflected and the "genteel tradition" it adhered to. "Puritans" always wanted music to point to a moral, said

Deems Taylor in 1922, and "if not," they ask, "will it help me to kill time without boring me." The music lovers of New England were "highbrows, defined as educated beyond [their] intelligence," with no sincere understanding of music.[4] Susman would have agreed with Kammen's conclusion: "It surely sounded as though all the other regions were ganging up on poor old New England." In most respects, these were a series of condemnations, political in nature and originating in New York. New York's younger cultural leaders were in revolt against what seemed New England's hegemony over American literature and art. Whatever this hegemony might have been, it would disappear in the twentieth century.

The native New England composers often looked at themselves and their region with unjaundiced eyes. They recognized New England's cultural inadequacies and waning artistic authority. George Chadwick, in an address before the University Club of Norfolk, Connecticut, given in June 1909, admitted to many shortcomings in New England, but said they were endemic to the entire nation. Beyond its urban areas, New England was "a musical desert," where one occasionally heard organs playing gospel hymns and talking machines playing popular music. In the cities, too, the overpaid quartet choir had replaced the volunteer church chorus. Urban areas had opera, symphony, chamber music, music schools, and musical theater—"everything to amuse and entertain the public, but not much which includes them in actual musical life." He worried that making music in the home and by the family was decreasing, "for without the interest of the people themselves in choral singing and in home music, the support of the general public is not to be expected."[5] His honesty is refreshing. His points about the role that amateur musicians played and his dismay at their thinning ranks were important ones.

At the same time, if asked, Chadwick would have called attention to the expertise of contemporary New England composers and the quality of their musical compositions. He would never have accused them of dour, narrow-minded genteelness. In 1909 they were as progressive as most composers in America, including New Yorkers. It was only after the mid-1920s that most of them would generally be thought more technically conservative than New York's composers. Also, the Boston musical scene was busily astir. Community orchestras, often conducted by members of the Boston Symphony, were becoming established. The Boston Orchestral Club, as much social as musical, was an amateur orchestra begun in 1884 with Callahan Perkins as president. Later Bernhard Listemann, then Chadwick, and then Georges Longy would conduct it. The MacDowell

Club was a similar group, founded in 1896. Among its conductors were Longy and Arthur Fiedler. Members of the Boston Symphony who had gone on strike and been fired formed the People's Symphony Orchestra in 1920 and were conducted by Emil Mollenhauer, later by Fabien Sevitzky (Koussevitzky's nephew). In 1925 Joseph Wagner would start the Boston Civic Symphony as a community and training ensemble. Many other ensembles were formed throughout New England, especially in the 1920s, under the aegis of the WPA Music Project.

The Boston Pops was and is prominent among the orchestras in New England. It was meant to attract less-sophisticated music lovers to music and others who wished an evening of easy diversion. Henry Higginson, when he founded the Boston Symphony, felt that his belief in cultural democracy required another orchestra to provide more relaxed musical fare, which in the late nineteenth century meant Johann Strauss, Jacques Offenbach, Franz Lehár, Franz Suppé, and the like. He wished also to allow symphony players to earn extra income. To this end, in 1885 he founded the Boston Symphony Promenade Concerts, led by Adolf Neuendorff. To create an atmosphere of informality, he had the rows of seats replaced with tables and chairs and served light refreshments to the audience. When the Boston Symphony moved into the new Symphony Hall in 1900, so also did the adjunct orchestra, its name now changed to the Symphony Hall Pops. Even though the earnings of the Pops helped defray the deficit of the senior orchestra, the Pops never received proper appreciation from the Boston Symphony's conductors. The many symphony players who performed in it frequently found what they played to be beneath them. After Arthur Fiedler took over the Pops in 1930, he won tremendous popularity for the orchestra and an equal measure of dislike from Serge Koussevitzky. Whether in favor or not with the Boston Symphony proper, the Boston Pops has continued to be regarded with affection by the general public and to attract a large following.

Another ongoing twentieth-century commitment was to early music. In 1905 Arnold Dolmetsch commenced making replicas of "original instruments" for the Chickering firm, and some instrumentalists took to them, including members of the Boston Symphony. Interest strengthened in playing music of and before the eighteenth century on instruments that approximated the original sounds. At last, in 1938, Alfred Zighera and some Boston Symphony players launched the Boston Society of Ancient Instruments, although the society continued to employ unfretted fingerboards and nonauthentic bows. Shortly, Putnam Aldrich, Willi Apel, and

Erwin Bodky were contributing their services to the society. Then, in 1942, Bodky founded the Cambridge Collegium Musicum. The Cambridge Society for Early Music, which replaced this group, tried to establish more bona fide criteria for performance.

In Peterborough, New Hampshire, Mrs. MacDowell converted the MacDowell farm, immediately after the composer's death in 1908, into the MacDowell Colony, as a memorial to her husband. It consisted of six hundred acres, secluded studios, and a few central buildings. Her inspiration owed a great deal to the American Academy in Rome. She set up the MacDowell Colony so that a selected group of writers, painters, sculptors, and composers could come each year and live for a while in retreat, free to create without interruptions impeding their work. The MacDowell Colony continues as the oldest art colony in America, of which now there are about eighty.

New England had also one grand failure to report, the Boston Opera Company. It was in the area of opera that New Yorkers were most justified in feeling superior. They, after all, had the Metropolitan Opera Company and, later, the New York Opera Company. New England music lovers were not as receptive as New Yorkers to music drama sung in a language other than English. The erotic, out-of-wedlock love illustrated in many operas and the rumors about the irregular lives led by opera singers repelled them even more. There was something outré about the snobbishness of the well-to-do class of New Yorkers who frequented the opera house that inevitably tainted opera itself. On the other hand, New Englanders were proud of the highly gifted Geraldine Farrar, born in Melrose, Massachusetts, in 1882, who took the international opera world by storm.

Until 1907 Boston's opera aficionados had been kept happy with what New York offered them in opera. In that year, however, Henry Russell, son of the well-known singer-composer of the same name and a London impresario who had successfully toured with the San Carlo Opera Company, came to Boston. He approached Eben Jordan Jr., of Jordan Marsh Department Store fame, about helping to sponsor and giving financial support to a local opera company. Jordan agreed, and Russell took on the new company's artistic directorship. It was to be incorporated with $150,000 in cash, shares to be sold at $100 each, box subscriptions at $2,000 a year, and with a three-year lease on an opera house at a low rental. Russell called on Frederick Shepherd Converse for assistance, and together they organized a board of directors and attracted fifty-four box subscriptions.

Jordan was president, Converse was vice president, and Chadwick and Charles Loeffler were board members.

Remembering how New Englanders rallied around the Boston Symphony and contributed money for the building of the acoustically superb Symphony Hall in 1900, the opera board set about raising money for, and then building, a new opera house. Its construction was begun in August 1908. Planned to seat twenty-seven hundred people, it was opened in November 1909. For several years the company put on magnificent operatic productions with an orchestra, chorus, ballet corps, and soloists second to none. A Boston Opera School was started to increase the stock of American singers. Jordan met the deficit for the first three years. All appeared to be going well until World War I commenced in 1914, forcing the canceling of the next season. In 1915 the company declared bankruptcy. Although Max Rabinoff tried to take over its assets and keep going what he renamed the Boston National Opera Company, he had to give up after two years and dissolve the group. No opera group on the scale of the Boston Opera Company could be self-supporting. No governmental aid was forthcoming. Bostonians were not as ready as New Yorkers to meet the annual deficits.

On balance, the charge of Puritanism as something deadening was manifestly unfair when levied against New England, the failure to support grand opera notwithstanding. A tremendous amount of musical activity of substance and variety was going on. What is more, innovation was a part of this activity. Like all parts of America, New England had its share of affectedly polite people, marked by false delicacy and obsequiously reverencing only conventionally acceptable artistic works. But it also had its cultural stalwarts steadfast in their allegiance to fine music and ready to abet any undertaking that would enrich the region.

CHANGE

Regardless of the efforts of the older composers and the quality of their music, Americans in the long run had remained unwelcoming toward native compositions. Rupert Hughes still had to observe in the year 1900, "Aside from occasional attentions evoked by chance performances, it may be said in general that the growth of our music has been unloved and unheeded by anybody except a few plodding composers, their wives, and a retainer or two." He explained his reason for writing *Contemporary American Composers* as follows: "The only thing that inclines me to invade the privacy of the American composer and publish his secrets is my hearty belief . . . that some of the best music in the world is being written here at home, and that it only needs the light to win its meed of praise."[6]

Yet the possibilities for performance did increase after the year 1900. More competent ensembles came to exist because they found financial sponsors and ready audiences in the burgeoning urban centers. A composer like Frederick Shepherd Converse could anticipate performances not only from his local Boston Symphony but also from orchestras scattered throughout the United States. If fortunate, a European orchestra or two might give him a hearing. Nevertheless, native composers, even one as prominent as Converse, learned that after a premiere or within a few years of one, the composition was forgotten. The composers had to contend with foreign-born conductors and musicians who favored their own countrymen's music; with impresarios and managers who anticipated greater profit by offering European works; and with Europhilic boards of trustees, patrons, and writers for whom things American were by definition second rate and unprestigious.

In addition, although one or two or their works might have some success abroad, the native composers saw none of their music added to the international repertoire. Mabel Daniels testified in 1902 to the disturbing indifference toward American music that she discovered in Germany, stating, "It is a sad but true fact that American music has, as yet, won no footing in Germany." Carl Engel speaks of Alfredo Casella writing about American musical life in *La critica musicale* and praising only jazz; Engel then observed, "In regrettable, though characteristic, silence he passes over our serious composers, and not with a syllable does he betray whether or not he ever heard of Messrs. Chadwick, Loeffler or Gilbert." Aaron Copland, even in 1952, mentioned that all sorts of excellent composers had been active in America but were ignored in Europe: "I myself lose patience with the European music lover who wants our music to be all new, brand-new, absolutely different."[7] The problem continues today.

The majority of the younger New England composers that we will be looking at honored the past. Nevertheless, their grasp of it differed significantly from person to person. They relied upon it to steady them through the unsettling social, scientific, and cultural transformations going on in their own time. They let it supply them with a semblance of personal unity in a disorderly and worldly era and checked it for possible artistic revamping, each in his own way. They were beset by a further problem: the hostility of various modernists toward works that drew from the musical common practices and tonal-triadic conventions of the past. Music that observed these conventions was denigrated as threadbare. The competition from American "ultramodernists" for a place in the sun intensified as the years rolled by. Too many composers of all persuasions were chasing too few opportunities for performance, funding, and teaching positions.

Modernism was very much in the air after the year 1900. Abhorrence of the dehumanizing features of the industrial society gave it birth. Its advocates multiplied after World War I, whose horrors haunted memory and hastened the dissolution of long-standing societal bonds. Modernism represented an international trend in literature, painting, architecture, and music. It took hold in an America where the customary restraints of church and class had weakened and individuality had strengthened; where things French were gaining favor; where the cultural focus was shifting away from New England to New York; and where composers were no longer inevitably Yankee or Christian. Comfortable melodies went out of fashion. Harmonious triads gave way to the simultaneous clash of tones a second, fourth, and seventh apart. Rhythms grew jagged, sometimes disappearing altogether and sometimes pounding the ears with sledgehammer blows. Structures were individual and unpredictable.

Modernism's impact on the New England composers with whom we are concerned was twofold. First, all were influenced by the fresh modes of expression it made available, some slightly, others to a somewhat greater extent, none completely. Second, because these musicians refused to embrace modernism fully, they underwent sustained attack from critics in the up-to-date camps. The result would be the eventual elimination of their works from consideration as musical literature worthy of interest. Gertrude Stein, around whom several of the bolder, more future-looking American musicians clustered in Paris, insisted that tremendous events like World War I served to speed up change in artistic experiences. To her circle, "the 'pastness' of people and events was not so important as their relevance, and this relevance was tested in the light of its applicability to the present." As a result, "it led to the *isolation* of historical figures and happenings from their original context and to the evaluation of each in terms of contemporary relevance."[8]

From this perspective, we can understand Carl Van Vechten's attack on all New England's composers, from Paine to Gilbert. He asserted that they lacked inspiration. They catered to the genteel bourgeoisie and affluent upper class, for which they composed polite, syrupy, and superficial music. Their works lacked the vitality of popular music, ragtime, and jazz. For these reasons, Van Vechten had "no warm regard" for works like Gilbert's *Dance in Place Congo, Negro* Rhapsody, and *Comedy* Overture. He confessed that H. L. Mencken had "pointed out to" him that it was his "duty to write a book about the American composers, exposing their flaccid opera bar by bar. It was in vain that I urged that this would be but a sleeveless errand, arguing that I could not fight men of straw, that these our composers had no real standing in the concert halls and that pushing them over would be an easy exercise for a child of ten. On the contrary, he retorted, they belonged to the academies; a great many persons believed they were important; it was necessary to dislodge this belief."[9] Van Vechten was unsympathetic to the premises on which these composers based the legitimacy of their works. Opposed to this, we would put Robert Frost's observation in "The Black Cottage" (1914): "Most of the change we think we see in life / Is due to truths being in and out of favor."

In the brave new world of the twentieth century one found a rejection of cultural authority, revolt against convention, antiromanticism, cultural fragmentation, technical experimentation, and new theories about what art communicated. Novel aesthetic doctrines originating in Europe were given names like Naturalism, Symbolism, Impressionism, Surrealism, Futurism, Fauvism, Dada, Neoclassicism, and Expressionism. To most future-looking artists, originality headed the criteria for judging a work. The artist was to nurture individuality and spurn external controls as impositions. Artistic restraints stemmed either from sterile reactionism and psychological and sexual repression, or from outmoded moral codes. Edith Wharton writes that there was a "dread of doing what has been done before," a "fear of being unoriginal" that threatened to lead "to pure anarchy."[10]

Traditional ambiguities in music (such as instant changes in tonality, chords pointing in several tonal directions, unusual resolutions of dissonance, deceptive cadences, hemiola rhythms, surprising redirection of melodic phrases) had normally grown out of what was usually anticipated. Modern ambiguities in music (bitonality to atonality, polychordal to nontriadic harmony, constant dissonance, irregular meter and uneven rhythms, and avoidance of repetition) made it difficult to anticipate anything in the music and thus might make an entire piece unintelligible to the conventional listener.

NEW WINE IN OLD BOTTLES: CONVERSE, MASON, HADLEY

Because the New Englanders with whom we are dealing did not believe in revolution, their task was to select from the pile of assorted modernisms what was congenial to them and reconcile it with practices from the past, in the hope that they would create viable musical compositions. Some of the new possibilities in music that modernism prospected did excite them. For example, several composers testify to the weakening hold of Central Europe and the new attention paid to France, a change accelerated by World War I. César Franck and Vincent d'Indy, Claude Debussy and Maurice Ravel—each suggested a different way of looking at music. Earlier, George Chadwick and Arthur Foote, now, Daniel Gregory Mason, Frederick Shepherd Converse, and Edward Burlingame Hill felt the fresh cultural winds blowing out of Paris in particular.[11]

On the other hand, these composers did not believe that acceptability of a composition should hinge on the unusual or iconoclastic. They believed that genuine change was effected only slowly. While valuing tradition, they also recognized that "the process of tradition" was "a process of selection." Change was common to all periods in history, but total rebellion against the past was a modern cultural phenomenon heretofore unknown to mankind.[12] They would certainly have agreed with John Lowes's statement: "Our most permanent aesthetic satisfaction arises as a rule from things familiar enough to give the pleasure of recognition, yet not so trite as to rob us of the other pleasure of surprise. We are keen for the new, but we insist that it establish some connection with what is friendly and our own."[13]

The New England composers were genuine eclectics, selecting what seemed congenial from various musical styles and techniques and incorporating them into their own. Already mentioned was the French overlay to their Germanic base. In addition, there was the input of music from the Slavic world, the Anglo-Celtic American tradition, African Americans, and American Indians. Each composer showed his eclecticism in different way: Gilbert's rough-and-ready African-Americanisms; Hill's version of French Impressionism; Converse's philosophical and symbolic ideas; Hadley's picturesqueness and vivid colors; and Mason's staunch adherence to the musical conventions. In addition, no composer maintained allegiance to only one manner of utterance. Converse, for example, wrote classically structured nonprogrammatic symphonies and string quartets and freely episodic tone poems of high romantic content. He also wrote pictorial symphonic discourses on the Ford automobile, on California, and on America in general that used all sorts of popular and traditional music representative of America's diverse ethnic groups.

In their works, melody as a pleasurable sequence of tones, often vocal and lyric in nature, predominates over angular movement or rhythmic chant, except in certain country-fiddle or jazz-oriented works. It may appear expansive and fluid in phraseology after the late-Romantic German fashion (see Mason's Sonata for Clarinet and Piano), or extend itself in short clipped phrases in accord with American dance (see Gilbert's *Dance in Place Congo*). Some understandable rationale guides the laying out of melodic phrases and strains. If a traditional tune is used, whether British American, African American, or American Indian, its sound may derive from a gapped scale, the seventh tone missing or fourth and seventh tone missing; or from a modal framework, normally exhibiting a lowered seventh. As a case in point, Hadley's Symphony No. 2, *The Four Seasons,* includes a second movement whose tune, à la British American folk song, avoids the fourth and seventh, and a third movement whose tune, à la Indian music, sounds modal with a lowered seventh and missing sixth tone.

These musicians wished to capture all facets of existence and humanity in their sound, sometimes the earthy but more often the essential, fixed, or durable circumstances of life. Every one of them thought they had composed music worthy of rehearing and hoped at least some of their compositions would be cherished as valuable contributions to America's musical literature. Among these contributions one can cite Mason's *A Lincoln Symphony,* Hadley's *Four Seasons* Symphony, Converse's *Mystic Trumpeter,* Hill's two *Stevensoniana* Suites, and Gilbert's *Dance in Place Congo.*

Frederick Shepherd Converse

Frederick Shepherd Converse (1871–1940) wrote music driven at first by German academic precepts. In his own characteristic fashion, he devised thematic material, chordal combinations, and structural designs based on what he thought were sound and tested principles. He did not hesitate to create works with nonmusical references. In this regard, Converse moved away from the restrictions of the conservative musical world in which he lived and toward the freedoms in sound, structure, and orchestral colorings characteristic of the more forward-looking composers of the turn of the century. His works display learning, skill, inventiveness, and unique touches that add interest to the orthodox procedures. His music establishes a kinship with Chadwick, who also ventured beyond the limits set by conservatives like Dwight. Converse shared Chadwick's fondness for discreet experimentation, programmatic references, interest in Americana, and at times, moments of humor. Moreover, Converse studied composition under Chadwick. During the first two decades of the twentieth century the art music public regarded him as one of the foremost American composers. The few times his works were performed abroad, they won the respect, however reluctant, of European audiences and critics. Beyond doubt, he added vitally to America's musical literature and is an important figure in America's cultural past.

He was born in Newton, Massachusetts, a town just over the line from Boston, and close to Parker's birthplace. Neither his Yankee ancestry nor his immediate background can account for his early interest in music. Yet his parents seem to have abetted his musical pursuits. Converse explained: "My passion has been music, and all my tastes and surroundings were calculated to stimulate and encourage this passion. I began to study music when yet a mere boy, and my preferences were toward composition."[14] He studied music at Harvard under Paine, whom he found to be a considerate teacher and friend. Harvard granted him his B.A. with highest honors in 1893. At first, his merchant father pushed him into a business career. However, the son soon abandoned commerce for music. As Louis Elson wrote: "A few months of a commercial career convinced the young Converse that he was unsuited to business, and he then decided to make music his profession."[15] Chadwick and (after Converse's marriage) Josef Rheinberger in Munich furthered his education in music composition. Whether in Boston or Munich, prominent musicians lauded his musical gifts and expected much from him.

Converse taught at the New England Conservatory from 1900 through 1902 and at Harvard from 1903 through 1907. He then left teaching to devote himself to music composition alone. Fortunately for him, he had an independent income with which to support his musical activities. The year he left Harvard saw him, along with Eben Jordan, working to found the Boston Opera Company, whose vice president he became in 1909, when the opera company first opened its doors. In 1920 Converse returned to the New England Conservatory and became its dean of faculty in 1931. He continued there until 1938, two years before he died. Contemporaries described him as without airs, kind to students, and modest about his artistic merits. On the evidence of Ruth Severance, he was a successful teacher: "As one of his former pupils I can speak of his character and ability as a teacher. He is clear and thorough in the presentation of his subject, and has the faculty of making it interesting and attractive. He always encourages and stimulates the development of originality in his pupils."[16] Sponsored by Henry Hadley, Converse was elected to the American Academy of Arts and Letters in 1937.

An interview was granted an unnamed reporter from the *Christian Science Monitor* in 1910, when Converse was at the height of his fame. He admitted: "I do not believe in nationality in music, but I do believe in good music. I think that we will eventually infuse a new freshness and vitality into music in America; that we will not be hampered by traditions that the European writers have to cope with; that music will grow simpler—we will go back to less complex forms, to more originality."[17] Several late works would introduce some modern techniques and explore one or another national vein. Not least of these compositions would be *Flivver Ten Million* (1926), *California* (1927), and *American Sketches* (1928). By 1930 he was calling himself conservatively modern; yet toward the end of the decade he was declaring: "I am through with the extravagant elements of modern music. No more experimentation of that sort for me. It is already old-fashioned. What we need is deeper spiritual and emotional significance in our music. Given that, all the rest will take care of itself."[18]

One can safely say that he favored a disciplined romanticism touched by mysticism and a clear and personal poetic speech. His works stress orderly beauty but also look inward and now and again disclose a wistful yearning. Several compositions are meditations on human life. One or two are high-spirited larks, which are in their own way meditations on human life.

The Sonata for Violin and Piano in A Major and the Symphony No. 1 in D Minor contain appealing music. The former piece, his Harvard honors thesis, was heard at a commencement concert in 1893. Seventeen years later, Converse would say: "Today it seems very young, yet it has enthusiasm and freshness, but of course I had not arrived at any degree of originality. . . . Now I consider the sonata pretty bad, but it is still played a little."[19] The symphony was composed in 1898 under the guidance of Rheinberger. A few months later, Wilhelm Gericke and the Boston Symphony played it. Chadwick, who had conducted the symphony at the Worcester Festival, said, "It would have been hardly possible for any work which showed a radical departure from recognized forms and methods to be considered for performance in the Munich School, and this symphony is not the only American work which has been affected by such conservatism."[20] Nevertheless, more individuality in thematic invention and greater technical security is apparent here than in the sonata.

On his return from Germany, Chadwick says, Converse gave heed to his "imaginative and poetic nature" and "vigorous mind." An intense study of modern scores, heretofore forbidden him in Munich, resulted in a "radical departure" into the world of the symphonic poem.[21] A series of these works came out: *The Festival of Pan, Endymion's Narrative, Night and Day, The Mystic Trumpeter, Ormazd, Ave Atque Vale, Song of the Sea,* and *The Elegiac Poem,* to name eight. Orchestration grew more sonorous and varied, the harmony less predictable and more complex. Usually, he rejected what was preponderantly picturesque or a mere progression of events. He preferred dramatic moods and shifts in feeling, the delineation of character in an individual, and the analysis of the forces and ideals that drive humanity. Converse was also an intensely religious person who would seek expression for his beliefs in several of his works.

He departed from conformity with *The Festival of Pan,* a "Romance for Orchestra" completed in 1899 and performed by the Boston Symphony in 1900.[22] Converse drew his subject from Keats's poem *Endymion* (1818). The music owes nothing to Debussy's *Prélude à l'après midi d'un faune.* One does find an advance in orchestration, thanks to Berlioz, Wagner, and Strauss. It was not long, however, before he would admire the music of Debussy and Sibelius. The composer did not indicate what sections of the poem inspired him. He shows the contrast between Endymion's misery and the exhilarating splendor of the festival itself in several loosely connected episodes.[23]

Converse composed his second "Romance for Orchestra," entitled *Endymion's Narrative,* in 1901, scoring it for a large orchestra. The Boston Symphony gave the premier performance in 1903. Again, Converse drew on Keats's *Endymion.* In a letter to Hale, the composer wrote that he wanted the work to be judged as music, so had omitted quotations from the poem. Scenes from the poem "suggested" the music. He had in mind the dejected Endymion's withdrawal from the festival of Pan, and his sister Peona's trying to learn the reason for his despair. Converse continues: "He then related to her what seems to me the spiritual essence of the whole poem, the struggle of a mind possessed of an ideal beyond the common view, and yet bound by affection and devotion to conditions which confine and stifle its surging internal impulses,—one of the most painful spiritual struggles to which man is subject."[24] This second "Romance" is an improvement over the first. His craftsmanship is of a higher order, his discourse more assured and persuasive, his grasp on fantasy firmer. Strong feeling permeates the music. Critics of the time applauded the work's telling orchestration and expressivity.[25]

In 1902 Converse completed *La Belle Dame Sans Merci,* after the Keats poem (1820), subtitling it "Ballade for Baritone Solo and Orchestra." Converse described it as "a symphonic poem with voice part" and with "extended orchestral interludes expressive of the moods of the text."[26] The style is more secure in the purely instrumental portions. The music allotted to the singer seems secondary. The total musical structure does not coalesce into a persuasive entity.

At the same level of excellence as *Endymion's Narrative* is *Night and Day*, "Two Poems for Pianoforte and Orchestra," completed in 1904, first performed in 1905 by the Boston Symphony Orchestra, and published in 1906.[27] The piano is integrated into the orchestra and not given prominence. An unnamed interviewer reported in 1910 that the composer was now noted for his "symbolic musical poems" and that *Night and Day* disclosed a mature artist with a "more awakened individuality." He then quotes Converse himself about the work:

> It seems curious that I wrote this work first for small stringed instruments, five or six, and piano, but I found that these were inadequate to express what I felt from the text that inspired me, and the text? Well, it was not exactly Whitman, although I afterward added mottoes from the poet—such as, "This is thy hour, O soul, thy flight into the wordless" [to preface "Night"], and "Day, full-blown and splendid—day of the immense sun, action, ambition and laughter" [to preface "Day"], but these excerpts do not really express the essence of my music, as I intended it. I treated night as the ideal—the things we dream of—vaguely, reverently. Day is reality—or the sterner side which presents itself—yet there are moments of supreme joy. The one is a meditative, personal mood—the other indicates things as they are.

Converse also said that he composed music for four or five hours daily and tried to feel strongly what he was creating: "Very often while writing I seem to become an actual part of the expression itself—and then it is I know that I have felt real emotion."[28] Walt Whitman (1819–92) was then receiving wide recognition as one of America's foremost poets. He was considered a transcendent thinker and a champion of American democracy. Composers of Converse's time and later were inspired by his words or set his verses.

The first movement, "Night," is a warm, delicately orchestrated nocturne, more introspective than dynamic or imposing. The second movement, "Day," features a spirited first theme and a slower second idea. The movement unfolds episodically, with marked diversity from section to section. After three climaxes, the last being the most powerful, it concludes with a long animated coda.

Next came undoubtedly one of Converse's finest works, *The Mystic Trumpeter,* an "Orchestral Fantasy (after the Poem by Walt Whitman)."[29] Completed in 1904, it received its premiere with the Philadelphia Orchestra in 1905. Although the English composer Sir Hamilton Harty would have his *Mystic Trumpeter* for baritone solo, mixed chorus, and orchestra introduced at the Leeds Festival in 1913, no musical likenesses exist between the two works. Converse omitted the first episode of the poem, which refers to medieval pageantry, because he wanted "only to use the elemental phrases of the poem: mystery and peace, love, war or struggle, humiliation, and finally joy. So I divided the poem into five parts and my music follows this division. Each section is introduced or rather tied to the preceding one by characteristic phrases for trumpet."[30]

The work is a cycle of imaginary musical scenes expressing universal human feelings. The divisions are linked by means of a recurring trumpet song and its elaboration. The song is first heard sounding meditatively yet with an aura of cryptic questioning in the opening measures of the piece. (One wonders if Charles Ives had this work at all in mind when he composed "The Unanswered Question" in 1908.) The caption tells of hearing a trumpeter whose "song expands my numb'd, imbonded spirit." Later, the music discourses on "Love, that is pulse of all—the sustenance and the pang," first with a dreamlike melody in the strings, then the woodwinds joining in. This concluded, the full orchestra sings an eloquent paean to love. "War's wild alarms" are characterized by the sound of brass instruments and marching tunes, one of which is "Marching through Georgia." A *meno mosso* in the middle of the movement contains a sad English horn solo, possibly mourning those slain in battle. The caption to the fourth section, "I see the enslaved, the overthrown, the hurt, the opprest of the whole earth," is translated into an exalted lamentation, first in the bass clarinet alone, next in the strings, and eventually in the brasses. The last section, "Vouchsafe a higher strain than any yet; Sing to my soul—renew its languishing faith and hope," recycles snatches of themes from all previous sections but focuses on the trumpeter's song. The imposing peroration by the full orchestra provides a convincing close to the entire work. Most critics praised the work highly. Hill remarked on its advanced technique and psychological discourse, concluding that in its interpretation of inner human feeling and capture of poignant expression, *The Mystic Trumpeter* surpassed all of Converse's previous works.[31]

The symphonic poem *Ormazd* was completed in 1911 and premiered the next year in St. Louis. Again, Converse reveals his preferences in program music. *Ormazd* is the god of light in Persian mythology. He and his hosts contend with and eventually prevail over Ahriman, the god of darkness, and his forces. In *Ormazd* Converse inclines toward greater chromaticism, expanded use of altered chords, some employment of the whole-tone scale, and increased dissonance. No false Eastern exoticisms mar the score. One does hear emotional, eloquent passages mixed with meditative episodes.[32]

After *Ormazd,* a drop in inspiration affects Converse's symphonic poems. *Ave Atque Vale* (1916), "a subjective expression of the feelings of one who bids farewell at the call of duty to all that is infinitely loved and cherished," is too bleak in mood.[33] *Song of the Sea,* based on "On the Beach at Night" from Whitman's *Sea Drift,* opens mournfully and mysteriously and offers consolation and affirmation at its close. There are moments of exalted loveliness. Nevertheless, the vital force of the earlier symphonic poems is missing. The most engaging attribute of Converse's *The Elegiac Poem* (1925) is its folklike musical character. Otherwise, the sound of sorrow parallels music already heard in Converse's other works. *Prophecy,* a symphonic poem for soprano and orchestra (1932), involves a text from Isaiah, "Come near, ye nations, to hear. . . . For the indignation of the Lord is upon all nations, and his fury upon all their armies." Of large scope, the work proceeds with a grand seriousness. It has imaginative touches but seems overly somber.

One other work needs mention here, although not a symphonic poem, the *Jeanne d'Arc,* "Dramatic Scenes for Orchestra." It originally comprised an overture and incidental music for a play by Percy MacKaye, which was mounted in Philadelphia in 1906. Converse extracted a suite from this music, orchestrated it for a large ensemble, and heard its premiere performance in 1907 at New England Conservatory's Jordan Hall. He then revised the score, which version the Boston Symphony performed in 1908.

The first scene, "In Domrémy," is a prelude to the whole work. It describes Jeanne d'Arc's early life with music of carefree innocence, though with intimations of future conflict. The second scene, "Pastoral Reverie," enlarges the idyllic image. "Battle Hymn," the third scene, announces imminent conflict to the sound of the ancient hymn "Veni, Creator," and the battles begin. With victory, the hymn returns exultantly in the trumpets. "Night Vision" centers on the sleeping Jeanne's vision of

St. Michael. Finally, "The Maid of God" reviews her past and closes with her pathetic death and ascension to heaven. The total effect is dramatic. The suite has a wealth of first-rate tunes. Unusual harmonies and harmonic progressions, several of them bold for Converse, are introduced for some striking effects. The handling of orchestral color is sure. It reveals Converse at the height of his powers.

Converse had written a first string quartet while a student. A second string quartet came out in 1904, about the time of *The Mystic Trumpeter.* Skillfully made and likable, its three slight movements do not amount to a major statement. For the most part, his later chamber pieces share the same strengths and drawbacks as the quartet. The two movements of the Sonata for Cello and Piano (1922) are cut from the same cloth. The same is true of the Piano Trio (1932) and the String Quartet (1935). Both works benefit from the composer's greater expertise. Polyphony is definitely to the fore. Yet, for all the attractiveness of these and other of his chamber works, Converse's efforts in this genre are of much less import than his orchestral works.

The composer's Symphony in C Minor, his second, received its initial performance from the Boston Symphony under Pierre Monteux in 1920. Converse said that the composition expressed the moods and emotions called up by the recently concluded world war. He warned the listener: "The point-of-view is subjective and human, rather than impersonal and epic." Converse added: "I have used the symphonic form because it suited my needs of expression; not from my especial desire to write a conventional symphony." He meant the two main themes of the fast opening movement to suggest the fortitude of the men and the compassionate feelings of the women on the home front. A brief *adagio misterioso* introduction "crystallizes into a stern and determined mood which dominates the whole movement, except for the contrasting feminine quality of the second theme." The slow movement that follows is a serene nocturne involving moonlight on a lake's waters, with one episode suggesting the meeting of lovers. The *scherzando* third movement delineates happy and insouciant youth. Nevertheless, one section sounds ominous. The last movement is warlike, but interrupted by a passage in a solemn, almost religious mood. It concludes with a jubilant celebration of the men's reunion with their loved ones.[34]

The symphony's reception was generally enthusiastic. Praised as singularly beautiful were the mysterious start of the first movement, the imaginatively realized nocturnal atmosphere of the second movement, and the conflict of feelings in the concise and vibrant third movement. Hill applauded the music's vitality, so much like "the immeasurable outpouring of energy which this country brought to bear on entering the war." The composer is a "spokesman of his country's heart. It [the symphony] is a concrete expression of 'the American spirit' from a new angle, which as far as I know has not been approached in this country. . . . [Mr. Converse] has become more universal but none the less eloquent."[35] Reservations were few and involved the length of the piece, the dense textures, and the frequent climactic passages.[36]

The next symphony, in E minor, came out in 1922 and was also well liked but thought to lack striking individuality and boldness. At the time of its premiere, Converse gave a modest evaluation of the work, saying it was a succession of universal moods—suffering, defiance, consolation, hope, and joy. He cut down the percussion instruments to kettledrums only, "because I am tired of the cheap, conventional effects obtained by their use."[37] Engaging melodies are plentiful. Harmonies seem natural. Orchestrations glow with rich detail. Structures unfold clearly.

In 1922, also, Converse finished a Fantasy for Piano and Orchestra. Not a major effort, this sunny work makes cautious use of jazz-influenced melodies and rhythms for the first time—two years before George Gershwin's *Rhapsody in Blue*. Ten years later, a Concertino for Piano and Orchestra saw the light. By this time the New England composers, including Converse, were being dismissed out of hand and their music seldom performed. In August 1939, the year before his death, the piece remained unpublished, and the composer complained that it had never received a "first rate performance," though "it is one of my best pieces."[38]

His Symphony No. 4 in F Major, completed in 1934, waited until the end of 1936 for a first performance at a concert, not of the Boston Symphony, but of a WPA sponsored ensemble, the Massachusetts State Symphony Orchestra. It is a conservative work, although with hints of popular song, African American music, and jazz. The work delights us with its honest, straightforward, down-to-earth character and its enjoyable melody, harmony, and rhythm.[39] Just before he died he completed a last symphony, in F minor, which Fabien Sevitz premiered in Indianapolis at the end of the same year. Pleasantly tuneful, the work reaches no great heights. His second and third symphonies remain Converse's most compelling abstract works. In workmanship and appeal they can challenge most other symphonies of their era.

One of the most arresting events in the history of American art music was the performance of Converse's opera *The Pipe of Desire* by the Metropolitan Opera. This "Romantic Grand Opera in One Act" was composed in 1904–5 to a libretto by George Edward Burton, a Boston architect.[40] Wallace Goodrich, fifty players from the Boston Symphony, and a chorus from the New England Conservatory of Music premiered it on 31 January 1906. Then, amazingly enough, the Metropolitan Opera Company produced the work on 18 March 1910. According to a report in the *Boston Evening Transcript,* 10 October 1908, it was Gustav Mahler, the great Viennese composer and conductor, who was responsible for the selection of this opera over those of other Americans for performance at the Metropolitan. Romantic symbolism congenial to Converse abounds in this stage work. Two days after the first Metropolitan staging, Converse was quoted as saying that too many contemporary operas dwelt on the sexual emotions. These feelings had their place (he said that he admired Strauss's *Salome* and *Elektra*), but there were others of some importance that he felt music should idealize.[41]

Iolan, the protagonist, represents common man, aware only of his own appetites, and without thought about the consequences of his actions. He challenges a fundamental principle affecting all humanity, prevails for an instant, but ultimately brings the sentence of death on his beloved, Naoia, and himself. The plot would have pleased Nathaniel Hawthorne. At the end the moral of the opera is heard:

> There is a God whose laws unchanging,
> No one may hope to disobey:
> Man's own desires forced upon the ordained way.
> He for a moment triumphs,
> He has his will:
> He pays the penalty.

The opera closes on haunting music that lingers in one's consciousness after the last measure is completed. Poetic leading motives and their transformations convey the changing symbolic expressions, one moment vehement, another rhapsodic, still another lightly tuneful, and so forth. A great deal of chromaticism enters the score. Unfortunately, the stilted language of Burton's libretto stifles the potentially dramatic moments with excess verbiage and inaction. Most critics on balance lauded the music. Hale, for example, found the libretto undramatic, with no connection to actual men and women, while the music showed a bona fide feel for the theater: "The human interest and the dramatic life of this opera are wholly in the music." The imaginative music "broadens, enlarges, italicizes the text; it gives character to the inherently characterless. It is written in the ultra-modern manner." Speech receives a natural setting. Clever orchestral tricks are absent. The dance music is delightful. The scenes where Iolan expresses his longing, Naoia describes her peaceful cottage life, and Naoia finds death are sustained skillfully. Without question, Hale concludes, Converse has sincerely felt the emotions he portrays.[42]

Converse tried again with another opera, *The Sacrifice,* in three acts, which the Boston Opera Company premiered on 3 March 1911. This time the composer wrote his own libretto, based on Henry Wise's "Dolores," contained in Wise's book of memoirs, *Los Gringos* (1849). He tried to stay within operatic tradition and insure scenes with color, movement, drama, and contrast. In addition, he allowed himself plenty of opportunity for featuring the voice as a lyrical instrument. The music intended for philosophical symbolism that characterized *The Pipe of Desire* is gone. The setting is Southern California in 1846. Chonita and Bernal, both Mexican Americans, love each other. Burton, an officer in the U.S. Army, loves Chonita. Hating Burton because he is part of a foreign army of occupation and also because he dares to love Chonita, Bernal assaults him. Chonita rushes to separate the two men and receives a serious wound. The stricken Chonita begs Burton to save Bernal's life. This the noble Burton does at the expense of his own, during a clash between his men and the Mexicans.

Leading motives are again employed to represent the various characters but do not dominate the music. Instead, ample room is made for complete melodies. Among the characters is Tomasa, a heroic Indian who represents her patiently enduring people. She grieves over the former grandeur of her race with music that is dignified and fervent in its description of tragedy. The first act contains a fine love duet. The second act has swaggering soldiers' music, a winsome song from a flower girl, and Chonita's innocent and affecting prayer. In the last act, Bernal and Chonita pledge themselves to each other with music of great warmth, and Burton's sacrifice is given a worthy musical rendition. Like a master chef, Converse flavors the score with a variety of contrasting tunes—American Indian chants, Spanish American dances, Catholic religious hymns, gypsy music, hints of "The Star-Spangled Banner" and "Yankee Doodle." All in all, *The Sacrifice* is a well-realized musical drama. Unfortunately, the Boston Opera Company was soon no more, and no other opera company took it up.

Converse wrote a third opera, *The Immigrant,* possibly influenced by Chadwick's *The Padrone.* Meant for production by the Boston Opera Company, *The Immigrant,* on its completion in 1914, found the opera company defunct. It was shelved, as was another Converse opera, *Sinbad, the Sailor.* The famous American prima donna Louise Homer gave an interview to Sylvester Rawlings of the *New York Evening World* in March 1910 to talk about Converse's *The Pipe of Desire.* Her statement is applicable to all American composers laboring, like Converse, to write operas acceptable to critics and audiences as well as to themselves:

> If native composers are to be encouraged we must enlarge our vision and become more lenient in our vision and become more lenient in our judgment. Musically, whatever foreigners think of us, we are a spoiled people. We set the highest standards of artistic excellence. A composer must be a Beethoven, or a Mozart, or a Wagner. . . . Do you think if such were the attitude of the people of France or of Italy, there would have been founded the new schools represented by Debussy and D'Indy, or by Puccini and Mascagni? Why not give the native genius a chance to find itself in whatever direction it may take?
>
> In literature we are far more broad. While we may not have developed a Shakespeare, we are producing, because of our larger tolerance, a school of writers, graphic, realistic, distinct and characteristically American. Give our composers a chance to be heard. Let their fancy find flight in any direction. Schools of music are not made by the scores that are never printed [and never performed].[43]

One final vocal work needs mention, the oratorio *Job,* for solo voices, chorus, and orchestra, commissioned by the Worcester Musical Association and premiered at the Worcester Music Festival on 12 October 1907. John Hays Gardner assisted Converse in readying a Latin text taken from *Job* and *Psalms,* and John Albert Macy prepared an English version. Converse explained that he was attempting a new departure by turning to a distinctive compositional method and form, neither theatrical like opera nor discontinuous like oratorio. *Job* was an attempt at an "epic." The troubled Job comes through as a flesh-and-blood everyman striving to approach and grasp the meaning of divinity. The principal moods are contemplative. Job is a tenor; Jehovah, a bass or a few basses singing in unison. The chorus normally engages in prayer to Jehovah. Converse's melodic resourcefulness is sure. Up-to-date chromaticisms appear alongside ancient modes and plainsong. The music sounds vital and fresh, especially to a listener attuned to late Romanticism.

Most of the works already discussed have a direct relation to what New England thinkers, if not most thoughtful Americans, considered intrinsically worthwhile, because they embodied ideals toward which humans should aspire. In this regard, Converse was plausibly American in spirit. However, three conspicuous compositions relate directly to an American setting and receive a specific American musical cast: *Flivver Ten Million, California,* and *American Sketches.* Completed in 1926, *Flivver Ten Million* had a first performance with the Boston Symphony the next year. Converse states that he was commemorating the building of the ten-millionth Ford car: "The ancients had their Scylla and Charybdis; we have our semaphore and 'traffic cop,' all equally perilous to pass; and I believe that the moon shines as tenderly on the roadside of Westwood [where Converse was living], as ever it did on the banks of the Euphrates. Hearing and admiring 'Pacific 231' [of Arthur Honegger], I said to myself, 'I too must try something of this kind for the "Flivver."'" He created the score for his own amusement and with the view that humor was an essential part of American life. The form is free and made up of short episodes. A few motives undergo thematic development.[44]

Converse was not the first composer to deal programmatically with some aspect of the United States, but he was one of the first New England composers to attempt a musical depiction of contemporary America. To do so, he included a greater amount of modernisms than usual for him. Possibly his admiration for Honegger's *Pacific 231,* a description of a railroad locomotive on the move, depicted in astringent harmonies and machine rhythms, influenced him in this direction. Escape chords, non-triadic harmony, bitonality, and just plain noise run through the score. [45]

The first episode, "Dawn in Detroit," opens softly. A muted trumpet crows like a lazy cock. Volume builds. The second episode, "Sunrise," flares out with a resplendent *fortissimo* sunburst. "The City Stirs" rouses itself to action. Next comes a "Call to Labor," complete with factory whistle. The "March of the Toilers" opens on a low pizzicato figuration in the strings. Muted trumpets call. The fugal fifth episode, "The Din of the Builders," is loud and features thumping eighth and quarter notes. This section puts an anvil to use as well as "Yankee Doodle." The next episode announces the "Birth of the Hero," and "The Hero" emerges marvelously and ludicrously to the honk of a Ford automobile horn. "He wanders forth . . . in search of adventure," in motor-rhythmic fashion. Episode 8, "May Night by the

Roadside—America's Romance," is an expressive *adagio* with considerable charm. The mood abruptly changes with "The Joy Riders," with its jazzlike sounds and rhythms and hints of "Dixie." Then come "The Collision" and the flivver's demolition. The eleventh and last episode, "Phoenix Americanus (The Hero righted and shaken)," sees the car's resurrection. Quickly, the flivver chugs away. The horn honks. Snippets of popular tunes add to the perkiness, and the piece closes. In *Flivver,* Converse unveils the roguish side of his personality. Yet the musical result is both poetic and imaginative. This antidote to puffed-up profundity won over the music public and immediately became his most celebrated work.

Flivver was followed by *California,* "Festival Scenes for Orchestra," completed in 1927 and first performed in April 1928 by the Boston Symphony. He had witnessed the colorful celebration of the fiesta in Santa Barbara, California, in 1927 and wished to give his musical impression of the historical procession of Indians, priests, explorers, conquistadors, Spanish women, and gringos that he had witnessed, and of his dining at the café El Paseo, under the stars. We hear a vigorous Indian "Victory Dance" and music for the "Spanish Padres and Explorers." "The March of Civilization" describes the foundation of the missions. "Land of Poco Tiempo" features a habanera-like dance to the Spanish tune "Chata cara de bale," which he found in a song collection of Charles Lummis. The "Invasion of the Gringos" is rowdy when using the traditional "Cape Cod Chanty" and tender when an Iowa traditional song, "The Unconstant Lover," is introduced. The final movement, "Midnight at 'El Paseo,' 1927," introduces Spanish melodies ("El Capotin" in waltz time) and lighthearted tunes of the Jazz age.[46] Like *Flivver, California* is light but delightful music. The orchestration is brilliant; melody, fetching; rhythm, supple and nicely varied; overall conception, fresh; sound, full and rich. It is no wonder that the work, too, proved popular with the public.

American Sketches, a "Symphonic Suite for Orchestra," was completed in 1928, orchestrated in 1929, and first performed by the Boston Symphony in 1935. A few themes left over from *California* found their way into the score. The pop- and jazz-tinged "Manhattan," which starts off the composition, "expresses the activity and turmoil of a great city; the grandeur, as well as the sinister sordidness of its varied scenes. Through it runs a thread of loneliness which is often felt by sensitive souls in such overpowering surroundings," says Converse. Next comes "The Father of Waters," in which a broad tranquil tune represents the placid flow of the Mississippi. At intervals one hears an old African American melody, "The Levee

Moan," taken from Carl Sandburg's *American Song Bag.* The third movement is "The Chicken Reel," whose fiddler's tune also comes from the
Sandburg book. The final movement, "Bright Angel Trail," investigates
the mysterious depths of the Grand Canyon and the legendary birth of the
Hopi Indians in its abyss.[47]

That Converse was sincere and wrote music of integrity cannot be
contested. That he was a capable artistic spokesman for his time and place
is obvious. He was able to impress the music public and the most astute
music critics during the first thirty years of the century. To appreciate him,
we must accept that he preferred to work mainly within the commonly
accepted musical idiom of his time. He was certain its language was not
exhausted and that he could find something fresh to say in it.

Daniel Gregory Mason

Daniel Gregory Mason (1873–1953), like Converse, grew up in the
greater Boston area. He agreed with Converse about eliminating the tasteless and sensational from music, and about including the enduring. Mason
was the most conservative of the three composers taken up in this chapter.
Revolt and experimentation were not in his nature. He started his musical
education with Paine and Chadwick. By following the long-standing canons inherited from his mentors, he alienated the younger composers residing elsewhere, and particularly in New York. It is ironic that Mason would
spend his adult life in New York, teaching at Columbia University.

Mason was born in Brookline, Massachusetts, a town adjacent to
Boston. His grandfather was Lowell Mason, of hymn-writing and music
education fame; his uncle was William Mason, concert pianist and composer mainly of piano works; his father was Henry Mason, founder of the
Mason and Hamlin piano and organ manufacturing firm. He credits his
family with his turn to music: "As I consider the old problem of heredity
and environment, then, in the light of my own experience, I feel sure that
friendly environment in the form of my grandfather, father, uncles, brothers and companions did for my music what no heredity could have done
alone. . . . It was because I heard music daily from piano, organ, glee club,
or music-box—it was because my family entertained musicians and discussed their problems . . . it was for all these environmental reasons that
music became for me so early the most vivid thing in the world."[48]

Mason composed his opus 1, *Birthday Waltzes* for piano, in 1894, and
published his first book, *From Grieg to Brahms,* in 1902. He came to teach at
Columbia University in 1905 and would remain there until 1942.

Through these years, he would remain a conservative New Englander in his outlook and values. He traveled to Paris in 1913 to study under Vincent d'Indy. In Mason's early works, Johannes Brahms, and in his post-1913 works, Brahms and d'Indy were the main influences. He also valued the Romanticism of Beethoven, Schumann, and Franck. Most program music bored him, except for a handful of works that he considered "of a high order," like Strauss's *Death and Transfiguration,* d'Indy's *Istar,* Dukas's *The Sorcerer's Apprentice,* and Rachmaninoff's *Isle of the Dead.*

Mason disliked the music of Wagner, Bruckner, and Mahler. He enjoyed a few works of Tchaikovsky, Strauss, and Debussy, when he thought they did not sound exaggerated. The modernists who rejected common-practice procedures he found abominable. Among the younger American composers he favored John Powell, Samuel Barber, and Douglas Moore.[49] Mason avoided ragtime, jazz, and blues-influenced songs and dance music, as well as the dissonant and jazz-oriented works of American avant-gardists, who were located principally in New York. Because so many of them were Jewish, an anti-Semitic tone mars his earlier writings, especially *Tune In, America* (1931). However, a letter that he sent to the *New York Times* in 1933, which the newspaper did not publish, expressed Mason's appreciation for the Jewish influence in music.[50] Five years later, in *Music in My Time,* he admitted his error and said that the corrupting influences he opposed were not confined to one group but were widespread. It is possible that Mason's deplorable anti-Semitism and drift to the right was occasioned in part by the offensiveness of some advocates of complete freedom from traditional practices, whom he saw as condoning irresponsible license.

He believed that music's appeal was equally intellectual, sensuous, and emotional, conveyed principally through melody and rhythm. Creating fine melody and stimulating rhythm, he said, was a matter of self-discipline founded on a tradition going back at a minimum to Beethoven: "You can no more write a solid sonata without knowing Beethoven than you can work efficiently in biology in ignorance of Darwin. Yet on the other hand this assimilation of the past has to produce not an academic and sterile complacency with what is, but an equipped and curious advance upon what is to be: the artist, like the scientist, brings all his learning to the test in acts of creative imagination, leaps in the dark. . . . The great artist is bound to the past by love and docility, to the future by a faith that over-leaps convention."[51]

In addition, Mason said, an American composer achieves individuality not through employing the musical peculiarities associated with the New World but through knowledge of the beliefs and values lodged in him and his fellow Americans "and taking his stand unflinchingly upon them." Among these beliefs are "the reserve, the dislike of ostentation, the repressed but strong emotion masked by dry humor, that belong to our New England type. . . . In our literature the type is immortally enshrined in the work of Emerson and Thoreau and, in our own day, of Robinson and Frost. We hear it often in the music of Chadwick, sometimes in MacDowell and in Hill (a sort of tender reticence), in Kelly's *New England Symphony,* and in Powell's overture *In Old Virginia* (for it belongs to the old South as well as to New England). The essence of it is a kind of moderation—not negative . . . but strongly positive."[52]

His was not a "go-as-you-please eclecticism" but one guided by the imperative to seek out the best models, especially from the musical classics.[53] He employed music characteristic of the United States rarely and cautiously. Singularly little that he composed betrays that he lived in the twentieth century. His boldest sallies were dabbling with the whole-tone and modal scales, the hesitant use of open fourths and fifths, chromaticism, and altered chords, and the dissonant piled-on dominant and nondominant constructions of late Romanticism. Highly critical of himself, he often reworked and polished compositions after their first presentation to the public.

The Sonata for Violin and Piano, op. 5, dates from the years 1907–8 and bases itself on the style of Brahms. One hears expansive melodies, compact development of motives, malleable rhythms, amiable harmonies, and a nicely calculated dialogue between the two instruments. In 1909–11 Mason composed a Quartet for Piano and Strings, op. 7, whose derivation and virtues are similar to those of the sonata.[54]

Between 1912 and 1915 he worked on a Pastorale for clarinet, violin, and piano, op. 8. Much of it, he says, came to him while vacationing in the Berkshire Hills of Massachusetts. His own description of what he was trying to express helps explain the limits he set on programmatic expression:

> The first theme (violin, D major), voiced the morning mood that filled one in that bright upland field, vocal with birds, steeped in sunshine and aromatic fragrance. Then with the change to minor and the entrance of the plaintive clarinet melody over the murmuring piano accompaniment I tried to suggest the change of mood that comes as a cloud passes over the sun. . . . There would come a sense of pause, of

something both melancholy and ominous that is as characteristic of those Berkshire uplands as the gayer mood of full sunlight. I used the violin rather than the cello which more usually accompanies a clarinet in chamber music, because its brilliance gave just the contrast I wanted with the deeper liquid tones of the clarinet.[55]

Burnett Tuthill thought highly of the Pastorale and urged Mason to compose another clarinet piece. The result was the Sonata for Clarinet and Piano, op. 14, written between 1912 and 1915. Tuthill says he loved "its three graceful movements," which were "well contrasted with the central scherzo characterized by the augmented triad and the whole-tone scale."[56] The first movement captures a warm twilight mood deepened by impassioned climaxes reminiscent of the late chamber works of Brahms. The second movement mixes wry liveliness with nostalgic tenderness. The finale reverts to the moods of the first movement. At times, the music leans toward the French, as in the augmented-fifth harmonies that enter shortly after the opening of the first movement.[57] Whatever its influences, the sonata is comfortable to play and gratifying to hear.

The most ambitious work of his early period was the Symphony No. 1 in C Minor, op. 11, composed in 1913–14 and premiered in Philadelphia in 1916. Mason then overhauled it, with some complexities eliminated. This revision was first done in New York in 1922. Mason tells us that he spent a great deal of money, time, and worry on it, only to achieve discouragingly infrequent performances and modest success.[58] Twelve years would elapse before he would venture again into orchestral composition. Some time later, when he conducted a revival of the symphony, Howard Hanson stated that he considered Mason "the last of the distinguished American romantic-classicists carrying on in the Brahms tradition in this country," and "found [in] this early symphony . . . remarkably fresh and impelling music, which may well defy the ravages of time."[59]

The Intermezzo for string quartet, which Mason composed in 1916, has a great deal of charm and confident writing. When Elliott Carter, by no means a conservative composer, heard it played almost twenty-five years later, he thought it one of Mason's best pieces, though lacking the personal quality of the *Lincoln* Symphony, his third.[60] Among Mason's finest works is *Russians,* a song cycle for low voice and piano, op. 18, written in 1916–17. It was later arranged for baritone and orchestra.[61] The Chicago Orchestra gave the premier of this last version in 1918. Arresting settings of five ungenteel poems by Mason's friend Witter Bynner make up the cycle. Ostensibly Russian characters speak out in the first-person singular. For example, the first song, "The Drunkard," starts off with:

> They ask me what I sing about.
> Who knows?
> Vodka bakes me in my innards.
> Drops of it are on my beard.

For a change, Mason overcame his reticence and produced a vivid score that is emotionally varied from song to song, dramatically telling when necessary, and running the gamut of feeling from warm poignancy to stony pessimism. Greater boldness of expression replaces the customary caution. The sound can be somewhat assertive, even vehement or grating, but usually convincing.

Russians possibly helped reduce a variety of restraints previously noticeable in his style. His next significant composition, the *String-Quartet on Negro Themes,* op. 19, composed in 1918–19, take a glance at African American spirituals and Impressionistic techniques. In the first movement, "You May Bury Me in the East" sounds; in the second, "Deep River"; in the third, "Shine, Shine," "Oh, Holy Lord," and "Oh, What Do You Say, Seekers." Dvořák had already pointed the way to the use of African American traditional music. Claude Debussy's Impressionistic style proved too charged with fresh compositional possibilities for Mason to ignore it. Arthur Shepherd applauded Mason's handling of the spirituals. To transplant material like this into art music was a matter of controversy; success depended on skill and good taste, Shepherd stated. To him, Mason had plenty of both qualities, for he realized "the great potentialities of these tunes, particularly in the way of mood and rhythms." Shepherd enjoyed especially the vitality and profound expressiveness in the handling of "Deep River." The composer effortlessly and tellingly counterpoises the spirituals, at the same time evoking "ample sonorities and piquant color-effects," which emerge "naturally and idiomatically" from the instruments.[62] Mason's friend Tuthill tells us that Mason used spirituals not because he was a nationalist but because he loved "beautiful simple tunes" of this sort.[63]

As for the Impressionistic measures, Mason admits to finding Debussy's harmonies enticing: "Debussy's harmonies, especially his sliding, clamped-together ninth chords reproducing a single melody at five levels simultaneously and thus virtually reducing harmony to zero, proved so seductive to the merely sensuous ear, that I used some of them with really startling inappropriateness, in the first version of my *Quartet on Negro Themes,* and only came to my senses [ten years later] in time to expunge them in a later edition. So slow was I to find my own musical ailment, and to perceive what, though food for others, was poison to me." He credits Hill with calling his attention to the neglect of the original character of the tunes.[64] Even in the revised version, Debussy-like sensuous qualities, freedoms in voice leading, and coloristic touches persist.[65]

The year 1920 witnessed the completion of the Prelude and Fugue for Pianoforte and Orchestra, op. 20, a work dedicated to and premiered by John Powell with the Chicago Symphony in 1921. No Americanisms appear in this thoroughly Romantic score. One hears sentiment but little sentimentality. The prelude opens with the orchestra in unison playing an eleven-note "motto-theme" tersely and portentously. The piano enters, its lyricism being the personal voice of the composer himself. The fugue, more truly a fantasy in fugal vein, behaves like a continuation of the prelude's music rather than as a separate movement. The subject and the counterideas in the episodes are skillfully deployed, and Mason supplies a monumental peroration.

The composer had always admired Thoreau. By twenty-five years of age, Mason hero-worshiped Thoreau as ardently as he did Brahms.[66] In July 1900 Mason was entertaining the thought of writing a biography of Thoreau: "I desire to make Thoreau vivid to the reader as a man among men, which means a great deal of description." A month later, he had written about nine thousand words and had a publisher, Beacon Biographies, awaiting the finished manuscript. Yet he kept on putting off the completion of the biography. He gave it up altogether in September 1908, when he suggested letting Edward H. Russell take on the assignment.[67] Thoreau, nevertheless, was not forgotten.

Mason finally paid his tribute to the philosopher of Walden Pond in the best way he knew how, the *Chanticleer* Overture of 1926, his opus 27. It is one of the composer's most successful pieces. In it, he makes an important side of Thoreau vivid to the listener. That the portrayal Mason attempts is not merely a literal one he makes clear in a comment on what he was attempting to capture:

> "All health and success," says Thoreau in *Walden,* "does me good, however far off and withdrawn it may appear; all disease and failure helps to make me sad and does me evil, however much sympathy it may have with me or I with it. If, then, we would indeed restore

mankind by truly Indian, botanic, magnetic, or natural means, let us first be as simple and well as Nature ourselves, dispel the clouds which hang over our own brows, and take up a little life into our pores." *Chanticleer,* an attempt to give musical expression to this same mood, bears as a motto the sentences Thoreau placed at the beginning of *Walden:* "I do not propose to write an ode to dejection but to brag as lustily as chanticleer in the morning, standing on his roost, if only to wake my neighbors up."[68]

The principal idea that opens this composition in sonata form centers on an approximation of a cock's crow heard in the trumpet. Above the music is a *Walden* quotation: "All climates agree with brave Chanticleer. He is more indigenous even than natives. His health is ever good, his lungs are sound, his spirits never flag."[69] This first part of the overture suggests the happiness in nature and the joy it brings to mankind. Dynamics grow softer and cackling bassoons chatter away on a contrasting "hen" theme. Thoreau's *Winter* is quoted: "Bless the Lord, O my soul, bless Him for wildness . . . and bless Him for hens, too, that croak and cackle." The tune is more chromatic and syncopated than the first one and hints at American popular song. Eventually, the recapitulation brings back the lusty crow of Chanticleer and the answering chatter of the hens, and then continues until a stirring conclusion is achieved.

No musical Americanisms are heard, yet the music encompasses the American vital force that Mason had hoped all native composers would eventually capture. One detects neither Brahms nor d'Indy peering over Mason's shoulder. Instead he gives us a thoroughly American soundscape. The overture has dynamic, cheery, and poetic attributes having no European parallels. The work quickly became a favorite with symphony audiences throughout the United States. Much to Mason's amazement, he made a net profit of $460.66 out of performance fees and royalties within a few years, instead of the usual net losses for each of his other works.[70] Reviewing a recording of the overture in 1985, Paul Snook considered it one of several works that proved American music did not originate with the compositions of Ives or the teaching of Nadia Boulanger. *Chanticleer* was "delectably brash and bumptious." The music struck him as harmonically free, open, and optimistic. The piece was "a kind of symphonic parallel to the self-assertive spirituality which animated Emerson, Whitman, and Thoreau . . . during America's cultural-democratic coming-of-age."[71]

After years of avoiding the genre, Mason composed his Symphony

No. 2 in A Major, op. 30, in 1928–29 and made revisions in the score in 1941, 1942, and 1948. No program accompanies the music. The composer himself described the composition as Romantic in tendency and style.[72] The piece strikes the ear as somber music, masculine in tone and weighty in texture. The exuberance of *Chanticleer* is gone. Conflict, meditation, and resignation are the symphony's dominant moods. Mason deals with the four movements cyclically, with ideas traveling across movements. The most prominent idea of the entire symphony, a descending chromatic passage of three tones, *tutti,* launches the symphony on its way. An aura of brooding dwells in the tones. Tuthill believes that a comment of Randall Thompson on the "sinister and foreboding pessimism" and "dour and bitter irony in Mason's music" is appropriate to this work.[73] The austerity and the impression of holding back one's feelings that one notes in the previous symphony are still apparent here. However, this second symphony is the surefooted work of a mature musician.

A much less consequential piece, the Serenade for string quartet, op. 31, in three short movements, was completed in 1931. Fugato passages are tucked into all the movements—the first, a sonata structure sans a real development; the second, a rondo that thrives on two English folk songs; the third, variational.

The *Suite after English Folk Songs,* op. 32, which he composed in 1933–34, is a delightful change from the stiffer Serenade. Fabien Sevitzky and the People's Symphony Orchestra premiered it in Boston in 1935. Mason keeps in mind his belief that the characteristic tunes and rhythms of a nation could serve as ingredients in a composer's music, but if allowed to dominate a composer's thinking, they could prove disasterous.[74] He appears comfortable with his material. The management of the tunes sounds right. We discover the restraint and matter-of-fact banter that stem directly from his New England upbringing. However, we also appreciate the rhythmic verve of folk dance and the warmth of personal feeling. The drawing power of the music stems from the attractive melodies, the composition's homespun atmosphere, and the plain discourse.

The next and grandest of Mason's compositions, the Symphony No. 3, *A Lincoln Symphony,* took shape in 1935–36 and had its premiere in New York in 1937. The musical depiction of Lincoln is tragic as it imparts, through him, the contradictory and incongruous nature of humankind's striving against evil and its sometimes fatal consequences. The tragedy embraces the events surrounding the Civil War, which brought Lincoln's compatriots and America's values into conflict. Mason possibly wanted to show that the aftermath of the struggle, in particular against slavery, had ended in the reassertion of human worth and liberty. Regardless of the destructive power of evil, as seen in the suffering and dying of thousands of people and the assassination of Lincoln, this reassertion comprises a triumph, if only a nervous one, as history has proved. The music does not follow a storyline. Its intent is to capture the moods of a discordant time and the fortitude of a leader seeking a common good.

When first heard, the symphony addressed the problem of American identity in the face of a devastating economic depression that was pulling society apart during the 1930s. It called attention to the convictions and standards, and the travail and sacrifice, that have allowed democracy to function. Lincoln, a figure from our heroic past, the war to save the Union and emancipate the slaves, and the heroism that showed itself in the soldiers at Gettysburg have always fascinated Americans.

The composer states:

> The only traditional theme is the *Quaboag Quickstep,* an actual popular tune of the 1860 period, used to suggest the thoughtless, restless, trivial people Lincoln had to inspire. The theme of the slow movement, *Massa Linkum,* it is true, is also conceived in the vein of the Negro spirituals, but is not based on any actual tune. Also my own are the themes of the serious Lincoln, of the humorous, gawky, yet tender Lincoln of the scherzo *Old Abe's Yarns,* and of the funeral march made from the *Quaboag Quickstep* in the finale, *1865.* I felt, and Douglas Moore, Chalmers Clifton, and other friends agreed, that this was a step in the right direction, away from the letter and toward the spirit.[75]

The first movement, "The Candidate from Springfield," begins slowly with the Lincoln motive, a downward skip of a fifth and an upward skip of a tenth.[76] Most measures of the symphony grow from this motive. Gradually Mason portrays Lincoln's character, his outward cheer and inward struggles, and feelings from serious to comical. Interchange between gaiety and heavyheartedness characterizes the movement.

The second movement, "Massa Linkum," is slow and sad. It opens on an English horn solo playing a modal-minor tune, the seventh tone of the scale lowered. An oboe and a flute continue with the tune. Shortly, a solo cello plays in the manner of a recitative and brings in the serious-Lincoln motive. The strings then swell into an eloquent *maestoso,* at which point the first theme returns in counterpoint with the Lincoln motive. The close is tranquil. The enjoyable third movement, "Old Abe's Yarns," has the Lincoln motive take on the character of a country bumpkin, a teller of cracker-barrel tales. Gawky yet appealing, it starts and stops in jerky manner. Playfulness marks the motive's reincarnations in inversion, retrograde inversion, and augmentation.

The finale, "1865," starts with the motive tonally unfocused and chromatic. A funeral march begins, its theme based on the first-movement quickstep, only with an opposite expressive impact. The movement combines dignity with poignancy and continues to unfold until an emotional peak is achieved. The music grows quieter. Allusions to themes from the three previous movements are made. A final augmented version of the Lincoln motive sounds grandly. The symphony has ended.

After listening to the symphony, Lawrence Gilman wrote in the *New York Herald Tribune,* 18 November 1937: "Mr. Mason . . . has demonstrated again and again throughout this work his depth of insight and of feeling, his power of salient and expressive utterance, his incorruptible honesty and dignity as an artist, his tact and sensibility as a poet and humanist in tones." Gilman praised the music's "lofty simplicity" and "noble austerity" that captured Lincoln's essence in concise fashion.[77]

Throughout his life, Mason tried to express his faith in the musical traditions and the Yankee vision of America. That he worked sincerely within that tradition and labored to encompass the ideals of New England within viable musical forms cannot be doubted. However unresponsive to twentieth-century innovation, he discoursed with some power and demonstrated not a little talent in those compositions that represent him at his best—the *String-Quartet on Negro Themes, Russians, Chanticleer,* the *Suite on English Folk-Songs,* and *A Lincoln Symphony.* Curiously, the compositions that have proved most rewarding to hear are outside his usual style in their references to African American, Anglo-American, and popular American music—or, in the case of *Chanticleer,* to an optimistic and typically American robustness unknown in his previous works.

Henry Hadley

Of all the composers taken up in this study, Henry Hadley (1871–1937) has been the most lambasted by later writers, when noticed at all. At least some vindication of his musical and aesthetic values would seem in order. His critics on the whole become apathetic to Hadley's accomplishments because he is not in accord with the sounds made, say, by Edgard Varèse, Carl Ruggles, Aaron Copland, and Wallingford Riegger. Was he an anachronism? He did resist the radical changes taking place in music and remained largely oriented toward the music styles of the common-practice tradition. Hadley knew that the public's musical taste was predominantly emotional and melody-prone and not receptive to music that faithfully reproduced the "machine age." His key works show partiality for picturesque tonal tints, theatrical gestures, and vocally oriented lyricism. Indeed, catchy tunes, lush harmonies, nicely realized orchestral colors, and soupçons of the strange and exciting were his stock in trade.

The most draining of his creative efforts was the composing of operas. While doing so, Hadley confronted the same puzzle that Paine, Chadwick, and Parker had faced. No American operatic traditions existed to guide him. Foreign-born operatic directors, singers, and instrumentalists had to be cultivated. The opera audience had as a standard the practices of Italy and, to a lesser degree, Germany and France. The composers found it difficult to surmount the problem of skeptical audiences and critics, of less than friendly opera companies, and of vocalists unattuned to native musical drama. Something uniquely American was already emerging from the popular musical stage: in the operettas of Sousa, the Broadway offerings of George M. Cohan, and the musical skits modeled after those of Harrigan and Hart and Weber and Fields. Regrettably, owing to the attitudes prevalent in the American operatic world, little of the ferment affecting the popular musical stage was transferrable to grand opera. If Hadley dared to write an aria sounding like a popular ditty, spokespeople for the operatic world called it trash. If he unveiled an American scene and featured ordinary men and women employing the American vernacular, critics claimed it nullified artistic standards. If he were rash enough to employ the syncopated rhythms of ragtime, jazz, and Broadway, the cognoscenti would decide that the utmost in vulgarity had been achieved. Hadley felt forced to stay with what he thought would work on the operatic stage.

Somerville, across the Charles River from Boston, was Hadley's birthplace. His father was a music teacher in the Somerville schools, and his mother was a singer and pianist. A great deal of chamber music was played at the Hadley home, with Henry Hadley on first violin, the composer Henry Gilbert (who was also born in Somerville) on second violin, his father on viola, and his brother Arthur on cello. Later, he would marry Inez Barbour, a professional vocalist. His father and Stephen Emery in theory and George Chadwick in composition provided his musical education. Although Hadley went on to complete his music studies with Eusebius Mandyczewski in Vienna and Ludwig Thuille in Munich, his friend and mentor for years continued to be Chadwick. While in Europe, Hadley met Brahms and heard him play. He also listened to Tchaikovsky's *Symphonie Pathétique* and "left the auditorium in such a state of agitation that, in spite of a blind snowstorm, he did not realize that he had forgotten his hat."[78]

During his life, Hadley conducted orchestras in the United States, Europe, and Japan. He also helped found the National Association for American Composers and Conductors. His main conducting posts were the Mainz (Germany) theater orchestra, the Seattle Symphony, and the San Francisco Symphony. During the 1920s he was associate conductor of the New York Philharmonic. In 1929 he organized the Manhattan Symphony and directed it until 1932. In the summers of 1934 and 1935 he led members of the New York Philharmonic in what was called the Berkshire Symphonic Festival, before Koussevitzky and the Boston Symphony superseded him and his players. As a conductor, Hadley devoted himself to the cause of the less radical American composers, championing the works of Chadwick, Converse, Taylor, and Gilbert, among others. Advanced and relentlessly dissonant works unsettled Hadley and were bypassed.

Converse had nothing but praise for Hadley's "generous, unselfish encouragement to other composers, young and old." He seems to have been free from envy and helped his contemporaries by bringing about performances of their works and by supporting the really talented among his younger colleagues. "His achievements in this direction, especially as assistant conductor of the New York Philharmonic Orchestra and later with the Manhattan Orchestra . . . were notable."[79]

Hadley's was a cosmopolitan musical approach that drew on the styles of composers he admired (Wagner, Strauss, Tchaikovsky, Chadwick, MacDowell), American song and dance, and to a lesser degree, the traditional music of some European countries, the Middle East, and the Far East. He would have agreed with John La Farge's statement, made in 1900, that American artists differed from Europeans: "We are not as they are—fixed in some tradition; and we can go where we choose—to the greatest influences, if we wish, and still be free for our future."[80]

On the other hand, savoring the cultural styles and traits of others might be at the expense of one's own identity, as some Hadley critics warned. Yet we should heed Allen Tate's counsel about John Peale Bishop's poetry and apply it to Hadley's music: "It has been said that Bishop has imitated all the chief modern poets. . . . But the observation is double-edged. In our age of personal expression the poet gets credit for what is 'his own': the art is not the thing, but rather the information conveyed about a unique personality. Applauding a poet only for what is uniquely his own, we lose thereby much that is good. If a poem in Yeats's manner appears in Bishop's book, and is as good as Yeats's, it is as good there as it is anywhere else."[81]

Herbert Boardman, Hadley's biographer, claims that Hadley's art was universal in scope but typically American as well, because his music reflected the drive, youthful enthusiasm, optimism, and idealism of contemporary America.[82] We also have the estimation of James P. Dunn, program annotator for the Manhattan Symphony, who wrote in 1918: "Generally speaking, I have always looked upon him as the foremost American composer in point of actual achievement. To me it has always seemed that he painted his musical canvases with such a colossal sweep, gave utterance to ideas of such deep significance and commanded such a gorgeous opulence of tonal expression as to dwarf into insignificance the efforts of most of his contemporaries."[83]

Hadley was a prolific composer and perhaps wrote too facilely. Yet his melodic creations once sounded fresh; his expression, sincere; his orchestral effects, striking; and his technical attainments, impressive to contemporary listeners. Hadley tried his hand at every genre, from songs and operettas to symphonies and operas. Assuredly, several of his around two hundred songs are among the best written in the United States during the early twentieth century. Amy Lowell felt honored when he set her poem "In a Taxi," saying that others had told her that the music was "very beautiful."[84] William Treat Upton praises the technical adroitness, fitting harmonization, and solid workmanship of Hadley's settings, singling out "The Time of Parting" (1921), the poem by Rabindrath Tagore, and "Colloque Sentimentale" (1923), the poem by Paul Verlaine, for special mention. The latter, he states, bears comparison with Debussy's setting: "While it lacks the eerie quality of the French song (particularly Debussy's organ point maintained with such uncanny effect throughout the entire ghostly conversation), [it] is in most respects . . . superior. Not so extreme in its characterization, it still obtains the appropriate atmosphere and is a fine, musicianly song. *The Time of Parting* is less involved, less dramatic in treatment, but no less effective."[85]

The first work to attract national attention was the Symphony No. 1 in D Minor, *Youth and Life* (1897). Enhancing its attractiveness for Hadley's generation were plentiful and frankly stated tunes, rhythmic vigor, and imaginative orchestration. As usual for Hadley, extramusical perceptions, here idealistic, inspired the work. He explained that when he sat down to

compose, emotional ideas came first, musical themes after. The first movement concerns the good and evil in life; the second, the remorse felt over
wrongdoing, "then a sound of bells, bringing solace with the thought of
aspiration and redemption, then a return of the gloom." In the third movement, young comrades bring happiness; the last movement expresses the
feeling of "achievement, of confidence, power, and hope—a strain that
speaks of love. The thought of gloom and despair is recalled for a moment—but hope and joy return."[86]

The year 1901 saw the birth of the *Herod* Overture and the Second
Symphony. The overture, written to preface a tragedy by Stephen Phillips,
dramatically contrasts a vehement main theme with a disarmingly soothing subsidiary theme. The title page to the score of the Symphony No. 2 in
F Minor, *The Four Seasons,* states that the music won the Paderewski and the
New England Conservatory Prizes.[87] It is an attractive work, completely
within the bounds of common practice, with some modal effects and
gapped-scale melodies. He says the idea of writing the music first came
during an Adirondacks hunting trip in October 1898. At first intended for
a symphonic poem, his thoughts were soon channeled into the "Autumn"
movement of the symphony. He wrote the other movements during their
respective seasons. For example, he was in an Indian canoe on Lake
Saranac on a summer night when the nocturnal material for "Summer"
occurred to him.[88] The premiere took place in New York in December
1901.

The first movement, "Winter," aims only for the moods, not a description, of the wintry season. A massive, passionate, Tchaikovsky-like first
theme, in full orchestra, evokes the stormy soul of winter. Afterward, four
horns introduce a melancholic subsidiary theme, including a number of
poignant appoggiaturas (a "longing for spring," perhaps?).[89] The ternary-
form second movement, "Spring," opens with a flute melody ("nature's
awakening"?) that suggests a British American folk connection. We hear
more than a little intimation of Chadwick's style. The affecting "Summer"
is slow and like something that Chadwick of the Second Symphony and
MacDowell of the *Indian* Suite might have written. Mysterious harmonies
of ambiguous tonality introduce the movement, followed by a flute, then
an oboe, on a syncopated melody featuring a Scotch snap. The program
notes state that the opening is an imagining of a midnight lake scene and
the tune an "Indian Love Song." "Autumn" completes the symphony. A
sadly singing legato theme ("destiny"?) in the lower instruments sounds
against a staccato sixteenth-note violin filigree (the "falling leaves"?). An

allegro molto brings cheer with hunting calls in the horns. The music expands the new theme, until three staccato chords halt the merriment and return the music to the grave opening (the "inevitability of the coming winter"?). Farwell praised the work, finding in it "a delicate balance, within the classical form, of romanticism, impressionism, and symbolism. It is romanticism that predominates, however, although such distinct impressions as those of wintry blasts and falling autumn leaves are happy and noteworthy features of the work. The languor and sun-warmed luxuriance of mid-summer finds poignant and beautiful expression."[90]

A relaxed and carefree *In Bohemia* Overture dates from 1902; the *Oriental* Suite, from the next year. The last is acceptably suggestive of the melodies and rhythms of the Eastern world, but of course is written in Hadley's manner.

Hadley wrote *Salome,* a tone poem for orchestra after Oscar Wilde's tragedy, in 1905–6. The Boston Symphony premiered it in 1907. Critics considered it his best work up to that time. Orchestras in America and Europe took it up. Hadley apparently completed the score before Richard Strauss's drama of the same name was produced. A preface to the published score gives the program: Salome hears the voice of John the Baptist. She sees and loves him and finds her love rejected. She dances the Dance of the Seven Veils for Herod, who grants her wish for the Baptist's head as a reward. Herod is repulsed by Salome's lovemaking to the severed head and has her executed.[91]

The piece begins slowly and peacefully, with a languid depiction of a moonlit site just outside Herod's palace. A theme pinpointing Salome's desire for John the Baptist sounds. The more animated second section centers on loud trombones declaiming the Baptist theme. The third section dramatically contrasts the two themes. Then comes "Salome's Dance," in triple time. Next, we hear Herod's trumpet theme, a brief reference to the Baptist's trombone theme, and again Salome's love theme. A fiery fast passage indicates her psychotic passion, soon followed by music marking her death.

His Symphony No. 3 in B Minor, op. 60, was written mostly in Italy in the summer of 1906 and premiered in Berlin in 1907. He attaches no program but admits that the second movement was suggested to him while hearing distant church bells near Monza.[92] Nothing in it matches the outsized fancies of the previous two symphonies. The first movement's sonata-allegro form shows the usual deployment of two themes, one intrepid, in strings and trumpets, the other quieter, in the strings. The moderately slow second movement depicts an engaging pastoral scene, with faraway bells chiming the announcement of a devotional hour. The third movement is a conventional scherzo but difficult to play. Its capricious principal theme incorporates a birdsong he heard in the Adirondack woodlands.[93] The compact finale sounds brilliant and affirmative in spirit.

Popular for several years after it was written in 1908, *The Culprit Fay*, a Rhapsody for Orchestra, op. 62, stems directly out of incidents related in Joseph Rodman Drake's poem of the same title. It won the thousand-dollar prize of the National Federation of Music Clubs in 1909. Its incidents take place on a summer midnight. A fairy has dared love a mortal maiden, and the fairy king sits in judgment. Tasks are assigned the prisoner in order to win redemption. He successfully completes his assignments and is welcomed back into the company of his peers. General merriment breaks out until the cock crows to signal the coming of dawn and the end of the festivities. The nighttime opening, including the motive assigned to the culprit fay, reminds us a little of *Salome*.[94] In a music review published in 1938, Elliott Carter praised both *The Culprit Fay* and *In Bohemia*, finding that "both achieve a real character and a deeply felt quality that in spite of their lack of strong individuality make them worth hearing more often in our orchestral concerts."[95]

Hadley's tone poem *Lucifer*, inspired by Joost van den Vondel's poem *Lucifer*, saw the light in 1910 but waited until June 1914 and the Norfolk (Connecticut) Festival for a first performance. Five themes supply its primary materials: (1) Gabriel's trumpet announcement of God's message of love; (2) Lucifer's theme of baleful cast; (3) a hymn from angelic voices; (4) music assuring peace and happiness; and (5) a theme of joy and victory during and after the battle with the forces of Lucifer. The work revolves around Lucifer's revolt and the heavenly hosts that gather, oppose the evil legions, and eventually prove triumphant.[96]

The Symphony No. 4 in D Minor, op. 64, *North, East, South and West*, of 1911, like *Lucifer*, received its premier performance at the Norfolk Festival, but three years earlier, in June 1911. It aims to capture the moods of the frozen North, the Far East, the southern black ragtime of the United States, and the American West and Pacific Coast. The profusion of well-known materials—shivery brass chords, picturesque exoticisms, syncopated rag, Indian tunes and rhythms—produce a carnival spirit designed to please listeners. Everything is expertly whipped together and served for the delectation of the audience. There is more of the pleasant suite, less of the serious symphony, about the music.

A competently written *Othello* Overture had its premiere in 1919. Classical in structure, earnest in character, and slightly daring in harmonic usage, it is a lesser work than *Salome*. A tone poem, *The Ocean,* came out in 1921. Hadley's music follows portions of the poem "Ocean Ode" by Louis Anspacher. Listening to it, one is reminded of Wagner and Strauss. The first part has an ocean motive of three chords. The motive returns throughout, normally sounding energetic and threatening, except at the conclusion, where the brass section plays it softly. The poetically charming second part introduces a "sea sprites" motive played by three flutes. The final part depicts the serene ocean that endures through all time. *The Ocean* has more satisfying and enjoyable music than have *Lucifer* and *Othello.*

The *Streets of Pekin* Suite, for orchestra, in seven short movements, was heard in 1930. Pleasant enough with its pseudo-Oriental music, it at times calls Puccini's *Madama Butterfly* to mind. The *San Francisco* Suite for orchestra followed in 1931. The three movements are labeled "The Harbor," "Chinese Quarters," and "Mardi Gras." Three years later came a bit of unabashed fluff, the *Scherzo Diabolique,* which entertains the listener with a depiction of a speeding automobile and the crash that follows.

A last major instrumental composition was completed in 1935, the Symphony No. 5 in C Minor, op. 140, *Connecticut-Tercentenary.* Hadley conducted it at the Norfolk Festival in June of that year. The initial movement has the title "1625" and makes reference to American Indian music and to the Doxology. The idyllic slow movement, "1735," features the chorale *Ein Feste Berg.* And the brilliant finale, "1935," brings the audience up to contemporary times. Competently written and highly listenable music results.

Hadley had no compelling desire to compose chamber music. He did produce a violin sonata, two string quartets, and two piano trios, all of them decently written, but his most noteworthy chamber effort was the Quintet in A Minor for Piano and Strings, op. 50, of 1919. The structures of the four movements are traditional ones; the style leans toward that of a slightly updated Brahms or Franck in the outer movements.[97] The zesty piano-led dash of the scherzo is similar to music by Chadwick.

With the one-act *Safie, the Persian,* based on a story by the Englishman Edward Oxenford, Hadley made a trial of operatic writing in 1909, while he was a music director in Mainz. When it was mounted in Mainz, a news item in the *New York Times* stated: "The piece is said to bristle with dramatic situations and Oriental color."[98]

He waited until 1914 to complete his first full-fledged, three-act opera, *Azora: The Daughter of Montezuma,* the libretto by David Stevens. The subject was the advent of Christianity among the Aztecs. The Metropolitan Opera refused to produce it. He tried other countries to no avail. Finally, Cleofante Campanini, director of the Chicago Opera, staged it in December 1917. As was usual in American opera, an inexperienced writer supplied a weak libretto. The Chicago audience heartily approved the work nonetheless. The orchestra is allotted much of the important music. The voices are allowed few set pieces. An occasional American Indian tune gains admittance. The lush harmonies and the discordant music at points of conflict indicate a Straussian influence. Otherwise the style leans toward contemporary Italian operatic styles.

With the one-act *Bianca* of 1917 Hadley went from tragedy to comedy. Carlo Goldini's *La locandiera* (The mistress of the inn) supplied the story, out of which Grant Stewart fashioned a libretto. Although the libretto could have been stronger, it does give greater opportunity for stage action than did that of *Azora*. The Society of American Singers sponsored the first production in New York in October 1918. The setting is a Florence inn; the year, 1670. Bianca is a headstrong young woman, courted by many suitors. She ultimately chooses her faithful servant Fabricio. The orchestra again has a dominant role. The motives allotted to people and situations are attention-grabbing yet have little development. The characters sing in recitative or brief melodic snatches, since much of the text calls for back-and-forth musical dialogue.

Probably his best endeavor at operatic composition was the two-act *Cleopatra's Night,* libretto by Alice Pollock, based on the Théophile Gautier story *Une Nuit de Cléopâtre*. Lafcadio Hearn had published a translation of the Gautier tale in 1882. The Metropolitan Opera Company gave the opera a first performance in January 1920. Chadwick's symphonic poem *Cleopatra* (1904) may have spurred Hadley's musico-dramatic treatment of the subject. In addition, the fashionable decadence of Strauss's opera *Salome* (1905) may have intrigued him. Hadley had visited Egypt and treasured the unusual ambience enveloping the Nile and its riverside cities and towns. Yet he excluded references to Egyptian music from the opera, explaining to William Guard: "I visited all the cafés chantants and native theatres in Cairo, determined to take down some material, but found it all so crude and primitive and atrociously out of tune that I fled the country to seek inspiration from nature."[99] Hadley reveals his lack of sympathy for and ignorance of Egyptian music in this statement.

In the opera, a love-besotted Meïamoun slips into Cleopatra's palace and confronts Cleopatra with the urgency of his passion. Intrigued, she conditionally accepts him: in exchange for one night of lovemaking, he must die at dawn. For the first time in American opera, erotic desire replaces sentimental love; sexual reality, idealized fantasy; Freudian drive, selfless concern for a beloved. The libretto, though weak, shows awareness of the requirements of the operatic stage. It provides Hadley with opportunities for dramatic activity heightened by orchestral scene painting, dance, and heated vocalizing. All of the musical paraphernalia of late Romanticism is brought to bear: chromatically slithering tones, acrid dissonances, augmented-fifth and diminished-fourth intervals, and elastic melodies that shrink or stretch out as needed.[100] Highly effective are Cleopatra's monologue, "My veins seem fill'd with flowing quicksilver," and her blazing song, "I love you." Pleasant contrast is afforded by a good-sized Intermezzo and the dances: one for solo ballerina, another, a sinuous "Dance of the Greek Maidens" and after this, a Middle Eastern–flavored "Dance of the Desert Girls." At the end of the second act, Cleopatra holds the dead Meïamoun to her breast and sings of her regret at his death and of her emptiness, "See, I keep my promise," the most melancholic song of the entire opera. Hadley would write other works for the musical stage, but none would come close to matching the excellence of *Cleopatra's Night*.

In 1922 *Resurgam,* an estimable oratorio for soloists, chorus, and orchestra, came from his pen. The heroic text is by Louise Ayres Garnett. The musical style owes something to Mendelssohn and Brahms, with an added dash of Elgar. The music is mostly convincing, theatrically telling, and one of his more conservative efforts.

His best works—the first four symphonies, *Salome, The Culprit Fay, The Ocean, Bianca, Cleopatra's Night*—won the admiration of his contemporaries and deserve respect in our time.

CHAPTER 10

REDEFINING TRADITION

A nation's traditional and popular music play an important role in defining its musical language. Many musical works have drawn on the songs and dances peculiar to one country: those of Mussorgsky and Russia, Grieg and Norway, Dvořák and Bohemia, Falla and Spain, and Vaughan Williams and England. At the end of the nineteenth century and the beginning of the twentieth, an interest in America's indigenous music aroused composers, performers, and writers on musical matters. *Slave Songs of the United States,* collected by William Francis Allen, Charles Pickard Ware, and Lucy McKim Garrison, came out in 1867. The Jubilee Singers of Fisk University, from 1872 on, were stirring the country with their African American spirituals. The novel sounds of minstrelsy, ragtime, and later blues and jazz were integral to the American scene. Theodore Baker advanced the study of American Indian music with his dissertation *Über die Musik der nordamerikanischen Wilden* (1882). Alice Fletcher's *The Hako: A Pawnee Ceremony* (1904) and Frances Densmore's *Chippewa Music* in two volumes (1910–13) and *Teton Sioux Music* (1918) signaled the concerted effort to collect Indian music. Collectors also occupied themselves with the folk songs of Appalachia and New England.

By the 1850s Louis Moreau Gottschalk had composed piano music that drew on African American, Creole, Latin American, and popular American song and dance. Chadwick was incorporating New England's vernacular idioms into his orchestral and chamber works in the 1880s. The Bohemian composer Dvořák had done the same with African American music while visiting the United States during the 1890s. Edward MacDowell had written an *Indian* Suite in 1895. Harry Burleigh, an African American student of Dvořák, collected minstrel tunes, arranged spirituals, and composed songs and other vocal pieces based on an African American idiom in the early part of the twentieth century. The previous chapter has mentioned Frederick Shepherd Converse and Daniel Gregory Mason as incorporating diverse Americanisms into some of their art music.

In addition, novelists, short-story writers, painters, sculptors, and entertainers were mining the same vein. William Sidney Mount commenced his striking paintings of black musicians in the 1850s. Joel Chandler Harris began to issue his Uncle Remus stories in 1881. Buffalo Bill's Wild West Show, organized in 1883, promoted the exploits of the plainsmen and American Indians. Starting in the 1830s, George Catlin, Karl Bodmer, and Alfred Jacob Miller were making portraits of Indian men and women and graphic portrayals of Indian life, thus bringing an unknown world to Americans of the eastern seaboard and to Europeans.

GILBERT IN PURSUIT OF A NATIONAL MUSIC

The composer Henry Gilbert (1868–1928) and his friend Arthur Farwell (1872–1952) were alert to this nativist movement. They aspired to a distinctively American music, identifiable by its spirit and by the unmistakably indigenous elements that permeated its melody and rhythm. They believed that a usable cultural past and present existed beyond the borders of New England, with Gilbert looking primarily into the lives and music of African Americans and, with Farwell, of American Indians.

They welcomed the invigorating naïveté that was wedded to this native music, in contrast to the world-wise sophistication shown in newer European works. Trying to explain composers like Gilbert and Farwell, Daniel Gregory Mason commented on how they "shared, I think, the intuitive conviction that American music must be more active, restless, humorous and sentimental than European; that to this end it must, or at least might, draw upon naïve elements of folk-song capable of answering and guiding its own naïveté; and that somehow the native style into which its elements were built must be simpler than European styles, more childlike in feeling, yet contented in its childlikeness—in short more naked and unashamed."[1]

A word about Arthur Farwell is necessary, since he and Gilbert worked closely together for several years. Farwell was born in St. Paul, Minnesota, to parents whose families had come originally from New England. Indeed, Farwell's mother was a distant relation of Ralph Waldo Emerson, and his father could trace his family tree back to the John Adams family. Farwell came to the Boston area to study engineering at the Massachusetts Institute of Technology. The playing of the Boston Symphony was a revelation to him. He got caught up in the local music scene and took some musical direction from MacDowell and Chadwick. Most revealing is the comment that Chadwick made in the spring of 1893, when the novice Farwell showed him a sonata he had written; according to Farwell, "Chadwick explained that he would rather have me take him something original like the sonata—not having studied—than to take him something technically perfect—but resembling Mendelssohn or other composers—having studied their works."[2]

Farwell went to Germany and France to continue his music studies, returning to America in 1899. In that year a clerk at Barrett's Old Cornhill Bookshop in Boston showed him a copy of Alice Fletcher's *Indian Story and Song,* and this started his strong interest in American Indian music. At the time that several publishers refused his composition *American Indian Melodies,* he moved to Newton Center, close to Boston, because his parents had relocated there. Bothered by the rejection of his music, he founded the Wa-Wan Press in Newton Center in 1901 to publish the "progressive" American works that standard publishers spurned. Soon thereafter he and Gilbert became friends. They shared their views on how to achieve a national musical identity. Farwell would go in the direction of American Indian music; Gilbert, of African American music. The Wa-Wan Press would continue life for ten years. Farwell moved away from Boston in 1909, when he began writing for *Musical America.*

Henry Gilbert and Arthur Farwell insisted on creative autonomy and displayed singular temperaments. However obstinately they traveled their own divergent roads and sought out their own manner of speaking, they never freed themselves completely from Germanic influences. Gilbert had a musical background. His mother sang, his father played keyboard instruments, and his birthplace was Hadley's Somerville, Massachusetts. Ole Bull's violin playing spurred Gilbert's study of that instrument. He studied theory and composition with George Elbridge Whiting, George H. Howard, and Edward MacDowell. According to Katherine Longyear, it was Gilbert who responded to MacDowell's request for Indian melodies for use in the *Indian* Suite by offering him a few from Theodore Baker's dissertation on American Indian music.[3]

Because Gilbert incompletely assimilated his learning, awkwardness shows in many compositions. Katherine Longyear reports that Arthur Shepherd once told her "that Gilbert realized that his lack of training was a handicap, but that Gilbert preferred to acquire the needed craftsmanship in his own way rather than to risk contamination of his own style." Clifton Furness, who considered Gilbert the first American composer whose work was individual and home-grown, quotes Gilbert as saying: "It has been my aim from the first to write some American, and un-European music: music which shall smack of our home-soil, even though it may be crude."[4]

The heart disease with which Gilbert was born drained his strength. It may have discouraged the field studies that might have followed his interest in the music of African Americans and American Indians. He did manage to visit the Chicago World's Columbian Exposition in 1893, supporting himself with menial work. Here he became acquainted with the music of Asia. At the exposition he also learned about Russian music from Prince Galitzin, a friend of Nicolai Rimsky-Korsakov. Joseph D. Whitney, of the Harvard faculty, sent Gilbert to Europe in 1894 to purchase music scores. In 1901 his legendary cattle boat trip to Paris took place, when he went there to hear Gustave Charpentier's *Louise*.

Gilbert was fortunate in his marriage to Helen Kalischer, for she made his domestic life peaceful and agreeable. Unfortunately, he was not very successful in earning a living. For a while he played the violin in pit orchestras, at dances, and for resort hotel entertainments. Factory work was tried and rejected. He also worked briefly for a printer, a real estate agency, and a music publisher. Eventually, he withdrew to Quincy, Massachusetts, where he tended farm animals.[5] The withdrawal was not a retreat from music. In addition to composing, Gilbert helped Farwell with the running of the Wa-Wan Press. The press would publish a half dozen of his piano pieces and over a dozen of his songs. Gilbert also transcribed Indian music that Edward S. Curtis had collected for volume 6 of *The North American Indian* (1911), acted as associate editor for *The Art of Music* (1916), and sent numerous articles to journals, including the *Musical Quarterly* and the *New Music Review*. Finally, Harvard called on him now and again for lectures on music.

In 1915 Gilbert wrote that though American composers had to learn their art from Europe, their failing was to accept European ideals of beauty. Moreover, most musicians in the United States were European-born, biased against American compositions, and preached only European ideas of beauty to the American public. Having in mind the reception of his own music, he says: "One always feels that music by an American is not wanted, especially if it happens to be *American music*. It is merely tolerated with a sort of good-natured contempt. It is true that American music as such is still very much in its infancy. But an unwelcome child always has a very hard time and sometimes fails to grow up."[6]

He defined himself as a nationalist composer, a seeker of "new rhythms, and piquant and unusual melodic turns, to express something which shall at least be different."[7] However, he cautioned against bizarre rhythms, freakish melodies, needless dissonances, and a cultivation of originality for its own sake, which he considered debilitating factors in most music by modernists. The works of Debussy and Ravel aside, "the musical world of today," he wrote in 1921, "is as prolific of tricksters, conjurors, and tone-jugglers as it ever was. . . . The majority of these lesser composers . . . [try to] astonish rather than delight . . . substitute pretense for worth, and . . . attain an attention-provoking eccentricity rather than to express a genuinely felt emotion."[8] Lastly, he came out forthrightly in favor of humor in music: "Personally I like to laugh, and my sense of humor I conceive to be one of my most precious possessions. . . . The sense of humor is not to be decried or by any means belittled, for, in its highest manifestation, it is at least a first cousin to philosophy. It is a great resource against the continuous ills of life, a shield against the too serious effect of the tragic, and a sovereign remedy and preventive of petty annoyance."[9]

Clifton Furness divides Gilbert's music into three periods.[10] The first period was one of free experimental use of existing musical resources within the confines of the styles that he knew, mainly Germanic, then French. The results are seen in works like the songs from the mid-1890s, on poems of Irish authorship, *Salammbô's Invocation to Tänith* (1902), and the Symphonic Prologue to Synge's *Riders to the Sea* (1904). Furness states that *Salammbô* gave Gilbert celebrity in Russia, where he became an admired American composer.

That Furness's three-period division needs modification is made clear when we come to his second stage. He states that Dvořák stimulated Gilbert to use native American matter, but leaves out the probable influence of the Americanist compositions that Chadwick commenced writing before Dvořák's Symphony *From the New World* (1892–93) and the influence of Chadwick himself, who lived near Gilbert. Moreover, there is an overlap of time between Furness's first two period designations. The *Two Episodes* ("Legend" and "Negro Episode") for orchestra date back to 1895–97. According to Furness, this work was praised by Jules Massenet and hailed in France as the first appearance of "autochthonous American orchestral writing." Subsequently, Gilbert composed the *Comedy Overture* on *Negro Themes* (ca. 1905–10); *The Dance in Place Congo* (ca. 1906–8); *Americanesque* (ca. 1903–8), later given the title of *Humoresque;* the *Negro Rhapsody* (ca. 1912), also known as *Shout;* and several ragtime- and jazz-influenced dances. To be added to Furness's list are two songs that became popular, "The Pirate Song" (1902) and "Fish Wharf Rhapsody" (1909), and some unfocused experimentation with American Indian material.

The last period, claims Furness, constitutes works in a mature, original style that proves that the composer had assimilated the various home-grown idioms. These pieces Gilbert "attempted to make expressive of American optimism, youthfulness, and buoyancy." Four compositions are cited: the opera *The Fantasy in Delft* (ca. 1915), *Symphonic Piece* (1925), *Strife* (1910–25), and *Nocturne, after Walt Whitman* (ca. 1925).

What distinguishes Gilbert's music after 1904 was his goal to speak with definiteness and honesty as he employed the vocabulary and rhythms of workaday musical sounds characteristic of America. The music tends to be spare, abrupt, rough, and out at elbows. He appears to be asserting a new and forceful point of view and to be pioneering the use of the vernacular in music. His friend Farwell points out that his technique, though resourceful and showing a rich imagination, often lacked finish—a failing, possibly, but also the source of its attractiveness. The unevenness was a direct outcome of what Farwell tells us was Gilbert's disdain for tradition and fashion, "whether in art, dress, or speech," and his struggle to attain artistic freedom.[11]

An examination of Gilbert's scores reveals melodies that are tonal, mostly diatonic, and normally suggesting a connection with the vernacular. Harmony is triadic, usually in accord with nineteenth-century practices. He occasionally uses tones of the ninth or the eleventh or chromatically altered chords. Rhythms are clear-cut. Duple time predominates; triple time is much less frequent. Modulations can be abrupt; sections of a movement are usually kept quite distinct. Orchestral pieces offer top-quality displays of instrumental color. The writing of descriptive rather than abstract compositions prevails.[12]

Salammbô's Invocation to Tänith, for voice and orchestra, op. 6, was composed in 1902 and builds on Flaubert's novel *Salammbô* (1863). With this piece, the composer reveals his awareness of contemporary French music—in calling up the atmosphere in Flaubert's novel, in the imaginative orchestration, and in the coloristic harmony. Gilbert's composition is impressive but does not try to capture the ambience of Flaubert's ancient Carthage. The piece was a serious attempt to discover alternatives to the Germanic style from which Gilbert was trying to break away.

Celticisms were another avenue of escape from the Germanic grid-lock. In this regard, he had the examples of MacDowell's Piano Sonata No. 4, *Keltic,* of 1901, and several characteristic piano pieces, such as "An Old Love Story," no. 1 of *Fireside Tales* (1902), to encourage him.[13] Songs like the pathetic "Lament of Deirdre" found him leaning in a Celtic direc-tion. The Symphonic Prologue to *Riders to the Sea,* a one-act play by John Millington Synge, was an ambitious effort. Composed in 1904, it was revised in 1913. He had first written a 94-measure prelude, requiring only a chamber ensemble, for a Twentieth-Century Club performance in 1905. He then expanded the music into the 164-measure Prologue of 1913, scored for a full orchestra and performed at the MacDowell Festival at Peterborough, New Hampshire, in 1914. Gilbert states that the music encompasses two dominant moods from the play: one elemental and remote like the ageless sea, the other, the representation of human lamen-tation.[14] He draws on an old Irish melody, which pervades most measures of the score, thus making the work almost monothematic. The mood of darkness, anguish, and surrender is always present. On balance, it is a stronger work than *Salammbô's Invocation.* After hearing the Prologue, Philip Hale wrote in the *Boston Herald* on 21 February 1919: "This Pro-logue is impressive music. It owes nothing to Munich or Paris. . . . He thinks for himself; he belongs to no school. . . . Even his crudities, show-ing a certain ruggedness that is not wholly displeasing, are those of a virile thinker."[15]

A third alternative to the Germanic style lay in the use of the Ameri-can vernacular. Gilbert believed that folk tunes were valuable musical ker-nels from which a significant work could develop. If the composer used these kernels well, Gilbert believed, he could present "in an intensified, enlarged, and extended manner the *spirit* of the original folk-tune."[16] He saw the futility in treating traditional music with scholarly respect. To cre-ate an artistically viable composition, the artist had to manipulate his material. After Gilbert tentatively tried Celtic folk song, he turned to indigenous American song. In January 1896 the Boston Ladies' Symphony Orchestra performed "Legend"; in December 1896 the Manuscript Soci-ety of New York performed "Legend" and "Negro Episode"; in 1897 Gilbert himself was the publisher of both pieces as *Two Episodes* for orches-tra.[17] "Legend" has lovely lyricism and is indebted to the music of MacDowell. (The first movement of MacDowell's *Indian* Suite is also enti-tled "Legend.") The composer's note prefacing the "Negro Episode" states that two Negro musical ideas are used, both taken from W. F. Allen's col-lection *Slave Songs of the United States.* The second, "Nobody Knows the

Trouble I See, Lord!," makes its initial appearance in measure 15. Both episodes are miniatures, satisfying in their own right, and the modest offerings of a still diffident composer.

Americanesque, so called at its initial appearance in 1903, was renamed *Humoresque on Negro-Minstrel Tunes,* op. 5, when published in 1913.[18] This pioneering attempt at a national music is constructed around three minstrel tunes: "Zip Coon," "Dearest May," and "Don't Be Foolish, Joe." The orchestral piece puts Gilbert's comic faculty on display. In the note that prefaces the score Gilbert writes of "the vigor and heart-touching qualities" of minstrel song, claiming it approaches "true folksong." He adds that he was trying for the comedy, pathos, and mirth inherent in the minstrel show of old.

The music from beginning to end can also be interpreted as poking fun at the decorum of priggish high-cultural compositions. It revels in vulgarities that genteel Americans condemned. The satirical mode, after all, had been a telling function of nineteenth-century minstrelsy, which had relished the drollness, the foolishness, and the piteousness in human behavior. At the time he was composing the *Humoresque,* the French and Russian figurative painters known as Les Fauves, the wild beasts, were active in Europe. Like a Fauvist painting, *Humoresque* sounds sturdy, clothes itself in starkly simple musical colors, and contains more than a modicum of energy. A slow middle section, where horns, later woodwinds, and still later violins intone a melody sounding like a sentimental plantation ballad of the 1850s, contrasts the robust dances of the outer sections.

As early as 1905 Gilbert was toiling on an opera based on the Uncle Remus tales of Joel Chandler Harris (1848–1908). The libretto came to him from Charles Johnston, who had been a member of the Bengal Civil Service but was now in retirement.[19] Gilbert, of course, was also aware of two MacDowell piano pieces: "From Uncle Remus," no. 7 of *Woodland Sketches,* and "Of Bre'r Rabbit," no. 2 of *Fireside Tales.* The Georgia-born Harris had worked on a plantation where he encountered a great deal of African American folklore. He was attracted by the animal legends through which southern blacks reconciled themselves to their circumstances. Interpreted by the sympathetic Harris, these tales tried to maintain the viewpoints, speech patterns, and traditional knowledge of African Americans. Unfortunately, Gilbert failed to acquire the musical rights for the opera because they were already assigned to another composer. He then recast the prelude to the opera into the *Comedy Overture on Negro Themes,* which was completed in 1909. It was heard at an Open-Air Mall

Concert in New York City in 1910, and then performed by the Boston Symphony in 1911.

The entire overture is in five sections and is built on three brief motives and one melody of eight measures taken from traditional African American song and dance.[20] The first section, featherweight and jocose, has music fashioned from two phrases found in Charles L. Edward's *Bahama Songs and Stories*. The leisurely second section contains the only complete melody, taken from a work song of Mississippi roustabouts and stevedores, "I'se Gwine to Alabammy, Oh," found in W. F. Allen's *Slave Songs of the United States*. The third section is an effervescent fugue on the start of the spiritual "Old Ship of Zion," from Jeanette Robinson Murphy's *Southern Thoughts for Northern Thinkers*. It ends with this theme played in augmentation by the brass and interwoven with "I'se Gwine to Alabammy, Oh." Next, a brief sixteen-measure passage returns the music to the mood of the beginning, followed by a return of the melody. The work closes on merry allusions to ragtime.

The syncopated rhythms and vivaciousness of the opening section, the entertaining fugue that describes Bre'r Fox's chasing after Bre'r Rabbit, the majestic restatement of the spiritual "Old Ship of Zion," and the spontaneous feeling of the whole did cause music circles to talk about Gilbert. A few people considered the piece undignified; most freely responded "to the youthful vigor, the racy humor and the romantic nature of this new music," states Olin Downes. Philip Hale writes: "The overture stirred the blood of the audience. All rejoiced in hearing a new voice with something to say and an original way of saying it. The fugue did not dampen the interest of the hearers, for the old form was used with dramatic spirit. No wonder that the audience, surprised and delighted, was for once in no hurry to leave the hall. . . . The overture is distinctively, but not bumptiously, not apologetically, American."[21]

Several orchestras in the United States took up the *Comedy Overture*. Moreover, the Russian composer Alexander Glazunov found the work "simple, original and powerful, well orchestrated and melodious" and recommended it to Reinhold Glière for performance in Russia.[22] Ivan Narodny states that when performed there it "struck a note absolutely new to Russian audiences. One Russian critic wrote: 'Gilbert is a composer who does not seek after artificial effects and forced phrases. . . . His music is spontaneous, natural and beautiful. One can feel the powerful individuality of the American composer in his direct and classic message. Though the work is based on negro music . . . it does not belong to the class of popular compositions.'" Later, Narodny quotes Glière as saying: "It is melodic, pleasing, and well orchestrated. America should be proud of a genius like Gilbert."[23]

The references to ragtime in the *Comedy Overture* are not isolated ones. Around 1906 he started writing a number of keyboard dances in ragtime rhythm, several of them originally intended for the Uncle Remus opera. Among the dances are the three in *American Dances* of 1906, the five in *Negro Dances* of 1914, and the six in *A Rag Bag* of 1927. They are close to the style of Scott Joplin. Thirty years after they were written, Elliott Carter reexamined the *American Dances* and *Negro Dances*. He found them "delightful," rich "in homey American humor," and "without pretence."[24]

Gilbert achieved his greatest success with *The Dance in Place Congo,* which New York's Metropolitan Opera premiered as a pantomime-ballet, alongside Cadman's opera *Shanewis,* on 23 March 1918. After this performance, it was usually presented as an orchestral tone poem at symphony concerts. Gilbert had enjoyed George Washington Cable's article "The Dance in the Place Congo," dealing with pre–Civil War life in New Orleans, published in *Century* magazine in February 1886. The Place Congo was a square where slaves had gathered once a week to enjoy themselves. The article's musical illustrations, especially of the "Bamboula" dance, excited Gilbert. He turned to writing a piece that would capture "certain dominant moods" he had garnered from his reading.[25] One wonders if Gilbert was familiar with Louis Moreau Gottschalk's piano work *Bamboula, danse de nègres,* published in 1849, based on the same tune.

The first section is somber and features a musical phrase from Cable's article that makes a protest against slavery. Little by little the rhythms of a dance invade the music until "the theme of the Bamboula is ripped out in its triumphant vulgarity by the full orchestra."[26] A climax results, followed by quiet lyric music, which depicts the tender activities, including love-making, of the slaves. This section, too, mounts to a climax. A barbaric free fantasy on the Bamboula music comes next, with the dance finally combining with the other musical motives. A bell sounds, calling the slaves back to their quarters. The dance disintegrates; a cry of protest rises, and with it, despair. Fragments of musical remembrances are heard until a pause interrupts the music. At the end, the tragic cry returns in the full orchestra. The bumpiness and seeming artlessness of Gilbert's music is present in this piece. Yet the rhythm is often complex. The harmony has a bite. Orchestration is brilliant.

Gilbert made a final use of African American music in a major work when he wrote the *Negro Rhapsody (Shout)* for performance at the Litchfield County Festival in Norfolk, Connecticut, on 5 June 1913. The "shout" was a powerfully felt religious dance of African American slaves, associated with hand clapping, foot stamping, and a shuffling gait executed to the music of exuberant spirituals. Gilbert's rhapsody starts off with a wild dance based on the spiritual "Where Do You Think I Found My Soul?" The second section uses the touching melody "I'll Hear the Trumpet Sound."[27] The "shout" recurs and achieves a feverish climax. An agitated drum roll sounds. At the end, wind instruments intone "I'll Hear the Trumpet Sound." The agitation subsides; grandeur increases as the music depicts a yearning for spiritual enlightenment.

The close of Gilbert's American period came not with an African American but an Indian piece, *Indian Sketches,* an orchestral suite in six movements: "Prelude," "Invocation," "Song of the Wolf," "Camp Dance," "Nocturne," and "Snake Dance." The work was started in 1911, but the premiere did not take place until March 1921, when the Boston Symphony Orchestra gave it a hearing. As mentioned earlier in the chapter, Gilbert had transcribed Indian music from the phonographic cylinders that Edward S. Curtis had collected for volume 6 of *The North American Indian*. He then examined other collections of Indian music. Although he considered most Indian music to be monotonous, he found some of it "striking and piquant." This work was intended to suggest the untamed primitivism of Indian life, in a series of mood pictures arising from fragments of Indian music.[28] The best of the suite is in the first three movements: the half-civilized emotion of the first, followed by the simple religiosity of the second, followed in turn by the sad call of the Kutenai. The last three movements are more conventional: a pleasant and predictable group dance, an amorphous waterside song of night, and a Hopi prayer dance.

Gilbert realized that the interest in works completely given over to traditional African American and Indian music was fading after 1915 and especially after 1920. Most of his music of this type he had begun before 1915. He himself was also looking for other avenues to explore. His new works now took a different orientation. He began a one-act opera in 1915 that had nothing to do with American Indians or African Americans, *The Fantasy in Delft*. He kept working at the music over the next four years. The libretto came from Thomas P. Robinson, an architect and writer-member of George Pierce Baker's "47 Workshop" at Harvard University, which was actively encouraging and producing plays by students.[29] The locale was Holland in the seventeenth century. The story involved two young women who were trying to get around their aunt in order to continue to see the young men they fancied. The finished composition was "delicate, poetic, and humorous," according to the several knowledgeable people who carefully read through the score.[30] Gilbert offered it to the Metropolitan Opera Company, which rejected it. Giuseppe Marinuzzi, the orchestra conductor of the Chicago Opera, in 1920 considered it the finest opera by an American that he had seen and wanted to produce it. He returned to Italy in 1921, and with his departure from Chicago any interest in producing the opera died. Otto Luening says that, when associated with the Opera in Our Language Foundation, he had studied the score of *The Fantasy in Delft* and found the music highly praiseworthy, but unfortunately, the Foundation "lacked the resources for production."[31] Gilbert never saw his opera produced on the stage.

In 1920 George Pierce Baker, who had originally urged Robinson to write the libretto for *The Fantasy in Delft,* was put in charge of the Pilgrim Tercentenary Pageant commemoration of the founding of Plymouth, Massachusetts. Along with Gilbert, other composers who were asked to write music for the celebration included Chadwick, Foote, Kelley, Converse, and Hill. Gilbert was responsible for the first of the pageant's four episodes. After fulfilling his commission, Gilbert reshaped his contribution into a concert composition for orchestra, Suite from *The Pilgrim Tercentenary Pageant.* The Boston Symphony performed it on 31 March 1922. In two parts, the first consists of a "Prelude and Norse Scene"; the second starts with a "French and Indian Pantomime," goes on to an "Indian Dance," and concludes with "Pestilence." The "Prelude," despite its brevity, communicates strength. The "Norse Scene" shows awareness of Grieg's music and MacDowell's Piano Sonata No. 3, *Norse.* At the same time, something definitely Gilbert's own is evident. Quite different, the "Pantomime" music brings joy to the listener, owing to its generous, forthright, and sincere expression. The "Dance" embodies a notable wildness of spirit.

Philip Hale reviewed the Boston Symphony concert in the *Boston Herald,* 1 April 1922. Gilbert is "singularly fortunate" in the "Pestilence" section, writes Hale, where he illustrates "desolation without falling into the abomination of desolation." Hale finds the suite to be "more than picturesque." It "conveys the feeling without the aid of any program; there is the hopeless, despairing, tragic note. There is this to be added: in these episodes Mr. Gilbert gains his effects concisely, with a few strokes. Only in the Norse episode does he grow somewhat diffuse."

During 1925 Gilbert was hard at work on the *Symphonic Piece,* whose Boston premiere came in February 1926. The composer said it was non-programmatic and originally intended to became the first movement of a symphony. Echoing the sentiments of Walt Whitman, he writes:

> My constant aim . . . has been to write some *American* music—i.e., some music which would not naturally have been written in any other country, and which should reflect, or express, certain aspects of the American character, or spirit, as felt by myself. That spirit, as I see it, is energetic—optimistic—nervous—impatient of restraint— and in its highest aspect, a mighty protest against the benumbing traditions of the past. This new birth—renaissance—of the human spirit, which is America, is a joyous, wildly shouting demonstration. Plenty of jingoism, vulgarity, and "Hurrah boys!" attaches to it, but the spirit of the new-birth underlies all, for him who can see it.

He says the first theme has a "Hurrah boys!" character; the second theme resembles, but only resembles, Foster's "Old Folks at Home," with suggestions of "The Arkansas Traveler" inserted at intervals.[32] The Boston audience responded enthusiastically to the music.

In all probability it was the Whitmanesque *Symphonic Piece* that the Boston Symphony performed in 1926 at New York's Carnegie Hall, where Daniel Gregory Mason says he encountered Gilbert: "He rose on my approach, and standing there in full sight and hearing of many neighbors began to tell me, in no measured terms, how inadequately his piece had been rehearsed. I tried to put on a little soft pedal, to make extenuations or qualifications, but in vain. It was an American piece, and he was telling the world it hadn't been rehearsed enough."[33] This Gilbert work possibly encouraged Mason to work on his *Chanticleer* Overture in 1926.

Gilbert was more explicit in acknowledging his regard for Whitman in his *Nocturne, after Walt Whitman* (1926). Pierre Monteux conducted its premiere in Philadelphia in March 1928. The Whitman passage he had in mind was:

> I am he that walks with the tender and growing night;
> I call to the earth and sea half-held by the night.
> Press close, bare-bosom'd night!
> Press close, magnetic, nourishing night!

> Night of south winds! Night of the large few stars!
> Still, nodding night! Mad, naked summer night![34]

Gilbert wrote a letter to Lawrence Gilman, saying: "My composition was written in 1926. I've always wanted to write something on that beautiful passage from Whitman. . . . That piece is filled with melody; in fact, it is one long melody from beginning to end. Melody is, I believe, about nine-tenths of music, anyway. . . . I have heard so many of the devilishly clever, uncannily ingenious, but dry and soulless musical concoctions which are all the style nowadays that I desired to give myself the satisfaction of making an individual protest against all this super-intellectual, modernistic tendency. So I wrote the *Nocturne*."[35]

The music has the effect of an idyll, charming in its simplicity. The listener hears a long hymnlike melody not unlike Paine's and Chadwick's workings in a psalmodic vein, and whose equivalent also occurs in the writing of the contemporary English school of composers. Now and again countermelodic activity takes place. However, no strong rhythms appear alongside the ever-expanding lyricism. When the composition arrives at the recapitulation, the passage reminds us of the early "Legend" of *Two Episodes*. Both have a similar gentle beauty and innocent tranquillity. Yet the "Legend" was a deed of youth, and here the composer is mature, technically secure, and individual.

A final work was completed just before his death, the Suite for Chamber Orchestra, commissioned by the Elizabeth Sprague Coolidge Foundation. Gilbert finished the music in 1927. Nicolas Slonimsky and the Chamber Orchestra of Boston played it for the first time in April 1928. The first movement, "Prelude," has little complexity and resembles a study for violins. The second movement, "Spiritual," draws on the style of an African American spiritual without actually quoting one. The last movement, "Fantasy," seems mostly a dance laced with popular tunes and ragtime rhythms. Gilbert died thirteen months after the premiere.

Gilbert revealed a great individuality in his compositions. His music can sound rough. He knew it did but would not change it. What naïveté it had he considered a virtue. Standing out in everything he wrote was its sincerity. He led the way in the use of African American music, ragtime, and jazz in artistic compositions. He experimented with American Indian material. With all his might, he tried to give an American character to a majority of his works; here, too, he led the way. Beginning with *The Fantasy in Delft,* a mature and distinctive style emerged, American to the hilt, but not dependent on any one native source.

HILL IN PURSUIT OF A FASTIDIOUS MUSIC

Edward Burlingame Hill (1872–1960) and Daniel Gregory Mason were students at Harvard when they engaged in an experimental activity similar to one engaged in by Charles Ives and his father. Charles Ives went on to employ what he had learned in his music. The experiment was of momentary interest to Hill and Mason, entertaining but not artistically manageable. Mason states:

> Hill and I would sometimes venture further afield, into Boston drawing rooms or studios, to regale our friends with music, two-hand or four—serious or frivolous. One of our favorite battle-horses was *Between Two Bands,* a graphic representation of one march (E. B. H. in the treble) beginning very near and loud, and gradually disappearing into space and *pianissimo,* while a different march (D. G. M. in the bass) would begin very far and soft and equally gradually approach into deafening *fortissimo.* There was a crucial moment when both bands were about equidistant, supremely relished by us if not always by our audience.[36]

When Hill spoke artistically, he wished not to recreate the clash of two unregulated independent musical streams but to employ a more precise language and to adhere to disciplined techniques.

Hill was born in Cambridge, Massachusetts. His grandfather, Thomas Hill, had been president of Harvard. His father was a Harvard professor of chemistry. Music making was constant at his home as he grew up. W. F. Apthorp, the music critic, came there to play the German masterpieces, especially Bach's; his father loved to sing the lieder of Schubert and Franz. His father was a friend of John Knowles Paine. Paine became Hill's teacher in music composition, and it was Paine's and MacDowell's influence that he felt strongly at first. Some dabbling in Russian and African American music also took place. He later studied with Chadwick at the New England Conservatory, Arthur Whiting in New York, and Charles-Marie Widor in Paris. Perhaps it was during the course of his sojourn in Paris (1898) that Hill initially felt the influence of Claude Debussy and Maurice Ravel.

Several home influences would also direct his attention toward French music, both as he grew up and after he returned from Europe to join the Harvard faculty. Charles Martin Loeffler, born in 1861, possibly in Alsace, joined the Boston Symphony as a violinist in 1881 and over several decades composed music in a Russian-leaning French style. To name one work, *La*

Mort de Tintagiles (1897) used an advanced harmonic language, delicately realized orchestral textures, and a viola d'amore to capture the atmosphere of an eerie play by the Symbolist writer Maurice Maeterlinck. Georges Longy arrived from France in 1898 to play oboe with the Boston Symphony. He organized the Longy Club in 1900 to provide Greater Boston audiences with excellently performed French wind music. Longy conducted the Boston Orchestral Club from 1899 to 1913, introducing many new French compositions. The Boston Opera Company put on several French operas, as well as Debussy's cantata *L'Enfant prodigue*. After World War I arrived, Karl Muck was forced to relinquish the conductorship of the Boston Symphony and a players' strike caused the dismissal of more than thirty players. Two French conductors, Henri Rabaud (1918–19) and Pierre Monteux (1919–24), came after Muck. Monteux especially made a major effort to rebuild the orchestra, as did Serge Koussevitzky, who took over in 1924. Orchestral membership ceased to be dominated by Central Europeans, and orchestral programs featured much more French and Russian music, not least being the works of Debussy, Ravel, and Stravinsky.

Edward Ballantine, Hill's associate in the Harvard music department, wrote in the *Boston Evening Transcript,* 25 May 1940, that Hill was one of the first Americans to study thoroughly the advanced contemporary composers of France and to value the teaching abilities of Nadia Boulanger. After he joined the Harvard music faculty, he urged his students to continue their music studies with her in Paris, and thus set in motion the departure of young American composers for Paris, beginning with Virgil Thomson. Hill himself stated: "I was interested in French music when it was regarded as intensely radical, and trust that I have a liberal attitude towards Stravinsky, Schönberg and Hindemith."[37] Such a point of view distinguishes him from Converse, Mason, Hadley, and Gilbert. At Harvard he gave courses on orchestration, about which he was expert, and on modern French music (d'Indy, Fauré, Debussy, and Ravel). Among his students were Virgil Thomson, Randall Thompson, Walter Piston, Elliott Carter, Ross Lee Finney, Irving Fine, Arthur Berger, and Leonard Bernstein.

As a teacher and composer, Hill played a significant role in promoting a more receptive attitude toward non-German twentieth-century styles. He constructed his own works clearly and logically, even to the smallest detail. At the same time, the emotional substance of the music came across as warm and expressive, however fastidious his approach. French Impressionism was a springboard for his creativity, not the central focus of his efforts. He eventually adapted what he learned from the French to American usages, especially after 1920. By the time he composed *Lilacs,* in 1927, whatever Impressionism still lingered seems more American and personal than French. By then, his music with its judiciously conceived merging of tones and feeling was emanating from a nature that was essentially contemplative.

The earliest compositions, written for piano, show the influence of MacDowell. In 1907 he completed his cantata *Nuns of the Perpetual Adoration,* for women's voices and orchestra, to a poem by Ernest Dowson. It proceeds from beginning to end almost entirely in lockstep homophony. After hearing an English performance in 1911, Ernest Newman praised its orchestration, "delicately poetical inspiration," and "half mystic, half passionate mood."[38] *Jack Frost in Mid-Summer,* a "pantomime" for orchestra, came out in 1908, and *Pan and the Star,* a "pantomime" for orchestra and women's voices, in 1914. Both works were praised for their expert orchestration, rich sound, and imaginative design.

Hill really broke out on his own with the symphonic poem based on a work by Stephen Phillips, *The Parting of Lancelot and Guinevere,* op. 22, completed in 1915 and premiered in St. Louis on 31 December 1915. MacDowell's symphonic poem *Lancelot and Elaine,* composed in 1888, may have tempted Hill to try his hand. Its lean, incisive, concentrated, and to-the-point language sounds very different from the MacDowell work and reveals the influence of French music and aesthetics. After a brief introduction, the English horn plays Guinevere's motive of painful longing. The motive is expanded upon with increasing urgency up to the onset of Lancelot's robust theme in the trumpets. An episode based on the Guinevere motive follows, containing Lancelot's reflections about his love for the queen.[39] Dramatic conflict begins with the parting of the lovers and reaches a climax. The music quiets down and changes into an epilogue with the melody given to the clarinets over triplet figures in the cellos and violas.

Abbreviated motives slowly come together to form larger sections. The resultant mosaiclike patterns struck critics as representative of an ultramodern musical style. H. T. Parker writes:

> Short and impinging motives characterize Lancelot, Guinevere and, as it seems in the epilogue, their fate. These motives are not developed and interwoven in intricate polyphony, saturated with harmonic elaboration or drenched in instrumental color in the fashion

of . . . the Straussian generation. In the newer and current mode, which flows out of Paris rather than Munich, they are wrought, bit by bit, into a fabric of tones that is more sensitive and incisive, that seeks harmonic subtlety rather than opulence; that prefers sharp or shaded instrumental tints to ornate vesture; that relies more upon adroit modulation and sharp-set juxtaposition than upon large and emphatic manipulation of the musical mass; that addresses itself to the comprehending mind and the sympathetic imagination of the hearer rather than to his nervous excitement.[40]

If *The Parting of Lancelot and Guinevere* showed Hill modifying his style toward general French musical practices, the two *Stevensoniana* Suites demonstrate that he has definitely gone over to the methods pioneered by Debussy and Ravel. The suites, nevertheless, are not imitations but independent artistic entities. Poems from Robert Louis Stevenson's *A Child's Garden of Verses* supplied the stimulation. The colorful instrumental combinations, the textural clarity, the warmth of feeling, and the naïveté of manner gratify the ear. The first suite, op. 24, was written in 1916–17; the second, op. 29, in 1921–22.[41] Both of them won a large following and gained Hill a name as one of America's outstanding composers. Scarcely any other contemporary American composers wrote for orchestra with such lively intelligence and awareness of instrumental possibilities, or wrote harmonies of such piquancy and with such convincing an expression of character. Only John Alden Carpenter's *Adventures in a Perambulator* and Deems Taylor's *Through the Looking Glass* come to mind as offering anything equivalent.

The first suite's movements are captioned "Marching Song," "The Land of Nod," "Where Go the Boats?" and "The Unseen Playmate." After its premiere at Boston's Jordan Hall in 1918, an unnamed reviewer in the *Christian Science Monitor* wrote:

The music made a favorable impression. The interest in the four pieces, march, lullaby—'The Land of Nod'—scherzo, and 'The Unseen Playmate,' is cumulative; and the last seems by far the best written of the four. The lullaby is frankly in the style of the modern French writers, particularly Debussy; and one suspects that Mr. Hill was especially interested in the last lines of the poem:

Nor can remember plain and clear
The curious music that I hear.[42]

Critics praised the suite's sophistication, tender wit, and kindly interpretation of the verse. The last movement was praised most. The march, though pleasant enough, was thought too modulatory and too complicated in its manipulation of instrumental combinations to project a childlike image.

The second suite received its premiere in New York in March 1923 and turned out even more popular than the first. In three movements—"Armies in the Night," "The Dumb Soldier," and "Pirate Story"—it has all of the virtues and fine qualities of its predecessor. The outer movements sound brilliant, rhythmically stimulating, and somewhat theatrical. The middle movement is a charming and whimsical reverie. No expression is inflated, no movement too long. Hill himself insisted that the music was not descriptive but an attempt to catch the moods of the poems.[43]

Between composing the two suites, Hill wrote *The Fall of the House of Usher,* Poem for Orchestra (after the story by Poe), op. 27. It is at the opposite expressive extreme from the suites. Composed in the summer of 1919 and revised in the fall and winter of 1919–20, it tells no story, according to Hill, but tries to capture the macabre atmosphere of the tale as a whole. Two themes, however, are associated with the morose Roderick and the dying Madeline Usher, respectively.[44] The structure is an abridged sonata form, with a brief introduction and coda. The music does suggest subdued horror, changing to frantic apprehension, changing to impending disaster—with economy and no sensationalism. At the end, the music touches on the destruction of the house and the dreadful end of the Ushers. Yet Hill's fastidiousness prevents him from creating the completely oppressive atmosphere and overhang of excruciating horror conveyed by the original. He appeals to the mind rather than whips up the emotions.

One suspects that for a few years Hill was fishing within himself to bring to the surface a fresh route for his creativity. Nine Waltzes for Orchestra, op. 28, came out in 1921. The unequivocally light music departs from the pictorial humor of the suites and the sinister passions of the symphonic poem. It features a set of suave dances, melodically rich, harmonically delicious, and smoothly orchestrated. The next year he worked on the shrewdly conceived *Jazz Studies* for two pianos (more jazz studies would come out in 1935).

In 1924 Koussevitzky and the Boston Symphony played his new Scherzo for Two Pianos and Orchestra. The audience loved the syncopated rhythms and the abundance of bracing nondominant seventh chords. Conservative critics found it coarse; devotees of jazz complained that it did not go far enough. After Oswald Villard wrote about how much pleasure the Scherzo had given him, Hill replied: "I fear it shares the fate of all *mulattos,* in that it is too lowly for the purists, and not positive enough for the 'jazz fiends.'"[45] The next year, two abstract works completely in the traditional mainstream appeared, the Flute Sonata and the Clarinet Sonata. Both are captivating works. For example, one of Hill's best tunes inhabits the second movement of the Clarinet Sonata.

His efforts met with unqualified success in *Lilacs,* Poem for Orchestra, op. 33 (after Amy Lowell), which the Boston Symphony performed in 1927. The composition is dedicated to the memory of the dead poet, once a dear friend. Hill states that he had long admired Lowell's poetry and thought her "Lilacs" an "excellent subject for musical treatment by one of New England ancestry." He chose not to follow the poem in his musical depiction. Instead he gave his impressions of its images, especially those in the beginning and end.[46] Almost twenty minutes long, the piece begins with a short Impressionistic introduction. One hears delicate sounds coming from a small number of muted violins and a celesta against abbreviated woodwind phrases.[47] Woodwinds, strings, and full orchestra follow each other in giving out the main melody, swelling in volume from soft to loud, then back to soft again. The music is profoundly felt. The orchestra sings with a sincere and convincing simplicity. A contrasting middle section follows, soon arriving at a broad *largamente* section, where Hill spins out the music in the high strings and woodwinds. Then the main theme returns, now restated in different fashion. The music of the coda quiets to a *tranquillo* and makes brief allusions to all of the ideas that have gone before. The final measures return to the *tempo dell' Introduzione,* and the material of the opening forms a fitting ending. The tones in the last measure fade away to nothing.

In *Lilacs* Hill accommodates readily to the position of poetic scenic painter who is unambiguously conveying an American ambience, a musical approach inaugurated by Chadwick and MacDowell. For all too brief a length of time, he sings tones filled with nostalgia, sadness, loneliness, and affection to transmit the loveliness of his native New England. It is an expression of the nobility in garden-variety things, a nobility that in the decade of the 1920s, when America seemed to be loosing its social and moral bearings, seemed more precious than ever to Hill. Amy Lowell's poem chronicles people, places, and activities with insightful images.

Eventually the reader arrives at an understanding of her principal subject—that the lilacs from their roots to their flowers represent both her
native soil and herself. George Boas writes about the poem: "When one
stops to think, it appears to be of no importance whether Miss Lowell was
of New England or not. . . . As an individual she will have disappeared
completely in a generation or two. But her ecstatic cry of identity with
New England seems important to you hearing it and I wonder whether
any poem, whether any work of art, ever seems important (except historically) unless its pattern takes on significance."[48]

It was Hill's "cry of identity," too. He too saw the lilacs as symbols of
his home and country. He reveals his feelings about the region he loved.
He conceives songlike lines that increase in fervor until they are discharged in a climax of sentiment. The intensity of expression is unusual
for Hill. Taken in its entirety, it seems the music of someone alienated
from the hedonistic social behavior of contemporary life. The composition
is neither epic nor long-winded, but intimate and reduced to essentials.
He has composed fresh music in an idiom that honors the traditional mainstream.

In the year that he completed *Lilacs,* Hill chose to put aside the writing
of program pieces in favor of absolute music. Three symphonies followed,
dating from 1927, 1929, and 1937. A Violin Concerto was premiered in
1938; the Music for English Horn and Orchestra, in 1945. In all of them,
the composer wishes only to express musical ideas. The style is less adventurous than that of younger colleagues like Walter Piston and Aaron
Copland, more so than that of Mason. The structures are indebted to the
Classical period. The designs are faultlessly shaped; the contents are
unambiguous in expression. It is music that addresses the senses and emotions of listeners. The same qualities apply to his late chamber music—the
Sextet for Piano and Winds of 1934, the Quartet for Strings of 1935, and
the Quartet for Piano and Strings, also from around 1935.

On the lighter side, he wrote a one-movement Concertino for Piano
and Orchestra in 1931, a Sinfonietta in One Movement in 1932, and a
Concertino for String Orchestra in 1940. All three are well-made and
entertaining works.

Hill always maintained throughout his creative life that the music itself
had to come first, not emotional or programmatic assertions. Personal
expression of feeling was an objective, but a composer like Hill had to see
to the musical logic first. He had no tolerance for the artistic betrayal that

came with reaching for superficially facile effects and disliked compositions that did away with time-honored practices in order to be in agree-
ment with the latest fashions or simply to shock. He strove to give his
music substance, even as he tried to preserve his artistic integrity amid the
confusing cross-currents of his day.

CHAPTER

11

THE COMPOSERS OF THE POST–WORLD WAR I PERIOD

Four composers loom large in New England's post–World War I years: Carl Ruggles (1876–1971), Walter Piston (1894–1976), Quincy Porter (1897–1966), and Randall Thompson (1899–1984). These men began their creative careers in the 1920s. It is ironic that the oldest composer wrote the most radical music, and each progressively younger composer veered more and more toward traditional idioms. However advanced or temperate, their writing is a part of the twentieth-century world of sound.

During the 1920s New England, like the rest of the country, was much taken with jazz, Broadway musicals, and the music of Tin Pan Alley. For many people, these vernacular styles constituted an authentic American musical language. A huge audience willingly paid money to hear the new popular music. In contrast, the music of American art composers, as always, had a much harder time gaining a hearing. Not that those composers dreamed of winning over a huge public. Rather, they hoped to find more than one or two hearings for their works and to have them achieve some parity with the contemporary European compositions—good, bad, and indifferent—that American art ensembles performed. The more dissonant the piece, the more likely that it would be ignored. Confronted by the repudiation of his efforts, Ruggles, in particular, was persuaded that the American music public was essentially philistine in taste and smugly commonplace in its thinking. In this regard, he sided with the many sophisticated critics of American society in the 1920s who were bent on searching for and exposing stupidity and fraud in our national culture. They argued that industry and money dominated an acquisitive society incapable of nourishing any art worthy of respect. According to their view, however talented American musicians might appear to be, most of them reflected the sterility of their native land. The very few who successfully resisted this sterility did so by living on the fringes of society and rebelling against it. These few defined themselves as artists by trying to ward off the debasing impact of the masses and writing to win understanding from musically perceptive listeners.

Ruggles grew so keen on recent German music that he changed his name from Charles to Carl. For two of the other composers, Paris was the lodestone that attracted them. As the composer and novelist Paul Bowles explained, Paris allowed American composers "the most pleasant of all possible lives"; for Bowles, "each day lived through" in Paris "was one more day spent outside [the American] prison." Aaron Copland agreed that he found the Paris atmosphere the most sympathetic to American artists. Germany no longer was a "must" for aspiring composers, and why go there when Ravel and Stravinsky were in Paris?[1] Moreover, in Paris was a remarkable teacher of music theory and composition, Nadia Boulanger. Walter Piston benefited from her teaching, as did several distinguished American composers from other parts of the country—Virgil Thomson, Aaron Copland, Roy Harris, Elie Siegmeister, David Diamond, and Elliott Carter. Quincy Porter also went to Paris but studied with Vincent d'Indy. Randall Thompson began his studies with Spalding and Hill at Harvard and continued them with Ernest Bloch in New York. His European destination was Italy. The Italian government would name him "Cavaliere ufficiale al merito della Repubblica Italiana" in 1959.

CREATIVE CONDITIONS AFTER WORLD WAR I

During the 1920s the need to battle one's way out of the restrictions of the past seemed pressing to some writers, artists, and composers. The new world emerging after the war had dethroned the past and seemed to demand a different approach to artistic expression. Their training concluded, the composers found themselves living and creating in an America in the midst of immense industrial growth and societal change. Romantic softness and sentiment, honeyed consonances, and soothing melodiousness did not appear appropriate to a modern era that had become hard-edged. Absorbing and making use of the spirit of lively individualism that reigned, they desired freedom to test novel ideas and to move creatively along whatever road they wished, liberated from compliance to any code devised by others. If someone like Thompson appeared more conservative than, say, Ruggles, it was because of individual choice, not because he was mechanically consenting to commonly accepted rules.

The end results of artistic liberation were not totally auspicious for composers, especially those who cultivated styles different from the customary. They soon found themselves laboring on their own, with little encouragement from the public. Only when a novel piece with some shock value was announced would the adventurous segment of the music public and the radical fashionables turn up at a performance. Once curiosity was satisfied and a declaration of cultural emancipation was made, even this audience dwindled away, leaving behind no more than a tiny cadre of true believers. Scarcely any sponsors arose to back the advanced artist. Scarcely any performing groups accepted his works to play, and when they did, scarcely any music lovers turned out to hear them. Music publishers lost money when they published the new "modern" music. Recording companies found few buyers for its recorded examples.

As usual, federal and local governments remained aloof from all things artistic and offered no financial support to musicians. Opera companies and symphony orchestras had rapidly changed into "big business" establishments, more costly to maintain and more pressed to address a larger and larger clientele. However sincere and talented the innovating artist, he or she would get short shrift from major musical organizations. The possibility was that the younger art composers, as yet with no reputations, might fail to be noticed at all.

Art composers tried to unite into associations that would promote the performance and publication of their music. Carl Ruggles, for example, would join the Composers' Guild, formed in 1921, which later metamorphosed into the Pan-American Association of Composers. This group, ultramodern in its musical ideas and techniques, made a great effort to organize concerts despite inadequate capital and halfhearted assistance from the music people in power. Walter Piston, to give another example, would belong to the League of Composers, founded in 1924. The more successful of the two groups, the league published the periodical *Modern Music* and succeeded, under Aaron Copland's guidance, in mounting some concerts, highly regarded at least by advanced musicians—the Copland-Sessions Concerts of 1928–31, and the Yaddo Festivals, which began in 1932. The league came to be formed, according to John Briggs, because Carl Ruggles and Edgard Varèse, who led the Composers' Guild, would put up with no one who disagreed with them, not even people on the board of directors: "Once when there were complaints that Composers' Guild programs were 'too advanced,' Messrs. Varèse and Ruggles telephoned each member of the board of directors and told him he was fired. That was how the League of Composers came to be formed by the ex-directors."[2]

Neither group tried hard to accommodate the general music public, certainly not before the mid-1930s. The antagonism of most music lovers toward both was inevitable. Claire Reis, a founder of the League of Composers, admitted: "Because our 'inner group' was somewhat inclined to be fanatic in the cause of modern music, we did not always sympathize quickly with those who did seem actually to suffer."[3]

The Great Depression that began with the stock market collapse in 1929 would bring changes in some composers' attitudes. Its long duration and the miseries it inflicted on the American people were unprecedented. Composers found their means of support, always precarious at best, now shriveling to nothing. Whatever commissions, prizes, and patrons there had been now were disappearing over the horizon. Ruggles, it is true, would continue going his own crusty way, unchanged in attitude or musical style. The other three men, however, whether they admitted it or not, were affected by the crisis. They did not subscribe to the inflexibly tough individualism of Ruggles. They felt that art could not survive for long if it remained completely exclusive and uncaring. Joshua Taylor, of the Smithsonian Institution, explains that the hardships of the American people stunned the artistic community and obliterated "what patronage the American artists enjoyed," even as "talk of 'pure' art and of conflicting isms had begun to wear thin." The notion "of an art community with its special values and private heroes," and of the artistic individual "as a professional living apart" from society died away. "More and more the artist wished to identify himself with society as a whole, to find his place in a broadly based culture."[4]

In 1932 Randall Thompson was telling his fellow composers to stop working in isolation and adhering to attitudes acquired from Europeans. In the hard times of the 1930s, their position was indefensible. Besides, they had no money to continue as they were. They should rejoin America in spirit, modify their styles, and try to address more than a few Americans with their music. "The European yardstick is no measure for the things we do," he said. It imprisons the American artist and encourages "a tyranny of opinion under which we struggle to please Europe but only succeed in displeasing and aping it. The value that a given work has for us," he writes, "is the important thing, and that value is only to be estimated by its relation to other works of our own."[5]

With the election of Franklin Delano Roosevelt to the presidency and his launching of the Four Arts Project of the WPA in 1935, composers benefited in several ways. Those that needed employment found it. Orchestras all over New England were formed, as they were in the rest of the nation. Performing groups financed by the Music Project began playing new works by American composers as part of their mandate. Admission was free or at only nominal cost, so attendance was high. Instructional classes in singing, instrumental playing, and music appreciation were offered the public, thus creating a huge new audience for art music. To cite one instance, a resident of Boston said her aunt, a coloratura soprano, belonged to a WPA vocal ensemble that toured New England during the late 1930s. A concert, held in Fenway Park, "filled all the seats to overflowing." Harry Ellis Dickson, director of the WPA Music Project in Massachusetts, wrote: "At one point, there were about five hundred musicians on my 'payroll.' We had a State Symphony Orchestra, a Commonwealth Symphony, and a whole opera company. I'd say that forty percent of the current BSO players came out of those WPA orchestras."[6] Boston soon had a Composers' Forum Laboratory, one of several throughout the nation sponsored by the Music Project, where new compositions were tried out and composers were expected to field questions from the audience.

Leonard Bernstein has acknowledged the impact of the Roosevelt years on American composers in a talk given to Tanglewood students in Lenox, Massachusetts, on 8 July 1970: "We . . . in 1940 were a generation of hopers. We came out of the Roosevelt decade, the thirties, educated by the Great Depression, the National Recovery effort, which was a great social spasm in our history."[7] As a result, many composers wished to write uplifting works that the general public could connect with.

The Music Project was phased out when World War II began, but quite a few of the orchestras continued to survive under different auspices. At the same time, the war roused patriotic fervor in composers, and they grew more eager to write compositions that could communicate with a broad public.

During the late 1930s public enthusiasm for symphonic music burgeoned. Art music had become less and less a recreation for the wealthy and highly educated. A poor factory worker, for one, became "interested in learning about the unknown," according to a report that his son relayed to the author. He took advantage of the concerts and musical instruction provided by the Music Project and "began to read and learn about the so-called great composers." He was also enjoying symphonies, especially those of Beethoven. His son said that the music alleviated the bleak existence he was enduring in the 1930s. "After a long day's work he would come home and listen to good music played on the radio." A very old woman told the author that her husband was studying in a Catholic seminary when he met her and abandoned preparation for the priesthood in order to marry and supported his family by working as a carpenter. In the 1930s, thanks to the opportunities to study music without cost, he learned to play the violin and cornet, and by means of the free concerts he came to appreciate "classical and operatic music." Every week, she said, "on Saturday we'd all [she and her six children] go out and Dad would listen to that opera all afternoon. Dad would listen to the Saturday afternoon opera program and through the pre-show explanations, the performance, and whatever commentary followed, would allow no noise at all. To avoid tempting fate, the family would leave for the duration of the show."[8] A woman whose parents had lived on a Midwest farm said that the family had discovered the world of symphony and opera through the radio broadcasts beamed into their area. Whether factory worker, carpenter, or farmer, Americans with a newfound taste for art music would find the music of Beethoven, Schubert, Verdi, and Tchaikovsky to be a fresh experience. There was no guarantee that the interest thus awakened would extend to contemporary American works. Much depended on how successfully a work communicated feeling and gave pleasure to the senses of inexperienced listeners.

By the 1940s writer after writer was reporting on the huge new audiences created by radio and the increase of the art music offerings broadcast to them. In part, the increase was owing to the federal government's insistence on such contributions as a prerequisite for a license to operate. Radio, too, was bringing art music to America's armed forces. A survey of soldiers' likes and dislikes in music was published in *Broadcasting* magazine on 5 October 1942. It revealed that though many rejected art music, a significant 32 percent enjoyed and wanted to hear more of it.[9] Piston's friend Aaron Copland was speaking the mind of most composers, save for diehards like Ruggles, when he said:

> The radio and phonograph have given us listeners whose sheer numbers in themselves create a special problem. They can't be ignored if musical creation is to flourish. More and more we shall have to find a musical style and language which satisfies both us and them. That is

the job of the forties. . . . I do not advocate "writing-down" to the public. . . . Composers, too, sometimes talk as if they really were convinced that nothing but pure inspiration goes into the making of a work. The truth is, of course, that it is far from easy to throw off old composing habits, to think afresh on the subject of the purpose and function of music in relation to the musical idiom used and the audience one is trying to reach.[10]

Minna Lederman was stating in 1940: "A jubilant press has hailed the announcement that there are now nearly three hundred symphony orchestras in the country. Half, it seems, were born since 1929 and of the sixteen with annual budgets of $120,000 to $750,000 not one died in the depression."[11] Orchestras had formed throughout New England, with or without WPA assistance. For example, in 1939 some music lovers of northwestern Massachusetts started up a Young People's Symphony. Interest in the project increased considerably. The next year, an adult orchestra was formed, the Pioneer Valley Orchestra, with Harold Leslie as conductor. Amateur players and what professional instrumentalists were available joined the group. The Kiwanis Club of Greenfield volunteered to take on the financial management. Using public facilities for rehearsals and performances held down expenses. During its first year of existence, the seventy-five to eighty players gave concerts in Greenfield, Northfield, and over the Vermont border, in Brattleboro.

Contemporary American composers, and New England composers in particular, found they had an influential champion in Serge Koussevitzky (1874–1951), the famous Russian conductor, when he arrived to direct the Boston Symphony Orchestra—that is to say, if their music corresponded to his tastes. His partiality was for French and Russian composers, Stravinsky especially, and not for Germanic composers like Schoenberg and Berg. The conductor's preferences would benefit Piston most, Ruggles least. Koussevitzky started as a double-bass player of considerable ability. He married wealthy Natalie Ushkov in 1905 and established his own symphony orchestra in Moscow in 1909. When the Russian Revolution took place, he left Russia (1920) and eventually ended up in Paris, where he again started his own orchestra and began directing the Concerts Koussevitzky. In 1924 he won the Boston Symphony post and remained as the orchestra's conductor until 1949.

An important action he took in 1935 was the start of the summer concerts of the Berkshire Festival, actually a supplanting of Henry Hadley's Berkshire Symphony Festival of 1934. Each summer Koussevitzky brought the Boston Symphony to western Massachusetts to present old and new music under relaxed festive conditions. The concerts at Tanglewood, in Lenox, Massachusetts, became an annual fixture, eagerly anticipated by visitors from around the country. The Berkshire Music Center, the prestigious instructional adjunct to the symphony's summer concerts, was opened in 1940. Here, advanced training was offered in singing, instrumental playing, conducting, and composition, under the most renowned international instructors.

As an advocate of contemporary American composers Koussevitzky had no match, provided he liked their music. The Boston audience was sympathetic to his advocacy. As Winthrop Tryon said of Koussevitzky's Boston concerts: "Speaking of the regular Friday afternoon and Saturday evening pairs in Symphony Hall, his audiences will take more unknown and lately-written works than he himself can prepare for them."[12] Fortunate composers received commissions to create major symphonic works. When he heard of a piece that might suit him and the Boston Symphony, he asked to see it. During the first two decades of his Boston tenure, he would premiere sixty-six American compositions. His zeal in presenting unknown compositions to audiences and the serious attention he gave to rehearsing them served to convince listeners and music critics of their merit. Yet, on one occasion, he pushed aside his strong ego and admitted the Americans "would never understand American orchestral compositions until they heard them conducted by American-born conductors."[13]

Nevertheless, his ego remained deep-seated and he often behaved despotically. When a musician opposed Koussevitzky, there were serious consequences. His nephew Fabien Sevitzky took on the directorship of the People's Symphony Orchestra of Boston in 1933, despite his uncle's objections. The result was estrangement between the two men. American composers who allowed Sevitzky to perform one of their works could expect Koussevitzky to banish their compositions from Boston's Symphony Hall.[14] American composers who kept their record clean and had a work scheduled for performance by Koussevitzky were still likely to suffer some humiliation. Vladimir Dukelsky had a work accepted for performance, to his delight, but had to endure the liabilities that went with Koussevitzky's acceptance. As he tells it:

> Rehearsals in Symphony Hall were closely guarded secrets with only special appointees permitted to attend. . . . Composers, troublesome and nosy creatures, were relegated to the first balcony and tol-

erated on condition that they remained silent and respectful. To correct a glaring mistake in the orchestra parts, or an erroneous tempo by the conductor, meant standing up and shouting—a daring feat attempted by few. I remember leaping to my feet when the coda of the finale was tackled *twice* too fast, and screaming: "No, no! slower, please." Koussevitzky stopped the orchestra, turned to me with a terrifying scowl, screamed back: "If too slow, I play faster!" and did. I screamed louder this time, in genuine anguish. Sergei Alexandrovitch rapped his stand with his baton and hissed: "*Personne* play!" (which was his way of saying: "Nobody plays."), then added in tragic tones, addressing me: "You conduct," and crossed his arms on his chest. "But I cannot conduct, Sergei Alexandrovitch," I wailed. "Then you compose and I conduct and you—SILENCE!" Koussevitzky summed up grandiosely and resumed the offending coda. It was now taken at the correct tempo, but the episode looked like a Koussevitzky victory.[15]

THE MAVERICK: CARL RUGGLES

Carl Ruggles was not a favorite composer of Koussevitzky. Ruggles was fired up by a modernism that conductors like Koussevitzky, their orchestras, and their audiences would refuse to accept. Although he gave painstaking attention to planning and to detail in his music, he failed to convince the general music public that his sound was anything except chaotic and unpleasant. Only a very small audience appreciated what he was attempting to do. Ruggles's musical discrimination grew so advanced that it made impossible a supportive two-way exchange with ordinary creatures. Ruggles insisted that he was artistically always in the right. Rigidity in attitude often gave way to arrogance. Pride vied with prejudice, stubbornness with insecurity, and touchiness with easygoing interaction with others. He used foul language and loved to regale visitors with racy, rambunctious tales.[16] Anti-Semitism was one of his worst traits. He ranted against "that filthy bunch of Juillard [*sic*] Jews" in a 1933 letter to Henry Cowell, and said Jews were "cheap, without dignity, and with little or no talent."[17] Ruggles, of course, was certain of his own personal and artistic superiority.

Ruggles subscribed completely to the concepts of artist and genius that had gathered strength in the nineteenth century and become dominant in the twentieth century. He thought that the work of art was the creation of an autonomous individual and that this personage surmounted tradition, general musical principles, and restraints of any kind. Charles Seeger, though he acclaimed the composer and greatly commended his music, remarked that Ruggles maintained that "musical value and the expression and communication of it is primarily the function of the composer." Not only did Ruggles know best, but he "knows he knows best." He felt no concern over "the social usefulness of his aims or deeds." He voiced "conviction—sheer arrogant assertion—of value" in his music. Throughout the 1920s and early 1930s a "Jehovah-complex" urged Ruggles to search for what "he preferred to call the 'Sublime.'" At all times, he displayed "a narrow taste, very particular, and quite of the absolutist type, with no gradations."[18]

Ruggles held fast to an exclusive array of convictions deriving from his own vision, approach to writing, and likes and dislikes. He was hobbled when it came to commenting on music different from his own. Consequently, Ruggles downgraded Tchaikovsky to the status of a hack musician and belittled the newly deceased Henry Hadley at a public lecture, indifferent to the presence of Hadley's widow in the audience: "I thought that music had reached the lowest possible point when I heard the works of John Alden Carpenter. Now, however, I have been examining the scores of Mr. Henry Hadley" and found them shoddier.[19] He thought Stravinsky was "overrated," Hindemith "a bore," and Walter Piston "a dreary jerk." Koussevitzky was "a stinker" who surrounded himself with "dirty little rats."[20]

Throughout his life even those who knew him well found it impossible to reconcile the intolerant, prejudiced person with the music that aimed to transcend ordinary human experience. He would complete less than a dozen compositions, but the finest of these contains music of such elevated quality (read Ruggles's "sublime") that it secured him a spot among the most significant American composers of the twentieth century. *Mystic* and *prophetic* are two terms often applied to his works. Ruggles's compositions are not for the fainthearted. He offers the listener no pleasant tunes. His music sounds jarring and attacks cherished traditional beliefs. It is marked by great energy and depth of feeling. It can generate a high degree of emotional excitement. His scores display resolutely independent lines, a plethora of chromatic tones, and structures that rarely resort to literal repetition. Interestingly, the instrumental combinations he composed for were less important considerations.

Ruggles was born in Marion, Massachusetts, and would die in Bennington, Vermont, at the age of ninety-five. His family had deep roots in

New England, and several of his ancestors were seafarers. At the age of six he constructed a cigar-box "violin" for himself and attempted to play it. He then studied the violin under George Hill and, before he was ten years of age, had played for visitors to Cape Cod, including President and Mrs. Cleveland. In 1890 his family moved to the Boston area (to Lexington, Belmont, and then Watertown). At first he wished to learn ship design and enter the business of ship construction. When he arrived in Boston, however, he abandoned his plans in favor of musical study—violin with Felix Winternitz and composition with Josef Claus. In 1903 he was a special student at Harvard, where John Knowles Paine and Walter Spalding became his instructors. Four years later, he was a music teacher at the Mar D'Mar School in Winona, Minnesota, and shortly organized and directed a local orchestra. Among the works he conducted were a few operas in concert form. He also met and married Charlotte Snell, a singer from New England, and augmented his income by playing in theater orchestras. For her entire married life Charlotte would lead an oppressive existence, wondering how to making ends meet, dressing herself and her son, Micah, mostly in hand-me-down clothing, and enduring her husband's constant rant against the world.

The year 1917 found him and his family leaving Winona and coming to stay in New York City. Some private financial backing came his way, and he also gave lessons in composition. For a while he was music director at the Rand School of Social Science. Ruggles quickly made new acquaintances among the most advanced composers living in New York, especially Ives and Varèse, and helped form the avant-garde International Composers Guild (1921) and Pan-American Association (1928). One of his earliest surviving work, *Toys* (1919), for voice, was written for the fourth birthday of his son, Micah. With *Men and Angels* for five trumpets and bass trumpet (1920), he was introducing more jarringly dissonant sounds within a constantly shifting atonal framework. The guild presented it in New York in 1922 and at a 1925 concert of the International Society for Contemporary Music in Venice. Thirteen years later, he would arrange part of it for four trumpets and three trombones and call it *Angels*. Chromaticism abounds in the music, and a certain amount of psychological stress is produced by constant dissonances from beginning to end. Yet the sound comes across as also straightforward and dignified. It demonstrates Ruggles's awareness of the innovative works of the Viennese composers Schoenberg and Berg, although he would travel along a different track from theirs.

Between 1912 and 1923 he had worked on an opera, *The Sunken Bell,* and had even moved to New York to get the Metropolitan Opera to mount it. The libretto, which Ruggles himself prepared, was based on a drama by Gerhart Hauptmann. The music did not come easily to him, however, and the road to the work's completion grew more and more difficult. Ruggles became certain that the opera was not worthy of performance and destroyed the score. Only sketches have survived.

Vox Clamans in Deserto, for soprano and chamber orchestra, came out in 1924. *Men and Mountains,* a three-movement suite for chamber orchestra, was completed and performed in the same year. William Blake's sentence "Great things are done when men and mountains meet" provided the title. Some years later he arranged the music for a larger orchestra, and it received a New York performance in this new format in 1936. Ruggles, by means of this music, was trying to encompass the huge, afflicted figures in Blake's mind and the poet's searching probe for meaning behind human existence. Nicolas Slonimsky claimed that it pictured "his country's stern landscapes" with sounds "entangled in Schoenbergian formulas." He praised the "powerful strings in unison for striding men and bulky discords for marching mountains." A second commentator, Lazare Saminsky, related the work to "New England spirituality," however "crude and clumsy" the means to achieve it. When the work was performed again, this time in the 1936 scoring for large orchestra, many in the audience found the music intolerable, and at least one critic suggested it was an example of post–World War I experimentation that now seemed dated.[21]

Greater complexity and increased contrapuntal movement entered with *Portals* (1925), written at first for thirteen strings but later for string orchestra. Ruggles had in mind the Whitman sentence "What are those of the known but to ascend and enter the Unknown." Note repetition is avoided until a sequence of seven to ten different notes are heard.[22] He does not subscribe to the serial procedures of the contemporary Viennese composers, however. A modus operandi that seemed highly individual to some reviewers seemed awkward to others. The work is notable for its simplicity and economy of means, and its strong impact, as the composer attempts to convey a rapturous experience rising above the merely human.

From 1927 to 1932 Ruggles labored to complete *Sun-Treader,* for large orchestra, which was by far his most ambitious and longest composition (it lasts about seventeen minutes). The title is borrowed from Robert Browning's "Sun-treader, light and life be thine forever." Nicolas Slonimsky presented the premiere in Paris and conducted the composition again in Berlin in 1936. It failed to get a performance in the United States until 1966, when Jean Martinon and the Chicago Symphony finally let Americans hear it at a concert in Portland, Maine. The music conveys extraordinarily concentrated power, starting with the startling opening of clamorous brass pronouncements, pounding timpani, and accelerating tempo. The jarring clash of tones a second and seventh apart is a constant, as is a brief motive that runs through the softer sections. A tone row of about nine or ten different pitches is employed, though not consistently. Rarely are more than three real parts heard at once. Currents of tightly organized and interdependent lines and a mélange of discordant sounds swell in loudness and intensity and subside into quietness until the culmination of the piece at the end. Instruments are made to play at their outermost ranges. The work has an epic effect and is best described as an ecstatic manifestation of feeling, akin to the transcendental musical images of Ives. Elliott Carter heard "a very thin but intense texture, contrapuntally speaking." He found the music "extremely sophisticated for its time in its use of dissonances but very primitive in its textual layout. This dissociation makes the piece seem un-European." Carter followed this with a statement of great significance when it comes to understanding Ruggles in relation to the American music public: "Of course, this kind of thing is symptomatic of the free attitude that American composers have often brought to the writing of music—an interest in trying things that in Europe would be considered dangerously out of line with proven esthetic standards. American composers have felt free to do this, partly because they have not been able to write for a ready-made audience for new music. . . . In a way, American works have been of necessity 'private works.'"[23]

In 1937 Ruggles left New York to teach at the University of Miami, where he stayed until 1943. It was about this time that he decided also to become a serious painter, working mainly in a nonfigurative style. He was soon devoting so much of his time to painting that he had little left over for musical composition. Some three hundred canvases would be executed. The dearth of new musical works can be attributed to how painstakingly he composed and, at least in part, to how discouraging it was that few performers and listeners cared to hear what he had to say. Fortunately for his financial well-being, he met Harriet Miller. She began to study painting with him. They soon became close friends and, before long, she took on the role of patron, subsidizing him and freeing him from the need to earn a living. He had purchased a house in Arlington, Vermont, and at first, after he left Miami, he divided his time between Arlington and New York. After his wife died in 1957, however, he stayed permanently in Arlington. Owing principally to Ives's advocacy, he was elected to the National Institute of Arts and Letters in 1954. Six years later, the University of Vermont honored him with a D.Mus.

During the last thirty-four years of his life he would complete only three works: *Evocations* (1937–42), for piano; *Organum* (1944–49), for orchestra; and *Exaltation* (1958), a textless hymn for unison voices and organ, written in memory of his wife.

His final years were passed in near isolation in his Vermont home. Owing to his disagreeable character, Ruggles was not someone many people wished to know. With its off-putting dissonance and idiosyncratic twists and turns, his music was not apt to get many hearings. Yet he held fast to his personal vision of what his music should be about and persisted in repudiating any turn to a more acceptable style, which, he felt, would compromise what he saw as his artistic integrity and independence. His compositions remain monuments to New England creativity. To hear a work like *Sun-Treader* is to experience a power that rises above the deficiencies of personality. Its problem is that unlike the multileveled appeal of a work by Mozart or Brahms, it addresses the listener at only one level—the realm of sound that inspires wonderment and sometimes awe. The paradox between the censurable remarks of his salacious tongue and the goal of sublimity in his music continued to the end.

THE CIRCUMSPECT MODERNIST:
WALTER PISTON

Walter Piston was the second art composer of consequence to come from Maine, the first being John Knowles Paine. During several decades of creative work, he produced mainly instrumental pieces for chamber groups and orchestra. A couple of choral numbers and a dance composition were the main exceptions. Opera was never attempted.

His music evidenced a good deal of dissonance, though never as off-putting as Ruggles's, and some avoidance of key, though rarely the comprehensive atonality found in Ruggles's music. At all times, the dissonance was related to harmonic function, and a tonal center of some sort usually helped structure a work. Especially after World War II, Piston experimented gingerly with serialism, but his heart was not in it. In short, unlike Ruggles, he was more a mainstreamer and retained several practices from the past. He even wrote some major works where the music has decided

Walter Piston conducting, with Jesús Maria Sanromá at the piano.

tonal quality, communicative lyricism, and only judicious chromaticism. Throughout his career he employed Baroque and Classic forms—fugue, passacaglia, sonata allegro, rondo—and abstract layouts—concerto, symphony, string quartet, and the like. He had a profound knowledge of contrapuntal practices, motivic development, and thematic metamorphosis. Not a note was wasted, not a measure was written that could not be explained in terms of logic and the purpose that it aimed to perform. He regarded poetic titles, literary quotations, and programmatic explanations with disfavor. Music to him had to stand on its own two feet.[24]

Born in Rockland, Maine, Piston moved with his family to Boston when he was ten years of age. Originally his family name had been Pistone, after his seafaring Italian grandfather, Antonio Pistone. His grandfather married a dyed-in-the-wool New Englander, established himself in Rockland, and dropped the -e from his name. The grandson at first studied draftsmanship at Boston's Mechanic Arts High School, graduating in 1912. He then enrolled at the Normal Art School to learn how to draw and paint, remaining there until graduation in 1916. At the same time he studied piano and violin. In 1920 he would marry the painter Kathryn Mason, whom he had met as a student at the school. World War I found him in a navy band stationed in the Boston area, for which he swiftly taught himself to play the saxophone. At war's end he earned a living playing in hotels, restaurants, and ballrooms. He first entered Harvard as a music major in 1919 and graduated in 1924 *summa cum laude*. While at Harvard he conducted the orchestra of the Pierian Sodality.

Harvard granted him a Paine Traveling Fellowship, which permitted him to live in Paris for two years (1924–26) and study composition with Paul Dukas and, more important, Nadia Boulanger. Boulanger introduced him to music by Stravinsky and the young modern French composers. He built his own style on what he heard while under Boulanger's tutelage. While in Paris, he completed a Piano Sonata and Three Pieces for flute, clarinet, and bassoon. The Piano Sonata represents a coming-to-terms with the Stravinsky-French modernisms spinning about him in Paris. The first movement mostly resembles a fast, driving, motoric toccata. The slow movement, cool and objective, emphasizes a single meandering line punctuated with abrupt chords. The finale, after an introduction, turns into a fast brittle fugue. Evident in Three Pieces were five elements integral to his mature style: a few discernibly melodious moments, occasionally brittle passages, an absence of superfluity, a confident conduct of harmony, and a persuasive handling of form. When he returned to Boston, Piston went to teach at Harvard, where he remained until retirement in 1960. He was always reluctant to leave New England and traveled hardly at all. His students were impressed by his scholarship, kindness, good humor, and understanding of their problems. He forced no one to write as he did, although he was always averse to students' scores that sported the purple patches of harmony and over-the-top emotionality of late Romanticism. One precept advanced by John Dewey was constantly behind his teaching: "We naturally associate democracy . . . with freedom of action, but freedom of action without freed capacity of thought behind it is only chaos."[25] He published his *Harmonic Analysis* in 1933, *Harmony* in 1941, *Counterpoint* in 1947, and *Orchestration* in 1955. These instructional books found use in music departments throughout the United States.

There is no question that Piston was one of the most noteworthy teachers of his time. Among his students were the composers Elliott Carter, Leroy Anderson, Arthur Berger, Gail Kubik, Irving Fine, Leonard Bernstein, Daniel Pinkham, Harold Shapero, Frederic Rzewski, and John Harbison. Piston's Harvard colleagues Archibald Davison, A. Tillman

Merritt, and Randall Thompson also enriched these students' educations, as did such visiting lecturers as Boulanger, Hindemith, Stravinsky, and Copland. The students were also surrounded by the rich musical offerings of the Boston area, not least of which were those of Koussevitzky and the Boston Symphony. The author himself can bear witness to the Harvard benefits deriving from Piston's demand that his novices in composition explore all contemporary styles, however different from his own, from Merritt's requirement that his students be able to sing Gothic motets at sight, and from Thompson's insistence that one not only speak about a Beethoven quartet or Schubert piano sonata but also quote on paper or at the piano the passage referred to. Then, too, there were for this author the Copland lectures (published as *Music and Imagination*), a whole year of the Primrose Quartet playing all the Beethoven quartets in free Harvard concerts, and the Boston Symphony concert series in Sanders Theater.[26]

Koussevitzky deserves credit for actively encouraging unknown American composers such as the young Piston. After he took over the Boston Symphony, Koussevitzky was told by Edward Burlingame Hill that Walter Piston taught at Harvard and composed music that was known to only a handful of people. The conductor invited Piston to see him and learned that the young man composed only chamber music. "Why not for orchestra?" Koussevitzky asked. Piston replied, "Because nobody would play it." The conductor said, "I will play it." Piston's first composition for orchestra, the *Symphonic Piece,* was given a Boston Symphony premiere on 23 March 1928.[27] Unfortunately, it made no strong impression on the audience. This did not deter Koussevitzky, or Piston. From then on, Piston's new orchestral works were regularly played in Boston, either as first performances (eleven works) or immediately after first performances by other orchestras. The members of the orchestra enjoyed playing his compositions because they were well made, idiomatically written, and easily playable. "He made us sound good," Harry Ellis Dickson told the author.

The composer conducted the Boston Symphony in his Suite No. 1 for orchestra in 1930 and his Concerto for Orchestra in 1934. The suite had links with jazz, particularly the blues-flavored middle movement. Its final movement is a fugue on a lengthy, chromatic subject. It won him more attention than the previous piece and was heard in several cities. The concerto reveals an intimate knowledge of Baroque practices and forms, as does the Prelude and Fugue for orchestra, first performed in Cleveland in 1936. W. J. Henderson reviewed the concerto in the *New York Sun* in February 1935: "Mr. Piston has made a work which will add to his repute. It is music of his time, vigorous, compact, straightforward, firmly knit. . . . He writes with a mastery of basic principles of form, a clean and fluent logic of development and clear-cut devising always easy to follow. . . . It is made with well-placed boldness and assurance."[28] These were hallmarks of his style throughout his life.

A Flute Sonata in three movements came out in 1930 and was fairly successful. His First String Quartet was finished in 1933 and was regarded as expertly put together and worthy of respect but excited no great enthusiasm. The first movement of the quartet is full of short choppy notes, with some contrast provided in brief, emotionally noncommittal lyric episodes. The slow movement begins with two hauntingly lovely phrases, but what follows remains on a fairly even ruminative level and rarely heats up. The last movement is fast and briskly informal and creates an atmosphere of easy unconcern. Copland commended the composition: "A work like the First String Quartet, with its acidulous opening movement, the poetic mood painting of the second, and its breezy finale, sets a superb standard of taste and of expert string writing." He found nothing American in it. As a rebuttal, Piston on one occasion said, "Copland and I had a friendly war about American music. . . . He had hopes of producing an American music that was just as recognizable as French and German music. I told him that America had so many different nationalities that it would be nearly impossible. I felt the only definition of American music was that written by an American."[29]

He would write four more string quartets (1935, 1947, 1951, and 1962), the Piano Trio No. 1 (1935), Violin Sonata (1939), Flute Quintet (1942), Piano Quintet (1949) and Quartet (1964), String Sextet (1964), and the Piano Trio No. 2 (1966), thus making him a major contributor to American chamber literature. In all, he shows a confident sense of what is appropriate to each genre and an awareness of every instrument's potentialities. By the time he had arrived at the Flute Quintet and Piano Quintet, the melodic coefficient of his music had increased enormously. By the Fifth Quartet, however, he was abandoning his more direct, transparent tonal language in favor of a more opaque, discordant, and tonally elusive chromatic language that would be typical of his writing in the 1960s and 1970s.

A Guggenheim Fellowship enabled Piston to live in Paris during 1935, and a commission from the Coolidge Foundation resulted in the First Piano Trio. This was followed by the sparkling Concertino for Piano and Chamber Orchestra (1937) and serious First Symphony (1938). The Concertino, premiered by Jesús Maria Sanromà at the piano and Piston conducting the CBS Symphony in a radio broadcast, was his best-received work thus far. In one movement, it has a particularly attractive slow melody allotted to the cello. The symphony won respect for its obvious musical quality but awakened little interest in the public. All the ingredients of his early style are present: the carefully molded and restrained melody, clearly distinguished contrapuntal threads, extended key relationships within a tonality, harmonies usually built on major seconds, fourths, and fifths rather than thirds, and persistent rhythmic figures, all within a dispassionate expressive framework.[30] Piston was not one to wear his heart on his sleeve, and what emotions the work contains are subtly stated and need ferreting out.

Evident in all of his earlier works was a need to reconcile traditional form, in which he believed, with affective expression, which gives the impression of being submerged and running like an undercurrent below a surface of polished elegance. He was often described as a classicist writing in an international rather than an American style. In 1936 Israel Citkowitz wrote a critique of the music Piston had written up until that time. As a composer, this commentator said, Piston has taste, sense of structure, contrapuntal skill, and dexterity in manipulating chromatic-diatonic lines. Citkowitz found the counterpoint too crowded at times, however, and the chromaticism excessive, giving the music a turgid, strained quality. Piston's devotion to architectonics and structural construction, while admirable, was at the expense of expression and emotional content.[31]

Undoubtedly Piston's most popular and most atypical work was *The Incredible Flutist*, a ballet that the Hans Weiner [Jan Veen] Dancers and Arthur Fiedler presented at a Boston Pops concert on 30 May 1938. By means of it, Piston may have been acting to prove critics like Citkowitz wrong. Familiar dances and ear-catching melodies are the ballet's selling points. He left out complex counterpoint and steered clear of intricate structures in favor of simplicity and unambiguous expressive content. The suite, in twelve sections, which Piston extracted from the ballet in 1939, made the rounds of the major symphony orchestras and gave him national stature. Unusual for the composer, the music realizes a scenario of a circus and mysterious flutist coming to a town, bringing jollity, romance, and enchantment to the inhabitants. Dances with attention-grabbing tunes (tango, tarantella, Spanish waltz, siciliana, polka) and a bumptious circus march contrast with haunting mood pictures, especially the quiet opening depiction of the community at rest and the romantic evening episode between lovers. Beginning with this work, we find Piston employing simpler

and more consonant harmonies, more open textures, more winning melodiousness, and America-related dance rhythms.

The so-called Peace of Munich brought no peace at all, and concerned
Americans began reappraising every sphere of human endeavor after
1938. Warning was given: "From now on the musical life of the United
States will bear an ever increasing burden of responsibility as it becomes
more and more the sole repository of a free European musical tradition
and culture."[32] Piston was deeply committed to this tradition and culture
and was conscious of the need to give it an American face. A distinct musical nationalism was abhorrent to him; rather, he wanted an integration of
his European musical inheritance with the spirit of America. If Americanisms crept into his music, they were there because it was natural for him to
think and act as an American immersed in American life. A noticeable but
understated indigenous character appears in the Violin Concerto of 1939,
which Ruth Posselt premiered in March 1940. In it, the composer continues to explore an affecting melodious language. It is now given a direction
that will characterize his compositions over the next several years. Hints at
popular American dance and song occur; the textures that emerge are
transparent, with carefully spaced chords constructed in fourths and fifths;
the tunes sometimes are built on a folksy pentatonic scale—all of this suggesting what was then thought to be an "American" sound. Yet the style
remains personal and engages in an intricate use of counterpoint and a
masterly metamorphosis of themes. The recycling of ideas from the first
two movements in the finale is especially pleasing. He would write five
more concertos for one or more soloists and orchestra: the Viola Concerto (1957), Two-Piano Concerto (1959), Violin Concerto No. 2
(1960), Clarinet Concerto (1967), and Flute Concerto (1971). All of
them are sensitively worked compositions.

George Smith said in 1940 that Piston's art was more of New England
than of America, thereby implying a deficiency in his music.[33] Heretofore
his critics had accused him of internationalism; now it was provincialism.
Responding to such criticism, Piston said:

Is the Dust Bowl more American than, say, a corner in the Boston
Athenaeum? Would not a Vermont village furnish as American a
background for a composition as the Great Plains? The self-con-
scious striving for nationalism gets in the way of the establishment of
a strong school of composition and even of significant individual
expression. If the composers will increasingly strive to protect them-

selves in the art of music and will follow only those paths of expression which seem to take them the true way, the matter of a national
school will take care of itself. And who can predict the time of its
coming? Some say it is already here. Some say it has been here since
the turn of the century. Others feel it will take time to show the true
significance of the enormous development of these recent years. But
the composer cannot afford the wild-goose chase of trying to be
more American than he is.[34]

The Boston Symphony premiered Piston's Sinfonietta for orchestra on
10 March 1941. Its three movements frequently hint at the neoclassic
music of Stravinsky, with the introduction of erratic rhythms, nonlyric
treatment of strings, declamations from the trumpets, liberal use of
French horns, phrase patterns repeated three or more times at different
pitches, and ground basses and constantly recurring melodic fragments.
Stravinsky had been at Harvard in 1939–40 delivering the Norton lectures
and working on his Symphony in C. The Sinfonietta pays homage to the
Russian composer, whom Piston held in high respect and whom he was
seeing on almost a daily basis.

World War II had come to the United States in 1941. Piston soon
grew heartsick over the continuing slaughter and at first felt that composing music was a useless activity in the face of the horrible reality confronting humankind. He had no energy to put notes down on paper. Arthur
Berger said that Piston's students in the armed forces wrote to him and
begged him to continue writing, since it was one of the reasons for their
fighting.[35] This helped overcome his lethargy. The result was the heartfelt
Second Symphony, a gem of American musical literature, which was written in 1943 owing to a commission from the Alice Ditson Fund of Columbia University. It outshone all of his previous works. Hans Kindler, who
premiered it with the National Symphony Orchestra in Washington, D.C.,
on 5 March 1944, described it as "without even the shadow of a doubt one
of the half dozen great works written during the last ten years. It sings forever in my heart and in my consciousness, and does not want to leave me."
It was immediately granted the New York Music Critics Award and taken
up by orchestras throughout the country. After Erich Leinsdorf conducted
it with the Cleveland Orchestra in 1946, he wrote to Piston: "The performance of your Symphony, which took place last night, was, to me personally, the most gratifying experience with any score that has seen daylight
within the last ten or fifteen years."[36] By this time, Stravinsky had become

greatly impressed by Piston's and Copland's music and said so in an article entitled "Stravinsky—Darling of Moderns Lauds 2 Americans: Copland and Piston" in the *New York World Telegram,* 10 February 1945. He said that he admired both musicians for their excellent musical ideas and thorough knowledge of technique.

This noble work marvelously communicates the profound emotions called up within him by the wartime contest. The symphony refrains from musical jingoism and attains a universal expression of concern for and confidence in humankind. Its musical construction communicates a warmth and emotive power that had not been heard before in his music. The first movement begins with a somber, elegiac strain, but eventually the sad singing gives way to a zesty, rhythmically jagged idea, like a jaunty march, that seems to epitomize America's certainty that it was acting in the right. However, it is the first theme that dominates the movement. The slow second movement has an eloquent clarinet intone a quietly moving lamentation, which continues over many measures. The final movement comes across as compelling and thought-provoking. It opens on a highly rhythmic theme, vigorously set forth, and has a first contrasting section that moves along steadily with a march step, and a second contrasting section where English horn and clarinet engage in a warm expressive passage. At the end, the emphatic first theme returns and realizes a strong and bold conclusion to the entire work. The Second Symphony was "one of the few really distinguished, most highly accomplished symphonic scores so far written in America," claimed Hugo Leichtentritt.[37]

The Koussevitzky Music Foundation commissioned the Third Symphony, which was completed in 1947, premiered by Koussevitzky and the Boston Symphony in January 1948, and granted the Pulitzer Prize. It contains personal songfulness, full and rich tones, and emotional qualities like those in the previous symphony. The slow beginning of the first movement touches on the range of human feelings to be dwelt on in greater length in the rest of the work. The second movement, a scherzo, hints at Viennese angst with its abundant chromatics and unwillingness to settle down. The introspective slow movement reveals an awareness of tragedy that only Piston and one or two other contemporary composers could encompass. The finale is the conquest of darkness by comic lightness and blithe optimism.

With this work, Piston had firmed his symphonic style. Wide-ranging and lengthy melodies now start off his symphonies and inform his slow movements. Syncopation and unpredictable rhythms add fresh interest to the lines as they spin out. In the scherzo and final movements what may sound close to American dance and jazz teases the ear. There is always a sense of forward motion, as if harmony, melody, and rhythm know where they are going and expeditiously at that. Nothing overstays its welcome. A sure hand guides the orchestration. At the conclusion, no loose ends remain. All ideas have been tied neatly together. The listener finds an immense range of expression, from the meditative discourse of the initial movement and the intense, reflective looking inward of the slow movements to the vigor and wittiness of the scherzos and tumultuous forward propulsion of the finales.

He had never abandoned his love for the Baroque. Passages linked to Baroque dances, passacaglia, and fugue were constantly coming and going in his music. Some works were unabashedly connected with the Baroque. The Suite No. 2 for orchestra (1948), for example, has a prelude resembling the old French overture and a sarabande movement and finishes on a passacaglia and fugue. Of interest, too, are the Suite for Oboe and Piano consisting of Baroque dances (1931), the Passacaglia for piano (1943), *Fugue on a Victory Tune* for orchestra (1944), Partita for violin, viola, and organ (1944), Toccata for orchestra (1948), and Ricercare for orchestra (1967).

The Fourth Symphony, like the Second, became a celebrated work immediately on its premiere and was played everywhere in America. Commissioned by the University of Minnesota, it was finished in 1950 and premiered by Antal Dorati and the Minnesota Symphony in March 1951. A high degree of lyricism and naturalness characterize its measures. The delightful opening melody, marked *piacevole,* sounds calm and easy in manner. American waltz and country dance are heard in the scherzo (*balando*), a sort of dancing rondo. The slow movement (*contemplativo*) is spun out in effortless, tranquil fashion, often obscuring its tonal direction owing to the frequent chromaticism. The finale (*energico*) is quick-witted, well defined, and celebratory. Piston, in a letter sent to Donald Ferguson in 1954, wrote: "I feel that this symphony is melodic and expressive and perhaps nearer than my other works to the problem of balance between expression and formal design. It should not prove complex to the listener in any way."[38]

The author was studying with Piston in the years 1949–51 and recalls Piston showing him the manuscript score of the symphony with the rests still absent from those measures that had no music. Piston said that he was forever going over and debating what he had put down and wasn't sure until the last minute if he wanted to add anything, so left the measures blank. Pertinent to the matter at hand, Piston said in 1958: "The major problem for the composer must be to preserve his individuality. He must resist the constant temptation to follow this or that fashion. He must find what it is he wishes to say in music and how best to say it, subjecting his work to the severest self-criticism. . . . Strength of will and faith in one's creative gift are essential. . . . The composer must judge for himself in these matters, with self-reliance based on a thorough knowledge of his craft and a capacity for independent thinking as an individual creative artist."[39]

Tunbridge Fair, Intermezzo for Symphonic Band, was also written in 1950, commissioned by the League of Composers and premiered by Edwin Franko Goldman and his band. Piston spent his summers in Vermont, where the annual Tunbridge Fair was a long-standing occurrence that the composer prized. The piece makes a fine display with tunes that are cheerful and likable.

His Fifth Symphony was written in 1954 for the American Music Festival at the Juilliard School of Music in New York and was performed there in 1956. Sonata, variation, and rondo forms define the classical Piston. Yet the music itself is explorative, going from chromatic and diatonic fluctuations of the first movement, to the highly chromatic, if not incipiently serial, technique of the second movement, to the diatonic approach of the finale.

The Boston Symphony commissioned the Sixth Symphony and performed it in 1955, directed by Charles Munch. It is an exceptional composition, with a flowing, expressive first movement, a somewhat folksy second movement, a wonderfully serene slow movement, and a finale whose tunes reach out to ordinary people. Piston's sensitivity to the particular instrumentalists for whom he is writing is made clear in a statement he made about this symphony:

> It is known that no two orchestras sound alike, and that the same orchestra sounds differently under different conductors. The composer of orchestral music must be aware of this, and his mental image admit a certain flexibility. The image is in a sense a composite resulting from all his experience in hearing orchestral sound, whether produced by one or two instruments or by the entire orchestra in tutti.

While writing my Sixth Symphony, I came to realize that this was a rather special situation in that I was writing for one designated orchestra, one that I had grown up with, and that I knew intimately. Each note set down sounded in my mind with extraordinary clarity, as though played immediately by those who were to perform the work. On several occasions it seemed as though the melodies were being written by the instruments themselves as I followed along. I refrained from playing even a single note of this symphony on the piano.[40]

Piston's religion was a private matter, and he belonged to no church. He rejected dogma and the need to subscribe to any set of beliefs. He disliked the commercialization of religious holidays, especially Christmas. If he needed a minister, as he did when he married, he turned to the Unitarian-Universalist denomination. Religious music was anything but his forte. It was surprising, therefore, that he accepted a commission from Brandeis University and composed the *Psalm and Prayer of David,* for chorus and chamber ensemble, in 1958. The work creates a reverent and transported atmosphere.

One of the few works to receive a title, *Three New England Sketches,* was written in 1959 for the Worcester Music Festival. The depictions, entitled "Seaside," "Summer Evening," and "Mountains," achieve what effectiveness they have by evoking subjective and sensory impressions rather than by recreating physical places. He suggests only; he aims at no program. The *Sketches,* he says, are "impressions, reminiscences, even dreams that pervaded the otherwise musical thoughts of one New England composer." The first movement is an Impressionistic mood picture. The second movement is quiet with *tremelo* fluttering sounds, as if from birds averse to activity. The last movement is fascinating from one point of view—it emulates Ruggles's *Sun-Treader,* with the pounding percussion and powerful rising figure in the orchestra. Here, however, it is not music trying to burst its bounds; rather, it demonstrates how a compelling musical statement can be achieved through noniconoclastic means.

The Seventh Symphony was composed in 1960 for the Philadelphia Orchestra and has many passages that seem related thematically and in mood with the *Sketches.* The movements are labeled *con moto, adagio pastorale,* and *allego festevole.* Like the Third Symphony, it won a Pulitzer Prize. The Eighth Symphony, his last, was composed in 1965 and had such a liberal dose of chromaticism that it sounds a bit like serial music. Harry Ellis Dickson says that Piston, "the court composer for the Boston Symphony," was experimenting with all sorts of styles, including twelve-tone. However, "he once told me after listening to us play an ultramodern, crazy piece of music, that no matter how he tried to write like that, it always came out Piston. 'When I hear music like that,' he said, 'I feel like Papa Haydn!'"[41]

It's not that "Piston" was always the same sort of music, but it was never thoughtlessly bold and written to shock. Nor was it ever his goal to write ultramodern music as an end in itself. He was always open to the experiences around him, musical and otherwise. These experiences he took in and used after consideration, in accord with his predilections, integrating them with long-established components of musical discourse, and allowing both to advance his personal manner of expression.

Two more major works require mentioning: the Variations for Cello and Orchestra (1966) and the Concerto for String Quartet, Wind Instruments, and Percussion (1976). They are elegant compositions, with no notes wasted and all passages aiming at communication, though not necessarily on an easy level. To the end, Piston wrote with the timbre and techniques special to each instrument in mind, as is proven in these two compositions.

THE MODERATE: QUINCY PORTER

Born in New Haven, Connecticut, Quincy Porter was a descendent of the Reverend Jonathan Edwards of Great Awakening fame and the grandson and son of Yale professors. He grew up in a cultured and intellectual household. After he entered Yale as an undergraduate, he was the music student of Horatio Parker, whom he admired, and David Stanley Smith. He had begun the study of the violin at the age of ten. For graduation he composed a Violin Sonata, which was filled with the longing, tenderness, and sadness of Romanticism. It looked to Brahms and at times to Beethoven or Schubert. Although he was supposed to take up the study of law, Porter instead went to Paris in 1920–21 and studied musical composition with Vincent d'Indy and violin with Lucien Capet at the Schola Cantorum. He then returned to America and studied composition with Ernest Bloch in New York and in Cleveland, Ohio, after Bloch moved there to become director of the Cleveland Institute of Music in 1922. From 1923 to 1928 Porter would teach theory at the institute. He was married in 1926 to the violinist Lois Brown. While in Cleveland he also played the viola as a member of the Ribaupierre Quartet. He thus gained an intimate knowledge of the chamber genre from the inside, as it were, and a predisposition to concentrate mainly on chamber music composition.

During these years, he composed two string quartets (1923, 1925), the *Ukrainian* Suite for string orchestra (1925), the Violin Sonata No. 1 (1926), and the Piano Quintet (1927). In these meticulously constructed pieces he sounds like a late Romantic but frequently turns to harmonies and effects that link him to his contemporaries. The *Ukrainian* Suite is agreeably melodic, has a little color, and transgresses hardly any of the guidelines inherited from the previous century. After its premiere at Rochester in May 1925, important orchestras in other cities took it up. On the other hand, the elegant Violin Sonata No. 1, which is based on the key of E minor, begins conventionally in a warm, somewhat lyrical fashion but often disengages from a tonal anchor and meanders about in an evocative manner. The music in these latter moments is representative of more recent musical practices that get away from the conventions of traditional composers. While the piece is not on the cutting edge of innovation, it does at times convey a dissociative out-of-body sensation, as if early Bartók and Prokofiev procedures were grafted onto a Bloch style. As is always typical of Porter's writing, the violin part sounds completely idiomatic.

A Guggenheim Fellowship enabled him and his wife to live in Paris for three years. While abroad, he wrote the Violin Sonata No. 2 (1929), Clarinet Quintet (1929), Piano Sonata (1930), Suite for viola alone (1930) and two more string quartets (1930, 1931). In these works, Porter had arrived at his mature style. He sounds more individual and far less beholden to other composers. Quality is high. Form and content are nicely tailored to fit each other. Themes are carefully crafted and concisely laid out. Ideas are developed in a fashion indicative of thorough technical knowledge and superior creative ability. He is not afraid to sound lyrical, especially in his slow movements. Dissonant content has increased, but it is incorporated into mainstream textures and processes.

When his Paris stay was over in 1932, Porter went to Poughkeepsie, New York, to teach at Vassar College. While resident there, he ventured into orchestral music, composing the *Poem and Dance* (1932), Symphony No. 1 (1934), and *Dance in Three-Time* (1937). He also composed two more string quartets, no. 5 (1935) and no. 6 (1937). Expression has become smoother, verging on the glossy, and dignified, verging on the dry. Harmony has acquired more of the characteristics of music from recent and present times. One finds unforced polyphony, melody moving in easy progressions, comprehensible textures, and structures marked by deft and graceful transitions. No conflicts or strong feelings disturb the music. Fluency, intelligibility, and restrained beauty are the aim. The three works achieve their goal by persuading the listener of their merits, not by overpowering the ear. Dances assume sophisticated, stylized designs rather than patterns and rhythms that are naturally danceable.

In 1938 Porter replaced Converse as dean of the New England Conservatory of Music and became its director from 1942 to 1946. He also was a cofounder of the American Music Center in 1939. Otto Luening says the center was born after he, Porter, and Henry Moe had met in New York in 1938 to discuss how to resolve the problem of providing American composers with a central reference library and distribution facility for their compositions. They met again in 1939, at Aaron Copland's Sixty-third Street studio, to incorporate the center as a nonprofit educational corporation. Later, Porter would serve a term as chairman of the board.[42]

In 1946 Porter left for New Haven to serve at Yale as a professor of music and in 1958 also was a master of Pierson College. Following the example of MacDowell, Ives, Ruggles, and Piston, he purchased a summer home in New England, on Squaw Lake, New Hampshire, to which he and his wife Lois loved to retreat. Several of the finest compositions of his career were written during these years, most of them while residing at Squaw Lake. He retired from teaching in 1965. Outstanding compositions are the Viola Concerto (1948), String Quartets Nos. 7, 8, and 9 (1943, 1950, 1958), Concerto Concertante for Two Pianos and Orchestra (1953), *New England Episodes* for orchestra (1958), Harpsichord Concerto (1959), Second Symphony (1962), and Variations for Cello and Piano (1963). His final composed work was the Oboe Quintet (1966). The Viola Concerto reveals Porter's love for the instrument and contains marvelous music. It is a work of apt and pleasant expression, radiates lovely colors, and has the power to please. The Quartets Nos. 7 and 8 are substantial American chamber compositions. They have poise and majestic expression but, even so, are invitingly warm and genially lyric. They sing without hesitation and with some personal feeling. The Two-Piano Concerto is affectively compelling, orchestrally luminous, and contrapuntally active. There is close cooperation between soloists and orchestra, rather than competition and virtuosic display. It won the Pulitzer Prize in 1954.

New England Episodes makes reference to an earlier Puritan period, with its psalms, ideals, firmness, harsh living conditions, episodes of gloom, and instants of joy. The main theme is modeled after the New England psalm tunes. The starting place for *New England Episodes* may have been a movie score composed for the Yale Library, entitled "Pan-American Scenes," from which the music was taken. The probing Cello Variations explore new expressive areas, where introspection and agitation replace pleasantness and optimism.

To summarize his later style one must cite his ability to write music that flows smoothly from section to section and that shows penetrating rhythmic sense, a confident use of contrapuntal language, employment of sophisticated harmonic methods often resorting to discordantly polytonal structures, and in general a merging of components taken from the modern German and French with traditional approaches to composing music. In these several ways he had a great deal in common with Walter Piston. Like Piston, too, he was not a conscious "nationalist," though he thought and spoke as a New Englander and loved his corner of the United States. Talking about the American composer, Porter said:

> He should gather as much knowledge of music as he can from as many good musicians as he is able to get in touch with; from other composers, from performers on as many different instruments as possible, from historians, from conductors. He should hear as much music as he can, with a keenly critical mind. . . .
>
> If we grant that he has been given his tools, and has acquired a wide base as a musician, how does he go about writing American music? My feeling is that he makes no conscious effort whatever to be American, but that he writes whatever seems to ring the bell most resonantly to his own musical consciousness. If he has been brought up in this country he will be influenced by his environment to write in certain ways; listeners who hear his music may find that these ways of writing music strike a sympathetic note. There may be something fresh in his music which rings true to the listener.[43]

 Virgil Thomson was unfair when he gave Porter a backhanded compliment: "His string quartets are idiomatically conceived for the instruments, relaxed in structure, not unpleasing but not quite absorbing either."[44] Porter was always modest about his attainments. Like Arthur Foote, he would not blow his own horn, nor would he attempt to form a coterie of young musicians who would follow his lead. He never set out to bowl over the listener or impress his colleagues with his modernistic tendencies. His voice rarely rose to the fiery and passionate. Even in his most fervent moments, an element of restraint is noticeable. Merely to titillate the ear was a failing, he thought. His virtues were unqualified competence as a composer and natural ability as a creative artist. One must appreciate him for his musical subtleties, penetration into the faculty of feeling, and delicacy in discriminating between what is valid expression and what is only surface sensation. He never made the vivid impression left by the other composers taken up in this chapter. No orchestra conductor tried very hard to obtain a new work from Porter. As Howard Shanet said of him, Porter was an example of a "highly talented professional" composer who was more honored than heard in this country.[45]

THE CONSERVATIONIST: RANDALL THOMPSON

During his lifetime, Randall Thompson was a composer who endured continuous condemnation from people favoring advanced musical ideas and techniques. However dear he was to American audiences, respected by conductors and members of choruses and orchestras, granted membership in prestigious societies, and paid tribute to with honorary doctorates, he was scarcely mentioned in the most influential histories of American music. Their authors, chiming with the views of modernists, found his music too familiar in style. It did not make sufficient demands on the listener and courted popularity, his accusers said. His string quartets, symphonies, and choral compositions had not met the criterion of "originality," "Americanism," or "modernity" imposed by "enlightened" historians.

Indeed, he was a conservationist who felt that preferring tradition, clear tonal organization, cautious use of dissonance, and enjoyable melody was not a form of triteness or dishonesty, as his critics claimed. Like Piston, he refused to resort to language not suited to his personality just to follow an up-to-date trend. He spoke up for music with uncomplicated emotional attractiveness. He preferred to honor rather than despise the general music public.

Composers, he said, should operate inside carefully defined bounds and realize their artistic autonomy inside clearly outlined restrictions. He thus countered the temptation to cultivate cleverness and complication with no other purpose in mind. Furthermore, restrictions like writing for amateurs or for a specific commissioned purpose kept the composer creditable. Randall Thompson maintained that "a composer's first responsibility [is] to write music that will reach and move the hearts of its listeners in its own day." He loved writing for amateur choruses, and his finest choral compositions occupy a high position in American music. Choruses, even those of limited ability, sound grand when singing his works. The music handily maintains equilibrium between a call for concentrated listening and sympathy for the average listener's capacity. It is no wonder that his choral music has won such an enthusiastic following among church and community choruses. As Robert Sabin says, "No American composer has written for voices with more ease and effectiveness than Randall Thompson."[46]

Thompson would also have agreed with Walter Piston, who wrote in 1941: "An American school will be built by those men, living in America, knowing it, and partaking of it, who are true to themselves. . . . If the composers will increasingly strive to perfect themselves in the art of music and will follow only those paths of expression which seem to them the true way, the matter of a national school will take care of itself."[47]

Both his parents came from Augusta, Maine, but he was born in New York City. His father was an English teacher at the Lawrenceville School in New Jersey and enrolled his son at the school. Later, his father left for Boston with his family to head Roxbury Latin School. Randall Thompson's first musical influence came from his mother, an excellent pianist. He studied voice with Howard Wood and organ with Francis Van Dyck, receiving his grounding in Handel and Bach from these men. In 1916 he graduated from the Lawrenceville School and enrolled at Harvard University to pursue his musical interests under Edward Burlingame Hill, Walter Spalding, and Archibald Davison. He would also study for a while with Ernest Bloch. It was Davison who helped foster his abiding interest in vocal music. The B.A. degree was granted him in 1920, and the M.A. in 1922. He knew well the psalmodic tradition of New England. He later was also attracted by African American spirituals, the music of Duke Ellington, and Appalachian folk and sacred shape-note melody.

In 1922 Thompson composed and submitted *Pierrot and Cothurnus,* a prelude for orchestra based on the drama *Aria da Capo* by Edna St. Vincent Milay, for the Prix de Rome and succeeded in winning a residence in Rome. There, in May 1923, the Accadèmia de Santa Cecilia performed the prelude under his direction. Its enthusiastic reception was the final evidence he needed to convince him of his abilities as a composer. He then composed a Piano Sonata (1923), *Five Odes of Horace* for men's voices (1924), and *The Piper at the Gates of Dawn* (1924), a symphonic prelude. With these early efforts, his distinctive manner of musical expression was gradually taking shape. While in Italy, also, he began to rough out his First Symphony.

On his return home in 1925, he went to live in New York City and tried his hand at writing incidental music for *The Grand Street Follies* and *The Straw Hat Revue*. He came back to Massachusetts to teach at Wellesley College in 1927, staying there until 1929. In 1927, too, he married Margaret Whitney (they had met in Paris), finished his *Jazz Poem* for piano (arranged for piano and orchestra the next year), and continued work on his symphony. In 1929 he was a lecturer in music at Harvard. By the end of 1929 he had completed the symphony. Howard Hanson premiered it in February 1930. A Guggenheim Fellowship in 1929–30 enabled him to start on a Second Symphony, which was finished in 1931 and which Hanson premiered in 1932.

Both symphonies sound indisputably American with their sprightly rhythms, effortlessness of manner, easygoing harmonies, and melodies beholden to New England psalmody, Appalachian and New England folk and traditional song and dance, jazz, and popular music. Discard the "literal and empty imitation of European models" that have held back the rise of a truly American music, Thompson advised composers, and instead become stimulated by "our own genuine musical heritage in its every manifestation, every inflexion, every living example."[48] He argued that complete originality was an unrealizable dream, whatever the situation. He disparaged the "cult of individuality" advocated by leaders of the modernist movement, because it put off the creation of a possible American musical style that might win over more than a handful of adherents.[49]

The Second Symphony soon established itself as one of the most widely accepted American orchestral works and received scores of performances in the United States and Europe. No program, pictorial or expressive, was intended. No cyclical management of his material was planned. Infectious rhythms and alluring tunefulness were its primary strengths. He was just writing four contrasting movements that balanced each other and that would speak directly to his audience. He certainly does so in the elegiac, spiritual-like slow movement and the jazzy *vivace* that follows. The music is refined through the composer's sensibilities and given an individual eloquence. No showiness or affectation mars the pleasure he delivers to his audience. He does not write to satisfy learned or scholarly individuals, whom he regarded as lacking in common and practical wisdom. The aim is to cheer, not challenge, the listener. After a reviewer heard Bruno Walter and the New York Philharmonic play the work, he wrote in *Musical*

America, 10 November 1933: "Applause such as seldom greets new compositions, native or otherwise, was the portion of Randall Thompson's symphony, and the composer was summoned to the stage several times to receive it. The audience liked the symphony's freshness, vitality, humor, and clever orchestration." The commentator himself, however, had reservations: "Nothing profound, nothing groping for the soul of man in music was to be found."[50]

Thompson was moving about the country with some frequency during the 1930s and 1940s. From 1932 to 1935 he served as the director of an investigation into college musical studies, for the Association of American Colleges. One result was his *College Music,* published in 1935. Ceaselessly traveling from position to position, he was again teaching at Wellesley College from 1936 to 1937, teaching at the University of California at Berkeley from 1937 to 1939, director of Philadelphia's Curtis Institute of Music from 1939 to 1941, head of the music sector at the University of Virginia from 1941 to 1946, a professor at Princeton University from 1946 to 1948, and finally a member of the Harvard faculty from 1948 until his retirement in 1965. Obviously, music education had come to occupy a vital place in his life.

A Third Symphony in A Minor would come out in 1949, commissioned by the Ditson Fund of Columbia University and broadcast over CBS radio in a performance by Thor Johnson and the CBS Symphony on 15 May 1949. Thompson had actually begun the symphony in 1944, in a period when he was deeply caught up emotionally with World War II and the crucial battles being fought then. In large part it is an artistic expression of his wartime feelings. The composer tried to achieve a depth of feeling and even a sense of tragedy that was absent from his earlier symphonies. It starts off with a funereal lament, *largo elegiaco,* that acquires dissonances, some slightly disturbing, toward the end of the movement. "The prevailing mood is one of sadness," Thompson says. The second movement, in contrast, is rhythmically energetic and tunefully appealing. The music next croons a slow and gentle song, *lento tranquillo,* and falls into dreamy meditation. As one might expect with Thompson, the finale is bright, animated, melodic, and oftentimes comical. It ends on an optimistic note. Traditional American sounds permeate the music. The day after George Szell and the Cleveland Orchestra played the Third Symphony on 23 March 1950, a reviewer in the *Cleveland News* described the work as "colorful, brilliant and melodious. While it is at times rather despairing in mood, almost tragic in its implications, it rounds into a dazzling Scherzo and a close that has its enthusiastic heights and a concluding atmosphere of warmth and happiness."[51] However, the symphony did not succeed nearly as well with audiences as did the Second Symphony.

Thompson was conducting several choral groups when he wrote his spoofing *Americana* for chorus and piano or orchestra in 1932. The text came from H. L. Mencken's selections of newspaper absurdities reprinted in the *American Mercury* and satirizes religious fundamentalism, feather-brained spiritualism, narrow-minded temperance, capital punishment, and American optimism in its five movements. It is an exuberant work and delightfully mocking.

His first major choral work was *The Peaceable Kingdom* (1936) for unaccompanied chorus, after Edward Hicks's nineteenth-century painting showing William Penn and American Indians in amity with each other and Daniel, lions, and lamb peacefully coexisting. Hicks took his inspiration from Isaiah 11:6–9: "And the wolf will dwell with the lamb. For the earth will be full of the knowledge of the Lord as the waters cover the sea." Thompson once stated, "The lions in this part [of the painting] look as though they were trying to make peace with Daniel; they appear to be succeeding." The text is from *Isaiah* and warns reprobates of their approaching punishment for time without end and guarantees endless bliss in the future to the morally upright. All is kept simple and clear. As is usually the case in his choral music, diatonic passages prevail. Consummate skill is evident in the treatment of the chorus so that it cannot help sounding effective. Melodic phrases are elegantly formed and satisfying to vocalize. The normal rhythms of the English language are carefully observed. What dissonances assail the ear come only in those moments when the words call for them.

Perhaps the most famous choral piece ever written by an American is the *Alleluia* (1940) that Koussevitzky commissioned for the opening of the Berkshire Music Center at Tanglewood, in Lenox, Massachusetts. The center had anticipated a celebratory choral salute. Instead it received an internalized work of genius, possibly reflecting his anxiety over the raging world war and the collapse of France. Thompson's ability in employing his technical skills was certainly extraordinary. The quality of the writing is remarkable, and the unusual comprehension of what would make a chorus sound grand is everywhere in evidence. The result was the creation of one of the most distinguished choral pieces of the twentieth century.

In the next year he composed his First String Quartet in D Minor, an extremely engaging chamber piece. It was awarded the Coolidge Prize, and the Coolidge Quartet gave it a first performance in Washington, D.C., on 30 October 1941. The work was modeled on Beethoven's three opus 59 quartets. Nevertheless, the first movement owes a debt to American fiddle tunes. A slow and sad movement follows it. The next movement is a cheerful *vivace ma non troppo,* twice slowed down for some contrasting lyricism. The close is an *allegro appassionato.* Instead of a fiery final climax, however, it acts to reconcile everything that has gone before by means of a serene ending. Virgil Thomson loved the work "not only for its touching Appalachian Mountain Americanism but for its broader musical interest as well. It is one of the loveliest pieces our country has produced, that any country, indeed, has produced in our century."[52] Thompson would produce a Second String Quartet in G Major in 1967, written for the Harvard Music Association. It is a much less weighty work than the First Quartet. Charm, wit, and a subtle folksiness prevail almost throughout.

Thompson's one-act opera *Solomon and Balkis,* the libretto by the composer based on "The Butterfly That Stamped," a tale from Rudyard Kipling's *Just So Stories,* was broadcast over CBS radio in March 1942, in a concert performance given by Howard Barlow directing the Columbia Concert Orchestra. It was staged in Harvard's Lowell House dining hall in April 1942, with Malcolm Holmes conducting the Harvard Orchestra and Radcliffe Choral Society. In it, ingratiating melody is combined with burlesque eighteenth-century recitative and a witty plot. The plot involves a harried King Solomon who faces domestic problems caused by his several wives and calls on the wisdom of his wife Balkis to rescue him.

World War II and the life-and-death struggle between the forces of fascism and democracy were occupying every American's mind when Thompson composed *The Testament of Freedom* in 1943. The University of Virginia Glee Club commissioned it in honor of the two-hundredth anniversary of the birth of Thomas Jefferson. Thompson intended the composition as a paean to a free people and an American democracy in which the supreme power is vested in the ordinary citizenry. Four texts from Jefferson, written at different stages of his life, from young manhood to when he was seventy-eight years of age, were set for male chorus and piano or orchestra, drawing on the most undemanding musical resources. Unison singing or the simplest of part-singing was heard against a self-effacing accompaniment. It is in the vein of the psalmodic tradition but redeployed to suit contemporary times. The composition was broadcast throughout the country and to the armed forces across the oceans on 13 April 1943. It was an immediate sensation.

Among his later works are *The Last Words of David* (1949) for chorus and piano or orchestra, the orchestral fantasy *A Trip to Nahant* (1954), the "seven country songs" of *Frostiana* (1959) for three- to seven-voice choruses, and *The Nativity According to St. Luke* (1961) and *The Passion According to St. Luke* (1965), both for soloists, chorus, and orchestra. The first composition was commissioned by the Boston Symphony to celebrate the twenty-fifth anniversary of Koussevitzky's directorship and is a choral piece that makes a deep impression. The orchestral fantasy owes much to psalmody and to American country dance.[53] *Frostiana* was first performed in Amherst, New Jersey, with Robert Frost present. Enthused by the musical setting of his poetry, he sprang up at the close of the last number and yelled, "Sing that again!"

If Quincy Porter was a composer who was more honored than performed in this country, then Randall Thompson was a composer who was more performed than honored, until relegated to the sidelines in the mid-1960s. After World War II, commissions gradually dwindled in number, and his willingness to communicate with a broad public "was taken as a sign in some quarters that he was not 'serious,' or worse, that he was not to be taken seriously." His works for orchestra and chamber players disappeared from professional programs, although amateur choruses continued to favor his music. In the last years of his life he felt "a very real anger" at being "ignored by what he termed the 'highbrows' of American music."[54] Only in recent years are professional performers rediscovering his music, as well as Piston's. On the other hand, amateur choral singers have never forgotten him.

CHAPTER 12

THE SECOND HALF OF THE TWENTIETH CENTURY

After World War II, Americans found themselves quickly becoming members of a mass society. There appeared to be a growing absence of distinctive ideals, an unconsciousness of individual or social responsibility, and a readiness to be manipulated by the techniques developed by mass media. Their relations with each other were turning out to be culturally weaker and more compartmentalized than heretofore. They tended to socialize less and to become active in fewer community activities. The constant movement of families from place to place and frequent shifts in social status also encouraged a more impersonal and noncommittal approach to things. People were more of a mind to passively observe rather than actively participate in artistic events, and showed a stronger inclination to go along with popular standards and customs.

However steadfast New England had been in maintaining its social and cultural identity, a new era began where its unique values and noticeable personality traits faded. There seemed to be less a sense of personal or social commitment in New Englanders, and more a vulnerability to the techniques developed by mass advertisers. Moreover, new ethnic groups from Catholic Ireland, Latin America, nations on the Mediterranean rim, the countries of Eastern Europe, and the lands of the Far East were displacing the old Yankee stock and diluting its influence more than ever before. The cultural orientations of most of these newcomers were different. Those composers who took themselves seriously as artists had a new enemy to battle against—the indifference of a changing public toward the music they found moving and exciting. Of greatest significance, almost all of the well-known New England composers of the late twentieth century would either not have been born in New England or, if born here, not have

329

come from a family of Yankee ancestral descent. Their local roots would tend to be shallower or almost nonexistent.

Television came on the scene after the war, grew relatively inexpensive, and developed into the favorite pastime of a vast number of Americans, New Englanders included. In an attempt to attract even more viewers, the directors of commercial television programming deliberately lowered the level of challenge and intellectual content in their offerings in order to suit a huge, indiscriminate audience. As Frank Stanton, the former head of CBS, put it, "cultural democracy" meant giving the majority what it wanted, and "most of the people, most of the time, want entertainment from their mass media."[1] He did not consider it commercial television's job to take on the burden of building audiences for artistic creations. Unfortunately, neither public television nor cable "arts" networks ventured to present music beyond the favorite pieces that had become overly familiar or hackneyed through much repetition, thus excluding a great deal of twentieth-century art music, especially that of Americans. AM radio no longer bothered with the arts at all, and FM stations supposedly dedicated to "good music" were more inclined to let Beethoven's Fifth Symphony be heard a thousand times rather than Piston's Fifth Symphony once. Even supposed leaders in better programming like nonprofit public broadcasting stations, among them WGBH of Boston, were inclined to take a route that would attract more listeners and more financial contributions.

With more and more people living in a city's suburbs, there was the threat that potential music lovers might grow more inclined to stay put rather than trek into town, where the old buildings looked shabby, dark streets were threatening, and expenses for baby-sitters, ticket purchase, and parking made the effort untempting—whether that city was Boston, Springfield, Worcester, Hartford, Manchester, Portland, or Providence. The arts in general would subsequently receive less dedicated support than artists would have desired. This would particularly be so toward the very end of the century.

In response to the decline in appeal, newspapers and general-interest magazines cut down on their arts coverage. The number of music critics shrank drastically, concert reviews were infrequently encountered, and articles having a bearing on art music were few. This held true not only for the small community newspapers but also for most city papers. While the *Boston Globe* continued to cover the arts area, it did so with fewer resources devoted to art music events. At the same time, it increased its coverage of the pursuits of the go-go younger set. A number of New England newspapers ceased to exist or amalgamated with other newspapers, again shriveling what little arts coverage there had been. As for the general readership, for all practical purposes what was not reported on ceased to have life. When a concert went unannounced in the media, it did not exist in music lovers' minds. If it took place and got no coverage, only the audience was aware of its existence. This became the fate of most performances of art music.

For a while, a movement favorable to art music seemed to gather strength. Standards of living improved considerably after the war. Income remaining after deducting necessary expenditures increased. The LP, the cassette tape, and later the CD facilitated the recording and distribution of new and lesser-known compositions to the music public. Young people enrolled in huge numbers in New England's colleges and universities, and their exposure to literature, paintings, and art music was often facilitated by curriculum distribution requirements. Several commentators made the claim that symphony and opera audiences were growing enormously. Orchestras populated by amateurs and professionals appeared in a majority of cities and the larger towns. Urban centers such as Hartford, New Haven, Providence, Portland, and Worcester had a readily available supply of competent musicians to draw upon, many of them trained in local music schools, conservatories, and colleges. They were also able to draw on a sizable pool of excellent freelance professional musicians, trained and living in the Boston area, to fill out their ranks.

Cultural centers began to spring up in the 1960s because government officials, enlightened leaders, and directors of commercial and manufacturing enterprises considered them beneficial to society and business. In the Berkshires, for example, Tanglewood, the Williamstown Theater Festival, Music Mountain, and Jacob's Pillow benefited from this mind-set. The National Endowment for the Arts and various state and local arts committees funneled money to composers and performing groups. Private funding organizations, among them the Ford Foundation, Rockefeller Foundation, Koussevitzky Foundation, and Fromm Foundation, also supported art music institutions and commissioned new music from composers. For a while it seemed that the upsurge of interest in art music would offset the leveling pressures of mass culture.

An altered democratic ethos was also gathering strength, however, in which the tastes of ordinary people gained ascendancy among intellectuals. They spoke in favor of the cultural power of the masses that was supplanting the cultural authority of a fastidious few. Music historians and critics of antiestablishment and grassroots persuasion contended that the ways of life of ordinary people had appealing or compensating attributes. They claimed that no person pretending to advanced learning and taste had a right to tell Americans uneducated, uninterested, or uninvolved in art music pursuits that their discrimination was inferior. This development is charted in Michael Kammen's *American Culture, American Taste* (1999). According to Kammen, after the 1960s cultural criticism on the side of the arts fell off, and what there was of it no longer had weight. There were few clearly defined and widely accepted sources of cultural authority. These were now "replaced in part by the rising influence of populist sources of authority, such as opinion polls, television ratings, published statistics on movie attendance, and political preference polls."[2]

"Elitism" was a ubiquitous accusation hurled by cultural militants at anyone who thought a symphony was superior to a rock song. The youth revolt of the 1960s abetted the charge. The young leaders of the revolt saw art music as a reflection of the existing power structure of a society that needed to be destroyed. In the 1970s would come the finger pointing of activists advocating the preservation of different cultures and identities within American society. During these years, the agitation over the Vietnam War, the demands for African American justice and women's rights, and the rejection of the excesses of the capitalistic establishment were unsettling the general public and occasioning a new scrutiny of American civilization. New England, already under decades of attack for its alleged Puritanism, found its cultural history being completely repudiated. Led by John Cage and several composers from California, a New Left in American music "challenged intellectual standards" that had guided New England's music making. This New Left "declared artistic works requiring close attention and specialized knowledge to be elitist. They were lies, representing an age of oppression of minorities, of social inequality, and of catering to the rich and wellborn. Obviously they should be banished." Those subject to banishment included Beethoven, Chopin, Rembrandt, Shakespeare, and the New England composers from Paine to Piston. They were all "just so much 'bullshit.'"[3]

Then there were the new American populists who found artistic quality second to none in all of the plainest varieties of musical language that had been and were in everyday use by ordinary Americans. They refused to make fine distinctions or apply any kind of discriminating judgment to musical compositions. Jazz, too, came under a cloud. The perceptive swing band compositions of Duke Ellington and the challenging bop art of Charlie Parker and Dizzie Gillespie were criticized in some circles as too exacting in their demands and not in touch with the masses. Writing about "the state of our art," in *Keynote* magazine of New York City's station WNCN in 1982, Gunther Schuller claimed the setting of elitism against populism, though superficially justified, lacked real merit and was based on false assumptions. At this time he was director of the Berkshire Music Center. He said that it was an argument "used to pit the 'disadvantaged' against the 'advantaged,' and attempts to make people who cherish quality music look like autocrats, snobs, and eggheads, insinuating that there is something anti-democratic and un-American about considering Duke Ellington superior to the Plasmatics or Mozart greater than John Lennon." The "ignoramus anti-elitists" cited audience statistics or sales figures and equated quality with mass consumption. Yet a great deal of popular music "is trivial *as music* and not of lasting relevance." He had a further concern: "The truth is that most average Americans haven't the remotest chance of encountering quality music [whether art music or jazz] in their lives. That fact results in turn in widespread cultural illiteracy and, in turn again, to a serious lack of grass root support for quality arts institutions and activities." America did have a culturally pluralistic society with a diversity of musical tastes. To like certain styles and not others was not bad in itself "if those likes and dislikes were based on a free choice and if the commercial musics didn't have such a total stranglehold on our people. . . . With network [and cable] television as its henchman and primary distributor, the commercial establishment dominates and determines the musical tastes of the vast majority of Americans." At the same time, the primary and secondary public schools were eliminating "quality" music from their classrooms and producing "a virtual musical wasteland." Meanwhile, the home did no educating, nor did the art music establishments, with their limited repertoire and conductors and soloists who had turned into "jet-age superstars."[4]

During the last three decades of the twentieth century, the norms of the artistic community and those of the populist counterculture, at the same time that they enriched each other, were constantly clashing. Those clashes were continuously in the background of New England's musical history during the post–World War II period.

I do not contend that every art composition is automatically superior to any popular piece. Quality and unworthiness exist irrespective of genre or style. Every genre comes into being based on a special set of assumptions, exists for a particular reason, and has a distinctive meaning for its listeners. Nevertheless, the United States is a nation that recognizes its multiformity and believes in a system of cultural limits imposed on all subdivisions of society. The nation gives no subdivision the right to overpower another. Room must be made for artistic modes that fall short of winning massive popular backing if our democracy is to fulfill its promise.

MUSIC ORGANIZATIONS AFTER WORLD WAR II

After the war, several exemplary ensembles came into existence. Among these were the high-grade Boston Philharmonic under Benjamin Zander, the admirable Greater Boston Youth Symphony sponsored by Boston University and a similar group sponsored by the New England Conservatory, the Pro Arte Orchestra, and the Boston Classical Orchestra, plus numerous town and city orchestras throughout New England and a variety of instrumental ensembles affiliated with conservatories and colleges. These organizations would contain professional musicians, competent amateurs, and music students from the various music schools and college music departments. The mix varied from group to group. Not least were amateur performers related professionally in some way with each other who established ensembles reflecting their calling. One such has been the large Longwood Symphony Orchestra, established in 1982, where doctors, medical technicians, and staff from eighteen medical institutions appear in concerts whose proceeds go to medically related nonprofit organizations.

In the last half of the twentieth century, several annual music festivals, other than Tanglewood and the others already mentioned, have done well in New England. Foremost among these is the Marlboro Festival, in connection with the Marlboro Music School in Vermont, which started life at midcentury. Musicians come here to study and participate in the concert performance of chamber music. Monadnock Music, with concerts scheduled in a small number of southern New Hampshire towns, puts on exploratory programs of opera and instrumental music. Additional music festivals include the Newport (Rhode Island) Music Festival, the Dorothy Taubman Institute and International Piano Festival of Williams College (Williamstown, Massachusetts), and the Rockport (Massachusetts) Chamber Music Festival.

After the demise of the Boston Opera Company, no important local opera enterprise existed until 1942, when Boris Goldovsky began the New England Conservatory Opera Workshop and presented cost-effective opera productions of commendable quality. Later, John Moriarty replaced Goldovsky and continued giving exceptional presentations of opera. Emulating the New England Conservatory, Boston University's School of Music also established an opera workshop and put on fine opera productions. As for professional companies, the Boston Lyric Opera stands out. John Balme founded it in 1976 as a resident company that mounted fully staged operas featuring young singers of considerable ability. Its performances are enjoyable, its ticket prices are as reasonable as possible, and it continues to survive to this day. It has tried to integrate itself into the community by offering in-school and after-school programs for children. Less fortunate was the Opera Company of Boston that Sarah Caldwell (born 1924) founded in 1957, even though the instrumentalists and singers under her direction gained a high reputation for quality, innovative staging, and boldness in exploring lesser-known and twentieth-century repertoire. Sarah Caldwell had studied under Goldovsky at the New England Conservatory, served as his assistant for eleven years, and conducted her first opera, Ralph Vaughan Williams's *Riders to the Sea,* at Tanglewood in 1947. By 1952 she was directing Boston University's operatic division. In 1976 she became the first woman to conduct a performance of the Metropolitan Opera in New York. An inspired and daring conductor, Sarah Caldwell kept her Opera Company of Boston going until 1991, winning international acclaim for performing twentieth-century operas such as Arnold Schoenberg's *Moses und Aron,* Luigi Nono's *Intolleranza,* Paul Hindemith's *Mathis der Maler,* and Roger Sessions's *Montezuma.* Unfortunately, she was a hopeless administrator, inexpert in attracting patrons, and completely lacking in financial sense. After disaster struck her company, she left Boston to become a guest conductor of major orchestras around the world.[5]

The early music movement accelerated after midcentury throughout the nation, spurred by the use of period instruments and voice production modeled ostensibly after earlier practices. New York City and Boston were the leaders in this resurgence of interest. Noah Greenberg in 1953 founded the New York Pro Musica Antiqua, and New York soon was the home of the Waverly Consort, Aston Magna, the New York Cornet and Sackbut Ensemble, the Ensemble for Early Music, the New York Consort of Viols, and the Concert Royal. In Boston, Narcissa Williamson started the Boston Camerata in 1954. When Joel Cohen led the group, from 1968 onward, it quickly gained an international reputation for performances of music from the Middle Ages and more recently of early American music.

Cohen's ensemble featured unceremonious, laid-back presentations, after which listeners were encouraged to come backstage and talk to the performers. Cohen commented in 1983: "Early music was counter-cultural at first, and now there are a whole host of 'official' ways to do early music. But none of the very best performers of early music talks about 'authenticity' at all; Andrea von Ramm, who staged *The Play of Daniel* for us and sings the title role, goes bananas whenever she hears the word. It's only the third-rank talents that want to codify everything. In the Camerata we want to keep experimenting; I hope we never toe the line."[6]

Martin Pearlman founded Banchetto Musicale in 1973, later renamed Boston Baroque. It was the first permanent Baroque orchestra in the United States. Its repertoire included music from the Baroque and Classical period—instrumental works, operas, oratorios, and masses. Then there was the Museum of Fine Arts Trio playing on authentic early instruments. At last, in 1981, the Boston Early Music Festival and Exhibition was held for the first time. A devoted following for early music was the result of all four endeavors.

Also to be mentioned is a third group, the Boston Musical Theater, formerly named the Friends of Dr. Burney, which Charlotte Kaufman established in 1976. Between 1981 and 1987 the group was housed in Boston's Museum of Fine Arts, where it presented restored theater pieces of the eighteenth and nineteenth centuries, especially ballad operas popular in early America. A skilled harpsichordist, Ms. Kaufman has made her own knowledgeable restorations of these stage works. The Gay-Pepusch *Beggar's Opera* had been one of Ms. Kaufman's specialties. A noteworthy appearance took place in May 1995, when the group teamed with Harry Ellis Dickson and the Boston Classical Orchestra to mount Georg Philipp Telemann's singspiel *Hochzeit des Comancho.* Toward the end of the century, the Boston Musical Theater also began performing American song classics from the Civil War period and twentieth century.

Finally, there is the Society for Historically Informed Performance, established in 1991, which gives concerts in various New England towns. Painstaking care is given to turning out programs that draw on the best current thinking about the authentic presentation of early music.

At another end of the spectrum is New England's contribution to jazz. One recalls the rag and stride pianist of the 1920s Sid Reinberg, the dance band led by Leo Reisman that played the Brunswick Hotel, and the fine ensemble led by Mal Hallett whose players once included Jack Teagarden and Gene Krupa. Such extraordinary jazz artists as Johnny Hodges, born in Cambridge; Max Kaminsky, Harry Carney, Ruby Braff, Sonny Stitt, and Roy Haynes, born in Boston; and Jaki Byard, born in Worcester, all contributed to American culture. In the early 1970s Gunther Schuller put together his renowned New England Ragtime Ensemble, the jazz counterpart of the early music movement.

DIVISIONS WITHIN THE ART MUSIC WORLD

At an earlier time, almost all American art composers were of Yankee extraction and born in New England. They were also Protestant Christians and possessors of similar attitudes toward life and art. In the post–World War II period, in part because most of the talented and successful composers in New England were not of Yankee ancestry, or of New England birth, or Protestant Christians, their attitudes differed and they agreed less concerning musical style. Atonalism, serialism, neoclassicism, neoromanticism, reactionarism, indeterminacy, ethnicism, populism, mysticism, minimalism, cross-culturalism, and postmodernism vied for ascendancy in the music world. More than ever before, art composers began to populate the music departments of New England's colleges and universities, because they had no place else to go to make a living. A delighted composer, Earl Kim, spoke of his light teaching load at Harvard, adding, "I don't believe that starvation is conducive to creating music. The universities are the modern Esterhazys. You can count on one hand the twentieth-century composers who have lived by composing alone."[7]

The various composers brought with them their special points of view about music making and could not help handing these views down to their students, however objective some composers tried to be. A synthesis of styles was just not in the cards. Multiple ideas and conflicting tendencies meant composers often begged to differ. The many dissimilar artistic goals could not be reconciled with practicable stances vis-à-vis the public. All was muddle, and sometimes excess ruled.

To add to the cultural rift in higher education, musicologists advocating the scholarly study of music gained prominence after the war and started to guide the outlook of music departments and to lessen the academic influence of composers. This was especially true for the Ivy League, the group of colleges and universities in the Northeast consisting of Harvard, Yale, Princeton, Columbia, Dartmouth, Cornell, the University of Pennsylvania, and Brown, all of them boasting a reputation for scholastic achievement and holding high social prestige. Although respectable musical knowledge acquired through study had characterized musicians resident in New England such as Alexander Thayer, Louis Coerne, and Archibald Davison, music as a purported scientific study regulated by exact procedures had its inception in America with Otto Kinkeldey, who for a time taught at Harvard, and with the establishment of the American Musicological Society in 1934.

Owing to the political and social upheavals in Europe that began in the 1930s, several well-known musicologists, most of them from Germany and Austria, came to the United States and induced changes in the curricula. Karl Geiringer went to Boston University. Curt Sachs appeared for a while at Harvard. Willi Apel, Otto Gombosi, and, much later, Christoph Wolff settled in at Harvard. Leo Schrade joined the Yale faculty and also delivered the Norton lectures at Harvard in 1962–63. Alfred Einstein was at Smith College. They directed attention to European music of the past and sometimes to the present. These scholars normally treated America's composers, musical history, and musical life as if they did not exist, and this disregard was passed on to their American counterparts. Non-native composers, among them Pierre Boulez and Luciano Berio, also arrived in the United States and perpetuated their ignorance of American music of the past and disdain for American music of the present in the minds of young American musicians.

This was not the only cause of the plunge in music enrollment by the best students, beginning in the 1970s, although plunge it did. At the time that Schrade was delivering his Harvard lectures, three out of four of the brightest students were majoring in the arts and sciences. Twenty-five years later, it was one out of four. Harvard reported a precipitous 77 percent decrease in college seniors going on to graduate studies and the brightest of these were shunning the arts, especially music. The probable reason was that earning a living in the arts remained uncertain, the respect accorded people in art music had sunk even lower, and college students were promised far more attractive, secure, and better-paying positions in business and industry. By this time Michael Spence, Harvard's dean of arts and sciences, was disquieted by the lower quality of students majoring in the humanities and was concerned about correcting it.[8]

Some music historians had begun to wonder if one reason for the disenchantment with academic music studies had to do with its emphasis on Europe and lack of connection with America, its past and its achievements. A corrective movement had begun when Oscar Sonneck, born in New Jersey, became head of the Music Division of the Library of Congress and editor of the *Musical Quarterly*. He helped found the Society for the Publication of American Music, wrote important pioneering essays on American music, and published four books of impeccable scholarship: *A Bibliography of Early Secular American Music* (1905), *Early Concert Life in America* (1907), *Opera in America* (1915), and *Suum Cuique* (1916). A second influential scholar, John Tasker Howard, born in New York, editor of three magazines, and curator of the American Music Collection of the New York Public Library, published the influential *Our American Music* (1931) and *Our Contemporary Composers: American Music in the Twentieth Century* (1941). After World War II, two men were especially important to the progress of American music studies, Gilbert Chase and Irving Lowens. Other excellent scholars joined the cause of American music. Prominent among them were H. Wiley Hitchcock, Richard Crawford, and Charles Hamm. In the 1970s a small group of concerned scholars—Chase, Lowens, Alan Buechner, and Raoul Camus of New York, Arthur Schrader of Sturbridge Village, Massachusetts, Neely Bruce of Middletown, Connecticut, and I myself met in Sturbridge and Middletown to formulate a plan for a music society devoted to "the study of American music and music in America." The result was the establishment in 1975 of the Sonneck Society (later called the Society for American Music), named in honor of Oscar Sonneck. It issued a newsletter and a journal and sponsored activities and publications that advanced knowledge about music in America. Within twenty-five years it had over 800 individual members and over 125 institutional members. Courses in American music began to appear in the program of study of major universities. Moreover, the society's members were instrumental in changing the direction of the American Musicological Society, which at last began to give serious attention to the American musical field.

THE BOSTON SYMPHONY ORCHESTRA

After Koussevitzky retired as music director of the Boston Symphony in 1949, Charles Munch (1949–62), Erich Leinsdorf (1962–69), William Steinberg (1969–72), and Seiji Ozawa (from 1972), none of them an American, followed him. With Koussevitzky went the strong dedication to performing the works of American composers. None of the music directors was particularly sympathetic to the cause of American music and usually measured it by standards contrived in Europe. As might be expected, the compositions by Americans were frequently considered second-rate.

Leinsdorf, for one, explained that during his conductorship of the symphony he reluctantly performed a few American works, which he said were of uneven quality, because he had to be diplomatic. After World War II America had provided "few vintage harvests in symphonic music," he said. It was difficult for him to appear "liberal, progressive, and confident that we in the United States had the most gifted school of composition" where no talent existed.[9] The assessment was as patently inaccurate as it was sweeping.

Munch, to his credit, improved the lot of his players. He increased the weeks of performance so that the instrumentalists had employment lasting through the year. The Tanglewood summer concerts went from thirteen to twenty-four. The orchestra engaged in two transatlantic tours (1952, 1956) and one tour across the Pacific (1960). An annual series of youth concerts, under the direction of Harry Ellis Dickson, began in 1959. For the orchestra's seventy-fifth anniversary season (1955–56), thirteen new works were commissioned, seven of them from Americans, one from Piston. Under Leinsdorf music education received stronger emphasis at the Berkshire Music Center, and the Boston Symphony Chamber Players were inaugurated (1964). One must also add that it was during his directorship, in 1964, that the Tanglewood Festival of Contemporary Music would begin. It quickly won recognition as one of the most distinguished festivals of its kind in the nation. By the year 2000 it would comprise ten concerts given over a five-day period.

Seiji Ozawa was a brilliant orchestral conductor but a poor diplomat, often riling his players, the community, and the musicians responsible for keeping the Berkshire Music Center operational. During his long sojourn with the symphony he would replace around 80 percent of its personnel and take the orchestra on tours of Europe, Japan, Hong King, China, and South America. He would also see to the commissioning of new music for the symphony's centennial, in 1981, and for Tanglewood's fiftieth anniversary, in 1990. That did not mean he would play American music on a regular basis. Scarcely any American works appeared in his concerts. In 1981, when the announcement was made that the orchestra was to engage in a world tour, there was also an acknowledgment that Ozawa refused to perform any American compositions during the journey. Furthermore, by his own admission, Ozawa was anxious that his family not become absorbed by American culture. In addition, despite the orchestra's outreach attempts and concern with extending services to the Greater Boston area, the orchestra seemed more an appendage to rather than a part of the community.

After Ozawa took over in 1972, he and the staff guiding the symphony grew worried over the problem of attracting young people to concerts and building future audiences. Symphony Hall seemed to be populated by old-sters, a majority of them women. The average age of concert attendees was over fifty-five years of age. This elderly audience was declared to be unreceptive to any unfamiliar music, especially if it was modern and disso-nant. Lack of money for tickets was only part of the problem deterring attendance by younger people, who might be more daring in their tastes, according to Mark Volpe, managing director of the orchestra. He blamed the lessening interest in art music and low youthful attendance at sym-phonic concerts on the cutback in music programs offered in public schools and the decrease in amateur music making. This, coupled with reductions in federal and local funding, lack of television exposure, and fewer recordings offered the public, had hampered the ability of the orchestra to expand its offerings and develop further contacts with the community, or so he claimed.[10] He failed to take the zeitgeist into consideration.

The symphony tried to accommodate younger people impeded by a "sound bite" mentality, a short attention span, a desire to be amused and not put to the test, and a need not to just listen but to see a show. A tempt-ing strategy was to countenance rather than try to reverse this trend. Rock concerts were permitted at Tanglewood, with the hope that the people present would return for more artistic presentations. No one did. Al-though attendance records were broken, the headaches caused were unen-durable. Youths under the influence of alcohol and illicit drugs destroyed property and created bedlam on the grounds and in the area. The concerts were stopped.[11]

An additional quandary was the reduction of financial support from the wealthy and the turning to the rank-and-filers in the audience for money. Every year members of the general music public were solicited for voluntary contributions. The public exacted something in return—pro-grams containing the compositions it liked and featuring the soloists who enjoyed wide recognition and were esteemed for exceptional talent. The freedom to schedule novel compositions and to focus on music rather than personalities was thus severely limited.

Ozawa chose to act in other areas, in moves that had as many political as aesthetic overtones and resulted in prolonged public disputes. One was the widely and unfavorably viewed Vanessa Redgrave affair of 1982. A scheduled performance of Stravinsky's *Oedipus Rex,* in which Redgrave was to participate, was canceled because of her espousal of the Palestinian cause. Wealthy donors from the Jewish community had objected to her appearance. It resulted in an embarrassing court case, which was decided in Redgrave's favor.[12]

Another dispute involved Schuller, the respected director of the Berkshire Music Center, who was also administrator of the weeklong Tanglewood Contemporary Music Festival, which Paul Fromm had financed, since its start in 1964. He favored what he considered a reputable modernism based on post-triadic, atonal, and serial procedures. After Ozawa's accession to the conductorship of the Boston Symphony, Schuller felt increasing pressure from the conductor to expand the contemporary music selections to include styles not especially favored by Schuller, such as indeterminacy, minimalism, and a mélange of movements rejecting the practices of established modernism and the alleged International Style. Fromm suddenly and inexplicably withdrew his support of Schuller. Schuller felt Ozawa's interference was unwarranted. Refusing to comply, he resigned both of his positions in 1984. Oliver Knussen, an English composer, replaced him as contemporary music administrator and Leon Fleisher as Berkshire Music Center director. Knussen resigned in 1993, and Reinbert de Leeuw, a Dutch composer, took his place. Ozawa's shakeups continued. It was not always apparent what he was trying to accomplish by the constant upheaval other than asserting himself in the decision-making process. What was clear was his absence of commitment to American music and American composers, already evident in his Boston Symphony programming.

At the century's close, the Boston Symphony was like an unanchored ship drifting with little sense of direction and without a discernible mandate from the music public or community to guide it. Ozawa had announced his impending resignation as director of the orchestra. The question was whether the board of directors would continue to look only outside of the United States for a replacement.

ENSEMBLES FOR NEW MUSIC

As the century progressed toward its close, fewer and fewer traditional music organizations programmed contemporary music. At the same time, performers tired of the hackneyed pieces they were forced to play repeatedly. Many of them joined the composers left out in the cold to correct the situation. Throughout New England, a number of organizations were brought into existence principally for the performance of new music.

Music schools, colleges, universities, and museums provided space and support to ensembles dedicated to the performance of contemporary compositions. They accepted their responsibility to minister to current musical culture and acted accordingly. Cooperative composers' ventures, some lasting a single performance, others several decades, also aired works that otherwise might never have come before an audience. Boston, with its many schools, composers teaching at these schools, and concentration of whatever resources were available to new music groups, was at the center of New England enterprises in this direction.

In 1969 a noteworthy action took place: Richard Pittman founded Boston Musica Viva, the first professional ensemble in Boston committed to contemporary music. He has continued over the years as its only director. Boston Musica Viva quickly developed into one of the most favorably regarded new music ensembles in the country, winning praise for the quality of its performances, the constant introduction of the latest compositions, and the many revivals of older twentieth-century works. Furthermore, as awareness of the merits of performing new music increased, Boston Musica Viva acted as an exemplar for other groups specializing in contemporary music that have been starting up throughout America. Appreciative of the support the group has rendered to living composers, quite a few American musicians have written pieces especially for Viva's players. By century's end, Pittman and Boston Musica Viva had presented more than 500 compositions by over 220 composers, around 130 of the works presented in world premieres, and around sixty in Boston premieres. Local artists such as John Harbison and Michael Gandolfi have benefited greatly from Musica Viva's sponsorship. Pittman has consciously sought to include a variety of styles in his concerts—those linked to atonal or serial procedures, pieces involving varying degrees of indeterminacy, and others associated with dance or theater or visual presentations. A valuable service is rendered the greater Boston community through family concerts and school-outreach appearances, where the music heard is of the twentieth century and easily comprehended. Travels to various parts of the United States, transatlantic tours, and numerous recordings have brought the music of Americans to the attention of a multiplicity of publics.

During the mid-1970s a burgeoning number of new music ensembles formed in and around Boston. Frank Epstein founded the first of these, the Collage New Music Ensemble, in 1975. At that time, several musicians had felt exhilarated by the musical styles evolving around them and wished to lend a hand. Discussions took place between performers and composers. Collage was launched to funnel commission money to composers and give concerts of newly written works, with the composers sharing in whatever income was obtained through ticket sales. Local artists such as Gunther Schuller, Charles Fussell, Stephen Albert, and John Harbison have had pieces performed by Collage. A few players from the Boston Symphony, wearied by the standard fare of the orchestra, contributed their services to the enterprise. The first meetings took place at Boston's Museum of Fine Arts, but after the museum refurbished the room Collage was using, it started concertizing at Sanders Theater, the Longy School, the Tsai Center of Boston University, Symphony Hall, and, most recently, the Walsh Theater of Suffolk University, where Collage is the ensemble-in-residence. Under the presidency of Frank Coolidge, Nick Anagnostis, and Charles Blyth and the musical directorship of David Hoose, the group has attempted to build bridges to the more adventurous listeners. By century's end, those listeners had experienced the premieres of over two hundred compositions.

The New England Philharmonic came to life as the Mystic Valley Chamber Orchestra, founded by Michael Perrault and Gervasio de Chaves, with a first concert directed by Charles Ellis in 1977. A year after its establishment, the orchestra began its programming and commissioning of new music, in addition to its performance of older but unhackneyed works. In 1986 it was given space at Framingham State College, and the next year its name changed to the New England Philharmonic to indicate its fresh character and its ambition to reach a larger audience. Jeffrey Rink assumed the music directorship in 1988 and immediately set about improving the quality of the playing and expanding the mix of amateurs and professionals. Five times the orchestra received the ASCAP Award for Adventuresome Programming. Among the local composers performed were Leon Kirchner, Michael Gandolfi, and Alan Hovhaness. In 1996 the orchestra moved to a residency at Simmons College and welcomed a new conductor, Richard Pittman. During Pittman's tenure, several out-of-the-ordinary concerts have been given at the Tsai Center of Boston University.

Two other organizations remain to be named. The first is the interdisciplinary Mobius Artists Group, established in 1977, and run by way-out artists who freely experiment in all media. Members sometimes go it alone and sometimes pool their talents for combined productions. Since 1983 the group has operated as a tryout place for local artists experimenting at the borderline of their disciplines, making room for novel live performances using sound, video, and all sorts of installations. The second organization is Alea III, founded by the Greek composer Theodore Antoniou and in residence at Boston University since 1978. New music, though not necessarily of the uninhibited cutting-edge variety, is its forte. Its emphasis, unlike the four ensembles already mentioned, is more international than national or local. Professional musicians play pieces featuring a "multiplicity of musical directions, historical styles, and performance practices." Antoniou says that the reason for Alea III's existence "is not to please or satisfy an audience but to educate people, to show them what is going on in the world of music."[13]

THE COMPOSER'S DILEMMA

The postwar years were unlike those that had gone before. During the first half of the century, whatever advanced compositional practices they used, composers acted within a cultural context that had given them some direction. Though their public was not huge, it was substantial, and listeners did not usually revolt when confronted with the new—thus the success of Koussevitzky and the Boston Symphony in presenting contemporary American compositions to audiences.

In the second half of the century, the muddled milieu gave composers little creative direction. In New England, as elsewhere in the country, they confronted burning questions that required answers. Did composers write to please themselves as artists? Did they write to please a particular or a general audience? Should they write at the urgent prompting of some inner impulse? Should they adhere to a traditional style, or branch off into atonalism and free dissonance, or cast off all constraints and experiment independent of external controls? Some musicians tried to belong, to work within a traditional framework, but in what tradition? Others became eclectics, their works composed of elements drawn from two or more sources. More adventurous composers felt displaced, torn away from the customary ways of musical life. A few of them sought aggressively to remove themselves from any connection with normal music channels, at times choosing to withdraw to a solitary life of cultural seclusion. After World War II older composers such as Piston and Thompson persisted more or less in their own set ways, and a younger set continued along the ways they had pioneered. However, another batch of composers came into prominence in New England and elsewhere that found the pathways to creativity encumbered by problems with no easy solutions. Each solved them in his or her way. The stylistic homogeneity of a hundred years before had gradually unraveled, and now stylistic heterogeneity prevailed. The music being written went every which way and contained widely dissimilar elements.

Uprootedness, anomie, and a measure of self-indulgence characterized the era. More than a few musical novices of the 1950s did not feel that they had to follow the guidelines suggested by the more prominent American composers of the previous generation (whether the romanticism of Samuel Barber, the neoclassicism of Piston, the traditional Americanism of Thompson, or the advanced Americanism of Aaron Copland). Many of them tended to spurn what styles were prevalent in the United States and look to Europe for indications of future courses of action. The Harvard-educated Elliott Carter conceded in 1964 that America was again becoming "an outpost of that European world, which Americans have so often found more attractive than the reality of what they have at home."[14] His reading of the situation was that native composers thought it necessary to find acceptance in the European artistic world in order to win entry into American musical circles.

Arnold Schoenberg, who now lived and taught in the United States, represented the world of atonality, as did such visitors as Boulez, Stockhausen, and Berio. For a while all four (and Schoenberg's followers, Berg and Webern, in absentia) were the gods of quite a few neophyte composers. In addition, Roger Sessions came into his own as an influential teacher. He boasted a New England ancestry but was born in Brooklyn. He had received instruction from Horatio Parker at Yale but quickly cast off Parker's conservatism. Though a contemporary of Piston, Sessions had gone the direction of the atonalists, with compositions unanchored in a tonal center, unobligated to consonance, and displaying a complexity of thought unfathomable to ordinary listeners. Shocked by the nationalism that had brought on the Nazis and Fascists, Sessions warned his students about American nationalism as a creative guide.

A general depreciation of what went before in America's music took place, especially the works of the easier-to-understand composers. As postwar years went by, composers who alluded to American idioms were declared behind the times, and those who hinted at any form of nineteenth-century Romanticism were branded as tasteless, in the writings of au courant commentators, despite the music public's interest in their works. Thompson was found to write awful kitsch that catered to low-brow taste; Piston was declared rigidly academic and pedantic. Neither man was seen as willing to confront the past or sunder his allegiance to an inherited pattern of cultural beliefs and musical practices. Neither composer wrote to reflect the post–World War II years and therefore was open to criticism. Their failure to do so meant that both were dismissible. Only Ives and Ruggles, among the New England composers, seem to have come under the wire. As an example of the new thinking, a *Boston Globe* reviewer advised his readers, "Nothing is more important in the musical year than the emergence of new works that challenge tradition even as they lengthen it."[15]

There was protest, of course. At one time, when André Previn was still caught up in this sort of thinking, he was lecturing in this vein before a student audience at Tanglewood. One young listener voiced disapproval, saying that advanced composers did not meet standards for evaluating music that were set by the public: "People wanted to hear something melodic, with a certain structure," he maintained. Previn countered with a put-down: "A melody is just a succession of notes. I suspect you're saying that people like music to be relaxing, passive listening." Furthermore, Previn said, "Most audiences sit at a concert the way you sit in a warm bath. It's extremely pleasant. . . . If you *make* them listen, *make* them participate, they often grow tired very quickly."[16] These audiences merited no consideration because they wished to maintain the status quo and would not oppose convention, Previn concluded. An attitude like Previn's only got the music public's back up.

To bolster their cause and give encouragement to each other, the more radical composers and their supporters, especially those located in New York City, took to announcing the premiere of masterpiece after masterpiece, some of them said to be mightier than anything that had gone before. In many ways, it was like whistling in the dark, an attempt to summon up optimism in a difficult situation. New Englanders kept more level heads. Gunther Schuller in 1967 was located at the New England Conservatory of Music when he warned that the "irresistible masterpiece" syndrome was foolish. The music public was not convinced by such claims and had not asked for these "masterpieces." And in the end it was the public who decided what was noteworthy in music—something composers had to learn to accept.[17]

On the other hand, composers were confronting a situation inhospitable to truly dedicated artistic pursuits. Concerts and "good music" FM radio broadcasts usually revolved around a narrow list of works from the past, excluding contemporary contributions. New music remained ig

nored while "star" singers and instrumentalists, exploiting a few traditional pieces, were accorded superhuman reputations and generous
incomes. The tried-and-true brought in audiences and made money; the
out-of-the-ordinary put a damper on attendance and lost money. The public was giving up whatever sense of adventure it might have had and
showed no enthusiasm for crossing the border into unfamiliar musical
regions. Is it any wonder that some said a pox on the public and its brain-
less perceptions and then went their own way? The composer Earl Kim,
from his vantage point at Harvard University, spoke of the disappoint-
ments brought on by hardly any performances. Furthermore, what was
played received careless performance by poorly prepared musicians and
almost always before unreceptive listeners. Composing, he said, was "a
terrible taskmaster" and came with "sleepless nights and getting yourself
performed." After much effort and expense to copy out the parts and convince someone to put a piece on, Kim said, he would hear a composition
only once. No wonder he said, "One is not above being bitter sometimes."[18]

At first, serialism and totally organized abstract works held sway—a
system of tone relationships in which the twelve tones of an octave are not
directed toward any one tone but are linked through a selected order of
tones in a given composition. Then came various atonal and modified-
serial styles that were less rigid. Coming to the fore next were a confusing
number of percussive and electronic approaches to composition. Later
indeterminacy was advocated as an ideal, in which deliberate use was
made of chance, whether in the framing of a piece or in its execution. This
was followed by performance art or music that brought magical rites,
secret or specialized rituals, and Asian pursuits of wisdom into play. There
was music for meditation, for experiencing psychedelic states of mind, for
expressing the natural environment, and for symbolizing modern-day
turmoil.

Creative independence with no audience listening to one's music was
a difficult road to travel. By the late 1970s a few musicians were trying to
win over the general music public again with more approachable music.
Music as recreation and works of artistic excellence were less seen as dia-
metrically opposed. Jeff McLaughlin, in an article in the *Boston Globe*,
11 March 1984, wrote of this revisionist trend, saying that entertainment
was "in" again and serious composers were bent on producing agreeable
and understandable music.[19] Works were offered the public espousing
minimalism, neoromanticism, tonal and atonal sounds, the eclectic put-

ting together of old and new styles, and borrowings from earlier works placed in juxtaposition with original writing. The hope was somehow to break through to a larger audience.

Alan Hovhaness, a composer born in Somerville, Massachusetts, and of Armenian-Scottish decent, provides an example of an artist who was attempting the reconciliation of different, even opposing, styles and practices. We find him using Armenian song and dance, various Far Eastern idioms, procedures borrowed from the European Middle Ages, Renaissance, and Baroque, and a new-fashioned modal system. His was a creative philosophy that tried to translate mystical feelings into the reality of sound. At another extreme was the composer Frederic Rzewski, born in Westfield, Massachusetts, and of Polish descent. At various times he tried out serialism, electronic sounds, multimedia presentations, and indeterminacy. He developed a Leftist social and political philosophy that spurred him on to writing music to delineate a variety of oppressed peoples, whether inmates of American prisons or the underdog population of Chile. Another contrast is provided by Daniel Pinkham, born in Lynn, Massachusetts, to an old New England family. He was essentially a neoclassicist, although he dabbled in serial techniques, electronic sounds, and Baroque patterns of organization. Of the three, Pinkham was the only one who remained in New England throughout his adult life.

How to reconcile the styles of Hovhaness and Rzewski to that of Pinkham was not the least of the quandaries confronting music historians who found it impossible to sort out a New England identity in the second half of the twentieth century. In addition, if a native-born composer lived most of his life outside New England, was he or she to be considered truly representative of New England? Here was another difficulty facing music historians. Finally, what of composers born elsewhere, who had come to make their homes in New England and contributed importantly to New England education and music making—musicians such as Leon Kirchner and Gunther Schuller? Their styles were quite unlike those of the other three. When audiences heard works of all five composers, they listened to compositions that sounded highly different from each other. Where was New England in this music? All of America had grown into one open cultural society, with special regional identities much diminished.

Thus the composer's dilemma had its parallels in the music historian's perplexity and in the listener's bewilderment. There no longer seemed to be a "New England" coefficient in American music.

CHAPTER 13

COMPOSERS BRIEFLY OF NEW ENGLAND AFTER WORLD WAR II

A merican composers, good, bad, and indifferent, were being turned out by the hundreds after the war, owing to the expansion of educational institutions and governmental assistance to those who wished to enroll. What to do with themselves was a bothersome question for all music graduates. As for composers, it was not just job situations but also the conditions favorable for the realization of performances that were limited. These composers frequently moved from place to place during the latter half of the twentieth century. Neither family and community ties nor affection for their place of birth were sufficient to keep them home. Opportunity and the need to earn a living forced them to be constantly in motion.

To write art music was all well and good, but scarcely anyone could make money out of it. Artists usually had to find and travel to teaching positions wherever available and apply for and hope to receive grants or fellowships. If fortunate, they obtained commissions to write musical works, won posts as composers-in-residence with orchestras or at colleges and universities, or worked as music editors, or performed music. One or two were fortunate to have private incomes or wives willing to support them. New England composers were leaving home more than ever to become vital constituents in the cultural activities of other sections of the nation. Young composers-to-be, born elsewhere, came to New England to obtain a musical education, then left to work in a different place. Composers who already had a track record somewhere else sojourned for a while in New England before moving on again. The creative world was in a constant state of flux.

The styles that these composers adopted were quite unalike. More than ever before, no composer could be considered to be locked into one particular approach. The artist added to, subtracted from, and completely changed a manner, as he or she desired. Moreover, each composer had to create his or her own "tradition," one's own customary method of writing made up of various stylistic snippets from the past and present. Obviously, no such thing as a unified New England outlook could easily emerge, given these circumstances. Besides, New Englanders were now completely open to the world and experiencing a tremendous variety of different kinds of music, offered to them by composers, recordings, concerts, the broadcasting media, and immigrants from every corner of the earth.

Whose musical voice would this postwar music public respond to? Was there a composer who had worked out a style from a combination of the materials at hand, native or otherwise, that the New England public could fervently declare to be "New England" or "American" or a generator of masterpieces worthy of inclusion in musical literature? What quickly becomes obvious is that nowhere in the 150-year history of New England's art music can a single musician of this sort be found. Most times it seems that the whole—composers, say, from Paine to Piston and beyond—is greater than its sum of individual artists. There has been extravagant and excessive admiration for individual musical performers, both instrumentalists and singers, in New England, as elsewhere in the United States. A Pavarotti and Yo-Yo Ma are played up in newspapers, magazines, radio, and television. The audience goes wild when they take their first step onto the stage and even wilder when they finish performing. Scarcely an art composer, however impressive his or her musical contributions, has even remotely received the same adulation. That Paine was accorded such praise when he first came on the Boston scene is as much owing to the public's amazement that a local composer could play in the same ballpark as the European big boys, as it was that he had composed a major symphony. Whether someday one will win considerable acclaim for his music alone is still only a remote possibility. Meanwhile, as we examine the composers active in New England during the post–World War II decades, we should recognize that their best works are not merely documentations of the spirit of their time (whatever that is), but also artistic and nonmaterial supports that can bring joy into everyday lives and also help men and women to remain firm under misfortune without yielding, and eventually to win through. Unquestionably, the New England composers who have provided and still provide such music deserve celebration. This applies to both those native to the area and others who have come to make their homes here.

BORN IN NEW ENGLAND, GONE ELSEWHERE

What stands out, when we survey the native-born composers who chose not to live their adult lives in New England, is that each has gone his or her own creative way. After they had arrived at their mature styles, scarcely any have paid even lip service to the neoclassicism that has had a lasting effect on the styles of many of those who never moved away.

Alan Hovhaness (1911–2000), born Alan Vaness Chakmakjian, provides a case in point for all that was said above. He was born in Somerville, Massachusetts. His father was Armenian and his mother was Scottish. He studied under Frederick Converse at the New England Conservatory of Music and took instruction from Bohuslav Martinů at Tanglewood. From 1948 to 1951 he was teaching at the Boston Conservatory of Music. He then moved to New York, traveled for a while in Asia, and finally settled in Washington State.

By World War II he had written over one thousand pieces, all of which he destroyed. This can be attributed in part to his discovery, at age thirty, of his Armenian cultural roots, a discovery that reoriented his musical style. He would later broaden his studies to include pre-Classical music and the musical cultures of India and the Far East. To achieve his creative goals, Hovhaness would draw on these sources for his modal, rhythmically complicated, and lyrically oriented compositions. At the same time, he played down harmony. Offered a scholarship to study under Boulanger in Paris, he declined: "I said no. I felt I didn't want to be a part of contemporary music. I didn't want to be a part of this very intellectual approach. A very cold approach, I felt." About his own music, he said, "The greater the emotional intensity, the greater the simplicity. This is not intellectual music, but music of pure feeling."[1]

Exoticism and mysticism intermingle in many of his more than four hundred works, all readily accessible pieces and some popular successes. He wrote a Broadway show, *The Flowering Peach* (1954), with lyrics by Clifford Odets, and chamber operas such as *Blue Flame* (1959) and *Pilate* (1963). *Lousadzak* (The Coming of Light), for piano and strings (1945), is an early example of his "reborn" style. Symphony No. 9, *Saint Vartan* (1949–50) combines his Armenian and medieval inclinations. Each of its twenty-four sections is very brief. Hovhaness goes from stately intonations to frenetic dance, from homophonic lockstep to canonic movement. The splendid instrumental lines give the feeling of a sonic rug from the Middle East that abounds in orchestral colors. The music extends from merry, lively moods to distressed, passionate ones, from ceremonial religious rites to spiritual hymns meant to transcend ordinary understanding and bring on a state of ecstatic rapture.

Mysterious Mountain (1955) brought him into wide notice after Stokowski and the Houston Symphony premiered it. The piece sounds natural, unruffled, and sincerely sympathetic. A rich hymn begins the first movement, followed by a faster middle section. The movement ends with a return to the hymn. The next movement starts off with a quiet fugue in the strings then comes a fast section with strange tumbling passages in the strings; and finally a broadly stated religious song. The finale returns to the sort of hymning heard in the first movement, closing with a solemn peroration.

A painting from the mystic Hermon di Giovanno, whom he regarded as a spiritual forefather, inspired the Symphony No. 6, *Celestial Gate* (1959). Symphony No. 16 for strings and Korean percussion (1963) and *Ukiyo: Floating World* (1965), a symphonic poem, look to the Far East. He once said, "The reason I liked Oriental music is that everything has a firm center. All music with a center is tonal."[2] *And God Created Whales* for orchestra and recorded humpback whales (1970), like *Mysterious Mountain,* added to his fame. *Mt. Katahdin* (1987) is a piano sonata looking back at New England.

On balance, his best work was done while he was still living in New England and in the decade after. By the 1970s he was frequently repeating himself. Though agreeable enough, his newer compositions took on an excessively artificial or stilted character, and the music was simplified to the point where the expression lacked spontaneity and sounded contrived.

Hovhaness has been a more than usually prolific composer. The abundance of music has inevitably included works of lesser merit. His finest compositions sound unique and impressive, however, and are always audience-friendly. A large number of music lovers have been keen about several of his pieces. After he departed New England, little of his activities and music can be linked to Yankeedom. Nevertheless, he is a composer whose best works have brought pleasure and uplift into people's lives and therefore deserve commendation.

Seven years after Hovhaness, Leonard Bernstein (1918–1990) was born in Lawrence, Massachusetts. He also is worthy of commendation, but

to the extent that he was accorded fame, it was more for his activities as a
conductor and as writer of music for Broadway than it was for his art
works. In his roles as composer, conductor, writer, speaker, and television
celebrity, he would become one of the most prominent personages in art
music during the second half of the twentieth century. Like Hovhaness, he
was not attuned to New England's past and traditions. The Hebraic proph-
ets, rather than the Puritan divines, were a part of his ancestry. He
attended Boston Latin School and then Harvard, where he studied theory
and composition with Piston and Hill. While still a Harvard student, he
wrote in the *Harvard Advocate:* "Boston, you must remember, is not a city to
be trifled with. If it chooses to sleep it can be very nasty when forcefully
awakened. Its temper is like the weather, which is conducive to sleep; and
with all these naps, Boston is unusually strongly armed during its waking
hours. Its resistance to change and artistic progress is phenomenal."[3]

Later he studied conducting with Fritz Reiner and orchestration with
Randall Thompson. In 1940 he was at Tanglewood and working with
Serge Koussevitzky, whose conducting assistant he soon became. In 1943
he was assistant conductor of the New York Philharmonic and by 1958
was its permanent director. From then on he belonged to New York City
and, as a traveling jet-age conductor, to the world at large. New England
became mostly a memory, save for his appearances at Tanglewood and
Boston's Symphony Hall.

He treasured his Jewish identity and found he had more in common
with the music of Vienna's Gustav Mahler, Russia's Igor Stravinsky, and
New York's Aaron Copland than that of Paine, Chadwick, and Piston. In
remarks made to Tanglewood students on 8 July 1970, he tried to explain
his background and values:

> We [in 1940] were filled with causes: we had Spain, China, Czecho-
> slovakia, the labor movement, racial equality, antifascism. We were
> dedicated to social progress and to the end of fascism in all its
> forms. . . .
>
> In the decade surrounding 1940 the key musical expression was
> nobility. We still had a form called the symphony, the noble sym-
> phony. We had the Shostakovich *Fifth* for the first time; the Prokofiev
> *Fifth* for the first time; Copland's *Third;* towering symphonic works
> by Hindemith, Bartók, Roy Harris, Bill Schuman, and what may have
> been the best of them all, Stravinsky's great *Symphony in Three Move-*

ments. All this music was heroic music: it spoke of struggle and triumph; it reflected the basic nobility of man.[4]

The music of Bernstein does try to project heroism indicative of struggle, though not always of triumph. Flamboyant gestures and histrionics also enter in. There are many instances of his resorting to virtuosity in his instrumentation and exaggeration in his emotions to attract attention. This said, the Symphony No. 1, *Jeremiah* (1943), is one of his best works, embodying more of his virtues and less of his faults. The orchestration is luminous, the melodies are memorable, and the sections well integrated. Ashkenazic chant is introduced. "Prophecy" captures the emotional force of the prophet's entreaties to his society. "Profanation" dwells on the vices and the disarray brought on by paganism. "Lamentation," a vocal commentary, is the voice of Jeremiah grieving for Jerusalem.

Around the time that he composed his first symphony, Bernstein left Boston permanently. The two symphonies that followed are not as persuasive as the first. Both sound too indebted to other composers' styles. Flash supplants restraint and sincere self-examination. Symphony No. 2, *Age of Anxiety* (1949), indulges in too much emotional flailing about to no purpose. Symphony No. 3, *Kaddish* (1963), dwells on the nature of faith but also scolds God and sometimes verges on a temper tantrum.

In 1971 Bernstein wrote *Mass,* a "theater piece for singers, players, and dancers" that employs singers, a rock band and vocalist, a pit ensemble, marching music, dancers, and acting to portray the contemporary age's crisis of faith. The piece doesn't seem to gel, however, and, thirty years later, sounds outmoded. He is more successful in his two operas, *Trouble in Tahiti* (1950) and the sequel *A Quiet Place* (1983). The first exposes the failings of the suburban middle class; the second makes an attempt at resolution and reconciliation. Popular and jazz idioms join with art music to make vivid the predicaments of modern-day life. Also winning are the Serenade (1954), five episodes paying tribute to the love discoursed upon in Plato's *Symposium,* for violin, harp, percussion, and string orchestra, and the *Chichester Psalms* (1965), for boy soloist, mixed chorus, and orchestra that set forth religious beliefs through musical and textual images of guileless naïveté and trust.

Where Bernstein often showed real aptitude was in his music for Broadway: the ballet *Fancy Free* (1944), the musical comedy *On the Town* (1944), the musical show *Wonderful Town* (1952), the operetta *Candide*

(1956), and the wildly popular musical *West Side Story* (1957). Here his high-spirited and communicative talents are to the fore. His tunes are magical; his rhythms are irresistible; his invention is unfailing.

Not least among his contributions to American culture were his endeavors to educate the American people about music. Recognizing television's importance, he put together several programs for CBS's "Omnibus," where he explained the meaning of artistic compositions, then let his television audience hear them. He started the series with Beethoven's Fifth Symphony in 1954. He also gave several highly important "Young People's Concerts" over CBS, from 1958 to 1972. Bernstein's enthusiasm for the music he loved knew no bounds, and his impact on children was tremendous.

A third composer who would depart from New England is Frederic Rzewski, of Polish descent and born in Westfield, Massachusetts, in 1938. Like Hovhaness and Bernstein, he would feel no real bond with New England and depart permanently from Massachusetts early in his career. For much of his adult life, he would live in Europe.

Young Rzewski began his musical studies under Charles Mackey in nearby Springfield. He then attended Harvard and Princeton and had as teachers Piston, Thompson, Sessions, and Babbitt. In 1960 he was in Italy and had Luigi Dallapiccola as an instructor. He was also soon acquainted with the radical goings-on of John Cage and his like-minded associates. This hodgepodge of instructors and influences helps explain his command of a vast array of styles and casual jumping from manner to manner to suit the creative needs of the moment.

In the mid-1960s he took on the views of the political Left and was a cofounder of Musica Elettronica Viva, one of the first groups to present innovative compositions involving improvisation and live electronics. MEV looked with favor on experimental jazz and promoted music as a spur-of-the-moment collective operation. Since 1977 Rzewski has been a teacher at the Conservatoire Royal de Musique in Liège, Belgium.

He wrote *Coming Together* and *Attica,* both for narrator and variable ensemble, a year after the Attica Prison riots of 1971. They immediately won over an activist audience when it heard the militant recitation of prisoners' words against a percussively repetitious minimalist accompaniment. Minimalism mixes with jazz in the *Song and Dance* of 1977, for flute, clarinet, bass clarinet, contrabass, and vibraphone.

The piece that won Rzewski international fame, however, was his musical turn to "humanist realism" and the fusion of nineteenth-century

Romanticism with twentieth-century procedures: the extraordinary *The People United Will Never Be Defeated! 36 Variations on a Chilean Song,* composed in 1975 for solo piano. A gorgeous tune by Sergio Ortega and Quilapayun, identified with Chilean resistance to the dictatorship following Salvador Allende's deposition, receives virtuosic treatment, mostly through traditional handling, but at times with passages ranging from tempestuous discourse to subtle restraint, and from tuneless and shapeless discord to hypnotic jazzy rhythms. For fifty-five minutes, the listener sits mesmerized by the composer's eloquence. It is without question one of the finest American piano compositions of the twentieth century. If anything from Rzewski merits commendation, it is this astonishing work.

Out of the same matrix came the *Four North American Ballads:* "Winnsboro Cotton Mill Blues," "Dreadful Memories," "Down by the Riverside," and "Which Side Are You On" (1978–79), also for piano. A reviewer in *Fanfare* magazine called them "people's rhapsodies . . . almost Lisztian" in the working out of the melodies.[5]

One of his later works is an extensive two-hour oratorio, *The Triumph of Death* (1987–88). Nevertheless, it is in his populist piano pieces that he has made his greatest impression.

Like the previous three composers, Barbara Kolb is a New Englander whose adult years have been spent mostly outside of New England. She was born in Hartford, Connecticut, in 1939, attended the local Hartt College of Music and the University of Hartford, went to Tanglewood to study under Lukas Foss and Gunther Schuller, and spent a year in Vienna on a Fulbright Fellowship. She was the first woman to receive the American Prix de Rome in music composition (1969–71). From 1979 to 1982 she was the artistic director of contemporary music at the Third Street Music School Settlement in New York. From 1984 to 1985 she was at the Eastman School of Music. In 1986 the Library of Congress appointed her as programmer of music for the blind. Her musical language tends to atonality and may include some Impressionistic elements. *Soundings* (1972), written on a commission from the Koussevitzky Music Foundation, gave her stature. *Millefoglie* for chamber ensemble and computer tape (1984) brought her even more to the attention of the music public. *Voyants* for piano and chamber orchestra (1991), written in memory of Aaron Copland, has been performed far and wide. A late work, *Virgin Mother Creatrix* for a cappella chorus (1998), was motivated by the mysticism of Hildegard of Bingen. Although Kolb has not achieved the wide prominence accorded the other three composers, her compositions are well made, make individual statements, and deserve wider dissemination.

California eventually claimed the composer John Adams, although he was born in Worcester, Massachusetts, in 1947, grew up in Vermont and New Hampshire, and took his B.A. and M.A. degrees from Harvard, which he attended from 1965 to 1971. His teachers in music were Leon Kirchner, David Del Tredici, and Roger Sessions. As a student, he witnessed the clashes of atonality versus neoclassicism going on within Harvard and, for relief, turned to the several varieties of folk, protest, and popular music offered by street musicians and folksingers and pop performers in the various places of entertainment in and around Harvard Square.

At the end of his schooling, he left Cambridge to teach at the San Francisco Conservatory and has remained mainly in San Francisco ever since. He was for several years the composer-in-residence and music advisor to the San Francisco Symphony, and he also directed the New Music Ensemble there as well as taking a turn as director of the Ojai Music Festival. Minimalism, with its reductive style of music making, was a strong movement in California's music, exemplified in the works of La Monte Young and Terry Riley. Adams's creative career started with his employing only plain sonorities, a protracted repetition of rhythms and phrase patterns, and an avoidance of complexity, which combined to produce a throbbing, mesmerizing impression on listeners. His style would relax gradually as he introduced richer harmonies, less repetitious passages, and more identifiable melodies. His expression would grow warmer and more productive of emotion and less of hypnotic states.

Phyrigian Gates for piano and *Shaker Loops* for string septet (later orchestrated) caused the music public to sit up and listen. He followed these with *Harmonium* for chorus and orchestra in 1980 and *Grand Pianola Music* for two pianos, two singers, and chamber ensemble in 1982. In addition, two far-out, controversial, and static operas came from his pen: *Nixon in China* (1987) and *The Death of Klinghoffer* (1991). In both, plot is neglected and the people put on the stage are treated as artificial prototypes and not as actual men and women.

With the Violin Concerto of 1993, Adams was only slightly a minimalist and more a composer intent on synthesizing the gestures of Romanticism and the reviving effect of popular music into his compositions. Already, in *The Chairman Dances* (1985), Gershwinesque foxtrot rhythms had been tried out. Four years later, *Eros Piano* attempted jazz. In *Hoodoo*

Zephyr (1992) he was experimenting with the soft, soothing, unintrusive style of New Age music. The influence of exotic dance music is heard in *John's Book of Alleged Dances* (1994). Rock music enters *Lollapalooza* (1995). He is usually surefooted in what he writes, although he did stumble badly in his cliché-ridden try at a trendy theatrical style, *I Was at the Ceiling and Then I Saw the Sky* (1995). Yet, for the most part, he remains one of America's most important composers active at the turn of the century.

BORN ELSEWHERE, EDUCATED IN NEW ENGLAND

Ever since Paine and Chadwick began teaching, music students from other parts of the country came to the Boston area to study theory and composition at the New England Conservatory of Music or at Harvard. Among the most prominent composers who studied here in the earlier part of the twentieth century were Arthur Farwell, Arthur Shepherd, William Grant Still, and John Alden Carpenter. As examples of the more prominent composers who studied here later in the century, Robert Moevs, Samuel Adler, and Elliott Carter are representative of most.

Moevs provides an example of a composer educated in and teaching for a short while in New England and then leaving the area. Born in La Crosse, Wisconsin, in 1920, he studied with Piston at Harvard, earning his B.A. in 1942 and his M.A. in 1952. From 1947 to 1951 he was in Paris and receiving instruction from Nadia Boulanger. From 1955 to 1963 he was on the Harvard faculty. From 1964 onward, he taught at Rutgers University, in New Jersey. As a composer, he started off in the footsteps of Stravinsky and Piston but gradually increased his chromaticism to parallel that of Schoenberg's and his emotionality to parallel that of Bartók. Before Moevs left the Boston area he had written a string quartet (1957) that highlighted his growing emotionality, especially in its monumental climaxes. In 1960 the Boston Symphony presented his *Attis I* for tenor, chorus, percussion, and orchestra, which produced a local uproar owing to its intense dissonances and menacingly wild, passionate expression that seemed to lash out at the audience. He then left New England to pursue his career elsewhere.

Samuel Adler provides an example of a composer born elsewhere, growing up and educated in New England, and then leaving the area. Born in Mannheim, Germany, in 1928, he came with his family to live in Worcester, Massachusetts, in 1939. He took his B.M. from Boston University (1948) and M.A. from Harvard (1950). His principal teachers in theory and composition were Hugo Norden, Walter Piston, Randall Thompson, and Irving Fine. Adler also worked with Aaron Copland at Tanglewood during the summers of 1949 and 1950. In 1950 he was called up for military service and was sent to Germany, where he organized and conducted the Seventh Army Orchestra and gave a series of well-received concerts in Europe. On his return to the United States in 1952, he went to Dallas, Texas, and the position of music director at Temple Emanu-El. He would also teach at North Texas State University (1957–66). In 1966 he left for his final posting at Eastman School of Music in Rochester, New York, from which position he retired in 1994. New England saw little of him after 1950.

Adler was a productive composer, writing over four hundred works. Among them are six symphonies, eight concertos, three operas, and eight string quartets. His early pieces adhere to tonal frameworks, clear-cut thematic matter, intelligible textures, and balanced structures with a liberal addition of warm intonations deriving from Hebraic chant. After he left Texas, his style altered to include serial procedures and sometimes improvisation and elements of chance. Regrettably, save for a few recordings, New Englanders who may desire to do so know hardly any of his music, which appears only rarely in concerts.

Our next example is of a composer born elsewhere, educated in New England and then leaving the area, and at first manifesting his New England education in his creativity. Elliott Carter is without question the best known of the composers who came from elsewhere to study in New England. He was born in New York City in 1908. By the time he entered Harvard in 1926, he had met the experimental composers Varèse, Cowell, and Ives, and had also examined the scores of the Vienna serialists Schoenberg, Berg, and Webern. At Harvard he worked with Piston and the English composer Gustav Holst and, from there, went to Paris and Boulanger for three years. In 1935 he returned to America to reside briefly in Cambridge, Massachusetts. But a year later he had joined the Ballet Caravan as music director and was soon living and working outside of New England on a permanent basis. His early compositions, the *Pocahontas* ballet (1939), Pastoral for viola and piano, Symphony No. 1 (1942), and *Holiday* Overture (1944), reflect his studies with Piston, Holst, and Boulanger. Indeed, he called the Pastoral his "Walter Piston piece."[6] Yet the symphony was already pointing the way to the future with its modulatory refinement, contrapuntal knowledgeability, and sophisticated sonorities. Howard Pollack claims: "Carter's *Symphony* was inspired by the landscape and cultural heritage of New England; one could hear the chirping of birds at the close of the first movement (much as one could hear the shrieking of gulls in the much later *Symphony for Three Orchestras*), the singing of hymns in the second movement, and the stomping of country fiddlers in the finale."[7] The *Holiday* Overture also is a "Piston piece," although here and there its measures grow more delirious, harmonies sound harsher, and rhythms tangle more with one another than they do in his teacher's music.

Carter's stylistic departure from that of his Harvard mentor began with his Piano Sonata (1946) and Cello Sonata (1948). In the latter work, the dissimilarities of resonance and the differences between the attack and release of tones for cello and piano are used to good effect. The autonomy of each instrument is made clear, particularly in the course of rhythmic and tempo alterations in one instrument, while the other continues with an already established meter and speed. The use of a six-tone row comes close to the methods of the Vienna serialists. The intervals deployed in his lines and the recurring harmonic resonance that integrate the sections are drawn from this row.

He now found himself working deliberately and taking extreme care about the minutest details. At the age of forty-three, and with the String Quartet No. 1 (1951), his personal voice was truly beginning to sound. Its four movements run into each other. Atonality replaces tonality. All parts are persistently active and constantly altering. Rhythms have become so intricate as to be hard to understand. Virtuosic playing is necessary. Carter is arriving at his concept of metric modulation, where tiny or intricate partitions of the beat are used to correlate two separate tempi. Scores begin to look like scenarios—sequences of dramatic events, with the string players demonstrating distinct characters through the music written for their instruments. Commenting on the stylistic changes he was introducing into his music, Carter said:

> I had felt that it was my professional and social responsibility to write interesting, direct, and easily understood music. With this quartet, however, I decided to focus on what had always been one of my own musical interests, that of "advanced" music and to follow out, with a minimal concern for their reception, my own musical thoughts along these lines. . . . If a composer has been well taught and had had experience (as was true of me in 1950), then his private judgment of comprehensibility and quality is what he must rely on if he is to communicate importantly.[8]

It was with the Quartet No. 1 that Carter started to gain notoriety for being a cerebral, hard-to-understand composer. His intricate interrelation of parts, convoluted rhythmic combinations, fussily laid-out tempo transformations, and steadfast reliance on severe, choppy lines flummoxed people. These traits in Carter's music produced a powerful and often off-putting aftereffect. The four quartets (1959, 1971, 1986, 1995) that followed continued to have similar characteristics, as did the Double Concerto for Harpsichord and Piano (1961), the Concerto for Orchestra (1969), and the Symphony for Three Orchestras (1976). Even his chamber vocal cantatas *A Mirror on Which to Dwell* and *Syringa,* though more lyrical, display his typical tough-mindedness.

Nevertheless, even if the general music public has not taken his music to heart, Carter remains highly respected by the music academics, several advanced musicians in the atonal camp, and a handful of faithful adherents among the music public. Although music pundits and periodicals pay a great deal of enthusiastic lip service to Carter's music, whether the expressions of admiration will continue after he is gone remains a moot question.

BORN ELSEWHERE, WORKING A WHILE IN NEW ENGLAND

Any number of composers, born and mostly or entirely educated elsewhere in the nation, have lived briefly in New England. Ross Lee Finney (1906–97) is an early representative of this group. He was born in Wells, Minnesota, educated at the University of Minnesota and Carleton College, and spent a year at Harvard, another year in Paris with Boulanger, and an additional year in Vienna with Berg. He then went to teach at Smith College, in Northampton, Massachusetts, and at a couple of other nearby institutions (1929–49). While in Northampton, Finney founded the Valley Press to publish the music of American composers. At the same time he was a guitarist and a folk song aficionado. His earlier works, with their flexible rhythms, diatonic tonal colorings, and straightforward expressiveness, have a close kinship with the music of Piston and Copland. The *Variations, Fuguing, and Holiday* for orchestra (1943), based on music by the eighteenth-century Boston psalmodist William Billings, and the *Pilgrim Psalms* for vocal soloists, chorus, and orchestra (1945), employing the psalm verse of the Ainsworth Psalter, provide an excellent representation of his interests during this period. Other important works from these years include his first five string quartets and the Symphony No. 1.

World War II troubled him greatly, and his ongoing creative approach brought him less and less satisfaction. By the end of the war he felt an urge for change and had also grown edgy about his residence in Northampton. In 1949 he left Smith College to begin his long stay at the University of Michigan and commenced the recasting of his style to suit his new expressive needs. His music now veered toward the twelve-tone method he had studied under Berg. As in Berg's works, however, he never entirely discarded tonality. Finney tried to explain why he transformed his manner of writing: "I knew the technique and had been thinking about it for a long time. . . . Secondly, I was involved in the Second World War, and that was a devastating experience to me, as it was to a lot of people. I have such memories of the utter hopelessness of trying to express the feeling I had in the same way that I had done before the war. In other words, when I got back from this, I felt that I had to have more expressive stuff in my vocabulary. Then, in a certain work, I suddenly found myself writing twelve-tone techniques."[9]

Finney's removal from New England had converted him into a different artist. Nevertheless, his recognizable melodic phrases and vague sense of tonality tempered his serialism and made his music sound a little more approachable than that of other serialists. The listener can detect here and there a traditional consonant harmony. Three more symphonies, three more string quartets, a piano quintet, two works for stage, many songs, and an unfinished opera, *A Computer Marriage,* demonstrate the changeover. The accounting of their history belongs to the Midwest.

Like Finney, Earl Kim (1920–98) spent years in New England but was a weaker force in local musical affairs. Of Korean descent, Kim was born in Dinuba, California, and studied at the University of California with Schoenberg, Bloch, and Sessions. He taught at Princeton from 1952 to 1967 and at Harvard from 1967 until his retirement. Yet, except for his teaching at Harvard, he did not engage energetically and directly with the music public.

His completely realized style, starting with the 1960s, drew inspiration from the texts of Samuel Beckett and the structure of a Japanese stone garden. Kim's music eliminates all unnecessary notes, retains a fragile, evanescent quality, and changes its expressive meaning by subtle degrees. The composer engaged occasionally in twelve-tone discourse, but however atonal his direction, as with Finney, there was always the relief of tonal references. Word settings are stripped down to essentials and call up delicate, almost insubstantial, moods. Sounds take on shapes analogous to stone objects and are set off by "sandy" silences.

Kim wrote piano pieces, chamber works, songs, and a short opera, *Footfalls* (1981), based on Beckett's words. He also attempted multimedia theater works: *Exercises En Route* (1971) for soprano, chamber ensemble, dancers, three actresses, and film, and *Narratives* (1979), for woman's voice, soprano, teleprojected actor, chamber ensemble, television, and lighting. His last major work was *White Heat,* which was premiered in Boston just before his death. Although he lived in New England, he seems to have lived thousands of miles away in his music.

What is fascinating about David Del Tredici is that, though born in California (1937) and a student at the University of California and Princeton, he would completely change his style after arriving in New England. Milhaud, Sessions, and Kim had educated him, and serialism had governed much of his initial mode of writing. He came to teach at Harvard in 1966, then switched to Boston University in 1973, and finally located at City University of New York in 1984. One pre-arrival piece, *I Hear an Army* (1964) for soprano and string quartet, gives expressionistic treatment to a poem by James Joyce. In an imaginative, atonal fashion, Del Tredici captures the panicky mood of a sleeper subjected to feelings of desolation and isolation after awakening from a frightening dream.

Del Tredici's manner slowly moderated before his coming to Harvard. Not until 1968, however, did he sound genuinely different. His new musical persona was on exhibit when he started on his cycle of compositions based on Lewis Carroll's *Alice in Wonderland,* with *Pot-Pourri* for amplified soprano, rock ensemble, chorus, and orchestra. As he went on adding pieces to the "Alice" cycle, discord diminished, common-practice procedures increased, and audiences sat up and took notice. In these works, he no longer complied with the principles of the avant-garde. Instead, he was deliberately tonal, harmonious, and unafraid to include appealing songs, designed like popular ballads, that were anathema to his modernistic contemporaries. Two compositions generated the greatest enthusiasm among listeners: *Final Alice* (1976), requiring an amplified soprano narrator, a concertante folk-instrument ensemble, and a large orchestra, and *In Memory of a Summer Day* (1980), for amplified soprano and orchestra.

When *Final Alice* was first heard, it excited a great deal of notice from audiences. They enjoyed what Del Tredici described as an "opera written in concert form," which contained "elaborate arias interspersed by dramatic episodes from the last two chapters of *Alice's Adventures in Wonder-land.*" These pages relate the weird court trial and Alice's return to "dull reality." Contributing a great deal to the effectiveness of the work are the settings of new poetry, particularly a burlesque of the poem "Alice Gray" by the nineteenth-century poet William Mee, and the closing "Apotheosis" abstracted from *Through the Looking Glass.* Mingling with "the bizarre Wonderland happenings" is "the implied love story—the human side of Carroll."[10]

He was acutely aware of his status as renegade from the modern camp as he plunged more and more into the region of listener-friendly sounds. After writing *Final Alice,* he took stock of the distance he had traveled away from what he first had been composing:

> About halfway through the piece, I thought, "Oh my God, if I just leave it like this, my colleagues will think I'm crazy." . . . But then I thought, "What else can I do? If nothing else occurs to me, I can't go against my instincts." But I was *terrified* my colleagues would think I was an idiot. People think now that I wanted to be tonal and have a big audience. But that was just not true. I *didn't* want to be tonal. My world was my colleagues—my composing friends. The success of *Final Alice* was very defining as to who my real friends were. I think many composers regard success as a threat. It's really better, they think, if *nobody* has any success, to be all in one boat.[11]

Del Tredici maintained that in pieces like *Final Alice* the introduction of consonance, tonality, and attractive tunes was itself an unusual, fresh-sounding, and out-of-the-ordinary departure, indicative of a composer one step ahead of the modernists and without their rigidity of procedure.

His other well-favored piece, *In Memory of a Summer Day,* refers nostalgically to a day when the writer Carroll and the actual Alice boated down the Thames. Its music delves into the artless happiness of the girl over the watery excursion and the "rapture and regret" of the grownup as he surveys her happiness. Two songs are italicized in the music, the insouciantly stated "Simple Alice" (ending, "We are but older children, dear / Who fret to find our bedtime near") and the impassioned revamping of the Alice tune for "Ecstatic Alice" (climaxing on "The magic words shall hold thee fast: / Thou shalt not heed the raving blast").

After Del Tredici left Boston for New York, he immediately received two commissions from orchestras. In response he wrote, in 1988–90, *Steps* and *Tattoo.* Neither achieved the popularity of the *Alice* music. Nor did any subsequent pieces elicit so great an enthusiasm, whether *The Spider and the Fly* (1998), *Gay Life* (2000), or *Miz Inez Sez* (2000).

Several other very competent composers could be named as coming to New England but not making a profound impression on the public, among them Charles Fussell (born 1938) and Marjorie Merryman (born 1951). Both had located in the Boston area and become affiliated with Boston University. By the end of the century, Fussell had already written five symphonies, much chamber music, a chamber drama, *Cymbeline,* and an opera, *Caligula.* Merryman's works usually bore titles, such as the *Laments for Hektor* for high soprano and chamber ensemble, *Jonah,* a six-movement retelling of the Jonah story with singers and chamber group, and *Bending the Light* for cello, piano, and percussion.

Stephen Albert (1941–92) has made a much stronger impression on audiences than have Fussell and Merryman. He was born in New York City and grew up in Great Neck, New York. Music was always to be heard in the home of his parents. His mother played the piano. He himself played the trumpet. Recordings of art music ordinarily formed a part of the evening's entertainment.

He studied music with Elie Siegmeister, Bernard Rogers, Roy Harris, Joseph Castaldo, and George Rochberg, among others. He was granted the Prix de Rome (1965–67) and a Guggenheim Fellowship (1968–69). Albert taught at Stanford, Smith, Juilliard, and Boston University, and for a time was composer-in-residence with the Seattle Symphony. For several years, before his tragic death in a car accident in Truro, on Cape Cod, he was living in Newton, Massachusetts, next door to Boston, and making a living as a stamp dealer. He had moved there from Harvard, Massachusetts, in 1980.

The Berkshire Music Center and Fromm Foundation commissioned *Voices Within,* for pit band and orchestra, and Schuller gave its premiere at Tanglewood in 1975. In this piece, Albert calls up the memories of popular tunes he has encountered and remembered. He replicates and modifies them while setting the pit band in rivalry with the orchestra. Yet he does so without identifying any of the songwriters or songs that are referred to. While Albert's central argument and musical results were fascinating to musically educated listeners, they failed to engross the general music public.

Ten years later, his first symphony, *RiverRun* (1983), won a Pulitzer Prize. It was with *RiverRun* that Bostonians, and for that matter people outside Boston, became aware of Albert in a big way. The musical community would hold him in high respect not only for his music but also for his desire to be his own man and his refusal to ally himself with any modern school of composition. He left himself free to explore whatever techniques he wished and take advice from whatever composer he admired. The message, the communication of an underlining theme, was important, not consistency in his modus operandi.

Albert's approach to composing was down-to-earth and organized tonally and thematically, in addition to being selective of what appeared to him the best from various styles. For these reasons, his works are easy to enter into and enjoy. Some passages may be quiet and allow for subtle rhythms and unusual tonal colors, while others may be loud and propelled by sharp, driving dissonances. His music is always marked by the open expression of imagination and feeling. For a long while he was preoccupied with the writings of James Joyce. Joyce's *Finnegan's Wake* was behind Albert's song cycles, *To Wake the Dead* (1978) and *Tree Stone* (1982), and the first symphony, *RiverRun*. Joyce's *Ulysses* inspired *Distant Hills* (1989) for tenor, soprano, and orchestra.

RiverRun is in four movements, with the outer movements sounding ampler and richer than the delicately scored inner movements. Albert's title refers to Ireland's Liffey River, but poetically and not programmatically, as do the headings to the movements: "Rain Music," music to capture the moods generated by the origins of the stream; "Leafy Speafing," a succession of tone paintings illustrative of the gentle to vigorous flow of the river; "Beside the Rivering Waters," with melodies denoting the riverside play of children, carousing of adults, and blare of bands; and "RiversEnd," which recycles previously heard themes as the waters pour into the sea at the same time that nightfall closes in. The auditor has completed a lovely, satisfying journey.

In an interview, Albert was asked about his tendency to hold close the music of the past and whether anything new was in his compositions. He replied:

> Today, "new" has practically become synonymous with "innovative." But something innovative has no more value than a mere fashion unless it is supported by memorable ideas that seem timeless. What is really new historically has often been the amalgam of past and current practice drawn together into an unexpected context—a new synthesis—that produces a fresh response. And this complexity of feeling must be matched by a surface that is clear and accessible. I

think these criteria can be applied with equal assurance to Machaut and Monteverdi, Brahms and Stravinsky. To the degree my talent allows, this is the ideal towards which I am striving in my own work. If I succeed from time to time, others may decide that what I'm doing has merit and is "new."[12]

A Cello Concerto was completed in 1990. It is made up of a progression of lucid, arresting sections, mostly of them absorbed in gloomy reflection and wrapped within a tragic cloak. Extended melodies with tonal underpinnings are designed to warm listeners with their romantic glow. The cello is allowed to sing idiomatically and uninhibitedly. This lack of embarrassment over letting a string instrument sing its heart out harks back to Samuel Barber. This can also be said of an earlier work, a violin concerto, *In Concordiam,* composed in 1986 and presented in a revised version by Gerard Schwarz and the Seattle Symphony in 1988.

The New York Philharmonic premiered Albert's Symphony No. 2 in 1994. It is an attractive work and gratifying to hear. At the beginning, splendid melodies grow from stitching together horn and woodwind phrases, spinning them out, metamorphosing them, bringing them together, and then sending them off on their own way. Afterward, an elaborate, humorous, and sprightly movement replaces music of thoughtful meditation. The flow of emotion swells during a grandiose finale, as previously heard melodies come back altered so that they can blaze forth for a last time, like rays of the sun at day's end.

Albert's life was snuffed out when he was at the height of his powers and poised to turn out major compositions that sounded fresh and would succeed in making contact with the general music public. Even sadder, with his death he experienced the usual treatment for an American art composer, however successfully he had engaged his audience—a few years after his fatal accident, his compositions were put on the shelf.

CHAPTER 14

COMPOSERS RESIDENT IN NEW ENGLAND AFTER WORLD WAR II

C omposers in considerable numbers have worked creatively for most or their entire adult lives in New England during the last half of the twentieth century. They divide more or less equally between the native-born and those coming from elsewhere who have settled here permanently. More than a few colleges, universities, and music conservatories maintain one or more of these creative artists on the faculty. For example, at the turn of the century Dartmouth had Jon Appleton and Charles Dodge; Brown had Gerald Shapiro; Hartt School of Music, Robert Carl; University of Rhode Island, Geoffrey Gibbs; University of Vermont, Thomas Read; Bowdoin College, Elliott Schwarz; Bates College, William Matthews; and Wellesley College, Martin Brody. None had achieved anything close to real celebrity. The most talked about—Appleton, Dodge, and Shapiro—are known for their electro-acoustical compositions, although these have not resulted in widespread eminence for their composers.

Each year the many schools of music in the six northeastern states churn out additional young musicians with ambitions toward becoming recognized vocalists, instrumentalists, and composers. Scarcely any ever gets to occupy the light. To state what may be obvious, it helps greatly for a composer to live in a large urban area dedicated to music making, say, Chicago, San Francisco, Boston, or New York City. Large cities are the most likely to have many professional and amateur performing groups, some of them committed to playing contemporary music, and the means for an artist to make a living. Noteworthy vocal and instrumental soloists live nearby or visit frequently. Some soloists, too, may willingly schedule new pieces in their programs or can be induced to do so. The opportunity to conduct shop talk with more than one or two peers is a given in a large metropolitan environment. The more prominent chroniclers of current musical events live in these places, attend and write about new music performances, and publish their observations and critiques in major newspapers and periodicals. When a competent community orchestra gives a premiere presentation, the artist may feel gratified but unfortunately it may not further his reputation. When the Chicago Symphony, New York Philharmonic, or Boston Symphony does so, the artist can expect that more than local notice will result.

Therefore, is it not a surprise that most of the best-known composers in New England live in the Boston area? If artistic sustenance is to be had anywhere in the region, it is Boston that is most able to supply composers with what is necessary to carry on their physical and creative lives and nourish their talents so that they fully develop.

What is also of significance is the number of indigenous composers, except for Alvin Lucier and Michael Gandolfi, who have studied with Piston at Harvard and started off in his footsteps. To different degrees they have adhered to objectivity and expressive moderation and have written around tonal centers. All things considered, their music features balanced structures, see-through textures, recognizable motifs, and respect for older stylistic genres. Like Piston, they may experiment with twelve-tone techniques and even with electronics but usually with circumspection. More often than not, as they grow older, the composers loosen their styles in the direction of greater emotionality, more textual complexity, and freer structures. Yet they always exercise careful control over their materials.

BORN AND STAYING IN NEW ENGLAND

For years, Leroy Anderson (1908–75) has struck out as far as most music historians are concerned—they deemed his music too accessible, too popular, and too featherweight for serious consideration. However affectionately people in general received his pieces, however imaginative and, in its own way, inventive his creative approach, and however meticulously he crafted his structures, Anderson has been regarded and treated as a nobody. To the writers on music, he was classifiable neither as an art composer nor as a popular songwriter. He fitted nowhere; therefore he was forgettable. Yet Anderson should not have slipped between the cracks.

He was born in Cambridge, close by Harvard, and in due course studied at Harvard under Spalding, Ballantine, and Piston, taking his B.A. in 1929 and M.A. in 1930. However, he did not turn out to be a neoclassicist writing symphonies, string quartets, and sonatas. His ambition was of a humbler sort. From 1931 to 1935 he conducted the Harvard University Band and then worked as an arranger for the Boston Pops and other orchestras. He first won recognition as a composer with *Jazz Pizzicato,* which was an instant success in 1939. After military service in World War II, during which he acted as a translator and interpreter, and a short stopover in New York, he went to reside in Woodbury, Connecticut, where he lived until his death. After taking up his Woodbury residence, he penned a long string of hits, almost thirty of them written for the Boston Pops.

The Syncopated Clock of 1945 started the ball rolling. *Fiddle-Faddle* came out in 1947. The next year, he made public the *Saraband* and *Sleigh Ride.* The latter presented him with a huge triumph. In 1949 he wrote *A Trumpeter's Lullaby* for Roger Voisin of the Boston Symphony. *The Typewriter* was his 1950 offering. His biggest hit of all, *Blue Tango,* was premiered in 1951. The unusual *Sandpaper Ballet* was written in 1954. By this date Anderson's compositions had won immense favor with the public and were more frequently played than the music of Gershwin or Copland.[1] Audiences loved the cosmopolitan, unpredictable, and waggishly humorous compositions. They enjoyed the original touches and unorthodox devices for producing "music." Most of all, they delighted in the contagious tunes and popular dance beats. What is more, Anderson freely arranged his numbers for all sorts of instrumental combinations and made them available for amateur performance.

His orchestral music was a breath of fresh air during a time when many art composers were taking themselves far too seriously and hermetically sealing themselves off from the music public with their unrelenting serial and atonal techniques and compositions so complicated and intricate as to be hard to understand.

Another composer active about the same time as Anderson was Irving Fine (1914–62). He was born and died in Boston. Harvard, where he studied theory and composition under Hill and Piston, granted him a B.A. in 1937 and an M.A. in 1938. He also was a pupil of Nadia Boulanger both in Cambridge and Paris. He also studied conducting under Koussevitzky at the Berkshire Music Center. He directed the Harvard Glee Club from 1939 to 1946 and taught as an instructor at Harvard from 1942 to 1945 and an assistant professor from 1945 to 1950. For many years Fine regarded Piston as a surrogate father. In 1948 Piston reciprocated by resigning from the Harvard Musical Association when an individual opposed Fine's application for membership owing to his being Jewish. When he was denied tenure at Harvard, however, Fine felt that Piston had given him insufficient support, and coolness ensued.[2] In 1950 he left Harvard to join the faculty at Brandeis University, where he remained until his death.

Because he was a painstaking craftsman and lived only until forty-seven years of age, he left behind but a small number of works. Early on, he associated himself with the neoclassicism of Piston and, less directly, of Stravinsky. This involvement was modified through his fondness for Copland, Ravel, and Barber. He also felt a bona fide dedication to music from the eighteenth century. The Violin Sonata (1946), Music for Piano (1947), and Toccata Concertante for orchestra (1947) exemplify his initial manner. The Toccata, organized around two motives first announced in an introductory fanfare and structure in sonata form, was premiered by Munch and the Boston Symphony in 1948 and immediately attracted attention to the composer. Fine's reputation was increased further when his Partita for wind quintet received the New York Music Critics Circle Award, also in 1948. Singers were delighted with his three songs for mixed chorus, the words from *Alice in Wonderland,* which appeared in 1942. Another set of three songs for women's chorus came out in 1949. The six numbers evoke an air of naive simplicity coupled to witty satire. An affecting Notturno for harp and strings, written for the Zimbler Sinfonietta, was completed in 1951. Its warm lyricism and imaginative appeal charmed listeners.

Fine then briefly experimented with a personal form of serialism, which nevertheless made room for tonal statement and carefully tempered dissonance. The String Quartet (1952) and Fantasy for string trio (1952) represent this phase. However, he fitted uncomfortably into the serial circle. Although he was grateful for serialism's enrichment of his style, he abandoned it for a compositional mode that acknowledged tonality more and was committed to melody and clarity in contrapuntal passages. The music was full of rhythmic life and always generous in feeling. The change gave rise to two of his most significant works, *Serious Song, or Lament* for string orchestra (1955), which saw performance throughout the United States, and the Symphony (1960–62), which he conducted at Tanglewood on 12 August 1962, eleven days before his death. As Copland said in his eulogy, "All his compositions, from the lightest to the most serious, 'sound'; they have bounce and thrust and finesse; they are always a musical pleasure to hear."[3]

To Fine's credit, after he went to Brandeis he invited Arthur Berger and Harold Shapero to join the faculty and for a short while was also able to bring in Leonard Bernstein. What's more, he bolstered the twentieth-century music offerings in the curriculum and promoted a series of contemporary music concerts, especially the annual Festivals of Creative Arts (1952–57). Two of the works heard at the festivals were Bernstein's *Trouble in Tahiti* and Copland's *The Tender Land.*

Harold Shapero came to Brandeis in 1952 and remained there. He was born in Lynn, Massachusetts, in 1920, played jazz and studied with Nicolas Slonimsky while an adolescent, then went to Piston at Harvard. He would also work with Stravinsky, Krenek, Hindemith, and Boulanger. His first real recognition arrived when Bernstein and the Boston Symphony premiered his Symphony for Classical Orchestra in 1948. Its roots are in Beethoven's symphonies by way of Piston and Stravinsky. The work's four movements, distinguished by their dignity and regal design, exhibit nervous drive contrasted with warm tenderness. They also make allusions to folk, popular, and jazz elements. The Concerto for Orchestra (1955), from which he would extract his somber hymn *Credo,* was built on similar lines. On the other hand, Shapero acknowledged his Jewish heritage with *Hebrew Cantata* for soloists, chorus, and instrumental ensemble (1954), based on Jewish traditional music but in a style revealing a blend of Piston with Béla Bartók. He also composed a curious Partita for piano and orchestra (1960), which contains a twelve-tone Latin American "Ciaconna," a neoclassic "Scherzo" and "Burlesque," and a Baroque revival "Aria." In the late 1960s he began experimenting with electronic music but at the same time his compositions showed a gradual loss in strength and character. None met with any success and as a result there was a dropping off in production.

John Bavicchi, a composer whose style is a blend of Piston and Bartók, was born in Dedham, Massachusetts, in 1922, took his B.A. in music at the New England Conservatory in 1952, and then studied with Piston at Harvard. He teaches at the Berklee School of Music and has conducted choral groups and instrumental ensembles with excellent results. His first important work, the Concerto for Clarinet and String Orchestra (1954), sounds like a chromatic and expressive update of Piston's manner without Piston's urbanity and extraordinary polish. Eleven years later, his *Festival* Symphony for band was revealing chromaticism verging on serialism and a more opaque interrelation of parts. The resultant sound was made more palatable through a marked rhythmic pulse. Two late pieces, his Quintet for Clarinet and Strings (1995) and Four Madrigals for a cappella chorus (1997), would seem worth getting to know. However, he has not been able to make a big noise on the local, let alone national, scene. No well-known performing group has championed his music, and he is little written about as a composer.

Alvin Lucier, born in Nashua, New Hampshire, in 1931, has also had no one championing his music, but at one time he was much written about as a composer because what he proposed as music compositions seemed so extreme. He was educated at Yale and Brandeis (not with Piston at Harvard), and then spent two years in Rome on a Fulbright Fellowship. He taught at Brandeis from 1962 to 1969 before leaving for Wesleyan University in Middletown, Connecticut.

His early orthodox compositions caused no flurry of interest in the music world, and this worried him. He decided to try a more revolutionary approach that would provoke people into paying attention to him. His radical essay at "music" involved brain waves, room resonances, environmental acoustics, and sound installations. In *Music for Solo Performer* (1965) he had electrodes attached to his scalp, and the brain waves that were generated were sent through loudspeakers. They also activated percussion instruments and pretaped sounds. His first listeners either fled from the presentation room or stayed to boo and issue catcalls. *Solar Sounder I* (1979) offered electronic sounds induced and directed by sunlight. *Clocker* (1988) was written for an amplified clock, galvanic skin response sensor, and digital delay system. *Amplifier and Reflector I* (1991) calls for an open umbrella, ticking clock, and a glass oven dish, from which sounds are captured.

When *Sferics* was heard in 1983, the audience was supposed to recognize that "art needs no shape" and "music is where you find it." Here, the music had no shape whatsoever and was to be found in the radio-frequency emissions from the ionosphere. A reviewer who attended a performance expressed the opinion of most of the people who were there when he spoke up about the need for "shape" and for a more discriminate location for music. He said that the noises "provoked speculation about how such 'avant-garde' activities can be taken seriously. Mr. Lucier has been exploring similar regions for nearly two decades" and finds scarcely any taker for his concoctions.[4]

Lucier's abnormal deviation from established standards of music making was at one extreme; Daniel Pinkham's complete devotion to recognized norms was at the other. Unlike Lucier, Pinkham felt no need to reinvent himself. Of all the composers taken up in this chapter, he alone was of Yankee extraction, with an ancestry going back to Puritan times, and in addition had a private income through inheritance. He was born in Lynn, Massachusetts, in 1923 and attended Phillips Academy from 1937 to 1940. He graduated from Harvard College in 1943 and earned his Harvard M.A. in the next year. His teachers in music theory and composition included Piston, Copland, Boulanger, and Barber. E. Power Biggs taught him the organ, and Putnam Aldrich and Wanda Landowska taught him the harpsichord. Since the late 1950s he has been the music director at King's Chapel and a faculty member at the New England Conservatory of Music. Furthermore, he has appeared in concert as a keyboard performer with a penchant for music from the Baroque period.

His music started off as an offshoot of Piston's—neoclassical and emotionally reticent (the Concerto for Harpsichord and Celesta of 1955). Later, he would make gingerly attempts at serial composition (Symphony No. 2 of 1962). Still later, he would warily add electronics (*Daniel in the Lion's Den* for narrator, three solo vocalists, chorus, five instrumentalists, and tape of 1972). At all times, his structures have been clearly delineated, his rhythms have remained unambiguous and dynamic, and his melodies have continued to come across as richly eventful. Even when he sounds most chromatic, he conveys a sense of tonality. Also, one detects obeisance to Baroque music (the Partita for harpsichord of 1958, and the *Sonata da Chiesa* for viola and organ of 1988) and, in his choral writing, to the Renaissance (the *Christmas Cantata* for chorus and brass instruments of 1957, and *A Curse, a Lament, and a Vision* for chorus and piano ad libitum of 1984). Not surprisingly, one hears hints of eighteenth-century New England psalmody, especially in the choral music written for use at King's Chapel. Obvious, too, is his indifference to jazz, folk tunes, and popular music.

In the 1990s Pinkham demonstrated his unflagging creativity when he composed, among other pieces, an elegant and often powerfully felt String Quartet, the Nocturnes for flute and guitar, which sports a rare tango, and *Quarries* for four-hand piano, which glances back at neoclassicism.[5]

A final native-born composer needs mentioning. Michael Gandolfi saw his first light in Melrose, Massachusetts, in 1956. Unlike Pinkham, he grew up with rock music and jazz and taught himself to play the guitar. Later, he would make a study of West African music. All of these influences were later factored into his compositions. He attended the New

England Conservatory, not Harvard, where he earned a bachelor's and a master's degree. He also enrolled in the composition program at Tanglewood Music Center. He then proceeded to teach both at the conservatory and at Tanglewood.

Gandolfi came into his own during the 1990s. The increase of interest in his music was certainly unmistakable after Richard Pittman and Boston Musica Viva presented *Grooved Surfaces* in 1996. The work, which is intimately connected with Ghanian rhythmic practices, begins with "Frame Shifting," where shifting patterns in the vibraphone, pizzicato violin, and piano right hand are heard against a steady pulsation from pizzicato cello and piano left hand. At the same time solo parts are given to the flute and clarinet. In "Pitching Rotation" there is a pentatonic design heard at different pitches. "Flipside" maintains the same rhythmic pattern, but metrical accents change and the tempi alter.

In 1997 he completed *Points of Departure,* which enhanced his New England reputation when Robert Spano and the Boston Symphony took it up in April 1998. As is usual in his music, there was tremendous variety in instrumental colorations, rhythms, and textures. The initial movement, "Spirale," is a sequence of passages running continuously around a fixed point while constantly receding from or approaching it. Each of its remaining three movements starts with an exact reappearance of a segment from the previous movement as a point of departure. "Strati" is an interconnected chain of vivid musical ideas, one folding into another. "Visione" is like a series of images and emotions occurring during sleep. "Ritorno" ultimately goes back to the opening "spiral."

Conjuring up an unusual musical atmosphere is one of Gandolfi's major strengths. Abundant evidence for this conclusion is provided by two works performed in the 1998–99 concert season: *Design School,* which was presented by the Boston Symphony Chamber Players, and *Geppetto's Workshop,* commissioned and performed by Elizabeth Ostling, flutist with the Boston Symphony, accompanied at the piano by Hugh Hinton. The extraordinary effects the two instruments produced as they realized the plot of the Pinocchio story in *Geppetto's Workshop* left the audience in a state of amazement.[6]

Thus far, Gandolfi has given the impression of a composer more interested in evoking colorful impressions that fire the listener's imagination rather than someone intent on originating memorable thematic lines that the listener can carry away as music. Works of great and broadly inclusive significance have not yet resulted. Assuredly, they will come. What is refreshing to quite a few members of the music public is that his music strikes out on a different path and invites them to come along. What is still unclear is the goal to which his path will lead.

BORN ELSEWHERE, SETTLED IN NEW ENGLAND

Several of America's most eminent composers have chosen to live in New England. They have held teaching and other positions, established homes, formed personal relationships, and participated in local life to such an extent that the northeast region has become their rightful home.

Arthur Berger is the oldest of this group. Born in New York City in 1912, he took his B.S. from New York University and his M.A. from Harvard. He was a student of Piston and Boulanger. During the 1930s Berger was numbered among the New York intelligentsia that advanced a blending of twelve-tone with neoclassic concepts. It was at this time that he became a member of a young composers' group pledged to Copland. He took an interest in Ives and was a Stravinsky devotee, too. Articles on new music came from his pen as well as strong defenses of Copland and Stravinsky when their music was declared passé in the postwar years.

In 1939 he was teaching at Mills College (where Darius Milhaud also taught) but left the school in 1946 to become a music critic in New York. From 1954 on, Berger was in New England, teaching at Brandeis until he retired in 1980. He then worked with students at the New England Conservatory until the turn of the century. He has continued to live across the Charles River from the conservatory, in Cambridge.

His compositions are completed after slow, careful labor, and there are not many of them. Yet the results have not been pedantic and stiffly formal. Indeed, he bristles at the thought that he may be referred to as an academic, a term he associates with the "Princeton crowd," namely, Roger Sessions and Milton Babbitt. At the same time, he concedes that a composition such as *Chamber Music for Thirteen Players* (1956) could be described as "neoclassic twelve-tone."[7] Some find his music to be intellectual, polished, and without excess emotion. Others perceive pleasing, piquant, and jocose qualities. Commentators are on more solid ground when they ascribe elegant textures, temporary rhythmic displacements, and a high level of chromaticism to the music. In addition, a clashing interplay of lines and the conflicting harmonies this clashing produces are heard in Berger's compositions (as in *Polyphony* for orchestra, 1956). Melodies sound fragmented rather than fully stated, and hardly any motives return in recognizable fashion. The three *Collages* of 1990–95 provide examples. The first two are written for flute, clarinet, violin, cello, and piano; the third adds percussion. Oftentimes the listener gets no sense of continuity in a movement. This holds true even in the extremely well made Septet for winds and strings (1966). Musical pointillism takes hold in pieces like the Duo for cello and piano (1951) and the Trio for violin, guitar, and piano (1972). The overall effect is one of brittle choppiness.

An attractive early work is the Quartet for Winds (1941), whose three brief movements are rhythmically sportive, fetchingly melodious, and readily accessible. Another of his more successful works, the String Quartet (1958), received the New York Music Critics Circle award for 1962. In its measures, personal meaning and searching expressiveness displace objectivity. A similar observation can be made for the *Ninety-second Psalm (Tov lehodos)* for chorus a cappella, and the songs "When I am dead" (1978) and "Ode to Ronsard" (1987). Also rewarding to hear are the Duo No. 1 for violin and piano (1948), which is the first of five duos he composed between 1948 and 1956, and *Perspectives II* for chamber orchestra (1985). After all things are considered, however, his compositions are more for the connoisseur than for the general run of listeners. For all that, Berger's view, stated in the *Boston Review* in 1987, was that winning over the general music public was beside the point. He was speaking as much about himself as he was about other twelve-tone composers when he said, "If Serialism's detractors mean that it has not become big-time box office, they should be reminded that there are other audiences, not at all negligible, besides the big ones."[8] Unfortunately, these "other audiences" can be elusive indeed. He has made few bids to engage them. As things have stood, except for the times when his music was performed and for his interactions with his students, he has kept himself aloof from the New England music scene.

Leon Kirchner has made a far larger impression on the music public than has Berger, whether in New England or the rest of the United States. He has talent in conducting, a flair for the piano, and a gift as a composer. He was born in Brooklyn to Russian parents in 1919. His family moved to Los Angeles when he was not yet an adolescent and destined him to be a physician. At the same time, he had been studying the piano and experimenting with musical composition. Music won out over medicine, and Kirchner started music study at the University of California at Los Angeles, where Arnold Schoenberg was one of his teachers. He would also study under Ernest Bloch and, after war service, with Roger Sessions at the University of California at Berkeley. By 1947 he was teaching both at Berkeley and the San Francisco Conservatory of Music. Like so many other composers, he went from teaching position to teaching position, including two stints at the Berkshire Music Center at Tanglewood (1959, 1960), until Harvard brought him to Cambridge in 1961. Kirchner has been a member of Harvard's music faculty ever since. His pianism is sometimes on exhibit at concerts, especially when his own works are involved. He has also made a name for himself as an accomplished conductor. When he leads an orchestra at Sanders Theater or the Gardner Museum, the auditorium overflows.

Stravinsky, Hindemith, and Bartók were the masters who shaped his technique during his earliest years; then Bloch, Sessions, Schoenberg, and Berg. Kirchner's mature style is a unique synthesis of these conflicting influences. But he is neither a neoclassicist nor a serialist, however much he adheres to the critical standards of balance and proportion of the former, and allows the ultrachromaticism of the latter to enter his measures. To him, what he has to say is as important as how he says it, and freedom of treatment comes before any strict theoretical system. Moreover, imagination is given full sway, even as introspective sentiment is explored. His music may also sound dramatic, rapturous, or highly agitated. Absence of key sometimes makes room for flashes of discernable tonality. Harmony based on clashing intervals of the second and seventh occasionally allows for the appearance of thirds and sixths. Extended declamation or warm-hearted, outgoing melodies ameliorate vigorously active rhythms.

The first work to give him some national prominence was the Duo for violin and piano (1947). It unleashed a personal eloquence that won him admirers even among composers, one of them Aaron Copland. He followed this the next year with the String Quartet No. 1, which confirmed his status as a major new composer. Its core ideas were imposing and lyric, although clothed in opaque textures. The pungent expressiveness of the four strings permitted no respite from conflict and drama. Its scherzo allowed for no smiling. In the final measures of the work, the grave advance of the instruments, utterly lacking in animation, suggested bleak despondency. His Sonata Concertante for violin and piano (1952), Piano Concerto No. 1 (1953), and Trio for violin, cello, and piano (1954) were built along similar lines.

Commenting on the Kirchner style that had emerged after the 1950s, Eric Salzman noted that the opening sounds of a piece provide the material for all of the music that follows. He quotes the composer as saying, "A few measures, an idea, constitute a gesture; the purpose of the work as a whole is to extend this in time. A phrase sets up the need for balance and extension, which is satisfied by what follows. This then constitutes a larger complex which sets up still more implications. The entire piece is built up and forms an entity with infinite implications."[9] Although he wrote without fretting over audience reactions, Kirchner did recognize that listeners had to get something out of hearing a composition. He felt that the least the composer could do was to insure that the audience was able to remember what had already taken place in order to follow what came next.

Almost two decades of effort went into writing his grandest work, the opera *Lily,* which he began in 1959 and completed in 1977. Saul Bellow's novel *Henderson the Rain King* supplied the libretto's subject matter, which warned of the alleged reformers of society whose zealotry might bring about the ruin of those whom they wished to improve. The music's virtues included many fine dramatic gestures, the colorful establishment of atmosphere, and expressive melodies. Unfortunately, as spectacle, the opera failed. Little action took place, and only one or two theatrical gestures grabbed the audience's attention.[10] Nevertheless, the quality of the music is high and a great deal of the score is agreeable to listen to.

Kirchner's songs fortunately require no outlay other than a singer and accompanist. Impressive is his song cycle *The Twilight Stood* (1983) to poetry of Emily Dickinson. The music embarks bravely and forcefully on an exploration of subjective emotions arising from the anxious intensity projected by the poetry. The piano part is tricky; the voice must venture into the limits of its range and accommodate widely different shades of expression. In a review of a performance of the cycle, Richard Dyer called it "bold, expressionistic music that captures the desperate subtext of the poet, the screaming behind the appearances of gentility."[11] Four years later, Kirchner adapted the songs, save for one, for solo piano as Five Pieces for Piano. Another vocal composition, *Of Things Exactly as They Are,* for baritone, chorus, and orchestra, was commissioned to celebrate the twenty-fifth anniversary of the Tanglewood Festival Chorus and received a Boston Symphony premiere in September 1997. Five American poets supplied the text. It is a chip off the same block as the song cycle with its thick, vigorous, potent, and emotional musical idiom that glances back at the close of the Romantic era.

Spurred on by his former student Yo-Yo Ma, Kirchner has composed some telling cello works. The *Triptych* for violin and cello (1988) was compiled from two pieces, "Cello Solo" and a transcription of "For Solo Violin," followed by "Duo for Violin and Cello." Then came the *Music for Cello and Orchestra* (1992) that for several years was a fitting vehicle for Ma's talents as a cellist. A comment by John Adams, another Kirchner student, is illuminating in regard to what has just been said:

> Somehow the sight of Kirchner in the environs of a university music building suggested a caged beast to me, and I eventually took the cue and left academia for good. Kirchner himself, although possessing a quick intellect, has always distrusted "intellectuals" and seems happiest in the company of performing musicians, the more naturally gifted the better. He appears to be more stimulated by a Yo-Yo Ma or a Peter Serkin than by another composer. . . . He is . . . a "natural" as a performer.[12]

Music for Cello and Orchestra is cast in one movement. Several painstakingly worked-out divisions in different speeds are interconnected. Within divisions, the pace continually varies, with several accelerandos and ritardandos. The music can pass as Romantic, with its rich subjective perception of conflict, abundant orchestral colorations, and rhapsodic torrent of affecting lyricism. His earlier Concerto for Violin, Cello, Ten Winds, and Percussion (1960) and Piano Concerto No. 2 (1963) are treated in similar fashion, as is his *Music for Orchestra* (1967) and *Orchestral Piece (Music for Orchestra II)* (1990). Another intriguing composition, *Music for 12* (1985) is atonal, yet not aggressively so, and lyrical, as if Kirchner were trying to discover a more agreeable reconciliation of the two. He ventured into electronic sound with the String Quartet No. 3 (1966), which won a Pulitzer Prize. In it, taped sound augments the strings and, at the close, dominates them.

Kirchner's music is not everyone's cup of tea. It tends to be unremittingly serious, with little lightening up. For the knowledgeable music lover willing to meet Kirchner halfway and listen attentively to his offerings, however, the music yields countless rewards, both as sound ultimately pleasurable to hear and as meditations on the inner workings of the psyche.

Even more than Kirchner, Gunther Schuller has an intimate knowledge of, and made notable contributions to, New England's and the nation's music. He has kept alive works from New England's past, reviving, conducting, and recording them, and has called attention to music from contemporary contributors. He has made a name for himself as a

major orchestral director and educator. Many radio and television programs have featured his talks on twentieth-century music. He has written
and lectured about conducting, technical matters, music education, musical culture, American music of the past, and the state of music today. In
1970 he was granted the Ditson Conducting Award for his generous support of other composers. Publishing and recording firms in which he has
had more than a finger include Margun, GunMar, and GM Recordings.

Schuller's tastes cover a wide range of diverse styles and genres, including jazz, ragtime, dance, traditional songs, popular music, and Third
World cultures. He has made a major effort to erase the divisions separat-
ing jazz, art music, and popular song and dance. Bebop artists such as
Charlie Parker, Dizzy Gillespie, Miles Davis, and John Lewis have had reason to be grateful for his assistance. In 1975 he revived Scott Joplin's opera
Treemonisha in Houston. After arriving at the New England Conservatory
of Music, he inaugurated a jazz department there and assembled an outstanding ragtime ensemble. He was also the initiator of the Third Stream,
a series of works that used features of both jazz and classical music in an
endeavor to develop a new and distinctive musical idiom.

Schuller was born in New York City in 1925, the son of German
immigrants. His father was a violinist with the New York Philharmonic. At
age seventeen Schuller was playing French horn in the Cincinnati Symphony. Two years later he joined the Metropolitan Opera Orchestra. He
also added his French horn to jazz groups and was a participant, with Miles
Davis, in Gil Evans's classic jazz recording *Birth of the Cool*. In the early
1960s he gave up his horn playing in order to devote his energies to his
other musical activities. He started his teaching career at the Manhattan
School of Music when he was twenty-five. Among other posts he held was
an assistant professorship at Yale, where he went in 1964. In 1967 he
became president of the New England Conservatory, and in the ten years
he held that position he gave the school a new lease on life by putting it on
a sound financial footing, boosting its artistic stature, and doubling its
enrollment.

Schuller was teaching at Tanglewood in 1963. In 1965 Paul Fromm
asked him to take charge of the annual Festival of Contemporary Music at
Tanglewood. By 1969 he had become codirector with Seiji Ozawa of the
Tanglewood Music Center. A crisis occurred in 1983, however, when
without notice Fromm made known his dissatisfaction with Schuller's programming of only the music he approved and excluding particularly the
minimalists. At the same time, Ozawa was apparently usurping Schuller's

Gunther Schuller and his ragtime ensemble.

prerogatives by making arbitrary decisions without consulting his codirector of the center. This led to Schuller's resignation in 1984, despite the wide backing he had received from the other musicians at Tangle-wood.[13] He has been artistic director of the Sandpoint (Idaho) Festival, advisor and conductor of the Spokane Symphony and the Pro Arte Chamber Orchestra of Boston, and has made guest appearances with orchestras throughout the United States and Europe.

While still a boy he enrolled in the St. Thomas Church Choir School and took up music theory with T. Tertius Noble. As an adolescent he continued studying music theory and composition at the Manhattan School of Music. He had no further formal lessons in music other than those on the French horn. He did listen assiduously to whatever music came his way and was particularly attracted to the work of Duke Ellington, Ravel, Scriabin, Schoenberg, Stravinsky, Messiaen, and Webern, all of which influences found their way into his own music. By the turn of the century he had written around 170 music compositions and four valuable books: *Early Jazz* (1968), *Musings: The Musical Worlds of Gunther Schuller* (1986), *The Swing Era* (1988), and *The Compleat Conductor* (1997).

His early *Symphonic Study* (1948) owes a great deal to Schoenberg. In 1950 Schuller completed a Symphony for Brass and Percussion that injected serialism into time-honored formats. Paul Fromm commissioned the String Quartet, premiered in 1957. *Variants* for jazz quartet and orchestra (1960) invigorated the symphonic fabric with a jazz vernacular generated by the vibraphone, piano, double bass, and piano.

Not surprisingly, jazz, blues, brilliant orchestration after Ravel, twelve-tone rows following Schoenberg, rhythmic manipulation à la Stravinsky, and pointillism like Webern's may all pop up in the same work, as they do in his extremely successful *Seven Studies on Themes of Paul Klee* (1959). The seven musical elucidations of the Klee pictures are short. A variety of orchestral colors and textures are applied with a sure hand. The music ranges from atonal, some of it twelve-tone, to tonal. One encounters jazz and Arabic melody. Harmony ranges from the medieval doubling of parts at intervals of a fourth, a fifth, or an octave only (known as organum) to late twentieth-century combinations based on a tone row without regard for traditional tonality. Mood can be generated by subtle and mysterious whispers to piercing tone clashes. One piece is no-nonsense serious; another provokes mirth.

The first movement, "Antike Harmonien" (Antique Harmonies), sounds expressionistic and atonal and moves at a slow pulse rate. Open fifths and medieval cadences add to the tone painting. "Abstrakte Trio" (Abstract Trio) is in three parts, lean, and subdued. The music is "abstracted" from feeling. "Kleiner Blauteufel" (Little Blue Devil) is a bit of cool jazz, with a blues-tinged trumpet melody over a pizzicato walking bass. "Die Twitschermaschine" (The Twittering Machine) is pointillistic twelve-tone music full of chirping sounds. "Arabische Stadt" (Arab Village) suspends the listener in the evening air, while below a sorrowful flute, pulsating percussion, and a nasal oboe play exotic dance tunes. "Eine Unheimlicher Moment" (An Eerie Moment) sounds disquietingly creepy, like a scene enveloped in menacing darkness. The final "Pastorale" presents high clashing notes in the strings and disconcerting phrases in the woodwinds and French horn. The simplicity, charm, and serenity normally associated with a pastoral atmosphere are not invoked. *Seven Studies on Themes of Paul Klee* illustrates Edwin London's conclusions about Schuller's treatment of the orchestra: "Schuller's approach to the orchestra is unstrained and instinctive, combining an intimate knowledge of the technical possibilities of the various instruments with an insight into the psychological makeup of orchestral players. He often treats the orchestra as a huge group of soloists capable of subtle and exquisite as well as grandiose and massive splotches of color and contour."[14]

Schuller's Symphony (1965) has a go at the total control of all musical parameters somewhat similar to the serial approach of Milton Babbitt. It caused scarcely a ruffle among the music public. However, a furor in music circles was occasioned by his 1966 opera *The Visitation,* commissioned by the Hamburg Opera. Moved by the ongoing African American struggle for justice and taking his cue from Kafka's mind-deranging *The Trial,* Schuller depicts a black man cast off from American society and experiencing complete anomie. Atonal expressionistic writing is interlaced with jazz, blues, spirituals, and gospel song. Bessie Smith sings "Nobody Knows You When You're Down and Out." One also hears electronic-generated sounds. Schuller, in a 1968 article on *The Visitation,* said there was no dichotomy between twelve-tone music and jazz, and that he had based the music on a single primary tone row and a group of derived ones from it, after the manner of Babbitt.[15] The singers declaimed mostly in unmelodic recitative. Critics complained that Schuller perceived American life as sterile, American culture as without merit. The Hamburg Opera presented the opera in New York, and another production of it was given in San Francisco, both in 1967. In 1969 London's BBC televised *The Visitation.* Listeners, particularly Europeans, of advanced taste lauded the work; others, particularly illiberal Americans, took offense at what they perceived as an unfair caricature of the United States.[16]

Schuller bounced back and proved his versatility when, in 1970, he composed *Museum Piece* for the Boston Museum of Fine Arts, which featured early music performers, and also an opera for children based on a Grimm fairy tale, *The Fisherman and His Wife,* with a libretto by John Updike. Eight years later, in "Toward a New Classicism," a lecture delivered at Goucher College, in Baltimore, he was saying that he realized art music could not survive without an audience. Otherwise, it was merely a laboratory or research-station production: "We composers should remember that after all the artistic, aesthetic battles have been fought and all the injustices to misunderstood composers rectified, the audience—the large over-all audience, in short, the culture—is the final arbiter of that which survives." The belief had existed that the radically new in art, if rejected at first, would eventually win over the audience. This was an illusion. Sixty years into the century, Schoenberg, Webern, and Ives had won few converts. By casting off tradition, tonality, and common practices for freedom and originality, more had been lost than gained. Composers needed to balance their art "with a commensurate infusion of emotion, simplicity, comprehensibility, and humanism." It was a mistake to think that "in order to accept something new, we must totally reject something old. . . . The conservatives reasoned the same way, only in reverse." He advocated more music education, both formal and informal, more meaningful melody and harmony, more simplicity, and the viewing of music as an uninterrupted continuity through the decades that bore a relationship to the life of the contemporary world.[17]

One consequence of Schuller's new reasoning was his Symphony No. 3, *In Praise of Winds* (1981), which comprises four traditional movements. The first movement starts off gravely and then speeds up as it develops the opening ideas, sometimes in the full orchestra and sometimes in passages having scarcely any weight. The slow second movement has full-sized communicative melodies that glance back at the idioms cultivated at the start of the century. The next movement is a true scherzo filled with sounds that impatiently dash forward, except in the more subdued trio section. The finale starts with a fanfare and later introduces a waltz and a jazzy tune as subordinate themes. Yet he was not aiming at merely resurrecting the past. He hoped to fashion his own identifiable musical idiom that would convey numerous facets of expressivity. At the same time he trusted that listeners would not write off his contributions as new modernist attacks on sensibility. To this end, he wrote a piano quartet, *On Light Wings* (1984), with movements entitled "Impromptu," "Scherzo," "Fantasia," and "Bagatelle (with Swing)." The main heading was to indicate that he meant the music to come over as "light," not "heavy."

The next year saw the Concerto for Orchestra No. 3, *Farbenspiel,* joining his previous two, of 1966 and 1978. The play of colors mentioned in the title referred to the interaction of soloists, small groups, and large choirs of instruments, in movements labeled "Chorisch," "Solistisch," and "Orchestral." He continued with *Of Reminiscences and Reflections* for orchestra (1993), which won a Pulitzer Prize, and *The Past Is in the Present* for orchestra (1994), which he dedicated to his late and much-loved wife, Marjorie. In 1996 Schuller composed *An Arc Ascending* for orchestra, drawing on the photographs of Alice Watson: "A Winter Marker," "A Tale of Spring and Fall," and "The First Gleam of Summer." The sections paint musical pictures that mingle Impressionism, tonality, atonality, and neoclassic rhythmic vigor.

Schuller has been trying with might and main to make music a viable art form that will again attract the general music public. His efforts have involved education, writing, conducting, publishing, sound recordings, lecturing, appearances on radio and television, and of course musical composition. The twenty-first century finds him continuing in these efforts with few pauses for rest. Without question, he has made a tremendous mark on musical life in New England. The two dozen or so major awards and honors accorded him testify to that.

Until his retirement in 1990, T. J. Anderson Jr. taught at Tufts and composed music somewhat similar in style to that of Schuller. His musical idiom is up to date, lyrical, tonal, and made tense by discordant harmony. Jazz, blues, and other aspects of his African American heritage find their way into his works. He was born in Coatesville, Pennsylvania, in 1928, the son of schoolteachers. Educated at Pennsylvania State University and University of Iowa, he came to Tufts in 1972. Some of his compositions are Symphony in Three Movements (1964), *Spirituals* for narrator, tenor, children's choir, jazz quartet, and orchestra (1979), *Egyptian Diary* for soprano and two percussionists (1991), the chamber opera *Walker* (1992), the song cycle *Words My Mother Taught Me* (2000), and *Notes for a Friend* for clarinet, viola, and piano (2000). He occupies a respectable place among New England's composers.

Yehudi Wyner, who was born in Calgary, Alberta, in 1929 and grew up in New York City, attended Yale and Harvard and studied with Richard Donovan, Paul Hindemith, and Walter Piston. He started teaching at Yale in 1963 and at the Berkshire Music Center in 1978. Wyner joined the Brandeis faculty in 1986. As a composer, Wyner has not been locked into any one style. At first a neoclassicist, as in the Partita for piano (1952), he afterward adopted a more open, chromatic style, with hints of jazz, blues, and Jewish cantillation, as in the Concert Duo for violin and piano (1957). An out-and-out Jewish idiom is evident in his *Friday Evening Service* (1963).[18] *Fragments from Antiquity* for soprano and orchestra has added Chinese and Greek flavorings (1981). Also important in his output is *On This Most Voluptuous Night* for soprano and seven instruments (1982). More recent are the piano miniatures *New Fantasies* (1991) and *Post Fantasies* (1995). These are occasional pieces of an improvisatory nature that run the gamut of expression. "Addio, Addio Roma," for example, imparts the despairing feelings of an empress exiled from the city. "Mano a Mano (con fuga frugale)" craftily transmits an opposite set of feelings.

Two composers who have made names for themselves in electronic music are Robert Ceeley (born 1930) and Tod Machover (born 1953). They have taught at the New England Conservatory of Music and Massachusetts Institute of Technology, respectively. The latter's *Brain Opera* was a hotly debated musical and technological event in 1996. In producing the opera, Machover invited the public to experiment with a complex electronic installation featuring a number of novel interactive "hyper-instruments." The results of the interventions went into a computer and became components of the composition. A similar approach was made in a two-act opera based on Leo Tolstoy's *Resurrection* (1999), where the voices and orchestra were modified through "hyperelectronic" enrichment.

After Gunther Schuller, John Harbison is the composer who has made the greatest impression on the national, and especially New England, music public during the last quarter of the twentieth century. He was born in Orange, New Jersey, in 1938. His father was a historian on the Princeton faculty, and his mother was a writer. From both parents he learned a love for music—jazz, popular, and art music. Harbison studied with Piston at Harvard, earning his B.A. in 1960, and later worked with Sessions and Kim. He was not really sold on Piston's musical style, finding it too cool, and decided also that he should shun Boulanger's teaching. In 1969 he joined the faculty of the Massachusetts Institute of Technology, where he has remained, save for several brief interruptions, usually as composer-in-residence to orchestras in other places. He regards New England as his home territory. Anthony Tommasini wrote of him in the *New York Times:* "He says it doesn't bother him that he had been dubbed a 'New England composer,' which he defined as reserved, conscious of craft, and comfortable with religious themes."[19] He is best known for his three symphonies, three string quartets, three operas, the several concertos, and the cantata *The Flight into Egypt,* which earned a Pulitzer Prize in 1987. He has also won admiration for his conducting.

In his first compositions, Harbison avoided key centers. The instruments scurry about in busy textures, combining mostly in disturbingly discordant and unresolved chords, but kept within composer-defined limits through a rather formal treatment of his material. The occasional appearance of jazzlike measures did not take the edge off the largely off-putting effect of the music. No real headway in his career was being realized. Like many other American composers, he had a change of heart in the 1970s, deciding he was tired of "personal *angst*" and "empty gesture" and the "unexamined inheritance from Viennese Expressionism" in music.[20] The obvious reference was to the serialism practiced by Schoenberg, Berg, Webern, and his teacher Sessions. This did not mean a total repudiation, however, as can be gathered from the Sonata for Piano No. 1, *Roger Sessions in Memoriam.*

The opera *Winter's Tale* (1974) lets us hear the adjustments he was trying to accomplish. Functional harmony and identifiable lyricism dilute the rigors of Viennese expressionism, which no longer dominates. Practices from the Classical and Romantic period appear. Songs hopefully to an audience's liking are sprinkled about in the score. *Flower-Fed Buffaloes* for baritone, chorus, and chamber ensemble, including jazz percussion instruments, came out almost two years later and stirred jazz into the art music mix. Allusions to American songs such as "Always" and "America, the Beautiful" and some jazz licks relieve the measures in *Sprechstimme.* Nevertheless, the music showed that stylistic changes were still in progress. Nothing had jelled yet.

His breakthrough came with *Diotima,* a twenty-minute piece written for the Boston Symphony in 1976. Diotima was a priestess whose name appears in Plato's *Symposium.* She had taught Socrates her theory of love, of the way it grew through an appreciation of the beauty in bodies, in souls, and in the structure of all things. At times the music suggests ceremonial or mystic events. Harbison conveys these meanings through a constantly metamorphosing melody, which eventually climaxes in a delirium of sentiment. From the premier of *Diotima* on, he had a worldwide reputation. He was invited to make appearances in various parts of the United States and received many commissions for new works. Yet his main allegiance was given to daily activities in the Boston musical community.[21] He achieved a further advance with his Wind Quintet (1978), which was difficult to play but easy to enjoy.

After Harbison achieved his mature style, his music revealed an extraordinary inventiveness and a wide sweep of feeling. One was likely to encounter frankly tonal passages contrasted with judiciously written atonal sections, strict triadic euphony with some secundal pile-ups of dissonance, rhythms out of Bach with those of jazz or Stravinsky, and blatant extroversion with subtle introspection. The music can sound identifiably melodic, appealing to the ear, charming or dark, joyous or poignant, artistically exalted or like a slice of pop art, but more often than not, coherent and enjoyable. Harbison's revamped manner can be heard in his several concertos: for piano (1978), violin (1980), viola (1989), oboe (1991), cello (1993), and flute (1996). What Andrew Porter had to say about the Violin Concerto might well apply to all. Porter found the concerto "like all his music, hard to categorize and easy to enjoy. It pleases the mind but is composed with a freedom properly called 'romantic.' Harbison is a poetic, civilized, courteous composer. His fancy ranges, but he doesn't shout and stamp."[22]

There is something for the listener to like in every one of these concertos. The least easy of all to assimilate is the first, the Piano Concerto. Yet there is also much to take pleasure in. With regard to the Viola Concerto, Harbison brought out the instrument's capacity for pensive or exalted statement and also gave it space to exercise its faculty for going readily from music of dignified restraint to outbursts of furious passion.[23] Harbison exchanged somberness for exuberance with the Oboe Concerto. It was written for William Bennett, oboist with the San Francisco Symphony, who had requested a wildly unrestrained "swing number." It came off sounding as if Bach was sitting in with the Benny Goodman Quartet. Finally, the Flute Concerto was well liked from the beginning because it sounded luminous, colorful, and replete with memorable melody, occasionally angular and occasionally songlike. At all times, the composer's expertise showed through, as did his full command of his musical idiom.

The First String Quartet (1985) was stripped down to essentials and wrought up by an excess of feeling. From beginning to end, it offered little emotional relief. His Second String Quartet (1987) comes across as a modernized version of a Renaissance piece for a consort of viols— "Fantasia," "Concertino," "Aria and Recitative," "Sonata," and "Ricercare." A certain calmness prevails. Further demonstrating Harbison's unpredictability, the Third String Quartet (1993) reveals his acquaintance with New England psalmody, with its ambiance of meetinghouse worship, varying from intimate to general devotion. One moment it is quietly prayerful, the next, fervently affirming.

One could not foresee how he would write symphonies either. The First Symphony (1981), in four traditional movements, lets off a romantic glow, with its rich harmonizations, warm melodies, and dynamic rhythms. In contrast, the Second Symphony (1986) is in four sections—"Dawn," "Daylight," "Dusk," and "Darkness"—to be played without interruption. The piece is much more complex, technically and expressively. The world of nature epitomizes the shifting conditions of the human spirit. From an opening imitation of the cry of a bird, it goes through alternating hopeful, desolated, and agitated periods until it reaches a peroration that sounds like a wild animal's bellow. The Third Symphony (1991) makes its own individual expressive statement as it too fathoms the human spirit. Listening to it reminds us of a comment made by Andrew Pincus that, like one or two other composers of his time, Harbison recognizes that "it is impossible . . . to remove the traditional elements of transcendence and awe without losing music's most redemptive, most human qualities. It is those qualities that all people in all times have sought in art, whether cave dwellers with their wall drawings, ancient Greeks with their ritual dramas, or medieval worshipers with their cathedrals."[24]

The fifty-five-minute *Motetti di Montale,* for soprano and piano (1980), moderated the demands he had previously made on lovers of vocal music. There were even less problems of accessibility in the six *Mirabai Songs* (1982) for soprano and chamber ensemble, and the people who heard them came away delighted. Mirabai, who sang as she danced along the thoroughfares of India's villages and cities in the sixteenth century, was the author of these rapturous paeans to the god Krishna. The music also advances rhythmically, is unashamedly melodious, and pulsates with a blaze of feeling. It set the stage for the vocal music that came after: *The Flight Into Egypt: Sacred Ricercar* (1986), *Emerson* (1995), and *Four Psalms* (1999). The last was written on a commission from the Israeli Consulate of Chicago to commemorate the fiftieth anniversary of Israel. It provides another example of Harbison's unfettered approach to composing. Psalms 114, 146, 133, and 137 supplied the major texts for a work that was ostensibly a cantata for four soloists, chorus, and orchestra. However, much of the piece approaches theater. Harbison mingled sections for the soloists with English settings of conversations he had had with fifteen people in and outside of Israel, including a Palestinian and a Bedouin. The outcome was a multifaceted, formal and informal, many-sided and incompatible view of Israel—in short, a present-day commentary on the psalms. The music was expertly written in a widely variable style to accommodate the different viewpoints. Sometimes extravagantly histrionic, sometimes discomposing, and oftentimes genuinely affecting, the work concludes softly with words of hope and a devout petition for reconciliation.[25]

Finally to be mentioned is Harbison's opera *The Great Gatsby* (1999), in two acts and ten scenes, based on F. Scott Fitzgerald's Jazz Age novel. Newly composed pop songs in the style of the 1920s are interwoven with operatic music whose tradition goes back to Wagner, Verdi, and Mozart. Perhaps it is best to end the discussion of Harbison with a layperson's reaction to the opera, when she heard its premiere:

The music was semi-tonal (as if combining Barber and Schoenberg, I'm not a musician so I can't evoke technicalities) with some lyric breakthrough arias. The created 1920s songs were very effective as were the party dance scenes. . . . The first act could have used about 20 minutes of cuts of repeated lines, but the second act tightened up nicely in dramatic cohesiveness. . . . The opera did convey the tragedy of Gatsby and made it seem timeless. . . . The funeral scene with Gatsby's father was heartbreaking. The audience reaction was more than polite if not overwhelming.[26]

The quotation describes some of the features of Harbison's music at the turn of the century from the general public's viewpoint. That public has accepted the way his works shift from tonality to atonality, from lyrical poetry to angular lines, from relaxed looseness to terse integration of structure, and from pleasant entertainment to intensely anguished passages. And most listeners' responses have indicated a genuine response to his music's emotional and intellectual content rather than merely a well-mannered reception of sounds that are essentially beyond them.

CHAPTER

15

A FINAL WORD

J ohn Harbison has summed up what it means to be called a "New England composer." To him, the term stands for an artist who exercises restraint in any demonstration of his knowledge when he composes and who is reserved in voicing his musical opinions when with others. The New England musician is always mindful of the manner in which he employs his technical skills to produce a finished composition and can aim at evoking the transcendental and spiritual without feeling embarrassment.[1] Furthermore, the New England composer has a respect for the time-honored mandate to go beyond ordinary experience. He tries to call forth wonder, since in this way music emancipates the vital force and brings out the more elevated part of human nature.[2]

Perhaps his definition is too high flown, and he overstates his case; yet there are elements of truth in it. Almost all New England composers, starting with John Knowles Paine, practiced restraint in their speech and creativity, except for the exuberant Ives, contentious Ruggles, and bizarre Lucier. To achieve the transcendental was on the minds of most of these artists. Certainly Ives and Ruggles made it one of their major creative goals, while wonder akin to amazement was a part of Lucier's agenda. A majority of them, in the twentieth century, started off as neoclassicists, introduced atonal and twelve-tone techniques into their works, and looked over electronic possibilities. None was a strict adherent to any compositional creed. Jazz, traditional song and dance, and popular music are traceable in some of their compositions. The closer they drew to the year 2000, the more eclectic their styles became. The different musical sources from which they chose ranged from the medieval period to the present, from musical cultures throughout the globe, and from every artistic and vernacular standpoint. The use of two or more different cultural identities within a unified composition grew almost routine, especially in the last two decades of the century.

There were composers, of course, from every section of the nation who followed a parallel road to the New Englanders. In the latter half of the century, however, the neoclassicism of a composer such as Copland seemed a thing of the past to up-and-coming composers in the two main centers for new music—California and New York. Instead, younger Californians became identified with much looser or more experimental methods, from indeterminacy to minimalism, and younger New Yorkers cast their lot with highly structured atonal or serial methods, positing an entire work on the use of a *klang* (an initial combination of tones) or a tone row. When the California-leaning musicians established a bastion in lower Manhattan, New Yorkers employed the terms "downtown" and "uptown," respectively, to identify the two camps. Nevertheless, throughout the nation there were composers who refused to be pigeonholed as belonging to one circle or another. Most of them were disposed to preserve time-proven ways of composing music and to limit change—John La Montaine, Ned Rorem, Lee Hoiby, John Corigliano, Carlisle Floyd, Joseph Schwantner, and Arnold Rosner, to name seven. In short, despite the cries of revolution and the death of the old in the arts, there was a continuum in art music between past and present, a cohesive whole whose elements altered slowly and by minute degrees.

All this said, at the start of the twenty-first century the new direction for the several musical styles was a sort of convergence. Coming more to the fore was a tendency to combine various historical modes of writing with recent elements, the goal being to bring together the excellences of many styles and to boost the amount of expressive references. It grew more and more difficult to identify or speak of a regional or national music. Every area was now open to the world and imbibed its influences.

THE LEGACY OF THE 1990S

What caused, indeed forced, art composers to reconsider their activities? In the 1990s the struggle for artistic survival came to a head—a sure way to concentrate composers' intentions. The proliferation of different cultures in the United States, each attracting its own adherents, diluted the impact of the arts. The confusion concerning what art was all about elicited a comment by Neil Rudenstine, president of Harvard University, in 1999: "Marx, Freud, anthropological studies, various forms of cultural studies, new theories of gender-related or ethnicity-related analysis: all of these stress very different aspects of works of art. Aesthetics isn't high on the list."[3] That is to say, music had to pass tests not related to its appeal as pure sound and its evocation of a sense of the beautiful.

Ethnic festivals and ethnic music in all six New England states spread the gospel of diversity. The entertainment business—radio, television, motion pictures, recordings, and concert giving—geared itself to whatever diversions would attract the greatest number—quiz and talk shows, crime- and sex-drenched serial dramas, and euphoric theatrical productions by under-thirty popular singers and instrumentalists. Among those attracted were men and women who might possibly have joined the audience for art music. When art music got coverage, it was because something outrageous or otherwise completely divorced from normal practices was being purveyed to the public.

Art music offerings on radio and television by vendors of high culture were rare. Classical music FM stations disappeared, shrank the time allotted to art music, or in the case of a station such as Boston's WCRB, became an "easy listening" classical station limited to playing only what time had tested and found to reliably please auditors. Public television and FM stations such as WGBH drummed up a clientele that favored the umpteenth repetition of a Three Tenor concert over a performance by a string quartet. Especially during their frequent fund-raising periods, broadcasters took no risks and, after bouts of sophistic rationalization about their reasons for doing so, introduced programs that compromised their image of cultural excellence.

Educators were bent on eliminating the teaching of music in the public schools because it was considered a frill, a frivolous subject of study. Budget constraints forced them to cut back on programs. Music was an easy victim because it could not be put into operation as a classroom subject or as an applied program without problems of space, equipment, and soundproofing. Nor could it prove its usefulness. Whatever cultural eminence art music had was now gone. Music departments disappeared or were downsized and music teachers dismissed in Boston, Hartford, Manchester, Providence, Burlington, and Portland. In the music classes that remained at the turn of the century, multiculturalism and popular mores prevailed to the exclusion of the artistic.

Nor did it help to advance the cause of art music in the schools by claiming it had not so much value in itself but value owing to its beneficial effects on the intellect, the body, and psychic apparatus. (This echoes similar assertions made by Lowell Mason more than 150 years ago.) The claim detracted from the real worth of the arts and was easily contested. For example, Lois Hetland, a psychologist affiliated with Harvard's Graduate School of Education, after reviewing 188 educational studies made over the past fifty years, found slight evidence that music improved special thinking and less that it helped students read better. Hetland said that she herself enthusiastically championed music classes and insisted that they warranted space in the curriculum on their own merits: "We don't ask history to justify itself on the basis of whether it raises English scores. It's valuable on its own."[4]

Congress tried time and again to stop funding for the National Endowment for the Arts, the supposition being that the serious arts meant nothing to Americans. They were also outraged by the confrontational antics of a few people working on the fringes of the art world and not representative of artists as a whole. Some congressmen who granted composers some significance considered the arts fit only for the personal amusement of a small select group. Art music carried no weight for them and was just another divertissement to while away an hour or two. The political right wing led by Jesse Helms and Rush Limbaugh mounted a continuous attack on the NEA, as in a message posted on the Internet from the "Rush Limbaugh Institute for Illogical, but Emotionally Satisfying Thinking," which claimed that the average taxpayer was cheated of 38 cents a year by funding for the NEA and that it was better to buy one-half a cup of coffee than give to "some tutti-frutti ballet company." Jim Lehrer interviewed William Ivey, the new chair of the NEA, in 1998 and was told that the foundation was still recovering from the attempts of the Reagan administration to wipe it out. In order to make it more politically acceptable, Ivey said, the NEA had to look at "a wide spectrum of artistic endeavor" and at "our many diverse traditions," whether folk, popular, or classical—in short, less funding for art music. It is significant that Ivey's background was not in the world of high art but as director of the Country Music Foundation.[5]

Again and again, stingy members of Congress suggested that the private sector would more than make up whatever cuts were made in public appropriations for the arts. That did not take place. Instead, the private giving decreased. Individuals, corporations, and nonprofit foundations began to direct a larger portion of their donations to social service organizations. Moreover, by the year 2000 it was clear that New England, and Massachusetts in particular, was "at the bottom of the Generosity Index again [according to the annually released "Catalogue for Philanthropy"]. The state is keeping sad company with regional neighbors New Hampshire, Connecticut, and Rhode Island, which also fall near the bottom."[6] Winning support for the arts among the public and the politicians of New England was difficult, concluded Michael Crowley in 1999. On the other hand, football and baseball had no such problems. (Witness the competition for, and monetary enticements offered to, the New England Patriots to relocate in Connecticut and to remain in Foxboro.) In Massachusetts, seventy million dollars were allocated to a new stadium for the New England Patriots, and additional millions were going to the Red Sox. At the same time, wrote Crowley, a thirty-five-million-dollar proposal to repair museums, arts centers, and historic sites won lukewarm support in the state legislature:

> "It's just unthinkable that we can find a way of doing major facilities for major sports organizations, but we can't find a way of helping nonprofit cultural organizations," said state Senator Stanley Rosenberg.
>
> "Cultural institutions are the place where that essential discourse is going on about our democracy and what it means to be an American," said Susan Hartnett, director of the Boston Center for the Arts.[7]

Crowley was painting an embarrassing picture of New England.

Looking over the situation in the 1990s, Michael Kammen suggested that it was of vital interest to a democracy to regard culture that aimed high to be a necessity rather than a luxury and that "there simply has to be sufficient governmental support for such an agenda":

> What our historical experience has shown, beyond any doubt, is that public money spent on cultural programs has a multiplier effect—in terms of *participation by people* as well as in economic terms. What the critics of state support for culture dismally fail to understand is that a diminution or elimination of public support will not prompt an increase in private support. Quite the contrary, it leads to a loss of private support. That, in turn, impoverishes the nation, with implications and outcomes that are truly lamentable.[8]

Obviously, owing to the nature of their enterprise, people engaged in making and producing popular music exist to make a profit and have no need for subsidies. After speaking to several directors of New England's art music organizations and to individual composers, however, I learned that what monies had come their way in, say, the 1970s had now diminished to an alarmingly low level, and getting the community to make contributions demanded year-round solicitations via telephone, mail, meetings, and pleadings at concerts. Richard Pittman, for example, said he had to devote a tremendous amount of time and energy to raising sufficient funds to keep Boston Musica Viva's head above water, and he was barely succeeding.

Tanglewood, with a reputation for upholding serious-mindedness in music, like many other such festivals, fell back on publicity, special festal celebrations, hackneyed programming, and famous soloists to serve as crowd pullers. Reviewing the Tanglewood Music Festival for the summer of 2000 in the *Boston Globe,* Andrew Pincus, who usually wrote for the *Berkshire Eagle,* spoke of the same overly familiar pieces requiring little rehearsal that were repeatedly played ad nauseum. He mentioned, too, the worn-out and over-the-hill singers, pianists, and violinists who were featured because they had drawing power, of the considerable hoopla that attended their appearances, and the consequent attendance of indiscriminating audiences who gave everyone a standing ovation whether they deserved one or not: "We pay jacked-up prices to hear second-rate attractions while first-rate ones at regular prices go begging. And people accuse Tanglewood of commercialism and selling out."[9] This was Tanglewood's dilemma—to replenish its audience without seeming to be "dumbing down."

What was said of Tanglewood applied also to the regular symphony concerts, although to a lesser extent. Contemporary composers during the 1990s were difficult to fit into the cultural equation. Heads of recognized professional ensembles claimed that much of the new writing sounded like a hodgepodge of this and that and was therefore transitory, rather than the result of thoughtful eclecticism and being capable of lasting value. Not enough listeners identified with the new music, however much the composers tried to make their pieces attractive. The economic survival of performing groups had to come first.

Despite the commissioning and performance of new works, the basic repertoire remained the same. Classical and Romantic composers provided the bulk of the programming. The language of Beethoven, Brahms, and Tchaikovsky continued to appeal strongly to what listeners for art music were left. For all the enthusiastic reception and extensive mention in the news media and other means of communication that some contemporary works received at their first appearance, no mechanism was in place to sustain their presence in future concerts. This, Schuller, Del Tredici, Rzewski, and Harbison quickly found out. All four men had produced exceptionally fine pieces that audiences had immediately enjoyed and presumably would have continued to enjoy. However, all had seen these pieces relegated to the closet shelf. Contemporary composers were the stepchildren of the music world and had to recognize that after a premiere and, if fortunate, a few additional performances, a composition disappeared from view.

A part of the problem was the constant dissension between composers, musical institutions, and devotees of music as to what music should be supported. Without shared standards to refer to, intellectuals and aesthetes were all over the cultural map. Divisiveness watered down what strength the art music community had. The state of cultural affairs was such that by 1985 Charles Newman was able to comment, "We are witness to continual internecine warfare and spasmodic changes in fashion, the simultaneous display of all past styles in their infinite mutations, and the continuous circulation of diverse and contradictory intellectual elites, which signal the reign of the cult of *creativity* in all areas of behavior, an unprecedented nonjudgmental receptivity to Art, a tolerance finally amounting to indifference."[10]

Whether we are willing to accept it or not, our nation has not realized the musical prestige in the world's eye that we hoped would result in a government by, of, and for the people. A high standing in music seemed imminent after the start given by the New England composers of the nineteenth century and the excitement accompanying the formation of one excellent musical institution after another throughout the country. Unfortunately, we soon developed the habit of rejecting our past and sending older works into exile, whatever their excellence. Unlike Europe, American governmental bodies, federal and state, gave piddling sums, and these only reluctantly, to the arts, and always there was the threatening talk about cutting taxes and economizing. The noblesse oblige that caused Henry Lee Higginson, Isabella Stewart Gardner, Eben Jordan, and Elizabeth Sprague Coolidge to give liberally to music had almost faded from sight at the end of the twentieth century. "Meanwhile, some of our cultural heritage" seemed "to be headed for extinction, and those who lamented that trend" were "likely to be labeled as snobs."[11]

CONJECTURES ABOUT THE PRESENT

In what follows, the intention is to offer some thoughts based on the evidence of the last few years.

It would appear that the present-day fluidity between social classes, the indulgence of assorted tastes at all class levels, and the wide multiplication of cultural choices have affected the arts adversely. The so-called highbrows now have an inclination to listen arbitrarily to any music from any number of sources, high and low—that is to say, if they listen to music at all. Nevertheless, one good result may have arisen. Critics can no longer equate high art solely with a highbrow class. In recent years, people from every social rank are more likely to be cruising the entire cultural sphere and sampling what is on offer than had been true fifty years ago.

Conceivably, art music is not necessarily wasting away. The door has opened wider for people from every part of society. The music-loving public may cherish the works from one to two hundred years ago. They may have rejected what the twentieth-century avant-garde had to offer. However, what they will want in the future is not the ceaseless repetition of the Beethoven Fifth Symphony and its like, or its pale imitation in new works. What they need are fresh contemporary compositions that can communicate with them. In response to this need, music may be altering into what it now must be. The eclecticism noted in the last chapter is but another name given the search for previously unemployed sounds that New England composers believe will meet the new requirements. Art music is not and never can be in a frozen state. Change is constantly taking place.

Change is in the air not only in New England but also in the rest of the nation. Paul Griffiths, in an article of December 1999, said that he detected change ready to occur wherever he looked. The present economic situation was endangering musical life. A new generation of composers was unhappy over the increasing marginalization of creative artists. They were becoming nothings. Hardly anyone was ready to welcome or listen to their works. Performing groups could not meet the expense of sponsoring them. The audience was showing itself able to manage without new music. Expression, they realized, must again come to the fore, but not as it was presently defined. Their problem was to create something fresh that was viable.[12]

Nevertheless, art music's principal allies continue to be men and women of liberal education. The dependable audiences in concert halls, such as they are, still include lawyers, the clergy, schoolteachers, college faculty members, medical doctors, and people learned in one of the sciences. Because of New England's strong position in education and medicine, it continues to produce large numbers of potentially faithful listeners. Regrettably, the preponderance of present-day music lovers is over fifty years of age. The under-thirty men and women of some education, in particular, are in the minority, oftentimes because the demands on young families shrink leisure time or because young people can least afford the cost of concert attendance. High ticket prices, exorbitant parking fees, baby-sitting expenses, and commuting from the suburbs make them think twice about attending music presentations. As has been true in the past, the politicians, engineers, and business people are scarcely to be seen in concert halls.

There is hope for building new audiences. One sign is the return of the concept of beauty in the arts, something listeners have insisted upon and modern artists have until now claimed is nonsense. Its long banishment to the artistic sidelines appears over. No longer is the term regarded as elitist, ethnocentric, and the creation of white males of fuddy-duddy mentality. Nor are there many composers of modern outlook left who repudiate beauty for reasons connected with Dadaism or expression-ism. They had formerly attached no meaning to the word, which they insisted was only a value judgment no more serious than "it clicks with me." Now, they think differently.

Actually, the general music public, whether today or two hundred years ago, has always upheld the criterion of beauty. It has regularly sustained the idea that beauty is a quality looked for, even necessary, in music that is pleasurably communicated to a person—and artists are agreeing more and more with the public. A sense of beauty results from the intense gratification given to the senses and deep satisfaction given to the mind of the listener. It arises from the appeal of sheer sound, the underlying scheme that governs the way a work reveals itself, and the notion that high spiritual qualities are being manifested. At concerts, I hear men and women invariably describe the music they have just heard and enjoyed as being beautiful. I now hear an increasing number of New England composers speak of it without embarrassment. Whether scholars find the word difficult to define or not and whether some people in the arts still dismiss it as irrelevant, people insist upon it and appreciate works that exhibit it, however elusive thinkers find its elucidation. Pertinent is the recent course "On Beauty" that Elaine Scarry teaches at Harvard to eager students who are open to and willingly absorb art works so designated. In them, "it's like a hunger," she says.[13] As one listener recently put it, fine music "is precious because its power does not lie [only] in the *thing* itself but to what that *thing* tells us about who we are in the most high quality (*beauty*) manner possible." Its value is "inherent within its function as an artistic product."[14]

The "noble" and "spiritual" in music has also had a rebirth in artistic circles that had once felt uncomfortable about the concepts. It may be true that we live in a worldly, hardheaded, irreligious, solution directed, anti-artistic world that shows few inclinations toward high-mindedness in music. For several years to think "young" and animalistic has been in vogue. However, a resurgence of interest in the incorporeal and deeply feeling sides of our humanity has started to filter through our society. It has manifested itself as a reemphasis on music's original and time-honored roots in exalted expression and lucid melody, harmony, and rhythm. In fewer instances it becomes a giving way to a self-effacing, unruffled representation of sounds that amalgamate art, jazz, and rock into a sort of New Age pabulum for the spirit.

Nobility is not a form of elitism or a buzzword for cultural snobs. It resides in the many examples of notable music that go beyond the stripped-down explicitness of songs adapted to the understanding and taste of the masses. It is discovered in compositions open to several possible interpretations and allows a revelation of our vital force in its endless permutations.

New England has had more than its share of composers who honor nobility and spirituality. Far back in Puritan times, the psalms were believed to harbor these virtues. One hundred years later, William Billings hoped to inject them into his hymns, anthems, and fuging pieces. Still later, Paine's Mass and two symphonies lived up to them. Ives, Converse, and Ruggles were not far behind in their advocacy. I have heard Walter Piston, Leon Kirchner, and Gunther Schuller speak in praise of music that is elevated in character. It makes one suspect that whatever traits appear in music of the future, they may, in some respects, be continuations from musical qualities honored in the past and present.

Andrew Pincus adds that composers such as the last two agree that, though all music may be created equal, not all of it has equal expressive capacities. Ruggles's stupendous *Sun-Treader* conveys something quite different from Vincent Youman's lightsome "Tea for Two." Nor do all New Englanders respond equally to deeply expressive music. One listener may be overwhelmed by the former and find the latter insipid; another may hear only obnoxious noise in the former and a catching lilt in the latter. That is to be expected. Curiously, some advocates of currently popular music advance the belief that the Beatles or an Elvis Presley is the equivalent of a Mozart or a Walter Piston, therefore making

Mozart and Piston unnecessary. But this is a flawed reasoning, anti-intellectual, dismissive of the past and future, and interested only in the here and now.[15]

Nor is it reasonable for spokespersons from the local African American, Latin American, and other communities to suggest that art music is so irrelevant to today's New England inhabitants that it should stand to one side and let the music of the "real world" take over.[16] They are generalizing from particulars pertinent to their constituency alone.

ARGUING FOR A NEW ENGLAND IDENTITY

Mention New England to a stranger and what is called to mind is a town green ringed with pleasingly old-fashioned homes, an inviting inn, and a steepled white meetinghouse, out of whose windows floats the sound of psalmody. The locals in this picture lead upright if somewhat eccentric lives and are certain of who they are and what their region's place is in the American scheme. This conception is so prevalent among Americans that it has entered our nation's mythology. Motion pictures and television dramas draw on the myth when they send their despondent urban protagonists off to a Vermont country hamlet or a Maine seaport village to "get in touch" with their true selves and "get their act together." Burned-out business people buy into the myth when they reject the pressures of their dog-eat-dog existence, resign their tension-laden positions, and elect to lead what they expect to be the tranquil life of a New England farm or settlement. Not to be left behind, the cities spruce themselves up and boost their historical connections. In the Greater Boston area we have freedom trails, the Faneuil Hall marketplace, the Pilgrim sites in Plymouth, the sacrificial stand for liberty on the Lexington green, the Concord bridge where the adamant minutemen stood, and the scattered homes of the eminent nineteenth-century writers and thinkers nearby.

Yet there is more to northeastern America than scenery, buildings, and historic events. There is the life of the mind and the search of the spirit that continue to distinguish and call up the area in American minds. Emerson and Thoreau have international readerships. Hawthorne's plumbing of the good and evil experienced by New Englanders is evergreen in people's thoughts. The brothers William and Henry James have made lasting written contributions to philosophy and psychology and to literature, respectively.[17]

What has all of this to do with art music? It has bolstered a New England sense of self that provided artists with a usable past. Composers from Paine on drew directly on the New England saga in songs, operas, and symphonic poems. The same staunch seriousness of purpose shown by the writers also underpinned their chamber music and symphonies. It is only in recent years that the links have become tenuous, as composers have ranged over a much wider cultural landscape. Yet the links still hold.

Knowing our music gives us an awareness of history and the ability to feel as if we belong somewhere. It also reaches into our deepest sensibilities. Billings's hopes and fears, in pieces like "When Jesus Wept," "Chester," and "By the Rivers of Watertown," are inseparable from the troubled times of the Revolutionary War, as are Julia Ward Howe's "Battle Hymn of the Republic" and George Root's "Battle Cry of Freedom" from those of the Civil War. And all five pieces can move us profoundly.

The initiation of singing schools, music in public schools, academic musical instruction, conservatories of music, music festivals, and above all, a welcoming climate for musical endeavors are all a part of the New England makeup. Then there are the capturing of the New England essence in so many of Charles Ives's compositions, the Puritanical unyielding in Ruggles's music, the Yankee straightforwardness in Piston's symphonies, and the evocations of the Yankee singing masters in Pinkham's choral works that grow in American minds, converting New England from matters that belonged just in a regional long-ago into perceptions that belong to a nation.

The ongoing societal transformations taking place in the six states are also characteristic. They have enriched the New England identity even as they remade it. Immediately after the first English settlements on Massachusetts Bay, there was an influx of French Huguenots, Irish Catholics, and Scottish Presbyterians. Later came Germans, Italians, Cape Verdeans, Greeks, African Americans from the South, and immigrants from Poland, the Slavic countries, the Middle East, China, and Latin America. No one religion stood for New England—Christian, Jew, Muslim, and Buddhist worship side by side. Atheists, agnostics, and ethicists are everywhere. Even Puritan worship was ameliorated and changed into Congregationalism and Unitarianism.

After Francis Latour examined the many changes brought about through immigration, he wrote:

> In spite of the changes many say have eroded the sense of place that was once sacred to New England's most revered writers, many who have made New England their home say that the place may mean something altogether different, but it still *means*.

"This is still a place where people go to protect their integrity as writers," says [Gish] Jen. "In that way, New England is still the place where people come to connect with themselves, just like Thoreau."[18]

No one music has ever stood for New England, at least not for long. Psalms, hymns, and folk music were soon modified through the addition of products of the native eighteenth-century singing masters and by secular songs from the British Isles. Then came the vast outpouring of new hymns, gospel songs, and popular music by New England composers in the first half of the nineteenth century. In the second half of the century, art composers whose compositions were based on Germanic styles marked a new departure. Meanwhile, New York took over as the center for popular music. By the first decade of the twentieth century, French and Russian influences began to supplant the German, and native vernacular music— British American, African American, and American Indian—found its way into artistic works. After World War I, New England's art music changed again, with input from Schoenberg and Stravinsky. After World War II, a welter of styles arose, no two alike, followed more recently by what seems to be an incipient convergence among composers, a tendency to combine a range of historical procedures with current ones, to blend tradition with innovation.

The changing forms of music have also enriched the New England identity even as they remade it. What is certain, too, is that music will gain as it continues to change now and in the future. Into the New England mix that we call art music should come additions from all the new people who are coming to inhabit the six states. This is as it should be. However, what the musical outcome will be awaits the future.

In conclusion, I would conjecture that New England's musical culture can no longer consider itself to be a single line of creative endeavor, or one conducted by a small group of individuals. Nevertheless, it cannot remain a representation of a splintered civilization in which members of dissimilar racial, ethnic, social, and religious sets remain independent, with each centered on its customary music and musical interests within the limits of geographical New England. Actually, the reverse is being seen. I suspect that we will find the supposedly dissimilar groups have been sharing and combining their music without our noticing. They are coming together and forming new coalitions in inexorable fashion. The cultural certainties that one absorbed from birth and that unified the region no long apply. On the other hand, all of us require antecedents. But today, at the beginning of the twenty-first century, we need to come upon them on our own.

We have to select and organize them so that we can perceive ourselves to be the most recent in a lengthy succession of musicians and music lovers. To find out how to accomplish the task with discretion, discernment, and consideration for all our neighbors, old and new, is essential. Tolerance and accommodation must grow within us and become the prescribed obligation for all of us, including the New England composers of the new century. This task must be accomplished; otherwise we will bequeath to the future a collection of isolated, marginalized, and exotically distinct subcultures, each one speaking its own private language, each one warring with another. If we succeed, we will continue to have a New England identity, however differently the future wishes to define it.

NOTES

NOTES TO CHAPTER 1

1. Michael Kammen, *In the Past Lane* (New York: Oxford University Press, 1997), 190.

2. Thomas Ryan, *Recollections of an Old Musician* (New York: Dutton, 1899), 96.

3. Perry Miller, *The New England Mind: The Seventeenth Century* (Cambridge, Mass.: Harvard University Press, 1967), 75.

4. Perry Miller and Thomas H. Johnson, *The Puritans,* rev. ed. (New York: Harper & Row, 1963), 1:22.

5. Neil Postman, *Building a Bridge to the Eighteenth Century* (New York: Knopf, 1999), 19.

6. Miller and Johnson, *The Puritans* 1:137.

7. Ibid., 233.

8. Samuel Sewall, *Samuel Sewall's Diary,* ed. Mark Van Doren (New York: Russell & Russell, 1963), 24–25, 27–28, 40.

9. The quotation is from Eloise Hubbard Linscott, *Folk Songs of Old New England,* 2d ed. (1962; reprint, New York: Dover, 1993), 2–3. The songs quoted are on pp. 6, 8, and 9, respectively.

10. Thomas Symmes, *The Reasonableness of Regular Singing, or Singing by Note* (Boston: B. Green for Samuel Gerrish, 1720), 6, 38.

11. Alan C. Buechner, "Thomas Walter and the Society for Promoting Regular Singing in the Worship of God: Boston, 1720–1723," in *New England Music: The Public Sphere, 1600–1900,* ed. Peter Benes (Boston: Boston University, 1998), 51.

12. Miller and Johnson, *The Puritans* 2:712–13; Walter Raymond Spalding, *Music at Harvard* (New York: Coward-McCann, 1935), 13.

13. Cotton Mather, *Directions for a Candidate of the Ministry* (Boston: Thomas Hancock, 1726), 57.

14. Barbara Lambert, "Social Music, Musicians, and Their Musical Instruments in and around Colonial Boston," in *Music in Colonial Massachusetts, 1630–1820,* ed. Barbara Lambert (Boston: Colonial Society of Massachusetts, 1985), 2:415–21.

15. For instruments in New England homes, see Barbara Lambert, "The Musical Puritans," *Bulletin of the Society for the Preservation of New England Antiquities*

62 (Boston: The Society, 1972), 66–75. The quotation from the *Boston News-Letter* may be found in Howard, *Our American Music,* 22; see also pp. 4 and 21.

16. Gilbert Chase, *America's Music,* 3d ed. (Urbana: University of Illinois Press, 1987), 14–15.

17. Helen Hartness Flanders and Marguerite Olney, *Ballads Migrant in New England* (New York: Farrar, Straus & Young, 1953), 28, 123.

18. Lambert, ed., *Music in Colonial Massachusetts, 1630–1820* (Boston: Colonial Society of Massachusetts, 1980), 1:162, 170–71.

19. Howard, *Our American Music,* 5.

20. George Hood, *A History of Music in New England* (Boston: Wilkins, Carter, 1846), 35–38.

21. Percy A. Scholes, *The Puritans and Music* (London: Oxford University Press, 1934), 265.

22. Louis C. Elson, *The History of American Music,* revised to 1925 by Arthur Elson (New York: Macmillan, 1925), 6–7.

23. Irving Lowens, *Music and Musicians in Early America* (New York: Norton, 1964), 37–38.

NOTES TO CHAPTER 2

1. Thomas Symmes, *The Reasonableness of Regular Singing, or Singing by Note* (Boston: B. Green for Samuel Gerrish, 1720), 8–9.

2. Thomas Walter, *The Grounds and Rules of Musick Explained* (Boston: J. Franklin for Samuel Gerrish, 1721), 3–5.

3. Quoted in Thomas Jefferson Wertenberger, *The Puritan Oligarchy* (New York: Scribner's, 1970), 130.

4. William Arms Fischer, *Notes on Music in Old Boston* (Boston: Ditson, 1918), 6–7.

5. Henry Wilder Foote, *Three Centuries of American Hymnody* (Cambridge, Mass.: Harvard University Press, 1940), 383–85.

6. Symmes, *Reasonableness of Regular Singing,* 20.

7. Perry Miller and Thomas H. Johnson, *The Puritans,* rev. ed. (New York: Harper & Row, 1963), 2:451–52.

8. Quoted in Irving Lowens, *Music and Musicians in Early America* (New York: Norton, 1964), 41.

9. Fisher, *Notes on Music in Old Boston,* 8.

10. Alan C. Buechner, "Thomas Walter and the Society for Promoting Regular Singing in the Worship of God: Boston, 1720–1723," in *New England Music: The Public Sphere, 1600–1900,* ed. Peter Benes (Boston: Boston University, 1998), 48–60.

11. Ibid.

12. Lowens, *Music and Musicians in Early America,* 192.

13. From a sermon delivered in 1741, entitled "Sinners in the Hands of an Angry God."

14. The Rowley information may be found in Foote, *Three Centuries of American Hymnody,* 380; the Worcester information, in George Hood, *A History of Music in New England* (Boston: Wilkins, Carter, 1846), 183–84.

15. David P. McKay and Richard Crawford, *William Billings of Boston* (Princeton, N.J.: Princeton University Press, 1975), 22.

16. Louis C. Elson, *The History of American Music,* revised to 1925 by Arthur Elson (New York: Macmillan, 1925), 27–28.

17. William Bentley, *The Diary of William Bentley, D.D., Pastor of East Church, Salem, Massachusetts* (Salem: Essex Institute, 1905–14), 2:350–51.

18. Ibid., 36.

19. Henry M. Brooks, *Olden-Time Music* (Boston: Ticknor, 1888), 263–64.

20. William Billings, *The Continental Harmony* (Boston: Isaiah Thomas and Ebenezer T. Andrews, 1794), xxviii.

21. Ibid., xxxi.

22. McKay and Crawford, *William Billings of Boston,* 152, 154.

23. Richard Crawford, *Andrew Law, American Psalmodist* (Evanston, Ill.: Northwestern University Press, 1968), 36, 121, 158–60.

24. Both letters are reprinted in Lowens, *Music and Musicians in Early America,* 167.

NOTES TO CHAPTER 3

1. See Irving Lowens, "Eighteenth-Century Massachusetts Songsters," in *Music in Colonial Massachusetts, 1630–1820* (Boston: Colonial Society of Massachusetts, 1985), 547–55.

2. Thomas Paine, who later changed his name to that of his father, Robert Treat Paine, Jr., because he did not wish to be confused with the freethinking Thomas Paine of England.

3. *The American Musical Miscellany* (Northampton, Mass.: Wright, 1798), 212–15.

4. Ibid., 82–83.

5. Increase Mather, "A Cloud of Witnesses" (Boston, n.d.), quoted in Gilbert Chase, *America's Music,* 3d ed. (Urbana: University of Illinois Press, 1987), 13.

6. [Alexander Hamilton], *Gentleman's Progress: The Itenerarium of Dr. Alexander Hamilton, 1744,* ed. Carl Bridenbaugh (1948; reprint, Westport, Conn.: Greenwood Press, 1973), 146.

7. Louis Pichierri, *Music in New Hampshire, 1623–1800* (New York: Columbia University Press, 1960), 56. Nine years later, Thomas Jefferson would make a similar request to a friend in Paris.

8. Henry M. Brooks, *Olden-Time Music* (Boston: Ticknor, 1888), 58.

9. Ibid., 63.

10. For information on Brattle and his organ, and instruments in church, see Henry Wilder Foote, *Three Centuries of American Hymnody* (Cambridge, Mass.: Harvard University Press, 1940), 77–81; Barbara Owen, *The Organ in New England* (Raleigh, N.C.: Sunbury Press, 1979), 2–5; and John Tasker Howard, *Our American Music,* 4th ed. (New York: Crowell, 1965), 17–18.

11. Foote, *Three Centuries of American Hymnody,* 84–85; Howard, *Our American Music,* 19.

12. F. O. Jones, ed., *A Handbook of American Music and Musicians* (Canaseraga, N.Y.: Jones, 1886), s.v. "Organ, History of in America." Also see Owen, *Organ in New England,* 23–25, and George Hood, *A History of Music in New England* (Boston: Wilkins, Carter, 1846), 152.

13. W. Dermot Darby, in *Music in America,* ed. Arthur Farwell and W. Dermot Darby, vol. 4 of *The Art of Music* (New York: National Society of Music, 1915), 24–25.

14. [Hamilton], *Gentleman's Progress,* 110.

15. Brooks, *Olden-Time Music,* 84.

16. Oscar G. Sonneck, *Early Concert-Life in America, 1731–1800* (Leipzig: Breitkopf & Härtel, 1907), 270–73.

17. The information on Portsmouth may be found in Pichierri, *Music in New Hampshire,* 181–89, 58; that on Newport, in Brooks, *Olden-Time Music,* 58–59.

18. Sonneck, *Early Concert-Life in America,* 250–51; Howard, *Our American Music,* 22–23.

19. Sonneck, *Early Concert-Life in America,* 262.

20. Ibid., 275, 283; Brooks, *Olden-Time Music,* 89–90.

21. Its origin may be with the Dutch of New York.

22. Arthur Loesser, *Men, Women, and Pianos* (New York: Simon & Schuster, 1954), 444–45.

23. Susanna Rowson, *Miscellaneous Poems* (Boston: Gilbert & Dean, 1804), 109–10.

24. John Adams, *Letters from John Adams, Addressed to His Wife,* vol. 2, ed. Charles Francis Adams (Boston: Little & Brown, 1841), 67–68.

25. Darby, in *Music in America,* 58–59.

26. For a more detailed discussion of opera in Boston, see Oscar G. Sonneck, *Early Opera in America* (New York: Schirmer, 1915), 134–47.

27. See, respectively, Pichierri, *Music in New Hampshire,* 81, 92; Brooks, *Olden-Time Music,* 60–61.

28. William Arms Fisher, *Notes on Music in Old Boston* (Boston: Ditson, 1918), 18–19.

29. Ibid., 22–23.

30. Quoted in Howard, *Our American Music,* 132.

31. Howard, *Our American Music,* 131.

32. H. Earle Johnson, *Hallelujah, Amen!* (Boston: Humphries, 1965), 13–14.

33. Edwards, *Music and Musicians of Maine,* 34.

34. Johnson, *Hallelujah, Amen!,* 31–33.

35. Thomas Ryan, *Recollections of an Old Musician* (New York: Dutton, 1899), 77.

36. Johnson, *Hallelujah, Amen!,* 47.

37. George Thornton Edwards, *The Music and Musicians of Maine* (Portland, Me.: Southworth Press, 1928), 38, 42–43, 71, 73.

NOTES TO CHAPTER 4

1. Irving Lowens, *Music and Musicians in Early America* (New York: Norton, 1964), 249, 256–57.

2. Van Wyck Brooks, *The Flowering of New England* (New York: Dutton, 1936), 188, 191.

3. Ibid., 179.

4. From "The Political Destination of America and the Signs of the Times," written in 1852 and quoted in Perry Miller, ed., *The American Transcendentalists* (Garden City, N.Y.: Doubleday, 1957), 353.

5. Mortimer Smith, *The Life of Ole Bull* (Princeton, N.J.: Princeton University Press, 1943), 59–61.

6. Miller, ed., *American Transcendentalists,* 405–6.

7. Ibid., 99–100.

8. Thomas Ryan, *Recollections of an Old Musician* (New York: Dutton, 1899), 135–41.

9. Ibid., 93.

10. Ibid., 20–21.

11. Ibid., 17–18.

12. William Foster Apthorp, *By the Way* (Boston: Copeland & Day, 1898), 2:55–57.

13. This was the range of ages in a band I listened to, in 1995, at an Independence Day celebration on a Maine village green.

14. George Thornton Edwards, *Music and Musicians of Maine* (Portland, Me.: Southworth Press, 1928), 34.

15. For a discussion of these collections, see Nicholas E. Tawa, *Sweet Songs for Gentle Americans* (Bowling Green, Ohio: Bowling Green University Popular Press, 1980), 15–63.

16. Reprinted in Gilbert Chase, *America's Music,* 3d ed. (Urbana: University of Illinois Press, 1987), 157.

17. George Root, *The Story of a Musical Life* (Cincinnati: Church, 1891), 54–55.

18. Ibid., 55.

19. Andrew Law, *Musical Primer* (Philadelphia: Robert & William Carr, 1793), 8.

20. Thomas Hastings, *Dissertation on Musical Taste* (Albany: Websters & Skinners, 1822), 74–75.

21. Ibid., 194.

22. Root, *The Story of a Musical Life,* 51–52.

23. Ibid., 9–10.

24. Pemberton, *Lowell Mason,* 30.

25. John W. Moore, *Complete Encyclopaedia of Music* (Boston: Ditson, 1854), s.v. "Musical Convention."

26. Louis C. Elson, *The History of American Music,* revised to 1925 by Arthur Elson (New York: Macmillan, 1925), 78–79.

27. Ryan, *Recollections of an Old Musician,* 44.

28. Samuel Eliot, *Ninth Annual Report, July, 1841* of the Boston Academy of Music (Boston: Marvin, 1841), 3–4.

29. Ryan, *Recollections of an Old Musician,* 46–47.

30. Carol A. Pemberton, *Lowell Mason* (Westport, Conn.: Greenwood Press, 1988), 20. By the 1830s it was a time-honored custom for music leaders to sell their publications to students, as apparently Mason was doing.

31. Arthur Lowndes Rich, *Lowell Mason* (Chapel Hill: University of North Carolina Press, 1946), 60–64.

32. Ibid., 24–25.

33. Pemberton, *Lowell Mason,* 36.

34. Ryan, *Recollections of an Old Musician,* 49–55.

35. John Tasker Howard, *Our American Music,* 4th ed. (New York: Crowell, 1965), 214.

36. Apthorp, *By the Way* 2:48–49.

37. Ibid., 47–48; William Arms Fisher, *Notes on Music in Old Boston* (Boston: Ditson, 1918), 41–42.

38. Apthorp, *By the Way* 2:51.

39. Walter Raymond Spalding, *Music at Harvard* (New York: Coward-McCann, 1935), 35.

40. Apthorp, *By the Way* 2:77.

NOTES TO CHAPTER 5

1. George Bancroft, "On the Progress of Civilization," *Boston Quarterly Review* 1 (October 1838): 390.

2. The history of early piano manufacture in the Boston area is given in detail in Arthur Loesser, *Men, Women, and Pianos* (New York: Simon & Schuster, 1954), 461–62.

3. Louis Moreau Gottschalk, *Notes of a Pianist,* ed. Jeanne Behrend (New York: Knopf, 1964), 76.

4. F. O. Jones, ed., *A Handbook of American Music and Musicians* (Canaseraga, N.Y.: Jones, 1886), s.v. "Mason & Hamlin Organ and Piano Company."

5. Nicholas E. Tawa, *Sweet Songs for Gentle Americans* (Bowling Green, Ohio: Bowling Green Popular Press, 1980), 105–6.

6. W. Thomas Marrocco and Mark Jacobs, in *The New Grove Dictionary of American Music,* ed. H. Wiley Hitchcock and Stanley Sadie (London: Macmillan, 1986), s.v. "Ditson, Oliver."

7. Nicholas E. Tawa, "Buckingham's Musical Commentaries in Boston," *New England Quarterly* 51 (1978): 335–37.

8. Ibid., 344.

9. Ibid., 338.

10. From the "Aesthetic Papers" of 1849; reprinted in Perry Miller, ed., *The Transcendentalists* (Cambridge, Mass.: Harvard University Press, 1967), 411.

11. George Willis Cooke, *John Sullivan Dwight* (Boston: Small, Maynard, 1898), 147.

12. William Foster Apthorp, *Musicians and Music-Lovers* (New York: Scribner's, 1894), 283–84.

13. Thomas Ryan, *Recollections of an Old Musician* (New York: Dutton, 1899), 119.

14. Sir George Henschel, *Musings and Memories of a Musician* (New York: Macmillan, 1919), 248–49.

15. Gottschalk, *Notes of a Pianist,* 157.

16. William K. Kearns, *Horatio Parker, 1863–1919* (Metuchen, N.J.: Scarecrow Press, 1990), 236.

17. Charles Hamm, *Music in the New World* (New York: Norton, 1983), 307–8.

18. Cooke, *John Sullivan Dwight,* 189–91.

19. Ryan, *Recollections of an Old Musician,* 197–98.

20. Ibid., 194–95.

21. Nicholas E. Tawa, *Arthur Foote* (Latham, Md.: Scarecrow Press, 1997), 28–29.

22. Louis C. Elson, *The History of American Music,* revised to 1925 by Arthur Elson (New York: Macmillan, 1925), 88.

23. *Music and Dance in the New England States,* ed. Sigmund Spaeth (New York: Bureau of Musical Research, 1953), 112–13.

24. *American Supplement,* vol. 6 of *Grove's Dictionary of Music and Musicians,* ed. Waldo Selden Pratt (Philadelphia: Presser, 1926), s.v. "Springfield Music Festival Association, The."

25. Francis Turgeon Wiggin, *Maine Composers and Their Music* (Rockland: Maine Federation of Music Clubs, 1959), 16–17; George Thornton Edwards, *Music and Musicians of Maine* (Portland, Me.: Southworth Press, 1928), 220–21.

26. J. H. Vaill, comp., *Litchfield Choral Union, 1900–1912* (Norfolk, Conn.: Litchfield County University Club, 1912), 1:14–15, 35–37.

27. Ryan, *Recollections of an Old Musician,* 84–85.

28. Ibid., 261; for a more recent and informative article, see Steven Ledbetter, in vol. 3 of *The New Grove Dictionary of American Music,* ed. H. Wiley Hitchcock and Stanley Sadie (London: Macmillan, 1986), s.v. "Lang, B(enjamin) J(ohnson)."

29. Arthur Foote, "A Near View of Mr. Lang," *Boston Evening Transcript,* 1 May 1909, pt. 3, p. 4.

30. Daniel Gregory Mason, *Music as a Humanity* (New York: Gray, 1921), 59.

31. M. A. DeWolfe, *The Boston Symphony Orchestra, 1881–1931,* revised and extended by John N. Burk (Boston: Houghton, Mifflin, 1931), 13.

32. Ibid., 16.

33. John H. Mueller, *The American Symphony Orchestra* (Bloomington: Indiana University Press, 1951), 35.

34. Ibid., 21.

35. Howe, *Boston Symphony Orchestra,* 85.

36. Clara Kathleen Rogers, *The Story of Two Lives* (Boston: Plimpton Press, 1932), 30; Lilian Whiting, *Louise Chandler Moulton, Poet and Friend* (Boston: Little, Brown, 1910), 124–25.

37. William Mason, *Memories of a Musical Life* (New York: Century, 1901), 253–56.

38. John Spencer Clark, *The Life and Letters of John Fiske* (Boston: Houghton Mifflin, 1917), 1:206, 418–20, 2:83.

39. William Kearns, "Horatio Parker and the English Choral Societies," *American Music* 1 (1986): 21; Adrienne Fried Block, in *American Grove,* s.v. "Beach, Amy Marcy (Cheney)"; Henry T. Finck, *Songs and Song Writers* (New York: Scribner's, 1900), 233; David Ewen, *American Composers* (New York: Putnam, 1982), s.v. "Foote, Arthur William"; Elson, *History of American Music,* 182–83.

40. Sidney Homer, *My Wife and I* (New York: Macmillan, 1939), 217.

41. Isabel Parker Semler, in collaboration with Pierson Underwood, *Horatio Parker* (New York: Putnam, 1942), 40; T. P. Currier, "Edward MacDowell as I Knew Him," *Musical Quarterly* 1 (1915): 26.

42. Morris Carter, *Isabella Stewart Gardner and Fenway Court* (Boston: Houghton Mifflin, 1925), 112–13; Honor McCusker, *Fifty Years of Music in Boston* (Boston: Trustees of the Public Library, 1938), 40; Rogers, *Two Lives,* 187–88.

43. Foote, *Autobiography,* 32; Sumner Salter, "Early Encouragements to American Composers," *Musical Quarterly* 18 (1932): 78–79.

44. George Willis Cooke, *John Sullivan Dwight* (Boston: Small, Maynard, 1898), 223.

45. Apthorp, *Musicians and Music-Lovers,* 279.

46. Maude Howe Elliott, *Three Generations* (Boston: Little, Brown, 1923), 41, 42–43; Cooke, *John Sullivan Dwight,* 216–17; Schmidt, *John Knowles Paine,* 121–22.

47. Foote, *Autobiography,* 51–52; Arthur Foote, "A Bostonian Remembers," *Musical Quarterly* 23 (1937): 41; George W. Wilson, program notes for the concert of the Boston Symphony, 6–7 February 1891.

48. "A. P. Schmidt, Pioneer Publisher of American Music, Is Dead," *Musical America,* 14 May 1921, 55. The writer of the article, who quotes Foote, is unidentified.

49. Foote, *Autobiography,* 45–46.

NOTES TO CHAPTER 6

1. See William Foster Apthorp, *By the Way* (Boston: Copeland & Day, 1898), 1:12.

2. Richard Aldrich, in *DAB,* s.v. "Paine, John Knowles."

3. Daniel Gregory Mason, *Music in My Time and Other Reminiscences* (New York: Macmillan, 1938), 39.

4. "Music in Philadelphia," dated 26 July 1876, *Dwight's Journal of Music* 36 (1876): 280; "American Composers," *Music* 4 (1893): 257; Rupert Hughes, *Contemporary American Composers* (Boston: Page, 1900), 146; Louis C. Elson, *The History of American Music,* revised to 1925 by Arthur Elson (New York: Macmillan, 1925), 169.

5. Karl Krueger, album notes to recording MIA 120.

6. John Lathrop Mathews, "In Harvard University," *Music* 9 (1896): 645–46.

7. Henry T. Finck, *My Adventures in the Golden Age of Music* (New York: Funk & Wagnalls, 1926), 79.

8. M. A. DeWolfe Howe, handwritten notes on Paine, in Houghton Library, Harvard University, shelf no. bMS 1826 (419).

9. Aldrich, "Paine, John Knowles."

10. Mathews, "In Harvard University," 648.

11. Louis C. Elson, in *Music and Drama,* 3 June 1882, supplement, 5.

12. William Treat Upton, *Art-Song in America* (Boston: Ditson, 1930), 78.

13. Hughes, *Contemporary American Composers,* 163.

14. Barbara Owen, album notes to the recording New World NW280.

15. New York: Beer & Schirmer, 1865.

16. "Music," *Atlantic Monthly* 30 (1872): 505. I have not seen the music of opus 11.

17. Boston: Koppitz, Prüfer, 1869.

18. John C. Schmidt, *The Life and Works of John Knowles Paine* (Ann Arbor, Mich.: UMI Research Press, 1980), 261, claims this tune is pentatonic. How-

ever, before two measures have gone by, the melody touches on every note of the scale except for the leading tone, and nowhere does the sound suggest the pentatonic.

19. Four Characteristic Pieces, in *Album of Piano Pieces* (Boston: Ditson, 1876).

20. Published with a copyright date of 1876 by G. D. Russell, they were reissued in the *Album of Pianoforte Pieces,* published by Ditson.

21. Spalding, *Music at Harvard,* 193, describes it as a street tune entitled "Rafferty's Lost His Pig."

22. *Boston Musical Herald* 11 (1890): 47.

23. [John Fiske], *The Letters of John Fiske,* ed. Ethel F. Fisk (New York: Macmillan, 1940), 334–35.

24. Schmidt, *John Knowles Paine,* 316.

25. H. E. Krehbiel, *Review of the New York Musical Season, 1887–1888* (New York: Novello, Ewer, 1888), 36.

26. The two newspaper items are in the Allan A. Brown Collection, scrapbook of clippings, **M304.1, vol. 2, Boston Public Library; the comment by "H. H." is among the notes of M. A. DeWolfe Howe, in Harvard's Houghton Library, shelf no. bMS Am 1826 (419).

27. W. S. B. Mathews, ed., *A Hundred Years of Music in America* (Chicago: Howe, 1889), 676; George Thornton Edwards, *Music and Musicians of Maine* (Portland, Me.: Southworth, 1928), 124; Schmidt, *John Knowles Paine,* 63–64, 71–72.

28. John Knowles Paine, *Mass in D* (New York: Beer & Schirmer, 1866).

29. Gunther Schuller, "Comments," in the album notes to the recording New World NW 262/63.

30. *Atlantic Monthly* 31 (1873): 506–8.

31. Ibid., 249–50.

32. Hughes, *Contemporary American Composers,* 146.

33. Elson, *History of American Music,* 166. See also Aldrich, "Paine, John Knowles."

34. *Atlantic Monthly* 37 (1876): 763–64.

35. Reprinted in *Dwight's Journal of Music* 35 (1876): 181.

36. George W. Chadwick, "American Composers," in *History of American Music,* ed. W. L. Hubbard, *The American History and Encyclopedia of Music,* vol. 8 (Toledo, Ohio: Squire, 1908), 2.

37. John Knowles Paine, *Symphony No. 1 für Orchester,* op. 23 (Leipzig: Breitkopf & Härtel, 1908).

38. Allan A. Brown Collection, scrapbook of clippings, **M371.11, Boston Public Library.

39. *Dwight's Journal of Music* 36 (1876): 350; see also 37 (1877): 7, for a comment on a later presentation of the work.

40. *Dwight's Journal of Music* 37 (1877): 128, 135.

41. Letter of John Fiske, printed in ibid., 148.

42. Allan A. Brown Collection, scrapbook of clippings, **M125.5, vol. 5, Boston Public Library; John Knowles Paine, Symphonic Poem: *Shakespeare's Tempest,* op. 31 (Leipzig: Breitkopf & Härtel, 1907).

43. *Dwight's Journal of Music* 38 (1878): 229–30.

44. Aldrich, "Paine, John Knowles"; *Dwight's Journal of Music* 40 (1880): 53–54; Allan A. Brown Collection, scrapbook of clippings, **M125.2, vol. 2, **M125.5, vol. 3, Boston Public Library; Program notes for the Chicago Orchestra, conducted by Theodore Thomas, 8–9 April 1892.

45. John Knowles Paine, *Im Frühling.* Symphonie No. 2 in A für Grosses Orchester, op. 34 (Boston: Schmidt, 1880).

46. Alfred John Goodrich, *Complete Musical Analysis* (Cincinnati: Church, 1889), 285.

47. The motive has some resemblance to that of the *adagio espressivo* slow movement of Schumann's Second Symphony.

48. Hughes, *Contemporary American Composers,* 47–48.

49. *Boston Advertiser,* 5 May 1881, reprinted in *Dwight's Journal of Music* 41 (1881): 82–83.

50. See the many newspaper reports in the Allan A. Brown Collection, scrapbooks of clippings, **M125.5, vols. 1, 13, 18, and **M304.1, vol. 2, Boston Public Library. The quotations come mainly from the *Boston Transcript* for 15 February 1882, 13 March 1882, 22 April 1894, and 24 April 1899.

51. Amy Fay, *More Letters of Amy Fay: The American Years, 1879–1916,* ed. S. Margaret William McCarthy (Detroit: Information Coordinators, 1986), 70.

52. Daniel Gregory Mason, *The Dilemma of American Music* (New York: Macmillan, 1928), 3–4.

53. Schmidt, *The Life and Works of John Knowles Paine,* 560–61. A synopsis of the French fable may be found in *Benét's Reader's Encyclopedia,* 3d ed. (New York: Harper & Row, 1987), s.v. "Aucassin and Nicolette."

54. Edward Ellsworth Hipsher, *American Opera and Its Composers* (Philadelphia: Presser, 1927), 306. The account of Paine's attempts may be found in Fay, *More Letters,* 42.

55. For further commentary on the idealized woman of the times, see Richard Guy Wilson, "The Great Civilization," in *The American Renaissance, 1876–1917* (New York: Brooklyn Museum, 1979), 46–51.

56. Richard Loucks, *Arthur Shepherd, American Composer* (Provo, Utah: Brigham Young University Press, 1980), 6.

57. John Tasker Howard, "Chadwick, George Whitefield," in *DAB;* also in John Tasker Howard, with the assistance of Arthur Mendel, *Our Contemporary Composers* (New York: Crowell, 1941), 11.

58. *Grove's Dictionary of Music and Musicians,* 2d ed., vol. 6, *American Supplement,* ed. Waldon Selden Pratt (Philadelphia: Presser, 1926), 158.

59. Carl Engel, "George W. Chadwick," *Musical Quarterly* 10 (1924): 440.

60. Rupert Hughes, *Contemporary American Composers* (Boston: Page, 1900), 214; I have discussed at length the musical characteristics of the semi-artistic songs that achieved popularity in Nicholas E. Tawa, *The Way to Tin Pan Alley* (New York: Schirmer, 1990), chapter 9.

61. *Boston Musical Herald* 12 (1891): 38.

62. Victor Yellin, "The Life and Operatic Works of George Whitefield Chadwick" (Ph.D. diss., Harvard University, 1957), 46.

63. Carl Engel, "Chadwick, George Whitefield," in *Cobbett's Cyclopedic Survey of Chamber Music,* 2d ed., vol. 1, ed. Walter Willson Cobbett (London: Oxford University Press, 1963), 237.

64. Steven Ledbetter, album notes to recording Northeastern NR 236 CD.

65. Ibid.

66. Allan A. Brown Collection, scrapbook of clippings, **M371.4, Boston Public Library.

67. Ibid.; Krehbiel, *Review of the New York Musical Season, 1887–1888,* 36.

68. Olin Downes, "American Chamber Music," in *Cobbett's Cyclopedic Survey of Chamber Music,* 2d ed., Vol. 1, ed. Walter Willson Cobbett (London: Oxford University Press, 1963), 12.

69. George W. Chadwick, String Quartet No. 4 in E Minor, parts only (Boston: Schmidt, 1902).

70. This and other commentaries on the Chadwick Fourth Quartet are found in the Allan A. Brown Collection, scrapbook of clippings, **M. Cab. 1.38, Boston Public Library.

71. Steven Ledbetter, album notes to recording Northeastern 234 CD.

72. Scrapbook of clippings, **M. Cab. 1.38.

73. Hughes, *Contemporary American Composers,* 212, 213; see also Allan A. Brown, scrapbook of clippings, **M304.1, vol. 2, for reviews of its first performance.

74. Allan A. Brown Collection, scrapbook of clippings, *M122.5 and **M165.8, vol. 2, Boston Public Library.

75. *New England Conservatory Magazine-Review* 7 (1917): 84.

76. Engel, "George W. Chadwick," 448.

77. Steven Ledbetter and Victor Fell Yellin, in *American Grove,* s.v. "Chadwick, George Whitefield."

78. Elson, *History of American Music,* 175.

79. Allan Lincoln Langley, "Chadwick and the New England Conservatory of Music," *Musical Quarterly* 21 (1935): 51.

80. Engel, "George W. Chadwick," 452.

81. "Music in Boston," *Dwight's Journal of Music* 39 (1879): 205.

82. Allan A. Brown Collection, scrapbook of clippings, M125.2, vol. 2, Boston Public Library.

83. Allan A. Brown Collection, scrapbook of clippings, **M165.9, vols. 3, 6, 10, Boston Public Library.

84. George W. Chadwick, Symphony No. 2 in B Flat (Boston: Schmidt, 1888).

85. Allan A. Brown Collection, scrapbook of clippings, **M125.5, vol. 15, Boston Public Library. For other reviews, see vols. 7, 8, 18.

86. George W. Chadwick, *Symphonic Sketches,* Suite for Orchestra (New York: Kalmus, n.d.).

87. Victor Fell Yellin, "Chadwick, American Musical Realist," *Musical Quarterly* 61 (1975): 91.

88. Oscar G. Sonneck, *Suum Cuique: Essays in Music* (1916; reprint, Freeport, N.Y.: Books for Libraries, 1969), 33.

89. George W. Chadwick, *Aphrodite,* Symphonic Fantasie (Boston: Schmidt, 1912).

90. George W. Chadwick, *Tam O'Shanter,* Symphonic Ballade (Boston: Boston Music, 1917).

91. Reprinted in the *New England Conservatory Magazine-Review* 6 (1916): 76–77.

NOTES TO CHAPTER 7

1. H. E. Krehbiel, in *Grove's Dictionary,* 2d ed., vol. 3, s.v. "Parker, Horatio William."

2. George W. Chadwick, *Horatio Parker* (New Haven, Conn.: Yale University Press, 1921), 7.

3. Henry Cowell and Sidney Cowell, *Charles Ives and His Music* (New York: Oxford University Press, 1969), 33–34.

4. William Kay Kearns, "Horatio Parker" (Ph.D. diss., University of Illinois, 1965), 16, 476.

5. Allan A. Brown Collection, scrapbook of clippings, **M.165.8, vol. 3, Boston Public Library.

6. Rupert Hughes, *Contemporary American Composers* (Boston: Page, 1900), 176. Hughes includes the songs in this assessment. One must keep in mind that he was writing before the appearance of Parker's operas.

7. Barbara Owen, liner notes to Horatio Parker, *Fugues, Fantasia, and Variations* (New World NW 280).

8. The suite was published in New York by Schirmer in 1904.

9. "Night Piece to Julia," words by Robert Heinck, music by Horatio W. Parker (Boston: Schmidt, 1886).

10. Allan A. Brown Collection, scrapbook of clippings, **M.371.9, Boston Public Library.

11. Chadwick, *Horatio Parker,* 22–23.

12. Kearns, "Horatio Parker," 681.

13. The score that I have seen is the reduced one published by Novello in London, copyright 1903.

14. Karl Krueger, liner notes to MIA 138, on which director Krueger has recorded the composition.

15. Kearns, "Horatio Parker," 583.

16. Chadwick, *Horatio Parker,* 12.

17. Quoted in Hughes, *Contemporary American Composers,* 186.

18. *Mona,* "an opera in three acts, the poem by Brian Hooker, the music by Horatio Parker" (New York: Schirmer, 1911).

19. Semler, Isabel Parker, with Pierson Underwood, *Horatio Parker* (New York: Putnam, 1942), 224, 227.

20. Chadwick, *Horatio Parker,* 18.

21. Semler, *Horatio Parker,* 245

22. Arthur Foote, *An Autobiography,* with a new introduction and notes by Wilma Reid Cipolla (1927; reprint, New York: Da Capo, 1979), 22–23.

23. Arthur Foote, "A Bostonian Remembers," *Musical Quarterly* 23 (1937): 37–44.

24. Allan A. Brown Collection, scrapbook of clippings, **ML 46.B6F6, Boston Public Library.

25. Other songs praised for their excellence are "It Was a Lover and His Lass," "The Night Has a Thousand Eyes," "When You Become a Nun, Dear," "A Ditty," "The Road to Kew," "I Know a Little Garden Patch," "In Picardie," "In a Bower," "Ho, Pretty Page," "Constancy," "A Twilight Fear," "A Roumanian Song," "The Hawthorn Wins the Damask Rose," "The Red Rose Whispers of Passion," "Sweet Is True Love," "Tranquility," "How Many Times Do I Love Thee," and "Ashes of Roses."

26. Foote, *Autobiography,* 45.

27. Allan A. Brown Collection, scrapbook of clippings, **ML46.B6F6 and **M371.4, Boston Public Library.

28. Arthur Foote, Quintet in A Minor for Piano and Strings, op. 38 (Boston: Schmidt, 1898). On the title page of the copy of the score that I have seen at Harvard University is the handwritten inscription: "To John K. Paine. This as well as the quartet. Arthur Foote, March '99."

29. Foote revised the work in 1910.

30. Allan A. Brown Collection, scrapbook of clippings, **M125.5, vol. 6, Boston Public Library.

31. George H. Wilson, "Music in Boston," *Boston Musical Herald,* March 1891, 46.

32. Its principal champion has been the cellist Douglas Moore of Williams College, who has prepared a performing version of the work and performed it on several occasions.

33. Karl Krueger, liner notes to the recording MIA 122.

34. Arthur Foote, Suite in E Major for String Orchestra, op. 63 (Boston: Schmidt, 1909).

35. Arthur Foote, A Night Piece (Boston: Schmidt, 1934).

36. Waldo Selden Pratt, ed., American Supplement to Grove's Dictionary, 2d ed. (1920), s.v. "Foote, Arthur William."

37. Lawrence Gilman, Edward MacDowell (New York: Lane, 1909), 72, 75.

38. John Tasker Howard, Our American Music, 4th ed. (New York: Crowell, 1965), 325.

39. John Erskine, The Memory of Certain Persons (Philadelphia: Lippincott, 1947), 76–77.

40. Allan A. Brown Collection, scrapbook of clippings, *M.165.8, vol. 8, Boston Public Library.

41. Marian MacDowell, Random Notes on Edward MacDowell and His Music (Boston: Schmidt, 1950), v, 34.

42. Gilman, Edward MacDowell, 80–81.

43. Henry T. Finck, Songs and Song Writers (New York: Scribner's, 1900), 242.

44. See the newspaper reviews collected in the Allan A. Brown Collection, scrapbook of clippings, **M.125.5, vols. 8, 18, Boston Public Library; Richard Aldrich, Concert Life in New York, 1902–1923 (New York: Putnam, 1941), 136–37.

45. Quoted in David Ewen, American Composers (New York: Putnam, 1982), s.v. "MacDowell, Edward Alexander."

46. Edward MacDowell, Suite for Large Orchestra, op. 42 (Boston: Schmidt, 1891); "In October," Supplement to the First Suite for Large Orchestra, to be placed between the second and third movement (Boston: Schmidt, 1893).

47. H. E. Krehbiel, in Grove's Dictionary, 2d ed., s.v. "MacDowell, Edward"; T. P. Currier, "Edward MacDowell as I Knew Him," Musical Quarterly 1 (1915): 37.

48. Abbie Farwell Brown, The Boyhood of Edward MacDowell (New York: Stokes, 1924), 191.

49. Allan A. Brown Collection, scrapbook of clippings, **M.125.5, vol. 15, Boston Public Library.

50. Edward MacDowell, Second ("Indian") Suite for Large Orchestra, op. 48 (Leipzig: Breitkopf & Härtel, 1897).

51. Charles Wakefield Cadman, "The 'Idealization' of Indian Music," Musical Quarterly 1 (1915): 390.

52. Gilman, *Edward MacDowell,* 70–71.

53. Philip Hale, *Philip Hale's Boston Symphony Programme Notes,* ed. John N. Burk (Garden City, N.Y.: Doubleday, Doran, 1935), 186.

54. Currier, "Edward MacDowell," 43.

55. Ibid., 30.

56. Marian MacDowell, *Random Notes,* 8.

57. Lawrence Gilman, *Phases of Modern Music* (New York: Harper, 1904), 34.

58. Marian MacDowell, *Random Notes,* 10–11. John Porte, in *Edward MacDowell* (New York: Dutton, 1922), 118, claims the melody was based on a tune of the Brotherton Indians.

59. Marian MacDowell, *Random Notes,* 11.

60. Ibid., 12–13.

61. Ibid., 14.

62. Howard, *Our American Music,* 344.

63. See, for example, Gilman, *Edward MacDowell,* 152; Howard, *Our American Music,* 328; and Percy A. Scholes, *Everyman and His Music* (1917; reprint, Freeport, N.Y.: Books for Libraries, 1969), 166.

64. Edward MacDowell, Sonata *Tragica* in G Minor, op. 45, for the Piano (New York: Schirmer, 1922).

65. Gilman, *Edward MacDowell,* 149.

66. Scholes, *Everyman and His Music,* 166.

67. Edward MacDowell, Sonata *Eroica* in G Minor, op. 50, for Pianoforte (New York: Schirmer, 1924).

68. Gilman, *Edward MacDowell,* 151.

69. Edward MacDowell, Third Sonata for Piano, op. 57 (Boston: Schmidt, 1900). The designation "Norse" does not appear on the title page.

70. Marian MacDowell, *Random Notes,* 20; Gilman, *Edward MacDowell,* 159.

71. Edward MacDowell, Fourth Sonata (*Keltic*) for Piano, op. 59 (Boston: Schmidt, 1901).

72. Gilman, *Edward MacDowell,* 156, 158.

73. Ibid., 71.

NOTES TO CHAPTER 8

1. "New Music," *Musical America,* 28 March 1914, 30.

2. David Ewen, *American Composers* (New York: Putnam, 1982), s.v. "Daniels, Mabel Wheeler."

3. Program book for the concert of the Boston Symphony Orchestra, 16–17 April 1937, 1101–2.

4. Christine Ammer, *Unsung: A History of Women in American Music* (Westport, Conn.: Greenwood Press, 1980), 91.

5. Arthur Elson, *Woman's Work in Music* (Boston: Page, 1904), 196.

6. Ibid., 234–35, 237, 239.

7. Richard Aldrich, *Concert Life in New York, 1902–1923* (New York: Putnam, 1941), 464–75.

8. Adrienne Fried Block, in *American Grove,* vol. 1, s.v. "Beach, Amy Marcy (Cheney)." For an excellent discussion of the changing role of women in music, see Judith Tick, "Passed Away Is the Piano Girl: Changes in American Musical Life, 1870–1900," in *Women Making Music,* ed. Jane Bowers and Judith Tick (Urbana: University of Illinois Press, 1986), 325–48.

9. Neither writer nor publication is identified in the clipping dated 19 March 1903. It may be found in the Allan A. Brown Collection, scrapbook of clippings, **M.165.9, vol. 3, Boston Public Library.

10. Arthur P. Schmidt of Boston published it in 1890.

11. Cobbett, Walter Willson, ed., *Cobbett's Cyclopedic Survey of Chamber Music,* 2d ed. (London: Oxford, 1963), 1:770.

12. Mrs. H. H. A. Beach, Quintet in F-sharp Minor for Piano and Strings, op. 67 (Boston: Schmidt, 1909).

13. Allan A. Brown Collection, scrapbook of clippings, **M125.5, vols. 16 and 17, Boston Public Library.

14. Ibid., vol. 19.

15. Mrs. H. H. A. Beach, Concerto in C-sharp Minor for Piano and Orchestra, op. 45 (Boston: Schmidt, 1900).

16. For a thorough discussion of Ives's relation to his older peers, see Nicholas E. Tawa, "Ives and the New England School," in *Charles Ives and the Classical Tradition,* ed. Geoffrey Block and J. Peter Burkholder (New Haven, Conn.: Yale University Press, 1996), 51–74.

17. Charles E. Ives, *Memos,* ed. John Kirkpatrick (New York: Norton, 1972), 49.

18. Ibid., 131.

19. Rosalie Sandra Perry, *Charles Ives and the American Mind* (Kent, Ohio: Kent State University Press, 1974), 1.

20. See Barbara Zuck, *A History of Musical Americanism* (Ann Arbor, Mich.: UMI Research Press, 1980), 72–73.

21. Charles E. Ives, *Essays before a Sonata and Other Writings,* ed. Howard Boatright (New York: Norton, 1962), 97–98.

22. John Kirkpatrick, in *The New Grove Dictionary of American Music,* ed. H. Wiley Hitchcock and Stanley Sadie (New York: Macmillan, 1986), s.v. "Ives, Charles (Edward)."

23. Aaron Copland, "One Hundred and Fourteen Songs," *Musical Quarterly* 11 (1934): 59.

24. Ives, *Memos,* 75.

25. Gilbert Chase, *America's Music,* 3d ed. (Urbana: University of Illinois Press, 1987), 443.

26. Ives, *Memos,* 87–88.

27. From John Kirkpatrick's preface to the score (New York: Associated Music, 1965), viii.

28. Chase, *America's Music,* 444.

NOTES TO CHAPTER 9

1. Arthur Farwell, Introduction, in Arthur Farwell and W. Dermot Darby, eds., *Music in America,* The Art of Music 4 (New York: National Society of Music, 1915), vii.

2. Marion Bauer, "Author's Foreword," *Twentieth Century Music* (New York: Putnam, 1933), ix.

3. Ralph P. Locke, "Living with Music," in Ralph P. Locke and Cyrilla Bar, eds., *Cultivating Music in America* (Berkeley: University of California Press, 1997), 110–11.

4. Michael Kammen, *Mystic Chords of Memory* (New York: Vintage Books, 1993), 210, 390; Warren I. Susman, *Culture as History* (New York: Pantheon, 1984), 45; Deems Taylor, in *Civilization in the United States,* ed. Harold E. Stearns (New York: Harcourt, Brace, 1922), 203–4, 208–9.

5. J. H. Vail, comp., *Litchfield County Choral Union, 1900–1912* (Norfolk, Conn.: Litchfield County University Club, 1912), 1:260–61.

6. Rupert Hughes, Foreword, in *Contemporary American Composers* (Boston: Page, 1900), viii–ix.

7. Mabel Wheeler Daniels, *An American Girl in Munich: Impressions of a Music Student* (Boston: Little, Brown, 1905), 47; Carl Engel, "Views and Reviews," *Musical Quarterly* 9 (1923): 149; Aaron Copland, *Music and Imagination* (New York: Mentor, 1959), 101.

8. Frederick J. Hoffman, *The Twenties* (New York: Free Press, 1962), 157–59.

9. Carl Van Vechten, *Red: Papers on Musical Subjects* (New York: Knopf, 1925), 27, n. 32.

10. Edith Wharton, *The Writing of Fiction* (New York: Scribner's, 1925), 14, 17.

11. Arthur Foote, "A Bostonian Remembers," *Musical Quarterly* 23 (1937), 37ff.; Daniel Gregory Mason, *The Dilemma of American Music* (New York: Macmillan, 1928), 5–6; Farwell, Introduction, *Music in America,* xvii; Virgil Thomson, *American Music since 1910* (New York: Holt, Rinehart & Winston, 1971), 5. When Hugo Leichtentritt cites Edward Burlingame Hill and Frederick Shepherd Converse as influenced by French Impressionism, we realize that no transitional composer was left untouched; see Hugo Leichtentritt, *Serge*

Koussevitzky, The Boston Symphony Orchestra, and the New American Music (Cambridge, Mass.: Harvard University Press, 1946), 45.

12. Douglas Moore concurs with these observations; see *From Madrigal to Modern Music* (New York: Norton, 1942), 254–56. The quotations come from Edward Shils, *Tradition* (Chicago: University of Chicago Press, 1981), 26.

13. John Livingston Lowes, *Convention and Revolt in Poetry* (Boston: Houghton Mifflin, 1930), 97.

14. Robert Joseph Garofalo, "The Life and Works of Frederick Shepherd Converse (1871–1940)" (Ph.D. diss., Catholic University of America, 1969), 5.

15. Louis C. Elson, *The History of American Music,* revised to 1925 by Arthur Elson (New York: Macmillan, 1925), 204.

16. Ruth Severance, "The Life and Work of Frederick Shepherd Converse" (M.A. thesis, Boston University, 1932), 8–9. See also Garofalo, "Life and Works of Frederick Shepherd Converse," 138.

17. "Music of Frederick S. Converse," *Christian Science Monitor,* 15 January 1910, 8.

18. John Tasker Howard, with Arthur Mendel, *Our Contemporary Music* (New York: Crowell, 1941), 56.

19. "Music of Frederick S. Converse," 8.

20. George Chadwick, "American Composers," in *The History of American Music,* ed. W. L. Hubbard, *The American History and Encyclopedia of Music,* vol. 8 (Toledo: Squire, 1908), 11.

21. Ibid., 11.

22. Frederick Shepherd Converse, *The Festival of Pan,* op. 9 (Boston: G. Schirmer Jr., the Boston Music Co., 1903).

23. William F. Apthorp, program book for the concerts of the Boston Symphony Orchestra on 21–22 December 1900, 294; Lawrence Gilman, *Stories of Symphonic Music* (New York: Harper, 1908), 65.

24. Philip Hale, program book for the concert of the Boston Symphony Orchestra on 11 April 1903, 1162, 1164, 1165.

25. See the clipping of the review by Philip Hale in the *Boston Journal,* 12 April 1903, in the Boston Public Library: microfilm no. ML 40.H3, roll 2. Also see the review by William F. Apthorp in the *Boston Evening Transcript,* 13 April 1903, 7. Louis Elson waxes enthusiastic over the composition in *The History of American Music,* 205.

26. Program book for the concerts of the Boston Symphony Orchestra on 2–3 March 1906, 1241.

27. Frederick Shepherd Converse, *Night and Day: Two Poems for Pianoforte and Orchestra,* op. 11 (Boston: Boston Music, G. Schirmer Jr., 1906).

28. "Music of Frederick S. Converse," 8.

29. Frederick Shepherd Converse, *The Mystic Trumpeter,* op. 19 (New York: Schirmer, 1907).

30. Program book for the concerts of the Boston Symphony Orchestra on 25–26 January 1907, 975.

31. Edward Burlingame Hill, "A New American Composer: Frederick S. Converse and His Career," *Boston Evening Transcript,* 29 January 1906; see the book of clippings in the Boston Public Library, shelf no. *M 165.8, vol. 7.

32. See Olin Downes, "New Work Played in Boston," *Musical America,* February 1912, 45, and also the report of "A. W. K.," *Musical America,* 24 November 1914, 1.

33. The Converse quotation is from the program book for the concerts of the Boston Symphony Orchestra on 27–28 April 1917, 1461.

34. Program book for the concerts of the Boston Symphony Orchestra on 30–31 January 1920, 892, 894.

35. From an article printed in the *Boston Evening Transcript,* 29 January 1920, and reproduced in Garofalo, "Life and Works of Frederick Shepherd Converse," 85.

36. See, for example, the several reservations that Philip Hale had about the music, although he was quite approving of the work as a whole, in "Play Symphony Inspired by War," clipping from the *Boston Herald,* 31 January 1920, in the Boston Public Library; see microfilm no. ML 40.H3, roll 5.

37. Program book for the concerts of the Boston Symphony Orchestra on 21–22 April 1922, 1423.

38. Garofalo, "Life and Works of Frederick Shepherd Converse," 115.

39. See "New Converse Symphony at WPA Concert," *Boston Evening Transcript,* 4 December 1936, 10.

40. Frederick Shepherd Converse, *The Pipe of Desire: Romantic Grand Opera in One Act,* op. 21 (New York: Gray, 1907).

41. "F. C. Converse, American Composer of Grand Opera in English," *New York Daily Tribune,* 20 March 1910, 7.

42. Clipping from the *Boston Herald,* 1 February 1906, in the Boston Public Library; see microfilm no. ML 46.H3, roll 2.

43. Sidney Homer, *My Wife and I* (New York: Macmillan, 1939), 202–3.

44. Program book for the concerts of the Boston Symphony Orchestra on 15–16 April 1927, 1792, 1794, 1796.

45. Frederick Shepherd Converse, *Flivver Ten Million* (Boston: Birchard, 1927).

46. Frederick Shepherd Converse, *California* (Boston: Birchard, 1929).

47. Converse provides this information in the program book for the concerts of the Boston Symphony Orchestra on 8–9 February 1935, 662, 664.

48. Daniel Gregory Mason, *Music in My Time and Other Reminiscences* (New York: Macmillan, 1938), 14–15.

49. Sister Mary Justina Klein, *The Contributions of Daniel Gregory Mason to American Music* (Washington, D.C.: Catholic University of America Press, 1957), 22.

50. Ibid., 19–20.

51. Daniel Gregory Mason, *Contemporary Composers* (New York: Macmillan, 1918), 39–40.

52. Daniel Gregory Mason, *Tune In, America* (New York: Knopf, 1931), 158–59.

53. Letter of Daniel Gregory Mason to Jay Chapman, 24 April 1903, Houghton Library, Harvard University, shelf no. bMS Am 1854 (1103).

54. Both works were published by Schirmer, in 1913 and 1917 respectively.

55. Mason, *Music in My Time,* 173.

56. Burnett C. Tuthill, "Daniel Gregory Mason," *Musical Quarterly* 34 (1948): 52.

57. Daniel Gregory Mason, *Sonata for Clarinet and Piano in C Minor,* op. 14 (Boston: Ditson, published by the Society for the Publication of American Music, 1920).

58. Mason, *Music in My Time,* 262.

59. Howard Hanson, *Music in Contemporary American Civilization* (Lincoln: University of Nebraska Press, 1951), 15.

60. Elliott Carter, in *Modern Music* 16 (1939): 101.

61. On 28 February 1918 Mason wrote to Bynner that he was scoring the Bynner songs and that he hoped to finish them soon in order to show them to Leopold Stokowski; the letter is in Houghton Library, Harvard University, shelf no. bMS Am 1891.28 (334).

62. Arthur Shepherd, in *Cobbett's Cyclopedic Survey of Chamber Music,* 2d edition, ed. Walter Willson Cobbett (London: Oxford University Press, 1963), s.v. "Mason, Daniel Gregory."

63. Tuthill, "Daniel Gregory Mason," 50.

64. Mason, *Music in My Time,* 167, 366.

65. Daniel Gregory Mason, *String Quartet on Negro Themes,* op. 19 (New York: Schirmer, published by the Society for the Publication of American Music, 1930).

66. Mason, *Music in My Time,* 98.

67. Letters of Daniel Gregory Mason to M. A. DeWolfe Howe, 26 July and 25 August 1900, 18 March 1908, Houghton Library, Harvard University, shelf nos. bMS Am 11524 (1984) and bMS 1524.1 (68).

68. Program notes for the concerts of the Cincinnati Symphony Orchestra on 23–24 November 1928, in the book of clippings in the Boston Public Library, shelf no. **M 481.267.

69. Daniel Gregory Mason, *Chanticleer: Festival Overture for Orchestra,* op. 27 (Boston: Birchard, for the Juilliard Musical Foundation, 1929).

70. Mason, *Music in My Time,* 386 n.

71. Paul Snook, review of New World NW 321, *Fanfare,* March/April 1985, 361.

72. Olin Downes, "Music in Review," *New York Times,* 19 February 1932, 15.

73. Tuthill, "Daniel Gregory Mason," 53.

74. Ralph B. Lewis, "The Life and Music of Daniel Gregory Mason" (Ph.D. diss., University of Rochester, 1957), 14.

75. Mason, *Music in My Time,* 387.

76. Daniel Gregory Mason, *A Lincoln Symphony* (New York: American Music Center, 1944).

77. Quoted in Howard, *Our Contemporary Music,* 44.

78. John Clair Canfield Jr., "Henry Kimball Hadley: His Life and Works (1871–1937)" (Ed.D. diss., Florida State University, 1960), 45.

79. Frederick Shepherd Converse, "Henry Hadley," included as appendix E in Garofalo, "Life and Works of Frederick Shepherd Converse," 236.

80. Richard Guy Wilson, "The Great Civilization," in *The American Renaissance, 1876–1917* (New York: Brooklyn Museum, 1979), 37.

81. Allen Tate, *Essays of Four Decades* (Chicago: Swallow, 1968), 351–52.

82. Herbert R. Boardman, *Henry Hadley* (Atlanta: Banner Press, 1932), 88.

83. Ibid., 78.

84. Letter of Amy Lowell to Henry Hadley, 9 June 1919, Houghton Library, Harvard University, shelf no. bMS Lowell 19.1 (579).

85. William Treat Upton, *Art-Song in America* (Boston: Ditson, 1930), 159.

86. Canfield, "Henry Kimball Hadley," 56–57.

87. Henry K. Hadley, *The Four Seasons: Symphony in F minor, No. 2,* op. 30 (Boston: Schmidt, 1902).

88. Canfield "Henry Kimball Hadley," 61–62.

89. In this and the other quotations within parenthesis, I follow the notes of Henry F. Krehbiel, prepared for the New York premier; they reappeared in the program book for the concerts of the Boston Symphony Orchestra on 14–15 April 1905, 1425, 1427, 1428, 1430. The *Boston Evening Transcript*'s "P.R.G.," who reviewed the Boston concert on 17 April 1905, said that the elaborate program furnished for the music was more Krehbiel's than Hadley's; see the book of clippings in the Boston Public Library, shelf no. **M 412.6.

90. Farwell, in *Music in America,* 376.

91. Henry Hadley, *Salome: Tone Poem for Large Orchestra after Oscar Wilde's Tragedy,* op. 55 (Berlin: Reis & Erler, 1906).

92. Program book for the concerts of the Boston Symphony Orchestra on 10–11 April 1908, 1604.

93. Boardman, *Henry Hadley,* 105.

94. Henry Hadley, *The Culprit Fay: A Rhapsody for Orchestra,* op. 62 (New York: Schirmer, 1910).

95. Elliott Carter, "Season's End, New York, Spring, 1938," *Modern Music* 15 (1938): 233.

96. Hadley gives these explanations in his score: Henry Hadley, *Lucifer: Tone Poem for Orchestra,* op. 66, after the poem by Vondel (Boston: Birchard, 1927).

97. Henry Hadley, *Quintet in A Minor for Piano and Strings,* op. 50 (New York: Schirmer, 1919).

98. *New York Times,* 14 March 1909, part 3, p. 2.

99. Quoted by Henry T. Finck in the *New York Post,* 2 February 1920; see the book of clippings in the Boston Public Library, shelf no. **M 422.45.

100. Henry Hadley, *Cleopatra's Night: An Opera in Two Acts,* op. 90, text by Alice L. Pollock (Boston: Ditson, 1920).

NOTES TO CHAPTER 10

1. Daniel Gregory Mason, *Music in My Time and Other Reminiscences* (New York: Macmillan, 1938), 365–66.

2. Evelyn Davis Culbertson, *He Heard America Singing: Arthur Farwell* (Metuchen, N.J.: Scarecrow Press, 1972), 30.

3. Katherine M. E. Longyear, "Henry F. Gilbert, His Life and Works" (Ph.D. diss., University of Rochester, 1968), 11.

4. Ibid., 43–44; Clifton Joseph Furness, in *DAB,* s.v. "Gilbert, Henry Franklin Belknap."

5. John Tasker Howard, *Our American Music,* 4th ed. (New York: Crowell, 1965), 355–56.

6. Henry F. Gilbert, "The American Composer," *Musical Quarterly* 1 (1915): 171.

7. Henry F. Gilbert, "Composer Gilbert on American Music," *New York Times,* 24 March 1918, section 4, p. 9.

8. Henry F. Gilbert, "Musical Hypocrites," *New Music Review* 20 (1921): 238–39.

9. Henry F. Gilbert, "Humor in Music," *Musical Quarterly* 12 (1926): 40.

10. Furness, "Gilbert, Henry Franklin Belknap."

11. See Farwell's estimate of Gilbert, in *Music in America,* ed. Arthur Farwell and W. Dermot Darby, The Art of Music 4 (New York: National Society of Music, 1915), 410.

12. Longyear reaches similar conclusions, in "Henry F. Gilbert," 69, 131, 218.

13. The MacDowell melody sounds very much like that of "Danny Boy," which Fred E. Weatherly had published in 1913.

14. The program notes of the MacDowell Festival concert, which contain Gilbert's explanation of the work's inception and moods, are quoted in the program book for the concerts of the Boston Symphony Orchestra on 21–22 February 1919, 804, 808. See also Henry F. Gilbert, Symphonic Prologue to J. M. Synge's Drama *Riders to the Sea* (New York: Schirmer, 1919).

15. Clipping from the *Boston Herald,* 21 February 1919, in the Boston Public Library, Microfilm no. ML 40.H3, roll 5.

16. Henry F. Gilbert, "Folk-Music in Art-Music: A Discussion and a Theory," *Musical Quarterly* 3 (1917): 577.

17. Henry F. Gilbert, *Two Episodes for Orchestra,* op. 2 (Boston: H. F. Gilbert, n.d.). He presented a copy to Harvard College, signed by him and dated 3 May 1897, now in the Music Library, shelf no. Mus 687.2.225.

18. Henry F. Gilbert, *Humoresque on Negro-Minstrel Tunes* (New York: Gray, 1913).

19. Johnston had also directed Gilbert's attention to Celtic literature and music.

20. Henry F. Gilbert, *Comedy Overture on Negro Themes* (New York: Gray, 1912).

21. Downes, "An American Composer," *Musical Quarterly* 4 (1918): 24; the Hale quotation is from a clipping from the *Boston Herald,* 14 April 1911, in the Boston Public Library, microfilm no. ML 40.H3, roll 4.

22. *Musical America,* 3 October 1914, 17.

23. Ivan Narodny, "An American Composer's Success in Russia," *Musical America,* 17 October 1914, 61.

24. Elliott Carter, "American Figure, with Landscape," *Modern Music* 20 (1943): 223.

25. Henry F. Gilbert, "Note" before the score of *The Dance in Place Congo,* Symphonic Poem (after George W. Cable), op. 15 (New York: Gray, 1922). The "Note" also is found in the program book for the concerts of the Boston Symphony Orchestra on 20–21 February 1920, 1086–87.

26. The quotation may be found in the "Note" preceding the score.

27. This spiritual is identified as "You May Bury Me in the East" by H.F.P. in *Musical America,* 20 December 1913, 21; and by Sear, "Henry Franklin Belknap Gilbert," 255.

28. See the program book for the concerts of the Boston Symphony Orchestra on 4–5 March 1921, 1072–75.

29. Longyear, "Henry F. Gilbert," 31.

30. See, for example, Edward Ellsworth Hipsher, *American Opera and Its Composers* (Philadelphia: Presser, 1927), 200; Otto Luening, *Odyssey of an American Composer* (New York: Scribner's, 1980), 240.

31. Luening, *Odyssey,* 240.

32. Gilbert's comments are contained in the program book for the concerts of the Boston Symphony Orchestra on 26–27 February 1926, 1356, 1358, 1360.

33. Mason, *Music in My Time,* 373.

34. Quoted by Karl Krueger, in the jacket notes to MIA 141, Krueger's recording of the work for the Society for the Preservation of the American Musical Heritage.

35. Ibid.

36. Mason, *Music in My Time,* 35–36.

37. David Ewen, *Composers of Today,* 2d ed. (New York: Wilson, 1934), 116.

38. George Lovett Smith, "Edward Burlingame Hill," *Modern Music* 16 (1938): 12–13.

39. Philip Hale, program book for the concerts of the Boston Symphony Orchestra on 24–25 January 1916, 1114.

40. H. T. Parker, "The Symphony Concert," *Boston Evening Transcript,* 25 March 1916, part 2, p. 10.

41. I have seen the first suite in a manuscript dated 1916–1917, which is now at the Boston Public Library, shelf no. **M 451.74; the score of the second suite that I have studied was published in New York by Schirmer in 1925.

42. "Hill Orchestral Piece," *Christian Science Monitor,* 13 April 1918; see the book of clippings in the Boston Public Library, shelf no. **M 451.74.

43. Program book for the concerts of the Boston Symphony Orchestra on 21–22 March 1924, 1366.

44. Program book for the concerts of the Boston Symphony Orchestra on 29–30 October 1920, 208.

45. Letter to Oswald G. Villard, 14 April 1925, Houghton Library, Harvard University, shelf no. bMS Am 1323 (1678).

46. Program book for the concert of the Boston Symphony Orchestra on 26 April 1927, 10.

47. Edward Burlingame Hill, *Lilacs: Poem for Orchestra,* op. 33 (New York: Cos Cob, 1931).

48. George Boas, *Philosophy and Poetry* (Norton, Mass.: Wheaton College Press, 1932), 14–15.

NOTES TO CHAPTER 11

1. Edward T. Cone, "Conversations with Aaron Copland," *Perspectives of New Music* (spring–summer 1968): 59.

2. John Briggs, "Crusty Composers," *New York Times,* 12 October 1958, sec. 2, p. 11.

3. Claire R. Reis, *Composers, Conductors, and Critics* (New York: Oxford University Press, 1951), 53.

4. Joshua C. Taylor, *The Fine Arts in America* (Chicago: University of Chicago Press, 1979), 192.

5. Randall Thompson, "The Contemporary Scene in American Music," *Musical Quarterly* 18 (1932): 12.

6. The Boston resident, who asked that her name be withheld, gave me an account of her aunt's activities in a written report. At the time she was an older student at the University of Massachusetts at Boston. The Dickson quote is from Robin Moore, *Fiedler, the Colorful Mr. Pops: The Man and His Music* (Boston: Little, Brown, 1968), 154–55.

7. Leonard Bernstein, *Findings* (New York: Simon & Schuster, 1982), 274.

8. Nicholas Tawa, *Serenading the Reluctant Eagle* (New York: Schirmer, 1984), 144–45.

9. John Peatman, "Non-Militant, Sentimental . . ." *Modern Music* 20 (March–April 1943): 153.

10. Aaron Copland, "From the '20's to the '40's and Beyond," *Modern Music* 20 (January–February 1943): 82.

11. Minna Lederman, "Star-Spangled Orchestras," *Modern Music* 17 (March–April, 1940): 194.

12. Winthrop Tryon, "First in Boston," *Modern Music* 20 (May–June 1943): 260.

13. Aaron Copland, *Music and Imagination* (New York: New American Library, 1959), 65–66.

14. Moses Smith, *Koussevitzky* (New York: Allen, Towne & Heath, 1947), 238–39.

15. Vernon Duke, *Passport to Paris* (Boston: Little, Brown, 1955), 102. "Vernon Duke" was Vladimir Dukelsky's pen name. A player in the symphony told me that even Stravinsky was not immune to the conductor's authoritarian rule. At one time, Stravinsky interrupted a rehearsal of one of his neoclassic pieces, waving his arms about and yelling, "Please, no expression!" Koussevitzky yelled back, "But there is expression," and continued conducting as before.

16. A fascinating story of his life and attitudes may be found in Marilyn Ziffrin, *Carl Ruggles* (Urbana: University of Illinois Press, 1994).

17. Ibid., 136.

18. Charles Seeger, "Carl Ruggles," *Musical Quarterly* 18 (1932): 579–80, 590; Seeger, "Carl Ruggles," in *American Composers on American Music,* ed. Henry Cowell (New York: Ungar, 1962), 15, 32.

19. Lou Harrison, *About Carl Ruggles* (Yonkers, N.Y.: Bardiansky, 1946), 2.

20. Ibid., 190–93.

21. See respectively, *Modern Music* 7, no. 2 (1929–30): 26; *Modern Music* 9 (1931–32): 39; and *Musical America,* 10 April 1936, 14.

22. Seeger, "Carl Ruggles," *Musical Quarterly* 18 (1932): 584.

23. Allen Edwards, *Flawed Words and Stubborn Sounds: A Conversation with Elliott Carter* (New York: Norton, 1971), 32–33.

24. I studied composition with Piston and recall his isolating a measure in a piece I was writing by covering each side of it with his hands, saying: "Defend that measure. Why did you write it?"

25. John Dewey, "Democracy in Education," in *The Elementary School Teacher* (December 1903).

26. Piston obtained an ushering job for me, which permitted free attendance at the concerts.

27. Smith, *Koussevitzky,* 206.

28. Reprinted in David Ewen, *American Composers* (New York: Putnam, 1982), s.v. "Piston, Walter Hamon."

29. Howard Pollack, *Aaron Copland* (New York: Holt, 1999), 175.

30. Elliott Carter, "Walter Piston," *Musical Quarterly* 32 (1946): 356, 361–62; Aaron Copland, *The New Music,* rev. ed. (New York: Norton, 1968), 131–33.

31. Israel Citkowitz, "Walter Piston—Classicist," *Modern Music* 13 (1936): 3–10.

32. Irving Weil, "The American Scene Changes," *Modern Music* 16 (November–December, 1938): 7.

33. George Smith, "Walter Piston: American Composer," *Magazine of Art* 33 (1940): 128.

34. Howard Pollack, *Walter Piston* (Ann Arbor, Mich.: UMI Research Press, 1982), 66.

35. Michael Steinberg, *The Symphony* (New York: Oxford University Press, 1995), 421.

36. Pollack, *Walter Piston,* 82–83.

37. Hugo Leichtentritt, *Serge Koussevitzky, the Boston Symphony Orchestra, and the New American Music* (Cambridge, Mass.: Harvard University Press, 1946), 121.

38. Ibid., 111.

39. Quoted by Steven C. Smith, in the notes to the compact disc recording, Delos DE 3106.

40. Quoted by Steven C. Smith, in the notes to the compact disc recording, Delos DE 3074.

41. Harry Ellis Dickson, *"Gentlemen, More Dolce Please!"* (Boston: Beacon Press, 1969), 101.

42. Otto Luening, *The Odyssey of an American Composer* (New York: Scribner's, 1980), 426–30.

43. Ewen, *American Composers,* s.v. "Porter, (William) Quincy."

44. Virgil Thomson, *American Music since 1910* (New York: Holt, Rinehart & Winston, 1971), 167.

45. Howard Shanet, *Philharmonic* (Garden City, N.Y.: Doubleday, 1975), 308.

46. Robin Sabin, "Twentieth-Century Americans," in *Choral Music,* ed. Arthur Jacobs (Baltimore: Penguin Books, 1963), 374.

47. From the program book of the Boston Symphony concert for 31 January 1941, reprinted in Leichtentritt, *Serge Koussevitzky,* 116–17.

48. Elliot Forbes, "The Music of Randall Thompson," *Musical Quarterly* 35 (1949): 1.

49. Thompson, "The Contemporary Scene in American Music," *Musical Quarterly* 18 (1932): 16.

50. *Musical America* contains further reviews of the symphony in the issues of 25 October 1939 (pp. 7 and 25) and 25 January 1940 (p. 21).

51. Caroline Cepin Benser and David Francis Urrows, *Randall Thompson: A Bio-Bibliography* (Westport, Conn.: Greenwood Press, 1991), 122.

52. Virgil Thomson, *The Art of Judging Music* (1948; reprint, Westport, Conn.: Greenwood Press, 1969), 77.

53. Where I have referred to New England psalmody, dance, and traditional song, other writers, unaware of or indifferent to this music, have explained the allusions in terms of southern Appalachia, the South, and the West. However, I do not mean to imply a strictly New England input, since Thompson, especially in the 1920s, had come to know a variety of American vernacular idioms.

54. Benser and Urrows, *Randall Thompson,* 31.

NOTES TO CHAPTER 12

1. Michael Kammen, *American Culture, American Taste* (New York: Knopf, 1999), 45.

2. Ibid., 258–59.

3. Nicholas E. Tawa, *A Most Wondrous Babble* (Westport, Conn.: Greenwood Press, 1987), 137.

4. Reprinted in Gunther Schuller, *Musings* (New York: Oxford University Press, 1986), 259, 260–61, 161–63.

5. For information on opera in Boston, see Robert J. Garofalo, *Frederick Shepherd Converse* (Metuchen, N.J.: Scarecrow, 1994), 33–34, 218–19; Warren Storey Smith, "Music and Dance in Boston," in *Music and Dance in the New England States,* ed. Sigmund Spaeth (New York: Bureau of Musical Research, 1953), 108–12.

6. Richard Dyer, "Keeping Time," *Boston Globe Magazine,* 22 May 1983, 64.

7. Janet Tassel, "Golden Silences," *Boston Globe Magazine,* 27 February 1983, 39.

8. Richard Higgins, "A Warning to Academia," *Boston Globe,* 30 April 1985, 1, 6.

9. Erich Leinsdorf, *Cadenza* (Boston: Houghton Mifflin, 1976), 234.

10. Quoted in Arthur Berger, "Highbrow Havens of the Berkshires Hope to Woo a Younger Species," in the *New York Times,* 24 August 1999, posted on the Internet.

11. Andrew Pincus, *Tanglewood: The Clash between Tradition and Change* (Boston: Northeastern University Press, 1998), 133.

12. See Nicholas E. Tawa, *Art Music in the American Society* (Metuchen, N.J.: Scarecrow, 1987), 200–202.

13. Richard Dyer, "Concert Will Aid Alea III, Antoniou's Lifelong Classroom," *Boston Globe,* 7 April 2000, D15.

14. Benjamin Boretz and Edward T. Cone, eds. *Perspectives on American Composers* (New York: Norton, 1971), 217.

15. Richard Dyer, "Music," *Boston Globe,* 25 December 1983, A1.

16. Helen D. Ruttnecutter, in the *New Yorker,* 17 January 1983, 62.

17. Gunther Schuller, "Can Composer Divorce Public?" *New York Times,* 18 June 1967, sec. 2, p. 17. The composer Elie Siegmeister was saying the same

thing in New York City and, as a consequence, finding that his music was being denied performances in the city.

18. Tassel, "Golden Silences," 39.

19. Jeff McLaughlin, "New Music Making Waves," *Boston Globe,* 11 March 1984, B1.

NOTES TO CHAPTER 13

1. Peter Westbrook, "Alan Hovhaness, Angelic Cycles," *Downbeat,* March 1982, 27.

2. Gregory Battcock, ed., *Breaking the Sound Barrier: A Critical Anthology of the New Music* (New York: Dutton, 1981), 286.

3. Written in 1938; reprinted in Leonard Bernstein, *Findings* (New York: Simon & Schuster, 1982), 22.

4. Ibid., 274, 276.

5. Peter Frank, in *Fanfare* 4 (July–August 1981): 214.

6. Howard Pollack, *Harvard Composers* (Metuchen, N.J.: Scarecrow, 1992), 106.

7. Ibid., 110.

8. Quoted in the liner notes to the LP recording of Quartets No. 1 and 2, Nonesuch H 71249.

9. Cole Gagne and Tracy Caras, *Soundpieces: Interviews with American Composers* (Metuchen, N.J.: Scarecrow, 1982), 184.

10. The quotations come from Del Tredici's explanatory statement in the notes to the LP recording, London LDR 71018.

11. John Rockwell, *All American Music* (New York: Knopf, 1983), 82–83.

12. Quoted in the notes to the CD recording, Elektra/Nonesuch oo 7559-79153-2.

NOTES TO CHAPTER 14

1. Howard Pollack, *Harvard Composers* (Metuchen, N.J.: Scarecrow, 1992), 29.

2. Ibid., 139–40.

3. David Ewen, *American Composers* (New York: Putnam, 1982), s.v. "Fine, Irving Gifford."

4. Edward Rothstein, *New York Times,* 16 January 1983, 51.

5. These pieces were played at the New England Conservatory in March 2000.

6. This was the audience's reaction at a Tanglewood performance of the work given by the two instrumentalists, which I attended in the summer of 1999.

7. Pollack, *Harvard Composers,* 79–80.

8. Reprinted in Carol Oja's notes for the CD recording New World Records NW 360-2.

9. Eric Salzman, "No 'System' for Him," *New York Times,* 21 February 1960, sec. 2, p. 9.

10. Joan Peyser, "For Him, Music Is Its Own Compensation," *New York Times,* 1 January 1984, sec. 2, p. 13.

11. Richard Dyer, "NEC's Pinkham Premiere Demonstrates Composer's Gifts," *Boston Globe,* 8 March 2000, C7.

12. John Adams, "Leon Kirchner: A Snapshot," in the notes to the CD recording Elektra Nonesuch 79188-2.

13. Norbert Carnovale, *Gunther Schuller* (Westport, Conn.: Greenwood Press, 1987), 26–29.

14. Edwin London, in *Dictionary of Contemporary Music,* ed. John Vinton (New York: Dutton, 1971), s.v. "Schuller, Gunther."

15. The article, first published in the October 1968 issue of *Musik im Unterricht,* is reprinted in Gunther Schuller, *Musings* (New York: Oxford University Press, 1986), 233.

16. See Winthrop Sargeant, "Musical Events," *New Yorker,* 15 July 1967, 106.

17. Schuller, *Musings,* 174–81.

18. His father, Lazar Weiner, was called the "father of Yiddish song."

19. Anthony Tommasini, "'Gatsby' as Opera, Fox Trots and All," *New York Times on the Web,* 20 December 1999.

20. Janet Tassel, "A Homecoming for John Harbison," *Boston Globe Magazine,* 26 February 1984, 46.

21. David St. George, "John Harbison," online essay written in 1994 and updated 16 October 1997 for Associated Music Publishers.

22. Andrew Porter, "Tumult of Mighty Harmonies," *New Yorker,* 20 June 1983, 88.

23. See Ellen Pfeifer, "Profiles: New England Conservatory Spring Festival," *Boston Globe,* 8 March 2000, C4.

24. Andrew Pincus, *Tanglewood: The Clash between Tradition and Change* (Boston: Northeastern University Press, 1998), 133.

25. See Richard Dyer, "Chicago 'Psalms' Pure Harbison," *Boston Globe,* 21 May 1999, D15.

26. "Chuckmpr," posted in "Opera Forum," *New York Times on the Web,* 21 December 1999 at 3:31 P.M.

NOTES TO CHAPTER 15

1. Anthony Tommasini, "'Gatsby' as Opera, Fox Trots and All," *New York Times on the Web,* 20 December 1999.

2. Andrew Pincus, *Tanglewood: The Clash between Tradition and Change* (Boston: Northeastern University Press, 1998), 133.

3. Craig Lambert, "The Stirring of Sleeping Beauty," *Harvard Magazine,* September–October 1999, 48.

4. Scott S. Greenberger, "Music-Thinking Link Doubtful, Study Says," *Boston Globe,* 21 September 2000, B5.

5. "The News Hour with Jim Lehrer," Public Broadcasting System, 23 June 1998.

6. Editorial, "Boosting Giving," *Boston Globe,* 21 September 2000, A22.

7. Michael Crowley, "No Roaring Crowds to Fund Art Projects," *Boston Globe,* 29 June 1999, B1, 8.

8. Michael Kammen, *In the Past Lane* (New York: Oxford University Press, 1997), 91.

9. Andrew Pincus, "Has-Beens Hold Forth at Tanglewood," *Boston Globe,* 20 September 2000, A27.

10. Charles Newman, *The Post-Modern Era* (Evanston, Ill.: Northwestern University Press, 1985), 9.

11. Michael Kammen, *American Culture, American Tastes* (New York: Knopf, 1999), 46.

12. Paul Griffiths, "With a New Century, a Promise of New Sounds," *New York Times on the Web,* 19 December 1999.

13. Lambert, "The Stirring of Sleeping Beauty," 46–48.

14. "Mcore" writing in "Classical Music in the Radio," a web forum sponsored by the *New York Times,* and posted 5 August 1998 at 4:11 P.M.

15. Pincus, *Tanglewood,* 131.

16. I have heard this said at one or two Boston community meetings, once on television's Channel 2, and in the course of some social evenings. At one time, a heated argument started up in my own home after the assertion was made that Haiti's art and music, which was brought to New England, were equal in value to Picasso's paintings and Stravinsky's music.

17. For an informative article on the subject of New England identity, see David M. Shribman, "New(er) England," *Boston Globe Magazine,* 7 November 1999, 17–18, 36, 38.

18. Francis Latour, "Currents," *Boston Globe Magazine,* 7 November 1999, 10.

BIBLIOGRAPHY

Adams, James Truslow. *The Founding of New England*. Boston: Little, Brown, 1949.

Ainsworth, Henry. *The Book of Psalmes: Englished Both in Prose and Metre*. Amsterdam: Giles & Thorp, 1612.

Ammer, Christine. *Unsung: A History of Women in American Music*. Westport, Conn.: Greenwood Press, 1980.

Apthorp, William Foster. *By the Way*. 2 vols. Boston: Copeland & Day, 1898.

———. *Musicians and Music-Lovers*. New York: Scribner's, 1894.

Ardoin, John. "The American Composer: Underdog of American Orchestras." *Musical America,* June 1961, 12–13, 58–59.

———. "Leonard Bernstein at Sixty." *High Fidelity* 28 (August 1978): 53–58.

Barbour, J. Murray. *The Church Music of William Billings*. East Lansing, Mich.: Michigan State University Press, 1960.

Barzun, Jacques. *Critical Questions*. Edited by Bea Friedland. Chicago: University of Chicago Press, 1982.

Bauer, Marion. *Twentieth Century Music*. New York: Putnam, 1933.

The Bay Psalm Book. Facsimile reprint of *The Whole Booke of Psalmes Faithfully Translated into English Metre,* 1st ed. (Cambridge, Mass.: Stephen Day, 1640). New York: Lenox Hill, 1977.

Benser, Caroline Cepin, and David Francis Urrows. *Randall Thompson: A Bio-Bibliography*. Westport, Conn.: Greenwood Press, 1991.

Bernstein, Leonard. *Findings*. New York: Simon & Schuster, 1982.

Block, Geoffrey, and J. Peter Burkholder, eds. *Charles Ives and the Classical Tradition*. New Haven, Conn.: Yale University Press, 1996.

Boardman, Herbert R. *Henry Hadley*. Atlanta: Banner Press, 1932.

Boretz, Benjamin, and Edward T. Cone, eds. *Perspective on American Composers*. New York: Norton, 1971.

Bowers, Jane, and Judith Tick, eds. *Women Making Music*. Urbana: University of Illinois Press, 1986.

Brooks, Henry M. *Olden-Time Music*. Boston: Ticknor, 1888.

Brooks, Van Wyck. *The Flowering of New England*. New York: Dutton, 1936.

Brown, Abbie Farwell. *The Boyhood of Edward MacDowell*. New York: Stokes, 1924.

Brown, Jeanell Wise. *Amy Beach and Her Chamber Music*. Metuchen, N.J.: Scarecrow, 1994.

Brown, Royal S. "Leon Kirchner." *Musical America,* April 1977, 6–7, 39.

Buechner, Alan C. "An Exploratory Study of the History of the Early New England Singing Schools, 1720–1800." Special qualifying paper. Harvard University, 1955.

———. "Thomas Walter and the Society for Promoting Regular Singing in the Worship of God: Boston, 1720–1723." In *New England Music: The Public Sphere, 1600–1900,* edited by Peter Benes, 48–60. The Dublin Seminar for New England Folklife, Annual Proceedings, 21–23 June 1996. Boston: Boston University, 1998.

———. "Yankee Singing Schools and the Golden Age of Choral Music in New England, 1760–1800." Ed.D. diss., Harvard University, 1960.

Burkholder, J. Peter. *Charles Ives and His World.* Princeton, N.J.: Princeton University Press, 1996.

Cadman, Charles Wakefield. "The 'Idealization' of Indian Music." *Musical Quarterly* 1 (1915): 387–96.

Canfield, John Clair, Jr. "Henry Kimball Hadley: His Life and Works (1871–1937)." Ed.D. diss., Florida State University, 1960.

Carnovale, Norbert. *Gunther Schuller.* Westport, Conn.: Greenwood Press, 1987.

Carter, Elliott. "Walter Piston." *Musical Quarterly* 32 (1946): 354–73.

Carter, Morris. *Isabella Stewart Gardner and Fenway Court.* Boston: Houghton Mifflin, 1925.

Chadwick, George Whitefield. *Horatio Parker.* New Haven, Conn.: Yale University Press, 1921.

Chase, Gilbert. *America's Music.* 3d ed. Urbana: University of Illinois Press, 1987.

Citkowitz, Israel. "Walter Piston: Classicist." *Modern Music* 13 (1936): 3–10.

Clark, John Spencer. *The Life and Letters of John Fiske.* 2 vols. Boston: Houghton Mifflin, 1917.

Clarke, Garry E. *Essays on American Music.* Westport, Conn.: Greenwood Press, 1977.

Cobbett, Walter Willson, ed. *Cobbett's Cyclopedic Survey of Chamber Music.* 2d ed. 2 vols. London: Oxford University Press, 1963.

Cone, Edward T. "Conversations with Aaron Copland." *Perspective of New Music* 6 (spring–summer 1968): 557–72.

Cooke, George Willis. *John Sullivan Dwight.* Boston: Small, Maynard, 1898.

Copland, Aaron. *Music and Imagination.* New York: Mentor, 1959.

———. *The New Music.* Rev. ed. New York: Norton, 1968.

Cotter, Holland. "'The American Century': A Nation's Legacy, Icon by Icon." *New York Times on the Web,* 23 April 1999.

Cowell, Henry, ed. *American Composers on American Music.* New York: Ungar, 1962.

Cowell, Henry, and Sidney Cowell. *Charles Ives and His Music.* New York: Oxford University Press, 1969.

Crawford, Richard. *Andrew Law, American Psalmodist.* Evanston, Ill.: Northwestern University Press, 1968.

Culbertson, Evelyn Davis. *He Heard America Singing: Arthur Farwell.* Metuchen, N.J.: Scarecrow, 1992.

Currier, T. P. "Edward MacDowell as I Knew Him." *Musical Quarterly* 1 (1917): 17–51.

Daniel, Ralph T. *The Anthem in New England before 1800.* Evanston, Ill.: Northwestern University Press, 1966.

Daniels, Mabel Wheeler. *An American Girl in Munich: Impressions of a Music Student.* Boston: Little, Brown, 1905.

Dickson, Harry Ellis. *Arthur Fiedler and the Boston Pops.* Boston: Houghton Mifflin, 1981.

—————. *"Gentlemen, More Dolce Please!"* Boston: Beacon Press, 1969.

Downes, Olin. "An American Composer: Henry F. Gilbert." *Musical Quarterly* 4 (1918): 23–36.

Duke, Vernon. *Passport to Paris.* Boston: Little, Brown, 1955.

Dwight, John S. "The History of Music in Boston." In *The Memorial History of Boston,* ed. Justin Winsor, vol. 4. Boston: Ticknor, 1880.

Eaton, Quaintance. *The Boston Opera Company.* New York: Appleton-Century, 1965.

Edwards, Allen. *Flawed Words and Stubborn Sound: A Conversation with Elliott Carter.* New York: Norton, 1971.

Edwards, George Thornton. *Music and Musicians of Maine.* Portland, Me.: Southworth Press, 1928.

Eliot, T. S. *Selected Essays.* 2d ed. New York: Harcourt, Brace & World, 1964.

Elson, Arthur. *Women's Work in Music.* Boston: Page, 1904.

Elson, Louis C. *The History of American Music.* Revised to 1925 by Arthur Elson. New York: Macmillan, 1925.

Engel, Carl. "George W. Chadwick." *Musical Quarterly* 10 (1924): 438–57.

Erskine, John. *The Memory of Certain Persons.* Philadelphia: Lippincott, 1947.

Ewen, David. *American Composers.* New York: Putnam, 1982.

Farwell, Arthur. *Wanderjahre of a Revolutionist and Other Essays on American Music.* Edited by Thomas Stoner. Rochester: University of Rochester Press, 1995.

Farwell, Arthur, and W. Dermot Darby, eds. *Music in America.* The Art of Music 4. New York: National Society of Music, 1915.

Fay, Amy. *More Letters of Amy Fay: The American Years, 1879–1916.* Edited by S. Margaret William McCarthy. Detroit: Information Coordinators, 1986.

Fiedler, Johanna. *Arthur Fiedler.* New York: Doubleday, 1994.

Finck, Henry T. *My Adventures in the Golden Age of Music.* New York: Funk & Wagnalls, 1926.

—————. *Songs and Song Writers.* New York: Scribner's, 1900.

Fisher, William Arms. *Notes on Music in Old Boston.* Boston: Ditson, 1918.

—————. *Ye Olde New-England Psalm-Tunes, 1620–1820.* Boston: Ditson, 1930.

Fiske, John. *The Letters of John Fiske.* Edited by Ethel F. Fisk. New York: Macmillan, 1940.

Flagg, Josiah. *A Collection of the Best Psalm Tunes.* Boston: n.p., 1764.

Flanders, Helen Hartness, and Marguerite Olney. *Ballads Migrant in New England.* New York: Farrar, Straus & Young, 1953.

Foote, Arthur. *An Autobiography.* Introduction and notes by Wilma Reid Cipolla. 1946. Reprint. New York: Da Capo, 1979.

————. "A Bostonian Remembers." *Musical Quarterly* 23 (1937): 37–44.

Foote, Henry Wilder. *Three Centuries of American Hymnody.* Cambridge, Mass.: Harvard University Press, 1940.

Forbes, Elliot. "The Music of Randall Thompson." *Musical Quarterly* 35 (1949): 1–25.

Gagne, Cole, and Tracy Caras. *Soundpieces: Interviews with American Composers.* Metuchen, N.J.: Scarecrow, 1982.

Garofalo, Robert J. *Frederick Shepherd Converse.* Metuchen, N.J.: Scarecrow, 1994.

————. "The Life and Works of Frederick Shepherd Converse (1871–1940)." Ph.D. diss. Catholic University of America, 1969.

Gilbert, Henry. "The American Composer." *Musical Quarterly* 1 (1915): 169–86.

————. "Folk-Music in Art-Music: A Discussion and a Theory." *Musical Quarterly* 3 (1917): 579–99.

————. "Humor in Music." *Musical Quarterly* 12 (1926): 40–55.

————. "Notes on a Trip to Frankfurt in the Summer of 1927." *Musical Quarterly* 16 (1930): 21–37.

————. "Originality." *Musical Quarterly* 5 (1919): 1–9.

Gilman, Lawrence. *Edward MacDowell.* New York: Lane, 1909.

————. *Phases of Modern Music.* New York: Harper, 1904.

————. *Stories of Symphonic Music.* New York: Harper, 1908.

Goodrich, Alfred John. *Complete Musical Analysis.* Cincinnati: Church, 1889.

Gotschalk, Louis Moreau. *Notes of a Pianist.* Edited by Jeanne Behrend. New York: Knopf, 1964.

Hale, Philip. *Philip Hale's Boston Symphony Programme Notes.* Edited by John N. Burk. Garden City, N.Y.: Doubleday, Doran, 1935.

Hamilton, Alexander. *Gentleman's Progress: The Itinerarium of Dr. Alexander Hamilton, 1744.* Edited by Carl Bridenbaugh. 1948. Reprint. Westport, Conn.: Greenwood Press, 1973.

Hamm, Charles. *Music in the New World.* New York: Norton, 1983.

Hanson, Howard. *Music in Contemporary American Civilization.* Lincoln: University of Nebraska Press, 1951.

Harlan, David. *The Degradation of American History.* Chicago: University of Chicago Press, 1997.

Harrison, Lou. *About Carl Ruggles.* Yonkers, N.Y.: Bardiansky, 1946.

Hastings, Thomas. *Dissertation on Musical Taste.* Albany: Websters & Skinners, 1822.

Heckscher, August. "Government and the Arts." *Music Journal* 21 (March 1963): 82–83.

Henschel, Sir George. *Musings and Memories of a Musician.* New York: Macmillan, 1919.

Hipsher, Edward Ellsworth. *American Opera and Its Composers.* Philadelphia: Presser, 1927.

Hitchcock, H. Wiley. *Music in the United States.* 3d ed. Englewood Cliffs, N.J.: Prentice-Hall, 1988.

Hoffman, Frederick J. *The Twenties.* New York: Free Press, 1962.

Homer, Sidney. *My Wife and I.* New York: Macmillan, 1939.

Hood, George. *A History of Music in New England.* Boston: Wilkins, Carter, 1846.

Howard, John Tasker. *Our American Music.* 4th ed. New York: Cowell, 1965.

Howe, M. A. DeWolfe. *The Boston Symphony Orchestra, 1881–1931.* Rev. and extended by John N. Burk. Boston: Houghton Mifflin, 1931.

Hubbard, John. *An Essay on Music.* Boston: Manning & Loring, 1808.

Hubbard, W. L., ed. *History of American Music.* The American History and Encyclopedia of Music 8. Toledo: Squire, 1908.

Hughes, Rupert. *Contemporary American Composers.* Boston: Page, 1900.

Ives, Charles E. *Essays before a Sonata and Other Writings.* Edited by Howard Boatwright. New York: Norton, 1962.

———. *Memos.* Edited by John Kirkpatrick. New York: Norton, 1972.

Johns, Clayton. *Reminiscences of a Musician.* Cambridge, Mass.: Washburn & Thomas, 1929.

Johnson, H. Earle. *Hallelujah, Amen!* Boston: Humphries, 1965.

———. *Musical Interludes in Boston, 1795–1830.* New York: Columbia University Press, 1943.

———. *Symphony Hall, Boston.* Boston: Little, Brown, 1950.

Jones, F. O., ed. *A Handbook of American Music and Musicians.* Canaseraga, N.Y.: Jones, 1886.

Kammen, Michael. *American Culture, American Taste.* New York: Knopf, 1999.

———. *In the Past Lane.* New York: Oxford University Press, 1997.

———. *Mystic Chords of Memory.* New York: Vintage Books, 1993.

Kearns, William K. "Horatio Parker." Ph.D. diss. University of Illinois, 1965.

———. *Horatio Parker, 1863–1919.* Metuchen, N.J.: Scarecrow, 1990.

Kingman, Daniel. *American Music: A Panorama.* 2d ed. New York: Schirmer, 1990.

Klein, Sister Mary Justina. *The Contributions of Daniel Gregory Mason to American Music.* Washington, D.C.: Catholic University of America Press, 1957.

Knight, Ellen. *Charles Martin Loeffler.* Urbana: University of Illinois Press, 1993.

Krehbiel, H. E. *Review of the New York Musical Season, 1887–1888.* New York: Novello, Ewer, 1888.

Lambert, Barbara, ed. *Music in Colonial Massachusetts, 1620–1820.* 2 vols. Boston: Colonial Society of Massachusetts, 1980, 1985.

Lambert, Craig. "The Stirring of *Sleeping Beauty.*" *Harvard Magazine,* September–October, 1999, 46–53.

Leichtentritt, Hugo. *Sege Koussevitzky, the Boston Symphony Orchestra, and the New American Music.* Cambridge, Mass.: Harvard University Press, 1946.

Leinsdorf, Erich. *Cadenza.* Boston: Houghton Mifflin, 1976.

Levy, Alan H. *Edward MacDowell.* Lanham, Md.: Scarecrow, 1998.

————. *Radical Aesthetics and Music Criticism in America, 1930–1950.* Lewiston, N.Y.: Mellen Press, 1991.

Lewis, Ralph B. "The Life and Music of Daniel Gregory Mason." Ph.D. diss. University of Rochester, 1957.

Linscott, Eloise Hubbard. *Folk Songs of Old New England.* 2d ed. 1962. Reprint. New York: Dover, 1993.

Locke, Ralph P., and Cyrilla Bar, eds. *Cultivating Music in America.* Berkeley: University of California Press, 1997.

Loesser, Arthur. *Men, Women, and Pianos.* New York: Simon & Schuster, 1954.

Longyear, Katherine M. E. "Henry F. Gilbert, His Life and Works." Ph.D. diss. University of Rochester, 1968.

Loucks, Richard. *Arthur Shepherd, American Composer.* Provo, Utah: Brigham Young University Press, 1980.

Lowens, Irving. *Music and Musicians in Early America.* New York: Norton, 1964.

Luening, Otto. *The Odyssey of an American Composer.* New York: Scribner's, 1980.

McCusker, Honor. *Fifty Years of Music in Boston.* Boston: Trustees of the Public Library, 1938.

MacDougall, Hamilton C. *New England Psalmody.* Brattleboro, Vt.: Daye, 1940.

MacDowell, Edward. *Critical and Historical Essays.* Edited by W. J. Baltzell. Boston: Schmidt, 1912.

MacDowell, Marion. *Random Notes on Edward MacDowell and His Music.* Boston: Schmidt, 1950.

McKay, David P., and Richard Crawford. *William Billings of Boston.* Princeton, N.J.: Princeton University Press, 1975.

Mangler, Joyce E. *Rhode Island Music and Musicians, 1733–1850.* Detroit: Information Service, 1965.

Mason, Daniel Gregory. *Contemporary Composers.* New York: Macmillan, 1918.

————. *The Dilemma of American Music.* New York: Macmillan, 1928.

————. *Music as a Humanity.* New York: Gray, 1921.

————. *Music in My Time and Other Reminiscences.* New York: Macmillan, 1938.

————. *Tune In, America.* New York: Knopf, 1931.

Mason, William. *Memories of a Musical Life.* New York: Century, 1901.

Mathews, W. S. B., ed. *A Hundred Years of Music in America.* Chicago: Howe, 1889.

Miller, Perry, ed. *The American Transcendentalists.* Garden City, N.Y.: Doubleday, 1957.

————. *The New England Mind: From Colony to Province.* Cambridge, Mass.: Harvard University Press, 1967.

————. *The New England Mind: The Seventeenth Century.* Cambridge, Mass.: Harvard University Press, 1967.

————. *The Transcendentalists: An Anthology.* Cambridge, Mass.: Harvard University Press, 1967.

Miller, Perry, and Thomas H. Johnson. *The Puritans.* Rev. ed. 2 vols. New York: Harper & Row, 1963.

Moore, Robin. *Fiedler, the Colorful Mr. Pops: The Man and His Music.* Boston: Little, Brown, 1968.

Morison, Samuel Eliot. *The Oxford History of the American People.* New York: Oxford University Press, 1965.

Mueller, John H. *The American Symphony Orchestra.* Bloomington: Indiana University Press, 1951.

"Music of Frederick S. Converse." *Christian Science Monitor,* 15 January 1910, 8.

Newman, Charles. *The Post-Modern Era.* Evanston, Ill.: Northwestern University Press, 1985.

Olmstead, Andrea. *Roger Sessions and His Music.* Ann Arbor, Mich.: UMI Research Press, 1985.

Offenbach, Jacques. *Orpheus in America: Offenbach's Diary of His Journey to the New World.* Translated by Lander McClintock. Bloomington: Indiana University Press, 1957.

Owen, Barbara. *The Organ in New England.* Raleigh, N.C.: Sunbury Press, 1979.

Pemberton, Carol A. *Lowell Mason.* Westport, Conn.: Greenwood Press, 1988.

Perkins, Charles C., and John S. Dwight. *History of the Handel and Haydn Society of Boston, Massachusetts.* 2 vols. in 3. Boston: Mudge, 1883–1934.

Perlis, Vivian. *Charles Ives Remembered: An Oral History.* New Haven, Conn.: Yale University Press, 1974.

Perry, Rosalie Sandra. *Charles Ives and the American Mind.* Kent, Ohio: Kent State University Press, 1974.

Pichierri, Louis. *Music in New Hampshire, 1623–1800.* New York: Columbia University Press, 1960.

Pincus, Andrew L. *Tanglewood: The Clash between Tradition and Change.* Boston: Northeastern University Press, 1998.

Pollack, Howard. *Aaron Copland.* New York: Holt, 1999.

————. *Harvard Composers.* Metuchen, N.J.: Scarecrow, 1992.

————. *Walter Piston.* Ann Arbor, Mich.: UMI Research Press, 1982.

Porte, John. *Edward MacDowell.* New York: Dutton, 1922.

Postman, Neil. *Building a Bridge to the Eighteenth Century.* New York: Knopf, 1999.

Pratt, Waldo Selden, ed. *American Supplement. Grove's Dictionary of Music and Musicians,* vol. 6. Philadelphia: Presser, 1926.

————. *The Music of the Pilgrims.* Boston: Ditson, 1921.

Reis, Claire R. *Composers, Conductors, and Critics.* New York: Oxford University Press, 1951.

Rich, Arthur Lowndes. *Lowell Mason.* Chapel Hill: University of North Carolina Press, 1946.

Rockwell, John. *All American Music: Composition in the Late Twentieth Century.* New York: Knopf, 1983.

Rogers, Clara Kathleen. *The Story of Two Lives.* Boston: privately printed at the Plimpton Press, 1932.

Root, George F. *The Story of a Musical Life.* Cincinnati: Church, 1891.

Ryan, Thomas. *Recollections of an Old Musician.* New York: Dutton, 1899.

Salter, Sumner. "Early Encouragements to American Composers." *Musical Quarterly* 18 (1932): 76–105.

Schiff, David. *The Music of Elliott Carter.* London: Eulenberg, 1983.

Schlesinger, Arthur M., Jr., and Morton White, eds. *Paths of American Thought.* Boston: Houghton Mifflin, 1963.

Schmidt, John C. *The Life and Works of John Knowles Paine.* Ann Arbor, Mich.: UMI Research Press, 1980.

Scholes, Percy A. *The Puritans and Music.* London: Oxford University Press, 1934.

Schuller, Gunther. "Can Composers Divorce the Public?" *New York Times,* 18 June 1967, sec. 2, p. 17.

————. *Musings.* New York: Oxford University Press, 1986.

Seeger, Charles. "Carl Ruggles." *Musical Quarterly* 18 (1932): 578–92.

Semler, Isabel Parker, in collaboration with Pierson Underwood. *Horatio Parker.* New York: Putnam, 1942.

Severance, Ruth. "The Life and Work of Frederick Shepherd Converse." M.A. thesis. Boston University, 1932.

Sewall, Samuel. *Samuel Sewall's Diary.* Edited by Mark Van Doren. New York: Russell & Russell, 1963.

————. *The Diary of Samuel Sewall.* Edited by M. Halsey Thomas. 2 vols. New York: Farrar, Straus & Giroux, 1973.

Shribman, David M. "New(er) England." *Boston Globe Magazine,* 7 November 1999, 17–18, 36, 38.

Smith, Mortimer. *The Life of Ole Bull.* Princeton, N.J.: Princeton University Press, 1943.

Smith, Moses. *Koussevitzky.* New York: Allen, Towne & Heath, 1947.

Snyder, Louis. *Community of Sound.* Boston: Beacon Press, 1979.

Sonneck, Oscar G. *Early Concert-Life in America, 1731–1800.* Leipzig: Breitkopf & Härtel, 1907.

————. *Early Opera in America.* New York: Schirmer, 1915.

————. *Suum Cuique: Essays in Music.* 1916. Reprint. Freeport, N.Y.: Books for Libraries, 1969.

Spaeth, Sigmund, ed. *Music and Dance in the New England States.* New York: Bureau of Musical Research, 1953.

Spalding, Walter Raymond. *Music at Harvard.* New York: Coward-McCann, 1935.

Stearns, Harold E., ed. *Civilization in the United States.* New York: Harcourt, Brace, 1922.

Steinberg, Michael. *The Symphony.* New York: Oxford University Press, 1995.

Sternhold, Thomas, and John Hopkins. *The Whole Booke of Psalmes Collected into English Metre.* London: John Day, 1578. Microfilm. Ann Arbor, Mich.: University Microfilms, 1984.

Susman, Warren I. *Culture as History.* New York: Pantheon Books, 1984.

———, ed. *Culture and Commitment, 1929–1945.* New York: Braziller, 1973.

Swafford, Jan. *Charles Ives: A Life with Music.* New York: Norton, 1996.

Swan, John C., ed. *Music in Boston.* Boston: Trustees of the Public Library of the City of Boston, 1977.

Symmes, Thomas. *The Reasonableness of Regular Singing, or Singing by Note.* Boston: B. Green for Samuel Gerrish. Microfiche. New York: Readex Microprint, 1985.

Tans'ur, William. *The American Harmony, or Royal Melody Complete.* 2 vols. 8th ed. Newburyport, Mass.: Daniel Bayley, 1773. Microfiche. New York: Readex Microprint, 1985.

———. *The Royal Melody Compleat, or The New Harmony of Sion.* 4th ed. Newburyport, Mass.: Daniel Bayley, 1768. Microfiche. New York: Readex Microprint, 1985.

Tawa, Nicholas E. *Art Music in the American Society.* Metuchen, N.J.: Scarecrow, 1987.

———. *Arthur Foote.* Lanham, Md.: Scarecrow, 1997.

———. *The Coming of Age of American Art Music: New England's Classical Romanticists.* Westport, Conn.: Greenwood Press, 1991.

———. *Mainstream Music of Early Twentieth Century America.* Westport, Conn.: Greenwood Press, 1992.

———. *A Most Wondrous Babble: American Composers and the American Scene 1950–1985.* Westport, Conn.: Greenwood Press, 1987.

———. *Serenading the Reluctant Eagle: American Musical Life, 1925–1945.* New York: Schirmer, 1984.

Thompson, Randall. "The Contemporary Scene in American Music." *Musical Quarterly* 18 (1932): 9–17.

Thomson, Virgil. *American Music since 1910.* New York: Holt, Rinehart & Winston, 1971.

———. *The Art of Judging Music.* 1948. Reprint. Westport, Conn.: Greenwood Press, 1969.

————. *Selected Letters of Virgil Thomson.* Edited by Tim Page and Vanessa Page. New York: Summit Books, 1988.

Tufts, John. *An Introduction to the Singing of Psalm-Tunes in a Plain and Easy Method.* 7th ed. Boston: Samuel Gerrish, 1728. Microfiche. New York: Readex Microprint, 1985.

Tuthill, Burnett C. "Daniel Gregory Mason." *Musical Quarterly* 34 (1948): 46–60.

Upton, William Treat. *Art-Song in America.* Boston: Ditson, 1930.

Vaill, J. H. *Litchfield County Choral Union, 1900–1912.* 2 vols. Norfolk, Conn.: Litchfield County University Club, 1912.

Walter, Thomas. *The Grounds and Rules of Musick Explained.* Boston: J. Franklin for Samuel Gerrish, 1721. Microfiche: New York: Readex Microprint, 1985.

Wertenberger, Thomas Jefferson. *The Puritan Oligarchy.* New York: Scribner's, 1970.

Whiting, Lilian. *Louise Chandler Moulton, Poet and Friend.* Boston: Little, Brown, 1910.

Wiggin, Frances Turgeon. *Maine Composers and Their Music.* Rockland, Me.: Federation of Music Clubs, 1959.

Winslow, Edward. *Hypocrisie Unmasked.* 1646. Reprint. Providence, R.I.: The Club for Colonial Reprints, 1916.

Woodridge, David. *From the Steeples and Mountains.* New York: Knopf, 1974.

Yellin, Victor Fell. "Chadwick, American Musical Realist." *Musical Quarterly* 61 (1975): 77–97.

————. *Chadwick, Yankee Composer.* Washington, D.C.: Smithsonian Institution Press, 1990.

————. "The Life and Operatic Works of George Whitefield Chadwick." Ph.D. diss. Harvard University, 1957.

Ziffrin, Marilyn J. *Carl Ruggles.* Urbana: University of Illinois Press, 1994.

Zuck, Barbara. *A History of Musical Americanism.* Ann Arbor, Mich.: UMI Research Press, 1980.

INDEX

Page numbers given in *italics* indicate illustrations.

Musical works can be located under the composer.

Books can be located under the title.

Abel, Frederick, 87

abolitionist movement, 81, 83

Accomplished Singer, The (Mather), 26

Adams, John (composer), 358–59; works: *The Chairman Dances,* 358; *The Death of Klinghoffer,* 358; *Eros Piano,* 358; *Hoodoo Zephyr,* 358–59; *John's Book of Alleged Dances,* 359; *Lollapalooza,* 359; *Nixon in China,* 358; *Violin Concerto,* 358

Adams, John (president), 57

Adams, Samuel, 36

Adler, Samuel, 359–60

African American influences, 113, 227, 271; on Beach, 209; on Converse, 246, 261; on Gilbert, 237, 272, 277–81, 284; on Thompson, 323

Ainsworth, Henry, 16, 19

Albee, Amos, 87

Albert, Stephen, 344, 366–68; works: Cello Concerto, 368; *RiverRun,* 367–68; Symphony No. 2, 368; *Voices Within,* 366

Aldrich, Putnam, 231–32

Aldrich, Richard, 209

Alea III, 345

ambiguities in music, 236

American Company (Old American Company), 57, 58

American Elementary Singing Book (Ives), 88

American Guild of Organists, 179

American Indian influences, 113, 227, 237, 271; on Beach, 209; on Farwell, 272, 273; on Gilbert, 281, 284; on MacDowell, 193–94

American Music Center, 320

American musical idioms, 227, 237, 271–72. *See also specific musical idioms*

American Musical Miscellany (Wright), 45

American Musicological Society, 338, 339

American national music. *See* national music

American Piano Company, 102

Ames, Evelyn, 124

Anderson, Leroy, 308, 370–71

Anderson, T. J., Jr., 387

Anleitung zum Gesang-Unterrichte in Schulen (Kuebler), 91

antebellum period: Boston Academy of Music, 90–94; cultural activity, 69–72; educational reform, 84–90; European influence on education, 72–78; formation of orchestras, 94–99; music periodicals, 104–110; music publishers, 103; piano manufacturers, 101–3; popular musical idioms, 78–84

Antes, John, 68

anthems, 33

anti-American prejudice, 110, 116, 234, 274–75, 338

anti–New England prejudice, 5, 228–30, 233, 235–36, 332

Antoniou, Theodore, 345

Apel, Willi, 231–32, 338

Apollo Club, 206

Apthorp, William Foster, 108, 125

Arnold, John, 32

Arrow Against Profane and Promiscuous Dancing, An (Mather), 10

art music: American vernacular in, 217–72, 434n53; audience for, 234,